PSYCHOLOGY IN PHYSICAL EDUCATION AND SPORT

(Sixth Revised and Updated Edition)

Dr. M.L. Kamlesh
M.A., M.Ed.(Phy. Edn)., Ph.D., D.Sc.(Honoraris Causa, Sri Lanka)
Fellow ASPASP
former Principal,
Lakhshmi National College of Physical Education,
Thiruvananthipuram.
&
former Dean, Faculty of Physical Education,
University of Kerala

KHEL SAHITYA KENDRA.
7/26, Ansari Road, Darya Ganj
New Delhi -110 002

Published by:
KHEL SAHITYA KENDRA
7/26, Basement, Ansari Road, Darya Ganj
New Delhi - 110 002.
Phones: 011- 65190343, 47090343, 43551324, (M) 9811088729,
8459074169
e-mail: khelsahitya@rediffmail.com, vivekthani@gmail.com
Website: www.khelsahitya.com

I.S.B.N. 978-81-7524-609-6

Printed and Published in India
First Edition: Metropolitan, 1983
Second Revised & Updated Edition : Metropolitan, 1988
Third Revised & Updated Edition : Metropolitan, 1998
Fourth Revised & Updated Edition : Metropolitan, 2002
Fifth Revised & Updated Edition : Metropolitan, 2010
Sixh Revised & Updated Edition : Khel Sahitya, 2015

Reprint: 2016, 2017, 2022, 2024

Laser Typeset by:
JAIN MEDIA GRAPHICS,
Delhi - 110035

Printed by:
ASIA OFFSET PRINTERS,
Delhi

This book is dedicated to the evergreen memory of the "master" teacher – **Prof. T.R. Sharma** *– who illumined hundreds of souls like mine with the light of knowledge and guided the destinies of education in the country like Zeus – the supreme Greek deity – who presided over the athletic contests at Olympia centuries ago.*

PREFACE

Horizons of exercise & sport psychology have been expanding fast for the last many decades. This hybrid science that took birth from the casual observations and experiences of physical educators, athletes and coaches in sixties of the 20th century, has now assumed the status of a critical performance-enhancement science measuring shoulders with biomechanics and exercise & sport physiology. In competitive sport today, people talk of sport psychology as a *buzz word* because the mental demands of sport are every bit as important as the physical demands. Athletes, individuals and teams, spend thousands of hours perfecting their physical performance but many often neglect their mental skills and fitness. The importance of sport psychology can be gauged from what Tiger Woods - the golf prodigy - like many top ranking athletes says: "My creative mind is my greatest weapon. It is a kind of inner vision that enables me to see things that others might not, like a certain way to play a shot. The psychology of golf can be complicated as it does entail mental toughness, self-confidence, conquering inner demons, instant recall of past successes and being able to purge failures. It is the game within the game, I developed my mental strength early and I cannot emphasize the importance of you developing yours now!"

Psychology has always been one of the major subjects of study in the theoretical framework of physical education as a teacher education programme since the inception and physical educators are supposed to be well-versed with the basic tenets of exercise and sport psychology for they have to address problems of students relating to motor learning, motivation, interest, attention, inter-personal relationships, group dynamics, competition, and so on in different settings. Further, of late tremendous stress has been placed on research in most crucial topics under sport & exercise psychology as a result of which not only has the haze been cleared from most psychological concepts that defied scientific solution but also new strategies of studying, understanding, training and conditioning athletic behaviour have been evolved especially from the viewpoint of performance-enhancement. This puts a greater responsibility on physical educators than ever before because they are the people who "catch children young", identify talent and lay a solid foundation for sport as a competitive endeavour. After a particular stage of teaching-training, the sports coaches take over from physical educators; their task is *specialized* and more focused, but not different as many, erroneously though, would believe. If physical educators are "masters", coaches are "grand masters". Both require a literary bent of mind, a scientific temper and managerial skills to accomplish their respective cherished goals both in education and outside it, in the wide world of sport.

Psychology in Physical Education and Sport, which now comes in fifth edition, is both for physical educators and sport coaches because both deal with human muscle and mind as experts in human engineering. The book is neither a treatise on psychological training of athletes, nor a manual of activity training; it is a unified approach to understanding man and his behaviour in activity and sport perspective. It has been revised and updated in the light of new information about activity and sport behaviour gathered from literary and Internet sources but not without assessing its authenticity and applicability on the anvil of personal knowledge and teacher experience of several decades. A thorough window-dressing has been given to almost all chapters and some chapters have been divided suitably in order to put some more stress on certain important points. The difference between the *the* and the *now* is clearly visible.

I am indeed indebted to the students and faculty of physical education and sport psychology in colleges and universities for their unstinted support to and appreciation for my literary works. I shall be failing in my duty if I do not profusely thank Shri Vivek Thani, propritor Khel Sahitya, New Delhi for his ever-readiness to publish quality physical education and sports texts like this for the benefit of all and sundary- whether within educational fold or outside of it.

Patiala, July, 2015

M.L. Kamlesh

CONTENTS

Psychology is the Science of Mental Life, both of its phenomena and of their conditions.
- William James

CHAPTER - 1

PSYCHOLOGY : AN OVERVIEW

Against a sound developmental background, psychology today is both an academic and applied discipline involving the scientific study of mental processes and behaviour. By over-viewing, understanding and analyzing such phenomena as perception, cognition, emotion, personality, behaviour, interpersonal relationships, and individual-environment interactions, modern psychologists try to understand why living beings act the way they do; how they grow up; how they learn and change; how they differ from one another; and even how they get into trouble or become disturbed. No doubt, psychology is primarily concerned with human beings, the behaviour and mental processes of animals is also an important part of psychological research, either as a subject in its own way or with strong emphasis about evolutionary links, and as a *limited* (and often controversial too) way of gaining an insight into human mind and behaviour by means of comparison or via animal models of emotional and behaviour systems as seen in neuroscience of psychology. Psychology also attempts to understand the role human behaviour plays in social dynamics while incorporating physiological and neurological processes into its conceptions of the mental functioning.

In its practical nuances, psychology refers to the application of such knowledge to various spheres of human activity, including issues related to daily life, e.g. family, education, and work, and the treatment of ever-increasing mental health problems especially those relating to psychosomatic disorders resulting mainly from ever-increasing life stresses and strains. Psychology has come to be recognized as one of the behavioral sciences - a broad field that spans the social and natural sciences.

ROOTS OF PSYCHOLOGY

Psychology have had its origin in the all-inclusive philosophy in the ancient times and gradually developed into a separate borderline science discipline. It is so because several areas falling within its purview are difficult to deal with by using scientific yardsticks.

Philosophic Roots

Psychology is well-known to emerge from two Greek words: psykhç (psyche) meaning "breath, spirit, soul" or "mind", and *logia* (logos) "study of" as explained in Aristotle's *De Anima* - a treatise on the soul. For the ancient Greek philosophers, soul was the essence of a living being - the cause and principle of life; so they often called its study a mental philosophy.... a legitimate province of metaphysical speculation (Wolman, 1979). In its philosophical context, the study of psychology dates back to the ancient great Civilizations of Egypt, Greece, China, India and Persia. For centuries the philosophers (or psychologists) strove to understand mind both in its observable (physical behaviour) non-observable (inner or mental aspects), and to disentangle the body-soul dichotomy, i.e. body and mind are separate entities - a view held by Plato, Aristotle, and *Sankhya* and *Yoga* schools of thought of the Hindu philosophy.

It was Rudolf Goeckel who in 1590, for the first time, used the word psychology, and attempted to justify *mind* as its major domain. Leaving soul to the purview of the philosopher, the Middle-age psychologist focused more on study of mental processes. Synonyms of mind include *intellect, intelligence, brain, wit, reason,* etc. These nouns denote nothing concrete but processes of thinking, reasoning, and acquiring and applying knowledge. So, *mind* refers broadly to the capacities for thought, perception, memory, and decision. It is a concept so complex, yet in a sense so amorphous, that over the ages it has resisted efforts to define it. It is through *human* thought, action and behaviour that philosophers and poets and scientists have sought to understand what mind is. Because *mind* could not be defined in clear and concrete terms, it continued to remain a mind-boggling puzzle. It simply was known to be a process of the brain and nervous system. According to McDougall (1949) mind "expresses itself in his (organism) experiences and in his behaviour". Once a laughing philosopher remarked, "What is mind? No matter? What is matter? Never mind".

Considering matter and mind to be substances with little natural connection between them, Rene Descartes (1590-1650) found consciousness as the essence of mind and so he regarded psychology as the *study of consciousness*. Consciousness is awareness, and is a matter of personal and private experiences, which originates in the brain and is manifested especially in thought, perception, emotion, will, memory, and imagination. Being largely subjective consciousness could neither be objectively dealt with nor generalized. We may be conscious of almost everything but we hardly can express our true feelings when passing through emotions like anxiety, fear, disgust, anger, pain etc. It seems probable that Descartes and his followers took no account of mind's subconscious and unconscious activities while making consciousness as the sole stuff of psychology. To philosopher John Searle, "*Consciousness is essential to mind. Any theory of the mind that does not make consciousness a central part of the investigation has missed the point*". But traditionally, scientists have been reluctant to study consciousness. The reluctance is based on the belief that consciousness is not "scientific"; instead it has something to do with mysticism or religion.

Scientific Roots

By the close of the nineteenth century, psychology branched off from its mother discipline philosophy and achieved the status of a borderline science as contemporary thinkers began to experiment with behaviours closely connected with mental processes. As a result the metaphysical and mental regions of the *soul* (mind) became two separate domains. Highlighting this point, Dr. Radhakrishnan observed:

> Our mental states, ideas, impressions and feelings are the subject matter of psychology but what we think is not a matter of what takes place in our minds; we think of reality, rightly or wrongly. A psychologist may be interested in the private experiences of individuals but a philosopher is investigating what our experiences mean. There is a difference between the vehicle of thought and the meaning of thought. Psychology is factual inquiry and philosophy is a conceptual analysis.

Structuralism

In 1879, when Wilhelm Maximilian Wundt (1832-1920) - a German physiologist and philosopher - founded the first laboratory dedicated exclusively to psychological research at Leipzig University in Germany, psychology became an independent experimental field of study. This made Wundt as the "*father of psychology*", and the year 1879 went down in history as the "birth date" of psychology especially as a science.

Making *introspection* as the chief source of data, Wundt sought to understand consciousness by breaking down such mental qualities as sensation, perception, reaction time, etc., into their basic elements and analyzing their inter-relationships. His approach is best known as *structuralism* or *experimental self-observation*. Wundt truly attempted to objectify the subjective procedures of studying mind. The popularity of structuralism began to wane as soon as the psychologists discovered that introspection often altered the nature of conscious mental process they wished to analyze.

Functionalism

Influenced greatly by Darwin's theory of *natural selection*, and at the same time without dissenting with Wundt's structural approach, William James (1842-1910), the truly first American psychologist, pioneered the *School of Functionalism* which aimed to understand the "fluid, functional, continually changing, personal nature of conscious experience". The functionalists wanted to learn how various mental processes such as perceiving, learning, and thinking helped people adapt. James made *observation* as the chief tool of enquiry and encouraged the application of psychology largely to education. He observed that *"human experience (consciousness) flowed like a stream and had continuity in time"* but it was purely personal and subjective in nature, so there were problems in investigating its nature objectively. Human beings may be able to describe what they *experience* but it is fairly difficult to ascertain the accuracy of their description. Words have different meaning for different people. James, therefore, sought to explain the functions of human mind (inner feelings) on the basis of physiological indices that accompanied emotional states. The physiological psychologists contested James' observations but these nevertheless served as a good model for describing the working of human mind. For James, psychology was "the *Science of Mental Life*, both of its phenomena (feelings, desires, cognitions, reasonings, decisions, and the like) and of their conditions".

Psychoanalysis

By the turn of the 20th century, Sigmund Freud (1856-1939), the Austrian physician, developed psychoanalysis, a psychotherapy method, on the basis of which he made startling revelations about sub-conscious and unconscious aspects of the human mind. As a leading light of the *School of Psychoanalysis,* he showed that the subconscious and the unconscious mental activities have an indelible imprint on man's observable behaviour. Using clinical observation and introspection, Freud systematically delved deep into the mind of the emotionally disturbed people and traced the causes of abnormal behaviour to hidden fears, repressed and suppressed desires, frustrations, conflicts, memories etc. His theories became very well-known for the interesting revelations about sexuality, repression and the unconscious mind as general aspects of psychological development, but they also shocked many and generated critical reactions in various quarters. However, they provided important insight into the emotional lives of people. Freud is best known for interpreting mind as consisting of Id, Ego and Super-ego representing biological, psychological and social aspects of human personality. His clinical innovations such as the method of free association and clinical interest in dreams added a new dimension to psychology and earned him great name and fame.

Carl Jung (whose analytical psychology became an alternative form of depth psychology), Erik Erikson, Melanie Klein, Karen Horney, John Bowlby, Erich Fromm, and others came under the influence of Freud. The Freudians declared in unequivocal terms that overt behaviour could not be understood without reference to 'unconscious springs of motivation'. Later psychologists asserted that Freudian theories were presented in "unstable form" and were not "scientifically oriented". Inconsistencies and incompatibilities, no doubt, are there in psychoanalysis theories, but psychology without Freud would find it difficult to justify its existence.

Behaviourism

The problems in studying abstract concepts like mind and consciousness were real. To overcome them, in the early part of the 20th century, John B. Watson (1878 -1958) and associates (who came to be known as behaviourists) began to concentrate on the observable aspect of behaviour in order to understand mind. The behaviourists argued that the contents of the mind were not open to scientific scrutiny and that scientific psychology should only be concerned with the study of observable behaviour for the covert (inner) behaviour indirectly reflected in overt (observable) activities, amply justifying the proposition *face is the index of mind.* Watson opposed introspection - the chief tool used by Wundt and James to scoop psychological data -

calling it unscientific. In his view, the real task of psychology was to observe and analyse the relationship stimuli and organism's response to them. This down-to-earth radical approach to the study of mind came to be known as *Behaviourism*, which enabled contemporary psychologists to deal with public phenomena as a biologist or a physicist would do. This stimulus-response (S-R) approach to the study of mind underscored reflexes and other observable responses as the central focus but discounted such creative processes of the mind as creative thinking, language acquisition etc. From this time onward psychology came to be known as *the study of behaviour*. Edward Thorndike, Clark Hull, Edward Tollman and B.F. Skinner carried forward the trails of behaviourism blazed by Watson.

Behaviourists attach great importance to behaviour-environment relations and analyze overt and covert (i.e., private) behavior as a function of the organism interacting with its environment. They do not reject the study of covert (inner) events such as dreaming. Concepts such as "mind" or "consciousness" are not used by behaviourists because such terms do not describe actual psychological events (such as imagining) but are used as explanatory entities hidden somewhere in the organism.

Gestalt School

Along with behaviorism and psychoanalysis, the "third force" within psychology, was the *Gestalt School* led by Max Wertheimer (1880-1943), Wolfgang Kohler (1887-1967), Kurt Kofka (1886-1941), and Fritz Perls. This new generation of scientists opposed structuralism and behaviourism on the ground that whole of an experience (Gestalt in German language means "overall whole") was different from the sum of its parts and it was erroneous to break psychological processes into basic components like elementary sensation or stimuli and responses. Gestaltists stressed on the relationship which exists amongst various components of behaviour and the way we perceive patterns and organize experiences. Gestalt psychology remains as an active force in our present day investigation of perceptual processes and learning.

Bringing the issue of evolution of psychology to some sort of logical conclusion, Woodworth (1948) remarked, though in a lighter vein, *"First psychology lost its soul, then it lost its mind, then it lost its consciousness, it still has behaviour of a kind"*. With behaviour as its central theme, psychology today takes into consideration everything that contributes directly or indirectly to the understanding of behaviour.

More Modern Approaches

Modern approaches to psychology are highly scientific and, of course, quite realistic, placing greater reliance on individual-environment interaction and cognitive processes which seem easy to study using experimental methodology. Precisely, these approaches are: Humanistic Approach and Cognitive Approach.

Humanistic Approach

With leaders Abraham Maslow (1908-1970) and Carl Rogers (1902-1987), the Humanistic Approach made its appearance during 1950s. By using phenomenology and inter-subjectivity and first person categories, this novel approach sought to glimpse the whole person not just the fragmented parts of the personality or cognitive functioning. It lays emphasis on the role of free-choice and man's ability to make conscious rational choices about how a person lives his life. The focus is on uniquely human issues and fundamental issues of life, such as self-identity, death, aloneness, freedom, and meaning. The founding theorists of humanistic approach believe in self-actualization, meaning that people have a natural inclination to strive to fulfil their potential. The distinguishing factors of this theory include the emphasis on subjective meaning, a rejection of determinism, and a concern for positive growth rather than pathology.

Cognitive Approach

The modern psychology is dominated by cognitive approach that challenged behaviourist approaches to explaining behaviour arbitrarily on the basis of 'stimulus', 'response' and 'reinforcement' which Skinner borrowed from animal experiments in the laboratory. In his 1959-review of the behaviourist approach, Noam Chomsky argued that Skinner's notions could only be applied to complex human behaviour, such as language acquisition, in a vague and superficial manner.

Information-processing model and neuro-psychology have emerged as the most exciting areas of modern psychology. The rise of computer science has made it easier for the scientists to understand and study information processing by human beings and information processing by machines. Increasingly more empirical evidence is being sought as to the mechanism of behaviour in its various aspects - physical, physiological, social, intellectual, environmental, cognitive and philosophic.

Cognitive psychology differs from other psychological perspectives in two key ways. First, it accepts the use of the scientific method, and generally rejects introspection as a method of investigation, unlike symbol-driven approaches such as Freudian psychodynamics. Second, it explicitly acknowledges the existence of internal mental states—such as belief, desire and motivation—whereas behaviourism does not.

Today, psychology has adopted an integrated perspective or what is more often called the ***bio-psycho-social approach*** towards understanding consciousness, behaviour, and social interaction. This new approach underlines a two-way interaction between behaviour (mental process) and dynamically interrelated biological, psychological and social factors that surround the organism. In other words, any given behavioural act affects and is affected by dynamic as well as interrelated external factors and forces, some perceptible, others inferred.

In terms of academics, research and application, the dimensions of modern psychology know no bounds, and yet to sum up the issue, it would be apt to precisely recapitulate the contributions its major perspectives make to the expanding of these dimensions.

- ***Behavioural Perspective***, with an emphasis on learning, whether animal and human, attempts to explain how behaviour changes under various conditions and with what consequences.
- ***Biological Perspective*** undertakes the study of the effects of genetics, brain structure, chemistry and hormones on behaviour and cognition.
- ***Cognitive Perspective*** takes insight into the mental processes such as thinking, sensing and perceiving.
- ***Psycho-dynamic Perspective*** investigates the influences of unconscious motivations on behaviour and cognition.
- ***Social Perspective*** takes care of social interactions amongst individuals under various conditions.

DEFINITION OF PSYCHOLOGY

Philosophers, biologists, physiologists, psychologists, sociologists and others have dealt with soul, mind, its consciousness and unconsciousness states, behaviour, cognition, and the like from a variety of perspectives as these all are so intimately connected with man –

the complex bio-psycho-social being. Each perspective, with its acknowledged merits and constraints contributes something to defining psychology and explaining what this expanding discipline is all about in the fast changing social, cultural and technological contexts.

Various schools of psychology have defined psychology in terms which they considered most apt in the context their leaders happened to work.

McDougall (1949) considered psychology "a science which aims to give us better understanding and control of behaviour of the organism as a whole". A psychologist today has assumed the status of a scientist whose task is to systematically study the processes and activities of the mind and explain and interpret human behaviour as a result of mental activity with reference to the context in which it happens to occur. Disiderto, Howieson & Jackson (1976) proposed it "as the investigation of human and animal behaviour and of the mental and psychological processes associated with the behaviour". Crooks & Stein (1988) defined psychology as the "scientific study of behaviour and mental processes of humans and other animals".

Undoubtedly, the tools and techniques of investigating mind and behaviour, over the decades have undergone a sea change. With the induction of computer technology, they have become more sophisticated, but interestingly no substantial change has occurred in the definition of psychology; it continues to be a *science of activities of an individual (organism) in relation to his environment,* as Woodworth (1948) said. Ross (1953) rightly said: "Mind is central notion of psychology, while behaviour is merely its subject of study".

Mellucci (2004) sums up the long-drawn debate over the definition and status of psychology thus:

> Those who practice and teach in the discipline (psychology) call it ***the science of study of mental processes and behaviour.*** Psychology is a "young science". It emerged from the combined influence of other scholarly and scientific fields, especially medicine, biology, and philosophy. It has grown rapidly over the last 150 years as a discipline in its own right. It has become an applied science that works alongside a wide variety of other fields: health sciences, education, management, and law just to name a few.

The three major fields of productive activity for the psychologists primarily are academic, research, and clinical (application). They have begun to intervene in several other areas unexpected of them.

Keywords in Psychology Definition

Woodworth's (1948) definition contains four important keywords that convey the crux of psychology. They are: (1) science, (2) activities or behaviour, (3) individual or organism, and (4) environment.

Psychology as a Science

Science, argued Aldous Huxley, is nothing but trained and organized common sense. Opposed to philosophy which is largely conceptual analysis, science is a systematic and organised factual enquiry of the natural phenomena primarily based on observation. It is, "objective, replicative, systematic, unbiased, principle and procedure centered and not result centered" (Magill, 1989). In the early part of the twentieth century, science referred essentially to techniques, findings and theories in the natural sciences - physics, chemistry and biology. Today scientists place greater emphasis on procedures innovated and adopted in the acquisition of knowledge than the field of knowledge they deal with. Irrespective of the field of knowledge under investigation, scientific method involves observation, description, explanation and prediction of phenomena.

Sciences are broadly classified as (1) *Matter Sciences* (physics, chemistry, astronomy, geology, etc.); (2) *Life Sciences* (biology, botany, zoology, physiology, anthropology, etc.); and (3) *Mind (behavioural) Sciences* - further categorized into *positive* behavioural sciences such as economics, political science, psychology, etc., and *normative* behavioural sciences such as ethics, aesthetics, etc. Behavioural sciences have numerous common areas of concern with philosophy. With largely subjective approach, normative sciences, in general, discuss and lay down standards and norms of human behaviour; positive behavioural sciences deal with mind or behaviour as product of complex interaction between myriad internal and external forces. Their approach, by and large, is objective.

Modern psychology is one of the positive behavioural sciences — a broad field that spans the social and natural sciences. It now claims to be more objective and less subjective, more experimental and less speculative. *What-ought-to-be* is of little concern to psychology; it simply attempts to investigate, discuss and explain as to how will a living being - man or animal – act, react and interact under a given set of circumstances. For many, psychology may be a matter of common sense but unorganised and untrained common sense helps no theories, hypotheses and principles to evolve as is the case with psychology today. Much of the content of modern psychology has emerged from a meticulous application of scientific method - observation, experimentation, and/or computer analysis. Research in most areas of psychology is conducted in broad accord with the standards of the scientific method, encompassing both qualitative ethological and quantitative statistical modalities to generate and evaluate explanatory hypotheses with regard to psychological phenomena.

With its roots in philosophy, physiology, and psychiatry, the relatively *new science of psychology* can be best understood as a federation of interests; an alliance of scholars, scientists and practitioners that is held together by a shared commitment to the systematic study of human and animal behaviour. Psychologists believe that animal movements and human mind can be examined as carefully and scientifically as astrophysicists study galaxies or biochemists study nucleic acids. All through psychology has maintained its breadth. It stretches from biological study at one border, through the examination of human beings in groups, which has much in common with sociology and anthropology out to the edges of clinical psychiatry and general medicine.

Hardcore scientists find psychology not as pure a science as chemistry and physics are. For them it is a "fuzzy" science because its several areas rely on research methods such as surveys and questionnaire. Besides, critics have asserted that psychology is least scientific due largely to correlational nature of survey research. Other phenomena like personality, thinking and emotion in which psychologists are interested cannot be directly measured and are often inferred from subjective self-reports, which may be problematic.

Activities (Behaviour)

All living beings are product of biological evolution. They are blessed with complex internally as well as externally directed and motivated activities - also called *normal powers of body and mind* behaviour. They are different from mechanical movements of man-made machines. While man's organic activities are inborn, involuntary, and largely reflex type, most activities - better known as skill-based behaviours - are acquired by experience, formal as well as informal learning-training process, and performed consciously. Irrespective of their basic nature, all activities need some stimulation - internal or external - for them to occur. Precisely, all behavioural activities have some purpose and are goal-directed. They enable living beings to 'adjust, maintain, preserve, and perpetuate themselves'.

Comprehensively, the term behaviour is applied to all internal and external activities performed by living beings voluntarily (consciously) and involuntarily (unconsciously). Behaviour does not mean simply observable activities, it also covers the entire gamut of highly complex action-reactions and interactions taking place inside the body and the brain. No activity of the body and mind can be discounted from the overall discussion on behaviour. Mind, which is an organised system of mental or purposive forces, plays a key role in the internal mechanism governing behaviour and shaping the kind, intensity, and extensity of observable behaviour. In order to understand an organism's activities it would be necessary to know, understand and analyze various inter-related body-mind processes - physical, physiological, morphological, neurological etc. Susan Butt rightly observed: "Behaviour is not movement and to specify an action in terms of muscle activity or extension-flexion of limbs is not a specification in terms of behaviour. Categories of behaviour are defined both morphologically and functionally i.e. in terms of their appearance as well as their effect or context". Interestingly, physical or physiological reactions falling within the purview of natural sciences are precise and predictable and can be studied objectively where as those constituting *psychic* behaviour are variable and unpredictable; they can be studied subjectively only. Behaviour, therefore, shall have to be seen in its totality; fragmenting it into physical (external) behaviour and mental (internal) behaviour would mean destroying it

Psycho-physiologists consider behaviour a highly complex nerve-muscle activity-continuum characterized by Cognitive, Affective and Conative phases.

Cognitive Phase refers to sensory input mechanism in which the organism receives information from the external environment through visual (sight), auditory (hearing) olfactory (smell), taste (taste), and tactile (touch) sense - also known as *Gateways of Knowledge*. Depending upon the type of stimulus, the highly specialized receptors embedded in each of the sense organs make the brain aware of what is happening, where and how. Psychologists call it *knowing experience* i.e. acquisition, or organisation and use of knowledge. The mechanism involves both sensory and perceptual processes. While sensory experiences are immediate and simple caused by physical stimuli, perceptual experiences indicate mechanism by which the brain organizes and interprets sensations. For example, a child seeing a cat; a 100m sprinter hearing the gun sound; and a dog sniffing a rotten food stuff; and each one recognizing what all these are, constitutes cognitive activity or knowing experience.

Affective Phase is that condition in which the organized and duly interpreted sensory-perceptual information causes affective (psycho-physiological) actions-reactions in the visceral, glandular and nervous systems. The reference obviously is to the feelings catalyzed by the knowing experience. Affective phase is truly called the *feeling experience*. The quickest possible decisions are taken at this stage with regard to the observable *fight, flight* or *freeze* responses the organism would be expected to give depending upon the nature and intensity of stimulus. Importantly, all affective experience is accompanied by emotional responses such as screaming, shouting, crying, weeping, laughing, crawling, cringing etc., which gives rise to physiochemical reactions on the one hand and intense feelings of pleasure, pain, disgust, repulsion, etc., on the other hand and both together initiate, energize and intensify the muscular activity that follows.

Conative Phase (also called motor phase) is a performing phase and is better labelled as *striving* or *doing experience*. Depending upon the circumstance, the duly brain-directed internal feelings cause the muscles, bones and joints to react to the situation and perform motor movements such as walking, running, moving body part(s), fighting, postural adjustments etc., in most befitting patterns and with desired intensity, thereby facilitating the accomplishment of pre-conceived goals at the optimal speed. In nutshell, motor movements and the resultant bodily changes, both overt and covert, are significant features of the striving experience, which is purposeful and goal-directed. Nevertheless, external conditions and internal states instantly decide the kind of adjustment organism would make. Cognitive and effective experiences culminate in motor activity. Though every stimulus, internal or external, catalyzes some response in the organism, numerous cognitive-affective experiences do not necessarily elicit any motor response.

The knowing, feeling and striving experiences are no terminates in themselves; they are different points of organism's unified response (integrated activity) to an impinging stimulus. On the whole, it is difficult to precisely pinpoint as to where one phase ends and the other begins. From the entry of the stimulus to occurrence of a motor response in the form of an observable movement, the entire mechanism is automatic and smooth. For example, we spot a wild dog or even hear it snarl (cognitive phase), we feel frightened (affective phase) for the situation is apprehended as dangerous to our existence, and we finally struggle to run (conative phase) for safety in whatever way possible. Similarly, we hear a stirring song (cognition), enjoy its melodious lilt (affection) and start tapping our foot or clap our hands (conation). Almost all observable activities of the organism are outcomes of various stimulus- response mechanisms - all quick, sudden and automatic. In this integrated circuit, we hardly can decipher as to what precedes what and what succeeds what.

Psychology does not simply address what goes on in our mind; it also takes cognizance of how internal states modify our external behaviour and vice versa. From a simple eye-blinking response to a highly complicated gymnastic somersault, the behavioural activity is a long chain of stimulus-response sequences, strengthened or weakened on the basis of quantitative and qualitative impact of the internal and external conditions.

Individual

Individual here means a human organism, a living being that thinks and behaves in an environment. The birth, growth, development, behaviour, etc., of the man are primarily governed by law of heredity which produces likes as well as variations. Both biologists and psychologists agree that every individual born is a unique creation of nature and no two individuals, even monozygotic twins, possess the same physical and psychological characteristics; they are simply different. Not only their shape, size, appearance and complexion, but also their ways of acting, reacting and interacting with each other and with their environment rarely resemble. Even though individuals in the given species are alike in most respects, differences in their biological attributes (size, strength, physiological actions-reactions) and their psychological characteristics (intelligence, mental makeup, sociability, and overt and covert behaviour) are clearly distinct, and unbridgeable. Individual variation exists at two levels. First, an individual's genetic make-up i.e. its genotype typically differs from that of his species members. Second, his physical appearance and behaviour i.e. its phenotype varies from his parents, brothers, sisters, relatives etc. Every individual's phenotype is the result of interaction between its genotype and the environment. This single fact of genetics makes the study of the mind and behaviour an uphill task and generalizations impossible. Homer, author of the Greek epics - Iliad and Odyssey- rightly remarked: 'To one man God has given deeds of war, and to another dance, to another lyre and song, and in another wide sounding Zeus puts a good mind". It is, therefore, been incumbent on the psychologists in association with biologists, sociologists and anthropologists to know, understand and analyze the behaviour of not only human beings species alone but also human beings as individuals. The focus has to be on the individual because individual alone is the measure of all things in this universe.

Environment

Behaviour occurs in an environment, not in vacuum. In psychology, environment is every thing that constitutes all external factors and forces, making the organism to act and react in peculiar ways under various settings. While the heredity supplies the hardware for behaviour, the environment programmes individual's mind to shape its behaviour in its own unique ways. Environment is categorized as physical (biological) and social. *Physical environment* is all that surrounds man and nurtures him as a unique being; it ranges from ultra-microscopic microbes to mighty physical objects such as mountains, rivers, fauna, flora, buildings, machines, etc., which play an important role in promoting or retarding man's health, growth, development, adjustment and life processes. *Social environment* refers to the human beings - their ideas, thoughts, beliefs, philosophies, customs, traditions, values, institutions, organizations, etc. One category of environment causes and maintains biological activity in man, and the other ensures man's development as a social being. Precisely, the one helps sustain and propagate life; the other adds quality to life by humanizing, socializing, and educating man so that he becomes an acceptable member of the human society. The child has to be lifted up from the state of animalism with which he is born. Social environment makes human behaviour complex, unpredictable and tricky.

The complex human behaviour may not easily be understood without reference to (a) the biological forces that impinge upon on the activities of the organism overtly or covertly to cause behaviour to take shape in a particular way, and (b) the socio-cultural milieu that makes the individual what he is and the way he behaves. Environment trims man's native behaviour by adding something to and/or subtracting from it. As a tree is known by its leaves, so is man known from the environment he happens to have been born and brought up in. The impact of environment on one's health, fitness, performance, life-style, intellect, knowledge, attitudes, habits, tastes, etc, is deep-rooted, indelible and, of course, dynamic. This makes the study of behaviour a difficult task. Skinner rightly said: "Environment acts in an inconspicuous way; it does not push or pull, it selects...... it is now clear that we must take into account what environment does to an organism not only before but after it responds. Behaviour is shaped and maintained by its consequences".

Though psychologists are harnessing sophisticated technology and using highly scientific techniques in an effort to come to grips with problems of studying behaviour systematically, several areas of human mind are still inaccessible to them. Being fairly comprehensive, Woodworth's definition of psychology seems to be quite close to what psychology is understood to mean in common parlance. Critics of this definition maintain that psychology without reference to mind - an interface between body and soul- is inconceivable. Ross (1953) observes:

> .... to say that psychology is the science of behaviour is no real escape from the difficult notion of mind, for the only intelligible and convincing account of behaviour that can be given must be in terms of mind, life and purpose. So the traditional definition of psychology as the science of mind, although temporarily discarded for the sake of clearness and objectivity, is the true one. Mind is the central notion of psychology, while behaviour is merely its subject of study. Psychology has never escaped from it and it never will.

Ross supported McDougall's assertion: "Mind, then, of the individual organism is that which expresses itself in his behaviour". Causes, mechanisms, dynamics and consequences of behaviour may be difficult to know, understand and deal with if mind is discounted from the discussion of psychology, no matter how so vague its concept is.

Goals of Psychology

While defining psychology as the *systematic, scientific study of behaviours and mental processes*, Plotnik (1999), prescribes the following goals for it:

- to describe different ways that organism behave.
- to explain the causes of behaviour.
- to predict how organisms will behave in certain situations.
- to control an organism's behaviour (for some psychologists).

DIMENSIONS (SUB-FIELDS) OF PSYCHOLOGY

Ever since its inception as a separate discipline, the dimensions of psychology have been expanding incredibly fast both in the areas of research and application. Today, hardly any aspect of human mind and activity seems to be outside the purview of psychology. Psychologists are commonly found working even in some places where they were least expected to, for example, industry, sport, management, etc. It is so because where there are human beings, there is bound to be some sort of behaviour, and enough scope for the psychologists to understand it in the settings in which it occurs and address the problems of adjustment confronting individuals and groups. The vast domain of psychology includes many different approaches to the study of mental processes and behaviour.

Following the tradition of most scientific disciplines, psychology has two aspects: fundamental (basic) and applied.

The *Fundamental or Pure Psychology* is primarily a limitless field of research and development. It supplies the theoretical frame-work and is concerned with the formulation of fundamental principles governing behaviour. It seeks to answer basic questions concerning mind, soul, behaviour and its causes, mechanisms, conditions, and the like through research using scientific methodology. Over the decades, this approach has assumed an inter-disciplinary status. The stress is on objective-description, explanation, analysis, assessment and measurement of behaviour in a variety of forms. In order to build up a strong theoretical knowledge base, psychologists now have to venture into the domains of disciplines not directly concerned with behaviour such as biology, physiology, sociology etc.

Applied Psychology is application of the principles of psychology to a particular field of knowledge or professional practice. When psychologists make use of the psychological theories and principles generated through observation, experimentation, and research in order to address issues concerning behaviour and accomplish certain goals in distinctly demarcated areas of human interaction such as education, medicine, industry, etc., they virtually transform fundamental psychology into applied psychology. Applied psychology, therefore, is a consumable field of knowledge, the major aim of which is no expansion of knowledge for knowledge's sake but to put it into practice to resolve various issues. Except for fundamental psychology, all other sub-fields of psychology come under the ever-expanding field of applied psychology. They are briefly explained below:

Abnormal Psychology

Abnormal psychology refers to the study of abnormal behaviour in order to describe, predict, explain, and change abnormal patterns of functioning. By studying the nature of psycho-pathology and its causes, psychologists apply this knowledge to clinical settings to treat patients with psychological disorders. (As distinguished from normal behaviour, the abnormal behaviour is generally maladaptive and causes an individual significant discomfort in order to be of clinical research interest. It is associated with disability, personal distress, the violation of social norms, or dysfunction).

Biological Psychology

Considering behaviour as an ultimate function of the nervous system, biological psychology, which includes physiology, neuroscience, neurophysiology, etc., is the scientific study of the biological substrates of behaviour and mental states. Therefore, the biological psychologists consider it sensible to study how the complex brain functions in order to understand behaviour. The thrust of research is on the physical and chemical changes that occur during stress, learning, and emotions, as well as how our genetic makeup and nervous system interact with our environments and influence our behaviours.

Educational Psychology

Educational psychology makes use of the general principles of psychology to understanding human behaviour in educational setting and improving learning and teaching processes by developing effective educational interventions and attempting methodological adjustments. Today, no teacher education programme is complete without educational psychology being a part of its curricula.

School Psychology

A combination of the principles of educational psychology and clinical psychology, the school psychology, is meant to (a) understand and treat students with learning disabilities, (b) foster the intellectual growth of "gifted" students, (c) facilitate pro-social behaviours in adolescents, and (d) otherwise to promote safe, supportive, and effective learning environments. School psychologists receive training in educational and behavioral assessment, intervention, prevention, and consultation. They may also take extensive training in research.

Clinical Psychology

Clinical psychology attempts to explain the causes and consequences of psycho-somatic disorders, mental illness, behavioural abnormalities and suggests relevant therapies there for. The major aim of is to understand, prevent, and relieve psychologically-based distress or dysfunction and to promote subjective well-being and personal development. Central to its practice are psychological assessment and psychotherapy. Clinical psychologists also engage in research, teaching, consultation, forensic testimony, and programme development.

Industrial and Organizational Psychology

Industrial and organizational psychology seeks to discuss and analyze human behaviour in the industrial and business setting or workplace environment with an objective to optimize human potential, increase productivity and ensure human welfare. Within in this subfield, while personnel psychology applies psychological principles in such processes as selection and evaluation of various kinds of personnel (workers), the organizational psychology examines the effects of work environments and management styles on the work motivation, job satisfaction and productivity.

Comparative Psychology

Comparative psychology is the study of the behaviour and mental life of animals other than human beings. Though human behaviour is primary focus of psychology, the animal behaviour and mental processes have a great import for the psychological research, for it helps to understand evolutionary links and gain an insight into the human physiology from the viewpoint of behaviour in its totality.

Cognitive Psychology

Associated with the Cognitivism School of Thought, the cognitive psychology addresses cognition and mental processes, with perception, learning, problem-solving, memory, attention, language and emotion being well-researched areas. In cognitive science/psychology, following the computational models, information-processing is the underlying principle of all mental functions and psychologists study the "software" of mental processes independent of the "hardware" it runs on. In nutshell, cognitive psychology involves how we process, store and retrieve information and how cognitive processes influence our behaviours.

Legal Psychology

As a recent innovation and research-oriented field, legal psychology with substantial inputs from social and cognitive psychology, explores such topics as crime, criminals, laws and procedures connected with social behaviour, jury decision-making, eyewitness memory, scientific evidence, and legal policy.

Developmental Psychology

Also known as child psychology, the developmental psychology has in its focus *the development of the human mind through various growth stages.* It examines moral, social, emotional, and cognitive development throughout a person's life. The idea is to understand how people come to perceive, understand, and act within the world and how these processes change as they move forward in age. Using variety of interesting but scientifically valid techniques and cleverly devised methods, the developmental researchers observe children both under natural settings and experimental conditions.

Social Psychology

Social psychology is study of the nature and causes of social behaviour as well as mental processes, with an emphasis on how people think about each other; how they relate to each other; and how they react to social situations. Of special interest to social psychologists are social interactions and relationships, group dynamics (nature and potential optimization of leadership, communication, etc), formation of beliefs, prejudices, attitudes, aggression, and stereotypes about other people.

Counselling Psychology

Counselling psychology purports to facilitate personal and interpersonal functioning across the lifespan with a focus on emotional, social, vocational, educational, health-related, developmental, and organizational concerns. Counsellors are basically clinicians, using psychotherapy and other interventions in order to treat clients. They are employed in a variety of settings, including universities, hospitals, schools, governmental organizations, businesses, private practice, and community mental health centers.

Health Psychology

Health psychology aims at application of psychological theory and research to health, illness and health care, with emphasis on the study of the wider range of health-related behaviour including healthy eating, the doctor-patient relationship, a patient's understanding of health information, and beliefs about illness. It is all about improving quality of life in its biomedical, mental, intellectual and social aspects.

Personality Psychology

Personality psychology has emerged as a new of area of study and research. The focus is on the study of personality development, personality change, assessment, and abnormal behaviours.

Experimental Psychology

Induction of experimental procedure has raised psychology to the status of science. On a few areas such as sensation, perception, learning, human performance, motivation, and emotion fall under experimental psychology.

Psychometrics

Psychometrics is a method that helps psychologists to give objectivity to their observations. In psychology, psychometrics focuses on the measurement of the people's abilities, skills, intelligence, personality and abnormal behaviours.

Sport & Exercise Psychology

An emerging subfield of psychology, sport & exercise psychology, is viewed as an attempt to understand, describe and explain the behaviour of exercisers and sportspersons in variety of settings with a view to help them enhance their performing ability in activity or sport event of their choice.

Fundamental psychology and applied subfields of psychology do not belong to two different genres. They are two sides of the same coin. No theories, laws and principles of science make sense unless their theoretical framework is very broad and sound, and they are capable of being applied to making things possibly better. Besides, the yardstick often used to categorize the basic and the applicative role of a principle or a theory is relative, not absolute. Theoretical principles and practices of psychology are two points on the same continuum.

Overview

Occupying a unique position as an academic discipline and an applied discipline in the fields of human interactions, psychology:

- deals with phenomena like perception, cognition, emotion, personality, behaviour, and interpersonal relationships;
- is a broad field of behavioural science that spans the social and natural science;
- also refers to issues related to daily life—e.g. family, education, and work—and the treatment of mental health problems;
- attempts to understand the role human behaviour plays in social dynamics while incorporating physiological and neurological processes into its conceptions of mental functioning;
- includes many sub-fields of study and application concerned with such areas as human development, education, sport, health, industry, law, and spirituality;
- describes and attempts to explain consciousness, behaviour, and social interaction; and
- has lately begun to examine the relationship between consciousness and the brain or nervous system.

SELECTED REFERENCES

Buskist, William & Gerbing, David W. *Psychology -- Boundaries and Frontiers*, Glenview, Ill: Scott Foreman/Little Brown Higher

Education, 1990

Crooks, Robert L. & Stein, Jean *Psychology - Science, Behaviour and Life*, New York: Holt, Rinehart and Winston, 1988

Desiderato, O., Howieson, D.B., & Jackson, J.H. *Investigating Behaviour - Principles of Psychology*, New York: Harper & Row. 1976

James, William, *The Principles of Psychology* (Vol. I), New York: Henry Holt & Co., 1890

Kamlesh, M.L. *Foundations of Physical Education*, New Delhi: Metropolitan, 2002

Magill, Richard A. *Motor-learning: Concepts and Applications* (4th Ed.), Dubuque, lowa: William C. Brown, 1993

McDougall, William *An Outline of Psychology*, Chapter-1, 1949

Melucci, Nancy J. *Psychology: The Easy Way*, New York: Barron, 2004

Munn, Norman.L, Fernald, L.Dodge, & Fernald, Peter S. *Introduction to Psychology*, New Delhi: Oxford & IBH, 1972

Plotnik, Rod *Introduction to Psychology*, (5th Ed.) Belmont; Brooks/Cole * Wardsworth, 1999

Restak, Richard M. *The Mind*, New York: Bantam Books, 1988

Ross, James S. *Ground Work of Educational Psychology*, London: George G, Harper, 1955

Williams, J.F. *Principles of Physical Education*, London: W.B. Saunders, 1964

Woodworth, R.S. *Dynamics of Behaviour*, New York: Henry Holt, 1984

Wolman, Benjamin N. *Contemporary Theories and Systems in Psychology*, Delhi: Freeman, 1979

Lexicon Universal Encyclopaedia *Psychology*: 593-595, 1986

Believe in the best, think your best, study your best, have a goal for your best; never be satisfied with less than your best, and in the long run things will turn out for the best. Always add up to the best.

- Henry Ford

CHAPTER - 2

PSYCHOLOGY IN ACTIVITY AND SPORT PERSPECTIVE

As instruments of character building, personality development and athletic excellence education, physical education and psychology make a perfect Triad. Any deficit in one makes the other two irrelevant, rather redundant. Often education is associated with classroom teaching and physical education with large-muscle activity on the fields of play or in the gymnasium; psychology assists the two to achieve their objectives. Both education and physical education aim at the optimal development of the child in body, mind and spirit, with the unflinching support of psychological principles underlying learning, motivation, intelligence, perception, cognitive, etc.

In the 21st century, physical education is not likely to be simply "...pushing and pulling .. ....running; jumping, ...falling and rolling and sweat", as Norman Steiner put it (Kamlesh,1988), but as a science of movement, a scientific art of teaching activity, and a potential field of research. The aim of education and that of physical education have little divergence. The two disciplines make a whole and share the same concerns and deal with almost similar issues. It is, therefore, important to briefly define the *field of knowledge* (education) and the *field of activity* (physical education) before proceeding to explain how psychology facilitates teaching-learning processes in both cases.

EDUCATION

Education is a very wide term which may mean many things to many people. It is naive to give it one single definition. Learning is basic to education, and it is a response to a demand to grow – to do something you could not before. In a restricted sense, it may mean a formal way of learning - *reading, writing* and *arithmetic* - as traditionally believed. In its broadest sense, education encompasses a vast array of abilities, attributes and skills, which we acquire during our life time, through formal and informal means and methods at home, at school, and in the wide the world. We may learn by self experience, inspiration, or by experimentation, but in formal educational process, there is some one to learn and there is some one to teach, i.e. a student and a teacher. Perhaps, it is much easier to receive than to give, for the receiver is single-mindedly concentrated on and concerned with receiving some thing new, something better in terms of behaviours or skills, but the giver has several considerations; for example, who is the learner – what age, sex, ability, experience etc., for what purpose and the context under which learning process proceeds; what strengths, constraints and limitations of his own and those of the learner are, etc. It hardly needs elaboration that learning, in any form, is far easier than teaching the other person who is not as good as you might be in perceptual, cognitive and motor domains, at least for the time being. You are the master of your mind (ability, skill, knowledge) and very well know what goes inside your mind, but you are at loss to know what goes in learner's mind. Synchronization between learning and teaching processes is always a matter of time. To define *teaching as the organization of learning* is an oversimplification of the term education.

Education without some vigorous muscular activity is no better than body without soul. By and large all educationists would cast their vote in favour of physical activity being part and parcel of school curricula for in the development of human personality it plays a very crucial role. Principles of psychology have uniform application in the processes of learning classroom lessons and acquiring athletic (motor) skills on the playing field.

PHYSICAL EDUCATION

Being an integral part of education, physical education is better known as movement or activity education, i.e. education through big muscle play activity such as sport, exercise, combative stunts, and dance, with a view to creating truly *physically educated individuals.* Characterized mainly by such basic activities such as running, jumping, pulling, pushing, falling, rolling, tumbling, throwing, kicking, hitting, stretching, swinging, and sweating, physical education is an important aspect of man's education in general. It is learning how to be aware of one's body and mind; how to discover the joy of moving and doing things; it is realizing one's potential through the medium of activity; and it is achieving perfection in body, mind and spirit. Divorcing physical education from education is not only naïve but dangerous too, for this would lead to negation of the integration of the human organism.

Through systematically organized exercise and activity programmes, physical education ensures for every participant at least a fairly good level of organic fitness, flowing health, emotional stability and physical wellbeing. It helps the child to grow optimally in body, mind and spirit and strengthen the apparatus of his intelligence – the brain, nerves and muscles – thus concretizing the age-old concept of *healthy mind in healthy body*. The quality of human growth, development, and productivity truly depend on the quality of physical activity people continue to do all through life. Importantly, skills of movement – motor skills, sport skills, work skills, professional skills, performance skills etc. – are acquired progressively through a well-organized effort, by following the basic principles and laws governing learning and growth processes in letter and spirit. It is in this sense that psychology plays a big role in physical education, as it does in general education.

From their earliest years at home and school children experience an overwhelming joy of participation and a sense of achievement through the medium of free play and organized physical activity, which contribute to the overall development of their personality, helping them prepare for an abundant, active and healthy life ahead. In final analysis, physical education is educating oneself physically, mentally, socially and emotionally through the medium of large muscle activity. For the ancient Greeks complete education consisted of *'aesthetics, ethics, mathematics and athletics'*.

Physical Activity and Exercise

Physical activity and exercise in particular are the essential processes of organized physical education. According to the US Department of Health and Health Services (1996), *"Physical activity" is a universal term defined as "bodily movement that is produced by the contraction of skeletal muscles and that substantially increases the amount of energy you expend"*. This covers a wide range of activities people perform in different contexts of life. Digging, tending plants, climbing, throwing, jumping, walking, running, bicycle or horseback riding, playing football or lawn tennis, rowing in a shell, or performing gymnastic stunts and thousands of activities human beings engage in as routines or in occasional contexts are comprehensively covered by the term activity. Multi-dimensional as it is, physical activity is the underlying principle of all sports, play, games, dance, and recreational activities, - some more organized than others.

Exercise is narrower in focus than activity and physical education as a whole. It is defined as *"one type of physical activity conducted with the intent of developing physical fitness"* (Corbin & Pangrazi, 1998). The term is typically used for callisthenics (free hand rhythmic exercises), resistance exercises, stretching exercises designed for flexibility, and aerobic exercises specifically designed to improve cardiovascular fitness. Exercise, in modern sense of the term, is more or less formal, systematic 'planned, structured and repetitive bodily movement done to improve or maintain one or more components of physical fitness'. Developmental effects of vigorous physical exercise, both aerobic and anaerobic, in terms of health, fitness and total wellbeing are well known.

Fitness

Fitness is the cumulative effect of nutrition, active lifestyle and regular exercise. Its definition and need might differ from individual to individual depending upon his/her age, vocation, state of health, and objective. Generally defined as *"a set of attributes that people have or achieve that relates to the ability to perform physical activity"*, fitness is an underlying principle for life, work and sport. Truly, fitness is more than being able to run a long distance or lift a lot of weight at the gym. Being fit is not defined only by what kind of activity you do, how long you do it, or at what level of intensity. While these are important measures of fitness, they only address single areas. Overall fitness is made up of such factors as cardiovascular endurance (aerobic endurance or aerobic fitness), strength, muscular endurance, body composition, and flexibility. Physical fitness is used in two meanings: ***general fitness*** (a state of health and wellbeing), and ***specific fitness*** (ability to perform specific aspects of sports or occupations). Some people also cite mental and emotional health as important part of overall fitness. Activity, fitness and health constitute a unified concept, and require a holistic approach in which body, mind and spirit are fully involved.

SPORT

Sport is the quintessence of physical education - the end-product of all activity effort. It is 'any physical activity which has the character of play and which involves a struggle with oneself or with others, or a confrontation with natural elements' (a UNESCO Committee). Both play and sport are household words. They have almost the same meaning and objective except that play is more relevant to infancy and childhood, and sport to youth span and adult life. Play is a formless "joyful spontaneous creative activity in which man finds fullest expression" (Ross, 1955), and "very important for the preservation, growth and development of the organism" (William McDougall). With a definite form, sport is 'a more formal, skillful and rule-governed highly organized competitive activity where the physical capabilities are the primary or sole determinant of the outcome, i.e. winning or losing. In the definition of sport are incorporated all forms of physical activity that snuggly contribute to physical fitness, mental wellbeing, and social development. These include play, recreation, organized or casual competitive sport, and indigenous sports or games. Sport is played for recreation as well as performance excellence, which has its focus on *prize, privilege, prestige* and *pride*' (Kamlesh, 2002). Since the dawn of civilization, sports and games have been pursued by countless generations of athletes and spectators for fun and for assessing strength, skill and stamina.

Physical exertion, skill, creativity, entertainment and competition are fundamental to sport. "Sports are institutionalized competitive activities that involve rigorous physical exertion or the use of relatively complex physical skills by participants motivated by personal enjoyment and external rewards", says Coakly (2001). Sport is about participation of people in it as actors and spectators, deriving thrill, excitement, fun and recreation. With Vandar-Zwaag (1998) sport is "a competitive physical activity, utilizing special equipment and facilities, with unique dimensions of time and space, in which the quest for records is of high significance". Loy (1968) listed the following basic characteristics of sport:

- Be play-like in nature (there is no true sports without the idea of fair play)
- Involve some element of competition and performed in a spirit of sportsmanship
- Be based on physical prowess
- Involve elements of skill, strategy, and chance
- Have an uncertain outcome

While the fast-track Olympic Movement has made sport intensely competitive, the induction of science and technology in preparation for and competing in it has changed the complexion of most sports altogether in terms of skill structure, fitness requirement and mental toughening. Sport as a competitive phenomenon places great premium on man's body, mind, emotions, learning process etc. It alters participant's behavioural dynamics, but sport as recreation carries with it greater educational value and is dealt with the educational psychology.

PSYCHOLOGY IN PHYSICAL EDUCATION AND SPORT

While activity is the bedrock of physical education, the gorgeous monument of sport stands on the foundation of physical education, which at the baseline is the function of school education. From an academic perspective physical education and sport make an art-science combine based on the fundamental concepts of movement, motion, activity, play, recreation, etc. In structure, they are activity-oriented behaviours; in function, they are instruments of good health and fitness; in objective, they are developmental to the hilt; in nature, they are joyful, recreating and relaxing; and in purpose, they are perfectly educational. Psychology is their guiding force.

The sub-discipline of psychology intimately connected with human behaviour on the playfield, in the gymnasium or in the swimming pool is activity or exercise psychology which derives its basic principles from educational or school psychology. It is thoroughly of applied nature. Physical education puts up a much wider perspective than does competitive sport. While activity is extensive and general, sport, today, is intensely performance-oriented and specific. There is no sport without physical education at the gross root level. Where physical education is milk, sport is butter churned out of it. It is difficult to think of butter when there is no milk. The physical educator and the athletic coach face the same problems of human behaviour and grapple with them almost in a similar fashion. Parameters of activity behaviour and those of sport behaviour have only a hairline distinction. It is no wisdom to put them in water-tight compartments. The application of psychological principles to understanding and conditioning behaviour in activity and sport is more a matter of degree than of kind. Psychology in physical education perspective focuses on general processes and procedures of learning, motivation, play, growth and development, etc; in sport perspective, its concerns become more intense and specific in consideration of the type of sport one plays and pursues what objectives beyond those of health and fitness. Psychological training, coping strategies, interventions, mental skills etc., have greater relevance in competitive sport than activity and recreational sport. Both in operational and psychological dimensions the sport-perspective is much more specific than is the activity perspective. However, the importance of psychology in the two cases is unequivocal, but for two different objectives. The psychological needs and problems of performing athletes are far more pointed, subtle, serious and complex than those of exercisers, fitness freaks and fun seekers. It is here we find sport behaviour to have been subjected to more extensive and vigorous research than activity behaviour.

Almost a century ago, psychology came to find an important place in teacher education curricula in physical education. It is no wonder that psychology entered education much before it did physical education. It was realized that educational processes could make no headway without the knowledge and application of the general principles of learning, motivation, cognition, etc., by the classroom subject teachers and physical educators. Broadly speaking, psychology in physical education addresses such important areas as growth and development, motor skill-acquisition, general innate tendencies, emotions, heredity and environment, individual differences, personality etc., with the objective to:

(1) understand the real springs of activity behaviour,
(2) guide behaviour into realizing one's potential through activity programmes,
(3) optimize benefits of physical activity in terms of growth and development, and
(4) ensure harmonious development of child's personality.

Psychology in physical education plays its role behind the curtain while psychology in top competitive sports has more explicit objective. In comparison to movement education at school, high profile sport requires more complex system of psychological management and intervention programmes for all kind of athletes.

In general teaching-learning context, psychology should be better understood as educational psychology rather than high sounding sport psychology intended to take care of highly complex behavioural issues and problems. Both physical education and sport fall on the same activity continuum except that the focus of one is on health, fitness and wellbeing, and that of other on performance leading to excellence.

EDUCATIONAL PSYCHOLOGY IN PHYSICAL EDUCATION

The need for *psychologizing* education was first stressed by a Swiss schoolmaster Pestallozi when education was undergoing tremendous change under the impact of Rousseau's powerful, rational and soul-stirring ideas almost two centuries ago. "...Pestallozi," says Ross (1955), "was first to emphasize the fact that mind of the pupil is the primary concern of the educator, and that the art of education must be based on an accurate knowledge of mental processes". These were the times when the structure and functions of mind were being studied using empirical methods and experimental techniques. From the philosophical writings, people knew quite a lot about the mind of the intellectual adult but very little about the mind of the impulsive child. Through his rational and experimental approach William James was instrumental in giving some concrete shape to educational psychology and finding a place for it in teacher education.

"Since the mid-nineteenth century psychology texts had become more and more 'scientific' and diverse in their content and titles. Separate branches of psychology were emerging including educational psychology, physiological psychology, studies of learning and memory, and clinical psychology" (Cratty, 1989). With the strengthening of teacher-training programme in the Western world, psychology became part and parcel of the curricula of teacher education. Significant ideas contributed by powerful psychologists like William James, Edward L. Thorndike, John Watson, B.F. Skinner and others enriched the content of educational psychology and made the application of its principles to the leaching-learning process a reality unknown to the contemporary world. Resultantly, teachers began to learn how to give better deal to the students with improved teaching methodology and behaviour management techniques. Today, educational psychology occupies an important place in education as well as in physical education.

In teacher education programme, physical education has more often than not followed the footprints of education. As a consequence relevant principles of educational psychology came to be incorporated in the physical educator's training programme. It is no wonder that in early development of teacher training curricula for physical educators, the trainees studied educational psychology with special reference to physical education, and not exercise and sport psychology, as is the fashion today. Stressing the need for psychology in pnysical education, Williams (1964) remarked:

> Physical education in its methods and materials should reflect modern psychology......This is true function of the teacher to use the native impulses of the young as a starting point for assimilation of knowledge, acquisition of skills and development of habits of the society into which youth comes.

Since then there has been no looking back for psychology as a curricular subject in physical education, developing its own modes of application of the principles of psychology and research in such areas as skill learning, teaching methodology, free play, motivational techniques, performance variables, behavioural control and change, cognitive processes, and so on. In activity scenario, psychology has continued to remain essentially educational in approach but in sport perspective, it has endeavoured to aim at "performance-enhancement of athletes at all levels of practice and competition" (Singer, 1984).

Psychology in physical education enables the teacher to act as a human engineer and become increasingly efficient in managing the human stuff and its behavioural problems in activity situations both on the field and in the classroom setting. At school, where students with varying backgrounds, social status and mental makeup are constantly seen influencing others and getting influenced by them, there are bound to be problems of behaviour, individual growth, social development, motivation, learning and adjustment. Psychology equips the teacher with tools and techniques that enable him to address these problems with increasing efficiency so that he can hit upon effective strategies to ensure harmonious development of child's personality and "social progress".

Content of Educational Psychology

Also known as ***academic psychology*** in some parts of the world, educational psychology benefits young prospective physical educators who train to take up teaching assignments at schools and colleges. With theoretical orientation, the content of educational psychology offers a small fraction of solution to practical problems teachers/physical educators encounter when discharging their duty at work place. Yet some content of academic psychology is directly adopted for use in the treatment and analysis of psychological states and describes how children behave in every day life – whether on the play field or outside it and in the classroom - and how their behaviour towards other children changes as they grow up.

Human behaviour is not always situation-specific. What happens in one situation, the impact is felt on other situations potentially. It would, therefore, be futile to talk in terms of specific content for psychology in physical education. However, by a general consensus, the content of educational psychology includes the following topics:

Individual Differences

The study of how and why individuals differ psychologically is an important area of understanding from educational viewpoint. This principally addresses two skills – intelligence and personality. Children of various age groups and of the two sexes differ greatly with one another in their capacities, abilities, capabilities, interests, aptitudes, level of intelligence, potential for growth and possibility of development, etc. This has serious implications for cognitive and motor skill teaching-learning process.

Social Psychology

The study of the psychology of social life, and in particular, how individuals behave in social situations is of immense value to teachers, physical educators and coaches. For example, how people behave in groups (athletic teams), how beliefs about people and events are formed, and how children become attracted towards one another etc., make significant reference points for curricular planning, construction and curricular transaction in education.

Developmental Psychology

The knowledge of the development of variety of skills and behaviours across the lifespan, i.e. various stages and growth and development, with particular emphasis on psychological and motor development during infancy and childhood, is of paramount importance to teachers. Developmental effects count a lot in sport talent identification.

Learning Theory

This is essentially the study of learning of information, how and when success is rewarded. Behaviourism has influenced the learning procedure and teaching methodology a great deal. It is imperative for the teachers to know how facilitative conditions can be created for learning things. The theories, laws, methods, factors and conditions of learning reflect the core of academic psychology.

Memory

Though closely related to learning, memory is always studied separately because of its peculiar nature and attributes. Its study occupies an important place in man's learning process. Examining various methods available for memorizing information, and the limits and limitations of these methods, is vital to psychology in education and physical education.

Biopsychology

The study of how mind controls working of the body and how physical functioning of the brain (and the rest of the body) is reflected in the mind's working forms the foundations of bio-educational psychology especially from the view-point of motor learning. Perception – its structure and dynamics – demonstrates further evidence of the close links between the brain and the rest of the body. In describing and explaining behaviour, biopsychology is of immense value to the teacher, physical educator and educational administrator.

Perception

The interpretation of environment through senses (or sensory data) constitutes perception, which is the gateway to information processing system in man. Great deal of research in the field of perception has concentrated on vision, although not exclusively. The value of perception lies in its strong emphasis on how our mental interpretation of sensory information manipulates our experience of 'reality'. In all learning, perception has a crucial role to play, hence its place in educational psychology.

Statistics, Measurement and Evaluation

Psychology also involves a lot of psychometric testing, measurement and evaluation pertaining to a variety of processes and procedures in learning, perception, attention, interest, personality, motivation, attitudes, aptitudes, and so on. Knowledge of statistics is necessary for teachers and physical educators to compare, judge, evaluate and monitor several psychological parameters. Psychology without statistics has a limited value.

Educational psychology is expanding at an incredible rate as it is assimilating new concepts and techniques of dealing with human behaviour in classroom, athletic and social settings. The induction of modern information technology and computer science, research in psychological aspects of education, physical education and sport has touched a new high in its methodological precision.

Lessons from School (Academic) Psychology

Psychology has been a great moving force in education. Following the footprints of education, physical education absorbed the wisdom of school (learning) psychology and built up the framework of its practices on a few fundamental truths about child's activity behaviour especially motor (and/or sport) skill-acquisition. These are best reflected in the psychological foundations of physical education.

- Child is a psycho-physical unity - a complete integration; there is no training of body or training of mind, it is educating the *whole* child. The involvement of the whole person in learning is well-established.
- *Readiness* of the individual to engage in some kind of movement is prerequisite to all learning - cognitive, affective and psychomotor.
- Motivation, satisfaction and practice together make for perfection in skill performance. Murphy (1947) says:

  Most learning springs from struggle. The motivated individual strives, blindly or intelligently, to find the means of satisfaction. As he strives, he discovers things and activities that bring him into contact with the source of satisfaction. These things and activities come to elicit, in their own right, part (or sometime all) of the responses made to the satisfier itself.
- Motor learning is *no* special kind of learning. It conforms in all essential respects to the same psychological principles which operate in all acquired reactions - physical, intellectual, emotions, social and inter-personal.
- Learning is dependent upon the attitude taken toward the activity, the set of the mind, and the motive behind

the act. Setting of right kind of motives is important, for only right motive promote right and enduring learning.

- Individual differences in motivation, social and physical factors and maturation determine many details relating to learning - its procedures, its effects, and over-learning of skills.
- Appropriate (suitable) methodology of teaching ensures satisfactory learning and adequate transfer-effect; however, unrelated skills cannot be expected to transfer.

Place of Psychology in Physical Education and Sport

In acquiring motor skills and perfecting fundamentals of games and sports, understanding people's motives for play, exercise and sport, explaining the impact of personality dynamics on athletic performance, decoding genetic and environmental influences on the growth and development, and in addressing a number of other issues like this, the knowledge of psychology is of immense value to teachers, physical educators and sport academics. Generalizations given below speak for place of psychology in activity and sport:

1. The knowledge of the principles of psychology enables physical education teachers and athletic coaches to *understand the real springs of activity behaviour* of the participants and enable them to match the right individual to the right sport or activity considering people's interests, aptitudes, personality traits and social attributes. Psychologically, it is important to fit in *round peg in round hole, and square peg in square hole.*
2. The aim of physical education is impossible to realize without adequate inputs from psychology. It needs no reminder that physical activity is only a facilitator of human growth and development provided all other factors – genetic potential, nutrition, learning environment etc. – do not fall short of requisite measure. Optimal benefits from activity programmes are derived only when enough psychological support is made available to both the participants and teachers.
3. Education and psychology are considered as monozygotic

twins. *Modification of behaviour* (education) is impossible without *study of behaviour* (psychology). Physical education is a perfect example of this principle. Play, exercise, sport, dance, etc., all require behaviour modification to occur in some way. Unless teachers know what it means to modify behaviour and how it can take place, it might as well be difficult for them succeed in their endeavours.

4. Psychology tells teachers/physical educators that every child is born with *some* unique potential, whether or not they are aware of it. Application of psychological principles facilitates understanding every child's potential and the extent to which it could be developed. In comparison to classroom subject teachers, physical educators are better equipped to provide opportunities to children to express their potential and develop their abilities in all kinds of activities.
5. In sport, the use of psychology goes beyond the academic objective; there it focuses on developing tough-minded individuals to face the tough competition with cool-headedness and utmost clarity of mind. The mansion of activity practices is built on the foundations of exercise and sport psychology.

SELECTED REFERENCES

Coakly, J.J. *Sport in society: Issues and controversies* (7th Ed.), St. Louis: Mosby. (p.20), 2001

Corbin, Charles, B. & Pangrazi, Robert B. *Encyclopaedia of Health: Physical Activity*, 1998

Cratty, Bryant J. *Psychology in Contemporary Sport* (3rd Edition), Englewood Cliffs; N.J. Prentice Hall, 1989

Loy, J.W. The nature of sport: A definitional effort, *Quest*: 10-1, 1968

Kamlesh, M.L. *Foundations of Physical Education*, New Delhi; Metropolitan, 2002.

Kamlesh, M.L. *Physical Education: Facts and Foundations*, Faridabad; P.B. publications, 1988.

Ross, James S. *Ground Work of Educational Psychology*, London; George G. Harper, 1955.

Singer, Robert N. What Sport Psychology can do for the athlete and coach? *Int. Jr. Sp. Psychol.* 15:52-61, 1984

Williams, J.F. *Principles of Physical Education*, Meerut: College book House, 2000.

Vandar-Zwaag, H.J. *Policy development in sports management* (2nd Ed.), West Port; C.T. Praege, 1998.

US Department of Health and Health Services, 1996.

"You need the game, you need the heart; you need the mind. Some guys have two of the three; some guys have a little bit of the three. In order to do it for six years, you need everything......"
- **Pete Sampras**, the US Tennis Star

CHAPTER - 3

SPORT PSYCHOLOGY

SCIENCE IN SPORT

Revival of the Olympic Games in 1896, heralded a new era of sport – an era of fierce competition – with consequential revolutionary changes in the approaches to athletic training. The age-old amateurish approach to training (rational thinking- based *trial-and-error* technique) was soon replaced by semi-professional approach (older athletes training the younger ones) and later professional approach (coaches training the athletes) during the first quarter of the 20th century. Up to this time, the two greatest assets for the disciplined athlete have been *genetic potential* and *a comprehensive training programme* to maximize his performance potential. The advancing surge of science brought several new sources of change and development of human potential. Sport too could not remain unaffected. The athletes and athletic trainers began to recognize and develop a new resource – the *sport science* - one that promises to revolutionize sport. Consequently, there began the ***Age of Scientific Approach*** to athletic training in the early 40s, and the athletic trainers began to selectively apply principles of science, especially those of physiology to begin with, in order to develop more ingenious techniques of training athletes with the sole objective of enhancing their performance potential. This effort paid rich dividends and by 1960's, the world of sport saw a host of sport sciences suddenly emerging and empowering athletes from several East European countries (especially those from erstwhile Soviet Union, German Democratic Republic, Czechoslovakia, Poland etc) to spring surprises in track & field, gymnastics, weight-lifting, swimming and other events at the Olympic Games, with "extensive as well as intensive sport science back-up" (Kamlesh, 2002). As time moved, the more enterprising coaches and smarter scientists in the areas of biomechanics, anthropometrics, physiology, psychology etc., join hands with the objective of developing more result-oriented training techniques, thereby facilitating identification, exploitation and manipulation of every single variable that could ensure success at athletic competitions. Though Baron Pierre de Coubertin – the Father of the Modern Olympic Games - was actually wary of using science to "build athletes" (Schrof et al, 1996), he wanted sport and sportspersons to be natural in their exploits, but the resistance did not last long. No one, in fact, could stop science from getting into the nerve-fibre of sport. Now sport has become all science in almost all its important aspects, e.g. training of athletes, management affairs, equipment manufacturing, developing of infrastructure, etc. Today, there is no sport without science being at the helm. Sport science is invariably a major feature of competition.

Due mainly to the intervention of science, the athletic records today seem to have *less* meaning than they had a few decades ago. Where as in the past a record may have stood for years, they are now crumbling and being re-written at an amazing speed. Dramatic change in athletic performance is generally attributed to the ever-increasing use of science and technology in the overall training process of athletes - from identification of athletic talent at a tender age, to grooming young athletes and grilling them into outstanding performers for years on end, and to giving them exposure in the progressively hard competitive situations in well-defined phases. At each of these watersheds, athletes are subjected to rigorous training regimens with due emphasis placed on innovative skill-acquisition, refined performance techniques, improved nutrition, top-notch sports-medicine backup (especially in injury prevention and treatment), maintaining optimal energy thresholds (through consistent physiological conditioning and hard weight-training), perfecting mental skills, etc.

Dichotomy of Sport Sciences

Sport science - an envelope term, embracing a cluster of disciplines, their derivatives and sub-disciplines, many of them having great practical import - uses the scientific principles from the mainstream biological and social sciences, and applies them to the sport and exercise environment in order to, for example, improve performance, reduce injury or increase motivation. It involves the systematic acquisition and objective evaluation of information about sport and those taking part in it as performers, trainers, and even as spectators. Sport science, therefore, includes any discipline (or branch of knowledge) that uses the scientific method and relies on observed information and experimentation, rather than biased judgment and vague impressions to explain and predict sports phenomena.

Over the decades, the universe of sport science has considerably expanded as more performance-related variables have been brought under the sceptre of scientific observation. At the same time it has also become clear that ***not*** all sciences are directly involved in the enhancement of human (athletic) performance process; some play more crucial role than others.

On the basis of their proximity to performance-enhancement objective, sports sciences are *dichotomized* into ***critical enhancement sports sciences*** and ***supportive sport sciences,*** as Rushall (1989) explained. Under the first category fall sport and exercise physiology, biomechanics and sport psychology. Performance-improvement is impossible to occur without their strong support. Listed under the category of supportive sport sciences are sports medicine (including physiotherapy and podiatry), sport nutrition, biochemistry, etc.

Rushall (1989) also points to a "pecking order" for sport sciences and their importance for training athletes. He says: "Performance improvements are mainly due to the application of principles of the enhancement sport science (physiology, bio-mechanics and sport psychology) .... In practical situations, it is difficult to determine whether improvements occur because of changed fitness levels (a physiological contribution) or improved behavioural/appraisal factors (a psychological contribution)". Physiology and bio-mechanics, though marked by measurability, objectivity and consistency, cannot penetrate the behavioural mechanism beyond certain limits. For instance, physiology develops the energy basis for performance but is limited and does not change its potential for effect after a relatively short period of time. The returns from bio-mechanics also diminish, if no innovative skills are introduced. With time, the ability to improve through mechanical efficiency also decreases. Psychology, although bogged by numerous methodological bottle-necks, has sky as the limit and *is the critical sport science for governing the level of performance that will occur.*

SPORT PSYCHOLOGY

Defining Sport Psychology

Supported by tremendous amount of research, sport psychology is now mature enough as an academic discipline to "stand alone as a scientific discipline". Competitive sport is a peculiar behaviour involving emotion, intense physical and mental struggle for supremacy, excellence, cooperation, achievement, and play. All these provide a rich area of experience to the participants and the spectators, and abundant opportunity for psychological research. People involved in sports attempt to master very difficult skills, often subjecting themselves to intense physical and mental stress as well as social pressure. The early focus of the psychologists studying sport behaviour had been on motor performance and motor skill acquisition. Soon it shifted to theories of social psychology. As sport psychology emerged as a prominent piece of athletic success, research began to be conducted in more crucial areas such as imagery training, hypnosis, relaxation training, motivation, socialization, conflict and competition, counseling, and coaching.

Today, sport psychology is recognized as the scientific study of people and their behaviours in sport contexts and the practical application of that knowledge. According to Richard Cox, "Sport psychology is a science in which principles of psychology are applied in sport setting, often (with a view) to enhance performance". Sport psychologists identify principles and guidelines that professionals can use to help adults and children participate in and benefit from sport and exercise activities in both team and individual sports. The two-fold aim of the sport psychologists is (a) to understand the effects of psychological factors on physical performance, and (b) to evaluate the effect of participation in sport activities on a person's psychological development, health and wellbeing.

A judicious mix of educational, social, developmental, experimental and, to some extent clinical psychology, sport psychology is legitimately a branch of sport science which trains its focus on the role of the mind in athletic performance and the application of the knowledge and skills gained from athletic performance to various other aspects of life and personal growth. Motivation, self-confidence, aggression, anxiety, team cohesion, etc. are of special interest to sport psychologists of the day. "Sport psychology", observe Browne and Mahoney (1984) "is the application of psychological principles to sport and physical activity at all levels of skill improvement". Continuing in the same strain, Singer (1986) viewed sport psychology as *"encompassing scholarly, educational and practical activities associated with understanding and influencing of selected behaviours of people involved in athletics, and exercise".*

As sport psychology became to be recognized as an academic field of study in 1970s, over the decades, its principles have begun to be applied to understanding and influencing behaviours in all kinds of activity - play, sport, recreation, and exercise - that have an impact on our performance. As a result this youngest of the sport sciences today is better known as ***sport and exercise psychology,*** rather than only sport psychology. Sport and exercise psychologists have expert knowledge and a research base in the psychology of sport and exercise and are familiar with other sport and exercise science disciplines (e.g. physiology, biomechanics), giving them an understanding of how sport and physical activity affect an individual's psychological health and well-being throughout their lifespan.

The major points of emphasis in a typical definition of sport and exercise psychology may be listed as under:

- Accepted as a critical performance-enhancement sport science, sport psychology is a multidimensional academic discipline.
- Resulting from research, experience and intellectual exercise, the principles and tents of sport psychology are scholarly.
- Activity (movement) teachers, physical educators, psychologists, practitioners and coaches potentially benefit from knowledge of sport psychology in influencing behaviour in different contexts.
- Sport psychology is a discipline of applied nature and practicability its marked characteristic.

Primary Roles for Contemporary Sport Psychologists

Keeping the objective of sport psychology in mind, Watson, an Australian sport psychologist expected his contemporary colleagues in sport psychology to fill three primarily roles:

(1) ***Player's self knowledge:*** As a contributor to performance-enhancement objective, a true sport psychologist must make sincere effort to enable a player to acquire a clear understanding of his or her psychological functioning, i.e. his or her mental strengths and weaknesses, to then be able to cope with the demands of social influences including competition, frustration of opposing players and teams, and the pursuit of achievement-oriented goals;

(2) ***Application***: It is now established beyond any shadow of doubt that the practical value of sport psychology lies in its applicability; therefore, the sport psychologist should be able to genuinely and intelligently apply the information acquired through observation and supported by psychological testing in the actual games situation. This means that as performance unfolds, the psychologist is able to act as a *support unit* in providing feedback to assist a player and coach to identify problem areas; and

(3) ***Research***: Finally, the area of research sport psychology is developing very fast. As such the primary role of a sport psychologist is to engage in some fruitful research in many areas so as to produce a body of knowledge which can explain and facilitate performance-enhancement in competitive situations. He must share his research findings with his colleagues especially coaches who should benefit the most from this research.

Besides the above, sport psychologists are also expected to (a) *teach and explain* the principles of educational psychology to the students and faculty at the institutes of physical education and sports, and (b) *engage in consultation process* and extend their valuable advice to the coaches and athletes regarding performance-enhancement skills. Some exercise and sport psychologists have also begun to work in the fitness industry designing programmes that maximise participation and promote psychological wellbeing.

Broad Areas of Study of Sport Psychology

Considering sport psychology to be "an applied psychology in the same way military and industrial psychology are", Singer (1981) pointed out that "it encompasses various branches of psychology as they are related to our ability to understand athletic performance, how to make it better, and how to influence favourable psychological outcomes from experiences in sport and exercise programs". In many countries the focus and practice of sport psychology is with elite athletes; *how to help make the best even better.* Being a systematic scholarly study of human thought, emotion, and behaviour in sport contexts, sport psychology consists of four main areas. First, the *relationship between personality and sport participation* is an extremely important area of study with the contemporary psychologists. Over the decades, the approach to the study of personality in exercise and sport context has undergone tremendous change with more sport-specific psychological tools and tests appearing on the scene. Research in personality is becoming more focused on performance variables operative at all age and competition levels. Second, the largest area of inquiry in sport psychology is attempting to understand *motivation* as the complex process that influences individuals to begin an activity and pursue it with vigour and persistence. Included in the broad category of motivation would be self-perceptions such as self-confidence, self-esteem, and stress that influence motivational behaviour in exercise and sport. Third, *interpersonal and group processes* that influence individuals' behaviours in sport such as the presence of spectators, group membership, and leadership, are crucially important areas of study in sport psychology. Included in this area are aggression and gender socialization, which are behaviours or characteristics that result from interpersonal social processes. Fourth, the area of mental training or *psychological-skills training* encompasses the use of intervention techniques to learn cognitive skills and behavioural strategies that can enhance sport performance and personal development. It refers to consistent practice of mental or psychological skills. Coaches and athletes know that physical skills need to be regularly practiced to become better. Similar to physical skills, psychological skills such as maintaining concentration and regulating arousal levels also need to be practiced. With the increasing emphasis on performance-enhancement and ascending competitive stress, it has now become all the more important that appropriate sport-specific psychological skills training programmes be wisely planned, as well as intelligently implemented and supervised by duly trained sport psychologists at all level of practice and competition for all kinds of athletes right from the beginning.

Summing up the issue and considering need of the hour, Singer (1993) felt that using more refined techniques of understanding and influencing athlete behaviour, sport psychology should endeavour to precisely focus on such important themes as exercise and health psychology for personal well-being, counselling and clinical approaches to help individuals to over-come personal problems and maladaptive behaviour, identifying processing mechanisms and conditions leading to the acquisition and maintenance of skill, performance enhancement techniques to contribute to performance potential, group situations leading to productivity, psychometrics to develop and administer tests for specific purposes, youth sport programs and the enrichment of experiences, and so on.

Typology (Subdivisions) of Sport Psychology

Over the decades, sport psychology has grown from strength to strength assimilating significant ideas from such diverse fields of human interaction as education, sport, physical activity, motor learning, play, exercise, research, psychology, etc., and in order to put up a distinct identity of its own as well as to create a niche for itself in the academe, it has sought to absorb philosopher's uncanny wisdom, scientist's astute objectivity, coach's keen training sense, physical educator's activity experience, and psychologist's art of mind exploring.

Looking at the expanding canvas of the sport psychologist's objectives and the diverse nature of the activities he is supposed to undertake in different contexts almost every where in the world, Cratty (1989) suggested three more or less categorical subdivisions for sport psychology, viz. educational sport psychology, experimental sport psychology, and clinical sport psychology.

Educational Sport Psychology covers learning, acquisition of motor and athletic skills, motivation, teaching-coaching techniques, teacher education and training, general theories of play, growth and development, developmental issues etc. Principles of psychology applied to play and physical activity at school constitutes the content of psychology of physical education. When these principles accomplish performance-enhancement in areas of fitness, health and competitive sport, the subdivision of psychology is better known as sport and exercise psychology. Educational sport psychology is highly relevant to sport activities in infancy and childhood and until the age of adolescence when inspired (motivated) children opt for competitive sport more seriously. The greatest consumers of educational sport psychology are movement teachers, physical educators and sports coaches who need to be informed and *educated* about human mind and behaviour in activity and sport contexts enabling them to address children's problems of learning, motivation, health and wellbeing.

Experimental Sport Psychology trains its research focus generally on such crucial areas of concern as human performance in athletic setting, psychomotor functions, psychological interventions, competitive behaviour and so on using laboratory techniques and field observations under controlled and natural conditions. Experimental sport psychologists are capable of coming to grips with a variety of problems relating to both tangible and intangible variables influencing human performance. They attempt to generate a fund of newest knowledge to be used to strengthen the foundations of sport psychology as an academic discipline and field of research so to facilitate the athletes, trainers and coaches improve their practices. Research, perhaps, is the most difficult aspect of sport psychology because the human mind and behaviour are not concrete materials to be experimented with as it happens in physical sciences. Investigating, understanding and influencing human behaviour under controlled (laboratory) conditions puts great premium on researchers' effort and energy due fluidity of human mind and nature of sport activity. Yet some useful guidelines are being derived from experimental endeavours in the applied aspect of sport psychology especially in motor learning.

Clinical Sport Psychology deals with the hidden springs/ motives of behaviour, meta-cognition (*thinking about thought* or *quality of thought*) and athletes' dream content, abnormalities in professional sport behaviour, counselling and guidance of athletes on private and personal matters, and the like. Using intervention strategies and inner mental training techniques (such as meditation, hypnosis, behavioural modification etc), the clinical sport psychologists, who are required to be essentially licensed, make athletes self-aware and teach them how to keep their *cool* and remain *relaxed* under the highly charged and emotionally disturbing situations during intense competition. They primarily record their observations, rather than engage in any kind of experimental research; teaching psychology is out of their purview.

Applied sport and exercise psychology has developed as an exclusively specialized branch of sport psychology, promoting research and examining professional issues in the areas of health psychology, intervention/performance enhancement, and social psychology of sports. It involves extending theory and research into the field to educate coaches, athletes, parents, exercisers, fitness professionals, and athletic trainers about the psychological aspects of their sport or activity. A primary goal of professionals in applied sport and exercise psychology is to facilitate optimal involvement, performance, and enjoyment in sport and exercise. The practice of applied sport and exercise psychology usually involves a combination of individual and group consulting or counselling depending on the style of the professional conducting the intervention and the needs of the client. AASP Certified Consultants and specially trained licensed psychologists are typically the most competent practitioners in applied sport and exercise psychology.

How and who does Sport Psychology help?

These days, sport has become extremely demanding in terms of skill, fitness and mental conditioning. While there has long been vast attention given to the physical aspect of performance, and what can be done to enhance it, only recently has the importance of the "mind game" been considered. Traditionally, athletes, individuals and teams spend thousands of hours perfecting their performance by putting in harder and still harder physical effort but many often neglect their mental skills and fitness. As sport psychology has emerged as a prominent piece of success in sport at all levels of performance, most athletes, coaches, trainers and other involved in sports would have seen the positive impact of psychological preparation or training on athlete's performance. Dick Frank, the former coach to Great Britain track & field team, says: 'It is the mental power that separates the exceptional from the very good...... there will be nothing to choose between them talent for talent, training for training. What separates them is what goes on behind the eyes.' Development of right mental skills is sure to enhance an athlete's physical and strategic skills and can make that all important difference between winning and participating in sport for the sake of it.

With more secrets of athletic training coming to limelight, athletes and coaches must know the worth of what top athlete Sally Gunnell said: 'Although you can train your body physically by sheer persistence, it's much harder to train your mind....all this visualisation did not come to me in a flash, I had to work at it, and learn how to use it.' Psychological part of athletic training is an intricate process, perhaps more intricate than the physical training part, and is closely connected with skill training and fitness-enhancement programmes. It constitutes of a variety of practical tasks such as clinical intervention, coping strategies, mental skills like imagining, concentrating, focusing etc., team-interaction and cohesion, which play a decisive role in both performance-enhancement and success at the competition. Modern competitive sport without psychological inputs is a headless horseman who runs in various directions purposelessly without accomplishing anything worth the name.

Psychology, as *the scientific study of mental processes and behavior* (Melucci, 2004), attempts to explode uncanny myths surrounding athletes, athletic behaviour, and training techniques. One of the goals of applied sport psychology is to investigate human performance (Schilling, 1992), to stabilize and to enhance sport performance (Seiler, 1992) by striking a balance between the physical and mental dimensions of performance. Sven Göran-Eriksson (2001) believes: 'So little is required to be successful in sport. It's certainly mostly a matter of psychology and in the end it's that psychological difference that decides whether you win or lose'.

Most athletes face a variety of problems such as inconsistent performance, worry about performance, performing below ability, making mental mistakes, difficulty in remaining concentrated, coping through injury, managing personal or team loss, transitioning out of competitive sports, balancing multiple roles, balancing multiple roles, and many more depending upon the context and situation during practice and competition. Sport psychology is effective across all sport-based activities and roles (players, coaches, trainers, referees, umpires, organizers, etc). Some areas where sport psychology plays a decisive role in overcoming these problems and enhancing athletes' performance include the following;

- Coping with competitive stress and performing under pressure
- Maintaining focus, concentration and attention
- Motivation
- Goal-setting
- Controlling and effective use of aggression
- Managing anxiety
- Team cohesion and dynamics
- Burnout
- Ability to get back into the field after injury

A Brief History of Sport Psychology

Sport psychology had a very humble beginning. History of sport psychology presents "a more mudded picture" (Singer, 1986). Those who inadvertently contributed to its development never intended to shape it as a sport science.

It was not until 1920 that the world's first sport psychology laboratory was founded by Carl Diem at the Deutsche Sporthochschule in Berlin Germany. Five years later, in 1925, A.Z. Puni opened a sport psychology laboratory at the Institute of Physical Culture in Leningrad. That same year, Coleman Robert Griffith of the University of Illinois established the first sport psychology laboratory in North America. He was interested in the effects on athletic performance of factors such as reaction time, mental awareness, muscular tension and relaxation, and personality. Regarded as "a prophet without disciples", Griffith established the first ever sport psychology laboratory at the University of Illinois; he wrote *The Psychology of Coaching* (1926) and *The Psychology of Athletics* (1928) containing information still very useful to coaches and athletes alike. His efforts went unnoticed and no one followed his footprints. At the University of Leipzig, Otto Klemm wrote several texts on the psychology of sport and physical activity including *The Twelve Principles in the Psychology of Physical Exercise* (1931) based on ten years of experimentation within a theoretical framework dominated by Gestalt learning theory. In 1942, scholars at the National Institute of Wushu, China (Wu Wengzhong & Tio Zhongho) wrote their first ever book, *The Psychology of Physical Education*. John Lawther's book - *The Psychology of Coaching* (1951) - signalled the separation between motor psychology (studies in motor learning) and sport psychology.

The following landmarks in the development of sport psychology as an area of academic exercise and research are worthy of note:

- By 1950s *Research Quarterly* (for Exercise and Sport) was flooded with articles dealing specifically with the psychology of athletics.
- Sport psychology began to take shape in German Democratic Republic (East Germany) in 1961 and that year the Institute for Sport Psychology was founded there under Dr. Paul Kunath who directed more than fifty theses dealing with various psychological parameters of sport there.
- In 1965, the International Society of Sport Psychology (ISSP) was formed by scientists from across Europe and in the same year the ***First International Congress of Sport Psychology*** was organized at Rome, with mostly physical educators from over sixteen countries a. participants. The presentations made there included essays heavily laden

with Freudian and Neo-Freudian influences, discourses in motor learning and motor performance, and both theoretical and practical data-based discourses focusing on development of superior athleticism. Representatives from Eastern Europe delivered papers particularly on *superior athleticism*.

- During 70s and 80s numerous scholarly texts from eminent sport psychologists appeared in the sport academics, generating tremendous global interest in sport psychology and facilitating formation of national societies of sport psychology in many countries. Several texts on motor learning and sport psychology authored by Bryant Jackson Cratty provided sport psychology with much wider publicity and gave it a firm foothold in the sport academia.
- From an applied-professional perspective, clinical psychologists Bruce Ogilvie and Thomas Tutko made sport psychology visible to their contemporary times. Their volume *Problem athletes and How to Handle them*, generated immense interest in the psychological aspects of competitors.
- While Cratty (1989) referred to three sub-divisions of sport psychology viz. educational sport psychology, experimental sport psychology, and clinical sport psychology, in the United States came up the *American Association for the Applied Sport Psychology* with focus on both theoretical and practical problems in the field, thereby expanding the horizons of sport psychology. This development triggered more interest in conducting research in sport psychology in setting outside laboratory and focused more directly on applied psychology in both the health field and sport contexts.
- In the meanwhile came up expanded version of sport psychology is ***Sport and Exercise Psychology***, which "has its roots in both psychology and sport science, it is somewhat unique science for it has the common intent to contribute to the understanding and maximizing of human performance and achievement, for example, to help an athlete be the best that he or she can be. The unique contribution is especially valued in the high-level sport, where the pressure to win is incredibly great", as Singer (1996), put it.

- Conceptualization of sport coaching as ***Instructional Sport Psychology*** - a combination of motor skill learning and sports pedagogy - is a recent phenomenon with the content in it amenable to empirical evaluation (Sherman et al, 1997).
- Further boost to sport psychology has come from the publication of the following important journals of sport psychology:
    - International Journal of Sport Psychology (1970)
    - Journal of Psychology of Sport and Exercise (1979)
    - The Sport Psychologist (1988)
    - Journal of Applied Sport Psychology (1989)
- The monumental ***Handbook of Research on Sport Psychology*** (1993) - the first of its kind - published by McMillan on behalf of the International Society of Sport Psychology is a yet another significant landmark in the development of sport psychology as an academic discipline and potential area of research.
- First authored by Salmela (1981, 1992), ***The World Sport Psychology Source Book*** (Lidor, Morris, Bardaxoglou & Becker, 2001) is a beacon light on the development of sport psychology across continents. It is a record book of the credentials of eminent sport psychologists in the world whose number has increased manifold since the First International Congress of Sport Psychology in 1965.

SPORT PSYCHOLOGY IN INDIA

Research and Publications in Sport Psychology

To begin with, global developments in sport sciences in general and sport psychology in particular generated a great deal of interest in India for this emerging discipline both as an academic discipline and a potential area of research. The declining standards of performance of the Indian sportspersons at the international level well-practiced sports like hockey, football, volleyball etc., further 'generated a great deal of concern and hastened the acceptance of sport psychology as one area to aid the performance of athletes' (Kamlesh & Mohan, 1987).

Scholars' interest in sport psychology research surfaced during 1970s primarily at the master of physical education degree level and grew further with a few doctoral studies. Most studies were either descriptive (analytical and/or comparative surveys) or correlational in nature, and conducted under severe constraints of literature scarcity, suitable instruments, and behavioural research methodology. Nevertheless, these humble efforts paved the way for bigger leaps. These studies, according to Kamlesh (1990) could be categorized as:

- *studies relating to personality* centered on athletic and non-athletic groups of junior, youth, senior and elite levels;
- *comparative studies relating to participants versus non-participants* in physical activity and exercise programmes at school, college and university levels;
- *correlation studies* involving selected psychological variables along with anthropometric, physiological and biomechanical parameters;
- studies in *cognitive behaviour;*
- studies in *motivation, interest, aptitude, intelligence* etc.; and
- *experimental studies* in reaction time, cognitive behaviour, motivation etc.

Creditably some studies conducted by sport psychology scholars, mostly physical educators could measure up to international standards and were well reported in national and international journals though flawed on account of design, instrumentation, data treatment and language. The research lacked professional approach; it was amateurish and non-directional. By and large, the research effort in India has been individualistic, with personal excellence as the major objective. There was no thrust on creating a strong theoretical base for sport psychology and establishing a behavioural data bank on various categories of athletes across sports so important for standard research. Prolific contributors to research in sport psychology in India have been M.L. Kamlesh, H.A. Khan, G.P. Thakur, Jitendra Mohan, Rajinder Singh, Agyajit Singh, (late) Sultan Akhtar, Jayahree Acharaya, Barid Bhattacharya, Anand Kumar, Avinash Sidhu, Reena Kaul, Jolley Roy, Anuradha Solanki, Sanjeev Sahni, and others.

Publication of ***sport psychology literature*** in India has been less prolific as compared to other countries. Kamlesh's *Psychology in Physical Education and Sports*-1983 (running in 5th edition) along with its *National Award-Winning* Hindi version (*Kreeda Manovigyan,* 1984, 1998) can claim to be the first text book of (educational) sport psychology for university courses of physical education and sports. Other publications that made sport psychology spread far and wide in country include *Athletic Personality: A Psychological Probe* (M.L. Kamlesh, 1990),

Sport Psychology (Sukumar Bose & Nrisingha K. Bhattacharya, 1988), *Psychology in Sport* (G.S. Sandhu, 1992), *Sport Psychology* (Agyajit Singh, 1992), *Sports Psychology* (P.M. Alegaonkar, 1997), *Sports Excellence: A Psychological Pursuit* (G.S. Sandhu & N.S. Mann, 2000), *Handbook of Sports Psychology* (Sanjiv P. Sahni, 2001), *Education Sport Psychology* (2006) and its Hindi rendering – *Shaikshik Kreeda Manovigyan* (M.L. Kamlesh, 2007). Besides this, several edited anthologies of selected papers presented by research scholars at the national conferences of sport psychology have helped disseminate knowledge of sport psychology and stimulate interest in research. Precisely, these publications include *Psychological Analysis of Sports Performance* (N.N. Mall & Jitendra Mohan, 1986), *Psychology and Sports Excellence* (L.A. Thakkar, Jitendra Mohan & M.L. Kamlesh, 1989), *Horizons in Sport Psychology* (M.L. Kamlesh & Jayashree Acharya, 1993), *Modern Trends in Sports Psychology* (B. Somalingam & M.L. Kamlesh, 1998), *Sport Psychology in Pursuit of Excellence* (M.L. Kamlesh & Jayashree Acharya, 1999), *Readings in Sport Psychology* (Jitendra Mohan & Meena Sehgal, 2005).

Team Interaction and International Exposure

The sport psychologists who, at one time or the other, have been associated with the training of national athletes across sports on part time basis included H.A. Khan (hockey, boxing, weight lifting, golf), Rajinder Singh (judo), M.L. Kamlesh (archery), Avinash Sidhu (women's field hockey), Jayashree Acharya (badminton, track & field), and others. H.A. Khan, Manoranjini Khan, Sanjiv Sahni, Jolley Roy, Reena Kaul, Anuradha Solanky, along with a few others, provided fulltime psychological backup to the national athletes, besides teaching sport psychology at the Netaji Subhas National Institute of Sports, Patiala and its regional centres.

The prominent Indian sports psychologists who have had the opportunity of representing the country at various International Congresses, Pre-Olympic Sport Science Congresses, Regional Congresses (Asian-South Pacific Association of Sport Psychology) over the years are G.P. Thakur, M.L. Kamlesh, H.A. Khan, Manoranjini Khan, Jitendra Mohan, P.M. Alegaonkar, Anand Kumar Srivastava, Jayashree Acharya, Sanjeev Sahni, Anuradha Solanky, Jolley Roy, Reena Roy, Avinash Sidhu, and others.

With channels of research communication as the *NIS Scientific Journal* (Netaji Subhas National Institute of Sports, Patiala), *Journal of*

Physical Education and Sports Sciences (LNCPE, Gwalior), *Research Biannual for Movement* (HVP Mandal, Amravati), *Indian Journal of Sport Science and Physical Education* (Department of Biology, Punjabi University, Patiala) etc., sport psychology is being well recognized as a potential area of research and academic activity.

Sports Psychology Association of India

In the mid-70s some enthusiastic physical educators and psychologists founded the *Indian Association of Sports Psychology* during a national seminar at Hyderabad. The society organized a national meeting and also published the first issue of the *Journal of Sports Psychology* but unknown reasons showed no further progress.

On 23rd February, 1985 during the first national conference of the embryonic Indian Association of Sports Scientists and Physical Educationists, a new body by the name of ***Sports Psychology Association of India*** was brought into existence by the efforts of M.L. Kamlesh, Avinash Sidhu, Rajinder Singh, Agyajit Singh, H.A. Khan, and others under the patronage of Dr. N.N. Mall, the then Dean, LNCPE, Gwalior. The first executive body of the Association was headed by Dr. Jitendra Mohan as President and M.L. Kamlesh as the Secretary General. The major objectives of the society were: (a) to promote advancement of sports psychology as an area of research, application and academics; (b) to facilitate communication among members and arrange scientific meetings and conferences; and (c) to make it possible to gather and communicate to the members and selected institutions/organizations latest information on the subject, and related concerns. Starting with a few members in the beginning, today the SPAI has cadre of more than 500 members from such diverse fields as physical education, sports, coaching, medicine, psychology, education, etc.

During the period of its existence, the SPAI has organized annual national conferences almost uninterruptedly and made possible the visit of the international stalwarts of sport psychology like Robert N. Singer, B.J. Cratty, Gerd Conzag, Dr. Hans Schellenberger, Peter T. Clarke, Mike Hughes, Keith Davids, and others over a period of time. The SPAI has facilitated the formation of the Asian South-Pacific Society of Sport Psychology and also hosted its meetings in India. In December, 2009, an International Conference of Sport Psychology was organized by the Laxmibai National University of Physical Education, Gwalior under the auspices of the Sport Psychology Association of India.

SELECETED REFERENCES

Browne, Margaret A. & Mahoney, Michael J. Sport Psychology. *Am. Rev. Psychol.* 35:605-625, 1984

Cratty, Bryant J. *Psychology in Contemporary Sport* (3rd Edition), Englewood Cliffs; N.J. Prentice Hall, 1989

Kamlesh, M.L. Sport Psychology in India. In Ronnie Lidor. Tony Morris, Nicole Bardaxoglou & Benno Beckor, Jr. (Eds.) *The World Sport Psychology Source Book* (2nd edition). International Society of Sport Psychology, 50-55, 2001

Kamlesh, M.L. *Foundations of Physical Education*, New Delhi; Metropolitan, 2002

Kamlesh, M.L. A review of research studies in sports psychology in India up to 1986. In L.A. Thakkar, Jitendra Mohan, and M.L. Kamlesh (Eds.) *Psychology and Sports Excellence.* Ahemdabad; Gujrat University , 227-256, 1990

Kamlesh, M.L. & Mohan, Jitendra The development of sport psychological research in India. *The Sport Psychologist,* 1, 257-261, 1987

Melucci, Nancy J. *Psychology: The Easy Way.* New York: Barron, 2004

Rushall, Brent S. Sport psychology: the key to sporting excellence. *Int. Jr. Sport Psycho;* 2:165-190, 1989.

Schrof, J.M. et al *The winning edge.* U.S. News & World Sport. 121 : 38-49, 1996.

Schilling, Guido Sport Psychology; *Sport Science Review,* 2, 29-45, 1992.

Seiler R. Performance enhancement - a psychological approach. In G Schilling (Ed.) Sport Psychology; *Sport Science Review,* 2, 29-45, 1992

Singer, Robert N. Future of sport and exercise psychology. In Judy L. Van Raalte & Britton W. Brewer (Eds); *Exploring Sport and Exercise Psychology,* Washington; American Psychological Association, 451-468, 1996

Singer, Robert N. Sport psychology: An Integrated Approach, *Proceeding of VIII World Congress of Sport Psychology;* Lisbon 131-146, 1993

Singer, Robert. N. Current perspectives on motor learning and sport psychology, In L. Unestahl (Ed.) *Sport Psychology in Theory and Practice;.* Orebro, Sweden, Veja, 1986

Singer, Robert N. Sport Psychology: Waves of the Future. *The Physician and Sports Medicine;* 9, 153-156, 1981

The mind which the psychologist studies, is the mind of distinct individuals inhabiting definite portions of a real space and of a real time. With any other sort of mind, absolute Intelligence, Mind unattached to a particular body, or Mind not subject to the course of time, the psychologist as such has nothing to do. - **William James**

CHAPTER - 4

METHODS OF (SPORT) PSYCHOLOGY

Human behaviour is a Gordian knot to detangle. Philosophers and scientists employ variety of methods and techniques to know, understand, analyze and explain behaviour, yet, in several ways it continues to be a mystery. Modern science and technology are a big help to the psychologists today to investigate human behaviour more scientifically and systematically than psychologists of earlier generation could possibly do. Discarding the rational approach, which is now considered primitive, scientists make a factual analysis of behaviour by taking due cognizance of all genetic and environmental factors that behaviour and direct it in different situations.

The behaviour canvas is very vast and multi-coloured, depicting behaviour in its various aspects - genetic, biological, mental, emotional and social. This makes the methods, means and techniques used by psychologists to unravel the mysteries of behaviour to be diverse - some subjective, some objective, some direct, some indirect, some scientific and some rational. Application of a particular method to understand the particular kind of behaviour in a particular context greatly depends on subjects' age and sex as well as the situation, objective, type of behaviour etc. Obviously, no single method or technique is good-enough to unravel secrets of behaviour in totality. Each method has its relative merits and demerits. Therefore, with a firm belief in a holistic approach and leaving nothing to chance, psychologists today make use of more than one method to understand behaviour both in a particular context and in totality.

COMMONLY USED METHODS OF PSYCHOLOGY

Explained below are some important methods, sometime also referred to as techniques, used by psychologists to investigate behaviour in various aspects of life and human interaction – growth, development, education, business, industry, work place, sport, etc.

Observation

Ordinarily observation may be simply noticing or perceiving something but in scientific nuance, it is 'an act of recognizing and noting a fact or an occurrence often involving measurement with instrument'. It refers to the accurate watching and noting of phenomena as they occur with regard to cause and effect of mutual relations without intervening in them. Today, psychologists observe behaviour scientifically, sometime using certain instruments, rather than causally having a bird's eye-view of it – a procedure which lacks pointed attention and is largely unreliable. They observe activities and movements including body language, facial expressions, gestures, eccentricities, attitudes etc., of an individual in natural situations without disturbing him. From this they infer, estimate and records facts about his or her thinking, cognition, motivation, attitude, aptitude, emotional reactivity, etc.

Besides in science and psychology, observation is an extremely important activity in education, management, sport and social life. Using observation as a handy tool, decision makers in different walks of life often engage in observation for different reasons. For instance, parents observe their kids at home, teachers observe students in the classroom, physical educators observe participants in activity classes, coaches and trainers observe athletes practicing and competing on the track, in the swimming pool and/or in the gymnasium, managers (supervisors) observe workers at the work place, and so on – objective in each case being specific. The basic premise here is that a person is in his real self when he is not conscious of being observed. Behaviours such as grinning, grunting, fist clinching, growling, howling, dry lips, shivering, shuddering etc., generally betray people's inner states of mind. Observation is considered a very effective instrument of behaviour investigation of young children, mentally disturbed individuals and introverted individuals. Sustained and repeated observation is a good device for making accurate and credible generalization about behaviour in any situation. Considered natural, flexible and economical, the observational method is quite useful in studying developmental characteristics, habits, aptitudes, interests and personality characteristics of people especially children.

Despite its merits, observation has certain *limitations*. First, the observer has to wait for a particular behavioural situation to occur. Efficacy of observation for longitudinal and cross-sectional behavioural studies is least questionable. Short-term observation is often baffling in behavioural analysis. Second, in order for the results of observation to be more reliable either the observational process is repeated over time or more than one observer are engaged to do observation simultaneously. Third, minute observation of certain behaviours as facial expressions in a dance sequence is not possible without keen and intelligent common sense. Similarly, reaction time cannot be recorded without RT apparatus, nor can 100m dash positions be decided without photo-finish camera at a world/Olympic meet. Fourth, a great deal of observational data either from the evaluation of an athlete's playing ability in a game or a dancer's performance, are qualitative. They are difficult to quantify and subjected to a statistical computation, thereby making the conclusions drawn from observational analysis comparatively less objective and least liable to generalize. Fifth, observer's advertent or inadvertent personal biases, for instance, his existing frame of mind or mood-state, often contaminate observational data. An already angry or prejudiced coach makes different observations than if he were happy or unprejudiced. Sixth, observation is known for its skin-deepness for the observer perceives and records external behaviour. What goes on in the subject's mind during observation is neither known nor monitored. Further, people behave differently when they sense they are being observed. They follow socially acceptable mores rather then revealing what actually they are wont to do, in other words, *faking good*. Seventh, it is difficult to establish cause-and-effect relationship on the basis of observation alone when two different behaviours are observed simultaneously for example, athletic achievement and motivation. The observer cannot jump to the conclusion whether high achievement in sport is due to high achievement motive or vice-versa. Finally, due to very broad and varied spectrum of behaviour, surveillance of all aspects of behaviour simultaneously is impossible unless too many expert observers are employed.

In sport and physical activity, observation facilitates vital decisions on player's status, selection, rejection, rank, discipline, conduct, suitability for awards, rewards etc. Human power of observation and judgement in such situations are considered far superior to objective data obtained through testing and measurement. In competitive diving, gymnastics, dance and rhythmic activities observation is the sole criterion of judgement.

However, it is important that while carrying out covert observation on the social, professional and family lives of people, observers (psychologists) must never overlook the ethical guidelines.

Introspection

Introspection, meaning *examination or observation of one's own mental and emotional processes*, is a highly subjective method, but rarely considered scientific. According to William James, it is *looking into our own minds and reporting what we there discover*, and it 'is what we have to rely on first and foremost and always'. Unlike animals human beings are blessed with the power to *look within*, i.e. to investigate their own mind. Introspection is a kind of reflection on an individual's own thought-processes, thought content and experiences stored in the memory. It is well established that problem-situations invariably leave a lot of ineffaceble impression on our mind, often making us pass through a variety of affective states (psycho-physiological experiences), setting us think hard and reason out things or the causes and effects to ourselves. During introspection, our perception turns inwards and we begin to probe the situation from a variety of angles often through the mind's eye. It matters little whether the experience under focus is predominantly physical, physiological, emotional, intellectual or spiritual.

Introspection is not necessarily carried out after experience; it may be during the experience itself. In order to go into the genesis of people's behavioural problems and grapple with them, the counselling psychologists help the subjects in one-to-one dialogue to delve into the influencing feelings, circumstances, factors and conditions and communicate as freely as possible. Variety of life problems can possibly be solved without much difficulty when people learn to systematically introspect themselves in a state of serenity.

Introspection also has certain ***limitations***. First, young children and mentally challenged individuals lack the ability to introspect themselves. Second, even normal people also find it difficult to introspect themselves with dead accuracy. Their attention fluctuates while concentrating on the ongoing experience i.e. the existing feeling. Third, certain psycho-physiological processes are so fluid that they cannot be observed instantly by means of introspection. Fourth, introspective data are purely personalized. It can neither be verified nor generalized. Fifth, even though good at introspection, most people would not reveal the life secrets so far as they concern sex, love, social relationship etc., for fear of shame, guilt, ill-fame and risk to life. Sixth, introspective information is often coloured by subjectivity, mood states fluctuation, personal prides and prejudices; so it cannot be wholly relied upon. Seventh, the natural flow of existing mental states vanishes when one tries to introspect them instantly. For example, when an emotionally aroused person tries to look within, analyse the situation and report, the situation gets modified. Eighth, well-established and highly automatized mental processes may not be subjected to introspection. Conscious analysis paralyzes them. Finally, for some psychologists introspection is an unscientific method because it does not test well on scientific criteria - objectivity, verifiability and experimental replicability.

In sport, athletes, officials, coaches, trainers, and administrators often search their own hearts when (a) performances do not improve, (b) repeated failures occur, (c) increasing incentives fail to sustain motivation, (d) burn-outs and drops-outs take place, (e) hostile aggression becomes more rampant, and so on. All elite athletes know the art of introspecting themselves skilfully and thoroughly. The secret of their performance-improvement lies in this only.

Experimentation

In scientific language, experimentation is observation of a phenomenon under controlled conditions. Experiments are conducted in a natural setting as well as in laboratory. (A *naturalistic setting* is a relatively normal environment in which researchers gather information by observing individuals' behaviours or phenomena without attempting to control or change the situation.) Research in experimental psychology is generally conducted in a laboratory under controlled conditions. This method of research relies on the application of the scientific method to understand behaviour. A *laboratory setting* involves studying individuals (phenomena) under systematic and controlled conditions with many of the real-world influences either controlled or eliminated. Precisely, a *laboratory experiment* is a technique to gather information (about a person, process, procedure, behaviour, things and their effects) about the brain, genes, or behaviour with the least error and bias by using a controlled environment that allows careful observation and measurement.

Experimental psychologists use variety of measurements

including response rate, reaction time, movement time, and also various psychometric measurements such as IQ. Experiments are designed to test specific hypotheses (deductive approach) or evaluate functional relationships (inductive approach). This allows the research scholars to establish cause-and-effect relationships among different aspects of behaviour and the environment. In an experiment, one or more variables of interest are controlled by the experimenter (independent variable) and another variable is measured in response to different conditions (dependent variable). Experiments are one of the primary research methods in many areas of psychology, particularly cognitive/psychonomics, mathematical psychology, psychophysiology, and biological psychology/cognitive neuroscience.

The ***salient features of experimental method*** in psychology need enumeration here. First, psychological experiments involve the experimenter and the subject (an animal or man) whose behaviour is to be studied. Second, experiments are conducted on "living organisms", and not objects or organic elements. Notably behaviour of living organisms is dynamic, variable and subject to modification not only due to the manipulation of independent variable but also internal and external intervening variables. Finally, laboratory conditions are largely artificial. The exact replica of field conditions, for example, competitive tennis situations, is difficult to reproduce in laboratory. The increasingly refined research techniques backed up by computer application are making it possible to simulate such conditions in the lab.

Undoubtedly objective and precise, the experimental technique has certain ***limitations*** when used in psychology. First, the mind and behaviour are studied under artificially created and strictly controlled conditions. Natural behaviour is not subject to any controls. As such the application of experimental technique produces questionable results as far as behaviour is concerned. Second, actual control over intervening and even independent variables, as required in experimental research, is difficult to exert. For instance, the subject's state of mind, level of motivation, willingness, anxiety etc., cannot be wholly kept under control. This makes behaviour unpredictable and the data unreliable. Third, experimental psychologists have generally used animals as subjects for study. Results obtained from experimental animal studies have often given rise to questionable theories and hypotheses. Now the use of human subjects is on ascendance. Fourth, experiments on humans have been put under some controls, namely informed and voluntary consent. Finally, solution of behavioural problems through experimentation is just not possible.

Experimental sport psychologists have now begun to study motor behaviour, perception, sensation, reaction time, reflex time, motivation etc., under experimental conditions. Effect of ergogenic aids, meditation, hypnosis etc., on athletic performance and psychological conditioning has been experimentally examined. And yet experimental studies on anxiety, aggression, motivation etc., have yielded no encouraging results. Physiological psychologists have arrived at reliable conclusions with regard to memorization, effect of various factors on learning, mental fatigue, axis of emotions etc. The computer aided experimentation is a big leap forward in objectifying behavioural data and obtaining more trustworthy facts.

Clinical Case Study

When dealing with problems of behavioural adjustment, psychiatrists and clinical psychologists use the clinical case study technique. First they diagnose the cause of maladjustment and then treat the individual cases through counselling and guidance. The method is both an art and a science. Using consummate skills of communication, psychologists attempt to reach the inaccessible areas of the human mind, systematically dig out vital information from the memory deposits of past events and experiences of their clients, and carefully monitor the signs and symptoms of deviant behaviour. Besides this, the study of patients' background, their developmental history, direct observation of behaviour, clinical interview with them, interviews with their relatives etc., are major sources of clinical data. The subjects may at times also be subjected to physical and mental check-up. The help of subject's parents, relatives and friends is sought to prepare the case history of the subject in order to prescribe further procedures to remedy the problem.

In educational setting, the clinical technique has been found effective particularly with delinquent and backward children. Depending upon the sensitivity as well as severity of the problem clinical psychologists prescribe different kinds of therapy (psycho-therapy, play therapy, group therapy, occupation therapy, attitude therapy etc); resort to psycho-analysis where necessary, offer guidance and counselling and apply auto-suggestion, hypnosis, psycho-drama and role-playing techniques singularly or in combination to bring the subject back to normal.

The approach of the clinical case study method is largely subjective. It is a lengthy process because studying and treating problematic and/or abnormal individuals is not a simple proposition. Only experienced and highly trained psychologists can handle this highly sensitive method. The scope of clinical technique in the field of activity and sport is limited. Physical educators and coaches deal with normal, healthy and mentally sound individuals. The technique may, however, be applied by clinical sport psychologists when dealing with variety of personal problems of athletes who continually perform under extremely stressful and emotionally charged conditions. "Primary problems", for example, says Cratty (1989) "revolve around gaining and maintaining the athletes' confidence while being seen by coaches as a helper, not an adversary".

Psycho-analysis

Evolved out primarily by Sigmund Freud, psycho-analysis is both a theory and method of studying human behaviour. Considering that all conscious activities are governed and determined by the "unconscious motives", psycho-analysts attempt to *freely* associate and communicate with the patient, get into his *psyche* to locate the cause of the behavioural abnormality, monitor its exact dynamics and finally prefer suitable advice/treatment to the subject so that he soon gets back on the track.

The basic assumption in psycho-analysis is that disordered behaviour results from unresolved unconscious conflicts and repressed urges, most of which are rooted in childhood experiences. A primary theme in many of these conflicts is the struggle between Id's sexual and aggressive impulses and the Super-ego's moralistic commands. These conflicts generate anxiety, which the ego's defence mechanism may not be able to manage successfully. 'As the subject tries more desperate strategies of coping with anxiety, symptoms of psychological disturbances such as phobias and conversion disorders begin to appear (Crooks & Stein, 1988).

Freud believed that the only way to assist people gain true relief from severe anxiety was to enter their unconscious, search out the anxiety causing conflict(s) and help them *gain insight* or conscious awareness of the repressed conflict. Classical Freudian psycho-analysts used *free association, dream analysis* and *interpretations of resistance* and *transference* as major techniques of psycho-therapy. Things have greatly changed since Freud's times but one thing that, perhaps, has not changed is the fact that psycho-analysis simply does not work with severely disturbed or uncommunicative people. The best candidates for this type of therapy more often than not may be relatively young, energetic, intelligent, successful, and highly verbal individuals who in the mad pursuit of materialistic philosophy live under variety of severe stresses and strains, generally emotional. Moving with the spirit of time, psycho-analysis has seen its processes and procedures modifying and refining in order to be more exact and result-oriented. More psychologists today have started tracing the causes of deviant, disordered or maladaptive behaviour to socio-cultural factors than purely to psychic ones as most Freudian psychologists did. As a result, psychology as witnessed a deluge of therapies including Humanistic therapy, Gestalt therapy, Cognitive therapy and Behaviour therapy, all meant to tackle and treat problematic behaviour.

Application of psycho-analysis in sport is severally limited because athletes are no psychic cases. Physically and mentally, they are the healthiest lot of people. In the highly competitive sport - both amateur and professional - the stakes on 'pride, prize, prestige, and privilege' are very high. This puts the human psyche under tremendous as well as constant stress. The sport atmosphere is replete with excessive aggression, anxiety, obsession and even mania. Only in rarest of the rare cases might psychoanalysis be used to understand and modify an athlete's behaviour. It might require the clinical sport psychologists to perfect this technique so as to make it very appropriate to the athletic context.

Genetic Method

Genetic method takes into account a person's growth and development patterns and attempts to locate the causes of complex human behaviour in the simplest beginning. The basic premise here is that the full appreciation of adult behaviour is unsatisfactory without study of the simple behaviour in one's childhood. It is widely known that early life experiences generally have long-lasting effect on an individual's behaviour later in life. The roots of certain habits, sentiments, tastes, aptitudes, interests, attitudes and complexes are traced to childhood. Geneticists take cognizance of physical, mental, intellectual and even social growth of the individual right from prenatal stage to adulthood. This enables them understand different constituents of mental behaviour such as feelings, desires, sentiments and emotions. Since growth and behaviour are hand in glove, importance of genetic method in psychological research is impossible to undermine. With the help of genetic method, psychologists are able to formulate general directive principles of growth and development, and predict the potential of each individual to a fairly accurate degree.

Genetic method, however, involves circuitous and cumbersome procedure, most often requiring the psychological researchers to be extremely patient and consistent in their efforts in an attempt to pinpoint to behavioural abnormalities and finally apply remedial measures. A genetic study is a longitudinal study in which psychologists have the advantage of seeing how a condition can affect individuals (sportspersons) over long time scales. The results from such studies are difficult to generalize.

Sports scientists in Eastern Europe and Russia have often used genetic method to a great advantage especially in their search for athletically talented children right from a tender age so as to groom them as star performers. By examining developmental pattern of hundreds of genetically healthy children, they have developed prototypes (anthropometric, bio-mechanic, physiologic, and to some extent psychological) that serve as scientific yardstick for segregating talented individuals from the mass of average. Success in this endeavour has been relative. Efforts are being made by sports scientists all over the world to find out a plausible explanation to the mind-boggling question: *are elite athletes made or born, being a special breed'*? If they really possess an inborn genetic potential, then what exactly is their genetic make-up and how do innate factors interact with environmental conditions to produce a sportsperson of an extraordinary status. In generalizations, the genetic method may be rewarding, in specifics, it has yet to prove its efficacy for an individual is a mystery and no scientific effort can unravel it.

Psychometrics

Psychometrics (psychological testing) is an objective, standardized and systematic technique of measuring, assessing and evaluating personal attributes generally thought to be important in describing or understanding the individual both from the view-point of innate traits and acquired behavioural characteristics. This semi-scientific procedure has added new dimension to psychology as an academic and research discipline. "Psychological measurement is the process of assigning numbers (e.g. test scores) to persons in such a way that some attributes of the persons being measured are faithfully reflected by some properties of the numbers", (Murphy & Davidshafer, 1991). Among the several methods used to measure the desired traits or characteristics of the subjects, a standardized instrument is perhaps the one most effective one. Technically, a *standardized test* is a technique to obtain information by administering a psychological test that has been standardized, which means that the test has been given to hundreds of people and shown to reliably measure thought patterns, personality traits, emotions or behaviours.

Psychological tests are used in a variety of situations with a variety of people in numerous contexts. For example, in *clinical psychology*, typical testing relates to assessment of intelligence, psychopathological states and neuropsychological processes; in *counselling psychology* assessment is made on career interests, skills and social adjustments; in *industrial/organizational psychology* assessment of managerial potential, training needs, cognitive and psychomotor ability is of great importance and in *school psychology* testing activities include assessment of ability and academic progress, maturity and readiness for school and assessment of handicapped children. Even though psychological tests are used to measure a variety of attributes their precision is severally constrained. They rarely, if ever, provide exact definitive measures of variables generally believed to have important effects on human behaviour. Although psychological tests are far from perfect (psychological testing has become a highly controversial issue), they represent the best, fairest and most accurate technology available for making important decisions about individuals (Murphy & Davidshafer, 1991).

Psychological tests are of two types: performance tests and paper-and-pencil tests (self-reports). In a ***performance test*** the subject is made to manipulate an object or a mechanical apparatus to register his response to a given stimulus. Reaction time, reflex time, depth perception, visual tracking etc., are tested through performance tests. Most psychomotor abilities are measured when the subjects are made to perform certain acts. When conducted under precisely controlled conditions, performance tests yield immensely valuable data on mental abilities, cognition and motor behaviour. There is a wide range of performance tests that can be used with diverse groups of subjects under varying conditions. ***Paper-and-pencil tests*** come either in the form of questionnaires, inventories or in drawings. The subject is provided with a prepared response sheet on which he is to register his response to each question, item or statement one by one in a given sequence. In ***drawing tests***, the respondent is not supposed to write or add anything on his own but to make certain mental calculations viz. additions, subtractions or multiplications. Standard Progressive Matrices (Ravens) is a culture-fair drawing test of intelligence. Eysenck Personality Questionnaire, Multiphasic Maudsley Personality Inventory, Sixteen Personality Factor Questionnaire, California Personality Inventory etc., are all well-known paper-and-pencil tests widely used in psychological research. While the performance tests are administered to one person at a time, paper-and-pencil tests can be administered both individually and in groups. The greatest advantage of these tests is that a large number of subjects can be tested simultaneously with no hassle. Unfortunately, the paper-and-pencil tests do not work well with young children and illiterate people. For administration of paper-and-pencil tests no special room or laboratory is required. Standard keys are available for each test which makes response evaluation comparatively easier. Usually psychological tests are available in standardized form for general use. They may also be tailored by research scholars themselves to serve certain specific purposes.

Collecting psychological data from athletic samples using performance tests, questionnaires, rating scales, inventories etc., has lately become an important research activity with physical educators, coaches and sport psychologists interested in understanding the psycho-dynamics, personality make-up and dynamics, motivational status, psychological skill training level, emotional response etc., of the participants, exercisers and athletes with a view to devise psychological conditioning and intervention programmes for their performance-enhancement. In the beginning, general psychological tests were used on athletic samples particularly for comparative purposes. This practice is still in vogue but problems arise in interpretation of results because the test authors, when standardizing tests were, perhaps, not aware of the specific nature of athletic populations. It needs to be noted that the most popular psychological tests were never standardized on athletic samples. According to Brent Rushall, for example, the Cattell's 16 Personality Factor Questionnaire (so frequently used in sport psychology research) was virtually useless in trying to uncover psychological characteristics associated with elite athletic performance, (Ostrow, 1990). Martens (1973) noted that despite more than 200 studies that had been conducted in sport psychology of the time, there was no information about the prediction of behaviour in sports'. He indicated that this problem stemmed from conceptual, methodological and interpretive problems in the sport personality research. By mid-1970s sensing that sport behaviour put up an entirely different scenario and posed peculiar problems than general psychometric environment, sport psychologists began to explore and examine a variety of situational and environmental factors which operated in and around sport context. This led to emergence of numerous sport-specific psychological tests. Martens' *Sports Competition Anxiety Test* (SCAT) seems to be the finest example of a new direction to sport psychometrics. Ostrow (1996) has documented 314 sport specific psychological tests covering achievement, aggression, anxiety, attention, aptitude, attitude towards exercise and sport, attribution, body-image, confidence cognitive, strategies, cohesion, imagery, sex role, locus of control etc.

THE CONCLUDING NOTE

There are inherent problems in psychological testing. First, unlike physical characteristics such as height, weight, limb measurement, etc., which are concrete, objectively and precisely measurable, psychological attributes are abstract and manifest only in individuals' behaviours, in which case psychological questionnaires and inventories may not prove reliable yardsticks for understanding behaviour faithfully. Second, numerous psychological characteristics are mere concepts and constructs. It is hard to define them in operational terms. This leaves enough scope for the people to raise fingers on the validity of a paper-and-pencil test unless the measure of a trait is supported by some other testing method. Third, subjectivity is inherent both in construction and in administration of self-report tests. The element of 'faking good' (true feeling being cleverly concealed) which contaminates data is difficult to sidetrack or account for. Even with strong statistical measures used, the construct and content validity of questionnaires, in many cases, remain far from satisfactory. Behaviour rarely reflects any one psychological attribute but rather a variety of physical, psychological, and social forces simultaneously. Finally, psychological tests do not attempt to measure the total person but only some specific attributes of his. Validated on specific samples, they are applied on specific chunks of populations. An intelligence test validated on children may not be fit to be administered to adults and vice versa. In sport and exercise where athletic samples and situations vary so greatly, this problem assumes greater significance.

Despite a variety of inherent strengths and weaknesses as well as constraints in their application, these methods have helped psychologists to create an inexhaustible fund of knowledge on which the glorious edifice of psychology as a scientific discipline so proudly stands. The use of one single method may be inefficacious, and, perhaps, questionable; a combination of several methods may not be.

SELECTED REFERENCES

Cratty, Bryant. J. *Psychology in Contemporary Sport* (3rd Edition), Englewood Cliffs, N.J. Prentice Hall, 1989

Kamlesh, M.L. *Methodology of Research in Physical Education and Sport,* New Delhi; Metropolitan, 2002

Martens, Reiner *Sport Competition Anxiety Test.* Champaign, III; Human Kinetics, 1993

Murphy, Kevin R. & Davidshafer, Charles O. *Psychological Testing: Principles and Applications* (2nd Edition), Englewood Cliffs, N.J; Prentice Hall, 1991

Ostrow, Andrew C. (Ed.) *Directory of Psychological Tests in the Sport and Exercise Sciences.* (2nd edition), Morgan Town, West Virginia; Fitness Information Technology inc., 1991

Behaviour is a phenomenon fundamentally different in kind from the action of any machine, however complicated. - James Ross

CHAPTER - 5

ORGANIC BASIS OF BEHAVIOUR

BEHAVIOUR

Organisms possess an innate ability to interact with the environment. This results in simple or complex movements depending upon their biological status and body structure. Behaviour is what organisms do. It is their chief characteristic. Organisms live because they behave and they behave because it is necessary for them to "struggle for existence". Through behaviour, they achieve various goals of life.

In order to behave, animals require two things: an integrated organic structure and environment. The ***integrated organic structure*** called body, which is a gift of nature (an outcome of sexual reproduction) to animals. The body possesses all the instruments, abilities and capabilities that enable animals to act, move, think, experience and learn skills so important to live purposefully. It represents all the internal natural forces which are subject to their own invisible laws. ***Environment*** is all that exists outside the body i.e. external forces, conditions, factors and other animal species that stimulate, reinforce or weaken, and regulate action-reaction patterns. Behaviour assumes special significance when it is discussed in the context of human beings, who unlike animals, "think and behave within a social environment" (Buskist & Gerbing, 1990). With this in mind, perhaps, Aristotle defined man as *a social animal.*

Behaviour is the central issue of psychology. It is not what we see animals doing overtly - the observable movements, but a highly complex phenomenon having genesis in organism's morphological structure and biological functions. Living organisms *behave;* they do not perform mechanical actions. Although the organism's structure and function are interrelated, one cannot be misled into believing that behaviour is merely "structure in action", which, surely, it is not. Organisms are evolved, so is their behaviour. Machines are manufactured; resultantly they simply perform mechanical actions, not behave; not even highly sophisticated robots or computers. Therefore, while explaining behaviour, two important facts need consideration. First, all living beings have some biologically evolved structure which is a whole and cannot be partitioned. For convenience sake, we may discuss an organism's structure part by part, however, not forgetting that the whole is greater and more complex than the sum of its parts. Second, all living organisms are self-reproducing, self-maintaining and self-sustaining beings. A precise reproductive procedure in each case brings them into existence. Once in the world, they struggle for existence by interacting with the environment, thereby growing more complex in their behaviour. Understanding behaviour would require us to have adequate knowledge about the organism's genetic make-up, biological history, bio-mechanics, physical structure, physiological functioning and neuromuscular sensitivity. Added to all this is man's socio-cultural, intellectual and spiritual attributes.

Characteristics of Behaviour

Behaviourists have listed the following characteristics of behaviour:

- Behaviour is *organism's response* to some form of stimulation - internal or external. Without stimulation no behaviour occurs. All living beings are naturally active. Stimulation for life is internal; it is Godly.
- Behaviour has a purpose. It is both goal-oriented and goal-directed. It helps organism in its *struggle for existence* as a result of which the organism adapts and adjusts in the environment. Herbert Spencer said: "Life is the continuous adjustment of internal relations to external relations". The most explicit purpose of behaviour is preservation of life. The organism's internally inspired and will to live is the basic motivating force behind behaviour. Precisely, motives primarily sustain life and determine the behavioural direction.
- Most stimuli for behaviour to occur come from the environment. Conditions outside the body are capable of modifying even the innate patterns of behaviour such as reflexes and instinctive actions.
- Apart from the visible bodily movements which an animal makes as a result of an external stimulus, the imperceptible

mental activity (what goes on in the brain and the nervous system) and body-kinaesthesia are also important constituents of behaviour. This is what makes behaviour a complex psycho-physiological phenomenon.

- Depending upon a species' biological status, the grade, level and quality of its behaviour become subject to variation. The higher the place of a species, the greater the behavioural complexity. Humans, primates, mammals, birds, orthropoda etc., are easily distinguishable by their respective behaviour. In terms of biology, "what is (structurally and) functionally higher is biologically higher".
- Structural and functional variation makes different organisms respond to the same stimulus differently; for example, the twilight that sends the rooks to the nests, makes the fox growl. A crashing (loud) sound makes a partridge freeze, a sparrow fly, and a man start.
- Depending upon the sort and strength of a stimulus and complexity of an organism's psycho-physical structure, the persistent movement resulting from stimulation varies in span and intensity. This means that all intense stimuli leave behind responses (residual effects) that have some carry-over value.
- Behaviour has internal and external aspects. Its internal aspect constitutes the nerve-impulse movement and visceral action-reactions that occur inside the body when a stimulus is applied. The external aspect of behaviour is exemplified in observable bodily movements (locomotion) of the organism. Both aspects are closely related and often interdependent.
- Behaviour is modifiable. Using classical or operant methods, behaviour can be modified. The classical conditioning takes place under contrived conditions and the operant conditioning occurs under unprompted or natural conditions.
- Within the limits and limitations of psycho-physiological make-up of the animal, the impress of the previous situation or movement is helpfully carried forward when dealing with the new situation. The previous experience plays a key-role in the animal's learning and behaviour.

Traits of behaviour, pre-suppose the presence of mind - an interface between the body and soul. *Movement is inherent in the organism itself and it is its life force.*

Human Behaviour

The three distinguishing features of man, as distinct from those of animals, are: (a) ***an upright posture,*** (b) ***an opposable thumb*** and (c) ***superior nervous system*** and cerebral cortex. Man's constant struggle to master environment resulting in the Cultural Revolution, have had a very close relationship with them. The special attributes of human behaviour that emerged there from include the following:

- Human behaviour is variable and greatly modifiable. Ability to learn and benefit from stored experiences does not allow man to remain a slave of his instinctive tendencies.
- As an outcome of a highly complicated information-processing system established in the superior nervous system and big brain, human behaviour is intelligent and creative.
- It is influenced, conditioned and shaped by social factors and forces. All formal learning, education and character formation take place in a social environment, thereby making human behaviour more complex.
- Depending upon quality of development and experience, the human response to a problem-situation shows great variability. With sustained environmental interaction, man acquires the ability to offer more varied options to a problem-situation.
- From birth to adulthood, patterns of human behaviour tend to change significantly across clearly demarcated stages of development. For instance, a child is significantly different from an infant, and an adolescent from a child.

BIOLOGICAL BASES OF BEHAVIOUR

Biologically structure and function are interdependent. They modify each other. Function of the organism cannot be discussed without reference to its structure. Although to a stimulus the organism responds as a whole, yet the role of nervous system in behavioural process is very crucial. The human behaviour, thoughts, memories, emotions, and even qualities such as intelligence and creativity are based on biological process that takes place within and between cells. The modern scientists, incredible as it would seem, are still not very clear as to how these enigmatic processes take place although they are fully aware of the anatomical structure of each type of cell and systems of the body.

Organization and Function of the Nervous System

If the human body were to be compared to a business corporation, the Nervous System would be its communication department. Every second our body is receiving information from our surroundings (such as temperature) and various parts of our body are sending their own pieces of information to add to that list too. Our stomach may be telling us that we really shouldn't have skipped breakfast, or our back is telling us that we really need to stretch out those muscles. All of this information is gathered, reviewed, and acted upon by our nervous system. In other words, all our activity - seeing, perceiving, moving, feeling, thinking or remembering – is basically a function of our nervous system, which is an extremely complex organization of neurons at the baseline, nerves and various parts of the brain.

The general organization of the human nervous system is shown in Fig. 5.1.

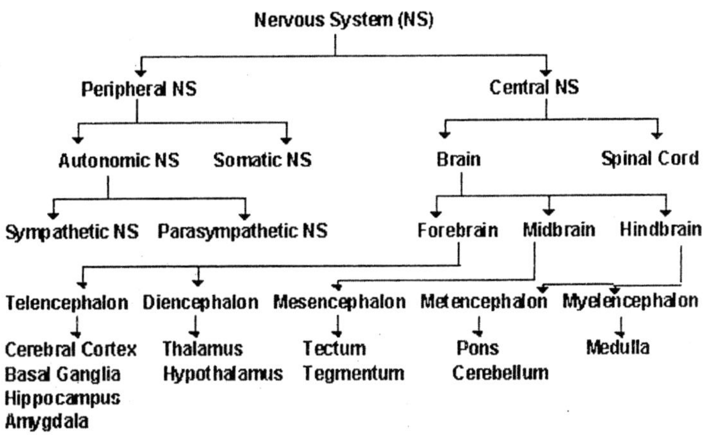

Fig. 5.1 General divisions of the nervous system

The nervous system can be divided into several connected systems that function together. However, in a simple division, the nervous system is categorized into the ***central nervous system*** and ***peripheral nervous system***, further subdivided into somatic and autonomic nervous systems.

Neurons

The building blocks of the nervous system are the Neurons, or nerve cells. They are highly specialized in nature and vary in shape, size, and characteristics. The level of concentration is according to their location and function in the nervous system. All neurons have a cell body containing the nucleus and processes (fibres) of two types; (1) axons (one per cell) typically generate and conduct impulses away from the cell body and release a neurotransmitter, and (2) dendrites (one to many per cell) typically carry electrical currents toward the cell body. Most large fibres are myelinated; myelin increases the rate of nerve impulse transmission.

On the basis of function (direction of impulse transmission) neurons are sensory (afferent), motor (efferent), and association neurons (inter-neurons). In brief:

- *Sensory neurons* are also known as afferent neurons. These neurons have receptors on the skin, in some organs, and in muscles and joints. These receptors gather information about our outside and inside environment and transmit that data to the central nervous system, which consists of the brain and the spinal cord.
- ***Connecting neurons***, also known as inter-neurons, are found only in the central nervous system. Their job is to receive and process the information from the sensory neurons and reach an appropriate reaction to send back.
- ***Motor neurons*** are also called efferent neurons. These carry the brain's instructions once again through the nerve pathway to the necessary part of the body.

Neurons communicate or send impulses (these are actually electrochemical events) through an action potential. This takes place from the dendrite and all the way to the axon ends. An action potential is a change of voltage within the axon. In other words, the negative state off the inner axon turns positive when the impulse comes by. The part of the neuron that receives most transmitted impulses is a collection of fibres called dendrites that extend out from the cell body like branches of a tree. Dendrites may receive information from a few to thousands of surrounding neurons. The more extensive the neurons' network of dendrites, the more connections can be made with other neurons. In the CNS, collections of neurons are called ***nuclei***. In the PNS, collections of neurons are called ***ganglia***. In the CNS, collections of axons are called ***tracts***. In the PNS, collections of axons are called ***nerves***.

The neural electrical activity involving electrical as well as chemical reactions is a very complex phenomenon and is dealt with by physiological psychologists in greater detail. However, it is important to note that neurons remain in a constant state of readiness to be activated by an impulse from an adjacent neuron. Further, once a nerve impulse is triggered within an axon, it is transmitted the entire length of the axon with no loss of intensity. Partial nerve impulses (action potentials) do not occur; thus, an axon is said to conduct without decrement. The nerve impulse follows the *all-or-none law* which denotes that if the sum of the graded potential reaches a threshold, there will be an impulse, if the threshold is not reached, an action potential will not occur. Very weak stimuli may trigger impulses in only a few neurons, whereas very strong stimuli may cause thousands of neurons to fire. The speed with which an impulse travels through a neuron varies with the properties of the axon ranging from less than one metre per minute to as fast as 100 metres per second.

When an electrical nerve impulse reaches the end of an axon, it cannot flow directly into other neurons because of the synaptic gap or cleft, which is no more than five millionth of an inch across. The electrical impulse does not bridge it alone. A chemical process is necessary in bridging the synaptic gap. With few exceptions, synapses transmit messages in only one direction, from the terminal button of one neuron to the dendrites or cell body of the next. Neurons communicate primarily through the release of certain chemicals. These chemical messengers, called ***neurotransmitters***, are contained within tiny sacs in the axon terminal buttons called synaptic vescicles. When the axon fires some of the synaptic vescicles migrate to the pre-synaptic membrane, where they release their contents into the synaptic gap. The total amount of neurotransmitters released is a function of how many times the axon fires. More intense stimulation produces a greater frequency of signals which in turn increases the amount of neurotransmitters released.

The entire process of neurotransmission is so complicated that the scientists are still in dark about many functions of the brain especially with regard to feelings, remembering etc.

Nerves

What we call nerves are actually bundles of many axons. Some of these nerves, such as the sciatic nerve, contain more axons and are therefore bigger than others. Nerves can vary in size from one inch thick to thinner than a human hair. Each nerve travels to or from one specific part of the body. The nerves which connect the receptors and the brain are called sensory or afferent nerves. They transmit the impulses from sense organs (sensory receptors) to the spinal cord and those that carry the message from the brain back to the spinal cord and muscles and glands, are known as motor or efferent nerves. It is possible for one nerve to have both sensory and motor neurons. This enables a single nerve to both carry information to the brain and from the brain. The human body contains an extremely complex network of sensory and motor nerves that keep the to-and-fro message transmission going ceaselessly.

DIVISIONS OF NERVOUS SYSTEM

Precisely, the nervous system comprises (1) Cerebrospinal Axis, (2) Peripheral Nerves, and (3) Autonomic Ganglia. In order to understand the internal mechanism of behaviour, it is necessary to have a bird's eye-view of the complex structure and function of various divisions of the nervous system.

Cerebro-Spinal Axis

The cerebro-spinal axis consists of the spinal cord and the brain.

Spinal Cord

Housed within a hollow tube-like structure composed of a series of bonds called vertebrae, the spinal cord (about 43 cm long in adult women and 45 cm long in adult men and weighs about 35-40 grams) looks something like a long, white smooth rope extending from the neck to the small of the back. The vertebral column is about 70 cm long. Therefore, the spinal cord is much shorter than the vertebral column. Along the length of the spinal cord are spinal nerves that branch out between pairs of vertebrae. These nerves connect with various sensory organs, muscles, and glands served by the peripheral nervous system. The spinal nerves occur in 31 matched pairs, with one nerve of each pair connected to the right side of the spinal cord and its counterpart connected to the left side of the body.

Even though the brain occupies a prime position in the CNS, the spinal cord nevertheless plays an extremely important role of conveying messages to and from the brain. Consisting of largely grey matter, ***the spinal cord is the centre of almost all reflex activity and a relaying station of impulses to and from the brain.*** In a reflex action (a highly automatic process) the receptors, through the afferent nerves, feed the impulses to the spinal cord; the spinal cord, in turn, activates the motor nerves to produce a reflex action without any mediation of the cerebral stimulation.

Spinal cord is the lower centre of the brain and is well-trained to dispose of stimuli which require fixed and automatic response. Impulses for an automatized action are initiated in the spinal cord. An automatized action is produced when an unaltered repetitive stimulation is given over a period of time consciously or unconsciously. But when the stimulus is modified, the automatic action is not produced; rather the higher centres of the brain are called upon to intervene and direct the response pattern. All complex behaviours require integration and coordination at the level of the brain. Certain organic or basic reflexive behaviours like eye-winking, knee-jerk, hand-withdrawal from a hot stove, sneezing, coughing etc., require no information processing at the brain level. They are fixed, automatic, rapid and naturally conditioned action patterns (reflexes), each one controlled by certain centres within the spinal cord. For example, hand withdrawal is controlled by the upper part of the spinal cord, whereas the knee jerk response by an area in the lower cord. No doubt, the brain is not directly involved in reflex phenomenon, it nevertheless is always aware of what goes on where in the body.

The Brain

The human brain is located within the cranial cavity of the skull. It consists of two cerebral hemispheres (forebrain), diencephalons, brain stem structures, and cerebellum. The adult human brain on average weighs 1.3 to 1.4 kg (approximately 3 pounds). The brain has about 100 billion nerve cells (neurons) and trillions of "support cells" called glia. It is divided into the Upper, the Hind, and the Lower Brain.

Cerebrum or the Upper Brain

The upper part of brain - the large convoluted mass of brain tissue located just beneath the skull - is cerebrum, which is divided in right and left hemispheres. The two cerebral hemispheres form the largest part of the brain. The thickness of the cerebral cortex varies from 2 to 6 mm. The right and left sides of the cerebral cortex are connected by a thick band of nerve fibers called the "corpus callosum." In higher mammals such as humans, the cerebral cortex looks like it has many bumps and grooves. A bump or bulge on the cortex is called a **gyrus** (the plural of the word gyrus is "gyri") and a groove is called a **sulcus** (the plural of the word sulcus is "sulci"). Lower mammals, such as rats and mice, have very few gyri and sulci.

The cortex consists of grey matter. The composition of the cerebrum is, in a way, reverse of the spinal cord. In the spinal cord, there is grey matter in the interior surrounded by whitish substance, in the cerebrum the interior comprises white substance and the outer surface layers are greenish in colour.

A deep tissue running from front to rear divides the cortex into right and left hemispheres. The hemispheres are symmetrical. In general, each hemisphere receives sensory information from and directs the muscular action of the opposite side of the body. The ***left hemisphere*** controls spontaneous speaking and writing, and memory of numbers and words. It co-ordinates complex sequences of movements, and is involved in feelings of anxiety and negative emotions. The ***right hemisphere*** is involved with recognition of faces, memory related to shapes and music, and it directs positive emotions and over-all emotional responses.

The cortex is where our memories are stored, where we make decisions, where we "see" a sunset or recognize and appreciate a melody, and where we organize our worlds, and plan for the future. Without a cortex we would cease to exist as unique, functioning individuals. This is not to say that the cortex acts alone in running our lives. Instead, it functions like an executive, interpreting incoming information and making decisions how to respond. As we go about our daily lives, our cerebral cortexes constantly analyse a vast array of incoming messages, evaluating against stored information about past experiences and then making decisions that are translated into messages that are sent to appropriate muscles and glands (Crooks & Stein, 1988).

Only a relatively small portion of the cerebral cortex is devoted to receiving sensory information and initiating motor responses. The remainder of the cortex, *the association* areas, are devoted to the so-called higher cognitive processes such as planning and decision-making. A comparison of the human cortex with that of different animals reveals interesting anatomical differences: as the behavioural complexity of the animal increases, so does proportion of the cerebral cortex devoted to association areas.

The cerebral hemispheres are "on duty" 24 hours a day, bustling with electrical activity even while asleep. However, the nature of the electrical activity changes over the course of each day and is related to our overall level of arousal or how awake we feel. To some degree, researchers have been able to localize a variety of functions within various regions of the two cortical hemispheres. Approximately 25 percent of the total area is involved in receiving sensory messages or transmitting movement messages to our muscles. These regions are called the *Sensory Cortex*, and the *Motor Cortex* respectively. The remaining 75 per cent of the cerebral cortex, called the Association Cortex is involved in interpreting sensory and motor messages, and in processing such higher mental functions as thinking, interpreting, remembering and planning.

The Lower Brain

Also known as the *reptilian brain*, the lower brain consists of Medulla Oblongata, Pons Varolii, and Cerebellum.

Medulla is the elongated part of the spinal cord which bulges slightly as it enters the cavity of the skull. This 'primitive lump' takes care of instinctive autonomic functions such as sleeping, breathing, swallowing, digestion and heart beat. It also controls movements of the muscles, joints and tendons, and maintenance of the body equilibrium. It marks the spot where axons ascending from the spinal cord and descending from the brain cross over so that left side of the brain is connected to the right side of the body. Even the slightest damage in the critical region of the medulla can cause death.

The ***Pons*** is a large bridge just above the medulla. It plays an important role in fine-tuning motor messages as they travel from the motor area of the cerebral cortex down through the pons to the cerebellum. It also plays part in arousal and dreaming and actually coordinates incoming sensory signals from the spinal cord and face, directing them to the proper area of the brain. The pons contains specialised nuclei.

The ***Cerebellum,*** also called '*little brain*', is a distinctive structure about the size of fist tucked beneath the back part of the cerebral hemispheres, and behind the brain stem. In some ways, the cerebrum is similar to the cerebral cortex and is divided into hemispheres and has a cortex that surrounds these hemispheres. Its primary function is to coordinate and regulate motor movements. It is instrumental in maintaining body balance and posture. The higher regions of the brain may initiate movements but their smooth execution is largely engineered by cerebellum, especially those required for rapid change of direction. Activities such as running, walking, or even standing may be accomplished but often only with great concentration on each component of motion.

The Hind Brain

The thalamus and hypothalamus comprise the "*brain of the ancestral mammal*".

The egg-shaped structure directly above the pons and medulla is ***Thalamus*** which serves as a "relaying station" for sensory information of vision, audition, taste and touch to the cerebral cortex. The cerebral cortex also sends information to the thalamus which then transmits this information to other areas of the brain and the spinal cord. Many of the cell nulei in the thalamus also perform initial data-processing before relaying information to the cortex. The thalamus also appears to work in conjunction with reticular formation to help regulate sleep cycles.

The ***Hypothalamus*** is composed of several different areas and is located at the base of the brain. Although it is the size of only a pea (about 1/300 of the brain weight), it plays a critical role in regulating very vital functions of the body such as hunger, thirst, body temperature and sexual arousal. It also monitors and controls the activity of the pituitary gland which, in turn, regulates and controls hormonal secretions of the endocrinal system. In short, the primary function of the hypothalamus is to maintain homeostasis - a relatively consistent balanced internal state. It acts as a "thermostat" by sensing changes in body temperature and then sending signals to adjust the temperature. For example, if you are too hot, the hypothalamus detects this and then sends a signal to expand the capillaries in your skin. This causes blood to be cooled faster. The hypothalamus also controls the pituitary.

Its role in controlling emotional expressions is significant. Being the hub of the endocrinal system, it has important place in different behaviours including sexual expression, reproduction, aggression and reaction to stress. In fact, hypothalamus is a part of the Limbic system of the brain which includes amygdala, hypocampus and septal area. The limbic system is most closely associated with emotional expression, and plays a role in motivation, learning and memory.

Peripheral Nervous System

The peripheral nervous system consists of contains 12 pairs of cranial nerves and 31 pairs of spinal nerves, connects the CNS to the rest of the body. In other words, it primarily serves the CNS by transmitting information to and from the spinal cord and brain. The sensory and motor nerves are spread all over the body like grass roots and conduct impulses to and from the brain very efficiently. The PNS has two divisions, the somatic and autonomic.

The ***Somatic Nervous System*** has the nerve pathways that take care of the voluntary muscles and all the senses such as hearing, vision, audition, etc. It controls the glands and the smooth muscles of the visceral organs - heart, lungs, stomach, intestines, blood vessels etc. The visceral organs, in fact, operate reflexively without voluntary stimulation. However, through long-time conditioning it is possible to have some sort of partial control over involuntary processes of the visceral organs.

The ***Autonomic Nervous System*** has the nerves that control the internal organs as well as the voluntary muscles. This system works well below our conscious level. It is categorized into ***sympathetic*** and ***parasympathetic***. In most cases each visceral organ has a separate set of connections with sympathetic and parasympathetic branches. The two subdivisions of the ANS operate differently, often having opposing effects on the organs they control. The sympathetic system is largely excitatory in nature and the parasympathetic system inhibitory. For example, the sympathetic system increases heart rate, dilates pupils, inhibits digestive activity, the parasympathetic system has the opposite effect in each case. Both systems do not operate in a counter-productive fashion, however. Instead, they work together to allow our bodies to function well when either relaxed or highly aroused. The normal state - somewhere in between extreme excitement and relaxation - is maintained by the balance between these two systems. However, under emergency conditions, for example, high emotional arousal, the sympathetic nervous system dominates the proceedings.

Precisely, the nervous system has three basic functions: (1) Gathering of inside and outside information (PNS), (2) Analyzing the information and determining appropriate response (CNS), and (3) Relaying that response to the required body part (PNS).

Muscles and Glands

Muscles and glands play a crucial role in behaviour. There are two types of muscles in the body - ***Skeletal Muscles*** and ***Smooth Muscles***.

The skeletal muscles are striped or striated muscles abundantly innervated by afferent and efferent nerves. They are attached to the bones and are voluntary in nature. They contract and flex/extend under stimulation from the brain and move the parts of the body to which they are attached. There are about 600 muscles in the human body and are placed in pairs i.e. *agonists and antagonists*. Under the control of the human mind, skeletal muscles perform big and/or fine movements of observable nature. Acquisition of motor skills and sports skills is fundamentally a function of muscle movement; the more efficient the muscle movement, the better the learning of skills. Proper conditioning of skeletal muscles leads to high level of skill and fitness. In fact, the muscular system acts as a fly-wheel in the human body. The smooth muscles make the visceral organs - intestines, stomach, etc. They are involuntary and their movements are controlled by the autonomic nervous system. They work non-stop but their activity is not visible from outside. Like striated muscles, they are contractible but their contractions are not violent.

Glands are small sac-like bodies which secrete liquid-like substance known as hormone. Hormones are poured direct into the blood stream. They control growth and development, regulate physiochemical activity, metabolism, and fuel the emotional reactivity through bio-chemical reactions. Glands make the endocrine system, the major endocrine glands being the pituitary, the thyroid, the parathyroid the adrenals, the pancreas and the gonads. They are all ductless glands. A single gland may produce several quite different hormones that perform virtually the same function. Like neurotransmitters, hormones act as chemical messengers. In fact, some important chemicals within the body can function both as neurotransmitters and hormones, Norpinephrine, for example, acts as a hormone when released by the adrenal glands and as a neurotransmitter when released by the neuron. There is, however, a key difference in the way these two classes of chemicals act. Because neurotransmitters need to travel only across a synaptic gap, they have a much more immediate effect upon behaviour than does the endocrine system

The endocrine system often works in tandem with the nervous system. For example, when a person is suddenly exposed to a frightful stimulus, his heat rate shoots up in response to sympathetic nervous system output. At the same time the adrenal glands secrete epinephrine, which has a similar effect on heart rate. This way, the two major behaviour-regulating systems of the body - the nervous systems and endocrine system - work in unison for the same objectives. Notably, hypothalamus is a key interface between the nervous system and the endocrine system. Importantly, endocrine glands do not produce a steady stream of hormones. Instead target-organs signal the secreting glands to either increase or decrease secretions. Hormones are not secreted until the target-organ is stimulated: at this point, the target-organ releases another substance that circulates back through the system to regulate hormonal activity in the initiating gland. This mechanism provides an internal control that limits its extremes of hormonal production.

Through these general mechanisms, the endocrine system influences many important physiological functions, mental processes and behaviour patterns, including disease-regulation, metabolism, emotional responses and motivation. The hormonal activity is also said to influence temperament, mood states, mental stability and even personality dynamics so important in the study of behaviour.

Stimulus-Response Phenomenon

Woodworth (1948) says "any force acting on a receptor and making it active is called stimulus". In physiology, a stimulus is an agent activating the receptors, i.e. a "physical agent of some sort which impinges upon excitable protoplasm". Light is a stimulus to the eye, sound to the ear and air to the skin. Further, "any activity aroused by a stimulus is a response to that stimulus". ***A stimulus is what arouses response and the response is what is aroused by stimulus.*** The stimulus and response are used in conjunction with each other. While response is an activity of the organism, stimulus is merely a passive force or agent. By analogy, the goad (the spiked stick used for driving cattle) itself does not push the ox forward; it stimulates it to react or move.

Response is no simple muscular activity; it is more than that. Operationally, it stands for psycho-physiological reactivity catalyzed by a stimulus. From the winking of our eye to a complex gymnastic somersault, the human organism makes a series of responses in quick succession under a stimulus situation. A visible motor movement in a body part is the result of a number of responses or action-reactions that take place internally even without our being conscious of them. The stimulus acts only on the living organism but all stimuli do not necessarily elicit muscular response. For example, a person hears noise; auditory receptors receive the stimulus, afferent nerves connected with audition inform the brain about noise, the brain analyzes that it is an aeroplane up in the sky; the individual makes no visible muscular movement but is reminded of his flight to Srinagar last summer; thus remembering is aroused by noise. Such a situation could be called an indirect response to the original stimulus - noise. The individual recollects how he wrote a letter to his friend prior to his flight to make arrangements for his stay; how he now plans to have some novel experiences, and so on. Life truly is an unending series of stimulus-response mechanisms.

Since behaviour comprises response or series of responses to one stimulus or numerous stimuli, the entire process is summed up in S-R the formula (stimulus shortened to S and response to R). To most of the natural stimuli, the responses are similar, uniform and non-variable but this may not necessarily apply to humans whose behaviour is greatly influenced by acquired and stored experiences. Except in infancy when the baby is wholly dependent on the parents for its needs, man's entire behaviour is variable, smart, intelligent, and unpredictable quite often unlike that of animals which is fixed and rigid. How will an individual behave in response to a stimulus is difficult to calculate instantly because human beings have more than one response-options readily available with them. Anger is a response but what stimulus is necessary to elicit such a response from an individual in similar and dissimilar situations is a difficult question to answer. Response to the same stimulus differs from person to person and from situation to situation depending upon one's age, experience, knowledge, training, education, and similar such factors.

S-R mechanism could be charted out as follows:

Stimulus → the physical agent or the goad
↓
Excitation → of the receptive apparatus or the sense organs
↓
Afferent Transmission → sensory nerves carry the impulses to the brain
↓
Central Adjustment → information processing at brain nerve centre and spinal cord
↓
Efferent Transmission → motor nerves transmit excitatory impulses to organs of response
↓
The Response → excitation of the effectors or response apparatus including muscles and glands, etc., which are no part of nervous system.

The mechanism is so well established and so swift that the individual is least conscious of it. When the same stimulus is repeated over time, a direct link is established between the afferent and motor pathways and reinforced, thereby circumventing higher brain centres, and resulting in automatization of the movement-pattern. This process is called S-R bond mechanism. A complex skill when automatised becomes a sort of reflex. In the acquisition of motor skills, forming habits and conditioning reflexes S-R bond plays an important role.

Response Influencing Factors

It is not necessary that two individuals give the same or similar response to the same stimulus. On repetition, even the same stimulus may evoke a different response from the individual. No discussion on 'response'. is complete without reference to the characteristics of the individual (organism), and the kind and quality of stimulus, for example, its intensity. Now the formula S-R may be modified and re-written S-O-R (O for organism). Individual's response to a given stimulus depends upon numerous internal and external factors.

In order to explain this phenomenon, at least three basic facts need consideration: (1) Structure of the organism, (2) State or situation in which the organism presently is, and (3) Activity already in progress.

Structure

Structure refers to the bodily characteristics of the organism, its structural and functional traits and qualities. Nature has provided peculiar physical structure to each animal species that enable them to respond to the environmental stimuli in their characteristic ways. For instance, in a danger situation, a bird will fly, a rabbit run, and a man may climb a tree, shut the door, or hit upon some other escape strategy. Upright position, opposable thumb and superior brain and complex nervous system (with power of differentiation and generalization), enable man to respond to various stimuli in different and diverse ways than animals. Importantly, some animals have a much keener sense of smell and sense of sight such as dog and eagle. As a result, their ability to respond to the same or similar stimuli differs from other animals. In several biological attributes, man is comparatively a weaker animal. He possesses neither a bull's horns nor an eagle's claws, nor a tiger's canine teeth, nor a cobra's sting, nor a monkey's agility as a protective shield in a danger-situation. What he has a superior brain to help him in his struggle for existence and to adapt to constantly changing environmental conditions by responding to various internal and external stimuli in his own characteristic ways. In addition, different growth stages bring about change in man's structure and function, which influences his ability to respond to the same stimuli in ways different from the previously tried ones. Consequently, the way an adult responds to the danger situation is qualitatively different from the way an infant or a child does. Response-variability is closely related to physical structure.

Temporary State

Response to a stimulus is also determined by the situation or state in which the organism is at a particular point of time. Drowsiness, hunger, intoxication, illness, emotional disturbance or excitement, depression, worry, happiness, etc., profoundly affect the response made to a situation. We know how an otherwise sane individual throws away all standards of decency when under the influence alcohol or drugs. When in a sad mood, a person thinks of the dew drops as tears of nature; in a happy state of mind, he considers them pearls. In an emotional upheaval, we hate listening to even the best of the musical numbers. A hungry cat struggles hard to get out of the cage; a satisfied one goes to sleep. Not withstanding our age, sex or status, we all react to situations according to our mood states and conditions of our body and mind. Therefore, happiness or sadness is a state of mind. A person suffering from severe headache will be ready to swallow the bitterest pill gladly; a healthy individual may spurn the idea of a food-supplement pill.

Activity in Progress

The activity in progress is another determinant of response. If the stimulus has no relevance to the activity in progress or it is mild in nature, the individual would take little notice of it. He will simply remain indifferent to it. If the new stimulus is impeding the progress of the on-going activity, the individual may expeditiously react to it keeping in view the exigency that prevails. Whether or not to react to the intervening stimulus will depend on the sense of urgency. On the other hand, if the new stimulus is conducive to the on-going activity, the response would become more intense. For instance, when seriously engrossed in reading, the pencil slips off our hand or a mosquito hums fiercely in our ears, interruption of reading either to retrieve the pencil or ward off the mosquito will be a matter of priority in relation to the on-going activity (reading) and intensity and propriety of the intervening stimulus.

When activities become, more or less, automatic with an individual's reasonable mastery over them, he might attend to more than one stimulus simultaneously without being vulnerable to interference from any quarter. Response to a stimulus is critically dependent on several personal and environmental factors. What response does a young maiden make to the advances of her first-love, shall depend upon her temperament, character, habits, present state, surroundings, time, place, experience, etc. The response of a new entrant to the school will be determined by factors like the school environment child's own socio-economic status, his experience, activities going on in the school at that time, etc. Therefore, impact of the environmental stimulus on the individual and that of individual's response on the environment are reciprocal and intimately related. With experience, training, and conditioning every individual becomes capable of making selective response. A priority principle is established when more than one stimulus is presented simultaneously. The urgency and meaningfulness of the stimulus are two major considerations for the response to occur in a selective manner.

Notably, strengthening or weakening of the already established responses or acquisition of new responses is invariably dependent upon the environment surrounding the individual and how he reacts with external forces, programming of the software of his mind especially in infancy and childhood.

TYPOLOGY OF BEHAVIOUR

Human behaviour is often categorized into (a) unlearnt and innate behaviour, and (b) learnt or acquired behaviour. The unlearnt behaviour constitutes those activities, movements and behavioural tendencies that are inborn, almost fixed and non-modifiable. The human organism has brought all these with him as it entered the world at birth. The learnt behaviour is one which the individual acquires either by design, choice and force of environment. It may be learnt by formal and informal means, consciously and unconsciously at home, at school, on the playfields or else where in the wide world. While the unlearnt behaviour - reflexes, instincts and general innate tendencies - is universal, the learnt behaviour – skills (conceptual, motor, management, and athletic skills), habits, customs, traditions etc - is typical of human beings. The innate behaviour is much more orthodox in operation; the learnt behaviour is intelligent, creative and diverse. However, there are points where it is impossible to distinguish between what is inherited and what is acquired because but for inherited equipment of behaviour and simple patterns, there could be no learning of the acquired behaviour. No one could learn kicking in football, shooting in basketball or running a marathon race unless one were blessed by nature in such motor movements as locomotion, walking, running, jumping or throwing actions. Overlapping between what one inherits and what one learns is closely related to the quality and frequency of individual-environment interaction. Man may not be a slave to his instincts yet emotions play a critical role in determining the direction of his development and behaviour. With education, he learns to manage himself emotionally but he cannot completely root out emotions from his behaviour.

UNLEARNT BEHAVIOUR

The core of unlearnt behaviour consists of reflexes, instincts and emotions. While reflexes are simple inborn action-reaction patterns, instincts are tendencies of behaviour, not behaviour as such, directing the organism to act in certain ways, emotions are a concrete expression of the instinctive tendencies when situations conducive to their arousal arise and impinge upon the organism.

Reflexes

Non-variable behaviour (reflexes) is best defined as those stimulus-responses patterns or processes which are inherited by the individual in the sense that they are determined by the innate organisation of structures. The most non-variable forms of behaviour are those physiological functions that directly control food intake, digestion, elimination, respiration, circulation and the like. To physiologists, they are better known as "*organic reflexes*". A reflex action may be a simple mode of behaviour or reaction of an organism to a stimulus – be it internal or external. The organic reflexes need little stimuli from the external environment; they are inborn and automatic - their control-centres lie within the organism itself. Since they are involuntary and within no conscious control of the individual, they are no stoppable in their operation. Sandiford (1933) believes that with training, operation of organic reflexes could be slightly modified. For example, stomach may be trained to respond effectively to different kinds of food, and constipation may be alleviated by regular habits of evacuation. In the process of learning motor skills and athletic skills in various games and sports, the operation of several organic reflexes has to be modified with some sort of training procedure; in other words, these reflexes have to be trained by connecting right stimulus to right response, engaging in repetitious action-reaction pattern, and adjusting focus of attention over time. For example, sprinters train start off race with the gun shot.

Simple reflexes (called tropisms in lower animals) are natural responses to light, temperature, sound, chemical stimulations, etc. They are perfect in operation, non-modifiable and least variable in pattern. Simple reflexes may include "pupillary" iris reflex, hand withdrawal (from heat and cold), mesenteric reflexes (working of the stomach and intestinal muscles in digestion), snoring, shuddering, startling (to sudden noise), trembling, shivering, rhythmic contraction (in epilepsy, paralytic agitations etc). They are different from organic reflexes. Organic reflexes may be trained and conditioned; simple reflexes are difficult to train as they are not under our conscious control. There is some visible or invisible reason behind every reflex action that occurs in the body. Unbearable light makes the eye wink, unwanted substance in the windpipe causes coughing, a boring situation results in yawning, titillation of the olfactory nerve makes us sneeze, sight or taste of food is a reason for salivation, a sudden stumble leads to a knee jerk, and a foreign material in food makes us vomit, and so on. All reflexes are involuntary and are marked by certain definite uni-directional response; they are controlled by unconscious processes of the nervous system and their aim is to preserve the 'self'.

By conducting experiments on dog, the Russian physiologist Pavlov showed that reflexes could be trained and modified if long term association could be established between the natural and the unnatural stimuli. Pavlov called this process as the conditioned reflex for the S-R connections that were acquired during the life time of the individual animal, could be trained to respond to a stimulus which itself is incomplete and inadequate to cause natural response. Conditioned reflexes are not to be confused with un-conditioned reflexes that are inborn and common to all species.

Instincts

The innate tendencies of behaviour common to all animals are known as instincts. They are spontaneous, natural and non-variable. The infant behaviour is instinctive all through. Crying when hungry or in discomfort, urge for limb movement is expression of instincts. Instincts are native tendencies or dispositions of stereotypic behaviour under natural situations. They are complex, specific and innate but modifiable as far as human beings are concerned. Only under specific conditions do the instincts operate. Also called as material potential forces of nature, they direct animal's growth and development. Ross (1955) considered an instinct as *an inherited or innate engram complex or disposition which determines its possessor to behave in certain specific ways in relation to certain specific objects.* William James says: "Instinct is an innate disposition which determines an organism to perceive or pay attention to any object of certain class and to experience in its presence a certain emotional excitement and impulse to action which finds expression in a specific mode of behaviour in relation to that object."

For McDougall, *an instinct is an innate or inherited mental structure which determines its possessor to perform certain specific actions in situations.*

Characteristics of Instincts

- An instinct is a natural, inherent, innate, unlearnt self-activity which man and animal have possessed during long biological evolution for the preservation of the 'self' and the 'species'.
- Remarkably, an instinct is a tendency or disposition and not behaviour itself. It is a force which imperceptibly directs and guides organism's internal and external activities. Instinct directs love between the mother and the child, and hostility between enemies.
- Instincts exist for organism's well-being. According to Ross (1955) ".....response is made to those objects of environment which are likely to affect the individual well-being: secondly those objects which are likely to affect the well-being of the species to which the animal belongs are attended to". For wellbeing only does the child do locomotion, and threat to life makes the mother attend to her infant's needs.
- Superior intellect, intelligence, experience and knowledge enable human beings to modify, adapt and canalize instinctive behaviour into ingenious ways. In infancy and childhood instinctive urges are difficult to resist or suppress, but as we grow we learn to sublimate instinctive energy.
- Some instincts appear earlier, others late and some may tend to get weakened as the individual grows up. Learning, experience, and environment tend to regulate our instinctive behaviour.
- Instincts are not regarded as separate faculties of the mind but local differentiations of the animal's general power to apprehend its environment and to be active with regard to it. They are merely branches of the original tree of mind's power. Thus, mind is more than a bundle of instincts: it is an essence of the organism, a unity of which instincts are merely aspects which can be thought of separately but have no discrete existence.

Comparing Reflexes and Instincts

Both reflexes and instincts are innate, inborn, almost fixed mechanisms. While reflexes are behaviours, instincts are tendencies or dispositions of behaviour, not behaviours. Reflexes are simple organic mechanisms; instincts are complex. Both are universally present in living beings. Their clear purpose is protection of life. They are facilitative reaction patterns catalyzed by some stimulus. Instinctive tendencies are expressed in emotional responses under specific conditions.

Being dispositions instincts are vastly modifiable, adaptable and trainable; reflexes are fixed and rigid in operation. Some reflexes can be conditioned. The instinct-operation is somewhat within the conscious control of the individual, reflex operation is not. With advancing age, reflexes become weak influencing motor movements and physiological functions, instinctive behaviour may not show traces of weakening. Finally, we are aware of hunger, thirst, sex urge, love, hate, etc., but not aware of eye-blink or knee-jerk reflex.

Innate Behaviour - Activity and Sport Perspective

Not only is the unlearnt behaviour the very foundation of learned behaviour, its implication in activity and sport is serious and significant. It is now well-understood that without strong instinctive "urge" no individual will participate in physical activity and sport, nor would people aim for excellence – improving or enhancing performance. Primarily, it is due to instinctive energy animals and human beings carry out the routines of life. All general theories of motivation derive their substance from instincts – the raw material of human behaviour. Once brought into play, instincts cut across all boundaries of conscious control and make the individual go all out for the achievement of a pre-determined objective even at risk of one's own life. Instincts, even though morbid and crude, are an undrying reservoir of vital energy. Instinctively reinforced athletes give out incredible performances in activity and sport.

Physical activity, play, recreation, etc., by nature are instinctive activities. Physical educators and athletic trainers need to understand that instincts and emotions are no foreign intrusions; they are an inbuilt aspect of human unitary system. Therefore, physical activity and sports programmes need to be planned and organised in such a manner that they offer adequate opportunity to all participants to put in supreme effort towards achieving excellence. It needs no reminder that to thwart a growing child in his motoric exploration would mean causing him frustration and throwing an open invitation to mental ill-health.

Reflexes form the bedrock of our skilled behaviour. The process of reflex training starts in infancy; it catches momentum during childhood all through and is at peak during adolescence. Most reflexes get automatically trained as the child interacts with the environment physically. The more intensely and purposefully is the child made to engage in self-learning, the better are its reflexes trained to perform various skills economically and efficiently. Children whose physical activities remain restricted during infancy and childhood and they get least opportunity to engage in varied vigorous sporting/recreational activities, often have uncoordinated movements later in life and their growth lacks the much desired quality. Reflex training not only results in a better biomechanical standard but also leads to development of multi-ability athletic personality. Children who had had intensive reflex training in childhood whether by design or by default are able to acquire athletic skills far better than others.

In physical activity and sport, it is impossible to acquire, establish and refine skills without training reflexes. The entire gamut of sports training underlines the need for reflex training. There is no sport skill worth the name - batting, bowling, catching, throwing, kicking, shooting, spiking, boosting, striking, hitting, rolling, sprinting, balancing, etc., to mention a few – that does not require training of various reflexes. This is generally important for two basic reasons: (a) to make a skill cost-effective energy-wise, and (b) to prevent injury as far as possible. It should, however, be noted that reflex training, especially from the viewpoint of sport, must start at appropriate growth stage and in regular physical activity classes through the medium of simple motor activities and minor games. Reflexes not properly trained in childhood, are hard to train later. This stands in the way of a person aspiring to be a good athletic performer.

SELECTED REFERENCES

Buskist, William & Gerbing, David W. *Psychology - Boundaries and Frontiers,* Glenview, Ill. Scott Foreman/Little Brown Higher and Education, 1990

Crooks. Robert L. & Stein, Jean *Psychology – Science, Behaviour and Life,* New York; Holt Rinehart and Winston, 1988

Ross, J.S *Groundwork of Educational Psychology.* London, George G. Harrap & Co. Ltd., 1955

Woodwork, R.S. *Dynamics of Behaviour,* New York, Henry Holt, 1948

Human beings are, of necessity, miracles with flaws.

- *from* **The Wisdom of the Body**

CHAPTER - 6

GROWTH, DEVELOPMENT AND PHYSICAL ACTIVITY

In nature, nothing seems to be more charismatic than the steady transformation of an almost speck-like zygote (a fertilized egg) into a multi-celled organism with all the native equipment of behaviour and characteristics that enable it to live, struggle for existence and attain certain objectives of life. It is a natural tendency with all the living beings to grow, become big within the limits and limitations of their potential, interact with the environment and develop patterns of behaviour that facilitate life activities.

Growth is an extremely complex biological phenomenon studied by geneticists, biologists, developmental psychologists, educationists, and others for a variety of reasons. In education and psychology, the study of human growth and development assumes special significance because human beings have to be provided with opportunities for learning and growing into physically and mentally well-equipped personalities. As children grow in years, their body and mind undergone tremendous irreversible change in structure, form and functions almost every moment, the cumulative effect of which we see in different well-demarcated stages of growth such as infancy, children, puberty, adolescence, etc. This advancement in time influences their ability to learn, acquire various physical and mental skills and carry out all important activities of life. Subject teachers and physical educators who feign unfamiliarity with the growth characteristics which children exhibit at various developmental stages, may not find it easy to provide satisfying curricular experiences to the students, whether in the classroom or on the playfields.

MEANING OF GROWTH AND DEVELOPMENT

All neonates are constitutionally complete at birth. They acquire no additional organs in life. Functionally they show greater maturity as they interact with the environment. This makes their behaviour increasingly more complex. Growth, whether pre-natal or post-natal, is simply no structural or physical change (change in phenotype); it is also a change in function and behaviour. Biologically, structure and function define and influence each other. Therefore, it is not uncommon for people to use the terms growth and development interchangeably, although the former is a part of the latter. While 'growth' often refers to change in body size, development is known to be a process by which the child develops his or her motor abilities and skills. It is important to make a distinction between growth and development in order to understand them fully.

Growth is one aspect of development and refers to the increase caused by biological process in which the organism becomes bigger in size, volume and heavier in weight. Starting its existence as a zygote – an almost invisible dot - the human organism grows to be more than five feet tall and more than 150 pounds in weight. Growth indicates enlargement of cells, fibres and muscles, skeletal elongation, in other words, increase in the general volume of the body. Growth is characterized by perceptible change in structure and form. Growth curves are used to measure growth. The distance curve is a measure of size over time; it records height as a function of age and gets higher with age. The velocity curve measures the rate of growth at a given time for a particular body feature (such as height or weight). In terms of the progressive development of adult proportions, growth is measured linearly (by height or length of limb bone); in the expansion of girth, or surface area (by quadratic measures); and in terms of volume, or mass (by cubic measures). Marked by physical transformation, an adolescent is easily distinguishable from an infant and an adult from an adolescent. The growth curve moves upward up to a certain age and stabilizes.

Development is a wider term and underlines advancement, more unfoldment, a progressive change, a sort of growing forward to greater maturity. On this issue Gesell (1949) says: "Development is more than a concept. It can be observed, appraised and even measured in three major manifestations: (a) anatomic, (b) physiologic, and (c) behavioural....... Behaviour signs, however, constitute a most comprehensive index of development states and developmental potential". Development specifically refers to characteristic change in the functionality of the organs and the systems. For instance, not only the skeleton elongates over time, it also ossifies and become strong-enough to bear more weight. Similarly, there is increase in the heart muscle size, which favourably affects cardiac out-put and stroke volume. According to Benedict, development is a "process in which the internal physiological change and the psychological processes stimulated by them are integrated (or responded to) in a way which enables the individual to master further and anew, environmental stimulations."

Often growth and development are used in conjunction. Mary & Kelly (1956) remark: "Physical development does not necessarily mean increase in size. There are modifications of the body-composition taking place constantly. In the body, for example, gain in weight comes partly from increase in neural, glandular, and muscle tissue; in childhood the gain comes principally from bone and muscle tissue, while in adult years, the gain is from and accumulation of fat tissue". Growth has a limited span; it usually reaches its dead-end as a boy or girl steps out of "teens". Development, on the other hand, continues even further. It has close relationship with a person's nutrition, life-style, vocation, environmental interactions, and so on. While growth is largely physical, development encompasses intellectual and social attributes viz. knowledge, skills and experiences. Growth is concrete, observable and measurable; development is an abstract concept only to be monitored and measured by indirect means. There is objectivity about growth, developmental indices are largely subjective. Girth and strength of a skeletal muscle may be directly measured, but its shapeliness and beauty are evaluated by indirect means. Scientists have devised a variety of tests of motor-ability, fitness, intellectual abilities, psychomotor qualities, etc., with a view to objectify the developmental changes a developing child undergoes over time.

GENERAL PRINCIPLES OF GROWTH AND DEVELOPMENT

Growth is a creative process. Growth begins with fertilization (means conception), the process by which the male gamete, the sperm cell, and the female gamete, the egg, fuse to produce a zygote. In pregnancy the three stages are commonly referred as Z.E.F. - meaning Zygote, Embryo, and Faetus. After birth, one is first a neonate, then a child, an adolescent and finally an adult. From conception to adulthood, the entire growth process is Nature's finest feat of creativity. As the individual moves from one clearly demarcated growth stage to another, something is added to his physical, mental, intellectual and performing abilities. Instinctive behaviour is gradually overshadowed by highly skillful and socio-culturally accepted behaviour. Growth is truly a building-up process so clearly manifest in each and every aspect of our personality.

Growth in some direction is inevitable. All living beings have to grow, for growth is the essence of their existence. Despite possible aberrations from genetic abnormalities or environmental stress in the form of malnutrition, disease, toxins, accidents, psychosocial stress, and/or other insults to the developing organism, every one has the potential to grow to the extent to which one's heredity has set limits. Human growth is so sensitive to environmental forces that it provides a reliable indicator of the quality of the environment, although even under stress the body maintains proportionality, in what has been called the "harmony of growth." Moreover, short-term or seasonal sources of stress need not permanently compromise the developing body, since humans possess the capacity for "catch-up" growth—a rapid increase in growth velocity that restores a child to predicted size—in weight and to a lesser degree in height. It is established that more favourable environmental factors such as nutrition, exercise, etc., ensure better growth in terms of quality and direction.

Mental growth is dependent upon changed structure. This growth principle indicates that unless a child grows bodily, he does not develop mentally; in other words, the physical growth and mental growth move hand in hand. When a child performs poorly on tasks of perception and comprehension, it is because his perceptual apparatus is not fully developed to understand the external cues; he also has deficit in the ability to discriminate between the important and the unimportant. The programming of mind's software is a gradual and steady process. Perception and performance of complex motor skills involving a very high degree of neuromuscular coordination are beyond the mental capacity of the child whereas an adult with a rich experience takes little time in picking up hints and reacting to the problem-situation quickly and successfully. A good quality mental activity is not possible without proper growth of the brain and the nervous system. In most cases, this process is generally synchronized; however, discrepancies in some cases cannot be ruled out.

By their very nature children are ego-centric and adults socio-centric. Child behaviour is motivated by instinctive drives that are instrumental in satisfying his biological needs. The child is amoral and the centre of gravity of all his activity is his ego which must be satisfied at all costs. As he steadily moves on the path of maturity, he comes to understand that there is something else beyond his own self (his ego)); people around him too need his attention as they attend to him through thick and thin. In contrast, adults, no doubt, are conscious of their self, but they are overtly more conscious of the society. Children may not share their possessions with others, but adults more often than not are conscious of their obligation towards children and guests first. The 'self' overshadows child behaviour, social norms and standards guide adult behaviour.

Growth is an outcome of interaction between the organism and its environment. In the matter of growth, except for the germ plasm, which is a gift of nature, all other factors that transform the tiny single fertilized cell (zygote) into an infant, a child and an adult individual are supplied by the environment. Interestingly, if the zygote were not set to interact with the environment, its transformation into a human would remain a distant dream. Francis Galton termed heredity as *nature* (seed) and environment as '*nurture*' (soil). Only through seed-soil interaction, i.e. germ plasm-environment interactivity does the growth take place. As a matter of fact, it takes place both at micro (internally) and macro (externally) level. The role of 'seed' and 'soil' in the growth and development of a human being is relative, still shrouded in mystery; for who knows whether the barking of the dog or the tan colour of its skin is due to heredity or environment. Scientists are trying to unravel this mystery.

Heredity sets limits for development in terms of potential. Despite availability of environmental factors such as nutrition, oxygen, activity etc., in more than adequate measure, no organism is likely to grow beyond the limits nature (heredity) has set upon various species in terms of their growth. As an over-simplification no mouse with the best environmental support, can grow as big as an elephant. The growth limits and limitations are put on species as well as on individuals. Even the monozygotic twins are not the same in their potential for growth. Some races are tall, others short; so are the individuals. This hard biological reality has far reaching implications in sport and physical activity. We are today well aware that Olympic athletes are 'genetically gifted' and that no environment, how so abundantly supplied, can singularly produce a star performer. Somato-type, for example, is an important factor in the making of a top athlete, but it is more a matter of genetic endowment than environmental support. Moreover, there hardly exists any strong evidence to show that somato-type undergoes significant change due to external factors. The morphological structure of the muscle is a limiting factor on the athlete's speed; it makes him either a long distance runner or a sprinter. In terms of potential, it is impossible to trespass hereditary limits and perform beyond genetic potential. A born imbecile can never become a genius.

Growth stages follow a patterned trajectory. Under normal circumstances, human growth and development from conception to maturity follow a patterned trajectory. This trajectory is characterized by a rapid velocity of post-natal growth (with growth rate at its fastest in the first year of life); a steady growth rate with a lower, decelerating velocity during childhood; a juvenile growth spurt around the age of seven or eight (in about two-thirds of healthy children); and the onset of adolescence, with a markedly accelerated growth spurt, beginning for girls at age ten, on average, and for boys at age eleven or twelve years. For example, the prenatal growth is terribly fast, i.e. within hours of fertilization, the egg begins to divide. Gradually that first cell becomes a ball of hundreds of cells, and within months it takes the shape of an embryo and then a faetus. The infantile growth is also too rapid but not as much as prenatal growth. The rate of growth begins to slow down as the baby moves forward chronologically. Tanner & Tayler (1963) observe: "The parents of a strapping teen-age son find it hard to believe that their offspring was once a tiny seven-pounder. In less than a score of years, he has increased in height about three and a half times and in weight more than 20 times, at the same time changing from an infant to a man. But this visible growth and transformation are infinitesimal compared with those that take place in the first two months he spends in his mother's womb. There, in eight brief weeks, he increases in length about 240 times and in weight one million times; he grows from a single fertilized egg into a miniature baby". Nature's ways of putting checks and brakes on the moving wheel of growth are difficult to figure out. Florance L. Good-Enough in *Development Psychology*, says: "A waggish mathematician has figured out that if the organism were to continue to double itself in size at the embryonic rate it would be as large as the whole solar system by the end of twenty one years. It is just as well that this tremendous rate of growth begins to slow down."

Patterns of behaviour tend to follow an orderly sequence. According to Gesell (1949), a child, "sits before he stands; he babbles before he talks; he fabricates before he tells the truth: he draws a circle before he draws a square; he is selfish before he is altruistic; he is dependent on others before he achieves dependence on self." In nature, there is pretty good order; first things happen first. The growth of physical characteristics and patterns of behaviour at each developmental stage is generally in a pre-sequenced order, individual variations notwithstanding, For instance, at birth, an infant is first sensitive to light than to sound. This sequence is never disturbed. There is an order in the learning of speech, formation of concepts and acquisition of motor skills. Motor and mental abilities come in large variety but an order is discernible in their development. Ability to throw a ball precedes the ability to catch it. Similarly the ability to add figures is acquired before the ability to make subtractions. The change in developmental behaviour is progressive, but well-sequenced.

Every child grows in his own unique way; he has his own rate of growth. Nature has made every individual different and so unique in almost every respect. No two children, even twins, have the same rate of growth. Gesell (1949) reported: "Some children are tall and some short; some slender, others stocky. Some are physically strong, others are weak; some are intellectually keen, others are dull. There are the energetic and the phlegmatic, agile and the awkward, the courageous and the fearful, the outgoing and the in-going in personality". Some children are "slow to catch on" at school for several years but overtake many later. The flash of promise, talent or giftedness at one point or period of growth does not necessarily guarantee excellence in life further, because becoming a philosopher or a mathematician, a soldier or an athlete is also a matter of certain interests and aptitudes which children happen to acquire in due course of time. The unique growth patterns which every individual child exhibits are at the root of individual differences so challenging in the educational process for parents and teachers alike. Individuality rather than the generality will always be a matter of greater importance for the educationist and the psychologist.

Growth is a gradual but continuous process. Right from conception through infancy, childhood and adolescence, growth remains a continuous affair. There are neither pauses nor rest periods. One growth stage fuses into the preceding one and the succeeding one so remarkably that the whole process looks like a continuum. What happens at one growth stage is carried over to and influences the following growth stage. Even sudden spurts in growth lead into and grow out of the quieter, less dramatic periods. During the slackened growth periods, possibly the child is mobilizing his energies for the following growth spurts. It takes about eighteen long years for a neonate after birth to become an adult. Biologically, the longer the life-span of a species, the slower and more gradual its growth and maturation, is the rule.

Different aspects of growth proceed at different speed. Growth has several aspects - physical, psycho-motor, psychological, intellectual, emotional and social. These rarely move in a synchronized way. Each one has its own characteristic speed and direction for they are influenced by variety of internal and external factors. Non-appearance of particular characteristic in a child at a particular time often worries parents. Let us take language development, for instance. Children characteristically speak three to five words at twelve months of age but in the next three or four months, they seldom acquire new words and often even forget those they knew. Language development slows down for the time being because the child's physical energy and enthusiasm for learning are thoroughly occupied with the thrills of upright locomotion. Physical growth is very rapid during puberty. Children learn more new things in the first five years of life than at any comparable period of life. Some children show signs of physical maturity earlier than others; conversely, others may look mentally more mature.

Each organ grows at a different rate and reaches the climax at different times. Chaos and order in growth go almost together. Something that looks disorderly may actually be a part of some definite sequence. Nothing is actually out of step even though each part of the body grows and develops in its own characteristic fashion and speed. The feet speed up first reaching their peak growth rate only after about three months after the adolescence spurt has begun. In another six months, it is the turn of the calf muscles and the thighs. Four months later hips and chest begin to swell at an accelerated rate followed by shoulders. In both sexes, the length of trunk and the depth of chest reach peak growth-speed last of all. Parents and teachers are often worried on account of the disproportionateness of child's body, causing temporary clumsiness. In some cases, torso looks much longer than the limbs and vice versa. Nose, ears, head, neck, extremities all grow at their own rate of speed. Near the end of adolescence, the whole thing settles down and the child's looks show perfect proportion.

Growth is characterised by fluctuation. The periods of accelerated growth and those of consolidation alternate. In general, infancy and pre-school growth stages are of accelerated growth whereas the later childhood and second half of adolescence are periods of slackened growth or consolidation. By 17th or 18th year, growth begins to taper off. No wonder, some people are found growing even at forty. Malnutrition, environmental stresses, pressures of school work, economic stringencies, etc., significantly influence rate of growth. Fluctuation in growth may also be traced to genetic factors. Fluctuation in growth is no drawback at all but a natural phenomenon. The growth-course is always undulated. Growth records maintained at school may reveal how growth proceeds in case of each child.

The rate and pattern of the growth are modifiable to an extent. At any point or period of development, the conditions within and without the body may cause modification in the rate and patterns of a child's growth, even though they are fairly definite for each child. The inadequacy of play and activity opportunities, mal-nutrition, academic pressures, scarcity of learning facilities, physical insecurity, environmental pollution, poor discipline at home and at school, etc., potentially influence the movement of growth-curve; these often put hurdles in the growth path. When children get freedom from such restraining factors, they show remarkable improvements in their growth rate and pattern. Good environment facilitates growth, the poor one retards it.

Growth brings differentiation and integration in behaviour. We can easily tell how an adolescent and a 5-year old child will respond to a danger situation at home or at school. The difference between the behaviours of the two is squarely due to growth influence including experience and knowledge. We can also understand how an adolescent has learned to integrate his knowledge, experience and intelligence, which the child has yet to do. The processes of differentiation and integration are like siblings. They stem from the same roots. It is impossible to understand the physical child without understanding, at the same time, the thinking, feeling and impulsive child. Likewise, it is hard to understand a mentally well-equipped child without reference to his social adjustment and better upbringing. There is a warm relationship, for example, between one's total adjustment at school and emotional growth, physical health and intellectual adequacy. Importantly, one's psychological status is dependent on one's physical well-being, physical growth and health, which are in close proximity with emotional development often influenced by the school success or failure. The totality of a child is the product of its family history, its personal history and its current satisfactions, dissatisfactions and pressures. Differentiation is a marked sign of growth; each organ, each aspect of child's personality reaches its fullness by the process of differentiation; integration synthesizes all developmental aspects giving a unique status to every individual.

The effect of training varies with stages of maturation. Children learn things only when they possess the ability for it. The child's behaviour pattern goes on varying from one growth stage to another. For instance, a young child gets easily bored from repetitious practice of sports skills due to his limited muscular strength and ability to concentrate; an adolescent, on the other had, is not tired of practicing skills for hours so for he is physically strong and mentally focused. He also understands the value of practice as the only means of skill improvement. This fact has a great import in motor-skill acquisition process. Complex motor skills involving precision, co-ordination and psycho-motor elements are learnt at an appropriate growth level. When complex motor skill training is introduced at a very early age, effects on growth may be negative. In fact, the activity programme should be designed in such a manner that it assists neuromuscular processes, improve general movement patterns, and develop confidence in children for performing variety of skills. Early maturing children in a class have an edge over late maturing peers in learning of motor skills because they possess better perceptual-cognitive abilities.

Experience, knowledge and skill influence growth; they never enhance innate potentially. Gesell (1949) believes that innate capacity for growth "is a gift of nature. It can be guided, but it cannot be transcended by an educational agency." Children studying in elite public schools may have an edge over those in studying in ordinary institutions in some respects, but this does not mean that their learning potential is abnormally increased. Experience, knowledge and skill come with education but education is an external factor which does not have the capacity to enhance any one's innate potential for development though it helps the individual in realizing his potential to the maximum.

Generalizations about growth, discussed above, are more than directive principles of programme-planning especially in physical education and sport where the objective is to provide optimal opportunities to every child to strive for self-actualization and excellence. It is important for physical educators and athletic trainers to adjust training loads in considerations of the hard facts about human growth and its processes.

STAGES OF GROWTH

Despite continuity, the period of human growth from birth to adolescence is commonly divided by psychologists into *Infancy* (from birth to weaning), *Childhood* (from weaning to the end of brain growth), *Juvenile* (from the end of childhood to adolescence), and *Adolescence* (from the start of growth spurt at puberty until sexual maturity). Each of these well-demarcated stages of growth is marked by conspicuous physical, mental, emotional and social characteristics. However, it is often difficult to tell when and where in a child's life does infancy end and childhood begin or childhood end and adolescence begin because the attributes, temperaments and physical and mental characteristics including aptitudes, interests, dispositions, etc., that appear at any point or period of time, have continuity in time and space all through.

The growth stages are defined as the series of changes which an organism undergoes from embryonic stage to maturity. Ross (1953) calls this as "the process of growing up in various phases by which the erratic, impulsive child becomes the steady reasoning adult." The span of each growth stage is arbitrarily set and differs from one psychologist to another.

Earnest Jones divided human growth into four stages.

Infancy	(11 to 5 years)
Late Childhood	(6 to 12 years)
Adolescence	(12 to 18 years)
Maturity	(18 years onward)

Ross (1953) listed five rather than four stages of development.

Infancy	(birth to 3 years)
Early Childhood	(3 to 6 years)
Later Childhood	(6 to 12 years)
Adolescence	(12 to 18 years)
Adulthood	(18 years onward)

Jones feels that 'we grow up twice achieving a pseudo-maturity before puberty'. At this age, nature seems to undo most of her pioneer work and begin the process of building up and consolidating. In his opinion, adolescence and adulthood are recapitulation of infancy and late childhood respectively. Interestingly, each pre-adolescent year of growth brings so rapid changes that it would be preposterous to call it as a separate stage of development. The span of each growth stage now is determined more realistically than ever before.

Infancy

Fertilization of the female ovum by the male sperm gives rise to a new life in the form of a Zygote (fertilized egg) in mother' womb, and in over nine months does a baby enter the world complete in all respects with attributes of a human being. This is where the infancy begins.

Physical Characteristics

At birth, the neonate has all its organs and organ-systems including nervous system functioning well. The infant weighs approximately 7.5 pounds and measures 19.5 inches. The male babies are slightly taller and heavier than female babies. The infant's average height increases by 30% by the age of five months, and by 50% by the age of one year. The height of a five-year-old usually doubles relative to that at birth. The limbs and arms grow faster than the trunk, so that body proportions undergo marked variation as an infant grows into an adolescent. Different body systems grow and develop at different rates. For example, if infants grew in height as quickly as they do in weight, the average one-year-old would be approximately 5 ft (1.5m) tall. Thus, weight increases faster than height—an average infant doubles his birth weight by the age of five months and triples it by the age of one year. At two years of age, the weight is usually four times the weight at birth.

The new-born has soft, small and uncontrolled muscles. Comparatively lesser development is seen in neck and leg muscles than in muscles of the upper limbs. Bones are soft and flexible composed chiefly of cartilage or gristle. The proportions between various parts of the body are very odd: for example, the baby's head is approximately one fourth of his body-length as compared with the adult height which is approximately one seventh of the total body-length. The neck is short and barely visible. The baby's eyes look very small and eye-muscles are too weak to allow him/her to have any controlled eye-movements.

The shoulders are narrow, but abdomen large and bulging. In proportion, infant's limbs are too short - hands and feet being miniature. The pulse rate of the infant ranges from 130 to 150 beats a minute but gradually tapers down to 118 within a few days. This compares with average adult-rate of seventy. Similarly, the respiration rate also drops down from 40-45 to 18 within several weeks. The brain-growth does not consist of the multiplication of neurons but increase in their size and the number of axons and dendrites. The nerve pathways become more and more complex after birth.

Infant's general movements are highly un-coordinated because of the immature condition of its nervous system. When a sensory stimulus is applied to any part of the body, activity occurs through out the body. When the left hand is stimulated, for example, the right hand also moves. Importantly, the infant is likely to kick his legs, twist his trunk, turn his head from side to side and if the stimulus is intense, he will cry otherwise he may simply sneeze or yawn. It takes long time before the infant has conscious control over his limbs. Differentiated movements are not seen at all. Much of baby's activity is reflex type; pupillary, lip movement, tongue movement, sucking, flexion, knee jerk, sneezing etc, are present at birth. Reflexes, in fact, occur in the specific areas of the body. Infant's general responses include visual fixation on light, spontaneous eye-movement, shuddering, shedding tears, feeding responses such as sucking, swallowing, tongue, cheek and lip movements, sucking of the fingers, yawning, hiccupping, rhythmic mouthing movements, frowning and wrinkling, leg and foot movements. All these movements are uncoordinated, undefined and mostly aimless. The first two years are very critical in infant's life as the baby is vulnerable to illness. The growth-pattern during infancy is the same for male and female. According to Krogman (1957), during the first year, the increase in weight is proportionally greater than the increase in height; in the second year, the reverse is true. Bones elongate more in the first year while in the second year their growth is slow. Muscles in the first two years develop fast and allow freedom to the child to show independence in movement. Muscle-control sweeps over the body from head to feet, with the muscles in the head-region coming under voluntary control first and those in the leg-regions last. Due to development in the nervous system, bones and muscles, the infant exhibits a co-ordinated pattern of movement. It has learnt now to walk and run after having gone through movement patterns of rolling, creeping, crawling, toddling, sitting with erect backbone, standing with assistance and standing by himself. Gesell (1952) says that the ability to maintain an upright posture comes only after a long series of preparatory co-ordination. Several variations may be found in infants' movement patterns: some can stand earlier while others take more time; some may learn to run earlier than others.

Sitting occurs at six months of age. Between nine and 10 months, the infant is able to pull himself to standing and takes his first steps. By the end of first year, the baby develops good head balance and can see objects directly in his line of vision. He learns how to reach for objects and how to transfer them from one hand to the other. At twelve months, an infant can hold a pencil or a crayon and scribble with it. He is able to seat himself in small chair; he can point at objects of interest, and can feed himself with a spoon. Before he is two year-old, he can open boxes, unscrew lids from bottles or jars, turn the leaves of a book, build tower with four or five blocks, insert pegs in peg-board, string beads, cut a gash in the paper with scissors and scribble with pencil or a crayon. Running, skipping, jumping etc., are in just rudimentary form. However, turning from back to side, kicking, bouncing, wriggling, reaching for his toes, and watching his fingers move are joyful physical experiences of an infant. In life's second year, the infant play does not remain solitary, but takes a definite form. The infant enjoys throwing objects and going after them. By the end of the third year, a baby can run, bounce, dance, skip and do all sorts of stunts. It can talk well, and understand the meaning of the things. It can fight well and is not much afraid of falling. The infant hits back when teased, and calls names. Its muscles and bones are well developed for its age. It can lift heavier objects and throw them at a distance though this kind of movement is still in crude form. The infant bubbles with energy and does not get tired of playing especially with objects which he uses as symbols. Still the fine muscles of the fingers are not under his control. While trying to scribble or draw a picture, the infant makes use of the whole fore-arm rather than fingers alone. However, it tires himself quickly when working persistently with pencils.

During next three years, the growth is somewhat even but it slows down considerably as compared to the growth in first two years. Good proportion in infant's height and weight is visible; he looks like a mini adult. His bones get harder and the possibility of their getting misshapen decreases. In several personal habits, the child becomes self-sufficient and needs no help. After running has been sufficiently practised, the child now turns to mastering hopping, skipping, galloping and jumping. Physical activity comprises aimless bouncing, running, going up the stairs, undifferentiated movement of limbs when louder noise is heard; kicking legs or trotting like a horse and flinging arms are very common in babies when rhythm is provided. A well-reared child is strong enough to resist disease and deformity.

Mental Characteristics

The brain of the newborn is not yet fully developed. It contains about 100 billion brain cells that have yet to be connected into functioning networks. But brain development up to age one is more rapid and extensive than was previously realized. At birth, infant's brain is 25% of the adult size. At the age of one year, infant's brain has grown to 75% of its adult size and to 80% by age three, reaching 90% by age seven. The influence of the early environment on brain development is crucial. Infants exposed to good nutrition, toys, and playmates have better brain function at age 12 than those raised in a less stimulating environment. Bower (1974) says ".... infancy is the critical period in cognitive development - the period when the greatest losses can occur. Further, the losses and gains that occur here become harder to off-set with increasing age". At birth, the infant's sense organs are complete but their functions are raw. For example, all infants at birth are either totally or partially blind to colour; hearing is almost negligible but senses of smell and taste are well-developed. Their skin is sensitive to touch, pressure, temperature and pinch. Kofka (1925) adds that "because the mind of the new-born infant is different from that of the older child, and because his experiences are linked to those of the intra-uterine life, the new-born infant is helpless psychologically".

Infant's emotional life is largely guided by pleasures and pains that arise either from non-fulfilment of biological needs instantly or from uncomfortable situations. To attract mother's attention, the infant loudly screams. Irrespective of the nature of stimulation, the resultant emotion is intense and sudden. Bakwin (1947) states: "The ability to respond emotionally is present in the new-born as part of the development process and does not have to be learnt. Maturing emotions require gratification if optimum health is to be attained". Emotional development, to a great extent, comes through mother's love, affection, favourable attitude towards the child. During the first two years, the child learns to understand a lot of things. By people's gestures he can make out whether he is being rebuked or cajoled.

At eighteen months, the mean number of different words used by babies is 10, and at twenty four months it is 29.1. Vocabulary-building depends on social interaction, intelligence, incentive and parental initiative. Generally, girls are ahead of boys in this respect. Marked individual differences in language development are found amongst children. Infant's emotional stability is closely related to his maturation and learning. Banham & Spitz observe: "With age, emotional responses become less diffuse, less random, and more differentiated. They likewise become more specialized and directed towards the situation in which they occur. From the general emotional excitement which appears at birth, fear, anger, disgust, distress, delight, elation and affection gradually develop".

A pre-school infant is conversant with its environment; it knows the meaning of some of the abstract things, has fairly good knowledge of language and faces no problem in expressing himself in ordinary ways. It can count numbers, make limited mental calculations and memorize things especially poems and rhymes. Children at fourth or fifth year are charged with high emotions; they are temperamental, obsessed with fears, show stubbornness, are fussy over trifles, weep and cry over trivialities. They rarely tolerate restrictions and consider themselves capable of doing more than elders can do for them. They over-estimate their energies and are overly aggressive and negativistic. Aggression is markedly reflected in their play activities. Finding an elder around, they tend to be aggressive in behaviour in order to attract his attention. As children cross fourth year, this tendency begins to decline. Self-assertion becomes very powerful during later half of infancy.

The child is self-possessive and does not tolerate any body's intrusion upon his activities and possessions especially toys. By the end of infancy, he can see through elder's designs and is capable of even retaliating with his speech or actions. The infant is largely restive. It cannot concentrate too long on one activity. Illustrated books and magazines attract him. This enables him to develop concepts about things, animals, places and people. For him abstractions are difficult to understand. He is inquisitive and curious about things and their functioning. The tendencies of construction and destruction are equally strong in his behaviour. The infant breaks toys to transform them into new objects. The child is often stubborn and makes parents yield to his whims. The effect of punishment is evanescent. He mixes up with his peers without distinction of colour, creed, caste and even language. His likes and dislikes develop through experience and environmental interaction.

Other Characteristics

Infants are largely solitary creatures, self-centred, impulsive, amoral and asocial. Their society is confined to their parents, siblings, household maids and servants and immediate neighbour-hood children. Their primary concern is fulfilment of bodily needs.

Freud considers infancy as the age of *Narcissism* (fixation on one's own body) or *Auto-eroticism* (natural sexual excitement), and age of *Oedipus* (attachment of the male child to the mother) and *Elektra* (attachment of the female child to the father) complexes. This seems to be a far-fetched idea, so difficult to understand. Freud believed that the personality development in infancy and childhood comes through three-staged sexual development: *Oral, Anal* and *Phallic*. Infants, according to Freud, derive sexual pleasure through oral activity (breast-sucking, bottle-feeding and taking every thing into mouth). Further, at Anal stage the pleasure comes through playing with faecal matter (urine, excreta) and external sexual parts almost unconsciously. At Phallic stage (puberty and beyond) children become fully aware of their sex organs the conscious or unconscious manipulation of which is a source of pleasure for them. Girls seem to feel jealous of boys because they find something amiss in their body perhaps external sex organs.

Infant's imagination is quite fertile. Fantasy, make-believe, day-dreaming and fairy tale play are essential ingredients of his imaginary world. The infant is generally unmindful of what happens around him. Sometime he is noticed playing with an imaginary friend.

Infants are generally quarrelsome. The quarrel, which begins over possession of toys, neither lasts long nor does it have permanent effect on their relationship. This tendency arises out of impulsiveness. When infants quarrel, they attempt to snatch away opponents' toys, destroy their works and resort to physical assault purely out of jealousy and spite. In the scuffle for toys, they scream, cry, hit, kick, scratch and bite.

Infant Play

Infant play is solitary and formless. Infants play with whatever they can lay hand on. They greatly enjoy throwing and later kicking and hitting toys, balls and other objects. They may even be seen talking to toys or themselves. For them toys and household objects are living things. Family's socio-economic status, peers, gender, play facilities such as open spaces, parks, gardens, wide courtyards, etc., have bearing on infant play. Bower (1947) says: "During infancy, the basic human motor skills are established, perceptual development is virtually completed, and the roots of the cognitive skills that will grow into a human intellect are laid." Children with better resources prefer dramatic play, creative activities and reading comics whereas others engage in running, jumping, climbing, playing with garbage, junk, etc., aimlessly. Boys seem to have a wider range of play interests than girls who prefer less vigorous activities. Dramatization occupies an important place in infant's play. Hurlock (1959) feels that "dolls, soldiers, or stuffed animals become living creatures; and wagons, doll-houses, and coaches, all of which are reproductions in miniature of the same equipment used for daily living, make it possible for the child to dramatize scenes from real life in his play. Dramatic play follows a definite pattern in which personification, such as talking to dolls or stuffed animals, predominates before the age of three years".

The use of mud, sand, clay, blocks, beads, paints, crayons, pastes, paper and things like these during play manifests infant's creativity and an urge for construction. Imagination and creativity guide the infant play, which is marked by freedom, spontaneity and urge for activity. By manipulating variety of objects, infants gain motor control over their limbs resulting in better coordination. Infants possess exuberant energy and they engage in an "aimless expenditure" of it in play. They acquire physical skills by observation, imitation or trial-and-error technique.

Childhood

Beginning with the fourth year, childhood extends roughly to twelfth year. During this period, growth moves in waves. There are at least two periods of accelerated growth and two periods of consolidation alternating during childhood, causing tremendous transformation in a child's behaviour and character. Stability in development is characteristic of the later part of childhood. Psychologists regard childhood as the period of "pseudo-maturity". The child at ten or eleven is very much "at home" in this world: he is capable of adapting to the environment. In Stanley Hall's view, childhood is "recapitulation" of pre-natal experiences.

With entry into the school, the child stays away from home for a substantial part of the day. The field of his activity and interaction widens as comes in contact with different kinds of other children. At school, a variety of social relationships develop, adding a new dimension to child's conduct and behaviour. He finds himself amidst a battlefield on one side of which is the infantile impulsiveness, and on the other life's socializing forces engaged in perpetual struggle for supremacy. This increases child's social awareness, and puts brakes on his instinctive gratification channels. Childhood is the entrance gate for formal education. The pulls and pressures of school discipline become instruments of repression and suppression of instinctive urges.

Physical Characteristics

From 4 years of age until the onset of rapid growth in puberty (the adolescent growth spurt) the average rate of growth for boys and girls is about 5-6 cm/year. During this time the 'typical' boy is slightly taller than the 'typical' girl. This situation is temporarily reversed when girls reach their adolescent growth spurt at around 11 years old, some two years earlier than boys. However, height-weight development, to a great degree, depends upon the intellectual and socio-economic status of the family, as claimed by Thompson (1954).

The child loses milk teeth and acquires permanent ones. This results in marked changes in his facial contours. Most children feel awkward and try to hide their mouth when talking. The forehead flattens, the lips fill out; the nose becomes larger and acquires clear shape owing to the development of the cartilage framework. To quote Thompson (1954): "As childhood progresses the trunk elongates, and becomes slimmer. The chest broadens and flattens. The neck becomes longer, thus permitting the shoulders to drop. The pelvis increases in size. By the age of eight years, the arms and legs are 50 percent longer than they were at two years and are very thin with no marked development in the musculature. This is responsible for the all-arms-all-legs look of the older child. The hands and feet grow very slowly in late childhood, though boy's hands and feet are generally larger than those of girls".

Year after year, varied physical abilities surface in infants, to quote a few examples. A child at four can stand heel to toe for a good 15 seconds with his eyes closed. He can perform the finger-to-nose test very well, also with eyes closed. He can jump in place on both feet. At five year, he can balance on tiptoe for a 10-second period, and hop on one foot, part his lips and clench his teeth. A six year old child can balance on one foot for a 10-second period. He can hit a target with a ball from 5 ft (1.5 m), and jump over a rope 8-inch (20 cm) high. At seven years, he can balance on tiptoes for a 10-second period, bend at the hips sideways, and walk a straight line, heel-to-toe for a distance of 6 ft (1.8 m). By eight years, the child can maintain a crouched position on tiptoes for a 10-second period, with arms extended and eyes closed. He is able to touch the fingertips of one hand with his thumb, starting with the little finger and repeating in reverse order.

The attractiveness of the early childhood-body almost vanishes and now the child seems to be growing out of proportions. The facial angularity makes the child temporarily unattractive. Consequently, he becomes negligent in his personal habits and appearance.

Motor Skill Development

Generally, children are energetic, restless, untiring and over-brim with energy, with a strong urge for out-door activity. Acquiring motor skills facilitates child's success at school and adjustment in the peer-group. As per their need, urge, inclination, and aptitude, all children attempt mastery over motor skills involving hand-eye, hand-foot coordination. Children deficient in essential motor-skills remain backwardness in sport and hesitate to participate in social activities for their movements are clumsy and awkward. They often develop sissiness and inferiority complex, which in the long run proves to be least effective in the harmonious development of their personality.

Quality motor development greatly depends on the opportunities and facilities children get for activity, free play, and sport - both organized and unorganized - at school, at home, at club and/or in the neighbourhood. Mastery over general skills of movement comes with repetitious participation in interesting and popular tag and 'It' games, relays, ball games, minor games, etc. It is natural for the boys to enjoy more vigorous games than do girls. Brackenridge & Vincent (1955) remark: "Girls, as a rule, surpass boys in skills involving finer muscles, such as painting, sewing, weaving and hemming while boys are superior to girls in skills involving the grosser muscles, such as baseball throw, soccer kick, and standing and running broad jump, for instance". Most children derive immense pleasure in running, chasing, kicking, climbing, hiding and seeking during free time, breaks and regular activity hours. In this endeavour, they are often unmindful of what happens to their appearance, and possessions such as books, bags, clothes, shoes, etc. This care-free attitude often lands them in trouble both at home and at school.

A child at seven has an unquenchable thirst for action. He is open, free and active. Inactivity is alien to him. Activity and its results interest him the most. With fast developing sense of equilibrium, the child can stand on one foot, hop and skip, keep time to music in his own characteristic style, bounce and catch a ball. He likes to climb trees or stairs and jump from a height. On getting tired, the child momentarily withdraws from play activity, but within minutes he returns to it. In next two years, marked changes are manifest in his body. He is sturdy, long-legged and rangy in appearance, and usually healthy and replete with vital energy. His sense of rhythm greatly improves and his skill-movements are consistent and smooth. After sufficient development in the large muscles, it is now the turn of the fine muscles to get desired attention and move on the path of progress more speedily than before. Manipulative skills multiply. The liking for vigorous activity in general is intense but not for a particular sport. Children cannot remain idle; they have to be doing something. When denied this opportunity, they develop disliking not for the activity but for the teacher. They often compare with one another the development of their muscles and power.

Mental Characteristics

The development of motor skills in the child goes hand in hand with the development of cognitive skills, a process called cognitive development. Cognitive development can be divided into four stages:

- *Sensory-motor Stage*: At this stage, infants discover their environment using a combination of sensory impressions (sight, smell, hearing, taste, and touch) and motor activities.
- *Preoperational Stage*: At this stage, children are not able to use information in rational and logical ways; rather they use images and symbols. They learn how to associate cause and effect and to represent something with something else. Speech development begins.
- *Concrete Operational Stage*: At this stage, children understand elementary logical principles that apply to concrete external objects. They learn to sort things into categories, reverse the direction of their thinking, and think about two

concepts (such as length and width) simultaneously.

- Formal Operational Stage: This stage is reached at adolescence. The individual can think in the abstract and speculate about probabilities and possibilities as well as reflect on their own thinking activities.

Appreciable improvement can be seen in child's mental growth. A great deal of independent thinking develops. The child can think about anything without physical presence of objects. Group-activity and social interaction with peers serve as catalysts for learning of proper language, communicative skills, and correct thought expression. The child acquires a fund of vocabulary by literature study.

Children use a secretive language - sometime by distorting their own speech - to communicate with one another especially when some mischief-mongering is the motive. The older children generally become boastful of their possessions rather than athletic skills. Through interpersonal interaction children internalize ethics, societal norms, and standards of behaviour. They become socio-centric. The school discipline and parental guidance assist children in exerting control over violent emotions. Hurlock (1959) says: "Characteristically emotional expressions in late childhood are pleasant. The child giggles or laughs uproariously, squirms, twitches, or even rolls on the floor, and in general shows a release of pent-up animal spirits". More often bursting into laughter at something or on some one for no reason or without context is indicative of some mischief.

Adequate opportunity for free interaction with peers, parents and teachers enhances children's knowledge and intellectual capacity. They tend to find deeper meaning in the social behaviour of elders and understand "what is what and who is who' at home, at school and outside. Children's likes and dislikes for certain teachers and relations are difficult to suppress. For fear of disapproval or punishment, they may not reveal them but they certainly discuss them among peers. Children put a name-tag to particular teachers for fun, which they thoroughly enjoy. Teachers generally have tough time with this age group. While the fears aroused by concrete objects decrease with age, imaginary fears continue to haunt children. Since children are well aware of their environment, they fear being jeered at or ridiculed in case their movements are awkward. Family and school problems and those of personal adjustment often worry children. They try to tackle them at their own level. Gesell (1949) points out that anger is the strongest of emotions during childhood. It is aroused when teacher makes unfavourable comparisons; he shows favouritism or unduly interferes with the activities of the children. Children aspire for good things; not getting them, upsets them. Most children are jealous of those acknowledged superior in intellect, skill and/or age. The expression of jealously is physical - usually in the form of "quarrelling, telling tales, ridiculing, teasing, bullying and even instigating quarrels." The simplicity and affectionateness of the early childhood is replaced by more serious and sobre expression of joy. The emotional flow is regulated by social norms. Children are often pulled up and even physically punished for not behaving in the classroom, and on the playfield.

Other Characteristics

In childhood the gregarious tendency overshadows behaviour. Children tolerate no monotony of solitariness; they enjoy themselves in the company of peers. They form gangs and organize them well, nominating captains, vice-captains and other leaders. Sometime, the strangers usurp the peer-group leadership by virtue of qualities of brain or brawn. The extreme gregariousness provides moral sanctions which govern their behaviour. The child behaviour is determined largely by anticipation of social praise and blame - the chief authority being the gang. The morals are ruled by public opinion.

Children's fidelity towards the gang is unflinching. Obedience to the 'gang leaders' is extracted at any cost. The *school-boy-morality* is at its peak, the boys cheating and lying to the teacher in the supposed interest of the gang. For children, home is merely a physical shelter. The gang-spirit enjoins a duty upon each member of the gang to make the gang bigger and stronger by motivation, persuasion or coercion. Inter-gang rivalry is common, the exhibition of which is seen in clashes, brawls, quarrels and fights among children outside school. Girls also have their cliques to serve their objectives as well as guard against mischievous male gangs.

The gang-affiliation is manifest during athletic competition, matches and tournaments at school and in the neighbourhood clubs. Where play facilities (open spaces, play grounds, sports gear, etc.) are scarce, children's energies are siphoned off into mischief-mongering and destructive acts such as annoying, abusing, and jeering at the older people, stealing fruit from the orchards of the neighbours, smoking, roaming aimlessly and loafing about in the streets and lanes till late evening, and the like. Cat-calling, whistling, stoning street lamps, damaging public property for fun, scribbling foul words on the roads, walls, railway wagons, public transport and in public toilets, etc., are peculiarities of later childhood behaviour. Haughurst (1953) feels that even laughter in children at this age is guided by group-whims e.g. "seeing others in a predicament, making faces, drawing caricatures of teachers and others in authority; playing practical jokes, and defying authority, even if this leads to punishment - all make the group laugh. Each individual child thinks these are funny situations and laughs too".

Female 'gangs' are milder in nature: they do not indulge in unsocial forms of behaviour. Crane (1957) says: "While gang activities may vary from community to community and among different social classes within a community, there is a marked similarity in their interest in games and sports, going to the movies or athletic contests, exploring the country or just sitting around to talk and eat. Boys, more often than girls, try to test the barriers imposed by adults, and as a result, may become noisy, troublesome and rowdy."

Depending upon avenues of expression, the gang-tendency influences character-formation. Properly directed gang-energy works wonders in sport and life, enabling children to be cooperative, obedient and responsible. As a matter of fact, gang-age serves as a life-line for the process of socialization. Physical educators and athletic coaches must draw maximally from this source of energy making children excellent performers. Play-fields are the best avenues for settling inter-gang rivalry for supremacy. Shifting gang loyalty is resented upon, often spelling disaster for children involved. For the weak and meek, the gang serves as a protective shield, and for the strong and the superior, it is a forum for expression of qualities of leadership and command. As children reach the threshold of adolescence, juvenile gangs begin to disappear.

Generally, children love to become members of neighbourhood sports teams or play groups. Their slide towards notorious gangs is natural when school fails to provide adequate opportunities play, recreation and sport activities. Dubuis (1952) observes: "When young people do not participate in sports ...... they frequently are headed for trouble because they have not had the opportunity to learn, to win humbly, to lose gracefully, and to endure physical discomfort to attain a goal". The later childhood is an ideal time-span for strengthening group-affiliation and team-cohesion through tours, picnics, camps, hikes, treks and tournaments.

Most children show extroverted behaviour. Ross (1953) admits: "The boy of ten or eleven is naturally an extrovert - that is, one who is concerned with objects outside himself rather than with his own mental life. He revels in out-door activities - in games and in camping. His interests are supremely practical; he is immensely curious as to how things work, and he picks up a mass of information on various tasks which is a matter of perceptual surprise to his elders" With a keen sense of colour and design, the child is selective about dress, toys, books, etc. He is fussy over trifles. Mother's love and father's firmness keep him on track. Children are very inquisitive about people, places and problems. They are argumentative too and try to thrust their opinion even on elders.

In early childhood, sex urge remains dormant. As children reach the brink of puberty, interest in sex is heightened. They look at sex differences both with awe and wonder. They try to know how a child is born. To satisfy their curiosity on this account, they either confide in older friends or read cheap literature. This might lead to sex-exploration, which according to Hurlock (1959) "takes many forms; the most common of which are peeping, direct observation of the reproductive anatomy, matching masculine prowess in the toilet, manual exploration, oral contact, masturbation, and attempts at intercourse. This is generally accompanied by provocative giggling, obscene language, and secrets". Children often are secretive on these matters and show a sense of guilt when caught red-handed.

In childhood, most children shape up well physically but those remaining bodily disproportionate, weak and reed-like have difficulty in adjusting socially. The athletically build children can easily be spotted from out a multitude of healthy and fit. Apart from this, a child's social adjustment also depends on interpersonal relationship at home, parental care and social attitude towards him. Indulgent parents who neglect their children let them slip out of their hands. On the other hand, the unduly strict and strong-willed parents make their children shy, inward-going, and weak-willed. Childhood is an impressionable age in which are laid the foundations for a promising personality through good efforts of the parents at home and teachers at school.

Children's Play Needs and Activities

Childhood is "play-age". A strong foundation for good health, fitness, skill-training, performance, competition and sport excellence, is laid during this period only. Most children tend to participate in activity and sport willingly and vigorously. Unfortunately, the burden of academic work allows them little freedom for this. When children are exposed to a range of physical activities, minor games, recreational sports, etc., the physical educators and sports coaches would find it easy to spot out the 'gifted' ones from out of the mass of ordinary ones. It is so because through participation alone do children's strengths and weaknesses come to surface and it is not difficult to know who is athletically endowed and who a part of the common crowd. This is right age when children should be introduced to major sports such as football, hockey, gymnastics, basketball, volleyball, athletics, etc.

When opportunities are scarce for organized play activities and sport, children do engage in such activities as pay no dividends in terms of skill, fitness, health and achievement. Simply playing modified cricket with improvised equipment at a street corner may be good as a leisure hour activity, but its outcomes are not commensurate with the objectives of physical education and sports in real sense of the term. Organized exercise and sport have a lasting effect on the development of motor-qualities, and physical, conceptual and social skills. Games of low organization have the potential to develop courage, coordination, posture and skill among children. Rhythmic activities such as set drills and folk dances are greatly valued for their ability to instil in children sense of rhythm, coordination, unity, uniformity and body-poise.

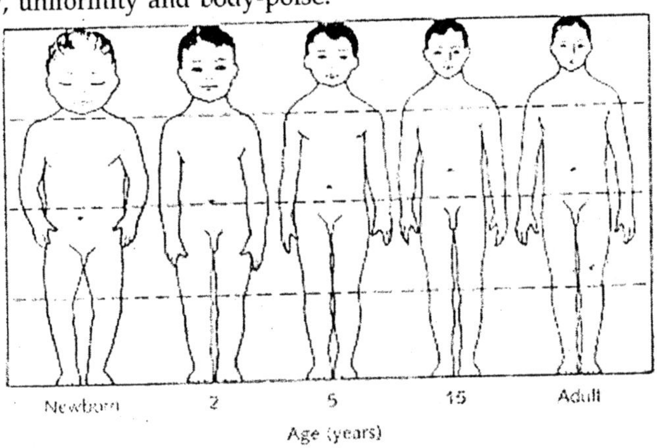

Fig. 6.1 The changing proportions of the growing body

Most children are usually healthy and abound in energy. They have a wide range of interests and longer attention span. They possess the ability to learn sports that take them to the path of excellence and achievement so essential for an amiable personality. However, too much adherence to rules and regulations may not produce desired effects. Talented children always require extra attention and care.

Adolescence

The term adolescence stems from 'adolesce' meaning 'grow to maturity'. The transitional period between childhood and adolescence is called puberty (from Pubertas meaning 'age of manhood') when a child gets transformed into an adult. Beginning with puberty and gradually submerging into adulthood, adolescence covers a period of 6 to 8 years, very crucial in the life of an individual. Ordinarily adolescence commences at twelve and ends with nineteenth year with variations in individual growth due to genetic or environmental factors causing children to be either early or late maturing individuals. In India, girls begin to mature by 10-11 years and boys 12-13 years. Geographical, socio-economic, nutritional and genetic factors play important role in the onset of adolescent growth-spurt.

While pre-adolescence (puberty) is referred to as a period of "predictabilities and unpredictabilities", adolescence is rightly labelled as an age of "great stress and strain, and storm and strife" (Stanley Hall). As the child crosses the threshold of puberty, he or she suddenly finds himself or herself caught in a physiological upsurge, psychological chaos and emotional upheaval. For first two or three years of adolescence, the human body and mind seem to be tossing on the high tide of stormy ocean of growth. Far reaching changes occur in his physiology and body-chemistry significantly influencing individual's behaviour, psychological make-up and social adjustment. The child is virtually unable to understand what is happening to him or her.

Physical Characteristics

Adolescence is a period of tremendously accelerated physical growth. Bayley (1956) observes that "between the ages of twelve and fourteen years, differences between the sexes are especially marked, with many more mature girls than mature boys. This difference is reflected in the large and more mature bodies of the girls and in their more aggressive, more sex-conscious, and more mature behaviour".

At puberty, a very considerable change in growth rate occurs. There is a swift increase in body size, a change in shape and body composition, and a rapid development of the ovaries and testes, the reproductive organs, and the characters signalling sexual maturity. The internal mechanism which leads to maturity of a child is explained by Tanner & Tayler (1963):

> The best evidence at present suggests that the whole process begins in the nervous system, in the small mass at the top of the brain stem that is called the Hypothalamus. (It) appears to act as a kind of biological timer; it turns on the hormonal processes that produce the adolescent growth-spurt and sexual maturity; at the proper moment it turns them off. This it does through its effect on the body's 'master' gland, the pituitary which lies immediately beneath the brain stem and which regulates activity of other endocrine glands. During childhood, it (hypothalamus) is apparently very sensitive to the small quantity of sex hormones present in the blood-stream even before birth. Responding to their presence, the hypothalamus prevents the pituitary from releasing its gonadotrophic hormones which would stimulate the sex glands to step up their hormone production. With the general growth and development .... the hypothalamus, at a certain time apparently becomes less sensitive to the sex hormones and ends its inhibition of the pituitary. Then the pituitary is free to release gonadotrophenes. These, in turn, prod the sex glands into stepping up their own out-put and sexual maturation begins. These interlinked processes continue until the sex hormones in the blood stream reach a level that can stimulate the hypothalamus which there upon calls halt to further sexual changes. Thus the level of development is stabilized.

Some of the changes are common to both sexes, but most are sex-specific. Some children grow slightly more slowly than others and reach puberty later than average. They do, in the end, reach a normal height, though children who have short parents tend to be short themselves. At puberty, boys have a great increase in muscle size and strength, together with a series of physiological changes making them more capable than girls of doing heavy physical work, and running faster and longer. Boys have lanky arms and legs, broad shoulders and an angular face characteristic of the masculine build: muscular strength and muscular weight increase considerably. In girls, secondary sex characteristics become pronounced. Their hips increase in width and rotundity caused partly by enlargement of the pelvic bone and partly by the development of the subcutaneous fat; breasts start elevating and protruding forward. During the adolescent growth spurt, for a year or more, the velocity of height increase approximately doubles; a boy is likely to be growing again at the rate he first experienced about age 2. As secondary characteristics become prominent, proportions of the adolescent body considerably change and a boy can easily be distinguished from a girl even they put unisex attire.

Practically all skeletal and muscular dimensions take part in the spurt, though not to an equal degree. Most of the spurt in height is due to acceleration of trunk length rather than length of legs. There is a fairly regular order in which the dimensions accelerate: leg length as a rule reaches its peak first, followed by trunk length and the body breadths, with shoulder width last amongst them. The earliest dimensions to reach their adult size are the head, hands, and feet. At adolescence, children, particularly girls, sometimes complain of having large hands and feet. They can be reassured that by the time they are fully grown their hands and feet will be a little smaller in proportion to their arms and legs, and considerably smaller in proportion to their trunk. The contours of the face, which have been altering gradually through out childhood, manifest sudden and marked changes. The whole profile becomes angular, the forehead more prominent, the chin more pointed, the nose longer. These changes, associated with the growth of facial bones, are accompanied by subtle changes in muscle size and in the distribution of fatty tissue under the skin. Consequently, adolescent's facial expressions exhibit ample seriousness, sobriety and definiteness.

The adolescent growth spurt in skeletal and muscular dimension is closely related to the rapid development of the reproductive system, which takes place at this time.

In boys, the first sign of puberty is usually an increase in the size of the testes and scrotum, with reddening and wrinkling of the scrotal skin. Slight growth of pubic hair may begin about the same time, but is usually a little later. The spurts in height and penile growth begin on average about a year after the first testicular acceleration. Axillary hair appears on average some two years after the beginning of pubic hair growth. In boys, facial hair begins to grow at about the same as the auxiliary hair appears. Breaking of the voice occurs relatively late in adolescence, and is often a gradual process and so not suitable as a criterion of puberty.

In girls, the appearance of the 'breast buds' is as a rule the first sign of puberty, though the appearance of pubic hair sometimes precedes it. The uterus and vagina develop simultaneously with the breasts. Menarche, the first menstrual period, is a late event in the sequence. It almost invariably occurs after the peak of the height spurt has been passed. Though it marks a definitive and probably mature stage of uterine development, it does not usually signify the attainment of full reproductive function.

The adolescent's sexual maturity is largely affected by his glandular functioning, socio-economic status and body-build. Children do not get suddenly sexually mature. It takes roughly three years for girls and two to four years for boys to exhibit signs of maturity. The looks, styles of locomotion and communication and patterns of interpersonal interaction conspicuously reveal changes that occur in adolescents.

Changes also occur in adolescent physiology. Organs of the digestive system change relatively in size; stomach becomes longer, intestines grow in length and circumference, the muscles in the stomach and intestinal walls become stronger and thicker. Adolescents consume more food than pre-adolescents. Their heart and blood vessels grow in size, becoming capable of transporting more blood to the tissues. Lung-increase keeps pace with the increase in width and depth of the chest which gets flattened optimally. Breathing becomes slower. Up to the age of fourteen, the two sexes do not differ in lung-capacity. After that boys surpass girls to a marked degree. Their bones get stronger - boys acquire flat bones while girls rounded ones. There is substantial improvement in adolescents' health standard. They are now strong-enough to resist diseases to which they were prone in childhood.

Dr. Jones believes that 'the adolescent is now recapitulating his infantile sexual history'. Psycho-analysts contend that the sexual impulse, which has been lying dormant all the years of childhood, suddenly becomes violent and as Slaughter put it, "Like the over-flow of a great river, it irrigates and fertilizes the tracts of human territory". Auto-eroticism, homosexuality and hetero-sexuality occur concurrently in adolescence.

In essence, the physical growth and behavioural transformation that occur in adolescence are second in magnitude to those which take place in pre-natal stage. As nine months of intra-uterine growth converts speck-like egg into a faetus, nine years of adolescence transforms a child into an adult capable of performing all functions and duties of life. Growth variation is a function of individual's own biological clocks.

Mental Characteristics

As a rule, physical growth and mental development go hand in hand. Late or early maturing in either aspect is, however, no exception. With wider mental outlook, and better intellectual capacity, adolescent boys and girls begin to think more rightly and find deeper meaning in things. Increased observation power makes adolescents examine objects, persons and ideals more critically than before. In the beginning, thinking lacks clarity. Adolescents hardly figure out why they react to the situations the way they do. To widen their mental horizon, adolescents read a great deal and generalize things. The "thrillers, fictions and saucy books" interest them the most. Adolescents do not accept ideas, ideals and principles on their face value but questions their validity - thus revolting explicitly against the authority of the literature and men. The sense of criticism, power of judgement and an eagerness to invent new ideas and ideals pervade the adolescent mind. At times, there is clash between adolescent's instinctive urges and the societal moral codes. The adolescent has a sharp memory and he is always curious to know about "people, places and principles".

In general, girls are more seriously affected by puberty than boys as they are subjected to more severe social controls. General physical well-being, socio-economic status of the family, peer groups, etc., affect adolescent's mental development and maturity. Stalz (1946) remarks: "Whenever, however, there is a marked discrepancy between social expectancy and a child's maturational readiness, there are likely to be problems for him and for society". Often the adolescent feels lonely, isolated, bored, restless and discontented with the prevailing social system. The pubescent child is antagonistic in his attitude towards his family, and the society in general. Characteristically, he goes 'around with a chip on his shoulder and a snarl on his face'. Not only does he seem to resent the happiness of others but also go out of way to spoil their fun by being as disagreeable, un-cooperative, and antagonistic. He resists authority and is often jealous of and hostile to the opposite sex. Lack of confidence generates in him negative attitude towards work. He derives psychological pleasure from out of the sensation emanating from manipulation and caressing of various body parts especially genitals. Wolman (1951) says that "masturbation usually reaches its peak between thirteen and fourteen years in boys and a year or two earlier in girls. This means that its peak coincides with the time of the greatest changes in the sex organs, when new sensations are appearing".

The adolescent is exuberantly imaginative. Ross (1953) feels that "the youth finds the world a difficult place and tends to live in the realm of fantasy that is nearer to his heart's desire". He builds castles in the air and indulges in day-dreaming. Often he is mentally absent in the class. Teachers do a lot of poking and prying to keep the adolescent awake and alert. His behaviour towards his class-mates, teachers and sometimes parents is strange and unpredictable. He laughs and cries in the same breath; he is self-confident and self-depreciative; selfish and altruistic; enthusiastic and indifferent at the same time. Academic burden and home work cause a little sense of insecurity and instability in his behaviour. Problems of personal safety, needs, adjustment, sexuality, education etc., often haunt adolescents. In appearance, a typical adolescent looks neither an adult nor a boy. This generates a great deal of anxiety. At times, he is so sensitive, adamant, and recalcitrant that even parents and teachers do not know what to do about him. His attention remains distracted and to wriggle out of the chaos surrounding him, the adolescent adopts variety of defence mechanisms.

The adolescent is usually in emotional turmoil. Discipline at school and restrictions at home cause annoyance and generate anger in him, which he is seen venting left and right. Adherence to rules is unbearable to him. Like a bird in the cage, the younger adolescent falls into tantrums to get his needs served but the older adolescent knows how to achieve his objectives without over-throwing the yoke of discipline. The adolescents' major problems pertain to social adjustment and peer acceptability, and not physical insecurity. Athletic adolescents may be worried about their selection on the school or club team.

Jealousy, though an infantile emotion, is now restricted to sexual promiscuity. The adolescent is jealous of a class mate or friend who receives more love, favours and privileges from teachers and peers. Taking liberty with the opposite sex is not uncommon. The adolescent's affection is reserved for such friends and peers as would stand by him through thick and thin, and assist him in pursuit of pleasurable experiences. Curiosity is mostly restricted to unexplored areas such as sex and general knowledge. The adolescent wants to know more about sex through books and discussion with his friends.

Other Characteristics

While the pre-adolescent child is dependant upon his parents and teachers for its personal needs, the adolescent leans towards heroes, leaders and great men and women for ideals and morals. Ross (1953) writes: "Young masters and mistresses especially must realize that they are peculiarly liable to be exalted into the position of a hero or a heroine, and seek to deal with situation in the best interest of their worshippers". The adolescent also finds outstanding school alumni as role models for studies and sports. The adolescent is often baffled with what society preaches and what it practices. This becomes the major cause of his resistance and even revolt against societal norms and standards. The arising psychological conflict makes him often aggressive in his behaviour in general. The perceived social inadequacies and prevailing injustice force him to play role of a reformer. Often far from stern realities of life, the adolescent considers himself to be a jack of all trades.

Adolescent interests, aptitudes and hobbies are diverse and subject to rapid change. A typical adolescent is showy, extrovert and extravagant. Fashionable clothes and cosmetics allure him a lot. Aping the mannerisms, modes of speech, dress, make-up, etc., of matinee heroes and heroines is so common with adolescent boys and girls these days. There is a constant search for an individual identity at school and at home in every adolescent. In peer-group gatherings, the leisure-time discussion centres on movies, actors, actresses, music, fashion, and the like.

In conduct, an adolescent is simply amoral. The conflict between his biological urges and harsh external realities is perpetual and persistent, and not so easy to resolve. The younger adolescent acts more impulsively than the does the older one. The sex urge is powerful but the adolescent finds it hard to express it openly. Social restrictions on this account are difficult to overthrow.

Some sense of right and wrong develops in adolescents through social interaction and personal experience. The role of parents and teachers in this matter is no less significant. The traditional attitude 'spare the rod and spoil the child', does not, in fact, work well with adolescents these days because the environmental influences on them are too strong to resist. The teachers and parents need to set moral standards for themselves first before they impress upon adolescents to assimilate them. After an initial struggle, the adolescent takes almost 2 to 3 years to set up a moral code for himself. Less council, greater peer interaction and influence play a more positive role in this difficult task.

Unless otherwise indoctrinated, most adolescents look at the religious beliefs with a sense of scepticism and criticality. They do not accept them without evaluating them on scientific standards. Being too orthodox and conservative or too liberal and enlightened depends upon what he inherits from family. It is often difficult for adolescents to be rational and scientific, and dogmatic at the same time.

Adolescent Sports and Play Activities

By 14-15 years, adolescents are physically tough, strong and resilient. They overflow with muscular energy. The most productive way to utilize their energy is to yoke them to vigorous physical activity and competitive sport. Even otherwise also, adolescents have a craze for "rough and rugged" activities that provide them avenues for the release of their pent up energies, and give a clean and clear image to their personality. Much of the rowdiness and negative behaviour that adolescents exhibit at school or outside is squarely due to denial of facilities for vigorous physical activity and sport.

A well-organized motor-skill training programme helps adolescents acquire more complex athletic skills so important for excellence in life and sport. In many advanced countries teen-agers have given out record-breaking performances at the Olympic Games because they have had a well-organized programme of sport and activity all through their school career. Adolescence is the right and, perhaps, the bright age for giving children an exposure to the world of competitive sport because (a) an adolescent on average is healthy; (b) he/she is strong-enough to resist disease; (c) he/she is capable of withstanding the rigours of hard conditioning training; (d) his/her recuperative power from fatigue and injury is fantastic; and finally, (e) he/she is very receptive to training. Research on adolescent growth has shown that children participating in organized sports have far better chances of achieving much higher goals in life surely and speedily than others. These days sport has become a great springboard for success - be it in education, technology, business, industry, management, or medicine.

Jones & Baylay (1957) remark: "At all ages after puberty, boys surpass girls in strength, and this superiority increases with age. The reason for this difference is that the muscles of the girls do not develop as much as those of the boys during adolescence. Girls generally attain their maximum strength at about seventeen years of age while boys do not attain their maximum strength until they are twenty one or twenty two years old". If strength - both physical and mental - is a major criterion of success in life, then a well-planned "required" programme of physical activities is a must for all adolescents irrespective of their physical or social status, aptitude and inclination. This is necessary to ensure their general well-being, good health and fitness, as well as some achievement in sport. Life is not likely to be comfortable for an adolescent without a reasonable amount of physical strength, body-control, endurance, speed, agility, etc. It is a sacred duty of the school to periodically assess health and fitness of every single student under their care, and help them improve upon them.

The physical activity programme for adolescents must be very vigorous and adventurous including mountaineering, camping, hiking, trekking, major sports, etc., since all these are helpful for building up qualities of character like self-reliance, resourcefulness, leadership, competitiveness, co-operation, courage, daring, pain-tolerance, risk-taking, etc. Swimming, dancing, gymnastics and athletics - being fundamental activity disciplines – need to be prescribed for both sexes because they provide both physical and psychological gratification.

GUIDELINES FOR PHYSICAL EDUCATORS/COACHES

Growth, by and large, is a genetic phenomenon. Psychologists, parents, teachers, and physical educators can do little to control or direct or change its course. They can provide facilities such as good nutrition, care and protection against health hazards, and more importantly physical activity helping it to maintain its natural flow. Sometimes, over-anxiety, over-enthusiasm or misconceptions about growth and the factors that influence it make parents and teachers take recourse to such practices as may impede growth without any one's being aware of it.

It is important to note that physical activity which includes play, formal exercise and sport, is one of the most important factors influencing growth all through one's life. However, unless genetic and environmental factors are in perfect order, physical activity is of little use in ensuring quality growth. It would be no wisdom to depend on physical activity as a panacea for all ills of growth. Physical activity is a means to health, fitness and skill. In this spirit alone, did Williams (1964) advocate the physical activity programme at all developmental stages to be "physically satisfying, mentally stimulating and socially sound."

In childhood and pre-adolescence, children are movement hungry as a result it is natural for them to over do and trespass the limits and limitations of their latent physical capacities even without formal motivation. Resultantly, their athletic performance at sub-junior and junior levels of competition is generally found to be enviable. However, as they cross high school, a good number of these budding athletes either burn out or drop out of sport leaving every one guessing. An important fact that needs attention is that the 'gifted' children, in their formative years, are overloaded with physical work-outs by the least psychological and unrealistic approach of the trainers and coaches. The deleterious effects of overloading or overdoing on the smooth flow of developmental processes may not be immediately known beguiling the over-zealous physical educators/coaches into believing that all is well with their training methodology. It requires activity-loading and competitive sport programmes to be intelligently planned in consideration of the educational objectives and the growth-potential of every young athlete.

Up to the later childhood, gender differences are of little consequence. As children cross the threshold of puberty, marked intra-gender and inter-gender differences in body build, strength, endurance, physiological capacities, mental maturity, psychological make-up, interests, aptitudes, etc., begin to surface giving distinct identity to boys and girls. So, the activity programme for the two sexes must move to such directions as are conducive to their individual growth and educational objectives. The boys have to grow into men and the girls into women, and play gender-roles in line with aspirations of the society. Not only is it unethical but also biologically improper to subject female children to the same hard activity regimens as meant for males and also motivate them to compete with and against males. The body-contact between adolescent boys and girls during sports activities has serious emotional and psychological implication giving rise to a variety of social problems, so difficult for physical educators and coaches to tackle. Often adolescent girls are inhibitive in opening up in front of the boys and the boys per force have to be restrictive in their actions so as to be a source of no physical, mental and emotional embarrassment to them. Physical activity and competition programme for boys and girls ought to be different and favourable to their development. Several physical activities are not at all conducive to female growth.

There is a significant change in the adolescent's psychological make-up, which the physical educators and coaches ought to know. Pre-adolescent children are generally more respectful and are scared of teacher's authority than adolescents because of their superiority in physical strength. The adolescent is capable of fighting back physically, so he is generally arrogant and less amenable to suggestion. He has scant respect for authority especially when he finds a big gap between what elders and/or teachers say and what they do. The inevitable result is ego-clash and strained teacher-taught relationship. Adolescents are often too critical of the parents and teachers for the ways they deal with them and their problems. So, they need more careful handling than do pre-adolescents.

In planning and conducting sports competitions, practice classes and skill-teaching periods, it is always rewarding to involve the older and intelligent adolescents as leaders, supervisors and guides. This will enhance their ego, make them feel important, raise their self-esteem and help them grow mentally and socially well. Adolescents act responsibly when placed in responsible positions. There is no better way of canalising their exuberant energies.

Physical educators and coaches must take an extended view of growth. No doubt, physical education aims at skill, health and fitness, its concomitant benefits are equally important. Physical activity and sport also must facilitate development of good character. The social aspect of growth is greatly dependent on the quality and frequency of social interaction children have on the playfields. It needs no reiteration that physical development is just one aspect of growth. The intellectual, emotional and social aspects of growth must progress concurrently with the physical growth. Sport and physical education will fail in their objectives if they simply produce athletic giants or 'muscular men' alone. Growth is to be seen in its totality and physical educators must take a comprehensive view of it.

In order to evaluate the effect of physical activity and sports programmes on growth, it will all the more be important for the physical educators and sports coaches to subject the students and young athletes to periodic skill and fitness testing and also provide them with adequate opportunities for participation in competitive sports and recreational activities inside and outside the institution. Proper records of students' physical measurements, skill status, performance and achievements in various academic and athletic activities must be maintained in order to assess their progress and the extent to which the pre-determined objectives are being realized. The records are the best means of knowing students' strengths and weaknesses and ensuring their smooth passage through the turbulent years of late childhood, pubescence and adolescence.

SELECTED REFERENCES

Bakwin, H. The Emotional States at Birth. *Amer.Jr. Dist Child*: 74: 373-376, 1974

Banham, K.M. The development of differential behaviour in infancy. *Jr Genetic, Psychol.* 76:283-289, 1950

Baylay, N. Individual patterns of development. *Child Develop*: 27: 45-74, 1956.

Bower, T.R.G. *Development in Infancy.* San Francisco, Freeman, 1974

Breckenridge, M.E. & Vincent, E.L. *Child Development* (3rd Ed), Philadelphia: Saunders, 1955

Crane, A.R. Pre-adolesent gangs: Personality Factors in middle childhood as revealed by parents ratings. *Child Devdopment,* 28: 439-458, 1957

Dubois, F.S. The Security of Discipline. *Ment.Hyg.* 36: 353-372, 1952

Gesell, A. Development Pedaetric. *Nerv Child,* 11 ; 225-227, 1952

Gesell, A. Growth Potentials of Human Infant. *Sci Mon,* New York, 68: 252-256, 1949

Haughurst, R.J. *Human Development and Education,* New York; Londgman's, 1953

Hurlock, E.B. *Development Psychology,* New York, McGraw-Hill Book Co. INC, 1959

Jones, M.C. & Baylay, N. Physical maturity among boys as related to behaviour. *Jr. Edu. Psychol.* 41 : 128-149, 1957

Kofka, K. *The Growth of the Mind,* New York; Harcourt, 1925

Krogman, W.M. The physical growth of the child. In M. Fishbein and R.J.R. Kennedy. (Eds) *Modern Marriage and Family Living.* New York:, Oxford University Press, 1957

Mary, I.G. & Kelly, H.J. Body composition in childhood. *Hum Biol.* 28: 289-308, 1956

Restak, Richard M. *The Mind,* New York: Bantam Books, 1988

Ross. J.S. *Groundwork of Educational Psychology,* London: George and Harrap, 1953

Stalz, R.A. The smiling response: A contribution to the ontogenesis social relations. *Genetic Psychol, Monog*: 34: 57-125, 1946

Tanner, J.M. & Tayler, G.R. *Growth.* Time Life International, Netherlands N.V, 1963

Thompson, H. Physical Growth In L. Cornnchail (ed) *Manual of Child Psychology.* (2nd. Ed.) New York; Willy, 1954

Williams, J.F. *Principles of Physical Education.* Philadelphia, W.B/ Saunders, 1964

Wolman, N. Sexual development in Israeli adolescents. *Amer. Jr. Psycho-ther,* 5: 531-559, 1951

Play is the highest expression of human development in childhood for it alone is the free expression of what is in a child's soul.

- Friederic Freobel

CHAPTER - 7

PHENOMENON OF PLAY

Philosophers, researchers, educationists, sociologists and psychologists have studied play, a general innate tendency, from various perspectives. Many of the most prominent researchers in psychology especially Jean Piaget, Williams James, Sigmund Freud, Carl Jung, Lev Vygotsky, etc., have viewed play as endemic to human species. Sally Jenkinson - the author of *Genius of Play* - considered play 'to be an intimate and integral part of childhood development.' The ***Convention on the Rights of the Child*** (adopted by the General Assembly of the United Nations on November, 29, 1989) explicitly recognized "the right of the child to rest and leisure, to engage in play and recreational activities appropriate to the age of the child and to participate freely in cultural life and the arts." The Convention participants resolved to "respect and promote the right of the child to participate fully in cultural and artistic life and shall encourage the provision of appropriate and equal opportunities for cultural, artistic, recreational and leisure activities". Once considered "at best a distraction and at worst sinful" (a Puritan attitude) i.e. 'a sheer waste of time and energy', play has now come to be understood as the most effective medium of child education - both formal and informal.

Education in ancient Greece was incomplete without athletics. Play or sport enjoyed equal status with aesthetics, mathematics and ethics in human education. "Life must be lived as play, playing certain games, making sacrifices, singing and dancing, and then a man will be able to propitiate the gods, and defend himself against his enemies, and win in the contests", mused Plato. In the *Laws,* he views 'play as a form of anticipatory socialization. If children were to become builders, he suggested, they should play at building houses. The teacher's role in this was to try to direct the children's inclinations and pleasures through play towards their final aim in life.'

MEANING AND DEFINITION OF PLAY

In dictionary, play is quoted as 'a recreational activity, especially the spontaneous activity of children.' Its origin is traced to an Anglo-Saxon expression *plega* meaning "to guarantee, stand for or take a risk for something and to risk danger or devote oneself to a single purpose." Play, according to Ulrich, is the single-most human activity which has a variety of connotations. In biological nuances, play is a bodily activity which the organism does in its characteristic way in order to be physically active, strong and healthy. In psychology, play activity is conspicuously marked by mental satisfaction, imagination, creativity, experience and ecstasy. Sociologically, play is an expression of gregarious instinct in man, interpersonal interaction and cohesive societal tendencies. What is playing in infancy and childhood turns out to be sport or recreation beyond adolescence.

Play may mean many things to many people, for example, "the natural unfolding of the germinal leaves of the child" (Froebel); as "a joyful spontaneous creative activity in which man finds his fullest expression," (Ross, 1953), or "an activity which is in itself free, aimless, amusing and diverting," (Lazarus). In William McDougall's view, play is "very important for the preservation, growth and development of the organism." Ruskin considered it as the "exertion of body and mind, made to please ourselves without a determined end". Gullick believed that "play is what we do when we are free to do what we like." While Stern found play to be a "voluntary self-constrained activity," T.P. Nunn considered it as a "profound manifestation of creative activities."

Play is for play sake only. It is a frivolous and non-serious activity; yet when watching children at play, one is impressed at their transfixed seriousness and entrancing absorption with which they engage in it. In 2004, play was precisely defined as *a physical or mental activity that has no purpose or objective outside of pure enjoyment or amusement*. Today, it is best envisioned as descriptive of a range of activities that may be ascribed to humans and non-humans. In general discourse, people use the word "play" as a contrast to other parts of their lives: sleep, eating, washing, work, rituals, etc.

In final analysis, play is defined as the process of partaking in an activity for amusement, pleasure and recreation. It can be imaginative or creative, limited or without boundaries. Play does not need to have rules and lets a child explore their surroundings in an unrestricted manner. Play can also consist of goals, this occurs in sports, where the aim is to compete against another team to achieve a winning score. Play is something that we all need and take part in, it is an important factor in everyday life and helps children to develop the skills in a fun and creative way.

Characteristics of Play

Though most characteristics of play are inherent in various definitions of play, Johan Huizinga and others, to be precise, have listed the following ones

1. Play is voluntary activity - a matter of choice
2. It is free and spontaneous activity (as natural as leaves to a tree)
3. Play is absorbing ("Play casts a spell over us" - Huizinga)
4. It is never imposed by physical necessity or moral duty
5. It is a means of expression (you do what you like to do)
6. Play is a quality of freedom, make believe, or escape (limitations of real world are eliminated through the mind)
7. It is intrinsically rewarding and self-contained (work for one person may be play for some one else)
8. Play is pleasurable (may be enjoyable or we won't do it)

Conditions for Play

Nature invented play to help young organisms to grow and become adults, for activity which is the essence of play, is a biological necessity. Play keeps the organisms activated; it preserves and propagates life. Play may also transcend species; the young of many other animals also exhibit behaviours that are similar to the play of children. However, while play is apparently universal, a number of necessary conditions need to be present for children's play to occur and be sustained. Among these are time and space, which, in turn, are frequently related to social, economic and environmental conditions. If, for example, children are engaged in labour (as most poverty-stricken children are) or overburdened with academic work (as most career-conscious urban children are), whether in their homes, at schools or outside them, the opportunities for play are much curtailed.

Adequate space for play at home, in the neighbourhood, at school or else where is very important for the human spirit to breathe in an atmosphere of freedom and joyous activity. As the growth of cities has led to a diminution in the availability of space in general and secure or safe space, in particular, space for play has become an issue. Most schools in the congested urban setting have hardly any space for children to have solace of free play.

A further necessary condition, that by its absence has occasionally disrupted the universality of play, is adult consent. Day by day parents and children too are becoming carer-conscious as a result great emphasis is being placed on studies, extra tutorials, home work, etc., at the cost of play and recreation. Children's lack of power in relation to adults has led to their play being curtailed when adults have disapproved of it.

Types of Play

Infant and child play is marked by spontaneity and universality. Johan Huizinga rightly observed that all children play and they play remarkably alike. No play is without some objective – whether implicit or explicit. On the basis of the objective, play could be categorized into functional play, dramatic play, socio-dramatic play and creative play.

Functional Play

It is predominantly movement-oriented in which an infant or child has to be performing some bodily movement. Play underlines activity, which is the very basis of life as well as growth. Without movement or activity no development worth the name takes place in an organism. All infants and children can rarely sit idle; they have to be moving, doing something or the other. With functional play the children will use the repetition of muscles to complete a task whether it is in creeping, crawling, clapping, jumping, bouncing, dancing, running, throwing and catching, or hammering an object. This repetition also enacts with the playing of toys. Children will repeatedly play with an object until they discover its correct use.

Dramatic Play

Dramatic play involves children manipulating their surroundings to create a make-believe world. By this they are able to use materials and objects around them to create something new. It explores their imagination to turn a rock into a magical dragon egg, a piece of cloth into a beautiful princess's gown, and so on. Children need dramatic play to develop their knowledge, sharpen intelligence and express their urge for gesticulation. According to Jean Piaget, 'One of the purest forms of symbolic thought available to young children, dramatic play contributes strongly to the intellectual development of children.'

Socio-dramatic Play

In socio-dramatic play, similar to dramatic play children use their imagination to create a role play that results in a specific task being formed. It helps the children explore a different reality where they could possibly be a vet that has to help a sick animal, or a doctor taking care or an injured child. They know they are not really a vet or a doctor but it lets them explore the possibility.

Constructive Play

This type of play involves the following of predetermined rules and set goals that are to be achieved. It is the making of three dimensional objects, such as cubby houses, Lego or blocks, knitting or sewing and model making. It requires the children to think creatively about a diagram they wish to make; problem solving skills as to how they are going to create what they wish and it also encourages children to design from an abstract thought and create something that may never have been seen before. Children learn how to follow instructions, work cooperatively and obey rules.

Work and Play

It is natural for play and work to be compared and contrasted. Mark Twain commented that play and work are words used to describe the same activity under different circumstances, but sociologist David Reisman preferred to consider play as a quality as different to an activity. Play and work are powerful binary oppositions that have attached to them a number of signifiers. Work, for example, is valued as a necessity that provides the material basis for life. It is also frequently seen as giving meaning to life. Play, in contrast, is often seen as frivolous and lacking the serious purpose of work. Play takes place in the time not given over to work and in some cultures, such time in school is called *playtime* to distinguish it from time devoted to lessons. These oppositions between play and work are organized not only in the present but also over the time of the life cycle as well. For example, in modern popular perception, childhood is a time for play, whereas adulthood is a time for work. Parallel to Froebel's thinking, Dewey wrote that play was an activity not consciously performed for any sake beyond itself whereas work was an activity in which the interest lies in its outcome. In Dewey's conception, play is subordinated to work. He poses this almost as a developmental task.

The social psychologists find play and work divided by a very thin line. For some people work is play; for others play, work. The professional boxers, wrestlers, or tennis, cricket, soccer, baseball and basketball players or top amateur athletes invest so much of time, energy and money in sport that play comes closer to work borderline. Apart from this, for an infant play and work have no distinction. The infant has no other serious business of life except play which, in the long run, serves as instrument of preparation for work. Mitchell & Mason remark: "Play is an activity; it is of interest to player; the same activity may be work or play according to the attitude taken towards it. An essential characteristic of play is satisfaction in the activity for its own sake with participation being voluntary."

For a realistic assessment of play and work, let us have a look at the following comparative chart.

	Play		Work
1.	Play is marked by freedom and spontaneity.	1.	Work is constrained and serious.
2.	Play is biological necessity.	2.	Work is social obligation.
3.	Interest and aptitude for play is innate.	3.	Aptitude for work has to be developed and reinforced.
4.	Pleasure and gratification are inherent in play.	4.	Work provides satisfaction only when there some substantial gain.
5.	Play is voluntary and frivolous with no serious aim.	5.	Work is a compulsion – a necessary condition for adult life.
6.	There is no ulterior end in play; we do what feel like doing.	6.	The objective in work is explicit; we have to go by work ethics and norms.
7.	Attention and interest in play are self-motivated.	7.	In work, interest and attention are divided between the task and its end-products.

Alderman (1974) commented: "As compared to work, play is natural and spontaneous. It is only later when play emerges into the more organised and complex games and sports that man begins to seek satisfaction of needs other than mere enjoyment of movements. Play in children, as a means and an end itself, must be considered separately and it is in the description of what constitutes play that its fundamental characteristics emerge".

Since the 1960s, the living standards across the Western world as else where having been rising as a result the boundaries between play and work have started to become more blurred and the notion that play is the work of the child has been disrupted by the realization, found in the work of the Dutch historian Johan Huizinga (1872–1945), that adults continue to play too. To this is added the growing convergence of children and adults by virtue of both sharing the same mediatized, cultural space.

BENEFITS OF PLAY

Playfulness is not only to be enjoyed but also to be accorded high value for its fundamental role in the success of all organisms, including humans. All healthy children tend to be playful. They indulge in play because they are naturally active and surcharged with life-energy. Rousseau remarked: "Children are always in motion; quiet and mediation are their aversion; a studious or sedentary life is injurious to their health and growth; neither their minds nor their bodies can bear constraint.....the body should be vigorous in order to obey the mind, just as a good servant should be robust..... The feebler the body, the more it rules: the stronger it is the more it obeys".

Commenting on the developmental values of play, Froebel said: 'Play is the highest phase of child development - of human development at this period: for it is self-active representation of the inner necessity and impulse..... Play is the purest, most spiritual activity of man at this stage and at the same time typical of human life as a whole of the inner hidden natural life in man and all things..... A child that plays thoroughly with self-active determination, perseveringly until physical fatigue forbids, will surely be a thorough determined man capable of self-sacrifice for the promotion of the welfare of himself and others".

Benefits of play in terms of physical, mental, emotional and social growth are well documented.

- Children develop and maintain gross motor skills by reaching, crawling, walking, running, climbing, jumping, throwing, catching and balancing; and fine motor skills by handling and manipulate toys with their fingers and hands.

- Repetition of basic physical skills and rough and tumble of active play facilitates improvement in children's bodily strength, flexibility and coordination.
- Play integrates and harmonizes various aspects of growth because play strengthens nerves, muscles and organs resulting in better cognition, health, fitness, physical efficiency and intellectual capacity.
- Play experiences allow children to internalize the skills they learn at school. In play, infants and children learn to discriminate between colours, shape, and sizes.
- Play allows for a healthier, more socially acceptable way of expressing one's feelings and opinions.
- In play the child experiences great pleasure, joy and freedom action, thought and expression, so necessary for the development of a healthy personality.
- It is through play that children grow and develop - individually, with others, and as part of a larger community.
- Play helps children recognize the need to prioritize as they are unable to play with every toy at the same time, which in turn teaches children to compromise and share.
- Children learn to initiate, sustain, and terminate social interactions through play. Through these interactions, children will also have the opportunity to develop and improve their communication skills, including the acquisition of alternative means of communication.
- Play is instrumental in building self-confidence, self-esteem and self-worth in children.
- Play takes the child away from the tedium of school work and helps him express his instinctive urges such as combat, construction, curiosity and creativity. Intellection and socialization are inherent in play itself.
- Increases in leisure skills helps to reduce or eliminate negative, excess, and 'high-risk' behaviours.
- Play provides opportunity to children to meet other kids in the neighbourhood and at school and to develop relationships and friendships. It is an excellent way to meet people, make friends, and sustain those friendships.

- It strengthens families. It is rightly said that the family that plays together, stays together.
- Play improves one's quality of life! Socrates argued that play, rather than force, should be used in training children.

THEORIES OF PLAY

Scholars have riddled for years, "Why do people (especially children) Play?" "Why is something so frivolous like play a cultural universal event"? "What useful function does play perform in our life"? "Is it a societal function that should be supported"? The answer to these and many more mind-boggling questions has come from some of the considered views and well-documented theories of play propounded by philosophers, biologists, psychologists, sociologists, educationists, and others over the millennia. The first known discussions of play and its relation to education made their appearance in the work of the ancient Greek philosophers Plato (427–348 B.C.) and Aristotle (384–322 B.C). The formal theories of play appeared on the scene much later especially from 18th century onward. These are generally categorized into conventional or early classical theories and 20th century and/or current theories.

The classical theories include the Surplus Energy Theory, the Relaxation Theory, the Preparation or Pre-Exercise (instinct/practice) Theory, the Recapitulation Theory, the Cathartic Theory, the Compensation Theory, the Competence/Effectance Theory, etc. Among the early 20th century and/or current theories of play the prominent ones are the Infantile Theory, the Cathartic Theory, the Psychoanalytic Theory, and the Cognitive Theory. Significantly, the Surplus Energy, the Recapitulation, and the Preparation Theory are known as Evolutionary Theories as they drew their substance from Darwin's postulates. These theories, however, gave rise to the first attempts to provide explanations for play, rather than observations of play or uses to which play could be put.

Surplus Energy Theory

The exponents of Surplus Energy Theory were the German philosopher Friedrich von Schiller (1759–1805) and the English philosopher and sociologist Herbert Spencer (1820–1903). Influenced by Darwin's "struggle for survival" principle, they expounded this theory to explain animal play, which, they termed "as the expression of surplus energy". According to them, once an animal no longer had to expend all its energy on survival, the surplus could be released in play. A lion sometimes roared not out of any necessity but to release "unemployed energy". Play is motivated by a need to release surplus energy, the authors believe. Popularly known as the Schiller-Spencer theory, it maintains that children play because "a quantity of energy is available to them; there is a tendency to expend energy" in some kind of activity such as play. Importantly, play is the result of surplus energy that exists because the young are freed from the business of self-preservation through the activities of their parents. Energy finds its release in the aimless exuberant activities of play.

Play is an expression similar to the collective singing of birds. Like young ones of the animals, children also are replete with more energy than they actually need for normal business of life. Play is "*letting off extra steam*". The organism is likened to a steam engine in which the boiler serves as a store-house for steam: the extra steam is let out through a safety valve attached to the boiler. Same way, the organism stores up more than required energy in its cells, muscles and nerves; it struggles for release. Nature, according to authors, has invented play as a 'safety valve letting out extra steam'. Just observe children at recess bell. Alderman (1974) remarks: "School children, who burst out of doors at recess to run and jump, climb and tussle, probably exhibit a combination of release from physical inactivity during classes and a psychological realisation of the situational stimulus. Their activity is both a biological and psychological explosion of energy". He continues: "Play in this sense, provides an opportunity for the discharge of the surplus energy and it would seem, in an age of decreasing work commitments and increasing leisure, man would be likely to have increasing surplus of energy and thus be involved in more playful pursuits".

Despite powerful appeal, the surplus energy theory seems to be "inadequate" in answering several important questions: Why play takes definite form instead of being a mere "formless discharge" of energy? Why children having little energy indulge in play activities, and why play-interests differ at different levels of age? Nunn remarks: "While we can imagine the surplus energy (steam) of an engine being turned to good ingenious ways, we cannot imagine it being used to make the engine itself a better engine but this is exactly what play does for the growing individual enabling him to find his own powers - physical, mental and moral". In infancy and childhood, play is the only means through which children acquire motor skills, cognitive skills, conceptual skills and performance skills. All this could not simply be termed as "aimless expenditure of exuberant energy".

Yet with all its inadequacies, this theory bridges the gap between the biological and psychological view-points. An important message the surplus energy gives is that all organisms generate more energy than they actually expend in life routines. For this they need some other avenue, perhaps, play.

Anticipation Theory

This theory is also known as *Preparation* or *'Pre-exercise'* Theory. Influenced by Darwin's views, Carl Groos (1861–1946) also presented a biological explanation for play in his two books - *The Play of Animals* and *The Play of Man*. He argued that play was the expression of an instinct necessary to the survival of the species. The young child, due to its prolonged dependency on adults, did not need the instinct. Hence play is the practice and development of capacities, like sex and fighting, to be used later in life. Thus, for Groos, the purpose of play was a preparation for life. Famously he claimed that, "instead of saying, the animals play because they are young, we must say, the animals have a youth in order that they may play" and thereby they practice skills necessary for their survival. Groos considered play as "a medium of bringing the instincts to surface, fixing them and then exercising them" and ensuring organisms' maturity.

The American psychologist James Mark Baldwin, who popularized Groos in USA, also concluded that play is a function of high utility. Play is the necessary practice for behaviours that are essential to later survival. The playful fighting of animals or the rough and tumble play of children are essentially the practice of skills that will later aid their survival. According to T.P. Nunn, "Nature invented play not merely for dispensing with the superfluous energy in the child but as device for using that energy to prepare him for serious business of life". Children play with toys, dolls, wooden or plastic animals and a variety of household objects. Enacting roles of a teacher, nurse, guard, husband, mother, wife, shopkeeper, doctor, engineer, policeman, etc., by young children shows their imitative tendency on the one hand, and reflects their future career on the other. The childhood play is believed to be a rehearsal of the real drama of life in which every child has to play an assigned role. Besides this, the repetitious play of imaginary role-models in childhood helps children to develop a sense of belonging to the society. Groos gives full credit to the Evolutionary Theory in this regard, for it considered play as means animals' struggle for existence.

This theory, unlike surplus energy theory, could explain not only why play was most prominent in young animals but also why it occurred in isolated animals that were not able to imitate others. The main objection to Pre-Exercise Theory, however, is that it explains play in the context of children only. Play is an important part of adult life also. Men, women, young and old engage in play without exception but they don't prepare themselves for any serious business of life nor do they find any workable solution to the life problems. Children, in fact, imitate what they see around and try to internalize it through play. This process also programmes the software of their mind so as to deal with life situations in future.

Instinct Practice Theory

In *Émile* (1762), Rousseau's famous treatise on education, Rousseau proposed the rather revolutionary theory that children went through distinct stages in their development and that education should primarily be tailored to those stages. Rousseau's comments on children's play were not in any way systematic but the text reveals that he held, albeit in sketch form, a theory of play. This consisted mainly in the view that play was instinctive and the means provided by nature for growth of the body as well as of the senses. Rousseau cited Locke, approvingly for the most part, throughout his book but when he came to consider the relation between play and education he turned only to Plato to support his belief that children should be taught through play. Rousseau thought that in all the games that children played, there could be found material for instruction. He held that what children learned from each other in play was worth far more than what they learned in the classroom. Later William McDougall contributed to this theory, considering play as a social phenomenon having roots in instincts, which are the prime movers of animal behaviour. Play is due to "pre-mature ripening of instincts" and in play, children make an uninhibited expression of the instincts of combat, construction, destruction, self-assertion, rivalry, pugnacity, etc. In childhood, instinctual energy finds release through play. During play children instinctively fight among themselves; they try to take possession of others' toys; construct their own and destroy others' works; struggle for physical and/or mental supremacy by engaging in such activities as races, jumps, throws or stunts; make a show of their physical prowess and possessions; and so on. All this facilitates ripening of their instincts.

Admittedly, urge for activity is innate which finds gratification in play. It would be naive to accept that all play activities are competitive only. The infant's play is hardly competitive. It is individualistic and instinctive.

Recreational (Relaxation) Theory

Contributions to the recreation or relaxation theory were made by Lazarus (1883), Lord Kames and G.T.W. Patrick (1916). The authors see play as a mode of dissipating the inhibitions built up from fatigue due to tasks that are relatively new to the organism. Thus, play is found more often in childhood. Play replenishes energy for as yet unfamiliar cognitive activities of the child and reflects deep-rooted race habits - racially acquired behaviours that are not therefore new to the organism.

Recreation is a rejuvenating and recharging device for energy which organisms expend in routines. Instead of discharging surplus energy, play rebuilds energy. Play removes fatigue and recharges power batteries. Change of activity breaks life's monotony, and keeps up interest. Patrick believes that life routines involve serious attention, acute concentration, abstract thinking, reasoning and over-use of fine muscles. All this is a potential cause for physical stress, mental strain and rapid fatigue. Play (recreation) is an antidote for all this. After day's strenuous routine, an executive finds a game of tennis or badminton exceedingly relaxing and rejuvenating. A game of cards, chess or carom has an embalming effect on physically tired industrial or farm workers. Recreational activities remove monotony and boredom.

If one went by this theory, then adults should be more playful than children. In fact, the opposite is true. A child is free and happy most time, whereas an adult is haunted by worries, anxieties and tensions. Even when tired, children do not quit play; they may switch over to some other activity and continue. While playing they are serious and focused. The child-play may be frivolous, but adult play sobre.

Recapitulation Theory

Based on the one of the most pervasive ideas of *race recapitulation* among psychologists, biologists, and educationalists of the late nineteenth century, this theory from G. Stanley Hall (1844-1924), holds that the development of the individual (ontogeny) recapitulates, or repeats the principal stages, the development of the human race (phylogeny), i.e. *'Ontogeny repeats phylogeny'*. Play is seen not as an activity that develops future instinctual skills, but rather, that it serves to rid the organism of primitive and unnecessary instinctual skills carried over by hereditary. Each child passes through a series of play stages corresponding to and recapitulating the cultural stages in the development of the race. Roots of play are in the ritual of the savage and his need for magic; in other words, play was the recapitulation of an earlier evolutionary state. "Such a view states that the child is an evolutionary link between animal and man, and that play is a re-living or re-capitulation of the history of his remote ancestors - both animal and man" (Alderman, 1974).

The Recapitulation and Anticipation theories run in opposite directions. For Hall, play is "the group of bodily habits of the past persisting in the present". When people play, they live over again "racial experiences" of the biological and social past. Labelling the Anticipatory Theory as "very partial, superficial and perverse considered biologically", Hall argued that the child does not rehearse his future but repeats the racial past and hence play is a "reminiscence" rather than "anticipation". Hunting, the use of bow and arrow, swimming, hide & seek, chasing, fishing, throwing, building caves and shelters, camping, playing with sand and mud, hiking and trekking, etc., are reflective of the linkages between the modern civilization and the bio-cultural and anthropological evolution of the human race. Activities that re-enact events from our history as a race are intrinsically more rewarding. Hall was of the considered view that man could not completely do away with the primitive tendencies of fighting, quarrelling, throwing, jumping, running, etc. Through play alone are these urges expressed in diverse ways. Hall was confident that play is a link between the savage and civilised man - a "vestige of the remote past persisting in the present". Aggressiveness, brutality, violence and pugnacity are man's legacy of the animal past. Even in the highly civilized life, these innate tendencies serve some purpose in man's struggle for existence. Play is a natural expression of these tendencies in milder and refined form.

The theory has been under attack mostly from behaviourists

who do not believe in the inheritance of acquired traits. A musician, they argue, does not necessarily have musical children. Same may be the case with an Olympic athlete. Social psychologists may find some substance in this theory; scientists consider it as a figment of imagination.

Cathartic Theory

Originally the idea of catharsis ("cleansing, or purging up") is found in Aristotle's writings. The Greek "catharsis" theatre (tragic drama) purged people of hostile emotions. While commenting on the qualities of a dramatic tragedy (literary composition), Aristotle said that "the effect of tragedy should be catharsis of the soul". By watching a true tragedy enacted on the stage, the chaotic emotions of the audience especially pity and fear get purged up with the release of their pent-up energies. As medicine purges the body, so does a tragic play cleanse the audience's soul as they project themselves into the characters of the suffering hero or heroine and go through an emotional conflict with them. In the same way, Aristotle considers play to be cathartic in effect.

The "catharsis" concept was adopted by Sigmund Freud to explain play tendencies of children. So, in some way cathartic theory serves as a backdrop to psychoanalytic theory. We play because we need to express disorganized or painful emotions in a harmless way. Children re-enact their punishments, for example, scolding a doll. Play represents an attempt to partially satisfy drives or to resolve conflicts when the child really doesn't have the means to do so. When a child works through a drive through play he has at least temporarily resolved it. T.P. Nunn writes "Men cannot shed all together the ancient tendencies of cruelty and mischief or vice but play is at once a means by which the mischief be taken out of them and a means by which they may be transformed into impulses of ethical value".

Behaviourists attach least importance to this theory because of too much of idealism in it on the one hand and too many ambiguities and absurdities on the other. It does not explain most recreation such as hiking, trekking, basketball, tennis, stamp collecting, angling, and so on. However, when juxtaposed with surplus energy, recreation and psychoanalytic theories, cathartic theory attains some significance.

Psychoanalytic Theory

The founder of psychoanalysis was Sigmund Freud (1856–

1939). His theory of play was outlined in his work *Beyond the Pleasure Principle* (1920), wherein he explicitly conceptualized play as the *repetition compulsion* whereby a child wishes to constantly repeat or re-enact an experience. This he saw as the working out of his pleasure principle; the reduction of tension produced by the life instincts; and, when the experience was unpleasant, of the death instinct. The replacement of the pleasure principle, of which play is part, by the reality principle takes place individually in Freudian theory as well as racially within the individual child when its instinctual drives give way to reason.

As a matter of fact, the psychoanalytic play theories were built by Buhler (1930), and Freud's daughter Anna Freud (1937) on Freud's postulates. These theories of play, which focused on the value of play for emotional development, gave rise to two developments; (1) the use of play as psychotherapy, and (2) founding of a few experimental schools on psychoanalytic principles in the early twentieth century. In psycho-analysts' view play represents not merely wish-fulfilling tendencies but also mastery - an attempt through repetition to cope with overwhelming anxiety-provoking situations. Play is defensive as well as adaptive in dealing with anxiety. It helps to relieve various forms of anxiety, for example, fear of the external world (objective anxiety), fear of its own instincts (instinctual anxiety), and anxiety of conscience (superego). With regard to objective anxiety, Anna Freud (1936) says, "During (infancy) the individual is still too weak to oppose the outside world actively, to defend himself against it by means of physical force or to modify it in accordance with his own will." And further, "The ego endeavors in all kinds of ways to defend itself against the objective unpleasure and dangers which menace it." During play, child's ego defends itself by denial in fantasy. It denies reality by means of fantasy. It transforms reality to suit his or her own purposes and fulfill his or her own wishes. Only then the child accepts reality. Child acts in a way that denies reality. "A small handbag or tiny umbrella is intended to help a little girl to pretend to be a "grown-up lady". Toy weapons of various sorts enable a little boy to ape manhood. Even dolls create the fiction of motherhood, while trains, cars, or blocks produce in the minds of children the agreeable fantasy that they can control the world", says Freud (1936). This element of make-believe seeks to make the child maintain balance between the real and ethereal worlds.

Considering play as a device to master one's ago, Erikson, the central figure amongst the Neo-Freudians, assumed that play was the "royal road to understanding infantile ego's efforts at synthesis". Finding that the individual-self and the social-self are hand in glove with each other, Erikson went on to say: "Play, then, is a function of the ego, an attempt to synchronize the bodily and the social processes within the self....the emphasis, I think, should be on the ego's need to master the various areas of life, and especially those in which the individual finds his self and his social role wanting. To hallucinate ego-mastery and yet also to practice it, an intermediate reality between fantasy and actuality is the purpose of play....." Making a clear distinction between a child's play and that of an adult, Erikson felt that the child's play has mastery objective while that of the adult is a "vacation" from reality, from seriousness, from consequences, and is quite light and un-evolved in nature. Children play because they have much more free time at their disposal and adults engage in play in order to escape from life's carking cares and corroding anxieties.

Several holes are discernible in the psychoanalysis theory. First, the theory basically centres round abnormal and unconscious mental states. It hardly offers convincing explanation for normal activities such as play. Second, play is a natural and spontaneous activity; it cannot be an expression of repressed and suppressed desires. What is true about psycho-pathological cases may not be true about normal people. Finally, modern behavioural scientists do not consider psychoanalysis as a scientific method of investigating behaviour for it is full of serious ambiguities and absurdities.

Cognitive Theory

Swiss psychologist Jean Piaget (1896-1980) found play closely related to the growth of human intelligence. He felt: "Play begins in the child's sensory-motor period of development. It is through play that the child associates himself with the external reality. Repetition, variation, experimentation and exploration are fundamental to child's play. Gradually these activities go on changing forms. In the course of time from individualistic and ego-centric level it raises itself to that of associational with his compeers and group-mates". In his view play has more of cognitive function than biological function as many other theorists had emphasized. Children derive "functional pleasure" through play.

Piaget emphasized the importance of play in symbolic representation and its contribution to socialization. According to him play provides a relaxed atmosphere in which learning can easily occur. He stressed that play is ***not*** the same as learning; cognitive development requires both assimilation and accommodation, while play is assimilation *without* accommodation. Play is derived from the child's working out of two fundamental characteristics of his mode of experience and development. These are accommodation and assimilation – the attempts to integrate new experiences into relatively limited number of motor and cognitive skills available at each age.

While ***accommodation*** *is an attempt to imitate and interact physically with the environment,* ***assimilation*** *is the attempt to integrate externally derived precepts or motor actions in a limited area of schemata.* Both these processes underlying human intelligence are biological, psychological and sociological at the same time.

Piaget categorized play into four types:

(1) *Sensory-Motor or Physical Play*: This is the kind of play in which the child repeats a physical activity, such as swinging its feet, throwing its head back, for the sheer enjoyment of doing it. Children perform hundreds of such activities including yelling, shouting, etc., for no reason except the pleasure that they drive from doing so.

(2) *Symbolic Play*: In symbolic play, this child mentally represents realities that are not present. On this Piaget says: "It is primarily affective conflicts that appear in symbolic play. If there is a scene at lunch, for example, one can be sure that an hour or two afterward it will be recreated with dolls and will be brought to a happier solution. If the child has been frightened by a dog, in a symbolic game things will be arranged so that dogs will no longer be mean or children will become brave".

(3) *Games of Construction:* Involve accidental learning emerging from symbolic play. According to Piaget (1962), these games are "initially imbued with play symbolism but tend later to constitute genuine adaptations or solution to problems and intelligent creations".

(4) *Games with Rules:* These games may involve two or more players, i.e. these are group games where rules

may be completely arbitrary. Board games (chess, carom, ludo, snakes and ladders, Chinese chakkar, draft board, etc), card games, and (minor) sports (such as "tag" or "It" games, relay races, etc.).

Ego Expanding Theory

Lange (1902) and Claparde (1911) came out with the idea that play is nature's way of completing the ego, an expressive exercising of the ego and the rest of the personality; an exercising that develops cognitive skills and aids in the emergence of additional skills.

'Play-is-life' Theory

This theory is associated with the educational philosophy of John Dewey who upheld that "all organic living beings are naturally active and their natural activities in the period of their growth and development are playful". Dewey points out that the organism is in a constant state of activity. Activity is the very essence of life, and it may take any form - physical, mental, intellectual, social, competitive or recreational.

EPILOGUE

Discussion of ***play in the twentieth century*** tended to be dominated by psychologists, a consequence of psychology having become the dominant discourse of nearly all aspects of childhood and education. The theories of Jean Piaget, Lev Vygotsky (a Russian psychologist), and Jerome Bruner (an American psychologist) differed from earlier explanatory theories in stressing cognitive rather than biological functions performed by play. While, Piaget emphasized the importance of play in symbolic representation and its contribution to socialization, Vygotsky described play as a "leading activity" and believed that play allows children opportunities to use language and to learn through role playing, as Plato believed, to "self-regulate" their behaviour by following rules. By these means they raise their own learning above the level they had attained previously. Bruner and his associates stressed the role of play in language acquisition and problem solving.

Important facts emerging from the overview of theories include the following:

- Play is due to a natural urge for activity, which may take any shape or form with the onward movement of an individual's growth.
- Play is spontaneous, not constrained; marked by freedom; and a pleasurable activity in a child expresses his "self" fully.
- People differ in their motives for play, and so are the benefits of play as varied as physical, mental, intellectual, emotional, and social.
- A play theory may be biologically, psychologically or sociologically oriented, but no theory singularly can explain all play behaviour, for each theory has its relative strong and weak points.
- We can understand people, their conflicts, and of course, their play better if we understand their motivations.
- Play can be a great motivator, helping to define people's lifestyles.

Whatever the theoretical jargon about play, no one can deny to it a significant place in human education, recreation and personality development. T.P. Nunn remarks: "It may be true that spontaneous play often derives its typical features from the adult life of distant ages, and also true that those racial memories still reawaken in each generation because they have direct value for the adult life for the present epoch".

SELECTED REFERENCES

Alderman, R.B. *Psychological Behaviour in Sport,* Philadelphia; W.B. Saunders Co., 1974

Dewey, John. *How We Think,* London; D.C. Heath, 1910

Dewey, John. *Democracy and Education,* New York; Macmillan, 1916

Freud, Sigmund *Beyond the Pleasure Principle,* New York; Norton, 1975 [1920].

Gerber, Ellen W. *Innovations and Institutions in Physical Education,* Philadelphia; Lea & Febiger, 1971

Groos, Karl. *The Play of Animal,* New York; Arno Press, 1976

Groos, Karl. *The Play of Man,* New York: Arno Press, 1976

Hall, G. Stanley. *Adolescence,* New York; D. Appleton, 1904

Huizinga, Johan *Homo Ludens: A Study of the Play-Element in Culture,* London: Routledge, 1998 [1949]

Layman, Emma. McCloy The contribution of play and sport to emotional health. In J.E. Kane (Ed.) *Psychological Aspects of Physical Education and Sport,* 1972.

Piaget, Jean. *Play, Dreams and Imitation in Childhood,* London; Routledge, 1999

Ross. J.S. *Groundwork of Educational Psychology,* London, George Harrep & Co., 1953.

Rousseau, Jean-Jacques *Émile.* Trans. London; J. M. Dent; C. E. Tuttle, 1993 [1762].

Schiller, Friedrich *On the Aesthetic Education of Man, in a Series of Letters.* Ed. Elizabeth M. Wilkinson and L. A. Willoughby. Oxford, UK: Clarendon Press; Oxford University Press, 1992 [1794]

Spencer, Herbert *Education: Intellectual, Moral, and Physical.* Paterson, NJ: Littlefield Adams 1963 [1861]

Spencer, Herbert *The Principles of Psychology.* Boston: Longwood Press, 1977 [1855]

Scholsberg, H. The concept of play, *Psychology. Rev.* 54 : 229-231

Ulritch, C. *The Social Matrix of Physical Education,* Englewood Cliffs, N.J. Prentice Hall, 1968

Vygotsky, Lev *Mind in Society.* Ed. Michael Cole. Cambridge, MA: Harvard University Press, 1978

Better to be unborn than to be untaught; better to be untaught than to be ill-taught.

- from **Upnishad**

CHAPTER - 8

LEARNING

It is impossible to explain behaviour without reference to learning - a process comprehensively covering all interactions, experiences and transformations (not present at birth), which an individual happens to have during his lifetime, and which leave, more or less, permanent effect on him. If learning were removed from human life, a person would be helpless like an infant who confronts hunger, thirst, and other basic drives of life, but knows not how to satisfy them. Besides this, there would be no such general characteristics of social behaviour as intolerance, hate, love, shame, envy, jealousy, sympathy, etc., because these are all learnt. Like animals, human beings inherit innate tendencies of behaviour - pugnacity, mating, gregariousness, repulsion, escape, self-assertion, self-abasement, etc. - but the activities which manifest them are learnt; for instance, hunger is inborn, tastes for various foods are developed. Learning has a significant impact on individual behaviour as it influences abilities, role perceptions and motivation. Learning is essential to perform activities that make man truly human - skilful, knowledgeable and significant. "If animals did not learn," says Melucci (2004), "they could not adapt successfully to changes in their environment, and they could not survive."

Human beings encounter learning situations every day. While most occur by chance happening, many are thrust upon us in situations where we have little or no control. Our learning starts right from the moment we enter the world. The first thing for us to learn is to breathe in the external environment and to suckle at our mother's breast to satisfy our hunger. Of course, locomotion is born with us, but many twists and turns have to be learnt. At each step of growth, learning situations go on multiplying and diversifying in form. We have to acquire hundreds of motor skills that facilitate our struggle for existence. We learn to talk, to express, to read, to write, to do sums, to cook, to wash clothes, to tuck button to our shirt or trousers, to bike to the school or market, to learn to play soccer or run a marathon, to tackle danger situations, to meet emergencies, and so on. From all this, we arrive at two important conclusions: (1) human learning is an unending process (it begins in the cradle and ends with the coffin); and (2) every situation that inspires or forces us to acquire a new behaviour is significant because the impression it leaves behind and also the experience we derive from it goes a long way in making our behaviour *per se* increasingly intelligent, ingenious and complex.

A human child has to learn much more in order to match the inherited "self-sufficiency" of the young one of an animal in the matter of fulfilling its biological needs. The great physical educator, Jay B. Nash remarks: "Man is really a weak organism. He does not have power of a bullock, the cunning of the deer, the dexterity of the monkey or even the sting of a cobra. What does he have is a brain and the ability to perform skill and pass on this skill on to the next generation." The ability to interact with the environment, store experiences, process information, create, assimilate and dissipate ideas; and to adapt to the rapidly changing environment enables man to emulate animals in all respects in due course of time. Learning, therefore, is neither a fad or frill, nor simply a biological necessity with man; it is a social attribute that makes man truly human. Just imagine man's plight if there were no learning.

General Assumptions about Learning

Psychologists make three important general assumptions about behaviour or learning (Buskist & Gerbing, 1990).

1. Organisms are first and foremost biological creatures, and *learning is a function of the characteristics of environmental setting.... all organisms and their behaviours are products of natural selection.* Behaviour analysts, however, contend that what organisms inherit is rather a capacity to be affected by the consequences of their behaviour.
2. *Learning, regardless of its capacity, is due to either classical conditioning, operant conditioning or both.* The simple associations learned through conditioning represent the foundation upon which subsequent and generally more complex learning rests. Indeed, differences in the complexity of learning are assumed to be attributable to the number and sequence or simple associations to be learnt...
3. *Learning, in all animal species including humans, can be more or*

less described by the same 'laws of learning". Hence the way humans learn to avoid an unpleasant stimulus in everyday life appears to be similar to that by which a rat learns to avoid electric shock in laboratory experiment.

DEFINITION OF LEARNING

'Acquisition of new behaviour and/or strengthening or weakening of old behaviour as a result of experience' is probably the earliest definition of learning. We know how behavioural changes take place in a developing child as it goes on acquiring increasingly varied and complex conceptual, motor and performance skills. Fernald & Fernald (1972) describe learning as the "process of having one's behaviour modified, more or less, permanently by what he does, and the consequences of his actions, or by what he observes. Learning is any change in behaviour that results from experience - except changes which are due to injury or physiological adjustments, such as sensory adaptation and muscular fatigue." In operational terms, learning is *'the stable performance changes caused by practice, as opposed to changes elicited by drugs, nutrients or some temporary motivation state'*. Learning is not confined to schooling or what happens formally at school, and informally at home but it spans over wide variety of physical, mental, intellectual, emotional and social skills, activities and behaviours which transcend all limits of time and place.

In psychology and, education learning is commonly defined as 'a process that brings together cognitive, emotional, and environmental influences and experiences for acquiring, enhancing, or making changes in one's knowledge, skills, values, and world views, (Illeris,2000; Ormorod, 1995). Learning as a process focuses on what happens when the learning takes place. Explanations of what happens constitute learning theories. Crooks & Stein (1988) project learning as "a relatively enduring change in potential behaviour that results from experience", and, of course, practice; it is not attributable to maturation. Emerging from this statement are three basic facts: (1) learning results from practice or experience; (2) learning is not directly observable; and (3) learning is an internal phenomenon and the change taking place in behaviour cannot be observed directly; it can only be inferred from the observation of a person's actions or activities (performance); for example, smile infers happiness, and crying infers sadness (or very happy), red face infers embarrassment (or anger), and a yawn in class infers a person is bored or tired. Most learning tends to produce lasting change in learner's behaviour, character and personality.

Some years ago Saljö (1979) carried out a simple, but very useful piece of research. He asked a number of adult students what they understood by learning. Their responses fell into five main categories: (1) *learning as a quantitative increase in knowledge,* i.e. acquiring information or 'knowing a lot'; (2) *learning as a memorizing exercise,* i.e. storing information that can be reproduced; (3) *learning as acquiring facts, skills and methods* that can be retained and used as necessary; (4) *learning as making sense or abstracting meaning* (Learning involves relating parts of the subject matter to each other and to the real world); and (5) *learning as interpreting and understanding reality in a different way.* Learning involves comprehending the world by reinterpreting knowledge.

The statement that learning is the modification of behaviour through practice, training or experience, is supplemented with the following important underlying facts:

- *Learning essentially involves change* - good or bad. The change, however, may not be evident until a situation arises in which a new behaviour can occur. Learning is not necessarily reflected in performance.
- *Not all changes reflect learning.* To constitute learning, change should be relatively permanent; temporary changes may be only reflective and fail to represent any learning. (Behavioural changes caused by fatigue or drugs constitute no part of learning).
- *Learning is reflected in behaviour.* A change in an individual's thought process or attitude, not accompanied by behaviour, is no learning. (However, an individual may learn but owing to lack of motivation, may not exhibit any changed behaviour).
- *The change in behaviour should occur as result of experience, practice or training* (not maturity, disease or physical damages).
- *The practice or experience must be reinforced in order for learning to occur.* If reinforcement does not accompany practice or experience, the behaviour will eventually disappear.
- *Thought not implied in any standard definition of learning.*

Contrary to popular belief, leaning is not confined to one's schooling; it occurs through out one's life.

Performance and Learning

Learning and performance are closely related concepts but not the same. While learning is the acquisition and development of memories and behaviours, including skills, knowledge, understanding, values, and wisdom as a result of experience and practice; performance is thought of simply as an observable behaviour, i.e. what we see a person doing when a (motor) skill is attempted.

Magill (1993) observes: "Learning....is an internal phenomenon that cannot be observed directly; it can only be inferred from the observation of a person's internal states based on what we observe from doing." He defines performance "most simply as observable behaviour such as hitting a baseball, running a mile, tracing through a maze, drinking from a cup, dancing a waltz or operating a lathe." Performance may include behaviours of greater magnitude than performing these and many more kinds of simple skills. For example, playing a "whole" game of basketball or cricket (which is much more than a few simple skills of throwing, catching, shooting etc.) may also be considered performance. While individual skills often can be evaluated more objectively, the whole game evaluation would require employment of more ingenious tools and techniques because performance involves a great deal of subjective content.

In sum, learning is acquiring a skill, a piece of information, or knowing what one did not before; performance is a doing phenomenon - an activity or a series of action resulting in some measurable or rated score. ***Typical measures used to assess performance and learning*** will include the following:

- *Amount of Response* – a number of repetitions, endurance; extraneous movements reduced.
- *Latency of Response* – reaction time (time elapse between presentation of a stimulus and the initiation of a response).
- *Rate of Response* – time that starts when the movement has been initiated and when movement is completed.
- *Errors* – kind of errors, number of errors, location of errors.
- *Reminiscence* – an increase in performance after a period of no practice.
- *Trials* – time per trial, number of trials necessary to reach

specified proficiency level.

- *Retention* - the" savings" of proficiency after a period of no practice and then tested and given another trial; it indicates how long and how much information that has been learnt can be retained.

KINDS OF LEARNING

Behaviour is an integration, and so is learning; neither can be categorized into purely physical or mental though for the sake of convenience and understanding, cognitive, affective and motor labels are given to certain behaviours/learning on the basis of the predominance of motor, mental or psychomotor elements.

Cognitive Learning

Cognition covers all mental activity commonly regarded as "*thinking, knowing, perceiving, recognizing, learning, conceptualizing, imagery, problem-solving, remembering, reasoning and judging*" (Guiness, 1990). Cognitive learning is viewed as change in an individual's behaviour in the areas of problem-solving, concept-formation, reasoning and acquisition of knowledge, through memory and/or understanding. The cognitive domain involves mental processes. The Taxonomy of categories arranged in ascending order of difficulty is:

- *Knowledge*: Recognition and recall of information.
- *Comprehension*: Interprets, translates or summarizes given information.
- *Application*: Uses information in a situation different from original learning context.
- *Analysis*: Separates wholes into parts until relationships are clear.
- *Synthesis*: Combines elements to form new entity from the original one.
- *Evaluation*: Involves acts of decision-making based on criteria or rationale.

Predominantly a mind game, the cognitive learning depends greatly on the cortical activity of the brain which deals with the conscious awareness of the external environment and acquisition and processing of all information. The individual-environment interaction during infancy and childhood facilitates motor development, simultaneously programming mind's software for a more mature and complex behaviour ahead.

Cognitive learning is a great continuum. At its low pole, lies simple observation of the external phenomenon through the sensory-perceptual processes, and at its high pole, the high intellectual activity (deep thinking, meta-cognition, reflection, etc). The study of history, geography, philosophy, mathematics, language, science, commerce, etc., falls with in the orbit of cognitive learning. Tollman conceptualized learning as 'an interaction of internal mental processes with the external events of environment'. According to him, behaviour is not learnt from trial and error but from thinking and considering alternatives.

Cognition is foundational to all human experience, in some form. Every stimulus impinging on the organism invokes mental and intellectual processes along with motor processes. *Efficient learning by all means depends on efficient cognition.*

Affective Learning

Affective domain is a classification of objectives that focus on the development of attitudes, beliefs, and values. Affective learning is about gaining new perceptions (e.g., self-confidence, responsibility, respect, dependability, and personal relations).

- Receiving: Aware of, passively attending to certain stimuli.
- Responding: Complies with given expectations by reacting to stimuli.
- Valuing: Displays behaviour consistent with single belief or attitude in situations where not forced to obey.
- Organizing: Committed to a set of values as displayed by behaviour.
- Characterizing: Total behaviour consistent with internalized values.

Affective learning is focused on 'change' in our attitudes, beliefs and values resulting from experience. In some way, all this is related to our sense of right and wrong and value-judgment. How we value an object, a thing, an individual, an event or a situation is generally a result of the amount and quality of association and interaction we happen to have with it. Attitudes and beliefs begin to form early in childhood and as one advances in age, they undergo change in view of experience. In the formation of attitudes and beliefs towards elders, parents, teachers, leaders, peers, athletic teams, academic subjects, etc., as well as development of values of life, external factors play a critical role. Once established, an attitude, whether positive or negative, is difficult to change. Attitudes formed from temporary associations or experiences change more rapidly, leaving little trace behind.

In the development of attitudes, our emotions and sentiments are equally important. Good parental guidance and positive emotional training – both structured and non-structured – facilitate formation of healthier attitudes. Left to themselves, children acquire attitudes according to what they themselves observe and experience. Affective learning has more serious psychosocial implication than either cognitive or motor learning. Our attitudes make life hell or heaven according to the substance they are made on.

Effective (Motor) Learning

Motor learning refers to acquisition of motor (movement) skills. The concept derives its substance from such processes as motor output, motor abilities, motor skills, motor performance etc. Our motor behaviour consists of a large variety of motor skills that help us carry out our life routines. A motor skill, writes Magill (1993), is "an action or task that has a goal and that requires voluntary body and/or limb movement to achieve the goal". Playing a piano, dancing, walking an artificial limb, throwing a baseball, hitting a squash ball, operating a wood lathe, driving an automobile (a car or a truck), piloting an aeroplane, and hundreds of other acts like these constitute a big universe of diverse and unique motor skills. Motor skill learning is both an unconscious process and a planned procedure. All simple motor skills such as crawling, creeping, lifting head and turning it side to side, moving limbs various ways, standing, walking, running, jumping, throwing, hitting, etc., are learnt unconsciously in natural way without our knowing it but complex motor skills such as tumbling, throwing dart, bowling, etc., are learnt by structured training.

Learning motor skills is squarely a muscle-mind game in which training reflexes both by classical conditioning and operant conditioning is necessary. Sherrington viewed muscle as "the cradle of recognizable mind" which "seems to have arisen in connection with the motor act; where motor integration progressed and where motor behaviour progressively evolved, mind progressively evolved". Motor learning is largely a practice-based phenomenon. Its aim is to establish and reinforce stimulus-response connections by constant conditioning process.

Viewed as a whole, learning is a continuum with overlapping cognitive, affective and motor elements as categorical points of emphasis. Perceptibly or imperceptibly, continuity in all these three learning phases is naturally maintained and is needed to be strengthened through educational endeavours.

Picking up important threads from variety of learning situations such as Thorndike's "animal association", Pavlov's "reflex conditioning", Kohler's "problem solving by animals", Ebbinghaus's "memorization of verbal lists", etc., representing leaning as whole, or at least in large part, the educational psychologist, Robert Gagné (1965) weaved a web of eight types (or classes of situations) of learning, (arranged in hierarchical order, being the lower level prerequisite to proceeding to higher levels) which all human beings use, or eight classes of situations in which human beings learn:

1. *Signal learning.* The individual learns to make a general diffuse response to a signal. This is the classical conditioned response of Pavlov. (Pavlov, 1927)
2. *Stimulus-response learning.* The learner acquires a precise response to a discriminated stimulus. What is learned is a connection or, in Skinnerian terms, a discriminated operant, sometimes called an instrumental response. (Thorndike, Skinner, and Kimball)
3. *Chaining.* What is acquired is a chain of two or more stimulus response connections. The conditions for such learning have also been described by Skinner. (Skinner, Gilbert)
4. *Verbal association.* Verbal association is the learning of chains that are verbal. Basically, the conditions resemble those for other (motor) chains. However, the presence of language in the human being makes this special type because internal links may be selected from the individual's previously learned repertoire of language. (Underwood)
5. *Multiple discrimination.* The individual learns to make a number of different identifying responses to many different stimuli, which may resemble each other in physical appearance to a greater or lesser degree. Although the learning of each stimulus-response connection is a simple occurrence, the connections tend to interfere with one another. (Postman)

6. *Concept learning*. The learner acquires the ability to make a common response to a class of stimuli even though the individual members of that class may differ widely from each other. The learner is able to make a response that identifies an entire class of objects or events. (Kendler)
7. *Principle learning*. In simplest terms, a principle is chain of two or more concepts. It functions to organize behaviour and experience. In Ausubel's terminology, a principle is a "subsumer" – a cluster of related concepts. (Gagne)
8. *Problem solving*. Problem solving is a kind of learning that requires the internal events usually referred to as "thinking". Previously acquired concepts and principles are combined in a conscious focus on an unresolved or ambiguous set of events. (Katona, Maier)

The first five types seem to fit easily into a behavioristic framework, while the last three are better explained by Ausubel's or Roger's theories of learning. In nutshell, human learning consists of motor skills, cognitive skills, intellectual skills, verbal information (skills) and attitudes.

THEORIES OF LEARNING

Human learning is a complex phenomenon because it is influenced by human needs (primary and secondary), maturation process, life motivations and host of other perceptible and imperceptible factors and forces. Learning-scientists are still in the dark about how genetic and environmental factors interact with one another to produce learning and how an individual at different growth stages learns a wide variety of skills and behaviours. Much of our knowledge about human learning comes from various theories based on observation of, rational experience with, and experimentation on animal and human subjects.

The theories (or methods) of learning so far known fall under three distinct categories: Association (Conditioning) or Behaviouristic Theories, Cognitive Theories or Cognitivism, and Observational Learning Theories or Social Constructivism.

ASSOCIATION (CONDITIONING) THEORIES

Association theories, which come under the framework of

behaviourism, attach immense importance to *stimulus-bond–response* sequence. The argument is that every stimulus (any event, situation, condition, signal or cue) that impinges upon the organism elicits some response (a behaviour resulting from a stimulus) and that *doing* or *undoing* of a response (pattern) is intimately related to the strength or weakness of this connection, very much dependent upon the frequency and strength of the stimulus. In simple words, when the stimulus is repeated over time, the bond between the stimulus and its response goes on strengthening, but when the frequency of the stimulus is decreased, the response starts weakening and ultimately get extinguished.

Edward Thorndike, John Watson, Charles Skinner, Tolman, Guthrie, Hull, etc., are behaviourist learning theorists. These theorists are known for three basic underlying assumptions about the process of learning:

1. Learning is manifested by a change in behaviour.
2. The environment shapes behaviour.
3. The principles of contiguity (how close in time, two events must be for a bond to be formed) and reinforcement (any means of increasing the likelihood that an event will be repeated) are central to explaining the learning process.

For behaviorism, learning is the acquisition of new behaviour through conditioning. There are two types of possible conditioning: Classical Conditioning and Operant Conditioning.

Classical Conditioning

In early psychology literature the classical conditioning theory is better known as ***Learning by Conditioned Reflex,*** and is based on the premise that a physical event (a stimulus) that initially does not elicit a particular response gradually acquires the capacity to elicit that response as a result of pairing (association) with a stimulus that elicits a reaction.

The first model, classical conditioning, was identified by Ivan Pavlov (a Russian physiologist) in the salivation reflex of dogs. According to him, a "conditioned reflex is a reflex produced by a stimulus that originally was incapable of causing this reaction but that has been substituted for the originally adequate stimulus by a process of long association". The process of conditioning reflexes (innate response patterns) may be defined as the 'automatization' of behaviour by repetition of stimuli which accompany a given response and which ultimately became causes for behaviour which formerly they accompanied. *Conditioning consists of substitution of what is called as inadequate stimulus for an adequate or natural stimulus for a given response.* When conditioning is accomplished the inadequate stimulus is sufficient to arouse activity as in the case of a dog.

An outstanding feature of conditioning is association i.e. "patterns of stimuli which are acting at the time of a response on their occurrence to occasion that response." Stimulus-response (S-R) bond is fundamental to conditioning. An inadequate (unnatural) stimulus is so cleverly placed between the adequate (natural) stimulus and its accompanying response that the outcome is a natural response even when the inadequate stimulus is removed from the scene after long association. Pavlov arrived at this conclusion after a series of laboratory experiments with animals especially dogs. This S-R situation may be summed up as under:

S_1 (meat)	-	R_1 (salivation, an original tendency)
S_2 (sound of the bell)	-	R_2 (alert response, an original response)
$S_1 + S_2$ (presented simultaneously)	-	R_1 (salivary response, several times)
S_2 (sound of the bell)	-	R_1 (salivation)

The salivary reflex is said to have got conditioned. The term "conditioned" could be briefly explained as under:

> When the response, for example, to food is natural, i.e. salivation, the reflex is said to be natural or unconditioned one. When, however, it functions in response to an arbitrary stimulus (sound of the bell) as outlined above, it is said to be artificial or conditioned. The unconditioned responses are natural, permanent, regular and racial form of responses due to the natural growth of inherited tendencies in the nervous system. On the contrary, the conditioned responses are temporary, individual and learnt forms of behaviour due to natural connections made and strengthened by force of environment during animal's life time; they are not innate, so they cannot be called as racial forms of behaviour. To put the matter straight, in the experimented illustrated above, salivation is an unconditioned response to food and conditioned response to the sound of the bell. The sound of the bell, on the other hand, is an unconditioned

stimulus for salivary response. Now, when the meat (natural stimulus) was removed, the salivary response, trial after trial, went on decreasing and ultimately came to a dead stop. It is significant to note, food (natural stimulus), as Pavlov stressed, must exist as a "reinforcer" and be placed in the middle of the conditioning process in order to effect conditioning of the reflex.

Learning of this type is quite common and seems to play an important role in such reactions as strong fears, taste aversions, some aspects of sexual behaviours, and even racial or ethnic prejudice.

Despite the theoretical possibility of the widespread application of classical conditioning, most theorists agree that it represents only a very small part of human learning. Skinner, in particular, felt that classical conditioning explains only respondent (reflexive) behaviours. These are the involuntary responses that are elicited by a stimulus. Skinner felt that the more complex human behaviour cannot be explained only by classical conditioning alone. He felt that most human behaviour affects, or operates on, environment. The latter type of behaviour is leant through operant conditioning.

Operant Conditioning

The formal discovery of operant conditioning was made by E.L. Thorndike (1849-1949) who also was the first behaviourist psychologist to emphasize a "voluntary" response while explaining how animals learn. His experiments with cats revealed that responses that produce positive outcomes tend to be repeated. He says that amount and rate of learning are dependent on temporal relationship between response and reinforcement stimulus. Continuous reinforcement stimulus after every correct response, enables the learner acquire the skill or activity in question. The situation remains natural and no attempt is made to manipulate behaviour. His Law of Effect is analogous to the concept of natural selection. Where as natural selection determines which members of an animal species will survive to reproduce, law of effect determines which responses will survive and become organism's behavioural repertoire. Charles Skinner proclaimed that "it is sort of selection by consequences".

Thorndike's trial and error or *hit and miss* learning is, by and large, a matter of connection between various stimuli and their responses under certain favourable conditions. While making an insight into the animal learning experimentally in a laboratory, Thorndike noted: "When confronted with a problem situation the animal in the earlier stages, makes a series of actions and movements to achieve the goal". Most of these movements are random, exploratory, blind and unnecessary. As the trials are repeated, the successful ones increase in number. Sandiford (1933) argued that calling this learning method 'trial-and-error' was misnomer; instead it should be called learning by "selection of successful variant" because it is by selection of the right way rather than by elimination of the wrong one that the new responses are acquired. Notably, the wrong response cannot exist in the presence of right one, and so it gets eliminated.

The trial and error learning justifiably explains how learning of basic motor skills takes place in the young ones of animals and human infants and children. Playing a skill-based activity like golf, billiards, baseball, hockey or basketball, typing, riding, writing, clay-modelling, driving a car, playing piano or flute, skating, plaining wood, paddling a canoe or performing any activity is primarily a trial-and-error procedure, involving repetitive stimulus-response process. Novices or players of lesser ability are seen attempting kicking, hitting, throwing, catching, tumbling or batting in several ways before succeeding to do it correctly, accurately, efficiently and economically. Factors like initial motivation, frequency of practice, learning outcome, goal clarity, etc., profoundly affect S-R bond strengthening and consequently learning.

Classical conditioning has also been shown to play a role in the development of certain emotional responses such as fear, anger and anxiety. This discovery is of paramount importance in helping people understand how such behaviours develop in human beings.

In real sense of the term, operant conditioning theory, also known as *Radical Behaviourism*, was developed by B.F. Skinner. In his view the operant conditioning is one where there is reinforcement of the behaviour by a reward or a punishment. The word *operant* refers to the way in which behaviour 'operates on the environment'. Precisely, a behaviour may result either in reinforcement, which increases the likelihood of the behaviour recurring, or punishment, which decreases the likelihood of the behaviour recurring. It is important to note that a punisher is not considered to be punishment if it does not result in the reduction of the behaviour, and so the terms punishment and reinforcement are determined as a result of the actions. Within this framework, behaviourists are particularly interested in measurable changes in behaviour.

In operant conditioning, a response occurs without any prompting by specific stimulus imposed by the experimenter, i.e. human beings or animals learn to associate their own behaviour with its consequences. When the desired response occurs, it is reinforced. This increases the likelihood of that response occurring when the stimulus is presented. For example, a child learns that pressing a button brings an elevator or puts the bulb on, a college student learns that answering questions in the class invites appreciation from the teacher and cheers from the peers, and so on.

In the tradition of Watson, the famous Skinner box demonstrated operant conditioning by placing a rat in the box in which the pressing of a small bar produces food. Skinner showed that the rat eventually learns to press the bar regularly to obtain food. He called Pavlovian conditioning *respondent conditioning* since it was concerned with respondent behaviour - that is, behaviour that is *elicited* by a preceding stimulus. Skinner's *operant conditioning* attempts to account for most of human learning and behaviour. According to Skinner, the events or stimuli – the reinforcer - that follow a response and that tend to strengthen behaviour or increase the probability of a recurrence of that response constitute a powerful factor in the control of human behaviour. Reinforcers are far stronger aspects of learning than mere association of a prior stimulus with a following response, as in the classical conditioning model.

Operants are classes of response; crying, sitting down, walking, and batting a baseball are operants. They are sets of responses that are *emitted* and governed by the consequences they produce. In contrast, *respondents* are sets of responses that are *elicited* by identifiable stimuli. The best method of extinction, said Skinner, is the absence of reinforcement entirely; however, the active reinforcement of alternate responses that hastens that extinction.

Operant conditioning emphasizes voluntary behaviours. Researchers call them "operant behaviour" – because they operate on the environment – they make the environment respond in ways we want. Operant conditioning has a great impact on human learning. It also explains much of generalization behaviour.

Basic Principles of Conditioning

Four basic principles governing conditioning; they are: (1) Acquisition, (2) Extinction, (3) Spontaneous Recovery, and (4) Stimulus Generalization and Discrimination.

Acquisition

The portion of a classical experiment in which a conditioned response first appears and increases in frequency or strength is referred to as acquisition.

Two factors influence the strength of conditioned response: (1) *intensity* of the unconditioned stimulus, and the (2) *temporal relationship* between the conditioned stimulus and the unconditioned stimulus. The intensity of the unconditioned stimulus (UCS) can also determine how quickly the conditioned response will be acquired; ***more intense UCS often produce more rapid learning***. The intensity of UCS determines both the speed of conditioning and the maximum or asymptomatic level of the conditioned response. Generally speaking, the intenser the UCS (natural stimulus), the stronger the conditioned response, is the rule. The second factor affecting the acquisition of the conditioned response is the *timing* of the CS and UCS. *In delay conditioning, the CS begins shortly before the UCS.* Delay conditioning produces the quickest and more powerful conditioning.... With longer delays between the CS and UCS, conditioning proceeds less rapidly and is usually weaker.

Extinction

Assuming that a response has been conditioned, what would happen to that response if the unconditioned stimulus no longer followed the conditioned response? This procedure which Pavlov referred to as extinction results in eventual elimination of the conditioned response.... Once conditioned responses are formed, they do not necessarily remain a part of organism's behaviour.

Spontaneous Recovery

Once a conditioned response has been extinguished, it may not disappear from the organism's behaviour permanently. Pavlov demonstrated that after conditioned responding has been extinguished, the response would often suddenly reappear on the next CS presentation following a "time-out" from the experimental procedure. Pavlov refereed to this impromptu reappearance of the conditioned response as spontaneous recovery. Although the conditioned response elicits fewer and fewer responses over the course of extinction, some conditioned responding will occur during the early portion of each session but not in after trials...This "returning" will be quicker than the original learning.

Stimulus Generalization and Discrimination

Once a response has been conditioned to a particular conditioned stimulus, other similar stimuli will also elicit that response, despite never having been explicitly paired with UCS; the more closely other stimuli resemble the CS, the more conditional responses they will elicit. This phenomenon called *generalization* explains why many organisms respond to unfamiliar stimuli that resemble familiar ones.

It makes good sense that responses generalize to stimuli that closely resemble certain unconditioned stimuli. The cat that does not avoid dogs resembling the very first one that chased it up a tree, and the person who does not avoid snakes that look and sound like a rattler that recently bit him, certainly are not behaving adaptively. On the other hand, it would be maladaptive for the cat to climb a tree every time it saw a creature that looked like a dog or for a human being to get frightened of all snakes. Fortunately, nature has also endowed many organisms with the capacity to respond to some but not other similar stimuli. This phenomenon called *discrimination*, is the opposite of generalization and involves distinguishing one stimulus from another. In an experiment, discrimination is conditioned by using two conditioned stimuli during training. On some trials, one CS is never followed by the UCS. On other trials, the other CS is never followed by the UCS.

Thus, generalization and discrimination are the obverse and reverse of the same process. Generalization occurs when responses are elicited by stimuli that resemble the conditioned stimuli, even though stimuli have been explicitly paired with the UCS. Buskist & Gerbing (1990) state that Pavlov's views about the continuity of CS and UCS remained unchallenged until Robert Rescorla and Allen Wagner of Yale University and Leon Kamin then at McMaster University in Canada changed our view of the classical conditioning. The quintessence of these new studies is that the ability of a conditioned stimulus to predict the unconditioned stimulus reliably rather than mere temporal contiguity between CS and UCS is the critical factor in classical conditioning. In other words, a contingency (in this case, a CS that reliably predicts the UCS) and not contiguity (closeness in time) between the CS and UCS is the key factor in classical conditioning. A contingency exists any time that the CS provides systematic or reliable information about the occurrence of the UCS. When the probability of the occurrence of the UCS is equally likely in both the presence and absence of the CS, no conditioning is required.

Operant (Instrumental) Conditioning is part and parcel of educational practices – both formal and informal. Responses learnt through operant conditioning operate on, or change the environment. *The central crux of the operant conditioning is that behaviour is affected by its consequences*, as explained above.

Reinforcement, (Punishment and Extinction)

Reinforcement, punishment and extinction play a key role in the entire learning process. Reinforcement is *any event that increases the probability that a response will occur* and is used to develop, strengthen or enhance desirable behaviour; punishment and extinction are employed to minimize undesirable behaviour.

Reinforcers are of many kinds. Primarily, the two types of reinforcement are positive and negative reinforcements.

A ***Positive Reinforcer*** is any stimulus or event, which when made dependent upon a response, increases the frequency of that response over time. The delivery of positive reinforcer following a response is called a positive reinforcer. Positive reinforcement strengthens and enhances behaviour by the presentation of positive reinforcers. There are *primary reinforcers* and *secondary reinforcers.* Primary reinforcers satisfy biological drives such as food, water, sex, sleep, etc. However, primary reinforcers do not always reinforce. For instance, food may not be reinforcer to some one who just completes a five course meal. Most behaviours in life, sport, management, and else where are influenced by secondary reinforcers, which include money, status, awards, rewards, grades, trophies and praise from others. Money, perhaps, is the strongest reinforcer in man's social dynamics. These become positive reinforcers because of their association with primary reinforcers and hence are called conditioned reinforcers.

Importantly, an event that functions as a positive reinforcer at one time or in one context may have a different effect on another occasion or at some other place. For example, food may serve as a positive reinforcer for a person who is hungry, but not when the person has had a large meal. Clearly, a stimulus that functions as a positive reinforcer for one person at one time, may fail to operate in a similar manner for another person.

Within itself positive reinforcement has several principles:

- The principle of ***contingent reinforcement*** states that the reinforcer must be administered only if the desired behaviour has occurred. If the desired behaviour has not occurred, the reinforcer becomes ineffective.
- By principle of ***immediate reinforcement*** is meant that the reinforcer will be most effective if administered immediately after the desired behaviour has occurred. The greater the time gap between occurrence of behaviour and preference of reinforcer, the less effective will the behaviour be.
- The principle of ***reinforcement size*** denotes that the larger the amount of reinforcement delivered after the desired behaviour, the greater effect the reinforcer will have on the frequency of the desire behaviour. The amount or size of reinforecer is relative. A reinforecer significant for one person may be insignificant for another. Thus, the size of reinforcer must be in relation to the behaviour and the individual both.
- The principle of ***reinforcement deprivation*** indicates that the more a person is deprived of the reinforcer, the greater effect it will have on the future occurrence of the desired behaviour. However, if an individual recently has had enough of a reinforcer and is satisfied, the reinforcer will be less effective.

A negative reinforcement involves the removal, reduction or prevention of a stimulus; it strengthens response on its presentation. ***Punishment***, on the other hand, decreases the probability of a response by virtue of its presentation. Yet there is a close relationship between negative reinforcement and punishment, which might be considered as the opposite side of the same principle. On one side, if a stimulus is delivered to an organism and the behaviour that caused delivery of that stimulus decreases the punishment is said to occur; for instance, if a child is scolded for writing on the wall and subsequently she stops doing this. On the other hand, if the delivery of the stimulus is prevented or postponed and the behaviour that prevented or postponed the delivery of that stimulus increases, negative reinforcement is said to occur. By definition, negative reinforcement is avoidance of or escape from a stimulus that is otherwise punishing. In any potentially aversive situation, the organism has only two response choices. It can either behave in a manner that results in delivery of the aversive stimulus (punishment) or it can behave in manner that results in avoidance of or escape from the aversive stimulus (negative reinforcement). Some negative reinforcers such as intense heat, extreme cold, or electric shock, unpleasant remarks, etc., exert their effects the first time they are encountered, whereas others acquire their impact through repeated association.

We see negative reinforcement in business, sport, social and religious organizations as well as in personal life. Supervisors apply negative reinforcement when they stop criticizing subordinates whose poor performance has improved. By withholding the criticism, the subordinates are more likely to repeat behaviours that enhance their performance. Negative reinforcement also occurs when parents give in to their children's tantrum - especially in public places, such as restaurants, and shopping malls. Over time the parent's tendency to give in may increase, because doing so stops screaming. Negative reinforcement is sometime confused with punishment, because both use unpleasant stimuli to influence behaviour. However, negative reinforcement is used to increase the frequency of a desired behaviour, where as punishment is used to decrease the frequency of an undesired behaviour.

Just as they distinguish between positive and negative reinforcers, psychologists also distinguish between primary and secondary reinforcers. A ***primary reinforcer*** is a stimulus that satisfies a biologically based drive or need such as hunger, thirst, sex, or sleep. The primary reinforcers are unconditioned reinforcers but they can also be successfully reinforced with a wide variety of stimuli (secondary reinforcers) such as money, a smile, a warm hug, a few kind words, and a pat on the back, an award or a prize. These stimuli acquire their reinforcing properties through association with primary reinforcers and are referred to as *conditioned reinforcers*. Money, perhaps, is said to be the strongest reinforcer in man's social dynamics. An important function of conditioned reinforcers is they bridge the temporal gap between behaviour and receipt of a primary reinforcer.

Thus, both positive and negative reinforcement are procedures that strengthen or increase behaviour. Positive reinforcement strengthens and increases behaviour by the presentation of desirable consequences. Negative reinforcement strengthens and increases behaviour by the treat of and use of an undesirable consequence or the termination or the withdrawal of an undesirable consequence.

Punishment is the attempt to eliminate or weaken undesirable behaviour. It is used in two ways. One way to punish a person is to apply a negative consequence called punisher - following an undesirable behaviour. For example, a player who is excessively offensive to an official or coach (undesirable behaviour) may be ejected from game (punished). The other way to punish a person is to withhold a positive consequence following an undesirable behaviour. For example, a salesman who makes a few visits to companies (undesirable behaviour) is likely to receive less commission (positive reinforcer) at the end of the month.

Punishment may end up in unintended results - mainly negative outcomes. Even though punishment may stop an undesirable behaviour of an employee or a sportsperson, the potential negative outcomes may be greater than the cost of undesirable behaviour. Punishment tends to minimize undesirable behaviour. But if repeated, punishment may result in undesirable emotions, hostility towards boss or coach, low performance and even high turnover and absenteeism.

An alternative to punishing undesirable behaviour is extinction. ***Extinction***, briefly explained above, is the weakening of behaviour by ignoring it or making sure it is not reinforced. The rationale for using extinction is that a behaviour not followed by any reinforces is weakened. In other words, if rewards are withdrawn for behaviour that was previously reinforced, the behaviours will probably become less frequent and die out. But extinction needs time and patience to be effective.

Efficacy of the Principle of Conditioning

As a result of his work, Pavlov (1927) observed that "different kinds of habits based on training, education and discipline of any sort are nothing but a long chain of conditioned reflexes". Today this generalization seems to be too sweeping but many psychologists believe that the principles of classical conditioning are applicable in many learning situations such as treatment of behavioural problems (e.g. control of bladder), study of sensory capacities (of infants, physically or mentally challenged individuals, and animals), and development of emotional reactions.

John Watson, the leader of the Behaviourist School of Psychology, considered conditioning extremely important from the view-point of making and breaking habits. In this context, Charles Skinner used the expression "*shaping*" to denote teaching new behaviour. Shaping involves reinforcing any behaviour that successfully approximates the desired response. This process seems to have been successfully used in training animals - pigeons, pigs and even young children - to perform certain skills that approximate the final level of behaviour.

In the acquisition of motor skills, the principle of conditioning plays a crucial role. Hitting, kicking, throwing, batting, shooting in basketball, spiking in volleyball, walking on the balancing beam, performing a somersault, and thousands of other athletic skills are acquired by constant and increasingly sustained conditioning. It needs to be known that conditioning in sport is not merely physical; it is mental too. Robb (1972) remarks:

> 'Critics of associationists' views point out that if behaviour is a result of forces exerted upon people, then learning is a matter of manipulating the forces exerted upon the learner. In order to use this theory effectively some one must know how people should behave if we assume there is a proper response. Then the teacher or experimenter, assuming he knows the proper response, must connect to a stimulus in order to change behaviour.

In activity and sport, the theory of learning by classical and/or operant conditioning has fairly wide application. Mastery over minor games, lead-up games, dribbling skills, throwing, catching, hitting, batting, shooting, etc., is acquired only by conditioning muscle and mind appropriately. Physical educators, athletic trainers and coaches adopt varieties of strategies and techniques to condition students' and/or athletes' body and mind. While physical conditioning improves fitness, reaction time, precision of movement and neuromuscular coordination, mental conditioning is necessary for building up self-confidence, ensuring toughness and strengthening determination keeping hard competitive situations in view. In sum, conditioning is adaptation to environmental situations in body, mind and spirit. Conditioning makes one fluent in action, economical in effort and smooth in performance. The ability to adjust behaviour to fit particular change in the environment is highly adaptive and is characteristic of organism possessing open genetic programmes. The more open the genetic programme, the greater the organism's capacity for behaviour modification through interaction with the environment. Thorndike very aptly wrote: "He who learns and runs away will have to learn another day".

COGNITIVE THEORIES OF LEARNING

The earliest challenge to the behaviourists came from gestalt psychologists, who criticized them for their too much dependence on overt behaviour to explain learning. They proposed looking at the patterns rather than isolated events. Gestalt views of learning have been incorporated into the *cognitive theories.* The two key assumptions underlying the cognitive approach are: (1) the memory system is an active organized processor of information, and (2) prior knowledge plays an important role in learning. Cognitive theories look beyond behaviour to explain brain-based learning. Their authors consider how human memory works to promote learning. For example, the physiological processes of sorting and encoding information and events into *short term memory* and *long term memory* are important to educators working under the cognitive theory. The major difference between gestaltists and behaviorists is the locus of control over the learning activity. For gestaltists, it lies with the individual learner; for behaviourists, it lies with the environment.

Once memory theories were established as a theoretical framework in cognitive psychology, new cognitive frameworks of learning began to emerge during the 1970s, 80s, and 90s. Today the research effort in learning psychology is directed towards topics like cognitive load and information processing theory. Contemporary perspective about learning is that it is a cognitive process, which assumes that people are conscious, active participant in how they learn. Cognitive theory of learning assumes that the organism learns the meaning of various objectives and events and learned responses depending on the meaning of the stimuli.

Prominent cognitive theorists like Kohler, Tollman, Levin, Comb, Ausubel, Rogers, and others believe that the organisms 'mentally process information about their environment; in other words, while going through novel experiences, they actually *'discover meaningful relationships in order to solve problems'*. From the cognitive viewpoint, behaviour is not due solely to environmental causes, but has an internal cause: processing information about the environment, storing it in the memory, and then manipulating it until a workable solution is found to the problem situation. The cognitive psychologists noted that the extent to which an organism can learn about its environment depends upon three things: (1) organism's capacity to form mental representation of its environment; (2) its ability to manipulate these representations; and (3) its ability to implement the results of such representation as it interacts with the environment.

Contrasted with S-R approach, the cognitive learning theories assume that the organism learns the meaning of various objects and events rather than a series of movements. Learned responses are not regarded as habits rather as acts made by the organism in terms of the meaning of stimuli. S-R relationship, argue cognitive psychologists, may be apt in describing animal behaviour; it is absolutely inadequate in explaining the complex human behaviour. The process of reception or interpretation of sensory stimuli and organization and reorganization of experience best explain the regulation of behaviour. Considering perception as the keynote in the learning process as a whole, the cognitive theorists firmly believe that the ultimate control of behaviour lies within the cognitive structure of the organism.

Insight Learning Theory

Wolfgang Kohler (1925), a German psychologist, showed that a protracted process of trial-and-error may be replaced by a sudden understanding that grasps the interrelationships of a problem. He called this process *insight*, which is more akin to piecing together a puzzle than responding to a stimulus. Sustained experimentation with chimpanzees made Kohler conclude that any discussion on learning was meaningless without reference to insight by which he meant *inner-sight* i.e. the ability of the animal to perceive the relationships among various aspects of the problem situation. Insight, said he, involves foresight as opposed to *hind-sight* as in trial-and-error learning. The central point in the trial-and-error learning is the "after thought"; in insight-learning it is the "prior thought". When thinking predominantly precedes action, the learning process may be called insight-learning.

The association learning does not account for all forms of learning nor is it possible for all learning to be reduced to conditioned associations. There is more to learning than mere association of factors in an event. Association leaders like Pavlov, Thorndike, Skinner, etc., do not seem to have trained their focus on non-observable mental processes like perception, thinking, memory etc. The cognitive theorists, conversely, consider individual's active participation in the process as a critical factor. They suggest that we learn by forming a *cognitive structure* in our memory that preserves and organizes information pertaining to the key elements in a situation. Thus, instead of simply responding to a stimulus, as suggested by the conditioning theorists, we make conscious choices that allow us to adapt to our environment.

Kohler's two classical experiments give us insight into his insight theory. In one – the "box problem" – chimps had to solve the problem of reaching a tantalizing bunch of bananas that just hung above their grasp. After some trial-an-error behaviour, the chimps suddenly arrived at the solution; they stacked the boxes one over the top of the other and got up to the banana bunch. In the second experiment, called the "stick problem", the fruit was placed out of reach outside the chimps' cage. A short stick (too short to reach the fruit) was well within the chimps' reach while a larger one lay outside the cage. The solution to both of these problems involved more than simple trial-and-error or association learning. Rather after pondering over the problem for some time, the chimpanzees suddenly seem to perceive the important relationships among the key elements.

In insight learning, the correct solution to the problem situation not only appears suddenly but also it is repeated readily on subsequent presentation of the problem. Once solved, the problem remains no longer a problem. Importantly, only the animals endowed with *generalization* and *discrimination* powers are capable of learning through insight. In the more highly evolved animal species, eventually a point is reached at which the subject invariably repeats its choice of object at the second trial if the first choice was correct and changes its choice if the first choice was incorrect. This type of learning is described as the formation of a learning-set because the organism develops a generalized approach to the problem. It can also be described as *transfer* because the subject profits from the previous experience. Another important factor in insight learning is presumably known as motivation. A well-motivated organism will go directly toward the observable goal or object, but when the most direct approach is blocked, the goal can be achieved only by taking an indirect or round-about route.

The cognitive view-point is illustrated in the following experiments: ***sign learning*** where specific cues are learnt; ***transposition experiments*** where cues are compared; ***instrumental problems*** where learning apparently occurs suddenly; and the ***formation of learning*** where the organism uses past experience to solve problem with increasing cues. Finally, insight learning depends upon the type of task involved, the subject's level of mental development, its prior experience, and its use of vicarious trial-and-error procedure. "*Fumbling and searching*", which cognitive psychologists call "*purposeful experimentation*" is, in fact, another name for trial-and-error.

Ausubel's Meaningful Learning

David Ausubel, in his Meaningful Learning Theory, contends that learning takes place in the human organism through a meaningful learning process of relating new events or items to already existing cognitive concepts or propositions - hanging new items on existing cognitive pegs. His viewpoint is, perhaps, best understood by contrasting *rote* and *meaningful* learning. Ausubel described rote learning as the process of acquiring material as "discrete and relatively isolated entities that are relatable to cognitive structure only in an *arbitrary and verbatim fashion,* not permitting the establishment of (meaningful) relationships". That is, rote learning involves the mental storage of items having little or no association with existing cognitive structure.

Meaningful learning, on the other hand, may be described as a process of relating and anchoring new material to relevant established entities in cognitive structure. If we think of cognitive structure as a system of building blocks, then the *rote learning* is the process of acquiring isolated blocks with no particular place in the building of structure, and therefore with no relationship to other blocks. *Meaningful learning* is the process whereby blocks become an integral part of already established categories or systematic clusters of blocks.

Any learning situation can be meaningful if (1) learners have a meaningful learning set i.e. a disposition to relate the new learning task to what they already know; and (2) the learning task itself is potentially meaningful to the learners i.e. relatable to the learners' structure of knowledge. William James (1890) described meaningful learning:

> In mental terms, the more other facts are associated within the mind, the better possession of it our memory retains. Each of its associates becomes a hook to which it hangs - a means to fish it up by when sunk beneath the surface. Together, they form a network of attachments by which it is woven into the entire issue of our thought. The "secret of good memory" is thus the secret of forming diverse and multiple associations with every fact we care to retain... Briefly, then, of two men with the same outward experiences and the same amount of mere native tenacity, the one who thinks over his experiences most, and weaves them into systematic relation with each other, will be the one with the best memory.

Latent Learning Theory

Edward Tolman (1886-1959) directly challenged B.F. Skinner's claim that consequences were essential for shaping behaviour. He supported his own view by allowing rats to spend time in mazes and then comparing the time it took to train these rats using rewards to the time necessary to train rats that were unfamiliar with the same mazes. The rats that had just "hung out" in the mazes learned to solve them correctly in a shorter time. He proposed that as animals explore environments, they form *cognitive maps* - mental representations of the features that allow them to know where they are and how to get from place to place. As an organism moves through an environment, each point passed serves as stimulus or reminder of the next step or turn. Cognitive maps also allow the formation of the alternative routes when a path is blocked off. Thus Tolman claimed that learning can take place in a *latent* fashion - in the absence of a reward or punishment. The learning will not be demonstrated until the reinforcement is presented, but that does not mean that it has not occurred. Left to themselves, rats will explore a maze. Students will hopefully read and study their physical education tests. But the rats won't run the maze for you unless you present the possibility of a positive reinforcement - a reward of food. Many students will not display their learning until the possibility of reinforcement exists - through a test, quiz, or assignment.

Tolman called this latent learning, and it has been suggested that the rats developed cognitive maps of the mazes that they were able to apply immediately when a reward was offered.

Information Processing Learning

Cybernetics is all about understanding *communication system in machine, man and animal.* As a theory, this branch of science takes into account man's capacities, limitations and adaptive "qualities" in his total performance. The impact of stimuli - external or internal - is not ruled out; rather it is argued that the way man's sensory-perceptual apparatus code the stimuli into 'patterns of neural energy and in the final motor response that results, is the key factor in learning'. Walford, Bartlet, Goody, Smith and others have contributed to the development of information processing theory of learning.

The cognitive scientists view the mind as a system that manipulates symbols, and they seek to model the algorithms - the precise and unambiguous set of instructions - that seem to guide it. Great importance is attached to the ***feedback loop*** as the basic building block of the nervous system. Feedback is recognized in the cybernetic theory as *error-information* and is one of the most important variables controlling and regulating human behaviour. It may be likened to an exaggerated form of the "law of effect or reinforcement" in association learning. It would be an over-simplification to say that the cybernetic scientists have hit upon a new model of learning entirely different from what associationists and cognitionists have suggested. They have, in fact, tried to analyze and assess the S-R and cognitive processes more scientifically and found deeper meaning in the behavioural mechanics from the view-point of psycho-neurological working of the human mind.

The information-processing theory is explained with the help of models (analogies). Fitts refers to three major models of learning: Communication Model, Control Model, and Composite Model.

Communication Model

In communication model, the learner perceives the activity as a whole studying it from all aspects. He initially processes information (sensory input) guided by central plan or goal. Elaborating on the process underlined in the model, Robb (1972) says:

Information arrives through the receptors and is coded or transformed into symbols by the central processing system. Listening to some one talk is a form of information processing. Learning to talk involves the learning of symbolic codes. When some one converses with you, you process the information by symbolic coding. The information is translated and either stored in the memory system or directed to the output area.

The retention of information, to a large extent, depends upon how that information has been encoded into *meaningful* chunks and groups. A person who can encode incoming stimuli better is able to retain impressions more vividly and, therefore, learn successfully. Information-processing theorists attribute slow learning or no-learning in some cases to such factors as poor or no-processing of sensory-perceptual information on individual's part, his inability to translate cues or signals effectively, and/or lack of storage chunk system which allows categorization of information appropriately.

Control Model

The control model system is related to the direction of behaviour. Two types of control models have been reported in literature: *regulatory system* and *follow-up system*. A fixed goal or fixed input, such as the temperature control system in our body, is at the central stage of the regulatory system. Learning to walk, encountering and overcoming stumbles and falls, maintaining a stable posture in standing, walking, sitting or sleeping or during different movements of the body, are good example of regulatory system. When the body equilibrium is disturbed or one is obliged to change the body position, anti-gravity controls go into action without the least knowledge of the individual how to *right* himself. In the follow-up system, there is no fixed goal of input. This may be thought of as an adaptive system where the procedure changes with the change of action or activity. The regulatory system is fixed and rigid; the follow-up system, flexible and fluid. In the process of learning, the individual makes use of both systems of internal controls. The function and operation of these systems is relative to the type of activity and goals underlying it. In several situations, the change of goal of an activity becomes necessary especially when it goes out of reach, though not initially so. The two systems work in perfect harmony. Both association and cognitive theorists agree that unless the goal of an activity is clear, learning may not proceed smoothly.

Composite Model

The composite model combines the communication and the control models. In motor skill learning both are involved. Without information processing, no motor movement could be performed with desired ease and effect. Good neuromuscular coordination is developed only when the two systems work in perfect unity. Precisely, a new S-R situation underlines sensory inputs to the higher centres of the brain – the cortex to be specific – information processing and motor output directing the neuromuscular system to initiate action. With repeated trials, the controls of the entire internal process are relegated to the lower centres of the brain i.e. the spinal cord that know their job well. With increasing repetition, intervention by the higher centres of the brain starts minimizing ultimately to get reduced to zero unless the action-plan is modified due to change in situation, requiring modified directions to the organs of effect – muscles, nerves and glands. While explaining the composite model, the cognitive theorists take cognizance of the hierarchical organization of behaviour, channel capacity for processing sensory-perceptual information and feedback loops.

The cognitive psychologists equate human brain with a sophisticated super computer. In their view, learning is analogous to the mechanics by which the computer generates outputs (solutions of the problems) based on the operations it performs on the inputs (information about the environment received through the sensory-perceptual processes). Behaviour analysts counter-argue that there is no valid evidence that internal representations actually exist in man's brain because they cannot be seen, but simply inferred from the observable actions. "Cognitive science is the study of the mind. It is an inter-disciplinary approach, an attempt to link research in six different fields – anthropology, linguistics, philosophy, psychology, neuroscience, and computer science – to discover what the mind is and how it works. The mind is a riddle and cognitive science is the mind exploring itself", (Rose, 1986).

Educational Implication of Information-Processing Theory

The information-processing theory, as it related to learning process, is still at an evolutionary stage. It has yet to establish its credentials because the scope for experimentation with mind's neuro-physiological mechanism has not widened too much. So drawing permanent conclusions from a few experiments conducted in this domain is fraught with danger. Moreover, the theory does not account for external influences on learning.

Viewed as a whole, learning is a continuum which underlines the fact that learned behaviour ranges from the simplest types of habits (called routines) apparently acquired through long conditioning to highly complex verbal and motor skills involving tremendous information processing. Cognitive skills have been described on the basis of extensions of conditioning phenomenon, but they also have been interpreted from the cognitive view-point which stresses symbolic processes, thinking and understanding.

In structured learning situations, the problem is so framed and presented that the learner can perceive its significant features and the relationships among them clearly; the confusing and distracting elements are kept in the background. As such, using his insight (inner eye), the learner gets at the solution not withstanding some initial "fumbling and searching". Infants and very young children are not mature-enough to perceive all aspects of the problem-situation. They require assistance (guidance) from the parents, elders or teachers. In general, parents and teachers are seem guiding, prompting, and motivating kids "how to do things" until the latter themselves are capable of "doing things" by themselves in their own ways. Once capable of *grasping* the right cues and/or significant elements of the problem-situation, kids resent external guidance or interference both in their physical exploits and mental explorations.

Cognitive theorists lay equal emphasis on formation of self-concept. Cognitive interaction, they suggest, enhance people's self-concept. Physical appearance, intellectual accomplishments, educational status, life experience, literacy, economic condition, social status, and several other factors are good correlates of self-concept. The cognitive theorists also stress the need for presentation of the problem as a whole, rather than in fragments. Educational thinkers believe in helping young children acquire the ability to "think correctly and act decisively" rather than to learn and perfect a good number of motor skills and/or assimilate important bits of knowledge alone. Self-actualization is an important aspect of cognitive learning.

Rogers's Humanistic Psychology

Roger's humanistic psychology has more of an affective focus than a cognitive one. In his classical work *Client-Centered Therapy* (1951),

Rogers carefully analyzed human behaviour in general, including the learning process, by means of presentation of nineteen formal principles of human behaviour. All nineteen principles are concerned with learning to some degree, from a "phenomenological" perspective, a perspective that is in sharp contrast to that of Skinner. Rogers studied the "whole person" as a physical and cognitive, but primarily emotional, being. His formal principles focused on the development of an individual's self-concept and of his or her personal sense of reality, those internal forces which cause a person to act.

The *"fully functioning person,"* according to Rogers, lives at peace with all of his feelings and reactions; he is able to be what he potentially is; he exists as a process of *being and becoming himself.* What is needed, according to Rogers, is real facilitators of learning, and one can only facilitate by establishing an interpersonal relationship with the learner. Teachers, to be facilitators, must *first* of all be real and genuine, discarding masks of superiority and omniscience. *Second,* teachers need to have genuine trust, acceptance, and a prizing of the other person (the student) as a worthy, valuable individual. And *third,* teachers need to communicate openly and emphatically with their students and vice versa.

SOCIAL (OBSERVATIONAL) LEARNING THEORY

Social learning theory, also called observational learning theory, is based on the premise that humans and many other animals are able to learn by watching the behaviour of others, as long as they can remember what they saw and are motivated to imitate those actions. For human beings the important models of observation may include parents, teachers, peers, television artists, bosses, matinee heroes, elite sportspersons, and significant others. An individual acquires new knowledge by observing what happens to his or her model. This is popularly known as *vicarious* learning. A learner acquires tacit knowledge and skills through vicarious learning. In real life, most people can identify cases in which they have learned directly either from watching role models or from watching the consequences experienced by other individuals.

According to Crooks & Stein, (1988), "children tend to behave in a manner similar to their parents both during their childhood and later on in life." There are strong cognitive components involved in learning by observation. People observe others' behaviours and store cognitive images of these acts in the memory where they remain until the right influence triggers the individual to enact that behaviour. Our brain processes all the stored memories of previously observed behaviours, selecting out those that seem appropriate in given situations. Once we follow an observed behaviour time and again, it becomes part of our own response system, getting subjected to rules of reinforcement as discussed earlier in these pages. In this manner, imitative behaviours become either *stamped in* or *stamped out*.

Using the work of Tolman and others, Albert Bandura formed a new theory of learning – that learning takes place primarily through observation of others' behaviour and also the consequences that other individuals experience in response to their behaviour. In his social learning theory, Bandura (1977, 1986) has explained at length the role of observation and imitation in learning. He and his associates performed a number of experiments demonstrating the mechanics and importance of observational learning in our lives. In one widely cited experiment, children observed adults beating on a five-foot inflated "Bobo" doll and were then placed in a similar situation. It was concluded that children who had observed this aggressive behaviour were more likely to act aggressively when placed in the same situation than did children in control condition who had observed quiet models (Bandura et al., 1983). Such results would not have been produced by classical or operant conditioning theory since neither responses nor reinforcement played a role in the learning process. On the basis of his study and other research, Bandura concluded that thinking is affected by observation, and that direct consequences are *not* necessary for learning – knowledge of the mere *possibility* of reinforcement or punishment may be enough to promote or suppress behaviour.

Bandura (1977) identified four key steps in observational learning. At first step, our attention is simply drawn to a modelled behaviour. Then, we store a mental image of the behaviour in our memory. At the third step, a specific type of situation triggers us to convert the remembered observation into actions. Finally, if our actions are reinforced, we add the said behaviour to our repertoire or responses.

Import of Social Learning Theory

Learning by imitation exerts a powerful influence on our lives. Everything cannot be learnt by conditioning alone. A smart repetitious demonstration, whether live or recorded, of an athletic skill, e.g. a gymnastic somersault, sweep pass in field hockey, chipping in soccer, ball lifting in volleyball, clear in badminton, or a three point shooting in basketball, goes a long way in impressing upon the learner's mind a correct image of the skill in question. In some situations, modelling may be even more effective than operant conditioning in shaping behaviour.

Social learning has considerable relevance in organizational behaviour. A great deal of what is learned about how to behave in groups, teams and organizations can be explained as the result of the process of observational learning. A young athlete acquires skills by observing what an experienced athlete or the coach does; in an organization a new employee will do what he sees others doing. Observational learning also occurs in a very informal, unarticulated manner. For instance, people who experience the norms and traditions of their organizations and who subsequently incorporate into their behaviour may be recognized as having learnt through observation.

Social learning is valuable because it enhances the self-efficacy of the learner. *Self-efficacy refers to a person's belief that he or she has the ability, motivation and situational contingencies to complete a task successfully.* People strong in self-efficacy have a 'can do' attitude towards a specific task and, more generally, with other challenges in life.

Social learning increases self-efficacy because people gain self-confidence after some one else to do it than if they are simply told to do.

Managers can shape employee behaviour by successfully reinforcing each successive step that moves individual closer to the desired response. If an employee, for example, who has been chronically a half-hour late for work comes in twenty minutes late, the boss can reinforce that improvement.

In sum, it is important to understand that all kinds of learning contribute in some way to producing significant learning effects and shaping our behaviours. While trial-and-error is another name for self-effort that makes us learn things in clueless situations, cognitive learning helps us form cognitive maps and structure that play an important role in latent learning through the establishment of experiences. With observational learning skills and behaviours are acquired effortlessly.

Principles of Learning

Several principles apply to learning depending upon the kind of learning or the task or skill to be learned. The major principles include motivation, reinforcement, whole versus part learning, learning curves, meaningfulness of material and learning styles (laws). Some of these principles have already been explained above while dwelling upon general nature of learning and various theories that govern its processes and procedures. They are highly useful for the teacher or trainer in order to impart maximum knowledge and skills to the students or trainees. However, blind adherence to these principles can cause more harm than good. Each one of these principles should be interpreted and applied carefully in full consideration of the particular task being learned as well as the time, context and place of its learning. For instance, all children may not be uniformly motivated and by the same motivational devices at all occasions; no two teachers have the same approach to and aptitude for teaching and their styles of teaching vary considerably – each teacher has his or her own unique style of teaching; human beings do not react to the reinforcement in the same way; dance teaching and teaching a dribbling or shooting skill in basketball are guided by different sets of teaching techniques and mastery methods; so on and so forth.

LAWS OF LEARNING

Educational psychologists have identified several laws or principles of learning, generally applicable to the learning process. In the early part of the 20th century, Thorndike developed the three basic laws of learning: *readiness, exercise,* and *effect.* Compared to learning theories, the laws are more firmly established because of their having been discovered, tested, and used in practical situations. They provide additional insight into what makes people learn most effectively.

Law of Readiness

"When any conduction unit is in readiness to conduct for it to do so is satisfying: when any conduction unit is not in readiness to conduct for it not to do so is annoying", said Thorndike. This brief statement explains learner's *readiness* (preparedness), both as a long-term process and a short-term measure. The long-term readiness is interpreted to mean *maturity* – physical, mental and emotional – which is a function of time. Being an element of growth, maturity is a natural process. Children learn to perform things only when they advance in age and their bones, muscles and nerves are strong, mature, and ready to tolerate learning load. There is time for everything we learn. What a child at five is able to learn, an infant can not; and what an adolescent is capable of learning, a child is not due to the level of maturity at each growth stage. Maturity and growth are directly related. Our limbs, muscles and nerves (the instrument of our mind) become mature with time provided the nutrition and movement experiences have been normal. Motor development (i.e. motor skill learning) stands on the foundation of physical readiness (maturity). With time only, an infant learns to crawl, stand, walk and run or babble and talk; a child gets admittance to school; a girl becomes a woman, and an adult becomes a parent. A child of three is not ready to enter formal school nor is a girl of ten ready to bear children. In each of these cases, readiness (maturity) has its own relative value.

While deciding activity load for children at different age levels, their maturity has to be the prime consideration for the teachers. Where muscle and mind lack maturity, inevitable outcomes of learning would be distress, disappointment and annoyance. The more mature the child, the easier it is for him or her to observe, understand and assimilate ideas, skills and abstract concepts, and so learn them. Maturity (readiness) is a prepotent factor in resisting injury and health hazards.

The second aspect of *readiness* is motivation or reinforcement, which is, more or less, situational. It refers to the environment or situation in which learning takes place. A highly motivated child is far more prepared to receive instruction, grasp the cues of the learning task, skill or situation and quickly get on to the task than a disinterested, unmotivated and unwilling child. While the external agents of motivation are awards, rewards, money or position, and other attractions, the internal motivation is intrinsic satisfaction accruing from completion of a task or performance of an activity. Interest and aptitude too have roots in internal motivation. The urge for activity, e.g. to walk, to talk, to struggle, to fight, etc., is due to internal impulsion and is closely related to an organism's instinctual motives, drives and needs. According to Thorndike, readiness involves not only maturation but also interest.

Mental maturity indicates perceptual-cognitive ability – largely a matter of experience due to organism-environment interaction. An experienced person gets on to the problem-solving process more quickly than a novice or an inexperienced individual. Readiness, then, is a relative term interpreted differently in different growth stages and in relation to different activities. Children of the same age differ in physical and/or mental maturity. Precisely, readiness is both a biological concept and a psychological phenomenon. At a certain point of growth, a child may be ready to learn one task but not another.

Readiness implies a degree of single-mindedness and eagerness. At school, getting the students ready to learn, creating interest in them by showing the value of the subject or the skill, and providing continuous mental or physical challenge, is usually the responsibility of the teacher, physical educator or the coach. If students have a strong purpose, a clear objective, and a definite reason for learning something, they make more progress than if they lack maturity, motivation, interest and aptitude. When students are ready to learn, they meet the teacher at least halfway, and this simplifies the teacher's job. Since learning is an active process, students must have adequate rest, health, and physical ability. Their basic needs must also be met.

Law of Effect

The principle of *effect* (outcome or consequence of an activity) is based on the emotional reaction of the student. It has a direct relationship to motivation. "Of several responses made to the same situation, those which are accompanied or closely followed by satisfaction to the animal will, other things being equal, be more firmly connected with the situation, so that, when it recurs, they will be more likely to recur; those which are accompanied or closely followed by discomfort to the animal will, other things being equal, have their connections with that situation weakened, so that, when it recurs, they will be less likely to occur", says Thorndike (1911). The principle holds that responses that produce a satisfying or pleasant state of affairs in a particular situation are more likely to occur again in a similar situation. Conversely, responses that produce a discomforting, annoying or unpleasant effect are less likely to occur again in the situation. According to Thorndike, "a satisfying state of affairs is one which the animal does nothing to avoid, often doing things, which put an end to it."

While satisfaction is a *reward* for the task or skill being learnt or performed with increasing ease or success; annoyance, discomfort or unpleasant feeling is a *punishment* for not doing it correctly or satisfactorily. Educationists and psychologists consider these outcomes as the obverse and reverse of the same process. From the first yell at birth (a natural instinctive action) to performing a complex triple somersault in gymnastics, whatever we do in life, generates either happiness or disgust or annoyance. Most biological activities having survival motive are pleasant in effect for they satisfy organism's basic needs and drives. So animals repeat them. Some activities do lead to distress, dissatisfaction and disgust; they endanger life; so organisms avoid them. John Watson did not agree with this kind of argument. He placed greater emphasis on the frequency (repetitiousness) of an activity rather than its effect or consequence as an important yardstick of its suitability for learning. In fact, satisfaction (pleasure) and annoyance (pain) as outcome of an activity are the two opposite poles of the continuum of an experience. Sometime an activity may produce pleasure at one point of time and pain at another. The difference in two lies more in degree than in kind. Making and breaking of habits is often painful.

Play is a pleasurable activity. All children play even without formal motivation. However, organized skill-learning often breeds boredom and monotony for its repetitious nature. So do un-innovative teaching techniques. Teacher's amiable personality, pleasant environs, attractive equipment, good infrastructure, etc., produce favourable effects on learner's mind. Conversely, teacher's rude behaviour, unimaginative teaching methodology, unattractive environment, etc., produce negative effects. Internally under-motivating and externally over-motivating conditions rarely produce positive effects. Sometime, physical activity and sport become a risky affair. A young boy who gets a punch on his nose and bleeds in a boxing class or a young girl who sprains her neck while doing a front roll will find it hard to return to the activity easily due to annoying experience.

One of the important obligations of the teacher or physical educator is to set up the learning situation in such a manner that each student is able to see evidence of progress and achieve some degree of success. Experiences that produce feelings of defeat, frustration, anger, confusion, or futility are unpleasant for the student. If, for example, a teacher attempts to teach advanced concepts, of gymnastics, on the initial engagement, the student is likely to feel inferior and be frustrated. Impressing upon students the difficulty of a task to be learned can make the teaching task difficult. Usually it is better to tell students that a problem or task, although difficult, is within their capability to understand or perform. Every learning experience does not have to be entirely successful, nor does the student have to master each lesson completely. However, every learning experience should contain elements that leave the student with some good feelings. A student's chance of success is definitely increased if the learning experience is a pleasant one.

Besides this, the law of effect is important in understanding learning especially as it relates to instrumental conditioning. However its status is controversial. Particularly in relation to animal learning, it is not obvious how to define a "satisfying state of affairs" or an "annoying state of affairs" independent of their ability to induce instrumental learning, and the law of effect has, therefore, been widely criticized as circular. In the study of operant conditioning, most psychologists have, therefore, adopted Skinner's proposal to define a reinforcer as any stimulus that, when presented after a response, leads to an increase in the future rate of that response. On that basis, the law of effect follows tautologically from the definition of a reinforcer.

Law of Exercise

Also known as *law of frequency*, this law denotes practice or repetition of a skill or activity. It is an extension of the *Law of Use and Disuse* in biology. Thorndike stated: "When a modifiable connection is made between a situation and a response, that connection's strength, other things being equal, is increased. When a modifiable connection is *not* made between a situation and a response over a length of time, that connection's strength is decreased." This principle underscores the fact that things or activities most often repeated are best remembered or learned. It is the basis of drill and practice. It has been proven that students learn best and retain information longer when they have meaningful practice and repetition. The key point here is that the practice must be meaningful. It is clear that practice leads to improvement only when it is followed by positive feedback.

The human memory is fallible. The mind can rarely retain, evaluate, and apply new concepts or practices after a single exposure. Students do not learn complex tasks in a single session. They learn by applying what they have been told and shown. Every time practice occurs, learning continues. These include student recall, review and summary and manual drill and physical applications. All of these serve to create learning habits. The physical educator must repeat important items of subject matter at reasonable intervals, and provide opportunities for students to practice while making sure that this process is directed toward a goal.

The law of exercise underlines the fact that when an action-sequence is repeated over time, the synaptic connections are strengthened making the repeated charge of a nerve impulse break down the resistance and smoothen the way for its speedy transmission. Juxtaposed with this is the biological principle that organs of the body which remain in constant use strengthen, and those not used over a period of time, atrophy. These two together illustrate that practice of an activity or skill is vital to perfecting its performance.

Repetition is another name for reinforcement. When an S-R connection is made, it ought to be strengthened by a process of repetition or practice. Importantly, a right connection made, and repeated in a right manner over time results in right result in the form of better performance. Conversely, once a wrong connection is made and repeated, any modification to be interpolated in it is likely to become counter productive. Learning of motor skills and later sports skills is largely a matter of right connections being developed in the neuromuscular system. Bucher (1972) remarks: "This law of learning in respect of development of skills in physical education means that practice makes for better coordination, more rhythmic movements, less expenditure of energy, more skill, and better performance". Highly complex gymnastic skills, juggling several balls simultaneously, acrobatics of a stuntman on the trapeze or piloting a plane is impossible to do without months and years of correct practice. Dancing, typing, cycling, driving, skating, kicking, hitting, jumping, throwing, etc., all require practice to achieve perfection. Practice of an activity or skill – whether physical or mental – leads to automatization, which would mean more output, speedy error-reduction, more efficiency, effort economy, and better performance. However, practice without feedback is like a headless horseman who knows not which direction to go.

"Both theory and practice need emphatic reminders that man's learning is fundamentally the action of these three laws of readiness, exercise and effect", remarked Thorndike.

ADDITIONAL PRINCIPLES OF LEARNING

While dwelling upon the three basic laws of learning, Thorndike also referred to certain conditions, which reveal how human beings learn various activities in various situations. These in due course came to be known as additional laws of learning.

Law of Primacy

Primacy is the state of being first and it often creates a strong, almost unshakable, impression. Things learned first create a strong impression in the mind that is difficult to erase. For the teacher it means that what is taught must be right the first time. For the student, it means that learning must be right. "Un-teaching" i.e. effacing wrong first impressions is harder than teaching them right the first time. If, for example, a student learns a faulty technique of serving in badminton or tennis, the coach will have hard time correcting bad habits and "re-teaching" correct ones.

The student's first experience should be positive, functional, and lay the foundation for all that is to follow. What the student learns must be procedurally correct and applied the very first time. The teacher must present subject matter in a logical order, step by step, making sure the students have already learned the preceding step. If the task is learned in isolation, is not initially applied to the overall performance, or if it must be relearned, the process can be confusing and time consuming. Preparing and following a lesson plan facilitates delivery of the subject matter correctly the first time.

Psychologists say that first impression is the last impression. Primary impressions always go a long way in forming attitudes towards people, things and life in general. A child's first day at school, a teacher's first session with the class and a bride's first meeting with groom have great significance as they largely determine the future course of events.

Law of Recency

The principle of recency states that things most recently learned are best remembered. In other words, last impression is the lasting impression. Conversely, the further a student is removed time-wise from a new fact or understanding, the more difficult it is to remember. For example, it is fairly easy to recall a telephone number dialed a few minutes ago, but it is usually impossible to recall a new number dialed last week. The closer the training or learning time is to the time of actual need to apply the training, the more apt the learner will be to perform successfully.

Information acquired last generally is remembered best; frequent review and summarization help fix in the mind the material covered. Teachers recognize the principle of recency when they carefully plan a summary for a lesson or learning situation. The teacher repeats, restates, or reemphasizes important points at the end of a lesson to help the student remember them. The principle of recency often determines the sequence of lectures within a course of instruction. The beginning and concluding parts of a speech are better remembered. In an activity lesson class, the warming-up and concluding recreational activity are better enjoyed than any other part(s). The taste of a dessert at the end of a meal lingers on both in the mouth and the mind for a longer time.

Law of Intensity of Stimulus

The strength or intensity of a stimulus determines how quickly and strongly would the response be made. The stronger the stimulus, the more intensethe response, is the rule. In a classroom setting, the more intensely is the material taught, the more likely it will be retained. A sharp, clear, vivid, dramatic, or exciting learning experience teaches more than a routine or boring experience. The principle of intensity implies that a student will learn more from the real thing than from a substitute. For example, a student can get more understanding and appreciation of a movie by watching it than by reading the script. Likewise, a student is likely to gain greater understanding of tasks or motor skills by performing them rather than merely watching them or reading about them. The more immediate and dramatic the learning is to a real situation, the more impressive the learning is upon the student. Real world applications that integrate procedures and tasks that students are capable of learning will make a vivid impression on them.

A crashing sound, a hard touch, a pungent taste, a strong stink etc., make one react to each of them more intensely and in peculiar ways. Stronger motivation may also elicit stronger response. However, there is always an optimal level at which the organism responds more effectively with an optimal level of performance. Beyond this, the more intense stimuli lead either to avoidance behaviour or freeze response. Higher performance or accomplishment comes only when the stimulus is optimal, rather than highly intense.

Law of Contiguity

Also known as the *Law of Association or Proximity*, the law of contiguity states that 'situations which occur together as parts of a whole either simultaneously or in close proximity (nearness) tend to revive one another'. For example, the Olympic Games remind us of the ancient Greek civilization and the Pan-Hellenic Festivals in which Olympics occupied a place of pride. They also bring to mind the memory of great athletes, heroes, monuments, artefacts, temples, palaces, etc., that had close association with the Olympic Games. This could be true in reverse order also i.e. when we learn something about Milo - the legendary Greek wrestler - or Plato as an athlete, we become aware of the pristine glory of the ancient Olympic Games.

For association theorists contiguity of experiences is extremely important in learning process. They argue that reward (positive reinforcement) may help the association process to proceed more rapidly and also strengthen the S-R connection, as association will occur regardless of reward if there is contiguity (continuity) between a stimulus and its response(s). This way, not will learning become a speedy process but also widen in dimensions. Lyrics, poems and songs are learnt more quickly than the prose chunks because each word in the composition is meaningfully associated with the other(s). The closer the proximity between the central figure and the peripheral details in a picture or a painting, the greater the clarity with which various aspects of it appear on the mind screen. Similarly, the greater the closeness among various skills of a game or a sport, the greater the chances of mastery over it is the rule.

Law of Multiple Responses

A living being responds to an external stimulus in more than one way simultaneously or in quick succession. A chance utterance or a sudden appearance of a stimulus sets off a train of thoughts or reactions which themselves serve as stimuli for some other responses. This is a situation of multiple responses. The desirable responses are made and the undesirable ones are suppressed. Human beings with higher biological status are capable of making multiple responses than animals.

The multiple-response situation may also be interpreted to mean that the individual, when confronted with a stimulus, attempts to respond to it in several related aspects of the situation, not just one. For instance, during an instructional class, the students do not only attend to what the teacher teaches but also to such things as teacher's turn-out, his gestures, his speech mode, teaching aids used, and the like. Academicians call it *concomitant (attendant) learning,* indicating that the subject acquires knowledge about several things at a time in a learning situation by chance or by design.

Law of Attitude, Set or Disposition

An *attitude* is a settled way of thinking; *set* refers to our state of body and mind; and *disposition* means our interest and inclination at a particular learning situation A person's response to a given stimulus depends a great deal on his attitude towards an activity or the condition (both physical and mental) he is in at the time of stimulus application. Even the continuance of an activity is closely related to one's state of body and mind at a given time. According to Thorndike, a well-fed caged cat goes to sleep while a hungry one would struggle to get out of it and reach out to food. This situational aspect has great bearing on learning. The elite and the ordinary athletes, the healthy and unhealthy persons, and the naïve and the intelligent individuals have altogether different attitude towards an activity or a sport. At a particular point of time their mind set may be different.

Law of Partial Activity

According to Thorndike: "A part or an element or an aspect of a situation may be pre-potent in causing a response and may have response bound more or less exclusively to it regardless of some or all of its accompaniments". The reference here is to learner's previous experience in a given task or activity. A person who has had some experience in some task, sport or activity and the one who already has had rub with the reasoning puzzles "will get on to the things" right away as compared to the one doing it for the first time. Apart from this, novices will handle the easier elements of a problem first and gradually move on to the harder and complex ones.

Law of Assimilation or Analogy

Learning situations that have no original or acquired response elicit response(s) made previously to *similar* situations. In other words, when a learner does not know how to handle a new situation, he attempts to do so with a response he made to some similar situation on some earlier occasion. A badminton player playing tennis for the first time will use soft grip on the racket, not the hard one.

Law of Associative Shifting

A conditioned response may be shifted from one situation to

another if the situations occur in succession. This is transfer-effect situation found in operant conditioning. In learning, the similar types of motor skills the learner benefits from are the consequences of an already established S-R connection. He uses his previous experience to face the new but similar situation. Conditioning is a universal phenomenon and it might be truly said that the teachers can elicit any response of which a pupil is capable, associated with any situation to which he is sensitive.

Law of Belongingness

If an S-R connection is natural, learning would be natural, effective and lasting. Motor skills involving natural running, jumping, throwing etc., are acquired rapidly because of the S-R connections in these cases are unconditioned and firmly established. There is little interference from any quarter when these connections are sought to be modified. The skills and activities that have no natural S-R connections take more time to learn and master. For example, in natural (forward) running, it is easier to interpolate modification than trying to run backward with the same arm-foot coordination.

LEARNING CURVE

Learning is *change in behaviour* occurring as a result of experience or practice. The learning process involves *accumulation* (of experiences), *consolidation* (of gains of experiences), *exploration* (of new fields of experience), articulation (communicating experiences) and *feedback* (knowing the efficacy of experiences gained). The major concern of the educationists, physical educators and psychologists, in their own field of knowledge and interaction, is to see that the educational process i.e. teaching-learning is not only carried on with least impediment and stumbling but also the learning outcomes are measured in some quantifiable form, assessed and evaluated using standard yardsticks, techniques and procedures for the benefit of the students, teachers and the administration. Precisely, the students must know what (and how much) they have learned (gained); the teachers, what and how they have taught; and the administrators, what objectives have been achieved, and to what extent.

In an unending process of individual-environment interaction, the child sheds some of its native modes of behaviour, modifies others and acquires a variety of new ones by impulsion, observation and initiation. Parents, teachers, physical educators and athletic coaches always remain eager to know what change has occurred in a child's behaviour, how much he has learned and how much his status in the subject, activity or skill has improved over time. Measurement of consequences (outcomes) of learning in some quantifiable form is an important function of all education including physical education and sport for the simple reason that it helps the educators to spot out abnormalities and/or drawbacks, i.e. strengths and weaknesses in a child's skills, knowledge, personality and character on the one hand, and evaluate teacher's own teaching techniques, styles, and procedures on the other hand in a given setting.

One way to accomplish this difficult task is to apply a very useful learning concept called learning curve which is valid for a wide range of situations in life - education, physical activity, sport and else where. For example, if a student is tested in a subject every week or every month, or his aerobic endurance is monitored every fortnight with increasing activity load, or his kicking skill in soccer is assessed every ten days for a period of six months or so, we can construct a performance (improvement) curve using graphical technique. Good teachers and athletic trainers make use of this technique very frequently to make an objective assessment of the teaching-learning situation. The learning curve was adapted from the historical observation that individuals who perform repetitive tasks exhibit an improvement in performance as the task is repeated a number of times.

Definition of a Learning Curve

A learning curve is a graphical representation of the changing rate of learning (in the average person) for a given activity or tool. In the learning process, this concept is used to measure how quickly a skill, a task, an activity or an idea can be mastered. Usually shown as a simple graph, a learning curve often depicts the combination of the time it takes to learn a new idea or skill set, combined with the rate at which mastery is achieved. Learning curves are often used to measure an individual's progress against an average. The concept of the learning curve is a powerful one and is applicable to all learning processes.

Learning of motor skills and improving performance in athletic events like sprinting, jumping or throwing is chiefly a matter of correct and constant practice. Apart from the motivation a child shows and the effort he or she puts in this process, acquisition of a skill and achieving mastery over (or perfection in) it, is a function of time. Depending upon its nature (simple or complex), each skill takes its own time to develop to a desired level of efficiency. Interestingly, almost all motor skills and athletic skills can be observed, tested and evaluated objectively for the data generated by these processes is quantifiable; it is easy to tabulate and plot on a graph for the purpose of comparison and analysis.

To illustrate the point, a boy or a girl is given the task of making ten direct shots in basketball from three different distances at the weekend after undergoing regular coaching for half an hour on week days. His or her performance in terms of successful shots made from each distance can be plotted on a graph using X axis as the performance (score) variable and Y axis as the time variable. By this strategy, the coach will be able to know whether or not coaching imparted by him improved performance; if yes, how much; and also at which distance? Similarly, trial scores could be monitored in sprints, standing broad jump, medicine ball put, sit-ups, and cricket ball throw. Sport and physical education abound in situations where trainees'/ students' performance in different activities can be monitored week after week or month after month and plotted on graphs for the purpose of comparison. Learning curve can be obtained from the scores in any physical activity like the ones mentioned above or mental attribute such as intelligence or aptitude where objective data are possible to generate over a period of time.

With repetition of almost any motor task, learning occurs, and the learner becomes more efficient or effective at carrying out the task or skill. In the pursuit of rotor tasks, time spent on the metal dot increases. In the mirror-tracing task, the tracing becomes more accurate.

Characteristics of a Learning Curve

In a learning curve, a diagrammatic presentation of the amount of activity or skill learned in relation to time is made. A typical learning curve will show on the Y-axis the amount learnt and the X-axis passage of time, as pointed at above. Autoimmunization in the performance of an activity or a skill is a function of time depending upon the frequency with which the stimulus is presented and/or the activity or skill is performed. Here it is important to note that progress in learning or improvement in performance of an activity or a skill is neither uniform nor consistent; it is marked by fluctuation – the path to progress is undulated. Progress in skill learning commonly follows an S-shaped curve, with some measure of skill on the Y axis and number of trials on the X-axis (Fig. 8.1). Cratty (1968) maintains that "the shape of a motor learning curve is a function of the spacing of the trials, and the capacities of the performer, as well as nature of the task". This brings to light a few characteristics of a learning curve.

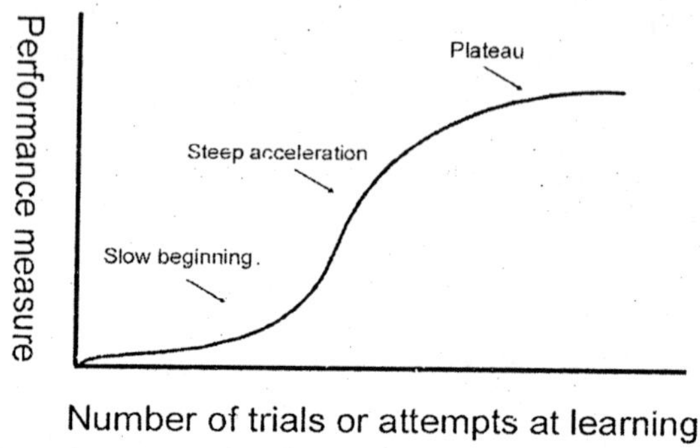

Fig. 8.1 The S-shaped "learning curve" typical of complex learning

Three characteristics are common to all learning curves: (1) initial spurt, (2) plateau, and (3) end (sudden) spurt.

The ***initial spurt*** occurs in the beginning. Here it is natural that the rate of learning exhibits spurt. When an athlete begins to learn a new skill, his learning curve shows an increasing gain-pattern. At this stage, apparently, the subject is highly motivated and seems to exhibit a significant surge of effort. Many experienced teachers and athletic trainers exploit this initial spurt by selecting the most important items to be communicated and presenting them as a package to the students at the beginning of the training unit. In many ways, it is possible to exemplify the initial spurt with the aphorism "the first step is the best step".

The initial rise is indicative of the rapid progress (increased retention of the information) generally attributed to novelty of the activity or skill, as well as interest and curiosity on the part of the learner which seems to generate greater energy that makes him put in harder effort right at the outset. The tremendous initial improvement in performance in the early phase may be explained on the basis of these facts only. With the increase in frequency of trial repetition, usually. the graph levels off at some stage, indicating that maximum performance has been achieved. Monotony sets in causing the interest and enthusiasm to wane, and less and less new information to retain after each repetition.

The second and, perhaps, the most crucial feature of the learning curve is the ***plateau***. At some point in the learning process, there is a flattening off in terms of improvement, the plateau. Frequently, the process of learning is marked by discontinuities and involves escalating from one plateau to another. Most learners are mostly too aware of the experience of finding themselves on a plateau, which manifests in the feeling that they are never going to get anywhere.

The third characteristic of the learning curve is the ***end spurt*** - a sharp upward lift. The end-spurt is preceded by fatigue which is likely to set in with the passage of time. When the training session draws nearer to an end and the subject realizes this, there occurs resurgence of interest and effort to learn more. This revival is called the end spurt.

Plateau - Genesis of Causes

Plateau – a state of flattened curve - indicates physical and mental fatigue, and shows the performance improvement almost arrested despite the learner making unabated effort. The learner seems to be disheartened, disgusted and discouraged. He is unable to know what is happening to him and why. Consequently, a feeling of guilt begins to overpower the learner. How long plateau continues to plague the situation and keep the learner guessing depends on several factors such as complexity of the activity or skill, ability of the player to put up with the situation, and skill of the teacher to help the student handle such a situation. Finally, with persistent effort and the patience displayed, the performance curve begins to suddenly shoot up.

Reasons often cited for the plateau in a learning situation include decline in interest, fluctuation in attention, inability of the learner to monitor right cues, boredom arising from repetitious skill practice, physical fatigue or exhaustion, absence of innovative teaching skills, physiological over-loading, etc. Psycho-physiologists trace the cause of plateau to the physiological limits a learner reaches after he puts in hardest effort to emulate others. It needs no reminder that each one of us is born with certain inherent physiological capacities, and our muscles, bones, nerves, receptors, effectors, glands, etc., have a fixed range of functionality well-defined in each case. Like an untrained runner, when a learner attempts to pump in all his energies at the outset and puts every thing at stake to achieve limited objectives, he is bound to face physical fatigue and mental blockades reflected in decreasing gains in the learning curve. Unfortunately, neither the teacher nor the learner is actually aware of these limits and limitations. Some scientists believe that physiological limits are rarely reached in normal circumstances because learning situations rarely are as intense as the competitive situations requiring a do-or-die effort.

With psychologists motivation is a significant factor in struggle against plateau. The truth of the matter is that learning curve cannot always be expected to move upward all the time; it has dip and rise every now and then because body and mind cannot always be functioning at a uniform level of efficiency and be conducive to the learning process. For example, bio-rhythms, energy output mechanism, interest, mind-set, mood state, attitude etc., never are the same; they fluctuate.

Individual differences also do matter in the learning process; not all individuals learn with the same speed, efficiency and effectiveness. In the light of this fact, a few important research findings on the learning curve (Cratty, 1968) include the following:

(1) Performance records of a task which is difficult for a performer who is immature or whose nervous system is impaired in some way, will generally produce a learning curve in which little initial improvement is evidenced.

(2) A capable and matured performer, learning a similar task to those with which he has had experience, will generally produce a learning curve in which quick initial improvement is evident, followed by a plateau.

(3) After an initial 'discovery phase' marked by rapid improvement, there is a tendency for an individual to improve at a decreasing rate and the regular curve to register irregularities in improvement due to the imposition of various motivating conditions.

Jumping from one plateau to another is called organization of learning. Organization of learning is achieved when the learner discovers a new and more effective method of performing particular tasks; for example, when he learns to apply boxing skills to tackle street though menace or to apply calculus to solve problems of business. Disorganization of learning is an actual falloff in performance. This arises when the subject has to choose between alternative methods of tackling a task.

Plateau-tackling Strategies

Occurrence of plateau in learning of a task or performance of an activity is inevitable and unavoidable. By-passing it is also impossible. Experts suggest several strategies of tackling plateau problem:

- First of all, it is important for a teacher to be sure whether plateau has naturally occurred or some change in learning (or teaching) style, injury or a mechanical defect in skill execution has caused it.
- Essential feedback on both performance and plateau helps the learner to face the "difficult" situation with courage, patience and firm resolution, rather than get bogged down under its weight.
- By a realistic approach only can a teacher/coach prepare the learner to fight plateau.
    - Since the cause of plateau in each activity and in each individual may not be the same, the remedial measure must also be different and individualistic.
    - When performance deteriorates due to muscular or physiological fatigue, scale down exercise (workout) loading, and provide proper rest and relaxation. Complete cessation of activity is not advisable, nor should it be encouraged.
    - Where mental fatigue characterized by monotony, boredom and inaptitude is the cause of plateau, switch over to some interesting activity or skill.
    - Make use of confidence-building measures like encouragement, motivation, inspiration, etc.
    - Innovative teaching techniques may not altogether banish plateau from the learning process, they soften down its impact on the students.

Some psychologists consider plateau to be a period of consolidation - a period of slackened progress when the learner consolidates the gains of initial spurt. It is a nature's way of providing compulsory rest to the learner after a hard initial effort. In a sense plateau may be likened to second-wind phenomenon, well-known to and experienced by the long distance athletes. As plateau period comes to a close, the learner feels relieved, settled and ready to carry on the activity with greater steam and strength.

SELECTED REFERENCES

Bandura, Albert *Social Learning Theory*, Englewood Cliffs, NJ; Prentice Hall, 1977

Bandura, Albert *Social Foundation of Thought and Action: A Social Cognitive Theory*, Englewood Cliffs; NJ, Prentice Hall, 1986

Bandura, A., Ross, D., & Ross, S. Imitation of film mediate aggressive models, *Jr. of Abnormal and Social Psychology*. 66; 3 -11, 1963

Bucher, Charles A. *Foundations of Physical Education*, St. Louis; Mosby, 1972

Buskist, William & Gerbing, David D. *Psychology: Boundaries and Frontiers*. Glenview III; Scott/Foreman/Little Brown Higher Education, 1990

Cratty, Bryant J. *Psychology and Physical Activity*, Englewood Cliffs, NJ; Prentice Hall, 1968

Crooks, Robert L., & Stein, Jean *Psychology - Science Behaviour and Life*, New York; Holt, Rinehart and Winston, 1988

Gagne, Robert M. *Essentials of Learning for Instruction*, New York: Holt, Rinehart and Winston, 1975

Gagné, Robert M. *The Conditions of Learning*, Holt, Rinehart and Winston, New York, 1965

Guiness, Alma E. (Ed) *ABC's of the Human Mind*, Peasant Ville, New York: the Reader's Digest Association Inc., 1990

Kohler, W. *The Mentality of Ape* (translated by E. Winter), New York; Harcourt Brace and World, 1925

Magill, Richard A. *Motor Learning: Concepts and Applications*, Madison, Wisconsin; WCB Brown & Benchmark, 1993

Melecci, Nancy J. *Psychology: The Easy Way,* New York; Barron, 2004

Munn, Norman L., Fernald, L. Lodge, & Fernald, Peter S. *Introduction to Psychology,* (Third Edition). New Delhi; Ford and IBM Publishing Co., 1972

Pavlov, Ivan *Conditioned Reflexes* (Translated by G.V. Anrep), New York University Press, 201-206, 1927

Robb, Margaret, D. *The Dynamics of Motor Skill Acquisition,* Englewood Cliffs, New Jersey; Prentice Hall Inc., 1992

Saljio quoted by Paul Ramsden [Ramsden, P. (1992). *Learning to Teaching in Higher Education,* London: Routledge.] P. 26, 1979)

Children explore their worlds through movement and make fundamental links between action and reality through movement.
- **Education Encyclopaedia**

CHAPTER - 9

SKILL-ACQUISITION PHENOMENON

Movement is the basis of life and muscles are the instruments of movement. Richly supplied with nerves and blood, muscles play a key role in movement both of the body and within it. Not only are we able to walk, run, jump and propel body through the space, but also to stand, sit, speak and blink and engage in hundreds of other gross and fine movements necessary for survival and achieving great things in life. But for movement, human beings would be just dull and drab as the dust. Human beings use movement to learn about their world, to function in the world as they grow and mature, and to maintain healthy bodies. Individuals must learn to move and at the same time move to learn. Children explore their worlds through movement and make fundamental links between action and reality through movement.

Play, activity and sport stand on the foundations of movement and most movement skills constituting them are learned by infants and children over time at various growth stages naturally or by an organized effort. Unless teachers, physical educators and sports coaches understand how children and youth acquire motor skills, whether building with blocks, learning to write or draw, effectively moving through space, or developing skills for sport or leisure activities, they would find it difficult to provide optimal learning experiences to them and optimize their capacity to perform creditable physical, mental and intellectual feats, so important for the life to progress and prosper.

MOTOR LEARNING

In animals and human beings, learning to perform some motor task in response to a given event or stimulus is motor learning. It involves a set of internal processes associated with practice or experience leading to relatively permanent changes in motor skill. Motor learning may be formally defined as 'a *process*, which is *inferred* rather than directly observed, which leads to *relatively permanent changes* in the *potential* for motor performance, as the result of *practice or exposure'*. This definition of motor learning differs least from the general definition of learning. The italicized words in the definition are a key to understanding the motor learning phenomenon. At first, motor learning is a process not a structure, and so dynamic in nature. Second, motor learning is difficult to observe directly except from observation of performance changes over time. Learning is essentially cognitive but it might reflect in motor activity. Third, any temporary change occurring in performance during a training session does not constitute learning; change must relatively be permanent or stable. Fourth, learning does not involve a monotonic increase in performance over time. Temporary states, such as distraction, illness, arousal, etc., can shift performance in one direction or another. Finally, motor learning is inferred only when performance changes are traceable to practice or exposure. If an individual's motor performance improves due to the use of a drug, for example, or worsens because of an accident or fatigue ("negative" performance change), we cannot attribute the changes to learning.

Underlining modification of motor behaviour, motor learning is the process of improving the motor skills, the smoothness and accuracy of movements. It is obviously necessary for complicated movements such as speaking, playing the piano, climbing trees and eating bananas but it is also important for calibrating simple movements like reflexes, as parameters of the body and environment change over time. The cerebellum and basal ganglia are critical for motor learning. From psychological viewpoint, motor learning process involves processing information, visual skills, practice, feedback, timing, etc.

Through motor learning the man is capable of achieving very skilled behaviour, and through repetitive training a degree of automation can be expected. To conclude, the concept of motor learning veers round motor skills, and the whole process is subject to certain well-documented procedures and principles.

Concept of a Skill

Skill is the *ability to bring about some end result with maximum outlay of energy, or of time and energy*. Characteristically, a skill, irrespective of its nature:

- requires movement and must be learnt.
- is marked by a high degree of precision and accuracy.
- is described through general terms as an act.

is an indicator of quality of performance, e.g. goal scored, foul shooting percentage, batting average, etc.

Skills are the tools we use to do our work or perform some activity with ease, efficiency and economy. The entire gamut of human learning consists of well-identified groups of skills such as motor skills, mental skills, intellectual skills, emotional skills, social skills, communication skills, conceptual skills, technical skills, team skills, leadership skills, self-management skills, and the like. Each of these groups of skills is learned in particular setting, in an appropriate and congenial environment using proper means, methods and techniques. A skill is called motor, mental or psychomotor on the basis of predominance of the element it emphasizes. However, the involvement of both muscle and mind in the learning of a skill cannot be rule out, meaning that no skill is purely physical or mental nor can it be acquired by body or mind alone, but the whole organism.

Motor Skill (Performance)

Motor skill is the *ability to execute movement in an optimal fashion.* It is a concept under a much wider area of motor behaviour. The motor behaviour study tries to find out how motor skill is produced. Importantly, all motor behaviour consists of three sub-specialities, viz. motor learning (defined above), motor control (how the human neurological system controls movement), and motor development (how the capacity of children to produce motor skills naturally matures). In order to understand how individuals learn motor skills (or how motor learning takes place), requires an appreciation of all these factors plus sport psychology (how to motivate individuals to learn motor skills and participate in sport and exercise), and pedagogy for physical education (i.e. how the learning environment can be organized to optimize the acquisition of motor skills).

Between 18 months and five years of age, children master many different physical skills. Large motor movements become coordinated, making it easier for children to move about quickly and smoothly. The ability to control their bodies gives young children freedom to choose how to move as well as the speed and direction of the movement. Large motor skills also play a role in upper body movements, such as pushing and pulling.

Skilled motor performance is a high quality movement meant

to accomplish a predetermined objective. Its unique characteristics include the following:

- It is an organized sequence of movements which require:
    - (a) *Spatial organization* – arranging effective movement patterns through the selection of appropriate muscle groups to execute the selected movement (batting in cricket, American football skills).
    - (b) *Temporal organization* – control of movement patterns through appropriate timings of muscle contractions and relaxations (as in water-skiing)
- Skilled motor performance involves accuracy and uniformity and is done with a purpose (shooting a basketball, catching in baseball).
- Sequence occurs whereby each muscle group functions or responds at the proper time (playing tennis strokes, jumping on the balancing beam, long jump).

Categorizing Motor Skills

Motor skills are movement skills – skills of moving body or its parts through the space and time. They result from the action of the nerves and muscles. From a simple eye-blink reflex to a highly complex gymnastic stunt or swimming stroke, the universe of motor skill is marked by variety and extensity. However, using various yardsticks, motor skills can be placed in different categories in order to understand each one of them in their proper perspective and know their implication as foundational drills for more complex activity such as soccer or hockey.

In physical activity and sport, motor skills are categorized as general motor skills and specific motor skills. While ***general motor skills*** are an essential ingredient of all human learning, ***specific motors skills*** are specific to individuals who specialize in specific tasks or jobs or pursue specialized objectives such as playing and excelling in sports. As a matter fact, life starts with motor activity and infants and children acquire a large variety of motor skills as they interact with the environment in hundred ways. The more intensive and extensive the individual-environment interaction, the greater would the possibility be of varied motor skills acquired by a child.

In psychology, motor skills are usually divided into gross motor skills and fine motor skills. ***Gross motor skills*** involve movement of large muscles of the body and they include lifting one's head, rolling over, sitting up, balancing, crawling, and walking. Gross motor development usually follows a pattern. Generally large muscles develop before smaller ones. Thus, gross motor development is the foundation for developing skills in other areas (such as fine motor skills). Development also generally moves from top to bottom. The first thing a baby usually learns is to control is it eyes. ***Fine motor skills*** include the ability to manipulate small objects, transfer things or objects from hand to hand, and various hand-eye coordination tasks. Fine motor skills may involve the use of very precise motor movement in order to achieve an especially delicate task. Some examples of fine motor skills include using the pincer grasp (thumb and forefinger) to pick up small objects, cutting, colouring and writing, and threading beads. Fine motor development refers to the development of skills involving the smaller muscle groups

Experts have used several yardsticks of classifying motor skills. For example, using *Precision of Movement* as a yardstick, Bryant J. Cratty favoured placing motor skills into two types: (a) ***Gross Motor Skills*** which require a great deal of muscular involvement - total body and or multi-limb movements such as running, chasing as in American Football; and (b) ***Fine Motor Skills*** in which very little movement is initiated and which usually involves the manipulation of tools or objects while sitting down, as putting in golf. This classification is based on the amount of muscular involvement necessary to complete/execute a skill.

The motor skill categorization by Richard A. Schmidt is based on the *Distinctiveness of Beginning and End Points*. By Schmidt's standards, motor skills fall into three distinct categories: (a) ***Discrete Skills*** which have a distinct beginning and ending, one which involves a single execution to complete the task such as shooting in archery, or javelin throw; (b) ***Continuous Skills*** that have no distinct beginning or end one which requires repetition of movement patterns; and (c) ***Serial Skills*** which require various steps or a series of movements in a sequence to complete the task, like bowling in cricket.

Stability of the Environment was the criterion used by E.C. Poulton; Margaret D. Robb; and John Drowatzky to categorize motor skills into open skills and closed skills. ***Open Skills*** require the performer to adjust to or regulate an environment containing objects which have spatial and/or temporal qualities; for example, soccer skills, water-skiing skills, etc. ***Closed Skills*** are the ones wherein performance can be planned in advance without fear of environmental changes or can be made to fit the environment predicted in advance, such as in swimming, gymnastics, balance beam, trampoline, etc.

CONCEPTS, CONDITIONS AND PRINCIPLES OF MOTOR SKILL LEARNING

The motor skill-acquisition phenomenon is governed and guided by several principles, conditions and factors. The study and understanding of the principles that under-grid motor skill learning provide the guidance and an underlying framework for (1) curricula of physical education programmes within schools; (2) the co-curricular sport programmes for the youth; (3) the pedagogical principles applied by physical education teachers and coaches; and (4) the clinical interventions of occupational and physical therapists for individuals of all ages.

Principles and generalizations explained below have resulted from long and diverse human experience, scientific research and application.

Maturity

Maturity or "readiness" in body and mind, as advocated by association theories, is a prerequisite for motor skill learning at each and every stage of growth. Maturity, no doubt, is a function of time, but its timing and quality are closely related to external conditions such as nutrition, peer group interaction, opportunity for activity and play, facilities for recreation, formal and informal instruction at home and at school, etc. Psychological readiness, though dependent on physical maturity in some way, has close relationship with environmental motivations, individual inclinations and aptitudes, as well as educational experience. Both intrinsic and extrinsic motivations combine well to prompt readiness in young children for special activities like sports, outdoor adventures, science Olympics, etc.

The maturity principle is of immense importance in determining activity, instructional, and athletic competition load for different age groups of children. Burnouts, drop-outs, and even stunted growth patterns may result where approach to activity-load is based not on maturity but on extraneous considerations. Physical educators and athletic coaches need to ensure utmost compatibility between skill-learning programmes and students' physical, mental and emotional readiness. A well prepared body can take physical overload with no distress, and a well prepared mind can easily grasp more complex ideas and concepts.

Cognitive Ability

All skill is to be learnt first at the mental level before it is performed physically. This denotes that unless a child is able to grasp the perceptual and cognitive elements of a skill adequately, it would be difficult for him to perform the skill with utmost precision. Therefore, the role of right perception and cognition in motor skill acquisition cannot be undermined. Various facets of this process include: learner's ability to perceive things correctly, to be adequately attentive to the on-going task or skill, to differentiate between relevant and irrelevant cues, to absorb important information about the learning situation, ability to translate important ideas into practical acts, and so on. As things stand, it is hard for young children to absorb too much of theoretical information about the activity in progress as they are naturally restive and eager to peremptorily get on to the skill performance without waiting for the teacher to finish instruction.

Better results can be expected from a repeatedly performed smart demonstration of a skill as a model. In contrast, too much theorizing breeds boredom and allows the instruction to fall flat on students' ear. Children who are able to master the gross elements of a skill are also able to process cognitive information about the skill, Therefore, skill demonstration - whether live or recorded - is an effective device in projecting skills as they actually need to be performed. It serves as a cognitive instrument for the students to observe and assimilate various elements of the skill by using their insight, understanding and experience.

Motor skill learning should need least theorizing. As a matter of principle, motor skills are practical activities, and involve a few precise procedures like observing the skill demonstration, imprinting skill image on the mind screen by keenly observing the movement-sequence, performing the skill part by part, switching over to complete skill-sequence and repeating it until it becomes an automatic procedure, eliminating errors and stumbling blocks in the internal transmission channels, and finally using feedback loop to engage in correct practice. Learning of gross motor-skills involves least cognitive ability but to master complex motor skills adequate perceptual and cognitive inputs are needed.

Practice

Practice is the lifeline of motor skill-acquisition. In fact, there is no skill learning without practice – correct and adequate. Irrespective of the status/nature of a task (skill), S-R connection will have to be established and reinforced by constant practice over a period of time in order for the skill to be acquired, mastered, and automatized. However, the amount of practice to perfect a skill greatly depends on the complexity, its importance in the total skill-structure of a sport, physical and mental ability of the learner and his or her previous experience with the sport in general and the skill in particular. Robb (1972) says:

> How good the performer wants be, that is, what skill level he sets for himself will determine how long and how hard he will need to practice. Persons of different age levels approach this (the practice) phase differently. Children practise to see what they can do. They seem to have no specific aspirations but they are extremely curious, and therefore, easily challenged. They seem to love practice. Adults on the other hand want result quickly and often seek to achieve without putting forth much effort.

Practicing motor skills correctly, regularly and intensively is essential for the learning to take place effectively and to the satisfaction of the student and the teacher alike. It is no half-truth that skill over-learning virtually depends on this single fact alone. In this connection physical educators and coaches need to be guided by several important procedures discussed below.

Student Variables

Skill practice is a thoroughly individual affair and must to be planned and carried out in consideration of the capacity of the learner, his level of motivation, previous experience in the activity/skill, his interest in the skill/activity, importance of the activity for him, the stage of skill training, and the like. A student's attitude toward learning a skill, a sport or an activity determines for the most part the amount and kind of learning that takes place.

Mass/Distributed Practice

Whether the skill practice should be mass or distributed is to be justified on he basis of following facts:

- Mass practice is used when the skill is complex, has many

elements, requires warm up, and/or is a new skill for the performer.

- Distributed practice is used when the skill is simple, repetitive, boring, demands intense concentration, is fatiguing, and/or demands close attention to detail.
- Mass practice is used when the learner is older or more mature, is able to concentrate for long periods of time, and/or has good ability to focus attention.
- Distributed practice is used when the learner is young or immature, has a short attention span, has poor concentration skills, and/or tires quickly.

Whole/Part Practice

Efficient skill-acquisition is closely related to the teaching style or technique adopted by the teacher. What is taught is no doubt important, but equally important is how it is taught. Optimal learning effects come from a smart combination of the two. The best teachers in the world are known for their teaching styles, not knowledge. In skill teaching, the use of whole or part method is not a matter of any guess work but of the teacher's ingenuity and skill. Nature of a skill, situation, students' maturity level, individual preference, etc., will largely determine which of the two methods is to be used. However, whether a skill is learnt in parts or in whole has no influence on the long-term retention of that skill.

- Most skills should be practiced as a whole in order to maintain the rhythm of the skill.
- If a skill is practiced in parts, it should be practiced as a whole as quickly as possible.
- Whole practice is used when the skill has highly dependent (integrated) parts, is simple, is not meaningful in parts, and/or is made up of simultaneously performed parts. Gymnastic stunts, bar exercises, jumping exercises, somersaults, etc., can, in no way, be taught in parts.
- Whole practice is used when the learner is highly skilled, is able to remember long sequences, and/or has a long attention span.
- Part practice is used when the skill has highly independent parts, is made up of individual skills, is very complex, and/or if limited work on certain parts is necessary. A swimming

stroke with such sequenced components as floating, arms and legs movements, inhaling-exhaling etc., is difficult to teach by a whole method.

- Part practice is used when the learner has a limited memory span, is unable to concentrate for a long period of time, is having difficulty with a particular part, and/or cannot succeed with the whole method.

Constant/Variable Practice

Whether the practice should be constant or variable is no matter of importance but of practical application.

- Variable practice involves practicing one skill in a variety of settings or conditions.
- Constant practice involves practicing one skill the same way for the entire practice session.
- Constant practice enhances the learning of open skills for beginners and closed skills for the advanced learners.
- Variable practice enhances learning of open skills for intermediate and advanced learners.

Blocked/Random Practice

The benefits of blocked or random practice in skill-acquisition are relative to skill sequence and objectives.

- Blocked practice refers to practice one skill for a certain amount of time, then a second skill for the same amount of time, and then the third skill for the same amount of time.
- Random practice refers to practicing one for a few minutes, then a second skill for a few minutes, then the first skill again, and then the third skill (or some other random order).
- Blocked practice leads to short-term success. Random practice leads to long-term success.

Mental/Physical Practice

In motor skill learning context, mental practice means *mental rehearsal* of the skill when it is being learnt as a whole. For example, performing a movement sequence from the take-off to landing in long jump or high jump several times mentally before the athlete actually attempts to perform this skill-sequence physically. Mental rehearsal of skills especially those complex and coordinative, is necessary for grasping vital cues of the skills being practiced and internalize them. This process facilitates strengthening S-R connections resulting in high neuromuscular coordination.

- Mental rehearsal can certainly increase skill performance provided it is used intelligently.
- Whether physical practice should be used before mental practice or vice versa will depend on the predominance of physical or cognitive element.
- Physical practice is better than mental practice alone. Neither should be preferred at the cost of the other.

While most coaches favour harder physical practice, psychologists put great emphasis on mental practice or rehearsal as a skill-improvement technique. The debate is inclusive but recent research indicates that mental rehearsal without physical practice is meaningless. It is true in reverse direction also. Whiting (1972) points out: ".... The designation motor skill is a misnomer since it would be difficult to think of skilled behaviour in which only efferent activity was involved". Mental practice and physical activity are like hand in glove.

Goal Setting

Goal setting occupies an important place in skill-acquisition process. It means establishing proper targets. With intelligent goal-setting, skill-learning proceeds speedily and efficiently. There is close relationship between goal-setting and level of aspiration. In general, goal-setting must be with reference to the objectives of the skill, learner ability, available time span and proficiency level desired. It must lead to some measurable achievement. Unrealistic goal-setting impedes learning; it brings down self-confidence especially when the goals set are hard to achieve. Important guidelines in this connection are given below:

- Setting goals based on current ability improves the learning of motor skills.
- Monitoring change in motor skill development based on the type of improvement desired (e.g., accuracy, distance, technique) improves the learning of motor skills.
- Goals should be clear, measurable and achievable.

Transfer of Learning

Application of the principle of transfer of learning facilitates speedy acquisition of skills. Important facts of this principle are enumerated below:

- Positive transfer occurs when previous learning has a favourable effect on new learning.
- Negative transfer occurs when prior learning interferes with learning new information or skills, or new skills interfere with previously learned tasks.
- The more closely related one skill is to another the more likely the transfer of learning (e.g. throwing a variety of objects). Unrelated skills present poor situation for transfer-effect.
- Greater positive transfer occurs when the first task is well learned. No major change in skill execution need be introduced until fairly high level of automatization has taken place in the current skill or performance sequence. Only such changes are to be interpolated as do not disturb the gross S-R connections.
- Greater positive transfer occurs when similarities are pointed out to the learner.
- Transfer from practice to the game is subject to the same identical element issues as transfer from skill to skill.

Skill teaching programme should be organized so efficiently that it optimizes transfer effect, making both the teacher and the student economical in the expenditure of energy and effort.

Feedback

Feedback refers to "error information" or knowledge of results about performance (practice) of an activity or skill. In the initial stage of skill learning, students (particularly novices) commit a variety of errors possibly because they lack concentration and conscious control over several unrelated body positions and movements. They cannot monitor "error information" correctly, which results either in delayed learning or prolonged wrong practice. This problem can be overcome by proving augmented (teacher) feedback. Robb (1972) argues that "practice alone is not sufficient; practice with feedback is necessary", for it has serious implications in skill acquisition procedure.

- Feedback improves the learning of motor skills by providing error deduction and motivation for the learner.
- Feedback should be based on the critical elements for each

skill.

- Only one or two corrections should be identified for each performance.
- Feedback should be delayed for a few seconds after the performance to give performer an opportunity to reflect on his or her own performance.
- Feedback should be given when the performer cannot see the result of the performance (e.g. technique).
- Feedback should not be given when the performer can see the result of the performance (e.g., accuracy, speed, or distance).
- Feedback is most helpful when it is specific and meaningful.
- Feedback should be given frequently in the early stages of learning and then tapered off.

Plateau

Plateau or *slump* in learning process is inevitable and unavoidable. There is no need to panic when skill learning slackens down on account of this. Rather the student and the teacher should learn to face this situation with courage and firm determination. At the sight of plateau, the over-dose of skill practice must at once stop. Attempt should be to downsize the activity load and re-do goal setting without downsizing motivation. Once the cause of performance slump is known, tackling plateau situation would not be difficult.

Progression

Progression is gradual movement or development from one stage to the next. In overload training and skill-acquisition, progression principle has immense utility. It is not advisable to adopt fast-track approach in teaching skills. Depending upon their nature, skills take their own time to be learned, perfected and mastered. Simple skills are learned faster, complex skills take longer to learn. Unless simple skills are mastered and performed satisfactorily, complex skills may not be acquired with the same strength and speed. Both motor skill and athletic skills are well-sequenced as far as complexity is concerned. A master physical educator or coach knows how to proceed from simple to complex, known to unknown, and informal to formal elements of skills. Progression also refers to proper practice load in relation to gender, age, ability, mental capacity, experience, etc., of the students. Both in intensity and extensity of the practice load, the movement forward-upward should be optimally gradual. Progressive approach facilitates physical conditioning, mental adaptation, skill automaticity, and motivational uplift.

Skill Retention

Consistent and correct practice of skill or movement sequence is instrumental in its retention longer. Too long a gap between two practice sessions especially in the initial stages of skill-acquisition weakens the S-R link causing forgetting and missing. In order that a particular skill is retained longer, it should be practiced to the point of over-learning or perfection. Retention of a skill also depends on the proficiency achieved in it over a period of time. Cratty (1968) stated that "placement of a skill in series of skills will influence its acquisition and retention". Skills in the initial part of series will be learnt first and retained best (primacy principle). Skills in the middle portion of series will be learnt last and retained least. Skills in the final portion of a series will be retained better than those placed in the middle as well as those placed near the initial portion of the series (recency principle).

Stages of Learning

Cratty (1968) observes: "The learning process relative to the acquisition of a motor skill, can be divided into several stages: preparation for the performance, obtaining initial cues, gaining insight and understanding of the task, practice, and competition". At each stage, a few important points have to be stressed in order for the skill learning to be a smooth affair.

Stage I

- Consistent practice should be given for both open and closed skills.
- Feedback should be provided on the intent of the skill.
- Model demonstrations and information related to the skill should be provided.
- Focus should be on success.

Stage II

- Feedback should be provided on the refinement of the movement.
- Focus should be on critical cues.
- Numerous practice opportunities should be provided.

- Distributed practice should be used.

Stage III

- Focus should be on the use of the skill in performance situations (e.g., offensive/defensive strategies).
- Focus should be on the refinement of skills.
- Focus should be on consistency for closed skills and flexibility for open skills.
- Variable practice should be used.

Apart from the principles explained above, there are two important considerations to which physical educators and coaches must pay proper attention. (1) When practicing skills where both ***speed and accuracy*** are important equal and simultaneous emphasis should be placed on speed and accuracy (e.g., moderate speed and moderate accuracy). Since achieving these two objectives will require long practice hours, it is important to make some provision for proper adequate rest breaks. (2) Some part of skill-practice session must necessarily be utilized for the *whole* game of which the skill under practice is a part. Apart from the freedom of movement this will give to the learner, there would be an attempt on his part to discern relationships among various skill elements of the game. The aim of skill-drills and lead-up games of a sport is to accomplish this objective.

Motor skill learning "is an organized coordinated activity in relation to an object or a situation which involves a whole series of sensory, central and motor mechanisms", say Argyle & Kendon (1967). It ought to be utmost satisfying in terms of its physical, psychological, and social outcomes for the entire mansion of human activity stands on it alone.

SELECTED REFERENCES

Argyle, M., & Kendon, A. The experimental analysis of social performance... In L. Berkowitz (Ed) *Advances in Experimental Social Psychology*. Vol.3, New York: Academic Press, 1967

Cratty, Bryant J. *Psychology and Physical Activity*. Englewood Cliffs; NJ, Prentice Hall, 1968

Crooks, Robert L., & Stein, Jean *Psychology - Science, Behaviour and Life*, New York; Holt, Rinehart and Winston, 1988

Gagne, Robert M. *Essentials of Learning for Instruction*, New York: Holt, Rinehart and Winston, 1975

Gagne, Robert & Driscoll, Marcy Perkins *Essentials of Learning for Instruction*, NJ: Prentice-Hall Inc., 1988

Keele, Steven W. "Movement Control in Skilled Motor Performance." *Psychological Bulletin* 70, 387 - 403, 1968

Magill, Richard A. *Motor Learning: Concepts and Applications*. Madison, Wisconsin; WCB Brown & Benchmark, 1993

Robb, Margaret, D. *The Dynamics of Motor Skill Acquisition*. Englewood Cliffs. New Jersey; Prentice Hall Inc., 1992

Schmidt, Richard A. "A Schema Theory of Discrete Motor Skill Learning." *Psychological Review* 82, 1975:225 - 260.

Woodworth, Robert S. "The Accuracy of Voluntary Movement." *Psychological Review* 3, 1899 :1 - 114.

"That almost magical link between classroom performance and something which is supposed to happen in the real world"

- J. M. Swinney

CHAPTER - 10

TRANSFER OF LEARNING

Experience is the essence of learning. Human beings are blessed with the ability to experience things, store experiences and transfer experiences from one situation to another in order to make learning a speedy, efficient and economical affair. Imagine that every time that people entered a new environment they had to learn how to behave or deal with situations without the guidance of prior experiences. For example, learning how to drive a car, a slightly novel task, after one has had enough experience in driving a motor bike, would be disorienting and dependent on trial-and-error tactics if one did not make use of the previous experience to tackle a situation somewhat different from the previous one. Munn, Fernald & Fernald (1972) noted: "One of the most important assumptions in formal education is that learning which occurs in school will be applied in situations outside school. Everything cannot be taught in the classroom but ideally concepts, principles and information can be acquired which will be useful in coping with new situation after one has left the classroom environment."

This phenomenon is pervasive in our everyday life at work, at home and in the community. Consciously or unconsciously, the experience-transfer takes place whenever our existing knowledge, abilities and skills affect the learning or performance of new tasks. For instance, very young children learn to speak in the very context in which they live or are brought up. Parents, care-givers, friends and siblings turn everything they touch into an opportunity for learning. Personal connections are formed between language and their ability to understand and manipulate the world around them. As they grow older and enter school or step into the neighbourhood society they are able to transfer this knowledge of language in to a very broad range of contexts and problems. This happens naturally and even with adults almost everywhere in the wide world. Simply put, transfer of learning is illustrated by the phrases "It reminds me of..." or "It's like..." or "It's the same as..."

Educators and educational psychologists recognize transfer of learning as perhaps the most significant issue in all fields of instruction including physical education and sport. Transfer of learning cuts across all educational domains, curricula, and methods.

The Transfer Concept

The concept of transfer of learning is not as complex as the concept of learning itself is. Learning is a very wide term, transfer an aspect of it. Transfer of learning or training is generally defined as *the application of skills, knowledge, and/or attitudes that were learned in one situation to another learning situation*. This increases the speed of learning. This important learning concept highlights how an individual transfers one's knowledge and skills from one problem-solving situation to another. By engaging in this exercise the individual widens the area of his or her experience and performs new tasks or skills with utmost economy in energy and effort. Gagne & Driscoll (1988) note: "The recall of what has been learned and its application to new situations or contexts is referred to as the transfer of learning, or, simply, transfer."

Transfer of learning is a commonplace phenomenon and often is done without any conscious thought. For example, suppose that when you were a child and learning to tie your shoes, all of your shoes had brown, cotton shoelaces. You mastered tying them. Then as you grew up, you got new shoes. The new shoes were a little bigger, and they had white, nylon shoe laces. The chances are that you had no trouble in transferring your childhood shoe-tying skills to the new larger shoes with the different shoelaces. In this case the application of skill and knowledge acquired in one situation has been applied in another situation. This way several situations come in our life almost daily where our previous experience facilitates our meeting the new but slightly different situations.

The Encyclopaedia of Education explains transfer thus: "*When a particular learning experience influences an individual's ability to respond effectively to stimuli different in some ways from the past experience, transfer of training is said to have taken place*". The transfer is almost spontaneous, automatic, and often unconscious mostly directed by exigencies of time, place and the skill or activity currently in progress.

Interestingly, the transfer concept holds somewhat different meaning in different disciplines of psychology. For example, in cognitive psychology perspective, it might mean how the semantic similarity of word pairs in one list affects time to learn on a second list (the transfer task). From this perspective, the original learning task and the "later activity" look very much alike. In organizational/ industrial psychology perspective, the psychologist might be interested in knowing how trainees' motivation to transfer is related to later job performance. The training domain (e.g., a web-based training programme) might be very different from the later "activity" domain (e.g., job performance). In sport psychology, transfer of learning may underline how a tennis player attempts to play badminton shots with the same dexterity using his previous experience in tennis.

The use of transfer of training in place of transfer of learning and vice versa is not uncommon though both are used in different contexts. J.M. Swinney considers ***transfer of training*** as an "....almost magical link between classroom performance and something which is supposed to happen in the real world." It is effectively and continuingly applying the skills, knowledge, and/or attitudes that were acquired in *a learning environment* to the job environment. ***Transfer of learning*** is the application of skills, knowledge, and/or attitudes that were learned in one situation to another learning situation such as learning trigonometry with the help of knowledge of geometry. This kind of transfer increases the speed of learning.

Types of Transfer of Learning

According to psychologists, the transfer capability comes from *generalization* (an important quality of human intelligence) and is related to *learning by analogy*. Learned information can be applied to other problem instances and possibly even other instances. Three specific types of learning transfer are normally identified:

- ***Within-Trial***: Learning applies immediately to the current situation; e.g. while practicing free throw shooting in basketball, a player makes use of his or her experience (error information) in each previous free throw to improve the next throw by concentrating more.
- ***Within-Task***: Learning is general enough that it may apply to different problem instances in the same domain; for example, learning to write with left hand when one got tired writing with right hand, or attempting to play tennis with left hand when one has already mastered playing it with the right hand.

- *Across-Task*: Learning applies to different domains; for instance, learning to understand history with one's knowledge in geography.

Further examples here include some types of *concept acquisition* in which a concept learned in one domain (e.g., blocks) can be related to other concepts (e.g., bricks) through similarities (e.g., stackable). Across-task learning is then strongly analogical.

Generalization

Generalization is the ability to apply knowledge and information gained in completing some task to other tasks and situations. Human beings generalize routinely. For example, knowing that one should always drive on the right on the road is a generalization from one's experience and observation in specific driving situations. However, in India or else where, driving on the right is not correct. This is an example of over-generalization, which human beings also do quite capably. Generalization can result from a number of different learning strategies including (a) explanation-based learning, (b) analogical learning, and (c) abstraction learning.

- *Explanation-based learning*: When an agent can utilize a worked example of a problem as a problem-solving method, the agent is said to have the capability of *explanation-based learning* (EBL). This is a type of *analytic* learning.
- *Analogical learning*: Reasoning by analogy generally involves abstracting details from a particular set of problems and resolving structural similarities between previously distinct problems. Analogical reasoning refers to this process of recognition and then applying the solution from the known problem to the new problem. Such a technique is often identified as *case-based reasoning*. Analogical learning generally involves developing a set of mappings between features of two instances.
- *Abstraction learning*: Contrasted with the conception of acquisition, *abstraction* is the ability to detect the relevant - or *critical* - information and action for a particular problem. Abstraction is often used in planning and problem solving in order to form a condition list for operators that lead from one complex state to another based on the criticality of the precondition.

For instance, in an office environment, a robot with a master key can effectively ignore doors if it knows how to open doors in general. Thus, the problem of considering doors in a larger plan may be abstracted from the problem solving. This can be performed by the agent repeatedly to obtain the most general result. Some architectures limit abstraction to avoid the problem of over-generalization, resulting in mistaken applications of the erroneously abstracted operator.

Inductive Learning and Concept Acquisition

In contrast to abstraction, *concept acquisition* refers to the ability of an agent to identify the discriminating properties of objects in the world, to generate labels for the objects and to use the labels in the condition list of operators, thereby associating operations with the concept. Concept acquisition normally proceeds from a set of positive and negative instances of some concept (or group of segregated concepts). With the presentation of the instances, the underlying algorithm makes correlations between the feature of the instances and their classification. The problem with this technique as it is described here is that it requires the specification of both relevant features and the possible concepts.

In general, as an *inductive* technique, concept acquisition should be able to generate new concepts spontaneously and to recognize the relevant features over the entire input domain.

While explaining his theory of learning, Thorndike argued that transfer-effect is either positive or negative. Based on this generalization, three types of transfer are mentioned in literature: (1) positive transfer, (2) negative transfer, and (3) zero or neutral transfer

Positive Transfer

When prior learning or training facilitates acquiring a new skill or reaching the solution to a new problem, psychologists call it positive transfer of learning or simply *facilitation*. In this situation the individual performs better than he would have without the prior training. In other words, if some one was assisted by his previous experience in a task or skill in responding to a new stimulus (activity) in some way, this is considered as positive transfer. For example, when a tennis player tries his hand at acquiring squash skills with no hassle or when a person fluent in French, Italian and Latin quickly learns Spanish; both are attempting positive transfer effect. Cratty (1968) argued that 'transfer of training may occur from limb to limb in the same individual. Practicing a task with one hand will facilitate its performance with the other..... when fatigue or other learning blocks occur, practice in a complex skill such as throwing, may at time be attempted with the non-dominant hand'.

Positive transfer is most likely to occur when the learner (a) recognizes common features among concepts, principles, or skills; (b) consciously links the information in memory; and (c) sees the value of using what was learned in one situation in another (Schunk, 1996b). Importantly, positive transfer plays a major role in encoding and in many higher order thinking skills. In addition to helping learners acquire specific information more easily, positive transfer helps learners function effectively in situations for which they have no previously acquired information. It enables learners to solve problems they have never seen before.

In a very real sense, no useful learning takes place unless positive transfer occurs. The only reason for teaching most topics in the classroom is to enable students to use what they learn in settings beyond the school. Knowledge that cannot be activated in new situations in which it is obviously applicable is referred to as *inert knowledge*.

Negative Transfer

Negative transfer occurs when prior learning or training hinders acquiring a new skill or reaching the solution to a new problem. In this situation the individual performs worse that he would have if had he not been exposed to the prior training or experience. Also called as *habit interference* or simply interference, the negative transfer is most likely to occur when the learner incorrectly believes there are common features, improperly links the information while encoding it, or incorrectly sees some value in using information from one setting in another. For example, knowledge of the Revolutionary War may actually confuse the student about events in the Civil War. Knowledge of French may confuse him with regard to Spanish. Skill at tennis may cause a person to make mistakes at racquetball. Negative transfer is usually detrimental to learning.

Learning to bat with left hand when one has already mastered the art of batting with the right hand exemplifies negative transfer effect. This type of learning "may prove beneficial in case of older children and adults who already have achieved dexterity", says (Cratty (1968), but in the case of inexperienced learners this might lead to habit interference, so common in life routines. Switching over from already well-established synaptic connections to new connections not yet properly made and established, will elicit negative transfer effect. Habit interference in verbal activities also occurs at times. After the end of the year, one may continue for sometime to write "May" after June has already arrived. Previous experience usually involves mixture of useful and hindering responses.

A *misconception* is a particularly important type of negative transfer. A person with a misconception is likely to assimilate new information through faulty structures and consequently make inappropriate accommodations within those structures. A person is likely to store the information incorrectly in long-term memory or retrieve the improper information from long-term to working memory, and will consequently be likely to deal ineffectively with the information at hand.

Whether the transfer effect is negative or positive will greatly depend upon whether one's learning as a whole is aided or hindered by the previous learning. Once certain habits have been formed, it is too expensive in terms of energy cost, time and effort to do away with them or bring about modification in them.

Zero (Neutral) Transfer

Some psychologists believe in ***neutral (zero) transfer effect*** meaning that learning of an activity/skill neither helps nor hinders learning of another. Where acquiring a new skill or reaching the solution of a new problem is neither enhanced or hindered due to past experience or training, indicates that the elements in the two sets of S-R connections are neither compatible nor incompatible; they are simply different. For example, learning to perform badminton neither assists nor hinders learning swimming strokes.

TRADITIONAL THEORIES OF TRANSFER EFFECT

Educational theorists have sought answers to explain the process of learning and transfer for centuries. Along with educational psychologists, they recognize transfer of learning as perhaps the most significant issue in all fields of instruction, but yet it has not been subjected to too rigorous experimentation unlike other aspects of learning. Most traditional theories of transfer of learning have emerged from rational experience and limited experimentation.

Formal Discipline Theory

Also known as the *Theory of Mental Discipline,* the Formal Discipline Theory considered human mind as "a bundle of faculties" such as intelligence, memory, reasoning, imagination, judgment, observation, etc. These powers of the mind, though inter-dependent, are capable of working independently. The formal discipline view is based on a general observation that training in Latin and mathematics serves to strengthen some particular aspects of memory or other psychological functions. The connection has been used to justify the inclusion of material or course in the curriculum which, although they have no apparent practical value for some students, are said to be useful in "improving memory", "strengthening the scientific intellect" or "giving elasticity to mental functions" (Munn, Fernald & Fernald, 1972). The early theorists argued that the Universe and the human brain were similar both in structure and function. The heavenly bodies - stars, planets, galaxies, etc. - have independent existence but are bound to one another by forces of attraction; so are the mental faculties - independent but connected to one another by mind's connective processes.

Later research proved the futility of the faculty hypothesis because no compatibility was found between learning of Latin and geometry on the one hand and development of power of reasoning on the other. No academic subject, art or science, can have a prior claim in the training of certain faculties and putting hurdles in the way of other(s). Even, memory, once considered a 'separate faculty', is now classified as auditory memory, visual memory, motor memory, musical memory, and so on. Training of auditory memory does not necessarily lead to improvement of the visual memory or memory on the whole.

The Two Factor Theory

The Two Factor Theory, propounded by Charles Spearman, is virtually an extension of the formal discipline doctrine. Variety of experiments with human intelligence led Spearman to conclude that every human child is born with certain abilities. Some of these abilities are general, others specific. General abilities (or general intelligence) which Spearman labelled as "g" factor, operate in learning activities of general nature, and specific abilities (specific intelligence), called "s" factor, are involved in learning specific activities. Spearman argued that "g" factor is universally present, and "s" factor differs from activity to activity and also from individual to individual. The likelihood of transfer is greater among activities of general nature, and it is minimal or negligible when learning experience shifts from its general position to specific position and vice versa. For example, history, geography, literature, science etc., are replete with "g" factor, while music, painting, sculpture, swimming, etc., contain too much of "s" factor allowing little generalization of transfer-effect.

L.L. Thurstone partially accepted this assertion. However, he argued that there was no central core factor common to all performances but a large number of specific abilities, which were represented as S_1, S_2, S_3, and so on. Thurstone claimed that an individual's performance in a particular task largely depended upon cluster(s) of these factors closely related in the same way as members of a family or a society are. Further research in this area, did not uphold the validity of "g" and "s" factors except that the probability of transfer was estimated to be greater when components of two tasks, ideas or skills possessed greater similarity. Moreover, in due course it became clear that the transfer-effect depended on many other inherent and environmental factors than merely functioning of the powers of mind.

Identical Element Theory

After series of experiments, Thorndike and Woodworth concluded that "spread of practice occurs only where identical elements are concerned in the influencing and influenced functions" – meaning that transfer occurs more readily when the content or procedures (or techniques) in the two tasks or skills are similar. For example, transfer on the basis of the content occurs when an individual familiar with card games learns the rules of another game quickly because many of the rules of the new game could possibly be like those of the games already known. He knows that a queen takes a jack, that there are only four aces in the pack, and so on. In academic setting, there is transfer from mathematical skills to mechanical engineering skills because both subjects involve the same symbols and symbolic operations, and from one language to another if the symbols and grammatical corrections are alike in some respects. In sport, learning of badminton could facilitate learning of tennis, and learning of basketball help learning handball because of the identical nature of skills in two sports.

Thorndike considered this kind of transfer of experience as positive. For him, identical elements had a very broad meaning. "Elements" could refer to general characteristics such as the purpose of response or the attitude related to the performance or to specific characteristics such as particular components of the skill being performed. Thorndike considered identical elements to be mental processes that shared the same brain cell action as the physical action correlate. His identical element theory seems to have some substance because out of millions of specific reactions each with their specific connections in the nervous system, quite a few of them are likely to be common to several situations.

Extending the limits of the identical element theory, the transfer approach principle places greater stress upon cognitive elements such as understanding and problem-solving rather than on characteristics of the learning situations. In some experiments the puzzle-solving in adults revealed that when subjects were taught the principle involved in one problem, they solved without error the other puzzles, involving the same principle. Those who did not learn basic principles failed to show much transfer. In geometry, for instance, those who have mastered solution of theorems could take on the related exercises without much difficulty.

It needs to be understood that transfer of principles involves understanding of how something works. Transfer through identical elements focuses upon the specific responses to make it do so. An automobile mechanic is able to repair machine engine because he understands the principles of combustion. Similarly, a person who can start his car, perhaps, is able to start a power boat also through transfer of identical element, without necessarily understanding the principles involved. An important thing to note in this approach is the fact that principles derived by the learner through the discovery process may be transferred more easily than principles learned as a result of guidance provided by the teacher. In such a kind of situation the motivating effect of discovery may lead the learner to raise his aspiration level, remember longer and show more success in solving related problems.

CONTEMPORARY APPROACHES TO TRANSFER

Researchers have worked to develop a general theory of transfer of learning - a theory that could help students get better at transfer. This has proven to be a difficult research challenge.

Near and Far Transfer

At one time, it was common to talk about transfer of learning in terms of near and far transfer. This "near and far" theory of transfer suggested that some problems and tasks are so nearly alike that transfer of learning occurs easily and naturally. A particular problem or task is studied and practiced to a high level of automaticity. When a nearly similar problem or task is encountered, it is automatically solved with little or no conscious thought.

Near Transfer

Near transfer of skills and knowledge are applied the same way every time the skills and knowledge are used. Near transfer training usually involves tasks that are procedural. Instructional designers need to design instruction that teaches the steps of a task which are always applied in the same order. Many examples can illustrate near transfer learning. A person who knows how to drive a car can transfer these existing skills to learn how to drive a bus (Clark, 1999). Similarly, a person who knows Hindi grammar can learn Sanskrit grammar with ease and a player who knows how to bat or catch in cricket, can transfer these skills to learn batting/catching in baseball.

The advantages of this type of training are that the skills and knowledge are easier to train and transfer of learning is usually a success. The disadvantage is that if the circumstances change, the learner is unlikely to be able to adapt their skills and knowledge to that change.

Far Transfer

Many potential transfer of learning situations do not lend themselves to the automaticity approach. There are many problems that are somewhat related, but that in some sense are relatively far removed from each other. A person attempting to make the transfer of learning between two distant problems or skills - for example, learning to type and play piano or learning play on the trombone and saxophone - does not automatically "see" or sense the connections between the two problems. Far transfer often requires careful analysis and deep thinking.

Far transfer tasks involve skills and knowledge being applied in situations that change. With far transfer tasks, instructional designers need to design instruction where learners are trained to adapt guidelines to changing situations or environments. One of the benefits of far transfer is that once the skills and knowledge are acquired, the learner is able to make judgements and adapt to different situations. The disadvantage of far transfer is that far transfer skills and knowledge are more difficult to instruct and transfer of learning is therefore less likely (Clark, 1999). A person who learned the principles of wind flow to design a windmill can transfer that knowledge to direct the sail on a sailboat

The theory of near and far transfer does not help us much in our teaching. We know that near and far transfer occurs. We know that some students readily accomplish far transfer tasks, while others do not. We know that far transfer does not readily occur for most students. The difficulty with this theory of near and far transfer is that it does not provide a foundation or a plan for helping a person to get better at far transfer and dealing with novel and complex problems. It does not tell us how to teach to increase far transfer.

Low-Road/High-Road Theory

Recently, Salomon & Perkins (1989) and Perkins & Salomon (1987) synthesized findings concerned with transfer by recognizing two distinct but related mechanisms, the "low road" and the "high road." Low road transfer happens when stimulus conditions in the transfer context are sufficiently similar to those in a prior context of learning to trigger well-developed semi-automatic responses, which need not be mediated by external or mental representations. A relatively reflexive process, low road transfer figures most often in near transfer, and refers to developing some knowledge/skill to a high level of automaticity. It usually requires a great deal of practice in varying settings. Shoe tying, keyboarding, steering a car, dribbling in soccer or basketball, and single-digit arithmetic facts are examples of areas in which such automaticity can be achieved and is quite useful. The practice of sports skills has to be to the level of automaticity.

High-road transfer involves cognitive understanding, purposeful and conscious analysis, mindfulness, and application of strategies that cut across disciplines. In high-road transfer, there is deliberate mindful abstraction of an idea that can transfer, and then conscious and deliberate application of the idea when faced by a problem where the idea may be useful. There is search for connections: What is the general pattern? What is needed? What principles might apply? What is known that might help? Such transfer is not in general reflexive. It demands time for exploration and the investment of mental effort. It can easily accomplish far transfer, bridging between contexts as remote as arteries and electrical networks or strategies of chess play and politics. For instance, a person new to politics but familiar with chess might carry over the chess principle of control of the centre, pondering what it would mean to control the political centre.

Transfer-effect in Physical Activity and Sport

The gigantic universe of sports and physical activities stands on the foundations of skills, at the baseline of which lie a large variety of motor and psychomotor skills which develop in human beings as a natural survival mechanism through infancy and childhood. Most motor skills develop without any organized effort on the part of the young child, his parents and others. However, sport or athletic skills, which draw their basic substance from simple motor skills of walking, running, jumping, throwing, catching, hitting, striking, etc., have to be acquired by "activity hungry" children both by an organized and/or unorganized effort at school and in the neighbourhood. While organized learning at school or a club facilitates a lot in grooming youngsters into great performers later in life, unorganized learning, which is more a matter of observational procedure, may not guarantee a brilliant sport career ahead for it is generally not backed up by scientific principles and procedures of learning. However, the principle of transfer plays an important role in all kinds of learning irrespective of its being organized, disorganized or unorganized.

In activity context, Magill (1990) defines transfer of learning *as the influence of having previously practiced skill or skills on the learning of a new skill or on performing the skill in a new context.* He believes that the principle of transfer of learning serves as the basis for educational curriculum development and instructional methodology. Ideally, the school curriculum, for example, in mathematics, numeral writing, numeral value identification, addition, subtraction, multiplication, and division must be presented in this specific sequence because each is based on the preceding concept. Algebra is not taught before basic arithmetic. Similarly trigonometry is not taught before geometry. In the same way, the teaching physical activity skills should be accomplished in consideration of the principle of transfer of learning to foundational movements in order to facilitate optimal learning effects. It is not difficult to understand why baseball would be taught before students have had ample experience in learning to throw, catch, and bat. The sequence of skills needs to be designed to take advantage of the transfer of learning principle. Basic or foundational skills should be learned before more complex skills that require mastery over certain basic skills or concepts, are introduced. The emphasis here is on a logical progression of skill experience where the decision of when to introduce a given skill should be made in terms of how it provides basis for transfer to succeeding skills.

From instructional view-point, when the instructor teaches students basic swimming strokes using dry land drills before allowing them practice strokes in water, he is assuming that there will be positive transfer-effect from land to water situation – the two situations being similar in some respects and, of course, dissimilar in others. The assumption here is that students will learn the swimming strokes quickly and more efficiently because of their dry-land drill experience. The transfer principle is invaluable when the skill to be learnt has strong element of danger in it such as gymnastics or diving. In activities like these, body harnesses are used in practicing certain skills to help the learner develop confidence in his ability to perform without fear of injury hindering learning process. The use of pitching machine to teach hitting in baseball or tennis and batting in cricket, and rebounding basketballs from a rebounder, is based on the assumption that practice with the machines will positively transfer to the "real" situations.

Learning a new skill can be speeded up, hindered or changed by previous instruction or it may not be affected at all. Often in preliminary learning stages, old skill will cause temporary interference but still enable the athlete to acquire new skill in a shorter time span than would otherwise be possible. Transfer is more likely to occur from relatively difficult skill to relatively easy skills and not vice versa. Transfer can occur by learning how to learn.

Sportsperson's tendency to revert to the old patterns of behaviour (skill performance) when the new situations seem to be more challenging, is common. This reversion is negative transfer. A section of motor learning psychologists does not subscribe to the view that there are negative transfer effects in motor learning. It is argued that what are typically observed as negative transfer effects are essentially cognitive rather than motor. The influence is not on the actual control parameters directing the movement. This view may be substantially correct yet negative transfer effects cannot be altogether discounted from the learning process. The most plausible explanation for the negative transfer effect phenomenon is that the negative transfer effects occur when a new response is required for an old stimulus. Two response conditions seem to be especially susceptible to negative transfer effects. They involve the *change in spatial locations of a response* to the same stimulus and the *change in timing characteristics* of the response to the same stimulus. It is contended that negative effects can be caused by condition created by equipment placement sequence or presentation of movement-sequence on repeated trials. Research has also revealed that negative transfer effects are typically temporary.

Physical educators and coaches ought to evolve such strategies and organize learning situations as facilitate greater positive transfer effect and minimize negative-effect. Citing experimental evidence, Cratty (1968) says:

> ..... a simple movement with a badminton racket such as hitting bird against a wall, will impede the learning of an apparently similar skill hitting tennis ball against the wall. In both skills, similar stimulus conditions are present – a racket, an object to be hit and a wall. However, responses required are different. In badminton, wrist action is primary requisite while relatively stiff wrist is desirable when wielding a tennis racket. The principle is also violated when attempting to improve the catching skill of a young child through the use of a bean bag than a ball, for the former literally 'sticks' when it comes in contact with hand.

Claiming that the myth of training transfer and generalization is strong and confused, Brent Rushall, believes that "there are three general forms of training adaptations that occur. They cause different benefits, or lack of benefits, for athletes who are exposed to "*modern*" coaching programs." The transfer of training effects at the physiological, neural, and symbolic levels differ. The greater the similarity of stimulation experienced at practice is to competitive settings, the greater will be the transfer of benefits derived from training and practice. This is a fundamental principle that is supported by the *Principle of Training Specificity* and cannot be ignored when exercising serious athletes. It can be ignored in untrained individuals but only up to a certain level of physical function and fitness. The importance of using competitive situations as training extensions, rather than always very important competitions cannot be overlooked. However, there are many sporting competitions that are all of equal importance. In those situations, performance improvements across the period of competitions should rarely be expected. At the same time performance inconsistencies should expected because of the lack of correlation between training/ practice demands and the requirements of competitive tasks.

Value of Transfer in Work and Sport

Transfer of learning is important in life especially in work environments and in programmes to educate people for those work environments. Whether it is welding, preparing for a courtroom presentation or calibrating an electronic device, it is important that students transfer their learning into the real world of things. We know that most students do not transfer classroom learning readily to the real world. Special effort must be made when designing assignments and learning environments, if students are to transfer their learning to the work world in a meaningful way. By becoming more aware of activities and contexts that create meaningful learning, instructional designers are better able to build programmes that prepare workers for the real world environment.

Robb (1972) states: "....the ability to apply previous learning from one situation to second situation is called transfer of learning. If there was no transfer of learning, man would be extremely hindered in acquiring knowledge and skills". The punching skill learnt in a boxing class at school may assist a student in tackling toughs in the neighbourhood or in the railway train. Here the student is transferring his learning experience in a physical education class to real life situations that resemble in some way. Seemingly the two situations are different, but the elements that call for transfer-effect among them are just alike. Bucher (1972) says: "The more meaningful an experience, the more likelihood of transfer. The more life-like the problems and activities, the greater possibility of transfer to life situations," is the rule.

The information-processing theorists generally agree that only meaningful experiences are stored in the memory and are retrieved quickly as the situations demand; others recede into the background. The chances of transfer are greater when experiences are similar and also meaningful. Cratty (1988) believes that "a verbal description of a skill prior to practice, is an attempt to elicit transfer. As a coach works on the fundamentals, he is attempting to promote the transfer of simple components to the performance of the complex whole. The young adult often attempts to transfer his past experience to the 'solution' of problems currently confronting him". In motor skill-acquisition, children greatly benefit from their previous experiences because no single skill is completely new; it is invariably a complex combination of several simple acts, actions, and skills in various degrees, which young learners have already mastered to some extent.

Promoting Positive Transfer

An important goal of all education including physical activity and sport should be to minimize inert knowledge by promoting positive transfer. The following are effective ways to promote positive transfer:

1. Teach subject matter in *meaningful* rather than rote contexts. This is a necessary but not a sufficient step in promoting positive transfer. It needs to be remembered that information that is not meaningful will not be associated with other information and will be forgotten quickly. All meaningful skills in a particular activity or sport have far grater chances of transfer to other sports and activities; for instance gripping the racquet in tennis, badminton, and squash; or holding waist/wrist in wrestling and kabaddi.
2. Employ *informed instruction*. That is, students should learn not only to describe a concept or strategy, but also to understand *when* and *why* the concept or strategy is useful. Delivering informed instruction by using scaffolding strategies will often be useful. Receiving theoretical instruction in biomechanics is not enough, the learner must also know what soccer or swimming skills can be improved by following biomechanical concepts, and how.
3. Teach subject matter in contexts as similar as possible to those in which it will be employed. To the extent that information is learned in settings similar to those in which it will be applied, learners can use clues from the learning situation to trigger the use of appropriate skills and information when they are later needed.
4. Provide opportunities to *practice* employing the subject matter in settings that represent the full range of eventual

applications. If all the practice takes place in a single, narrowly defined setting, then it should not be surprising that the learner will fail to apply it in settings that seem to be different. It is important to provide opportunities to practice in settings that represent an accurate sample of the full range of realistic applications that the learner is likely to encounter.

5. Provide opportunities for *distributed practice* after the information has been initially learned. Once information or skill has been initially learned, the additional opportunities for practice in a variety of realistic settings described in the preceding guideline should be spread out over a lengthy period of time, rather than combined into a single study or practice session.
6. Promote positive attitudes toward subject matter or skills so that students will feel inclined to deal with rather than avoid topics/skills when they are encountered elsewhere. When people need an idea to deal with a new problem or a novel situation, they are more likely to draw upon learning about which they have positive feelings than learning that evokes hostility or resentment. The development of proper attitude toward learning theoretical concepts of physical education and skills of various sports and physical activities is very helpful in facilitating positive transfer effect.

SELECTED REFERENCES

Bucher, Charles A. *Foundations of Physical Education*, St. Louis; Mosby, 1972

Cratty, Bryant J.*Psychology and Physical Activity*, Englewood Cliffs; NJ, Prentice Hall, 1968

Gagne, Robert M. *Essentials of Learning for Instruction*, New York: Holt, Rinehart and Winston, 1975

Gagne, Robert & Driscoll, Marcy Perkins *Essentials of Learning for Instruction*, NJ: Prentice-Hall Inc., 1988

Magill, Richard A. *Motor Learning: Concepts and Applications*. Madison, Wisconsin; WCB Brown & Benchmark, 1990

Munn, Norman L., Fernald, L. Lodge, & Fernald Peter S. *Introduction to Psychology*. (Third Edition). New Delhi; Ford and IBM Publishing Co., 1972

Perkins, David N. and Salomon, Gavriel *Transfer of Learning*: Contribution to the International Encyclopaedia of Education, Second Edition Oxford, England: Pergamon Press. [Online], 1992

Robb, Margaret, D. *The Dynamics of Motor Skill Acquisition*, Englewood Cliffs. New Jersey; Prentice Hall Inc., 1992

Saljio quoted by Paul Ramsden [Ramsden, P. (1992) *Learning to Teaching in Higher Education*, London; Routledge], 1979

Salomon, G. & Perkins, D. Teaching for transfer. *Educational Leadership*, 22-32, 1988

White, Richard T. Implications of Recent Research on Learning for Curriculum and Assessment, *Journal of Curriculum Studies*; Vol. 24, no 2, 153–164, 1992

Motivation is the art of getting people to do what you want them to do because they want to do it.
- Dwight D Eisenhower

CHAPTER - 11

MOTIVATION

The word motivation most likely comes from the word "motive," which stems from either the French *motiver* or the German *motivieren* or the Latin *movere* - all meaning "to move". It is viewed as an intervening variable that causes behaviour. Unlike physical variables, psychological variables like motivation are not seen nor touched but inferred from observable behaviour. An office clerk working overtime to earn his next promotion, a student burning midnight oil to get a good grade in the examination, and an athlete training hard to make it to the Olympic squad are all said to be motivated. In this sense, motivation is an internal condition (sometime described as need, desire or want) that serves to activate behaviour, energize it and give it a direction. The term is generally used for human motivation but, theoretically, it can be used to describe the causes for animal behaviour as well. Truly motivation is a process of 'inspiring, goading or coaxing' the organism to move in some direction. To motivate is to induce movement; so motivation is *"any condition that might energize and direct our actions"*, argue Crooks & Stein (1999). In nutshell, motivation refers to 'factors within a human being or animal that arouse and direct goal-oriented behaviour'. It is a complex process that influences individuals to begin, pursue, and persist in an activity.

Definition of Motivation

In psychology, motivation refers to *the initiation, direction, intensity, and persistence of behaviour.* It is a temporal and dynamic state that should not be confused with personality or emotion. It involves having the desire and willingness to do something. A motivated person can be reaching for a long-term goal such as becoming a professional athlete, a musician or a writer, or a more short-term goal like learning how to spell a particular word or play flute for fun. *Motivation* can be anything that arouses an organism toward action for a desired goal. It can be the reason for an action that directs some one to achieve some pre-determined goal. Essentially, motivation can be defined *as a general desire or willingness of an individual to do something or some action. The sources of this desire or willingness are said to be conscious or unconscious stimuli that may result from a range of psychological or social factors* (Oxford English Dictionary, 2000).

As a broad-based term, motivation encompasses several aspects of behaviour - individual, collective, internal and environmental. It can be designated as a tendency for the direction and selectivity of behaviour to be controlled by the conditions to the consequences, and the tendency of people's behaviour to persist at some task or job until some preset objective is achieved. At work, studies, in sport or else where people respond to external or internal stimulations, adapt to the changing conditions and struggle hard to achieve high standards of efficiency only when they are "adequately motivated, no matter whether the drive to move" is due to internal "push" (inspiration) or external "pull" (a desire to win awards or rewards).

To give evidence of the complex nature of motivation, human action is spurred by physiological drives or genetic instincts, habits, psychological needs, emotional information, social pressures, pain or pain avoidance, fear or anxiety, desire for possessions or other rewards, goal pursuit, and a variety of other factors. The unique interaction of these forces at a given point in time causes us to choose certain activities over others, engage in some activities with greater zeal, cease engagement in an activity at times or altogether, or persist in some behaviours even in difficult times. Primarily human motivations are biological, both psychological and social motivations develop later as individual-environment interaction advances in time and space. Munn, Fernald & Fernald (1972) explain this phenomenon thus:

> Initially our motivation is like that of other organisms and it has the same physio-chemical foundations. We share with them such physiological needs as hunger, thirst and sex. We are aroused much as they are when such needs arise and are not satisfied; like them we are driven to activity. There is, however, an important expression of such needs. Animals satisfy them more directly. When hungry, they seek food, where they have learned to find it. When excretory needs arise, they satisfy them immediately. When animals are frustrated by others, they fight, sometime killing their opponents. Men, on the other hand, satisfy their needs indirectly and in ways decreed only in part by nature and the immediate

> situation .... much of human motivation even though it stems from the so-called "animal needs" is influenced by customs, traditions or man-made laws.

Motivation reinforces behaviour. A motivated person is expected to do better at a task, achieve greater success and show improved performance at every stage. Human beings inherit the basic needs and drives but many associative activities are learned. For example, hunger for food is natural and unlearnt but tastes and preferences are acquired in a particular environment or setting. Biological needs and drives are no doubt foundational to motivation but cognitive conditions such as a desire to achieve or an ardent urge to be with friends and peers too have an important place in human motivations.

As the "cause of behaviour", say Buskist & Gerbing (1990) 'motivation is concerned with three major objectives: (1) the initiation and orientation of a behaviour toward a specific goal; (2) the intensity or strength of a behaviour; and (3) the cessation of a behaviour.

ROOTS OF MOTIVATION - MOTIVE, DRIVE AND NEED

Since motivation underlines the reason(s) for engaging in a particular behaviour, these reasons may include a drive, a need, a desire to achieve a goal, a state of being, or an ideal. In human beings, motivation involves both conscious and subconscious drives. We all have one ultimate motive in common – *to be happy*. This motive is the driving force behind everything we think, feel, and do from the time we wake in the morning until we go to sleep at night. In this context, it would not be inept to ultimately define motivation as simply *our desires, efforts, and attempts to be as happy as possible*. The term happiness does not necessarily refer to a feeling or emotion. Feelings come and go; so it is neither realistic nor desirable either to hope to remain exclusively in one emotional state. Understanding human motivation is impossible without understanding the psychological concepts of motive, drive and need.

Motive

A motive is a *reason* for doing something. Alderman (1974) defines motive as "a latent relatively stable personality characteristic which causes a person to be either attracted to or repulsed by the consequences of particular courses of action; it is tendency within the person directing his thoughts, feelings and actions towards the service of goals or function". Why living beings behave the way they do, is a question of motive(s). That way, motives are purposes or intentions directing the initiation and dynamics of behaviour. Biologically, the behaviour of all organisms is a motivated behaviour because it serves some inherent purpose. If behaviour is likened to a horse, motive is its rider. The rider makes the horse move, canter, trot or gallop as situation dictates. In other words, motive initiates and energizes organism's effort and directs it towards a predetermined goal.

While motivation is "a general level of arousal of action", motives are specific conditions, attached to particular courses of action and their consequences, resulting from that arousal state. Psychologists consider motives, more or less, stable innate tendencies of behaviour that direct energies of the organism either towards accomplishing a task or simply avoiding a situation in order to seek some kind of fulfilment. Motives are psychological abstractions; they are a high road to goals(s).

A motive has two aspects: the inner (the subjective), and the outer (the objective). The inner aspect is *visible tension* caused by the non-fulfilment of needs – especially the immediate physiological needs like hunger, thirst, urination, evacuation, etc. Apart from this, frustrations, anxieties, worries, failures etc., pervading the social environment also cause tension. The outer aspect of motive is *the goal* which the animal seeks. Tension eases or decreases when the goal is achieved. A motive is induced by a need, so needs serve as the springboard of motives. Needs being the prime initiators of motives create drive in the organism, and heighten the tone, tenor and tempo of action – a general response to stimulation. By and large, motives:

- mobilize organism's energy, and intensify drive for action;
- direct the resultant behaviour towards achievement of a predetermined goal; and
- determine such responses as would help organism maintain or regain homeostasis (internal equilibrium).

Depending upon the situation, motive to behave in a certain way is already there in the individual's mind or it may arise at the spur of the moment. For example, in normal situation, no one will dip his hand in water to escape pain but a sudden contact with the hot stove may unconsciously force a kitchen maid to do so. Intention to escape from pain, reinforced by the burning sensation, is the real motive (cause) behind this situation. A motive practically is the same as "set" in learning process because it "predisposes the individual for certain activities and for seeking certain goals." Motives arise and function in relation to the situation, and the process follows the selectivity or priority principle - first things to happen first.

Needs, drives and motives are classified as primary and secondary. ***Primary Motives*** are inborn and unlearnt. They are directly related to the organism's survival and biological activities. ***Secondary Motives*** are learnt, and dependent on external 'reinforcement'. They arise in man's socio-cultural environment and are concerned with nurturance. Apart from this, a motive may be partially instinctive and partially acquired because human experience adds or subtracts something even from the well-established behavioural processes and patterns as a person interacts with new situations. For example, hunger involves primary motive of food-seeking but what and how to seek food is learned. When hungry, the child instinctively cries, loudly expressing its food motive; when instantly fed, the child is satisfied, but if not, the food-seeking drive intensifies (the cry gets louder and still louder) with corresponding activities like screaming, kicking up arms and legs, turning, twisting, rolling on the floor, etc., start becoming increasingly violent. Similarly in the conditioning of a dog (Pavlov's experiments), the successful movements of the animal are reinforced by finding food. This way the dog learns how to act when motivated by hunger. The infant grabs the nipple or pushes it aside when sensations and perceptions arouse positive or negative responses depending upon the motive(s) aroused by pleasant or unpleasant feelings accompanying internal and/or external conditions. This ***Principle of Hedonism*** maintains that people maximize their gains and minimize losses depending upon what the situation offers by way of satisfaction or dissatisfaction. Underscoring the psychological significance of hedonism in life and sport, Alderman (1974) says:

> ....a person chooses those causes of action which are pleasurable to him. It is a principle fundamental to physical activity and sport especially today when people are doing what they want to do rather than what they are supposed to do. People are choosing those activities that are attractive to them in some manner and are disregarding those that are unattractive.

Freud considered 'libidinal' satisfaction and self-preservation as the central activity motives of all living beings. For him, instincts were a 'psychological representation of inner physiological stimulation' which energized and caused the organisms to interact with the external forces for achievement of certain goals. Instincts, therefore, are primary motivating force behind all life processes.

Siding with Freud, William McDougall argued that human behaviour was motivated by several types of motives such as organic motives, emergency motives, subjective motives, etc. ***Organic Motives*** include hunger, thirst, sex, respiratory, regulatory and eliminatory needs etc., which are controlled by the internal body states and stimulations. With age, human beings learn to modify or partially control these motives either by choice (training, education, discipline, suppression, etc.) or out of compulsion (necessity); this, in other words, is an automatic repression or suppression of natural urges. Organic motives aim to preserve life. ***Emergency Motives*** arise from external stimulations (situations in the environment). A sudden change in the situation (temperature, circumstance, air pressure, bright sun, darkness, rain or gale) forces the organism to quickly change stance, posture, on-going motion or activity, and make some adjustment. Emergency motives arise suddenly and call for an instantaneous grapple with the situation, which could endanger life. ***Objective Motives*** deal with man's active relationship with his environment and his efforts to gain mastery over it. They are further classified into exploratory motives and manipulative motives. ***Exploratory Motives*** have links with the acquisition of knowledge about environment. They involve perceptual and cognitive processes. Man by nature is curious about things, objectives, events, and people. He wants to know how things work and what deeper meaning they have. When children engage in exploration, they assimilate facts from the environment. ***Manipulative Motives*** involve manipulation of objects such as machines, toys, household objects, things around, etc. Through this process does a child become aware about their working and the manner he can use them for other purposes than they are intended for. When manipulation is at its best, development of relationship between man and his environment is at peak too. Both exploratory and manipulative motives enhance the child's quality of interaction with and knowledge about environment.

Need

A need is a necessity or want. It is a link between the motive and drive (action). In psychology, need is some sort of *vacuum* which must be filled by some activity. For Murray (1943) need was *a construct which stands for force in the brain region, a force which organizes perception, apperception, intellection, conation and action in such a way as to transform in a certain direction, an unsatisfactory situation.* Need is occasionally provoked directly by internal process of a certain kind... but more frequently, when one is in a state of readiness, by the occurrence of one or a few commonly effective (environmental) processes. In current literature, needs are now viewed as dispositions toward action (i.e., they create a condition that is predisposed towards taking action or making a change and moving in a certain direction).

Life is a chain-link of needs and they always keep us busy in a struggle for their fulfilment. Needs stem either from internal stimulations or external events. There is a need for oxygen, water, food, sex, etc., in order for us to survive and maintain life continuity; there is a need to work and earn livelihood; there is a need to belong to a family or a group and be recognized as some one important; there is a need to have conjugal relationship and have children, and so on. If there were *no* needs, life would be worth nothing with little struggle to sustain it. Man's behaviour, to a great extent, can be explained on the basis of the needs as their genesis lies in psycho-physiological activity of the organism. "Most needs", says Alderman (1974) "are accompanied by emotions and feelings and are associated with instrumental or goal-directed behaviour designed to produce the particular goal and reduce the need." An undue delay or non-fulfilment of needs leads to an upheaval-like situation, making the organism struggle for maintaining homeostasis (internal equilibrium). The effort is directed towards either fulfilling the need(s) or suppressing them as the circumstances dictates. Once a need has arisen, it seeks fulfilment either way.

The needs exist in an endless variety. They are generally categorized into basic needs and secondary needs. ***Basic needs*** are biological, ***secondary needs*** psychological or social. However, under all need conditions, the utmost effort of the organism is to seek adjustment whatever way possible. While primary needs of hunger, thirst, sex, love, etc., are universal and innate; secondary needs like need for achievement, attention, adjustment, recognition, etc., differ with individuals. Hall & Lindsey (1970) have listed twenty important needs of life: abasement, achievement, affection, aggression, autonomy, counteraction, dependence, dominance, defence, exhibition, harm-avoidance, nurturance, order, play, rejection, sentience, sex, succourrence, and understanding. The strength of each of these needs, and the capacity to achieve them differs from person to person and in the same person at different occasions. External conditions, state of individual's body and mind, mental capacity, inclination and interest go to determine what needs would require how much attention and when.

Drive

In psychology, *drive is an urgent need pressing for satisfaction, usually rocted in some physiological deficiency or imbalance (e.g., hunger and thirst) and impelling the organism to action* (Encyclopaedia Britannica, Ready Reference, 2009). Psychologists distinguish between drives that are innate and directly related to basic physiological needs (e.g., food, air, and water) and drives that are learned (e.g., drug addiction, sport excellence). Among the other drives psychologists have identified are achievement, affection, affiliation, exploration, manipulation, maternity, pain avoidance, sex, and sleep. "The basic motives revealed in animal behaviour usually called drives" (Woodworth, 1958) are manifest in physical and physiological movements. On the face of it, a drive is an impetus to action, "a thrust forward", or a force impelling the organism to move towards a predetermined goal. According to Alderman (1974): "Drive.... is seen as a psychological mechanism directed towards consumatory reactions, that is, reactions which bring immediate and direct value or satisfaction to the individual such as eating, drinking or scoring a goal." In simple words, a drive is a *propelling agent* - a vehicle of action, which originates either in the internal stimulation (life force from within the organism) or stresses existing outside the body (external situations). The hungry seeks food, the thirsty water, and a lonely person in a forest seeks protection against wild danger. Driven by the force of some need at the back, all the three engage in an activity that hopefully will fulfil their objectives. A drive, then, is essentially *an energizer of action*. The more acute the need, the more intense the drive to seek the objective; the more intense the drive, the stronger the effort and more persistent the activity towards the goal, is a psychological truism. The drive reinforces action-potential of the organism in a particular situation especially where danger to the organism is real and substantial.

Like motives and needs, drives are also classified as primary drives and secondary drives. *Primary Drives* are biological in orientation. They are innate and arise when instinctive tendencies such as hunger, thirst, sex, love, etc., are in operation. These drives aim to protect the organism and facilitate its survival. *Secondary Drives* are artificially created as noticed in Pavlovian conditioning processes. With repetitious occurrence of certain stimulus-response connections (behavioural patterns) secondary needs are produced and reinforced consciously or unconsciously so that there are corresponding drives "goading" the organism to move towards pre-set goals. These drives are not inherited but appear when secondary needs are at work. It is now well-established that secondary drives play an equally important role in human life as they mobilize people's action towards achieving excellence in chosen field of their knowledge – study, business, management or sport. While under-driving is least achievement-oriented, over-driving often causes avoidable stresses, strains and tensions that afflict people who are crazy in the pursuit of excellence. High achievers are known for their intense drive for action and accomplishment.

TYPES OF MOTIVATION

For motivation is *the communication to an internal force* that serves to put into motion a behaviour, thought process, action or reaction, it can come from any source, direction, event or individual. Since birth, we all have been involved in many types of motivation whether or not we were aware of it. Motivation is a hard fact of life and it will continue to affect us in some form or the other throughout our lifetime. Based upon several theoretical frameworks, motivation can take any form – primary, secondary, positive, negative, intrinsic or extrinsic. Different types of motivations can be more beneficial than others in various situations.

Primary Motivation

Biologically oriented primary motivation is the very basic function of self-preservation. The need to eat, drink, be warm, avoid pain and even participate in sex is driven by primary motivation. It is impossible to say how one would behave when placed in an extreme situation involving one of these fundamental needs. Many crimes have been reportedly carried out by those who feel "driven" to steal food or to kill another human being to stop inhumane treatment. Primary motivation is one of the types of motivation that we are all inclined to exercise under the right conditions, although few of us know how we would react in various situations because our actions and thoughts at a given point or period of time are guided by the circumstances then prevailing and motives working in the background. Primary motivation is instinctive and unlearnt; it carries a strong force of seething emotional energy inside us.

Secondary Motivation

Secondary motivation is considered to be a learned motivation, and is different for each person. These types of motivation are what propel us through life; a conscious desire for doing or accomplishing something specific, whether a goal or a result that makes us act in such a manner that achievement of it remains our sole focus of attention. Learning and perfecting a new skill can be a great example of this. For example, becoming proficient in French or Spanish brings in some psychological reward – an honour or prestige. The same could be said about participating in a sport like cricket, tennis or golf. Career-conscious students, who attach more importance to academic grade, naturally study very hard; and those who value sport for the incentives it provides, practice and perfect sport skills more than they practice academic skills. Parents, teachers, peers and significant others have a significant role to play in secondary motivations.

Intrinsic Motivation

Intrinsic motivation comes from within; it is fully self-determined and characterized by interest in, and enjoyment derived from, sports participation. It emanates from rewards inherent to a task or activity itself - the enjoyment of a puzzle or the love of playing. This form of motivation is usually associated with high achievement and enjoyment in a person's chosen field of activity – education, business, sport, acting, music, fine arts, etc. Intrinsic Motivation is geared toward internal rewards and reinforcers such as achievement, responsibility and competence. There are three types of intrinsic motivation viz. intrinsic motivation to know, intrinsic motivation to accomplish and intrinsic motivation to experience stimulation. We can celebrate our success when we do well at examination or sport and we can beat ourselves up when we don't. Some examples of internal rewards are enjoyment, achievement, a sense of competence. People are said to be intrinsically motivated if they:

- attribute the results of their activities/endeavours to internal factors that they can control (e.g. the amount of effort or practice they put in),
- believe they can be effective agents in reaching desired goals (i.e. the results are not determined by luck),
- are interested in mastering a topic, skill, or activity rather than just engage in rote-learning to achieve creditable success.

Intrinsically motivated individuals perform for their own achievement and satisfaction. If they come to believe that they are doing some job because of the pay or the working conditions or some other extrinsic reason, they begin to lose motivation. Intrinsic motivation is considered to be the healthiest type of motivation and reflects an athlete's motivation to perform an activity simply for the reward inherent in their participation. As per Hungarian psychologist Csikszentmihalyi (1975, 1990), 'the highest level of intrinsic motivation is flow state, which is characterized by complete immersion in an activity, to the degree that nothing else matters, and there is a perfect match between the perceived demands of an activity and an athlete's perceived ability or skills. During flow, self-consciousness is lost and athletes become one with the activity.'

Extrinsic motivation

Motivation that comes from outside of the performer is extrinsic motivation. It is geared toward external rewards and reinforcers. Some examples of external rewards are money, pay, promotion, praise, awards, rewards, feedback, working conditions, disciplinary action, boundary-setting, etc., - things that come from one's environment, and controlled by others. Money is the most obvious example of external motivation, but coercion and threat of punishment are also common extrinsic motivations. While running a 100m sprint at the world athletic meet, the crowd may cheer on a favourite performer, which may motivate him or her to win the race. Trophies, cups and medals are also extrinsic incentives. Competition is in general extrinsic because it encourages the performer to win and beat others, not to enjoy the intrinsic rewards of the activity. Too much importance to external means of motivation is likely to bring down intrinsic motivation. Extrinsic Motivation is said to be less effective because it comes from outside the person. External reinforcers, for instance, are usually in the form of control.

Addiction Motivation

When it is something we really like and happen to have or do it for long time we get attached to it terribly and feel driven to do it. In more direct language, we get addicted to it, whatever "it" is – a particular wine, woman, wealth, food, drink or even muscle building exercise. In other words, motivation does not always lead in a positive direction. The procedure has its genesis in habit formation. A habit, say the psychologists, is a "bad" habit how so good it might be.

An addiction is an unhealthy "love-and-trust" relationship with an object or an activity. Love and trust are very strong intrinsic rewards that are tied into our neural networks for survival. Survival needs, such as the need to eat, is an internal reinforcer because it causes pain in the form of hunger when we do not eat. We get an internal reward when we enjoy what we are eating.

The same is true when we resist something we are addicted to. The pain is in the form of cravings or withdrawal symptoms and the reward is in the feeling we get when we engage. However, in the late stages of addiction we no longer get the reward but the reinforcer gets stronger.

Subconscious Motivation

Addiction is an example of subconscious motivation...we may not know "why we do it" or "how that could happen" when we find ourselves in trouble again. This is because it would be too uncomfortable for us to know that we are dependent on an object or activity so our faithful servant - the subconscious mind - "protects us" from that reality with a system of defense mechanisms we refer to as *denial.*

Other subconscious types of motivations might include various neural networks created early in life which are now part of *Implicit Memory:* for example,

- An accident-prone person may have a subconscious desire to hurt or punish himself for guilt over some long-past misdeed or mistake.

- A person who uses food for comfort may have a subconscious "part" of themselves...a neural network...that learned early in life to substitute food for the nurturing that was not available.
- Someone who pushes others away may have a part of themselves that sabotages opportunities for intimacy in order to protect from abandonment.

It has long been known that the subconscious mind uses defense mechanisms to ward off pain and anxiety. These defensive strategies are learned programmes that run automatically from neural networks that we intuitively refer to as "parts". On many occasions, all of us have faced the "to be this (or have this) or to be that (or to have that)" situation, explaining that "one part of me wants to do X... but another part of me holds me back". These "parts" are programmes installed on conflicting neural networks. There are various forms of therapy for "integrating" these parts to resolve subconscious conflicts.

"Toward" or "Away From" Orientation Motivation

Most of us know about the "Carrot-or-Stick" types of motivation. Our common sense suggests that some people are motivated more by the stick and others by the carrot. "Stick People" respond better to external and internal *reinforcers* while "Carrot People" respond better to external and internal *rewards*. Another way saying this is the "Toward or Away From" orientation. Stick people are oriented to move *away from* pain. Carrot people move *toward* pleasure.

There are times when each orientation is necessary. For example, if your goal is to manage your weight it is more effective to adopt a "toward pleasure" orientation because the closer you get to your goal (e.g., a healthy lifestyle), the stronger your motivation becomes. If you take the "away from" orientation...the further you get away from a weight you do not like, the weaker your motivation becomes.

Carrot People tend to be idealists who can set the course, but Stick People are good at seeing the bumps in the road.

GENERAL THEORIES OF MOTIVATION

Motivation has long been an important subject of study in psychology. Early researchers, influenced by Darwin's postulates, ascribed much of animal and human behaviour to instinct. The Father of Psychoanalysis, Sigmund Freud believed that much of human behaviour was also based on irrational instinctive urges or unconscious motives. Walter B. Cannon proposed that basic human drives served homeostatic functions by directing energies toward the reduction of physiological tensions. Behavioural psychologists, in contrast, stress the importance of external goals in prompting action, while humanistic psychologists examine the role of felt needs. Cognitive psychologists have found that a motive sensitizes a person to information relating to that motive: a hungry subject, for example, will perceive food stimuli as larger than other stimuli.

Based on the perspectives of internal and external stimulation, theories of motivation have been categorized into (a) Internal Process Theories, and (b) External Process Theories.

INTERNAL PROCESS THEORIES

According to internal process theorists, motivation to live, to struggle to achieve something (some objective) is largely due to internal (from within the organism) "push". Behaviour is motivated because it serves several purposes in life. Numerous theories explain this viewpoint.

Instinct Theory

This theory is based on the belief that all living beings are born with *certain innate patterns (tendencies) of behaviour* called instincts, which motivate and direct species behaviour. Siding with Darwin's evolutionary hypothesis, William James (1890), William McDougal (1908), Sigmund Freud, and others upheld that instincts were the real cause of animal behaviour including man. James argued that human beings are even more influenced by instincts than are lower animals because they are motivated not only by biological instincts but also by psychological instincts like jealously, sympathy, sociability etc.

While Darwin and Freud had referred to (a) *struggle for existence*, and (b) *survival* as the two basic instincts, McDougall enumerated as many as fourteen instincts and James listed fifteen. In early 1920s, the Drive Theory was so influential that people proposed as many as 15,000 instincts to account for virtually every kind of human behaviour imaginable under the sun (Houston, 1985). Gradually, it became clear that instincts simply described behaviour; they did not explain it. Lack of empirical evidence, and increasing influence of behaviourism pushed the instinct (a tendency, not behaviour) theory on to the back stage.

Drive (Reduction) Theory

Drive Reduction Theory grew out of the concept that all living beings have certain biological needs such as hunger, thirst, etc. When these needs are not satisfied, the drive to satisfy them increases, and as they are satisfied by managing something to eat or to drink, the drive's strength is reduced. This way, a state of *homeostasis* (internal body equilibrium) is maintained. Hull (1943, 1952) was among the first psychologists in the modern research tradition to emphasize the importance of drive reduction for motivated or learned behaviour. Thus, Hull returned to the study of motivation to include *unobservable* states such as internal drive. He believed that behaviour is a result of human reaction to the environment in an attempt to survive or maintain homeostasis. Hull defined drive as *a stimulus, arising from bodily needs for survival, which stimulate behaviour*. People, when deprived of food or water, for example, will be driven to satisfy these needs by engaging in particular sets of behaviours that have allowed drive reduction in the past. Hull categorized drives into primary drives and secondary drives (as explained above).

Drive theory has some intuitive or folk validity. For instance when preparing food, the drive model appears to be compatible with sensations of rising hunger as the food is prepared, and, after the food has been consumed, a decrease in subjective hunger. Several problems, however, leave the validity of this theory open for debate. First, it does not explain how *Secondary Reinforcers* reduce drive. For example, money does not satisfy any biological or psychological need but reduces drive on a regular basis through a pay check second-order conditioning. Second, if the drive reduction theory is held true we would not be able to explain how a hungry person can prepare a meal without eating the food before he finished cooking it. In addition, it is clear that drive reduction theory cannot be a complete theory of behaviour. The ability of drive theory to cope with all kinds of behaviour, from not satisfying a drive (by adding on other traits such as restraint), or adding additional drives for "tasty" food, which combine with drives for "food" in order to explain cooking render it hard to test.

Need Theories

Several writers have based their motivation theory on need hypothesis. Prominent among these are Abraham Maslow, Henry Murray, David McClelland, and others.

Maslow's Hierarchy of Human Needs Theory

Human beings have variety of wants, needs and desires which cause certain behaviours and significantly influence them. Primary needs are biological; they are inborn and unlearnt. Secondary needs have environmental orientation and are learnt. Man's total life struggle is devoted to satisfying his needs. With his humanistic approach, Abraham Maslow, one of the most influential writers in the area of motivation, developed a Hierarchy of Human Needs Theory (1943, 1970), which came to be one of the most widely discussed theories of motivation in the recent times. Prior to him, researchers generally focused separately on such factors as biology, achievement, or power to explain what energizes, directs, and sustains human behaviour. Major points of emphasis in Maslow's theory can be summed up as follows:

- Human beings have wants and desires which influence their behaviour. Only unsatisfied needs influence behaviour, satisfied needs do not.
- Since needs are many, they are arranged in order of importance, from the basic to the complex (Fig. 11.1).

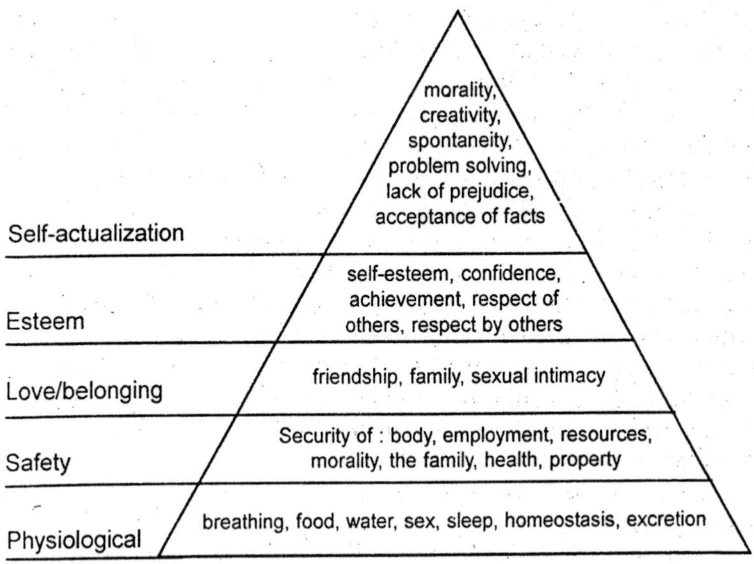

Fig. 11.1 Maslow's Hierarchical Structure (Pyramid) of needs

- The person advances to the next level of needs only after the lower level need is at least minimally satisfied.
- The further the progress up the hierarchy, the more individuality, humanness and psychological health a person will show.

In the Fig. 11.1, the lowest levels of the pyramid are made up of the most basic needs, while the more complex needs are located at the top of the pyramid. Needs at the bottom of the pyramid are basic physical requirements including the need for food, water, sleep and warmth. Once these lower-level needs have been met, people can move on to the next level of needs, which are for safety and security.

As people progress up the pyramid, needs become increasingly psychological and social. Soon, the need for love, friendship and intimacy become important. Further up the pyramid, the need for personal esteem and feelings of accomplishment take priority. Like Carl Rogers, Maslow emphasized the importance of self-actualization, which is a process of growing and developing as a person to achieve individual potential. Apart from describing what is meant by self-actualization, Maslow identified some of the key characteristics of self-actualized people. According to him, self-actualized individuals -

- have realistic perception of themselves, others and the world around.
- are problem-focused i.e. they are concerned with solving problems outside of themselves, including helping other, and finding solutions to problems in the external world.
- are spontaneous in their internal thoughts and outward behaviour. While they can conform to rules and social expectations, they also tend to be open and unconventional.
- have a concern about personal growth and the need for independence and privacy thought they enjoy the company of others.
- tend to view the world with a actual sense of appreciation. Even simple experiences continue to be source of inspiration and pleasure.
- often have *peak experiences*, or moments of intense joy, wonder, awe and ecstasy after which they feel inspired, strengthened, renewed or transformed.

Maslow believed that these needs are similar to instincts and play a major role in motivating behaviour. Physiological, security, social, and esteem needs are ***deficiency needs*** (or *D-needs*), meaning that these needs arise due to deprivation. Satisfying these lower-level needs is important in order to avoid unpleasant feelings or consequences. Maslow termed the highest-level of the pyramid as ***growth need*** (or *being needs* or *B-needs*). Growth needs do not stem from a lack of something, but rather from a desire to grow as a person. The needs placed in five different levels in Maslow's hierarchy of needs may be briefly described as given below:

1. ***Physiological Needs***: These include the most basic needs that are vital to survival, such as the need for water, air, food and sleep. Maslow believed that these needs are the most basic and instinctive needs in the hierarchy because all needs become secondary until these physiological needs are met.
2. ***Security Needs***: These include needs for safety and security. Security needs are important for survival, but they are not as demanding as the physiological needs. Examples of security needs include a desire for steady employment, health insurance, safe neighbourhoods and shelter from the environment.
3. ***Social Needs***: These include needs for belonging, love and affection. Maslow considered these needs to be less basic than physiological and security needs. Relationships such as friendships, romantic attachments and families help fulfill this need for companionship and acceptance as does involvement in social, community or religious groups.
4. ***Esteem Needs:*** After the first three kinds of needs have been satisfied, esteem needs become increasingly important. These include the need for things that reflect on self-esteem, personal worth, social recognition and accomplishment.
5. ***Self-actualizing Needs***: This is the highest level of Maslow's hierarchy of needs. *Self-actualizing* people are self-aware, concerned with personal growth, less concerned with the opinions of others and interested fulfilling their potential.

[*Note: Although Maslow referred to additional aspects of motivation, 'Cognitive' (knowledge, meaning, understand, explore etc.) and 'Aesthetic' (appreciation and search for symmetry, order, beauty, balance, form, etc.) he did not include them as levels or stages within his own expression of the Hierarchy of Needs. They were added to the hierarchy in 1970, making the pyramid a seven level structure. In 1990, 'Transcendence' needs i.e. helping others to achieve self-actualization was also added.*]

Maslow published his first conceptualization of his theory over seven decades ago and it has since become one of the most popular and often cited theories of human motivation. An interesting phenomenon related to this theory is that in spite of a lack of evidence to scientific and research support the need hierarchy, it enjoys wide acceptance and has a powerful intuitive appeal. Maslow's basic position is that as one becomes more self-actualized and self-transcendent, one becomes wiser and automatically knows what to do in a wide variety of situations. Daniels (2001) suggests that Maslow's ultimate conclusion that the highest levels of self-actualization are transcendent in their nature may be one of his most important contributions to the study of human behaviour and motivation.

Grand Theory of Motivation

Maslow's work lead to attempts to develop a grand theory of motivation; for example, Leonard, Beauvais & Scholl (1995) proposed five factors as the sources of motivation:

1. *Instrumental Motivation* (rewards and punishers),
2. *Intrinsic Process Motivation* (enjoyment, fun),
3. *Goal Internalization* (self-determined values and goals),
4. *Internal Self Concept-based Motivation* (matching behaviour with internally-developed ideal self), and
5. *External Self Concept-based Motivation* (matching behaviour with externally-developed ideal self).

Individuals are influenced by all five factors, though in varying degrees that can change in specific situations. Factors one and five are both externally-oriented. The main difference is that individuals who are instrumentally motivated are influenced more by immediate actions in the environment (e.g. operant conditioning) whereas individuals who are self-concept motivated are influenced more by their constructions of external demands and ideals (e.g., social cognition).

Factors two, three, and four are more internally-oriented. In the case of intrinsic process, the specific task is interesting and provides immediate internal reinforcement (e.g., cognitive or humanistic theory). The individual with a goal-internalization orientation is more task-oriented (e.g., humanistic or social cognition theory) whereas the person with an internal self-concept orientation is more influenced by individual constructions of the ideal self (humanistic or psychoanalytic theory).

Nohria, Lawrence, & Wilson (2001) provide evidence from a sociobiology theory of motivation that humans have four basic needs: (1) acquire objects and experiences; (2) bond with others in long-term relationships of mutual care and commitment; (3) learn and make sense of the world and of ourselves; and (4) to defend ourselves, our loved ones, beliefs and resources from harm. The Institute for Management Excellence (2001) suggests there are nine basic human needs: (1) security, (2) adventure, (3) freedom, (4) exchange, (5) power, (6) expansion, (7) acceptance, (8) community, and (9) expression.

Alderfer's ERG Theory

By expanding Maslow's need hierarchy theory, Alderfer (1972) developed a comparable hierarchy with his ERG (existence, relatedness and growth) theory in which physiological and safety, the lower order needs, are placed in the existence category, and love and self-esteem needs in the relatedness category. The growth category contained the self-actualization and self-esteem needs.

Alderfer's Hierarchy of Motivational Needs

Level of Need	*Definition*	*Properties*
Growth	Impel a person to make creative or productive effects on himself and his environment	Satisfied through using capabilities in engaging problems; creates a greater sense of wholeness and fullness as a human being
Relatedness	Involve relationship with significant others	Satisfied by mutually sharing thoughts and feelings; acceptance, confirmation, understanding and influence are elements
Existence	Includes all of the various forms of material and psychological desires	When divided among people one person's gain is another's loss if resources are limited

This hierarchy of needs is not much different from that of Maslow and can be seen as just collapsing into three tiers. It may be a bit more rational. For example, in Alderfer's model, sex does not need to be in the bottom category as it is in Maslow's model, since it is not crucial to (the individual's) existence. (Remember, this is about individual motivation, not species' survival.) So by moving sex, this theory does not predict that people have to have sex before they can think about going to school, like Maslow's theory does.

Henry Murray's Psychological Needs

Personality theorist Henry Murray (1938) argued that human motivation, at beast, comprised of a variety of psychological needs as listed below:

Achievement	:	To overcome obstacles, to exercise power, to strive to do something difficult as well as quickly as possible
Acquisition	:	To gain possession and property; to grasp, snatch or steal things, to bargain or gamble; to work for money or goods
Affiliation	:	To form friendship and associations; to greet, join and live with others; to cooperate and converse with others; to love, and join groups
Cognizance	:	To explore (moving and touching); to ask questions; to justify one's actions; to offer extenuations, explanations, and excuses; to resist "probing"
Deference	:	To admire and follow a superior or allied other; to cooperate with a leader; to serve gladly.
Nurturance	:	To nourish, and/or protect a helpless other; to express sympathy; to "mother" a child
Play	:	To relax, amuse oneself, seek diversion, and amusement; To have "fun", to play games; to laugh, joke, and be merry; to avoid serious tension
Recognition	:	To excite praise and commendation; to demand respect; to boast and exhibit one's accomplishments; to seek distinction, social prestige, honours or high office
Succorance	:	To seek aid, protection or sympathy; to cry for help; to plead for mercy; to adhere to an affectionate nurturant parent; to be dependent

Acquired Needs Theory

Also known as the *Three-Need Theory, Learned Need Theory* is actually built on Murray's hypothesis. David McClelland, Atkinson and others made an in-depth study of the origin of achievement motivation and how it prevailed across cultures (McClelland et al., 1976).

After making an in-depth study of needs hierarchy, McClelland et al., (1976) came to the conclusion that needs are not simply inherited but also shaped by our experiences over time. Most of these needs fall into three general categories: (1) Achievement (nAch), (2) Affiliation (nAff), and (3) Power (nPow), which means that in life we all seek power, achievement or affiliation.

The major argument in the theory is that we have different preferences, and will tend to have one of these needs that affects us more powerfully than others and thus affects our behaviours:

- *Achievers* seek to excel and appreciate frequent recognition of how well they are doing. They will avoid low risk activities that have no chance of gain. They also will avoid high risks where there is a significant chance of failure.
- *Affiliation seekers* look for harmonious relationships with other people. They will thus tend to conform and shy away from standing out. They seek approval rather than recognition.
- *Power seekers* want power either to control other people (for their own goals) or to achieve higher goals (for the greater good). They seek neither recognition nor approval from others — only agreement and compliance.

These needs can be measured using the TAT (thematic apperception test) which is a projection-style test based on interpreting stories that people tell about a set of pictures.

According to the theorists, achievement motivation is usually acquired in early childhood. Children high in n-Ach generally have parents who encourage them in positive ways to succeed at difficult tasks and who reward them for their success. The parents inspire them to be creative in accomplishing difficult task than urging them to quit. Further, the parents who place emphasis on achievement and success in school or at work tend to have children with the same kind of values. Family economics and culture in which people are born and brought have significant influence on their achievement motivation. For example, children who have strong economics generally read story books containing theories relating to achievement, such as hard work and productivity, and cultures in which there is civil unrest such as labour strikes and political protests, tend to have young people high in n-Ach.

The need theorists have undoubtedly been successful in generating research aimed at a better understanding of man's social behaviour. The approach assumed that motive-states are the main springs of action in sport. These are termed as the *motive to achieve success* and the *motive to avoid failure*; together they form the central constructs of this theory. McClelland believed that the motive interacts with the cues from the environment to arouse affective states, typically believed to be pride and shame, which then elicit approach or avoidance behaviour in achievement contexts.

Research has shown that individuals driven by the motive to achieve success select challenging tasks, take intermediate risk, and demonstrate improved performance, but those driven by the motive to avoid failure do not always avoid intermediate risk, or select either easy or extremely challenging tasks, or demonstrate low performance as predicted by the theory. Atkinson's research was mainly with children; it was not conducted in the sport context. Despite this, the need achievement approach has helped a great deal in understanding the motivation process fairly well. This theory has been criticized for the ethno-centric bias, the weight it places on elements of personality as the major energizing force of motivated states, and its failure to account for heightened performance of individuals with low achievement motivation in some situations.

Opponent-Process Theory

The motivational theorist, Richard Solomon bases his argument on the fact that 'every emotional experience, there is an opposite emotional and motivational state' (Solomon, 1980). In simple words, we have pairs of emotions that act in opposing pairs, such as happiness and sadness, fear and relief, pleasure and pain. When one of these is experienced, the other is temporarily suppressed. This opposite emotion, however, is likely to re-emerge strongly and may curtail or interact with the initial emotion. Thus activating one emotion also activates its opposite and they interact as a linked pair. This way we are motivated to maintain a relatively stable emotional state. The opposite emotion that develops in response to the initial emotion may persist longer than the initial condition, thereby reducing the strength of the first emotion. For instance, your fear of parachuting will diminish with every jump, but your elation with each safe landing will persist. In fact, Solomon & Corbit (1974) analyzed the emotions of skydivers. Beginners experienced extreme fear in their initial jump, which turned into great relief when they landed. With repeated jumps, the fear of jumping decreased and the post-jump pleasure increased.

Opponent processes also work in reverse direction. Pleasant emotional experiences such as a drug-high will be followed by an emotional let-down which, in turn, motivates drug-users to seek high again. For example, a person buys something to cheer himself up but later feels guilty at having spent so much. So he buys something else to cheer up again. Same way, a thrill seeker goes rafting. The excitement of the journey is a mix of fear of the next rapids and relief at having survived the last one. Sometimes these two conflicting emotions may be felt at the same time as the second emotion intrudes before the first emotion wanes. The result is a confusing combined experience of two emotions being felt at the same time that normally are mutually exclusive. Thus we can feel happy-sad, scared-relieved, love-hate, etc. This can be unpleasant but as an experiential thrill it can also have a strangely enjoyable element (and seems to be a basis of excitement).

Even with these arguments, Solomon fails to explain why people initially engage in different behaviours. The emotional reactivity to the same situation differs from person to person and in the same person to the same or similar situation on different occasions, and at different places. With experience, human beings learn to control their emotions, often with partial success because life is a mix of opponent processes in which maintaining a steady state is like walking on the sword edge.

Two Factor Theory

According to Herzberg, two kinds of factors affect motivation, and they do it in different ways:

- ***Hygiene factors***: These are factors the absence of which motivates, but the presence of which has no perceived effect. There are things that when you take them away, people become dissatisfied and act to get them back; for example, heroin to a heroin addict. Long term addicts do not shoot up to get high; they shoot up to stop being sick

– to get normal. Decent working conditions, security, pay, benefits (like health insurance), company policies, interpersonal relationships, etc., are also good examples of motivators. In general, these are extrinsic items low in the Maslow/Alderfer hierarchy.

- ***Motivators***: These are factors whose presence motivates, but their absence does not cause any particular dissatisfaction; it just fails to motivate. Examples are all the things at the top of the Maslow hierarchy, and the intrinsic motivators.

So hygiene factors determine dissatisfaction, and motivators determine satisfaction. The two scales are independent, and you can be high on both.

Reinforcement Theory

Skinner uses the term *Operant Conditioning* (already discussed under learning) to describe the effects of the consequences of a particular behaviour on the future occurrence of that behaviour. The four types of operant conditioning include: *positive reinforcement, negative reinforcement, punishment,* and *extinction*. While both positive and negative reinforcements strengthen behaviour, punishment and extinction weaken behaviour.

- *Positive Reinforcement*: It is strengthening a behaviour. It is the process of getting goodies as a consequence of a behaviour. You make a sale, you get a commission. You do a good job, you get a bonus and a promotion.
- *Negative Reinforcement*: It is also strengthening a behaviour. It is the process of having a stressor taken away as a consequence of a behaviour. Long-term sanctions are removed from players when their good conduct records improve.
- *Extinction*: Extinction is weakening a behaviour. It is the process of getting no goodies when doing a behaviour. So if a person does extra effort, but gets no thanks for it, they stop doing it.
- *Punishment*: It is weakening a behaviour. It is the process of getting a punishment as a consequence of a behaviour. For example, if a teacher does not teach a class and his pay is cut for absence from duty.

	Apply	Withhold
Reward	positive reinforcement (raise above baseline)	negative reinforcement (raise up to baseline)
Stressor	punishment (bring down below baseline)	extinction (stay at baseline)

The traditional reinforcement schedule is called *a continuous reinforcement schedule*. Each time the correct behaviour is performed it gets reinforced.

EXTERNAL PROCESS THEORIES

While the internal process theories explain the internal (intrinsic) sources of motivation (called "push)) for people to act in certain ways, the external process theories attach great importance to external factors and conditions such as awards, rewards, monetary gains, prizes, goals, etc., which attract or "pull" people to behave the way they do. Need, drive, and motive are abstractions (abstract concepts), awards, rewards, prizes, etc., are tangible reinforcing (or motivating) agents.

The external process of motivation is better explained by two recent theories: the Incentive Theory and the Expectancy Theory.

Incentive Theory

The incentive theory is based on the premise that external events (incentive goals) attract or "pull" people towards acting in typical ways. The theory stands on the foundation of behaviour-environment interactions and is an attempt to account for learned or acquired motivation. It holds the view that both positive and negative incentives motivate behaviour in a situation which means that we either act to obtain a pleasurable outcome (positive reinforcement) or attempt to avoid or escape from an unpleasant or un-pleasurable outcome (negative reinforcement).

A reward, tangible or intangible, is presented after the occurrence of an action (i.e. behaviour) with the intent to cause the behaviour to occur again. This is done by associating positive meaning to the behaviour. Research shows that if a person receives the reward immediately, the effect would be greater, and decreases as duration lengthens. Repetitive action-reward combination can cause the action to become a habit. Motivation comes from two sources: oneself, and other people. These two sources are called intrinsic motivation and extrinsic motivation, respectively. Importantly, a reinforcer is different from reward, in that reinforcement is intended to create a measured increase in the rate of a desirable behaviour following the addition of something to the environment. The incentive theory also lays emphasis on the role of learning in understanding motivated behaviour. It has some immediate practical implications for explaining a great variety of every day acts or routine activities.

Unfortunately, when people are given external incentives such as awards, rewards, material benefits, positions, jobs, promotions, increments; higher scales, etc., for doing things which are intrinsically (naturally) motivating, they begin to lose interest after sometime and even stop working with the same initial enthusiasm unless such reinforcers are not only continued, but intensified too. This way, the incentive theory fails to explain complex nature of the incentive system that does not always bring the same results under the same situations and with people coming from different socio-cultural backgrounds.

Expectancy Theory

Also called *Valence-Instrumentality-Expectancy Theory* or *VIE Theory*, the Expectancy Theory holds that we are motivated by desirable things we expect we can achieve. It underscores the perceived probability or perception of success. The idea is that when a person works hard to achieve something, he always expects to be rewarded with success or at least better performance. In other words, the person's assessment of the degree to which effort actually correlates with performance, defines expectancy. As we constantly are predicting likely futures, we create expectations about future events. If things seem reasonably likely and attractive, we know how to get there and we believe we can 'make the difference' then this will motivate us to act to make this future come true.

Motivation is thus a combination of:

- *Valence*: The value of the perceived outcome (What's in it for me?)
- *Instrumentality*: The belief that if I complete certain actions then I will achieve the outcome. (Clear path?)
- *Expectancy*: The belief that I am able to complete the actions. (My capability?)

Of course you can have an unpleasant outcome, in which case the motivation is now one of avoidance.

Expectancy theory attempts to mathematize motivation. In this theory, expectancy, instrumentality, and value must all exist in order for a person to take action, according to the formula:

M = E*I*V or Motivation = Expectancy * Instrumentality * Value

Or

Motivation = Perceived Probability of Success (Expectancy)*
Connection of Success and Reward (Instrumentality) *
Value of Obtaining Goal (Valance, Value)

M (motivation) is the amount a person will be motivated by the situation they find themselves in. It is a function of the following.

- *E (*expectancy*) = The person's perception that effort will result in performance. In other words, the person's assessment of the degree to which effort actually correlates with performance.
- *I (*instrumentality*) = The person's perception that performance will be rewarded/punished; i.e., the person's assessment of how well the amount of reward correlates with the quality of performance.
  (Note here that the model is phrased in terms of extrinsic motivation, in that it asks 'what are the chances I am going to get rewarded if I do good job?'. But for intrinsic situations, we can think of this as asking 'how good will I feel if I can pull this off?').
- *V (*valence*) = The perceived strength of the reward or punishment that will result from the performance. If the reward is small, the motivation will be small, even if expectancy and instrumentality are both perfect (high).

Since the formula given above states that the three factors of Expectancy, Instrumentality, and Valance or Value are to be multiplied by each other, a low value in one will result in a low value of motivation. Therefore, all three must be present in order for motivation to occur. That is, if an individual doesn't believe he or she can be successful at a task ***or*** the individual does not see a connection between his or her activity and success ***or*** the individual does not value the results of success, then the probability is lowered that the individual will engage in the required learning activity. From the perspective of this theory, all three variables must be high in order for motivation and the resulting behaviour to be high.

Cognitive Theories

There are several motivational theories that trace their roots to the information processing approach to learning. These approaches focus on the categories and labels people use help to identify thoughts, emotions, dispositions, and behaviours.

Goal-setting Theory

The goal-setting theory is based on the notion that individuals sometimes have a drive to reach a clearly defined end state. Often, this end state is a reward in itself. A goal's efficiency is affected by three features: proximity, difficulty and specificity. An ideal goal should present a situation where the time between the initiation of behaviour and the end state is close. This explains why some children are more motivated to learn how to ride a bike than mastering algebra. A goal should be moderate, not too hard or too easy to complete. In both cases, most people are not optimally motivated, as many want a challenge (which assumes some kind of insecurity of success). At the same time people want to feel that there is a substantial probability that they will succeed. Specificity concerns the description of the goal in their class. The goal should be objectively defined and intelligible for the individual. A classic example of a poorly specified goal is to get the highest possible grade. Most children have no idea how much effort they need to reach that goal.

Douglas Vermeeren, has done extensive research into why many people fail to get to their goals. The failure is directly attributed to motivating factors. Vermeeren states that unless an individual can clearly identify their motivating factor or their significant and meaningful reasons why they wish to attain the goal, they will never have the power to attain it.

Attribution Theory

The Attribution Theory (Heider, 1958; Weiner, 1974) proposes that every individual tries to explain success or failure of self and others by offering certain "attributions." These attributions are either internal or external and are either under control or not under control. The following chart shows the four attributions that result from a combination of internal or external locus of control and whether or not control is possible.

	Internal	*External*
No Control	Ability	Luck
Control	Effort	Task Difficulty

In a teaching/learning environment, it is important to assist the learner to develop a self-attribution explanation of effort (internal, control). If the person has an attribution of ability (internal, no control) as soon as the individual experiences some difficulties in the learning process, he or she will decrease appropriate learning behaviour (e.g. I am not good at this). If the person has an external attribution, then nothing the person can do will help the individual in a learning situation (i.e. responsibility for demonstrating what has been learned is completely outside the person). In this case, there is nothing to be done by the individual when learning problems occur.

Unconscious Motivation

Some psychologists believe that a significant portion of human behaviour is energized and directed by unconscious motives. "Psychoanalysis has often demonstrated that the relationship between a conscious desire and the ultimate unconscious aim that underlies it need not be at all direct," believes Maslow. In other words, stated motives do not always match those inferred by skilled observers. For example, it is possible that a person can be accident-prone because he has an unconscious desire to hurt himself and not because he is careless or ignorant of the safety rules. Similarly, some overweight people are not hungry at all for food but for fighting and kissing. Eating is merely a defensive reaction to lack of attention. Some workers damage more equipment than others do because they harbour unconscious feelings of aggression toward authority figures.

Psychotherapists point out that some behaviour is so automatic that the reasons for it are not available in the individual's conscious mind. Compulsive cigarette smoking is an example. Sometimes maintaining self-esteem is so important and the motive for an activity is so threatening that it is simply not recognized and, in fact, may be disguised or repressed. Rationalization, or "explaining away", is one such disguise, or defense mechanism, as it is called. Another is projecting or attributing one's own faults to others. "I feel I am to blame", becomes "It is her fault; she is selfish". Repression of powerful but socially unacceptable motives may result in outward behaviour that is the opposite of the repressed tendencies. An example of this would be the employee who hates his boss but overworks himself on the job to show that he holds him in high regard.

Unconscious motives add to the hazards of interpreting human behaviour and, to the extent that they are present, complicate the life of the administrator. On the other hand, knowledge that unconscious motives exist can lead to a more careful assessment of behavioural problems. Although few contemporary psychologists deny the existence of unconscious factors, many do believe that these are activated only in times of anxiety and stress, and that in the ordinary course of events, human behaviour - from the subject's point of view - is rationally purposeful.

SOURCES OF MOTIVATION

Based on the theories of motivation discussed above sources of human motivation can be categorized as either extrinsic (outside the person) or intrinsic (internal to the person). Intrinsic sources and corresponding theories can be further subcategorized as either body/physical, mind/mental (i.e., cognitive, affective, conative) or transpersonal/spiritual (Fig. 11.2).

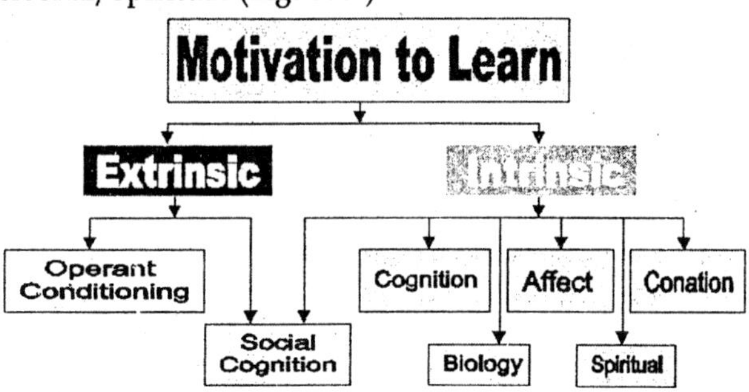

Fig. 11.2 : Sources of human motivation

In current literature, needs are now viewed as the root of all overt and covert human actions, reactions and interactions directed and devoted to accomplishing something. Action or overt behaviour may be initiated by either positive or negative incentives or a combination of both. The following chart provides a brief overview of the different sources of motivation (internal state) that have been studied both intensively and extensively. While initiation of action can be traced to each of these domains, it appears likely that initiation of behaviour may be more related to emotions and/or the affective area (optimism vs. pessimism; self- esteem; etc.) while persistence may be more related to conation (volition) or goal-orientation.

Source of Motivational Needs

Behavioural/External	• elicited by stimulus associated/ connected to innately connected stimulus • obtain desired, pleasant consequences (rewards) or escape/avoid undesired, unpleasant consequences
Social	• imitate positive models • be a part of a group or a valued member
Biological	• increase/decrease stimulation (arousal) • activate senses (taste, touch, smell, etc. • decrease hunger, thirst, discomfort, etc. • maintain homeostasis, balance
Cognitive	• maintain attention to something interesting or threatening • develop meaning or understanding • increase/decrease cognitive disequilibrium; uncertainty • solve a problem or make a decision • figure something out • eliminate threat or risk
Affective	• increase/decrease affective dissonance • increase feeling good • decrease feeling bad • increase security of or decrease threats to self-esteem • maintain levels of optimism and enthusiasm
Conative	• meet individually developed/selected goal • obtain personal dream • develop or maintain self-efficacy

	• take control of one's life • eliminate threats to meeting goal, obtaining dream • reduce others' control of one's life
Spiritual	• understand purpose of one's life • connect self to ultimate unknowns

Levels of Motivation in Life and Sport

From the study of various theories motivation discussed above, it is clear that phenomenon of human motivations is very wide. It may not be understood, explained, and guided by a single perspective Theoretical explanations given to it may be diagrammatically represented as given below (Fig. 11.3).

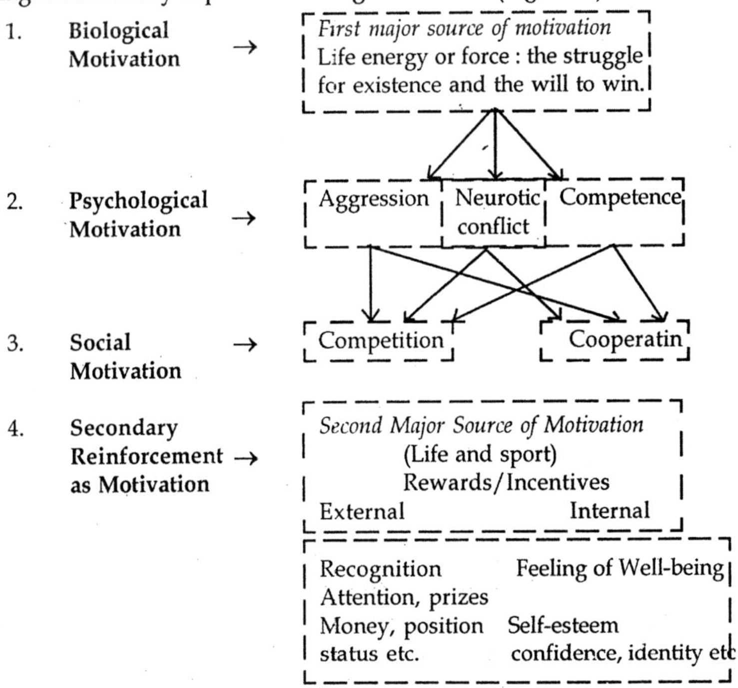

Fig. 11.3 Levels of motivation in life and sport

Man is a biological entity (an organism), a *thinking* machine, and a social animal - all in one - and yet a human being as a whole is much more than sum of their parts. So, any discussion on man, his behaviour and the factors and forces that motivate man to behave in a certain way, is not to be simply restricted to biological, psychological and social aspects of life but also those even beyond it. However, when it comes to analyzing the secrets and sources of human motivations (Fig. 11.3), we can markedly see that the baseline sources of human motivations consist of the basic life-energy (élan vital) manifest in each and every atom of the universe and each and every cell of the human body. Obviously, the survival activity (struggle for existence) of all living beings including man is powered by the cosmic energy - the implicit force in the matter to expand, to develop and to propagate life. By ***biological motivations*** do human beings grow, move and interact with the environment. We breathe, make locomotion, stand and walk, run, throw, catch, hit, and kick and perform all sorts of acrobatic movements because we are biologically motivated. Both life and human behaviour have a purpose. ***Psychological motivations*** stem from constant human struggle to resolve neurotic conflicts arising from stresses, strains and tensions generally caused by non-fulfilment or unduly delayed satisfaction of both basic and secondary needs of life as Freud and his followers asserted. For instance, aggression in man is linked to his biological struggle for existence, as in animals, but its expression will occur only when there are some powerful psychological reasons working at the back. In fact, psychological reasons add fuel to the flame. ***Social motivations*** have socio-cultural orientation and reflect competence and competition - the two processes of human struggle for adjustment. While biological and psychological motivations are individualistic, social motivation is always in relation to others - all those who matter in man's life.

Biological and psychological motivations are natural and primary motivations (reinforcers), generally intrinsic - arsing from 'within' the organism. Social motivations may be both primary (influenced by human thought and action), and secondary - those coming from outside the human body and are man-made and artificial such as tangible and intangible awards or rewards. Achieving an award or reward as an incentive for performance is no doubt motivating but its expectancy too is equally rewarding. While the external incentives, to be more precise, include recognition, attention, awards, rewards, money, status, etc., the internal motivational sources reflect feelings of well-being, self-esteem, confidence, identity, etc.

Irrespective of the source they come from, all motivations are potentially and legitimately, influenced by external forces especially the human experience. High achievers and successful individuals and groups differ from low achievers and less successful people both in the source and the level of their motivations in almost every walk of life - work, business, education, sport, etc.

EDUCATION AND MOTIVATION

Motivation is of great interest to the teachers and educational psychologists because of the crucial role it plays in student learning. A motivated child learns his or her lessons well and achieves better grade at the examination. However, the specific kind of motivation that is studied in the specialized setting of education differs qualitatively from the more general forms of motivation studied by psychologists in other fields such as industry, business, sport, etc. A child's motivation at school is qualitatively different from an adult's motivation at work or job.

Motivation in education (including sport and activity) can have several effects on how students learn and how they behave towards subject matter. It can:

- direct behaviour toward particular goals
- lead to increased effort and energy
- increase initiation of, and persistence in activities
- enhance cognitive processing
- determine what consequences are reinforcing
- lead to improved performance.

Because students are not always internally motivated, they sometimes need *situated motivation* (some praise, punishment, award, reward etc.), which is found in environmental conditions that the teacher himself creates.

Impacting Motivation in the Class

Stipek (1988) quotes a variety of reasons why individuals especially children may be lacking in motivation for academic work or sport. He provides a list of specific behaviours associated with high academic achievement. This is an excellent checklist to help students develop the conative component of their lives. In addition, teacher efficacy is a powerful input variable related to student achievement (Proctor, 1984).

There are several specific strategies that teachers can adopt to increase motivation on classroom and/or field tasks. In general, these fall into the two categories discussed above: intrinsic motivation and extrinsic motivation.

Intrinsic	*Extrinsic*
o Explain or show why learning of a particular content or skill is important	o Provide clear expectations
o Create and/or maintain curiosity	o Give corrective feedback
o Provide a variety of activities and sensory stimulations	o Provide valuable rewards
o Provide games and simulations	o Make rewards available
o Set goals for learning	
o Relate learning to student needs	

As a general rule, teachers need to use as much of the intrinsic suggestions as possible while recognizing that not all students will be appropriately motivated by them. The extrinsic suggestions will work, but it must be remembered that they do so only as long as the student is under the control of the teacher. When outside of that control, unless the desired goals and behaviours have been internalized, the learner will cease the desired behaviour and operate according to his or her internal standards or to other external factors.

SPORT MOTIVATION - A THEORETICAL EYEVIEW

Man by birth is physically active and sportive in nature. So both physical activity and sport are spontaneous, natural and enjoyable activities at the baseline. They are self-motivated and self-motivating. However, when they are viewed as social institutions and subjected to some kind of formal discipline and organization, i.e. play metamorphosing into sport and physical activity becoming physical exercise, they become procedure-based and are governed by general laws of learning and motivation. For instance, basic motor activity is natural and unlearnt, but all sport skills (based on simple motor skills) have to be acquired using appropriate methods and means including motivation. Similarly, physical activity is Nature's gift to all living beings as a survival reaction, but formal physical exercise as a means of keeping body healthy and fit and also to train for competitive sport has to be learnt through a meticulous educational process. It is so because all formal life business - work, business, study, training, sport, etc. - is subject to some discipline and so they look least interesting. But because life cannot go on without it, all of us are inspired, coaxed, cajoled and even coerced to acquire the required life skills in some measure to keep things moving at all cost. For instance, work is necessary to earn bread, and sport to enjoy life. Motivation is a prerequisite in both cases; to some people it comes from within and for others, some external attractions must exist to motivate them.

At the base level of organization, physical activity is all play – pure and simple - for which the motivation is chiefly intrinsic and its source biological. No one invites an infant and a child to play; they play because it is essential for them to do so, on biological and psychological grounds. Motivation for play is internal and unbounded. The motivational spectrum begins to dramatically change as soon as sport takes precedence over play and physical activity, and is judged in socio-cultural context as a means of performance and excellence.

In order to know, understand and explain sport motivation, it will be necessary to keep in mind the general theoretical framework of motivation (various motivational perspective), discussed above. However, there is something special, something different, about sport that needs consideration and it is that sport, since the revival of the Olympic Games in 1896, has increasingly become highly competitive potentially affecting systems of training athletes. The involvement of science and money in sport in a big way has altogether changed its nature, having serious implications for human health, happiness and psychology.

Sport motivation, which involves "inner life energies, and their forms of expression" is now being explained and interpreted from different sport-specific perspectives significantly those of Konard Lorenz's Theory of Aggression, Sigmund Freud's of Neurotic Conflict, and Robert White's Theory of Competence. All of them carry special significance for the sport psychologists as on this basis they have tried to pinpoint with astute precision why people engage in sport, and what makes sportspersons develop in themselves an unquenchable thirst for constant performance-improvement leading to breaking and creating athletic records.

Theory of Aggression

Aggression is as *any action, verbal or non-verbal (physical) that is intended to harm another individual*. It may be defensive or unprovoked; it is motivated. Lorenz's (1966) instinct-based theory holds that aggression serves as a defence mechanism in the survival of man and animals, and the expression of our instinctual energy is generally preceded by a specific stimulus in the environment. Without stimulus (a provocation) no aggression can possibly occur. The stimulus, called a sign stimulus, elicits a species-typical response. Several reasons are cited for animals including man being aggressive in their behaviour. For example, certain cerebral diseases play a significant role in generating aggression in man. In addition, evidence from physiological research suggests that the neurotransmitter serotonin may be involved in aggressive behaviour in man and animals. Amphetamine and testosterone, which block the release of serotonin, also increase the likelihood of aggressive behaviour.

Aggressive energy may find many targets for its expression, and sport among them may be an important one. The aggressive athlete is "eager, strong and highly motivated" and he will seek to vanquish the opponent, how so strong. Most athletic events require mobilization of *'stored-up'* (innate, inborn) aggressiveness in specific directions. Obviously an aggressive athlete will generally succeed and become a *superior* athlete with further intensified effort. In sport, aggression might be a cause of motivated behaviour as the "struggle" in sport is not for *existence*, but for achieving mastery over environment and establishing one's supremacy over other athletes.

Some sociologists feel that the savage tendency of being aggressive - a racially old form of behaviour - has persisted in man over hundreds of millennia of existence but neither civilization nor culture has diminished it. For example, "body to body fight experience" (a survival tendency) could also apparently disappear from man's life like many other "racial experiences of the past", but it has not (the reason may not be difficult to seek); it still continues to exist in the form of sanctioned aggression in activities like sport. The "militant enthusiasm" of a protesters' crowd, for example, at a football match, is an expression of a sanctioned form of aggression (the animal expression of aggressive energy). Were it not so, human beings would, perhaps, be more aggressive than they are even in everyday routines.

Like Sigmund Freud, Lorenz agreed that expression of

aggression has a cathartic (purgatory) effect on the animal. Just as all human beings are equipped with the innate aggressive responses and the energy to execute them, all athletes display drive and energy that seem directed toward maintaining athletic rank or defeating an opponent. This observation may vary with different athletes in different sports. There, however, is a common denominator - a firm determination (strong will) to win over Nature or an opponent. In some sports, the aggressive component is latent as in boxing or wrestling; in others, it is camouflaged by ritual and equipment as in tennis or badminton. In body-contact sports (wrestling, judo, boxing, etc.) aggression is prominently manifest, in non-contact sports (volleyball, tennis, badminton, etc.), it is directed at the opponent via equipment (instrumental aggression) or bodily movements, gestures, facial expressions and/or the body language as a whole. As a biological source of energy, aggression could be expected as a strong motivation in the early careers of athletes before secondary reinforcements begin to pervade the scene more prominently.

Individuals vary in the manifestation of aggressive energy probably for two major reasons. First, there are genetic and constitutional variations in the animals' potential for aggression. It is true about humans also. In one situation, one athlete may find himself over-brimming with aggressive energy; the other may simply remain helpless, passive, even lax and lethargic. Second, as children become increasingly socialized as a result of interaction with the environment, their pulsating energies are directed, and guided ingeniously into more constructive activities and creative impulses. By focussing aggressive energies upon sport, the athlete becomes greatly socialized by realizing that he or she must control and master the aggressive experience. As maturity sweeps over athletic experience, aggressive motivation also becomes less manifest. Aggressive behaviour in sport also begins to decline both in intensity and frequency as athletes mature. The moving wheel of age makes many biological processes either slide or slow down.

In competitive sport, prevailing conditions, situations and circumstances play a significant role in making athletes behave sometime more and sometime less aggressively. There are occasions when the humblest of the athletes may become too aggressive (even beyond expectations), and an overly aggressive athlete may cringe and crunch. Wordy brawls among players (among team-mates and also between opponents), resentments against referee's decisions, tiffs with the game officials, swearing and throwing invectives at the opponents, clenching fists, exhibiting intimidating gestures, jeering at players and/or officials, etc., is a profound manifestation of aggressive behaviour. However, aggressive instinct, i.e. an irrepressible desire to win at all costs is enough to mobilize an athlete's energy to engage in goal-directed behaviour with greater intensity, which might be labelled as aggressive assertion, but rowdiness during a game, may not be construed as bad behaviour.

Theory of Neurotic Conflict

Freud's Theory of Neurotic Conflict and White's Theory of Competence which underscore innate fund of energy and intrinsic motivations, also allow for inputs from the environment more than Lorenz Theory of Aggression does. Motivational feedings from neurotic conflict and competence sources are said to be largely modifiable through experience. Some athletes are excitable, unpredictable and difficult to deal with. Others keep their cool and are calm, mentally stable, and more dependable. This variation may be due to variation in their genetic makeup and, to some extent, to the socio-cultural milieu in which they live and train.

According to psycho-dynamic theory, which draws inspiration from instinct theory, aggression is due to pent-up energy that keeps on accumulating in an individual until it reaches a flash point. This situation is, more or less, akin to volcanic eruption or explosion. Freud called the release of pent-up energy through legitimate channels as catharsis, and asserted that many cultural and social activities provide socially acceptable means of expression of aggressive instincts. The cathartic outlets are *displacement* and *sublimation*. In displacement, aggressive tendencies are channelled toward objects other than the original source that arouses aggression. In sublimation, aggressive tendencies are transformed into socially acceptable activities such as athletic, academic or artistic pursuits.

Freud's insistence on neurotic conflict as the major reason for aggressive behaviour, both in life and sport, is possibly correct. The vulnerability of the serious athletes or high performers – whether amateur or professional – as is the case with most common people, to certain obsessions, parental indifference, insecurity, anxiety, etc., right from their childhood is a reality, not a far-fetched idea. This is the major reason for neurotic conflict in them. When athletes are not appreciated for themselves as human beings, but for their performances and achievements, they find their self-image getting de-shaped and their ego threatened. Against this sense of insecurity, do they fall back on a certain set of defences, common to the athletic ego that creates what is essentially a neurotic adjustment - a comparative drive to compete and be successful, a desire to play a heroic role and a need to indulge in sexual exploits over women. Under such situations, the athlete's own strengths and weaknesses determine what his or her own reactions would be toward life and sport.

Neurosis represents cultural values of society in which an athlete is born and brought up. This also has something to do with his attempts at adjustments in the society. The two important ways of coping with the problem of neurotic conflict in athletic context are: (1) to suggest a change in the social values surrounding the athletes and sport, and (2) to work with the individual athlete, assisting him to have a better adjustment in current circumstances. Sport psychologists believe that sport is an acceptable expression of adjustment mechanism and a direct channel through which sublimation of morbid instincts could be possible. Sport may represent either a healthy relationship with the authority or a challenge to it. Sports activities are an expression of a neurotic conflict to the degree the primary instinct is redirected from the original object to another for gratification. Further, disharmony and in-congruency between an athlete's physical growth and mental development could also cause a conflict as in the case of power-lifters who stand on two extremes of muscular development and psychological fitness.

Narcissism and exhibitionism are strong neurotic motivations in many top athletes. *Narcissism* refers to libidinal energy that is turned inward so that the self becomes the focus of sexual drive. The athlete is in love with *himself* and often obsessed with the aesthetics, powers and strengths of his own body. The degree of neurotic motivation in an athlete depends upon the level of psycho-sexual development he has reached and it is represented by the quality, level and frequency of participation in sport contests and competitions. Although neurotic conflict, in general, begins to appear early in childhood mainly due to internal and external repression and suppression of desires and urges, most neurotic adjustments in athletes stem from phallic developmental stage when Oedipal conflicts arise and the object of sexual urge is expressed through outlets other than those specifically sexual, such as identifications, activities, performances, attention-seeking behaviours, and the peer-group games.

Freud's theory offers both a genesis for sport motivation and explanation for individual differences. A strict application of this theory reveals that a human being struggles to maintain a balance between the demands of his Id and those of the Superego, resulting in a state of constant neurotic conflict. The society cannot tolerate man's aggressive and sexual urges which constantly struggle for outward expression directly or indirectly. Sport is a socially acceptable conduit for these urges, providing opportunities to the athletes to express them through legitimate means and maintain a steady state or equilibrium.

A typical athlete would manifest not only some form of aggression but also a degree of resolution as a result of sport participation. When such as athlete is primarily motivated by neurotic conflicts that quality will dominate his individual motivation all through. It is likely that such an athlete will suffer periodic spasms of psychological break-downs and require therapeutic measures. Most neurotically motivated athletes, it is argued, will drop out of sport competitions once their neurosis gets resolved. Freud suggests that higher the level of civilization, the greater the restrictions on the libidinal discharge of energies, will produce more neurosis.

The more mature and intrinsically motivated athletes seem to attach least importance to money, material gains, status, recognition, etc., in general, extrinsically motivated athletes and those with not very mature thinking would consider the external motivation to be more important than the intrinsic value of participation in sport and enjoy the solace of success. Freud's Theory of Neurotic Conflict, although beset with very complicated and, to some extent, contradictory explanations has, nevertheless, paved the way for understanding intrinsic springs of human motivation in athletic people to some extent. Lack of empirical evidence is a big hurdle in the way of giving scientific status to many inferences drawn from this theory.

Theory of Competence

White's Theory of Competence has had its origin in the Ego Psychology, which explains that the individual engages in continual manipulation of his environment in order to experience the effect it has upon him. The experience could be exciting, stimulating, pleasurable, disturbing or painful but the drive for competence is as significant for human development as is the necessity for satisfaction of basic needs of hunger, thirst, love, sex, etc. The purpose of sport activity, argue the competence theory theorists, is not to achieve a specific goal but to enable the participant to experience the effect of interaction between himself and his environment as well as to deal with it effectively. Athletic motivation, therefore, is largely an expression of the search for feeling of competence.

The competence-oriented athlete is easily distinguishable from the one who is emotionally motivated. He plays sport for intrinsic reasons and experiences feelings of self-fulfilment in his pursuit for excellence. The inherent satisfaction this athlete experiences, is a reward of competence motivation and is essential for the development of humans. The athlete runs, jumps, throws, hits or kicks because by doing so he derives an inner satisfaction, a sense of accomplishment. Even if he loses, he does not grieve over failure, and basks in the glory of thought of having competed well. In sport, athletes try to assert themselves on the environment and assert mastery over it as well as on their own actions and activities. For many an athlete, the glory of winning or breaking records is a secondary objective, and their primary objective is participation as a true competitor. This is what an intrinsically motivated athlete is.

White also argues for extension of Freud's concept of motivation in which the source of energy is traced to *libido* - the sex energy. According to White, there are independent ego energies that originate entirely in the autonomous part of personality. These are equipped with a drive toward "effectance", which induces motivation in the individual to interact with the environment and to assert dominance upon it (environment), which, in turn, feeds back into the experience of individuals especially young children as they pass through learning experiences about tasks which they will be required to perform in future.

Understandably, the major sources of energy - aggression, neurotic conflict and competence - are influenced by environmental interactions and individual differences. Primary motives, explained above, are at the root of achievement motivation; secondary motives simply reinforce them as situations demand. For example, play is not a commitment with children; it is an expression of their natural urge for activity, which takes many forms depending upon the environmental conditions. Sport, for many adults, especially professional sportspersons and serious amateurs, is a life-time commitment.

Competence, of course, provides most constructive reason for sport motivation. To maximize competence motivation and minimize aggression and neuroticism in sport, it would be necessary to define carefully what behaviours were constructive and which of them not, if not destructive, so to say, and then to develop a perfect model of identifying athletes who displayed those behaviours, and finally to link a system of denials and rewards with appropriate behaviour. Positive reinforcements could possibly be encouragement from the coach, material rewards, and spectator- or peer-group support. Negative reinforcement could be disapproval from the coach, denial of material rewards, peer-group rejection and spectator indifference.

SOCIAL COGNITIVE APPROACH

Historically, the social cognitive approach is the most recent approach explaining human motivation in social context in general and sport context in particular. It included research into perceived competence, self-efficacy, intrinsic motivation, and achievement goals.

The essential elements for a cognitive perspective on motivation is to study the way in which knowledge is acquired, represented and used by human beings. The emphasis is on how cognitive activity and/or thoughts govern achievement endeavours. The attempt here is to understand how individuals think and how the cognitive thoughts govern action (the human activity). The underlying message is that cognitions and beliefs mediate behaviour and it is up to the scientists to describe and explain what constellations of cognitions affect the on-going stream of achievement behaviours in sport.

Self-Efficacy

Bandura (1977) used the term self-efficacy (also used synonymously with self-confidence or self-esteem) to describe the conviction one has to successfully execute the behaviour necessary to produce a certain outcome. It is not concerned with the ability of the person per se with the assessment of what the individual can do with his or her competencies. Originally, self-efficacy was proposed as an explanation to various intervention procedures utilized in the treatment of anxiety; it is now being used in sport to explain the mediation of achievement behaviours. Recent research in this area has shown modest relationship between self-efficacy and sport performance in connection with other mechanisms of achievement.

Perceived Competence

Based on the work of White (1959), Harter (1978, 1980) made an attempt to explain why individuals feel impelled to engage in mastery attempts in achievement contexts. To Harter, perceived competence is a multi-dimensional motive that directs individuals in the cognitive, social and physical domains. Success and failure in these domains are evaluated by significant others (parents, teachers, peers, leaders, etc.) and the perceived competence and the intrinsic pleasure gained from these evaluations are seen to increase achievement-striving when success is realized. The perception of incompetence and displeasure are assumed to lead to anxiety and a decrease in achievement striving when failure is realized.

Several studies in this domain have shown some relationship between physical competence and success in sport. Simultaneously, it has also been suggested that children participate in sport for many reasons (Singer, 1984) other than to demonstrate competence. However, continued engagement in a contest where physical competence is a placed at a premium may favour those who wish to demonstrate competence as part of their motivational set. Researchers have found a variety of difficulties in using Harter's (1978) model of measuring competence in competitive sport contexts.

Achievement Goal Approach

This approach suggests that to understand motivation and achievement behaviour in all of its forms, the function and meaning of behaviour must be taken into account so that the goals of action may be identified. By doing so multiple goals for behaviour are identified, not just one. Variation in behaviour may not be the result of high or low motivation but rather than manifestation of different perceptions of what is the appropriate goal within that social context. For example, some children may strive to achieve in order to receive social approval from others, but other children may want to achieve in order to demonstrate competence to others (Roberts, 1993). Success and failure are psychological states based on the interpretation of the effectiveness of the person's achievement striving. If the outcome of achievement striving is seen to reflect desirable attributes of the self, such as high effect or high ability, then the outcome is interpreted as success. If the outcome is seen to reflect undesirable qualities of the self, such as laziness or poor ability, then the outcome must be regarded as failure. Success, failure, and achievement are only recognized in terms of the goal of behaviour for that individual.

The urge to compete, excel and achieve, in more or less measure, is common to all human beings. Consequently, people assert their motivated energies in a variety of fields such as science, art, sport and the like. The stimulus and strength for the urge to compete, excel and achieve are derived from the socio-cultural ecology. To understand the role of motivation in exercise and sport against the background of general theories of motivation, it is natural for a person to be tempted to seek answer to such mind-boggling questions as to why people engage in play and/or institutionalized sport; what causes competitive sport behaviour; what incentives does one receive from participation in physical activity and in competitive or recreational sport; what goals sportspersons pursue; what enhances activity drive in us; what creates performance-excellence motives; and so on. The study of motives for sport at comparative age levels makes an interesting reading because motives are subject to fast change with transition from growth stage to the next. According to Singer (1984), common motives of children in sport are:

- to develop skills and competence;
- to affiliate and make friends;
- to gain success and recognition;
- to exercise and be fit;
- to release energy and experience challenges; and
- to seek excitement.

It is likely that early experiences (with others) that are not satisfying physically and socially produce children who reject and withdraw from physical activity, and later from vigorous sport. Further, 'genetic predisposition, parental attitudes and social pressures are cited as important variables influencing youngsters' participation in exercise and sport', says Cratty (1989).

RESEARCH EVIDENCE ON SPORT MOTIVATION

Motivation is an internal energy force that determines all aspects of our behaviour; it also impacts on how we think, feel and interact with others. In sport, high motivation is widely accepted as an essential prerequisite in getting athletes to fulfill their potential. However, given its inherently abstract nature, it is a force that is often difficult to exploit fully. The fund of information available today about the motivational dynamics in sport comes to us from research and experience of athletes, coaches, trainers, sports academics, mangers and others. It is not always a fact that only superior athletes are a highly motivated; a young school athlete may be as strongly motivated as the superior adult athlete. This is what makes sport motivation a complex process.

Sport Motivation - A Prismatic View

Motivation influences individuals to begin, pursue, and persist in an activity. Intrinsic motivation is self-fuelling over the long term because it is based on controllable feelings of enjoyment and competence; extrinsic motivation relies on external reinforcers from the social environment. Current theory views motivation as a cognitive process in which our behaviour is a direct result of how we think and process information about ourselves and the world. The one common thread in several theories of motivation (discussed above) is that people are motivated to feel competent, worthy, and self-determining. From birth, we all try to be competent in our environment. As our lives continue, our need to be competent is channelled in various areas through socialization. Thus, people differ in their motivation to achieve certain things. Several important factors fuel this intrinsic motivation to be competent and self-determining. First, we all feel competent for different reasons.

Research in exercise and sport psychology has shown that individuals have different goals for achievement and that to truly understand motivation we must understand how each person defines success or competence for him or herself. Another important factor that influences motivation is what psychologists call perceptions of control. Humans are motivated to be self-determining, which means we want to be in control of our own actions and behaviour. Individuals with more internal perceptions of control are more motivated than individuals who feel others control them or that they are lucky. Two important psychological constructs that affect motivation are self-esteem and self-confidence. Self-esteem is our perception of personal worthiness and the emotional feelings associated with that perception.

Many psychologists view self-esteem as the most central core component of our identity, and thus it has a major influence on our motivation in sport and exercise. Self-worth or self-esteem is an important need for all individuals and it emanates from feeling competent and in control of our behaviour in an achievement area that is important to us. The literature emphasizes that self-esteem is the direct result of social interactions, so social support and positive reinforcement for individual mastery attempts are crucial to the development of self-esteem. Self-confidence is also a critical factor in motivation and is similar to perceived competence. Athletes who feel more competent and self-confident are motivated to work harder to perform better in their sport. As with self-esteem, if we lack confidence in our ability, we need elaborate extrinsic incentives to motivate us.

Feedback and reinforcement can be used in a positive way to enhance peoples' feelings of competence, which then increases their intrinsic motivation. This area, called behaviour modification, has been developed from animal research in psychology and deals with how the use of reinforcers influences human behaviour. The fundamental assumption of behaviour modification is that behaviours are strengthened when they are rewarded and weakened when they are punished or unrewarded. Extrinsic rewards are common in sport, such as trophies, medals, certificates, scholarships, and even large perks and fat salaries in professional sports. Research indicates that extrinsic rewards given in competition may serve to weaken or undermine existing intrinsic motivation. If the extrinsic rewards associated with competition are perceived as controlling by individuals, then intrinsic motivation decreases as individuals feel less self-determining. Motivation involves intensity of behaviour and the urge to be competent and successful. It is easy to see, then, that for some people this motivation, which was once positive and enjoyable, turns into anxiety and becomes stressful. The popular notion of "psyching up" by athletes refers to their levels of arousal, which is defined as physical and psychological readiness to perform. Think of arousal as a specific state of motivation in a particular situation. A popular misconception is that you can never be too motivated or highly aroused, but research has shown that high levels of arousal can hurt performance. Studies have shown that arousal is related to performance in a curvilinear or inverted-U model, which means that as arousal increases, performance increases to an optimal zone, after which further increases in arousal hurt performance. Optimal arousal is very personal—every individual has a unique optimal arousal zone. Another consideration in arousal is the type of task a person is performing. Complex and precise physical activities, such as putting in golf or shooting in archery, require lower levels of arousal for optimal performance as compared to those that use gross motor skills, such as football blocking or playing soccer.

Approaches to Sport Motivation

The two prominent approaches that give us a peep into the sport motivation process include (a) Incentive Motivation Approach, and (b) Achievement Motivation Approach. In order to effectively tackle the question of the intensity of athlete's behaviours (i.e. maximizing participants' effort) is (1) to determine why an athlete participates in sport; and (2) what he intends "to be" (i.e. achieve) through it.

Following a model of human incentive motivation systems in every day general situations by Birch & Veroff (1969), Alderman (1970) and Wood (1976) proclaimed that the incentive value of various goals that individuals perceived as valuable partially determines their motivation to participate in competitive sport. This they called Incentive Motivation in Sport (i.e. the athlete's major reasons for participating in particular sport). Alderman & Wood (1976) initially found seven major systems - sensation, curiosity, achievement, aggression, affiliation, power and independence - governing persistent kind of goal-directed behaviours of humans in sport. Later, Alderman's study (1978), however, showed that, in value of strength, *Affiliation, Excellence, Stress, Success, Aggression, Power,* and *Independence,* formed an orderly sequence which was consistent when his inventory was employed on several thousand athletes. Each system of incentive motivation, according to Wood (1980, 1982) has its focus on an important key concept as explained below:

Excellence: "Opportunities for athletes to do something extremely well or to be very good at something that is, to successfully compete against a standard of excellence".

Key Words: Being Very good at Something.

Power: "Opportunities for athletes to influence, change and control the opinion and attitudes of other people (primarily other athletes and coaches) have towards them".

Key Words: Influence and control Opinions.

Sensation: "Opportunities for athletes to have exciting, interesting and sensory experiences primarily in terms of novelty, uncertainty and complexity".

Key Words: Excitement of Sport.

Independence: "Opportunities for athletes to do things on their own without the advice and criticism of any other person (primarily athletes and coaches).

Key Words: Doing Things alone.

Success: "Opportunities for athletes to receive prestige, recognitions, status and social approval for their achievement".

Key Words: Recognition and Prestige.

Aggression: "Opportunities for athletes to physically dominate and intimidate other athletes and to psychologically humiliate and intimidate other athletes".

Key Words: Domination and Intimidation.

Affiliation: "Opportunities for athletes to attain, maintain, and consolidate warm interpersonal relationships (primarily with other athletes and coaches)".

Key Words: Close Interpersonal Relationships.

A few cross-cultural studies on incentive motivation of athletes have shown only four incentive systems – excellence, affiliation, success, and stress-seeking – as much more prominent and strong reasons for athletes to participate in competitive sport (Wood, 1980; Kamlesh 1993, 1984); Cratty, 1989, and Patial, 1991). However, Cratty (1989) contended that tests of motives for why people enter and persist at various sports are specific to (1) the age group studied; (2) the culture in which the data have been obtained; and most important (3) the sporting context in which research has been conducted.

After having reviewed studies on motivation conducted over several decades, Singer (1984) concluded that those who have a high need to achieve:

- "demonstrate an extremely high persistence at activities;
- exhibit exceptional quality in performance;
- complete activities at a high rate;
- are task rather than person oriented;
- take reasonable risks and look forward to challenges;
- like to take responsibility for their own action; and
- like to have knowledge of the results of the activity in which they are involved".

Research shows that highly related to sport motivation are such concepts as (1) goal-setting, (2) feeling of self-efficacy or competence, (3) flow - a state of extremely positive psychological wellbeing, (4) extrinsic awards and rewards, and (5) attributions of causes for relative success or failure in athletic competitions (Cratty, 1989). Summarily, high and low performers in sport are characterized by high and low motivational profiles. Male and female athletes vary little in motivational level though both participate in sport different reasons. Superior athletes *inter alia* possess an exceptionally strong need (drive) to achieve as compared to low calibre athletes.

CONDITIONS AND FACTORS FOR SPORT MOTIVATION

In sport, high motivation is widely accepted as an essential prerequisite in getting athletes to fulfill their potential. The quality, volume and strength of sport motivation are significantly affected by several factors and conditions with which physical educators and sports coaches ought to be familiar in order to enhance the motivational drive in subjects under their charge and stamp out negative influences.

Genetic Makeup

Human beings and animals behave in typical ways because they both have inherited the physical structure (shape, form) and mental equipment (intelligence, intellect) perfectly aligned to the kind of activities they are genetically programmed to perform. It is impossible to add to or subtract from an individual's genetic makeup (inheritance) or animal species though several possibilities are now being spelled out in genetic research. A healthy body and a powerful mind (strong guts and nerves of steel) that matter so much in superior athletic performance are inherited. That is why competitive sport is not every one's cup of tea; you need special muscle and special mind to be a champion. It is rightly said if one wished to be an Olympic athlete, they should choose their parents carefully, meaning that champions are born, not made. Without genetic endowment it is impossible to grow into a champion. Intrinsic motivation, which is generally a potential cause of superior performance and high achievement, is an inherited quality. Several physical, mental and emotional traits that feed the flame of sport motivation have genetic-orientation; for example, being robust in body and mind, dominant, assertive, aggressive and over-powering.

Environment

Except heredity, everything else surrounding us is environment - objects, things, animals and human beings. All of them, in their own characteristic ways, stimulate action in man and facilitate his genetic potential to grow, develop and prosper to its fullness. People realize their potential and attempt self-actualization only in the environment. While heredity is fixed, uncompromising and unalterable; environment is flexible, compensating and modifiable. Heredity is not man's making, though environment is. All external motivation (reinforcement) - money, awards, rewards, concrete incentives, etc. - is traced to the environment. A captivating environment acts as a very powerful force in motivating people to take to sport, making it possible to create what is called sport culture in a society. All nations that have excelled in sport in recent times have done so on the strength of improved environment, and not by changing people's genetic potential, which is impossible. Not all superior athletes are blessed with superior genetics; many among them are product of the environment they were born and brought up in. Of all external reinforcers, only the human beings - parents, teachers, trainers, coaches, spectators, sports fans, significant others - and their attitudes wield the magic wand to generate, guide and direct a person's energy ingeniously into channels that lead to excellence and high achievement in sport. All effort should be made to make the sport-environment athlete and performance friendly.

Facilities

Facilities refer to playfields, athletic tracks, playing surfaces, running courses, gymnasiums, swimming pools, equipment, sports gears, sports wears, etc. They influence both man and his motivations significantly. They attract people to engage in some form of physical activity, recreational and competitive sport offering such incentives as good health, fitness, pastime, exercise, performance, and excellence. Today, for almost all sports, facilities and equipment have become anchors of success. Synthetic surfaces for track & field athletics, hockey, tennis and badminton have become an essentiality. Archery, shooting, some track & field events carry no attraction if the latest sophisticated equipment is not placed at the disposal of the performing athletes, especially young sportspersons. These external motivators need to be provided in abundance during practice and during competition so as to keep sportspersons of all levels well-motivated. Several problems occur when standards are not maintained in constructing and providing facilities; for instance, dropouts, failure, low performance and increased incidence of injury.

Motivational Techniques

Several motivational techniques and strategies are used by experts - athletic coaches, sports academics, physical educators and others - to keep sportspersons motivated. Some of these techniques are universal, while others are event- and/or athlete-specific. While using them consideration shown to sportsperson's status, calibre, education, experience, and level of competition and situation will yield better results.

Goal-setting

- Encourage athletes to set a few ambitious but achievable long-term goals; perhaps to represent their country in a major championship in three or four years. Through empowering athletes to set their own goals, they are more likely to accept the challenges that lie ahead and pursue the goals with enthusiasm.
- To keep athletes on track with their long-term goals, they should also set appropriate medium-term goals. Setting too high goals often proves counter-productive. Elite athletes often set personal goals that are based on both self-determined and extrinsic motives. They have high belief in their ability to succeed.
- By far the most important goals in practical terms are those for the short-term, as it is these that keep athletes focused on the checkmarks which are seminal to achieving superior performance. Therefore, short-term goals should be

predominantly process-oriented such as daily physiotherapy sessions, remedial exercises in an oxygen chamber, non weight-bearing aerobic activities, monitoring of nutritional intake and so on, a short time before a big event.

- Goals need to be monitored and revised on a regular basis. One of the biggest mistakes that coaches make in setting goals is that they are often too rigid in their approach. The goal-setting process works best when there is some flexibility and the individual athlete or team take ownership of each goal. Thus, coaches and managers are better off exercising some democracy when setting goals, particularly if working with more experienced athletes.

Using Intrinsic-Extrinsic Motivation

Though the simultaneous presence of high extrinsic and high intrinsic motivation is likely to yield the most positive benefits for adult athletes, it is critical that extrinsic motives are nurtured on a firm foundation of high intrinsic motivation. Without high intrinsic motivation, athletes are likely to drop out when they encounter problems such as injury, non-selection or demotion. On the other hand, the key aspect in using extrinsic rewards effectively is that they reinforce an athlete's sense of competence and self-worth. Thus, a reward should be informational in nature rather than controlling. If a reward comes to be controlling, it can significantly undermine intrinsic motivation. For a reward to be informational, it is advisable that it has relatively little monetary worth (i.e. it is a token reward), such as a 'woman of the match' or 'athlete of the tour' title. Also, the reward should be presented to an athlete in front of all potential recipients with some emphasis placed on the prestige associated with it. Other popular ways of using token rewards include inscribing athletes' names on annual honours boards for their contributions, or awarding a special item of clothing.

Motivational Music

The value of music as an ergogenic aid is well-understood by athletes and coaches. It is a particularly good way to motivate athletes in training and prior to competition provided they perceive the music to be inspirational. Many top athletes and coaches use music to punctuate all of the indoor training sessions that they lead. Specifically, during circuit training or rowing ergometer intervals the use of loud/fast music, and during recovery periods playing soft/slow music has proved to be a great motivating device. Therefore, regulating work and recovery times by music has proved as an excellent technique of keeping athletes' motivational level constantly high. Several research studies corroborate the fact that this approach increases work output, reduces perceived exertion and improves in-task effect – the pleasure experienced during the activity.

Positive Self-talk

Positive self-talk is a technique which is now being increasingly used to enhance motivation across a wide range of achievement domains. It makes use of an athlete's powerful inner voice to reinforce their self-esteem or important aspects of their performance. With appropriate repetition, self-talk can positively alter an athlete's belief system and keep him moving despite stumbling blocks.

A skillful coach impresses upon his athletes to use three types of self-talk. The first type is known as *task-relevant self-talk,* which serves to focus an athlete's attention on the task at hand. The athlete may use a *mantra* 'pillar of power' to reinforce his strong posture. The second type is known as *mood-related self-talk,* which impacts on how athletes feel. This is the way by which an athlete can handle the 'butterflies in tummy situation' just before competition. The third type is known as a *positive self-affirmation statement* and the most famous exponent of these was the legendary boxer Mohammed Ali who repeated the claim, 'I am the greatest' so many times that even his opponents believed it.

SELECTED REFERENCES

Alderfer, C. *Existence, relatedness, & growth,* New York: Free Press, 1972

Alderman, R. B. Strategies for motivating young athletes, In W. Straub (Ed.) *Sport Psychology: An Analysis of Athletic Behaviour.* New York: Movement Publications, 1978

Alderman, R., B. *Psychological Behaviour in Sport.* Philadelphia; W.B. Saunders, 1974

Bandura, Albert *Social Foundation of Thought and Action: A Social Cognitive Theory,* Englewood Cliffs; NJ, Prentice Hall, 1986

Bandura, A. Self-efficacy: Toward a unifying theory of behaviour change. *Psychological Review*: 84, 191-215, 1977

Buskist, William & Gerbing, David D. *Psychology: Boundaries and Frontiers.* Glenview III; Scott/Foreman/Little Brown Higher Education, 1990.

Cratty, Bryant J. *Psychology in Contemporary Sport.* (Third Edition), Englewood Cliffs, New York: Prentice-Hall, 1989

Crooks, Robert L. & Stein, Jean *Psychology: Science, Behaviour and Life.* New York: Holt, Rinehart & Winston, Inc., 1988

Csikszentmihalyi, M. *Flow: The Psychology of Optimal Experience,* New York: Harper and Row, 1990

Csikszentmihalyi, M. *Beyond Boredom and Anxiety,* San Francisco, CA: Josey-Bass, 1975

Daniels, M. (2001). *Maslows's concept of self-actualization.* Retrieved February 2004, from http://www.mdani.demon.co.uk/archive/MDMaslow.htm

Freud, Sigmund *Beyond the pleasure principle.* New York: W. W. Norton & Company, 1990

Hall, C.S. & Lindsey, G. *Theories of Personality* (Second Edition), New York: John Wiley & Sons., 1970

Harter, S. (1980) The development of competence motivation in the mastery of cognitive and physical skills: Is there still a place of joy? In C.G. Roberts & D.M. Landers (Eds.) *Psychology of Motor Behaviour and Sport,* (P 3-29) Champaign, Ill: Human Kinetics., 1980

Heider, F. *The psychology of interpersonal relations.* New York: John Wiley & Sons., 1958

Hull, C.L. *Principles of Behaviour.* New York: Appleton Century-crafts., 1943.

James, William *The Principles of Psychology* (Vol. I), New York: Henry Holt & Co., 1890

Kamlesh, M.L. Indian athletes: A diagnosis of their incentive motivation. *Proceedings of the World Congress of Sport Psychology,* Singapore: 35-37, 1989

Kamlesh, M.L. Diagnosing incentive motivation in sport: A replicative study. Paper presented at the *8th World Congress of Sport Psychology,* Lisbon, 1993

Leonard, N., Beauvais, L., & Scholl, R. *A self-concept-based model on work motivation.* (1995). Paper presented at the Annual Meeting of the Academy of Management, August. Retrieved: December 1999, from http://www.cba.uri.edu/Scholl/Papers/Self_Concept_Motivation.HTM

Maslow, A. H. A Theory of Human Motivation, *Psychological Review* 50, 370-96., 1943

Maslow, A.H. *Motivation and personality,* New York: Harper., 1943

Maslow, A. *Motivation and personality (2nd Ed.),* New York: Harper & Row.,1970

McClelland, D.C *Human Motivation*, Glenview, Ill: Scott Foreman, 1985

McClelland, D.C. et al. *The Achievement Motive* (2nd Ed.) New York: Irvington, 1976.

McDougall, William *An introduction to social psychology*. Boston: Luce., 1926

Munn, Norman, L., Fernald, L., & Fernald, Peter, S. *Introduction to Psychology* (3rd Ed.), New Delhi: Oxford & IBM Publishing Co., 1972

Murray, Henry A. *Explorations in Personality*. New York: Harper & Row, 1938, 1943.

Nohria, N., Lawrence, P., & Wilson, E. *Driven How Human Nature Shapes our Choices*, San Francisco: Jossey-Bass, 2001

Patial, Om Kumari Study of selected psychological variables of female Indian hockey players. *Unpublished Doctoral Thesis.* Gwalior; Jiwaji University, 199

Proctor, C. Teacher expectations: A model for school improvement. *The Elementary School Journal*, 469-481., 1984, March

Roberts, Glyn Motivation in sport: Understanding and enhancing the motivation and achievement if children. In Robert N. Singer, Murphy M., & L. Keith Tennant (Eds.) *Handbook of Research on Sport Psychology*. New York: McMillan., 1993

Singer, Robert N. *Sustaining Motivation in Sport,* Tallahassee, Florida; Sport Consultants International, 1984

Stipek, D. *Motivation to learn: From theory to practice*. Englewood Cliffs, NJ: Prentice Hall, 1988

Solomon, Richard L. The opponent-process theory of motivation. *American Psychologist*, 35: 691-712, 1980

Veroff, J. Social comparison and the development of achievement. In C.P. Smith (Ed.), *Achievement Related Motives in Children*, New York: Russell Sage Foundation, 1969

Weiner, B. *Achievement motivation and attribution theory,* Morristown, NJ: General Learning Press, 1974

White, R.W. Motivation reconsidered: the concept of competence. *Psychological Review*, 66: 297-333, 1959

Wood, Nancy L. Incentive motivation in sport: A theoretical analysis and the development of a measuring instrument. *Unpublished Doctoral Dissertation*, The University of Alberta, Edmunton, Alberta, 1980

Wood, Nancy L. Improving the motivation of your athletes. *Coaching Science Update*. Rusdon: Victoria College of Physical Education, Australia, 1982.

Woodworth, R.S. *Dynamic Psychology*. New York, Columbia University Press, 1958.

Institute for Management Excellence. (2001). The nine basic human needs. *On line Newsletter*. Retrieved February 2004, from http: / / www.itstime.com / print / jun97p.htm

Emotion is love and hate, anger and fear, pride and jealousy. It's things we like to do (such as be in love). Yet it's also things we don't like to do - such as be angry or afraid.

- Unknown

CHAPTER - 12

EMOTION

Emotions are *our* feelings. Literally, we feel them in our bodies as tingles, hot spots and muscular tension. Shared with several species of animals, emotions are biologically based adaptations that assist us in responding to particular external stimuli. We win a soccer match, we jump with joy; we lose a dear one, we feel sad; we see a beggar, we sympathize with her; a good joke is told, we laugh, and so on. Almost every situation evokes some feeling, and as the situation becomes intense, it is expressed as emotion. No aspect of our mental life is more important to the quality and meaning of our existence than emotions, because emotions actually express our true feelings. They are what make life worth living, or sometimes ending. If there were no emotions, man would be deterred in expressing what life truly means. When passing through intense feelings of joy, happiness, hate, love, sadness, pity, fear, anger or disgust we consciously or unconsciously reveal what goes at the back of our mind as a reaction to the situation. During an emotional upsurge - pleasant or painful - we are neither normal nor natural in thought and action, often doing or saying things which sanity may not approve of. This is what makes emotions important to us all.

MEANING AND DEFINITION OF EMOTION

The English word 'emotion' is derived from the French word *émouvoir*. This is based on the Latin *emovere*, where *e-* (variant of *ex-*) means 'out' and *movere* means 'move'. The term "motivation" is also derived from *movere*. In this sense, an emotion may be *a mental and physiological state associated with a wide variety of feelings, thoughts,* and *behaviours* more conspicuously physiological actions-reactions. It is often said to be an excitational approach to coping with a powerful turbulent situation. Advanced Learner's English Dictionary defines emotion as 'a feeling (as opposed to thoughts), such as happiness, love, fear, anger, which can be caused by the situation that you are in or the people you are with.' A few definitions of emotions from prominent psychologists are as under:

> Emotions are actually disturbed states or processes which originate in psychological situations and which are revealed by marked bodily changes in the glands and smooth muscles.
>
> **- Young**
>
> Emotions are innate responses (hereditary reaction patterns) essentially chaotic in nature, involving the whole body in their expression but particularly the glandular and visceral systems and their nervous connections and having intimate relationship with the preservation of the individual and the species.
>
> **- Peter Sandiford**
>
> Emotions, in fact, are the psycho-physiological reactions through which instinctive organismic energy finds expression.
>
> **- William McDougall**
>
> (Emotion is) .... a reaction to a stimulus event (either actual or imagined). It involves changes in the viscera and musculature of the person, is experienced subjectively in characteristic ways, is expressed through such means as facial changes and action tendencies, and may mediate and energize subsequent behaviors.
>
> **- Deci**

An emotion, precisely, is defined as a state of arousal and an attempt to label it. Our *level of arousal* (intensity of psycho-physiological reactivity) directly affects how we behave. The arousal influences the efficiency of our behaviour with moderate levels leading to most efficient behaviour. Both low and high levels of arousal cause inefficient behaviour. The amorous kiss, the face turning red as beads of sweat form on the forehead, and the clenched fist (in a fight reaction) all share at least one thing in common: each is an outward sign of what is sometimes called inner turmoil or emotion. While motivation is easy to define with some precision, emotion is a much more difficult term to narrow down. We all know what it is like to *feel* emotion and express it outwardly.

Emotions sometimes create states within us that we would do anything to maintain. Other times they create negative feelings that fully occupy us until we can eliminate them. They are conscious experiences involving participative (private) feelings, physiological arousal, expressive reactions, and observable activities related to the experiences.

General Characteristics of Emotions

Based on various definitions, general characteristics of emotions may be briefly enumerated as given below:

- As vehicle of instincts (the general inherited tendencies and driving forces of behaviour), ***emotions are inborn and universal.*** Men, women, infants, children, adolescents, adults, and old people - all experience them inevitably in one or the other situation. The expression of emotion in animals is limited; in man it is varied and wide.
- Emotions have a ***wide range***. Depending upon the manner with which an external stimulus impacts the organism, the feelings generated range from mild to very intense. For example, the feelings of anger stretch between two extreme ends of simple resentment and rage, that of fear range from just apprehension to that of horror or terror, and of happiness from elation to ecstatic joy, and so on.
- Emotions are easily aroused but require varied stimuli for arousal. For example, an infant may be afraid of falling, and an adult, losing his job. Fear is normally aroused in young infants by sudden loud noise and by insecure body positions. Non-fulfillment of a desire may anger an adult, but a child may fall into a tantrum. Practically any situation can cause fear or anger and to any extent of reaction. The reaction to a fear or anger situation may depend upon intensity and seriousness of the situation.
- In emotional upsurge the urge for movement (motivation) or reactivity is instantaneous, and its impact felt in our body and mind both. Our muscles and mind get tense or relax; our blood vessels dilate or contract. Uncontrollable excitation of the vascular-muscular apparatus occurs setting the entire physiology on fire. Arousal typically happens when the body releases chemicals into the brain that act to stimulate emotions, reduce cortical functioning and subdue conscious control, and create physical agitation and 'readiness for action'. Emotional feeling of being comfortable or uncomfortable leads to coping activities. The response may be instantaneous (and often subconscious) and also more thoughtful handling of the aftermath of the

situation. The basic purpose in both cases is to regain homeostasis.

- Depending on the intensity of stimulus, emotions are characterized by a terrible arousal state in which our bodies experience heightened physiological activity and extremes of emotion. This can be both powerful and dangerous, both for ourselves and for others. Physiological changes, signs and symptoms that accompany emotional arousal, typically include dilation of eyes, redness or blush on the face, tenseness in muscles, tottering of legs in fear, clenching of fists etc. The endocrinal activity increases body-chemistry which is already on fire. For example, adrenalin secreted by adrenal glands during anger, produces agitational behaviour. Circulatory and respiratory mechanisms step their activity, involuntary movements either stop or get accelerated showing marked variations in muscular strength. The action-potential of the muscles either gets frozen or explodes into uncontrollable violent movements, largely involuntary.
- Emotions are typically conscious phenomena, yet they typically involve more pervasive bodily manifestations than other conscious states. We know that certain situations anger us or make us helpless, morose, disappointed, withdrawn, or over-brim with energy and we are conscious what happens to us during these states.
- Emotions are reputed to be antagonists of rationality, i.e. emotion and rational thinking are, to a certain extent, mutually exclusive. When we get emotional about something, our ability to make rational decisions has a strong tendency to fail. Consider the things we say. A person who is 'hot-headed' is considered to be rather emotional and likely to make rash decisions, whilst a person with a 'cool head' makes thoughtful, considered decisions. We talk about mental processes being 'clouded' by emotional states. Because they are visceral (i.e., we feel them physically), they cause a turbulence which tends to block out other contributors to, our decision-making processes - our rational thinking, our intuition, our common sense, our focus on the problem itself instead of the turbulence, etc.

This is perhaps what former U.S. President Franklin Roosevelt implied when he said that "we have nothing to fear but fear itself."

- Emotion is a chemical state in our brains which we experience as basic 'feelings'. Those same chemicals inhibit our higher cognitive capabilities and limiting what we call rational thought. Under the impact charged emotional state, we say and do things which sobre reflection declares to be stupid, unwise and even unethical. An angry son may abuse his mother, a disgusted player attack the umpire, and a lovelorn threaten suicide.
- Emotions and motivation come from the same root. They may not be the same but they are related to each other in three ways: (1) being product of behaviour, emotions serve as a motivator; (2) they serve as signals that tell us when to do something or refrain from doing it; and (3) emotions generally accompany our actions – reinforcing or restricting them (Buskist & Gerbing, 1990).

  [*Emotions and motivation don't always go together, however, for emotions may occur in the absence of motivation. Emotions can be produced by changes in the environment that we may have no conscious control over, such as when we learn of the death of a close friend.*]
- Recent research shows that emotions can be conditioned by classical and operant methods. For instance, using conditioning technique, adults train themselves to control their anger, shun hate, sublimate sexual energy; and children can be made overcome fear.

Value of Emotions

Emotions play an indispensable role in our life. They come straight from our heart, not head. Their value lies in determining the quality of our life. For example, if we allow anger or fear to take control of our self, we always have to sit on pins, incurring tremendous loss of vital energy, and possibility of becoming a prey to psychosomatic disorders. On the other hand, if we learn to keep cool and relaxed even under the worst of provocations, we can be confident of keeping healthy, happy and energetic through most part of our life.

Charles Darwin thought animals used facial expressions to communicate their intent - such as whether they intended to attack or approach. He suggested that human expressions might serve essentially the same purpose. So, emotions help us to communicate. They add force, depth, texture, and greater meaning to whatever we are saying. We generally wear our hearts on our sleeves as our inner emotions are displayed on our outer bodies. Emotions are generally conveyed through facial signals or body indicators. For example, our eyes behave differently under different emotional situations. In anxiety, they are damp; in fear they are wide; in anger, they are wide and staring; in sadness, eyes cast down; in happiness, they sparkle; and in surprise and desire, they wide open; and in shame, eyes and head turn down; and so on. The same way, our face, in boredom, is generally immobile, corners of mouth are turned down or lips pulled to the side, the head is propped up with hand, and eyes are looking away. Most of our emotions are conveyed with the sole purpose of signalling emotion to other people. These signals are generally very useful as they help others decide how to behave towards us. If someone is looking angry, then attacking them is probably not a good idea. If they are looking afraid then you could attack them or you could help them and thus earn their gratitude.

Emotions are 'e-motions', where *e-* (variant of *ex-*) means 'out' and *movere* means 'move'. They act to motivate us to be doing something - interacting with the environment so important to maintain and sustain life. Without emotions we would probably not do very much and hence would not survive - at least in the evolved form we are in now. Soldiers fight well when they are emotionally aroused; the poor fight for food when hunger haunts them; when afraid, people escape to safer havens, and so on. In fact, struggle for survival is motivated by emotions only. Were it not for love, animals and humans would not indulge in sex and keep up racial continuity.

The fine chords of our heart and mind are struck by emotions alone. When we think about something that contradicts our values, our emotions will tell us that it is bad. When we think about something that could hurt us, our emotions will tell us that this is not a good idea. Just by imagining what might happen, our emotions are still triggered and hence let us make better decisions. They contribute crucially to defining our ends and priorities. In an emotional state, first things happen first.

Further, emotions are the gateway to our self-knowledge. Descartes was right in his assumption that if anyone can know our emotions it is ourselves. In fact, emotions are one of our avenues to self-knowledge, since few kinds of self-knowledge could matter more than knowing one's own repertoire of emotional responses. At the same time, emotions are both the cause and the subject of many failures of self-knowledge. Their complexity entails much potential to mislead or be misled. In so far as most emotions involve belief, they inherit the susceptibility of the latter to self-deception. They push us out of comfortable complacency where we have settled into erroneous views about ourselves. "Negative" emotions force us to question our ego boundaries, our goals, our values, our self-concept, our archetypal-field elements, etc. For example, we might become angry or fearful about circumstances which are not truly dangerous to our well-being but seem to be so only because of incorrectly defined ego boundaries; i.e., we become upset about something which is "none of our business." Instead of viewing these challenges as unpleasant because they propel us out of our comforts (however stagnant they might be), we can choose to see the emotions' energy and demands as an exciting call to a life of vigour, exploration, and growth.

Emotions are a response which is characterized by the generation of energy within the body and psyche. They provide energy for us to confront challenges. The energy is given to us for the specific purpose of gearing us up for action (pleasant or unpleasant), such as fighting, or defending ourselves verbally, or interacting enthusiastically with another person, or running away, or working on a project. Some of this energy is provided physiologically through the release of adrenaline and other substances in the body. When emotionally charged, an individual becomes several times stronger than he ordinarily is. Emotional energy is far superior to any other energy in man. It is said that in 400m race a runner runs the first 100m stretch powered by his muscular energy, the next 100m by physiological energy, the third 100m by mental energy, and the last 100m by emotional energy.

CLASSIFICATION OF EMOTIONS

Over the years, psychologists have used different yardsticks to classify emotion. Not considering emotions as *distinctive discrete states,* Russell (1979) placed emotions along bi-polar dimensions of valence and arousal. Using bi-polar approach, Ekman (1972) divided emotions into basic and complex categories, where some emotions are considered foundational to the existence of others. As primary colours combined to make more varied colours, so could *primary emotions* blend together to form the full spectrum of human emotional experience; for example interpersonal anger and disgust blending to form contempt. Plutchik (1980) proposed a three-dimensional "circumplex model" which describes the relations among emotions. He posited eight primary emotion dimensions arranged as four pairs of opposites, such as love vs. hate, joy vs. sadness.

Another important approach towards distinguishing emotions concerns their occurrence in time. Some emotions occur over a period of seconds such as 'surprise', where others can last years, for example, love. The latter could be regarded as a long-term *tendency* to have an emotion regarding a certain object rather than an emotion proper (though this is disputed). A distinction is then made between emotion episodes and emotional dispositions (inherited trait like inclinations). Theorists like Scherer (2005)) placed emotions within a more general category of 'affective states', which can also include emotion-related phenomena such as pleasure and pain, motivational states (e.g. hunger or curiosity), moods, dispositions and traits. However, the most widely used criterion of classification has been difference in *purity* of feeling, i.e. an emotion may be primary or it may be secondary. This is considered to be a useful notion in understanding how we feel.

Primary Emotions

Primary emotions are those that we feel first, as a first response to a situation. Thus, if we are threatened, we may have a feeling of fear. When we hear of the death of some close to us, we may have a feeling of sadness. Such reactions are unthinking, instinctive responses. They are typically seen in animals also, which confirms our inference that they have an evolutionary basis.

Typical primary emotions are fear, anger, sadness, happiness, love, and surprise. Notably these can also be felt as secondary emotions;

for example, fear as nervousness or horror, anger as disgust or rage, sadness as disappointment or shame, happiness as contentment or optimism, love as affection or lust, and surprise as wonder. The problem sometimes with primary emotions is that they disappear as fast as they appear; for example, the mother's anxiety vanishes the moment she finds that the baby who fell off the bed is unhurt. The replacement of primary emotions by secondary emotions complicates the situation, making it difficult to understand what is really going on.

Secondary Emotions

Secondary emotions appear after primary emotions. They may be caused directly by them, for example where the fear of a threat turns to anger that fuels the body for a fight reaction. They may also come from more complex chains of thinking. Secondary emotions may be simple feelings or may be a mix as more emotions join the fray. Thus news of a wartime victory may start with feelings of joy, but then get tinged with sadness for the loss of life.

Emotion Associates

As subjective experience (or experienced from an individual viewpoint) emotion is often associated with distinct feeling states like temperament and mood, differentiated by time. In order to understand emotion, it is necessary to understand these associative terms.

Temperament

Temperament is usually considered a personality trait - something you are born with or acquire young. It seldom changes. Some people, by birth, have a sunny disposition; others are always nervous or irritable. A temperamental person changes his disposition little. Temperament thus lasts for the duration. It is a lifetime platform on which moods and emotions occur. If your temperament is negative, being happy may seem better to you, but it may yet be lower than being a naturally optimistic person almost always. Temperaments are often vague, diffused emotions, which may be contrasted with the more distinct mood and very specific emotions.

Mood

Moods are shorter-term sustained emotional states, typically lasting hours; they can last for days or longer. For example, you may wake up with a feeling of a bit down and stay that way for most of the day. We can be sent into a mood by an unexpected event, from the happiness of seeing an old friend to the anger of discovering betrayal by a partner. We may also just fall into a mood. Mood affects our judgment and changes how we process decisions. When in a happy mood, our perception of the falling rain is different from when we are in a sad mood.

Conditions like depression are not really moods; they are typically caused by a chemical imbalance in the brain. Moods can be caused by shorter-term chemical imbalances, for example brought up on by a poor diet.

Emotion

Emotions as commonly experienced and discussed are different from moods and temperament in several ways. First, emotions tend to last for much shorter periods. The delight at being given a birthday present may subside in minutes as it is replaced by disappointment about a useless gift. Emotions thus tend to replace one another and it can be difficult to be both happy and sad (although we may have a good go at it). Emotions also tend to be more extreme than moods and temperament, with higher highs and lower lows. We can become very angry very quickly, though it is difficult to stay very angry and it may subside into an irritable mood or be replaced by another completely different emotion.

Emotions tend to be very specific, triggered by noticeable events and are immediate reactions to these and which drive us to particular actions, for example running away from a snarling dog or going to chat up an attractive other person.

EMOTIONS - A BRIEF ACCOUNT

As to the number of basic emotions, there has been no agreement among theorists. For example, James (1894) talked of only four basic emotions (fear, grief, love, rage), McDougall (1926) listed seven (anger, disgust, elation, fear, subjection, tender-emotion, wonder), Watson (1930) mentioned just three (fear, love, rage), and Plutchik (1980) enumerated eight basic emotions (acceptance, anger, anticipation, disgust, joy, fear, sadness, surprise). A deeper list of emotions (categorized into a short tree structure) is provided by Parrot (2001) as given below:

List of Basic and Secondary Emotions

Primary Emotion	Secondary Emotion	Tertiary Emotions
Love	Affection	Adoration, affection, love, fondness, liking, attraction, caring, tenderness, compassion, sentimentality
	Lust	Arousal, desire, lust, passion, infatuation
	Longing	Longing
Joy	Cheerfulness	Amusement, bliss, cheerfulness, gaiety, glee, jolliness, joviality, joy, delight, enjoyment, gladness, happiness, jubilation, elation, satisfaction, ecstasy, euphoria
	Zest	Enthusiasm, zeal, zest, excitement, thrill, exhilaration
	Contentment	Contentment, pleasure
	Pride	Pride, triumph
	Optimism	Eagerness, hope, optimism
	Enthrallment	Enthrallment, rapture
	Relief	Relief
Surprise	Surprise	Amazement, surprise, astonishment
Anger	Irritation	Aggravation, irritation, agitation, annoyance, grouchiness, grumpiness
	Exasperation	Exasperation, frustration
	Rage	Anger, rage, outrage, fury, wrath, hostility, ferocity, bitterness, hate, loathing, scorn, spite, vengefulness, dislike, resentment
	Disgust	Disgust, revulsion, contempt
	Envy	Envy, jealousy
	Torment	Torment
Sadness	Suffering	Agony, suffering, hurt, anguish
	Sadness	Depression, despair, hopelessness, gloom, glumness, sadness, unhappiness, grief, sorrow, woe, misery, melancholy
	Disappointment	Dismay, disappointment, displeasure
	Shame	Guilt, shame, regret, remorse
	Neglect	Alienation, isolation, neglect, loneliness, rejection, homesickness, defeat, dejection, insecurity, embarrassment, humiliation, insult
	Sympathy	Pity, sympathy
Fear	Horror	Alarm, shock, fear, fright, horror, terror, panic, hysteria, mortification
	Nervousness	Anxiety, nervousness, tenseness, uneasiness, apprehension, worry, distress, dread

Each of these emotions can be defined primarily as a source of energy, in some of its cognitive aspects - associated thought processes - and the physiological changes it involves as well some other attributes so that it is easy to understand how they influence our life processes including health, happiness and welfare.

Anger

With its source in the instinct of *combat* or *aggressiveness*, anger reaction is caused by any situation which either interferes with the working of parental instinct, the pursuit of any instinctive goal, causes distress or poses perceived harm to our physical health or our ego boundaries (including everything which we ascribe with our human self - our family or home, our plans, our freedoms, etc). From simple resentment (very mild type of anger) or bitterness to rage, the range of anger varies a lot depending upon perception of the situation and stimulus intensity. The major purpose of anger is to give us a heightened sense of individuality and territoriality, and an increase of energy which is given to us specifically to deal with the threat.

In the socio-culturally evolved society, the combat instinct, in its pure and simple form, does not serve any biological purpose. Expression of anger may have cathartic effect on mind and personality development. The nature of human aggression has now altogether changed. When angered, an animal may straight away charge the opponent without thinking of the consequences but a human has several options up him sleeve to deal with the combat situation. Exploding population and fast depleting resources have made man's survival struggle more aggressive.

Fear

Fear has its roots in *escape* instinct. Like anger, fear is a reaction to a perceived threat. While anger is a response to damage which seems to have occurred already, but fear is a response to the *possible* damage which might occur. A sudden startling noise, danger-cry, body pain, and in general something mysterious and uncanny, can cause fear. The objective is to release energy so that we can confront the circumstance, in other words, to make attempt to seek shelter or to lie hid or to flee or escape from the situation. A threatening sight or sound usually makes the animals take to their heels simultaneously sending the warning signals to their species to escape. The roar of a lion puts all animals on fear alarm and creates a stampede amongst them. It is, in fact, the danger cry that does the trick in arousing fear response. The energy which is associated with fear stimulates our thinking processes (in contrast with anger's stimulation of the body), so that we can think more clearly to analyze the threat and devise a plan. (In practice, however, fear tends to "paralyze" us; the energy is present, but we do not use it, and so this lingering energy becomes an impediment to action and thought.) With human beings, fear takes various forms. A child may be afraid of falling and an adult losing a job: the child may cry only and the adult may look for another job to escape pains and pangs of the bad situation.

Love

Love takes its strength from *mating* instinct and is an outflow whose nature is to seek a productive connection to something. It is aroused by the presence of a suitable member of the opposite sex or perception of its sexual organs. In animals, the sex urge is seasonal having a fixed pattern and it leads to reproduction. In man, love takes varied forms. It may be aroused even by desire for sex and for display or perception of secondary sex characteristics of the opposite sex - a charming face, shapely breasts, or buttocks, an ornate musculature etc. In humans, emotion of love is perennial, and "conditional"; it is directed only toward particular people and things. Sigmund Freud considered sex instinct (libido) as the centre of gravity of all other instincts and the prime-mover of animal behaviour. Sex-gratification takes variety of forms in man and it has far reaching psycho-social implications.

Feeling of Loneliness

Loneliness has its genesis in the instinct of *gregariousness* – the tendency to stay together. This is not an emotion, but a default, characterized by the discomfort caused by the festering energy which we are not using in an effort to create social contacts. It is stimulated by the sight of the other members of the species. Normally specific cries or specific odours are sufficient to evoke this reaction. "United we survive and stand, divided we fall and die" is the essence of gregariousness. Staying together promotes and preserves common interests and objectives of life. Generally, herbivores are more gregarious than carnivores. To counter the feeling of loneliness, man has developed civilization.

Tender Emotion

Parental instinct gives rise to tender emotion, generally called affection. McDougall calls this instinct as 'Nature's brightest and most beautiful invention and as the mother of both intellect and morality". The most primitive key to this instinct is the sight, sound or smell of the animals' young ones. Especially their cry of distress immediately arouses this emotion in parents. As animals grow up, the parental instinct pales into insignificance but in human beings this continues to nurture filial love and strengthen family bonds.

Surprise (Wonder)

Curiosity is at the back of wonder. When an object or situation resembles one that would invoke activity of another instinct but is not apprehended sufficiently clear to do so, the instinct of curiosity starts operating in the form of surprise or wonder. The objective is to seek fuller understanding and complete knowledge of the object in view. While curiously exploring things, animals could get into trouble (curiosity killed the cat), but humans could discover and invent things that have changed man's life and face of the earth too. Curiosity is at its peak in infancy and childhood.

Default of Emotion

Psychologists do not categorize the following feelings as emotion proper but as default of emotion.

- *Anxiety:* Anxiety is an unrealistic fear. It is both a personality trait and a situational feeling. To distinguish it from fear we may say a tiger creates fear, a cat anxiety; fear is like a passing cloud, anxiety a lingering cloud. If we ignore the problem which is evoking fear, the energy remains as a vague anxiety. To resolve the anxiety, we have to backtrack through it to find the original fear and then confront the issue which frightens us.
- *Depression*: It is a default because of its failure to obey our impulses toward life and action. Emotions are characterized by a release of energy, and a drive toward action; depression is characterized by diminished energy and drive, because most of the original energy has already dissipated. As a feeling that badly impinges upon our energy rather than the one that energizer, depression is related to our thoughts.

In depression a person is severally handicapped in doing anything energetic.

- *Envy*: Envy is characterized by the festering energy which we are not using in an effort to acquire that which we envy, and it is characterized also by thoughts of hatred toward the owner of the envied object (as though his or her ownership is a threat to our ability to own something similar). A studious student may feel envy when he finds a sporty being honoured by the school.
- *Frustration:* This can be a blend of anger and sadness. Repeated failure to get a better grade at the exam, improve performance in high jump despite hard training, or get an urgently needed job, often leads to frustration. We are angry at the blockage in our movement, and sad that we have not yet achieved our goal.
- *Grief*: Grief is characterized by a gearing-down of a portion of the body's energy system; this gearing-down is a necessary action because the person or activity which was receiving the flow of energy and love is no longer there. The channels are being shut down; the energy which was to be directed is being dissipated. Loss of some one or some thing dear to us causes grief, which sometimes lingers longer than expected.
- *Guilt*: A feeling of guilt more often than not is characterized by the discomfort caused by the festering energy which we are not using in an effort to attain our goals. Aside from the energy aspect of guilt, it is a useful and vital alarm mechanism that informs us that we have violated our values – no matter what those values are. An adolescent's indulging in masturbation produces in him a feeling of guilt despite physical pleasure.
- *Happiness*: Dynamically, this is the opposite of grief instead of closing ourselves down, we are opening ourselves so that more energy can flow through us, for a fuller connection to the life around us. We feel happy when we achieve an objective or get something we desired for long. Happiness energizing mechanism. Happy, we feel up and doing.
- *Jealousy*: Jealousy is directed primarily toward a person

who owns a coveted object; envy is directed more toward the object itself, but the dynamic is the similar. In both cases, there is a festering energy because we are dwelling on our desire instead of using the energy in an effort to obtain the object which we desire. Overpowered by envy, a person tries to do better; when jealous, he tries to pull down other's leg and harm him.

- *Sadness*: Sadness is similar to grief; the energy festers because we have lost (or we *want*) a particular person, object, or activity with which to interact energetically. Sadness seems to be less severe in impact than grief.
- *Shame*: Shame is characterized by the discomfort and is caused by the festering energy which we are not using in an effort to attain our goals. We have stifled that energy because we have decided that we are unworthy of in attaining those goals. Children cry 'shame, shame' when they see some one in a semi-naked or nude position.
- *Shyness*: This is caused by the festering energy which is intended to be used for the acts of social contact. When we have no confidence, we often feel shy of expressing ourselves on a stage, in a group of people or in the company of peers thinking that others might laugh at us.
- *Worry*: Worry is characterized by the festering energy which was intended to be used for action to resolve the situation about which we are worrying. Career-conscious parents often worry about their children not studying well and getting no better grade at the examination.
- *Positive Self-feeling*: Backed up by the instinctive tendency of self-assertion, this is aroused by the presence of inferior fellow-creatures. Its result is show of strength. A person superior in size, strength, status or power, asserts himself on those inferior in these respects. Apart from this, primary factors of self-assertion are common to all animals. Human beings assert themselves on others in variety of ways, for example, by the power of their superior intellect, physical skill and strength, aesthetic qualities, athletic prowess and performance, money, position, wealth etc.
- *Negative Self-feeling:* It is a complimentary feeling evoked by the presence of a superior member of the species, and is

accompanied by submission and to crouch and cringe i.e. generally to adopt a posture of deference. Youngsters, either out of sheer respect or because of their inferior status, often submit to the will of the elders or stronger ones. When inferior feelings exist longer than usual, a person is likely to grow extremely meek and humble, often losing self-esteem. Persistent strong negative feelings lead to developing a crippled personality and ending up in suicide attempts.

THEORIES OF EMOTION

The questions why and how emotions are produced, what functions they serve and how they find expression in animals and humans is answered by several theories (approaches or perspectives) that have emerged over the last hundred years or so. Psychology and more recently evolutionary biology have offered a number of theories of emotions, stressing their function in the conduct of life. Philosophers have been especially partial to cognitivist theories, emphasizing analogies either with propositional judgments or with perception. But different theories implicitly posit different ontologies of emotion, and there has been some dispute about what emotions really are, and indeed whether they are any kind of thing at all.

Emotion theories are divided into 'cognitive' (psychological) and 'non-cognitive' (evolutionary) or instinctual theories.

Non-Cognitive or Somatic Approaches

Somatic theories of emotion claim that bodily responses rather than judgments are essential to emotions. The two most important pioneer somatic theories include James-Lange theory and Cannon-Bard theory.

James-Lange Theory

The earliest attempts to create a theory of emotions were actually two different attempts by two individuals in two different countries two years apart - neither apparently aware of the work of the other. James (1884) argued that emotional experience is largely due to the experience of bodily change. The Danish psychologist Carl Lange also proposed a similar theory at around the same time. The collective works were later combined into the *James-Lange Theory*. According to the theorists, we have experiences, and as a result, our autonomic nervous system creates physiological events such as muscular tension, heart rate increases, perspiration, dryness of the mouth, etc. This theory proposes that emotions happen *as a result* of these, rather than being the cause of them. Precisely, an emotional experience is composed of four events: (1) you notice a situation - there's a man with a gun, (2) you react to your observation - you put your hands in the air, (3) you notice your reaction - my hands are in the air, and that leads to (4) an emotion summarizing what you noticed, your response - I must be scared. The sequence thus is as follows:

Event ==> arousal ==> interpretation ==> emotion

For example: I see a bear. My muscles tense, my heart races. I feel afraid. The bodily sensation prepares us for action, as in the *fight-or-flight* reaction. James elucidated his concept as:

> My theory ... is that the bodily changes follow directly the perception of the exciting fact, and that our feeling of the same changes as they occur is the emotion. Common sense says we lose our fortune, are sorry and weep; we meet a bear, are frightened and run; we are insulted by a rival, are angry and strike. The hypothesis here to be defended says that this order of sequence is incorrect ... and that the more rational statement is that we feel sorry because we cry, angry because we strike, afraid because we tremble ... Without the bodily states following on the perception, the latter would be purely cognitive in form, pale, colorless, destitute of emotional warmth. We might then see the bear, and judge it best to run, receive the insult and deem it right to strike, but we should not actually feel afraid or angry.

The James-Lange theory is supported by experiments in which by manipulating the bodily state, a desired emotion is induced. Such experiments also have therapeutic implications (e.g. in laughter therapy, dance therapy). The theory is often misunderstood because it seems counter-intuitive. Most people believe that emotions give rise to emotion-specific actions: i.e. "I'm crying because I'm sad," or "I ran away because I was scared." The James-Lange theory, conversely, asserts that *first* we react to a situation (running away and crying happen before the emotion), and *then* we interpret our actions into an emotional response. In this way, emotions serve to explain and organize our own actions to us.

In the 1920s psychologists Walter Cannon and Philip Bard challenged this theory by arguing that physiological changes are caused by emotions. The viscera are largely unresponsive and react relatively slowly (i.e. - we 'feel' the emotion before the physiological changes have occurred.)

Cannon-Bard theory

Developed by physiologists Walter Cannon (1927) and Philip Bard (1934), this psychological theory suggests that people feel emotions first and then act upon them. These actions include changes in muscular tension, perspiration, etc. The basic argument of this theory against the James-Lange theory of Emotion is that emotion is the result of one's perception of their reaction, or "bodily change." The premise here is that one reacts to a specific stimulus and experiences the corresponding emotion simultaneously. Therefore, if one is afraid of heights and is travelling to the top of a skyscraper, they are likely to experience the emotion of fear. Subsequently, the perception of this emotion (fear) influences the person's reaction to the stimulus (heights). Cannon and Bard posited that one is able to react to a stimulus only after experiencing the related emotion. The sequence thus is as follows:

Event ==> *Simultaneous* arousal and emotion

For example: (1) I see a bear. I feel afraid. I tense in readiness to run away. (2) I see a man outside my window. I am afraid. I begin to perspire.

The Cannon-Bard theory assumes that (1) we detect what will be an emotion-arousing event through any of our senses - whether vision, or touch, etc. (2) That detection is relayed to the thalamus - viewed at the time as the "seat" of emotions - where the signal is split. (3) One signal is sent to the cortex. (4) Another signal causes whatever is the appropriate bodily reaction. (5) The sensors within the body detect the body's reaction and relay information regarding that reaction to the cortex where (6) the newly arriving information combines with the original signal (#3 above) to yield the appropriate emotional experience. The theory sparked much controversy in cognitive circles due to its suggestion that there is no mechanism to emotion, and many theorists attempted to provide explanations of emotion that suggested a mechanism.

These earliest theories were sophisticated for their time, but gave only a hint of work which leads to our modern theories of emotion.

Two-Factor Theory

When trying to understand what kind of person we are, we first watch what we do and feel and then deduce our nature from this. This means that the first step is to experience physiological arousal. We then try to find a label to explain our feelings, usually by looking at what we are doing and what else is happening at the time of the arousal. Thus we do not just feel angry, happy or whatever: we experience feeling and then decide what they mean. The sequence thus is as follows:

Event ==> arousal ==> reasoning ==> emotion

This is notable as it places emotion as a cognitive act (albeit subconscious) rather than a deeper state (this is the place of arousal). For example, when we are feeling unwell, we often will deduce the illness from the symptoms. From then on, hypochondria can take hold and further symptoms psychosomatically appear to confirm our conclusions.

Schachter & Singer (1962) gave some people a mild stimulant and others a placebo (on a pretence of testing vitamins). They then gave them a questionnaire containing rather personal questions. A stooge in the room got angry at the questionnaire and the people who had been given the stimulant (and who hence felt aroused) got even angrier (the people with the placebo were not that angry).

Activation Theory

This first modern Theory of Emotion, which combines elements of somatic and cognitive approaches on emotion, stresses that *arousal* underlies emotion; more arousal means more emotion, but that rather simple idea is based on a variety of observations - some confirmed, some now disputed. When we are emotionally aroused, our EEG brain waves show a certain loss of regularity. This irregular EEG pattern of arousal can be produced by stimulating or removing the portions of our central and autonomic nervous systems that help arouse or calm us.

Several research studies found that the limbic system and hypothalamus are involved in such diverse emotions as aggression and fear. Advocates of Activation Theory suggest that emotions are expressed in three ways. First, they are expressed through cortical activity such as thought, worry, or anxiety. Second, they are expressed through body activities such as sweating or crying - actions controlled by the autonomic nervous system. Finally, emotions are also expressed through facial expressions and muscle tension.

Thus, one mode of expressing emotion involves cortical arousal, a second involves brain-stem arousal, and a third involves body motor arousal. The tie between emotion and physiology seems fairly tight. This theory places heavy emphasis on physiological activities. However, it does not spend much time discussing the "thinking" or "feeling" parts of emotion. That is corrected in a later theory proposed in the 70's - Attribution Theory.

Attribution

In his Attribution Theory, Stanley Schachter asserts that our emotions result from the joint impact of our level of arousal and the interpretation we make of an existing situation. More recently, others have added the idea that to experience an emotion, we must also make a causal link between the arousal and the label we give it.

Our body's physiological reaction to arousal - be it loving or lying, fearing or fighting - is essentially the same. We name our *response* (that is, our emotion) by means of information we pick up from our environment. Thus, a given level of arousal may be labelled anger or love or any of the other emotions, based on what we think caused the arousal in the first place. For instance, what would you predict would happen if you were physiologically aroused but could not explain why? If this theory is correct, you should look for cues from your environment. Thus, as we change the environment (the cues), we ought to be able to change the "emotion" you will report you are experiencing.

Opponent-Process

A third attempt to develop a theoretical explanation for emotions tackled the issue by returning to one of the most basic processes of motivation - homeostasis. Solomon & Corbit (1974) analyzed the emotions of skydivers. Beginners experienced extreme fear in their initial jump, which turned into great relief when they landed. With repeated jumps, the fear of jumping decreased and the post-jump pleasure increased. To illustrate the point further examples may include: (1) A person buys something to cheer themselves up but later feels guilty at having spent so much. So they buy something else to cheer up again. (2) A thrill seeker goes rafting. The excitement of the journey is a mix of fear of the next rapids and relief at having survived the last one.

We have pairs of emotions that act in opposing pairs, such as happiness and sadness, fear and relief, pleasure and pain. When one of these is experienced, the other is temporarily suppressed. This opposite emotion, however, is likely to re-emerge strongly and may curtail or interact with the initial emotion.

Thus activating one emotion also activates its opposite and they interact as a linked pair. To some extent, this can be used to explain drug use and other addictive behaviour, as the pleasure of the high is used to suppress the pain of withdrawal.

Sometimes these two conflicting emotions may be felt at the same time as the second emotion intrudes before the first emotion wanes. The result is a confusing combined experience of two emotions being felt at the same time that normally are mutually exclusive. Thus we can feel happy-sad, scared-relieved, love-hate, etc. This can be unpleasant but as an experiential thrill it can also have a strangely enjoyable element (and seems to be a basis of excitement).

This Opponent Process Theory is based on *three* assumptions.

- First, being head over teacup in love is a very disabling experience. Great fun, it still makes it difficult to get things done. This theory is based on the assumption that we try to keep our arousal at a moderate level. We strive to keep it tolerable, and rather constant - kind of an emotional neutral.
- Second, the theory assumes that any change in our level of arousal will - with repeated stimulation - lead to the development of an internal opposing process. That internal process will eventually counteract the effects of the external stimulation in order to return the experienced level of arousal to a tolerable level.
- Third, since arousal may increase or decrease, it follows that the opposing process can either decrease or increase. Now this leads to a couple of rather interesting predictions. For example, if we can remove from your environment whatever it is that caused you to become aroused, then that should change how you perceive the environment. The theory also implies that your emotional experiences will change over time. Why? Because the opponent process will – through repeated classical conditioning experience - also change over time.

Cognitive Approaches

There are some theories on emotions arguing that cognitive activity in the form of judgments, evaluations, or thoughts is necessary in order for an emotion to occur. This, argued by Richard Lazarus, is necessary to capture the fact that emotions are about something or have intentionally. Such cognitive activity may be conscious or unconscious and may or may not take the form of conceptual processing. An influential theory here is that of Lazarus.

A crucial mandate of cognitivist theories is to avert the charge that emotions are merely "subjective." But propositional attitudes are not the only cognitive states. A more basic feature of cognition is that is has a "mind-to-world direction of fit." The expression is meant to sum up the contrast between cognition and the conative orientation, in which success is defined in terms of the opposite, world-to-mind, direction of fit (Searle 1983). We will or desire what does not yet exist, and deem ourselves successful if the world is brought into line with the mind's plan.

Cognitive Appraisal Theories of Emotion

In the absence of physiological arousal, we decide what to feel after interpreting or explaining what has just happened. Two things are important in this: whether we interpret the event as good or bad for us and what we believe is the cause of the event. The sequence thus is as follows:

Event ==> thinking ==> *Simultaneous* arousal and emotion

This challenges the two-factor separation of arousal and emotion, supporting the Cannon and Bard theory albeit with the addition of the thinking step.

In *primary appraisal*, we consider how the situation affects our personal well-being. In *secondary appraisal* we consider how we might cope with the situation. This is sometimes also called *Lazarus Theory*. For example, when a colleague gets promoted, I might feel resentful if I think I deserve the promotion more than they do.

Perceptual Theory

A recent hybrid of the somatic and cognitive theories of emotion is the perceptual theory. This theory is neo-Jamesian in arguing that bodily responses are central to emotions, yet it emphasizes the meaningfulness of emotions or the idea that emotions are about something, as is recognized by cognitive theories. The novel claim of this theory is that conceptually based cognition is unnecessary for such meaning. Rather the bodily changes themselves *perceive* the meaningful content of the emotion because of being causally triggered by certain situations. In this respect, emotions are held to be analogous to faculties such as vision or touch, which provide information about the relation between the subject and the world in various ways.

Affective Events Theory

This a communication-based theory developed by Howard M. Weiss and Russell Cropanzano (1996) that looks at the causes, structures, and consequences of emotional experience (especially in work contexts.) This theory suggests that emotions are influenced and caused by events which in turn influence attitudes and behaviours. This theoretical frame also emphasizes *time* in that human beings experience what they call emotion episodes - a "series of emotional states extended over time and organized around an underlying theme" This theory has been utilized by numerous researchers to better understand emotion from a communicative lens.

Robert Solomon (1980), Jerome Neu (2000) and Martha Nussbaum (2001) take this approach. My anger at someone simply is the judgment that I have been wronged by that person. Robert Solomon (1980) spurred both interest and opposition with his provocative thesis that emotions are judgments, albeit judgments of a particular kind, characterized by their mode of haste and their evaluative content. Under the influence of (Sartre 1948), he also adopted the view that emotions could be understood as strategic choices, collectively driven by the goal of protecting and enhancing self-esteem (Solomon 1984). In his more recent work he has also written about the emotional dimension of justice, and advocated an enrichment of emotion theory through cross-cultural perspectives and the integration of scientific perspectives (Solomon 1999).

Jerome Neu (1977) is sympathetic to psychoanalytic views of the mechanisms underlying the pathology of belief and desire frequently associated with emotion. But he remains among the staunchest defenders of a cognitivist view of the core of emotion, as attested by his book title borrowed from William Blake's line "A tear is an intellectual thing", (Neu 2000). Neu has repeatedly stressed, in particular, that what distinguishes one emotion from another is not how it feels, but what belief is embedded in the emotion about its target. Despite the unifying theoretical vision suggested by this doctrine, much of Neu's work explores the pervasively messy and multifarious ways in which emotions influence our lives.

Social Contagion

Emotion can spread rapidly through large crowds, as the massive social proof leads us into extreme states. This explains much of crowd behaviour, where 'normal' people act in ways they may later deeply regret.

Social contagion effects can also occur when people believe they have been infected by a disease. As more people show the (psychosomatic) symptoms, this is taken as proof that 'I am bound to get it'. Just watch football matches and see how the crowd reacts almost as one.

EMOTION REGULATION IN SPORT

Emotions play a central role in sport performance. Without being emotionally aroused an athlete's "psyching up" procedure is not complete. All winning performances are invariably a result of emotional upsurge in the athlete. From the theories of emotion discussed about, it has become amply clear that emotions – whether positive or negative – generate tremendous energy in the organism as they arise; rather they put the body and mind on fire. Sport may be recreation for some athletes; it is an emotional experience for many.

According to Richard Lazarus, irrespective of the status of the athlete and the nature of sport he or she plays, all sportspersons invariably pass through the following categories of emotions at one stage or the other during competition as well as during practice and preparation:

1. ***Emotions resulting from harms, losses, threats***: They include anger, anxiety, fear, guilt, shame, sadness, envy, jealousy, disgust, etc., and are called negative stress emotions.
2. ***Emotions resulting from benefits***: They include happiness, joy, pride, gratitude, love, etc. and are called positive emotions.
3. ***Borderline cases***, such as hope, contentment, relief, compassion, aesthetic and response.

4. ***Non-emotions***, including complex states such as grief, depression; ambiguous positive states, such as challenge, confidence, determination; negative states, such as frustration, disappointment, mental confusion.

Reasons for emotional experiences may be personal or environmental and could be as varied as the number of emotions.

Arousal and Anxiety

Of all the emotions, anxiety, arousal and aggression are the most critical ones from the viewpoint of sport because their implication in the performance of an athlete or a team is fairly serious and has far reaching consequences. Amongst athletes, coaches and sport psychologists, they are the most talked about emotions because more than 60% problems of athletes in any sport during competition chiefly relate to arousal, anxiety, or aggression.

Arousal and anxiety, though two separate terms, are related to each other down the line. ***Arousal*** is usually defined physiologically as the intensity of behaviours on a continuum from sleep to extensive excitement, which has come to be considered as a pre-requisite for optimal sport performance. It has an emotional component, caused by (1) positive feelings of excitation & confidence, or (2) negative feelings of fear, anxiety, or sadness. Physiologically, arousal is indicated by an increase in the body's level of activation. ***Anxiety*** is an emotion related to over-worry about a real/perceived threat. For example, anxiety reflects the athlete's feeling that something may go wrong, outcome may not be successful and performance failure may be experienced. In this way, anxiety is the cause, and arousal as the effect, so to say. It is established that rise in anxiety level causes the arousal curve to move up. Intense anxiety invariably leads to intense arousal. Anxiety is categorized into *trait anxiety* – a relatively stable and acquired behaviour disposition, and *state anxiety* – a transitory feeling which fluctuates over time. While trait anxiety is usually considered as a personality trait, state anxiety is episodic in nature. Some athletes by nature are anxious while most are influenced by state anxiety in way or other.

Dynamics of Emotion in Sport

All athletes invariably respond emotionally to the performance situation in their own characteristic ways both during and after the games. For instance, when a player (in badminton, tennis, basketball or volleyball) scores a point, he feels happy, and puts up a more confident, energetic and motivated appearance. Conversely, when he misses or loses a point, he feels disappointed, and seems over-attentive and often apprehensive about the next point or move; a more experienced player may also feel more resolute to handle the situation with more confidence. Transitory situations like these make the athlete's anxiety and arousal level move up and down, sometimes too fast, and with this his or her fortune also fluctuates until the game ends in a win for one and loss for the other.

Similarly, when a match is won, there is elation, jubilation and happiness all around; the player or team jump, squirm and shout with joy; every one including the team management is upbeat. With this, the level of expectancy moves up. On the other hand, when a match is lost, a feeling of despair takes over; unusual loss of energy is felt; every one accuses every one else but himself; and the spirit droops. Besides, a player also feel scared as he or she starts thinking that his or her opponent is more powerful than him or her. Much depends how the situation is perceived and how its impact is felt on the mind.

The role of cognition in the perception of the situation and expression of emotion has been considered central. Lazarus (1991, 2000) feels that 'emotion is a part of a changing person-environment relationship, and motivation and appraisal are central to this process'. The event appraisal and emotional response sequence could be depicted as follows:

> Event ?Primary appraisal (related to a person's well-being & goal achievement) ?secondary appraisal (concerns coping) ?emotional response (includes physiological changes) ?behaviours or performance

The characteristics of the emotional response in sport setting carries three basic elements as shown below:

- *Physiological Changes*: Precisely, there is increase in heart rate, blood pressure, and skin response, muscle tension, etc. In sport, an increase in arousal may accompany some emotions like anxiety and excitement, and a decrease in arousal may accompany other emotions like sadness & disappointment.
- *Subjective Experience*: The subjective feelings an athlete consciously experiences during the emotional episode in

sport setting generally include anger, happiness, fear (getting scarred), etc.

- *Action Tendencies*: There is attempt on the part of the athlete to run away or escape from the situation (when afraid). In a state of sadness, the athlete becomes motionless. When leading, one is conservative and there is decrease in performance.

Effects of Emotions on Sport Performance

Emotion has both facilitative and debilitative effect on athletic performance. In general, while positive emotions like joy, happiness, elation, etc., have facilitative effect on performance, negative emotions such as anger, fear, anxiety, over-arousal, etc., put hurdles in the way of performance. Research on this issue is full of contradiction and still inconclusive. However, several studies indicate that 'optimal emotions can initiate and maintain the required amount of effort for a task' (Hanin, 2000), meaning that when, for example, an athlete's anxiety level is optimal before and during competition, his or her chances of performing best are also optimal. Optimal emotions keep the athlete energized as a result of which his or her level of motivation level remains high. From a study on the relationship between emotions, coping and performance of athletes at the 2000, Olympic Games, Pensgaard & Duda (2003), concluded that optimizing emotions were related to coping effectiveness (objective & subjective) and is a positive predictor of objective competitive results, viz. Enthusiasm (P+), Ready (P+), Optimistic (P+), Safe (P+), Determined (P+), Happy (P+), Relaxed (P+), Anxious (N+), Tired (N+), Angry (P+), Scared (N+), and Pessimistic (P+).

High arousal due either to anxiety or aggression in sports like soccer, hockey, basketball, etc., may result in an increase of anaerobic power, but it possibly may reduce the level of accuracy and movement precision as emotional arousal is said to blur to vision and impinge upon concentration. Several studies indicate that high arousal coupled with some emotions impairs working memory (Parfitt et al., 1990) and narrowing of attentional focus so that the athlete finds it difficult to perform well (Moran, 1996). It also reduces cognitive resources available for the task or activity in hand.

Ways to Regulate Emotion

Regulation of emotions is important both in life and sport is important if one wished to perform at an optimal level of efficiency whether at work or in an athletic event for this is the only way of conserving and economizing on vital energy that we humans beings possess for keeping the wheel of live moving with optimal results. The two kinds of emotion regulating methods suggested in literature include:

(1) ***Cognitive Methods** (stress-management training, imagery, cognitive confirming/positive self-talk, problem-solving skills, vicarious learning/modeling, self-analysis (training log or competition journal); and

(2) ***Arousal Control Methods** (relaxation, viz. breathing, muscle relaxation, bio-feedback, etc., and raising arousal level through upbeat music, physical activity, arousing training, etc.)

*Discussed in detail in chapter on anxiety and aggression.

SELECTED REFERENCES

Buskist, William & Gerbing, David W. *Psychology - Boundaries and Frontiers.* Glenview, Ill. Scott Foreman/Little Brown Higher and Education, 1990

Cannon, Cannon, Walter. *Bodily Changes in Pain, Hunger, Fear and Rage* 2nd Ed. New York: Appleton, 1929

Ekman, Paul *Emotions in the Human Face.* New York: Pergamon Press., 1972

James, William. What is an emotion? *Mind*, 9, 188-205., 1884.

Lazarus, Richard. "Cognition and Motivation in Emotion." *American Psychologist*, 46: 362-67, 1991

McDougall, W. *An introduction to Social Psychology*. Boston: Luce, 1926

Neu, Jerome. *A Tear is an Intellectual Thing: the Meaning of Emotions.* Oxford, New York: Oxford University Press, 2000

Neu, Jerome. *Emotion, Thought and therapy: a Study of Hume and Spinoza and the Relationship of Philosophical Theories of the Emotions to Psychological Theories of Therapy.* London: Routledge and Kegan Paul, 1977

Nussbaum, Charles. *The Musical Representation: Meaning, Ontology, and Emotion.* Cambridge, MA: MIT Press, 2007

Parrott, W. *Emotions in Social Psychology*, Psychology Press, Philadelphia, 2001

Plutchik, Robert *Emotion: A Psycho-evolutionary Synthesis*. New York: Harper and Row. 1980

Plutchik, R. A general psycho-evolutionary theory of emotion. In R. Plutchik & H. Kellerman (Eds.), *Emotion: Theory, research, and experience: Vol. 1. Theories of emotion* (pp. 3-33). New York: Academic. 1980

Sartre, Jean-Paul. *The Emotions: Outline of a Theory*. New York: Philosophical Library, 1948

Solomon, Robert. "Emotions and Choice." In *Explaining Emotions*, edited by Amélie Rorty, 251-81. Los Angeles: University of California Press, 1980.

Solomon, Robert. *The Passions: The Myth and Nature of Human Emotions*. New York: Doubleday, 1984.

Russell, James A. "Core Affect and the Construction of Emotions." *Psychological Review*, 110: 145-72., 2003

Schacter, Stanley, and Jerome Singer. "Cognitive, Social and Physiological Determinants of Emotional States." *Psychological Review*, 69 : 379-99, 1962.

Scherer, Klaus R., A Schorr, & T. Johnstone, (Eds.) *Appraisal Processes in Emotion: Theory, Methods, Research*. Oxford: Oxford University Press., 2001

Scherer, Klaus R. "What are emotions? and how can they be measured?" *Social Science information*, 44 (4): 695-729, 2005

When an archer is shooting for enjoyment, he has all his skill; when he shoots for a brass buckle, he gets nervous; when he shoots for a prize of gold, he begins to see two targets.

- **Chuang Tzu** - a Chinese sage

CHAPTER - 13

SPORT COMPETITION AND PERFORMANCE ANXIETY

In our society sport, defined as *any activity, experience, or business enterprise focused on fitness, recreation, athletics or leisure*, fulfils important functions and is indeed indispensable. It offers opportunities for physical activity in a world where physical activity is increasingly diminishing; it promotes good health and well-being (when pursued in moderation); and it provides a means of social contact and ample opportunity for intensive experiences. Above all sport provides competition - a channel through which an athlete can test his or her performance potential and the spectators have a good pastime.

Ordinarily, sport may be "play-like in nature" (Loy, 1968), a leisure time activity and a means of relaxation but moving with the Olympic spirit, it is today better understood as "a competitive activity...., in which the quest for records is of high significance" (Vandar-Zwaag, 1998). Coakly (2001) considers sports as "institutionalized competitive activities" that involve rigorous physical exertion or the use of relatively complex physical skills by participants motivated by personal enjoyment and external rewards. Intensive proliferation of the Olympic Movement, rise of professionalism in sports, refinement in the coaching academics, induction of science and technology in the methodologies of athletic training in a big way, increasing media role in sport marketing, and steeply ascending spectator interest in watching sport have made sports intensely competitive, with serious psycho-social implications for the athletes and the society. If there were no competition, sport would be a lifeless activity, worth nothing.

However, over the decades, sport competition has become terribly intense and every one connected with sport, closely or remotely- the athlete, trainer, coach, manager, administrator, scientist, and the spectator - is joining the rat race for "winning" the *Olympic Gold* using every strategy up their sleeve. Innovative techniques of identifying sport talent, and grooming them into star performers and finally making them compete under all kind of stresses and conditions has become an order of the day. Sport has become all science, in which scientists from as diverse fields as sport & exercise physiology, sport psychology, sport biomechanics, sport anthropometry, nutritionists, sports medicine, etc., have come to play a central role, assisting the athletes and their trainers to overcome variety of problems relating to training and competition. Truly, preparing for and coping with competitive situations is becoming increasingly more complex than preparing for war.

COMPETITION

Rooted in the Latin *competere* meaning 'seek together', competition indicates some sort of 'contest with another or others' which enables a person or a group to assess their physical prowess, ability or mental strength on the basis of some comparable performance given. It is usually defined as *a conscious struggle or rivalry* in which an individual or a group seeks to excel others (usually opponents) in certain activity or attribute through performance. A competition situation existed or is created when there are two or more opponents desirous of contesting for something to prove their superiority or supremacy in it. Since any one can challenge any one, competition turns out to be *an open conflict* conducted according to laid down rules and regulations; it cannot be a free-for-all situation. Competition has sanctity as a social phenomenon present in almost every aspect of life – business, education, industry, economy, defence, health, fitness, sport, etc. Without it, no individual or society can march on the path of progress and prosperity.

In biology, competition is interpreted as "struggle for existence"; in economics, for control of wealth and resources; and in sport, for supremacy in terms of skill, strength and strategy. Science, economics, art, culture, technology, etc., pale into insignificance without competition. Frontiers of knowledge expand only when there is a constant strife among the intellectuals, scientists, educationists, philosophers and researchers to "ring in the new and ring out the old". Expressions like 'excelling', 'doing better than others or showing better performance every time one competes in some situation', 'dominating others or the environment', 'surpassing every on else', reflect competition.

Competition in Sport

Sans competition, sport is as dull and drab as dust; it breeds monotony and boredom. Competition makes sport thrilling; it makes hearts throb and brains burst with excitement. Since the mid-twentieth century, competitive sport spiral has been shooting up fast as a result of which human performance in sport has touched new heights both in amateur and professional sports

Competition could be direct or indirect. In ***direct competition*** two individuals face each other as in boxing, wrestling, judo, badminton, tennis etc., or two teams as in hockey, football, basketball, handball, volleyball, cricket, etc. In ***indirect competition*** individuals or sometimes groups compete against the standards of performance set by others or by themselves as in swimming, track & field, archery, shooting, golf, etc. In the latter situation, there is *no* physical confrontation among contestants. Performance standards to be emulated could be objective or subjective.

Sports competitions are generally so designed that contestants with lower ability or performance standard compete in the earlier rounds, and those succeeding to register win, move up the ladder so that the best of them confront each other at the end. In this arrangement, the intensity of competition and level of performance gradually increase at each stage; so does the psychological stress. To avoid contest among unequal competitors, individuals/teams are matched on the basis of their previous performance. As the competition level rises, matching of contestants becomes automatic, making the semi-finals and finals fixtures extremely stressful for competitors but thrilling for spectators.

Today, thus sports training procedure has undergone a sea change. From a simple art of *individualized* teaching, it has become a complex science in which inputs from training methodology, human engineering, information technology, and sport sciences like sport physiology, sport psychology, biomechanics, sports medicine, nutrition, etc., are given important place. Every single variable connected with performance is carefully identified, analyzed and manipulated by the coaching personnel and scientists for preparing training regimens and competition schedules for individual athletes and teams.

With high stakes involved in several sports like tennis, basketball, boxing, American football, soccer, billiards, golf, etc., and *winning* being the major objective for every one, sport is adopting a truly professional approach in each and every compartment connected with success - infrastructure, equipment, training, competition scheduling, performance appraisal, and management. Media intervention has taken sport to every doorstep.

Sport Competition – Merits and Demerits

Competition is a stark reality of modern sport. Its merit and demerit will squarely depend on the value society attaches to both sport and competition.

Merits

- Competition boosts performance. It spurs excellence.
- Athletes evaluate their strengths and weaknesses in skill, prowess, ability, strategy, achievement, etc., through competition objectively and plan out strategies for maximizing improvement.
- Through competition man satisfies urge for action; catharsis of emotions is achieved better through competition.
- Competition levels off inequalities of colour, caste, creed, language, race, etc., among people, recognizing only sportspersons in true sense.
- Competition is a big reinforcer of behaviour – a source of both intrinsic (love of activity) and extrinsic motivation (awards, rewards, prizes, privileges and prestige).
- Competition is a life-disciplining device for people play sport to rules.
- Toughening body and mind is achieved through competition. Good competitors learn how to take touch decisions at crucial moments.
- Competition offers avenues for building up a high level of health, fitness, recreation, skill and performance.
- Watching and/or participating in competition are excellent leisure-time activity wit no negative side effects.

Demerits

(1) Only a few talented, skilled and well-prepared individuals compete, the mass is left out.

(2) Athletes are trained for competition as soldiers for war or horses for races; this is really killing and is likely to have serious health and psychological implications later in life.

(3) With winning as the ultimate objective, the use of unfair

means such as doping at health risk, corrupting officials and buying and selling players at billions, are difficult to rule out.

(4) Sport competitions cause tremendous stress, anxiety, aggression, and violence. Overly 'psyched up' players damage their own mental health, and vitiate society and the environment.

(5) If success in sport is evaluated in terms of victory only, the merits of sport and competition are really too few.

(6) A highly competitive culture (society) tends to *reinforce* competitive behaviour among people, generating both instrumental and retaliatory or hostile aggression.

Human emotions, as explained in previous chapter, in general, play a central role in athletic performance, but the two highly significant psychological (emotional) variables that critically influence behaviour and competition outcomes (performance) are anxiety and aggression - both dealt with by psychologists as personality traits as well as situational variables in sport context. Interestingly, more than 50% of the content of sport psychology is pregnant with issues relating to these two.

ANXIETY

Anxiety is a uniquely commonplace experience that everyone experiences from time to time. It is an emotional state, represented by a feeling of dread, apprehension, or fear. Medical experts sometimes categorize anxiety as an emotion or an affect depending on whether it is being described by the person having it (emotion) or by an outside observer (affect). The word emotion is generally used to describe biochemical changes and feeling state that underlie a person's internal sense of anxiety. Affect is used to describe the person's emotional state from an observer's perspective. If a doctor says that a patient has an anxious affect, he or she means that the patient appears nervous or anxious, or responds to others in an anxious way (for example, the individual is shaky, tremulous, etc.).

Sometimes anxiety being experienced in the present may stem from an event or person that produced pain and fear in the past, but the anxious individual is not consciously aware of the original source of the feeling. It is remoteness aspect of anxiety that makes it hard for people to compare their experiences of it. Whereas most people will be fearful in physically dangerous situations, and can agree that fear is an appropriate response in the presence of danger, anxiety is often triggered by objects or events that are unique and specific to an individual. An individual might be anxious because of a unique meaning or memory being stimulated by present circumstances, not because of some immediate danger. Another individual looking at the anxious person from the outside may be truly puzzled as to the reason for the person's anxiety.

Definition of Anxiety

Anxiety is an abstract concept, so difficult to describe concretely because it has so many different potential causes and degrees of intensity, yet people have defined in several ways, for instance, as "a disturbed state" of the body (Johnson, 1951); "emotional reactivity" (Hardman & Johnson, 1952); "arousal" (Skubic, 1956); "nervousness" (Ekegami, 1970); "neuroticism" (Kane, 1970); "Unrealistic and unpleasant state" of body and mind (Pikunas, 1969); etc. In *Children's Health Encyclopaedia* anxiety is defined as "a condition of persistent and uncontrollable nervousness, stress, and worry that is triggered by anticipation of future events, memories of past events, or ruminations over day-to-day events, both trivial and major, with disproportionate fears of catastrophic consequences". In *Sport Science and Medicine Encyclopaedia*, anxiety is referred to as "a subjective feeling of apprehension and heightened physiological tension". *Psychoanalysis Theory* considers anxiety as 'an unpleasurable affect in which the individual experiences a feeling of danger whose cause is unconscious'. In *Wikipedia*, anxiety is described as 'a psychological and physiological state characterized by cognitive, somatic, emotional, and behavioural components'.

Distinction is often made between fear and anxiety. Anxiety is related to fear but it is not the same thing. Fear is a direct, focused response to a specific event or object, and the person is consciously aware of it. Fear has an obvious cause and once that cause is eliminated, fear will subside. Most people will feel fear if someone points a loaded gun at them or if they see a tornado forming on the horizon. They also will recognize that they are afraid. Anxiety, on the other hand, is often unfocused, vague, and hard to pin down to a specific cause. It is less clearly linked to specific events or stimuli. In this form it is called free-floating anxiety. It tends to be more pervasive and less responsive to changes in the environment (Crooks & Stein,

1988). Rethlingshafer (1963) makes a clear distinction between fear and anxiety: "A fear is a quickly passing cloud that moves across the sun, anxiety is the cloud that lingers and truly beclouds the man". Cratty (1989) sums up the issue:

> Fear is usually defined as a rational emotional reaction to danger or the anticipation of danger or harm from a real objective stimulus in the external environment. Moreover, the magnitude of the fear is directly proportional to the amount of danger that evokes it. In contrast, anxiety is an emotional reaction that is often irrational to conditions that may be unknown to others. Moreover, the intensity of the anxiety is often disproportionately greater than the magnitude of the objectively measured danger.

Causes, Symptoms and Dimensions of Anxiety

Spielberger (1966) believed: "Anxiety is a feeling that exists in people nature. It occurs under irritating conditions. Excess anxiety may result in abnormal functions for the body. Everybody feels different anxiety, and physiological properties play very important roles in this situation". Its mechanism is simple. Any thing, event, object or person can cause anxiety. Link (1993) explained: "Anxiety starts gradually and increases step by step. In case not to be controlled, it rises and irritates the people. The main reasons of anxiety are business travel, smoking, alcohol, over weight, failure, inappropriate physical appearance, competition etc. Anxiety indications may be bone pains, being tired, headache, nervous, poor sleeping, forgetting, hesitations, hypochondriacs etc."

Anxiety Causes

Causes of anxiety are numerous. Anxiety is a multidimensional response to internal, external and/or combination of both stimuli. The human nervous system is hard-wired to respond to dangers or threats. These responses are not subject to conscious control and are the same in man as in lower animals. They represent an evolutionary adaptation to dangers that all animals have to cope with.

The most familiar reaction of this type is the fight-or-flight reaction to a life-threatening situation. When people have fight-or-flight reactions, the level of stress hormones in their blood rises. They become more alert and attentive, their eyes dilate, their heartbeats increase, their breathing rates increase, and their digestion slows down, making more energy available to the muscles. This emergency reaction is regulated by a part of the nervous system called the *autonomic nervous system*, or ANS.

One problem with this arrangement is that the limbic system cannot tell the difference between a real physical threat and an anxiety-producing thought or idea. The hypothalamus may trigger the release of stress hormones from the pituitary gland even when there is no external danger.

A second problem is caused by the biochemical side effects of too many false alarms in the ANS. When a person responds to a real danger, his or her body relieves itself of the stress hormones by facing up to the danger or fleeing from it. In modern life, however, people often have fight-or-flight reactions in situations where they can neither run away nor lash out physically. As a result, their bodies have to absorb all the biochemical changes of hyper-arousal rather than release them. These biochemical changes can produce anxious feelings as well as muscle tension and other physical symptoms of anxiety.

In some cases, anxiety is produced by physical (triggers) responses to stress or by certain disease processes or medications.

Anxiety Symptoms

A person's genetics, biochemistry, environment, history, and psychological profile all seem to contribute to the development of anxiety disorders, which may be characterized by a variety of symptoms as given below:

- ***Somatic***: Physical symptoms of anxiety include rapid heart beat, muscle aches (from tension), headaches, dizziness or light-headedness, stomach distress, constipation, frequent urination, nausea and/or vomiting, diarrhoea, tingling, pale complexion, sweating, numbness, difficulty in breathing, sleep disturbances, fatigue, and sensations of tightness in the chest, neck, shoulders, or hands. These symptoms are produced by the hormonal, muscular, and cardiovascular reactions involved in the fight-or-flight reaction.
- ***Behavioural***: Behavioural symptoms of anxiety include pacing, trembling, general restlessness, decreased appetite or other changes in eating habits, hyperventilation, pressured speech, hand wringing, and finger tapping.

- *Cognitive*: Cognitive symptoms of anxiety include recurrent or obsessive thoughts, feelings of doom, morbid or fear-inducing thoughts or ideas, and confusion or inability to concentrate.
- *Emotional*: Emotional symptoms include feelings of tension, or nervousness, self-consciousness, self-doubt or questioning, feeling "hyper" or "keyed up," inability to control emotions, and feelings of unreality, panic, or terror.

Dimensions of Anxiety

Dimensions of anxiety are very wide. An anxiety situation, on the one hand, triggers variety of physiological actions-reactions causing the arousal (activation) level to shoot up, and on the other, it gives rise to a "feeling tone" - a cognitive experience causing serious psychological implications. Viewed as a cognitive label, anxiety may occur within various time-frames relative to the existence of a potentially stressful event.

Endler (1978) has suggested the following five facets of anxiety:

1. *Interpersonal ego-threat* (threat to self-esteem as result of failure)
2. *Physical danger* (threat of personal harm)
3. *Ambiguity* (unpredictability and the fear of the unknown)
4. *Disruption of daily routines* (fear of disruption of daily habits)
5. *Social evaluation* (fear being negatively evaluated by others)

Situation, time and context determine what facet of anxiety will dominate when. A mild stimulus may cause no physiological upheaval, but an intense stimulus may put the body and mind on fire. A still more intense stimulus may add emotional dimensions to it when everything could be seen going out of gear. Inbuilt coping mechanism tries to bring back homeostasis (internal equilibrium) but persistent or chronic anxiety may become a potential cause for psychosomatic disorders.

Anxiety is often deemed synonymous with *activation* and *arousal*, which may be misleading. In literature, anxiety is documented as a psychological state, which in an intense form is accompanied by such physiological symptoms as dry mouth, clammy palms, wet forehead, increased cardiac and respiratory functions, slow peristaltic movement, faster metabolic activity, etc. In this sense, equating activation-arousal with anxiety may be logical; in reality, anxiety is more than mere general activation-arousal level, which is normal state, not necessarily caused by anxiety.

Attempts have been made to draw parallels between *stress* and anxiety. Both indicate internal arousal situation, but both are different. Stress is a *general adaptation syndrome* denoting internal bodily changes due to exercise, a threatening psychological event, or from the impingement of disease or injury. Anxiety, as different from stress, comes from a concern over lack of control over circumstances. In some cases being anxious and worrying over a problem may generate a solution. Normally, however, it will just result in negative thinking. While stress is event related and specific, anxiety is non-specific and internal psychological condition. Stress may cause and anxiety, in turn, lead to strain – a bodily and psychological reaction to stress. The ability and the manner(s) in which people react to the stressful situations differ from person to person. Some may exhibit more prominent restlessness of body and mind, while others show tendency of heightened muscle tone or some unique pattern of muscular activity.

A certain level of stress is needed for optimum performance. While too little stress does not motivate athlete for good performance and is expressive of feelings of boredom and 'not being stretched', excessive stress damages performance and enjoyment of sport by promoting negative thinking, eroding self-confidence, narrowing attention and disrupting flow. Only at an optimum level of stress the athlete will get the benefits of alertness and activation that a good level of stress brings. Too much stress and too much anxiety can seriously affect an athlete's ability to focus on his or her skills and flow in a performance.

Perhaps, the notion of trait and state anxiety has direct relationship with external life stressors, which means that environmental situations produce the maximum stresses that cause anxiety and tension. Repeated exposure to stressful situations may lead to either of the two consequences or outcomes, says Cratty, (1989).

SPORT ANXIETY

Sport is littered with the broken dreams of those who wavered when they most needed to be in control of themselves and focused on the task at hand. When a competitor 'freezes' in the big moment or commits an inexplicable error, anxiety, in one of its many guises, is very often the root cause. This dreaded state is experienced by every athlete at one time or another. The pain of losing because of one's own mindset is perhaps the most frustrating loss of all. Sport anxiety is simply mind-body state that is marked by uneasiness, fear or worry. It is usually a conditioned response to a stimulus. The precise impact of anxiety on sporting performance depends on how an athlete interprets his or her world. Unfortunately, far too many athletes accept high levels of anxiety as an inevitable part of the total sporting experience and fail to reach their potential. Its dynamics in different sports and different competition situation is of great interest to the athletes and their trainers.

According to Kroll (1976) several specific symptoms and factors account for pre-competitive anxiety in athletes in general; for example:

(1) *Increased Physiological Activation*: (somatic complaints such as stomach upset, urge to urinate, trembling, ring in the ears, excessive yawning, etc);
(2) *Fear of Failure*: (perception of concerns about making a foolish mistake, losing, choking up, belying coach's expectation);
(3) *Feeling of Inadequacy*: (feeling of personal dissatisfaction with the matters of preparation, training, etc., inability to concentrate, general weakness or undesirable feeling of fatigue);
(4) *Loss of Control:* (not being able or confident to control what follows, perceiving luck or fate as the chief determinant of success or failure, thought of being jinxed, have a poor or unfair officials or performing on a poor playfield or with poor equipment); and
(5) *Guilt:* (feeling associated with issues of morality and aggression, concerns about hurting an opponent, playing dirty tricks or swearing too much).

Anxiety Dynamics in Sport

Sport places a wide variety of stressors upon participants; it can be physically exhausting; it pitches you against superior opponents; and hostile fans might verbally abuse you. These elements may need to be overcome and your emotional frailties are constantly laid bare for all to see. When the demands of training or competition exceed one's perceived ability, anxiety is the inevitable outcome.

Many athletes perform their best during training or practice and find that they choke during competition. Choking is described as a decrease in performance due to too much *perceived* stress, referring to the stress or "pressure" that may not be real but that lives only in athlete's mind and in the way he interprets the competitive situation. Ultimately, it is not the external situation that causes stress, but the way each one of us including the athlete thinks about that event that creates feelings of stress, anxiety and fear. For athletes who choke during competition it is important to understand that they can control the thoughts they have regarding the event; for example, thoughts of doubt, failure and a lack of confidence in their ability. Such negative thinking often breeds feelings of anxiety, nervousness, and tension in the performing athletes is a reality of the modern sport.

In sport psychology nuances, this is performance anxiety, which is so common, and is pretty much seen as normal, but it becomes a problem when it interferes with sporting performance. It is future orientated and produces many physiological symptoms. Significantly, it happens in all sports but is most prevalent in those sports with high motoric activity. Irrespective of their sex and age, athletes, in general, tend to have variety of fears (mildly expressed moments of anxiety) before, during and even after the competition situations sometimes frequently and sometimes occasionally. Fear of doing poorly in fundamental skills, apprehensions over low levels of physical fitness, uncertainty about outcomes of a competition (or series of competition), etc., are common anxiety situations which sportspersons encounter.

A few fears may be realistic, but most are unrealistic, unfounded and irrational. Some fears motivate the athlete to put in harder effort to resolve anxiety, but those not handled properly let his performance slide. Fear of competition is common (and in some cases it is real) among athletes, and is more or less, relative to their age, level of participation, quality and amount of exposure in sport competition, personality makeup, mind-set, and the psychological preparation at a point of time, etc. "The fear", says Cratty (1968), "can range from cognitive evaluations of the seriousness of an impending threatening competition to the experience of bodily changes as competition approaches". Although frequent exposure to competitive situations makes athletes adept in handling anxiety skilfully, yet its important coping strategies are taught to them right from the very beginning along with physical training.

Albert Ellis has listed five main unrealistic desires or beliefs that cause anxiety in sportspersons:

- The *desire always to have the love and admiration* of all people important to them. This is unrealistic because they have no control over other people's minds: people can have bad days, can see things in odd ways, can make mistakes, or can be plain disagreeable and awkward.
- The *desire to always be thoroughly competent.* This is unrealistic because sportspersons only achieve competence at a new level by making mistakes. Everybody has bad days and makes mistakes. One of the benefits of training with better athletes is that they can see themselves making mistakes and having bad days too.
- The *belief that external factors cause all misfortune.* Often negative events can be caused by an athlete's own negative attitudes. Similarly his own negative attitudes can cause him to view neutral events negatively. Another player might find something positive in something the athlete views as a problem.
- The *desire that events should always turn out the way that the athlete wants them to* and people should always do what he or she wants. Other people have their own agendas and do what they want to do.
- The *belief that everything that has happened in the past will inevitably condition and control what has happened in the future.* Very often things can be improved or changed if the athlete tries hard enough, or look at things in a different way.

Sports differ from one another in skill structure, play dynamics, competition procedure and the need for physical and psychological training. Therefore, not all sports generate the same kind and the same amount of anxiety in sportspersons. For instance, individual sport athletes (archers, shooters, wrestlers, track & field athletes, gymnasts, judokas, etc.) encounter and cope with anxiety is by and large different from the ways team players (footballers, basketball players, hockey players, handball players, cricketers, etc) do. In all probability, the individual sport athletes experience higher level of anxiety that team sport athletes. A possible explanation for this phenomenon could be that in individual sports the athlete alone bears the brunt of the situation, in team sports the stress shifts from one compartment to another, i.e. from one area to another, for example, from attack to defence or from right wing to left wing and vice-versa as in soccer. Similarly, in short duration activities (sprints in track & field and swimming) the athletes have to go all-out to finish the action in one breath, with no time left to manage anxiety deliberately. In point-based or long-duration sport events (marathon, volleyball, basketball, handball, etc.) sportspersons have enough opportunity to have a breather and plan next move, and so manage anxiety menace.

The impact of a competitive situation on an athlete depends upon how they make a cognitive appraisal of the situation, i.e. how they objectively or subjectively evaluate the consequences of the situation. When evaluation is negative (one foresees failure), one would try to wriggle out of the situation at once. However, this option may not always be readily available. If the situation cannot be avoided, a response must be executed. The nature and/or quality of the response can be evaluated at psychological, physiological, and behavioural levels. While psychological and physiological responses relate most directly to anxiety, behavioural response is most observable and is the one that is evaluated. The consequence of competitive event, on the face of it, is either success or failure. The public display of the consequences of sport-related response is most likely a major reason why such situations have potential to generate strong anxiety responses. Success or failure, whether perceived or actually encountered, goes a long way in determining the volume of anxiety the subsequent situation will generate in the sportspersons. Failure, in general, generates anxiety but strangely some people are said to be afraid of too much and too easy success either.

Traditional coaches and trainers may try to help the athlete understand why negative or anxiety-producing thoughts and feelings develop and then try to change or modify that process with limited amounts of success. Why such thoughts arise may be of interest, but knowing the answer is not always necessary to overcome them.

Specific Causes of Sport Anxiety

Cratty (1989) rightly said: "Conditions within the athlete combined with his or her cognitive evaluation of the threat of competition and with the objective nature of competition itself work together to produce anxiety in athletes". Causes of anxiety in life and in sport hardly differ but certain factors causing anxiety in athletes are specific to sport and its contexts.

- Sport is an area of challenge, stimulation and considerable uncertainty. At the precise moment an archer releases an arrow, a soccer right-winger kicks for goal, or a bowler bowls a Yorker in cricket, the outcome is unknown. The stress that sport provides therefore is inevitably linked with its inherent uncertainty. Sport is a cultural focal point because it is a theatre of unpredictability. So, anxiety is rooted in the dynamics of sport itself.
- While (some) stress and uncertainty may motivate some athletes, they induce anxiety in most athletes largely novices, less experienced and those practicing sport below pre-elite level. Several distinct factors like untested equipment, unfamiliar playing field, varying environmental conditions, competition officials, opponents, etc., can increase athletes' level of anxiety. Above all, the more important the contest the greater the stress, and the more likely it is that a competitor will be prone to anxiety.

  These days, spectators have a huge impact on how athletes feel. In fact, studies of the home advantage phenomenon show that teams playing at their home venue win on average, around 56-64% of the time, depending on the sport. The impressive medal count of host nations during Olympic Games is also notable, in particular the record-breaking haul of medals won by Australia in Sydney (2000), by Greece in Athens (2004), and China in Beijing (2008).
- Participants in individual sports have been shown generally to suffer more anxiety before, during and after competition than participants in team sports, presumably because the sense of isolation and exposure is much greater in sports such as triathlon, tennis, gymnastics, badminton, and snooker than in the relative anonymity of field sports.
- For athletes in high body-contact sports such as boxing, wrestling, judo and martial arts, the possibility of getting injured is a much greater source of anxiety than anything else. Typically, this anxiety causes some critical changes in technique. For example, anxious boxers will often lean too far forward, be clumsy in their leg movements or fight defensively, any of which may result in them getting knocked out.

- An additional anxiety causing factor is the expectation of success. When sportspersons themselves or their trainers/managers expect too high of them or they are given verbal reinforcers, their ability to play natural nosedives. Some athletes rise to the challenge imposed by public expectation while others can choke.

Types of (Sport) Anxiety

A variety of type-tags have been given to anxiety such as trait anxiety, state anxiety, manifest anxiety, chronic anxiety, specific anxiety, etc. Spielberger (1966) was the first anxiety theorist to distinguish between anxiety as a state and anxiety as trait. Later Burton (1970) and Martens (1971) also supported this concept.

According to Spielberger et al., (1970), ***State Anxiety*** (A-state), "is a transitory state and fluctuate over time and is characterized by subjective, consciously perceived feelings of apprehension and tension accompanied by or associated with activation or arousal of the autonomic nervous system". State anxiety is situational stress induced by situations in the game. A sportsperson's autonomic nervous system is aroused in this state which is the natural reaction of any individual.

Trait Anxiety (A-trait) is considered as an enduring personality characteristic defined as "a motive or acquired behavioural disposition that predisposes an individual to perceive a wide range of objectively non-dangerous circumstances as threatening and to respond to these with anxiety reactions disproportioned in intensity to the magnitude of the objective danger". This can be thought of as a world view that an individual uses when coping with stress.

From Spielberger's theoretical postulates about anxiety, arose the concept of ***Competitive Anxiety*** (generated in a sport competitive situation), which Bird & Cripe (1986) defined as a "specific form of anxiety that occurs as a function of the competitive situation". Using trait- and state-anxiety canvass, Martens (1977) developed the construct of sport-specific ***Competitive Trait Anxiety*** and ***Competitive State Anxiety***. He defined CTA (Competitive Trait Anxiety) "as a tendency to perceive competitive situations threatening and respond to these situations with feelings of apprehension or tension". In the same way, Competitive State Anxiety (CSA) maintains Martens, "is the anxiety reaction triggered by particular competitive situation. The concept is no different from general state anxiety except that CSA is specific to a sport situation. In sport, individuals who are state anxious and low on the trait anxiety in tough situations, often deliver good performances consistently. Whereas, athletes who have higher levels of trait anxiety, added with the state anxiety, tend to perform below expectations.

ANXIETY-PERFORMANCE RELATIONSHIP IN SPORTS

Sport is a means to achieving self-actualization, i.e. bringing out the best in an athlete. Every faculty of the body and mind is stretched to its limits when an athlete plays a sport on competitive basis. We know how steeply the performance curve has risen in sport over the years in recent times, making it almost impossible for the elite performers to sustain their dominance; they are toppled from their position much earlier than expected. Every moment more talented, more skilled and better trained individuals with tremendous mental toughness enter the competition arena more especially in sports like tennis, badminton, golf, track & field, swimming, cricket, soccer, and so on. Apart from the induction of more innovative science-oriented techniques of training, mental preparation of athletes is gaining greater importance than many other compartments of sport, with focus on anxiety management. The reasons for occurrence of anxiety are many and have been discussed above. Notably, however, anxiety sets in when an athlete begins to doubt his or her capacity to deal with a stressful situation. Often it is not the talent or the training factor that decides one's performance. It simply depends on how one has trained oneself to deal with the ups and downs of the game.

Research reports on the role of anxiety in exercise and sport, and the relationship between anxiety and athletic performance have been conflicting, and often confusing, chiefly due to inconsistent terminology used and lack of agreement among scientists over the very meaning and concept of anxiety, its dimensions and methods of its assessment, observed Kamlesh (1990). Despite contradictory findings, there is a general consensus among psychologists that (1) anxiety is both and affective state and a pleasurable emotional reaction in which autonomic nervous system and the glandular system play a crucial role; (2) the level of anxiety in a sportsperson tends to rise prior to the athletic contest; and (3) repeated participation in competitive sport enables athletes to understand their anxiety and manage it more efficiently.

There is always a pre-defined 'region of anxiety' in a sportsperson, before the start of any game, bout or a race. When this anxiety is at the optimum level, it can lead to a significantly better performance. If the level exceeds or falls below this 'region of anxiety', it can adversely affect performance. The dominant and elite sportspersons are well-versed with the strategy of converting their performance anxiety into excitement, which stimulates the positive hormones and internal body reactions, assisting winning performances. Experienced athletes are more efficient in handling anxiety states and their consequences than novices or athletes of lower calibre (or inexperienced athletes). They take the anxiety arousal as a facilitator to come up with a better performance. The secret of their success in doing so lies in their ability to keep anxiety under control and interact with the sport environment more purposefully and be always in state of readiness to handle the unpredictable and unforeseen exigencies and emergencies on the field of play skilfully and ingeniously. A sportsperson whose mind interprets anxiety as a debilitating force (agent) often ends up in defeat. The athlete-environment interaction is, perhaps, the most important single factor that enables athletes to come to grips with the moments of debilitating anxiety.

In most sport situations, relationship between anxiety and performance is reported to be linear; in others, it is curvilinear depending possibly on the kind of sub-component being under focus. Research results in this domain show no congruency. Worry and apprehension associated with cognitive state anxiety become a major hindrance in athletic performance. The lower levels of cognitive state anxiety, the better the athletes will perform, says Cox, (1994). Precisely, the relationship between somatic state anxiety and athletic performance takes the inverted-U shape, while the relationship between cognitive state anxiety and performance is normally linear and negative.

Anxiety-Performance Relationship Theories

Anxiety is a normal human emotion in the face of a threat. It is a state of high arousal and a feeling of discomfort. Anxiety has its benefits too. In sport it can help you to succeed by motivating you to beat your opponent - if you are afraid of failure you might push yourself harder. But too much anxiety can get in the way of your success. If you are too anxious you might get distracted, make mistakes or even give up. This paradoxical phenomenon called sport anxiety is explained, more or less logically, on the basis of a few theories that have come up over the decades.

Drive Theory

According to the *Drive Theory* (Hull, 1943), discussed briefly in the previous chapter, if an athlete is appropriately skilled then it will help them to perform well if their drive to compete is aroused - they are "psyched up".

Inverted-U hypothesis

An alternative approach to Drive Theory came up in the form of Inverted-U hypothesis that predicts a relationship between arousal and performance approximates to an inverted-U shape (Yerkes and Dodson, 1908). Competitive state-anxiety usually follows a pattern of subjective feelings of tension and inadequacy, combined with heightened arousal of the autonomic nervous system. The intensity and duration of the anxious state alternates according to; the amount of stressful stimuli the athlete encounters, and the period of subjective threat created by the stimuli. The hypothesis is that as arousal is increased then performance improves but only up to a certain point (top of the inverted-U). If the athlete's arousal is increased beyond this point then performance declines. In its simplistic nature, the theory stated that the best performance could be guaranteed with an average level of arousal (a) if the level of arousal was too low (b) or too high (c) poor performance would result (Fig.13.1).

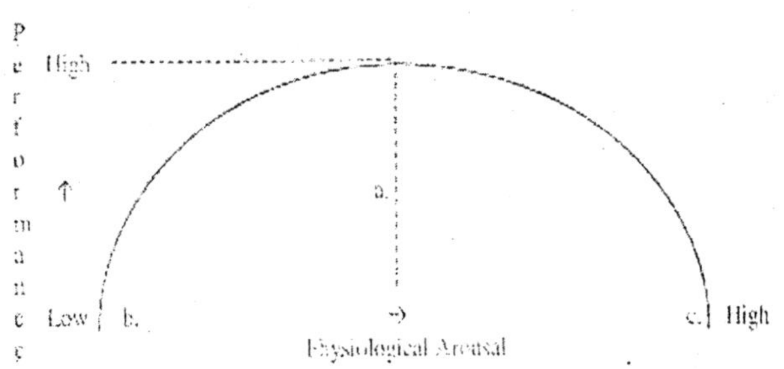

Fig. 1: The Inverted-U (Yerkes & Dodson, 1908) Hypothesis: The early explanation of the relationship between arousal and performance.

Fig. 13.1 The Inverted-U (Yorkes & Dodson, 1908)

Not being satisfied with the simple principle proposed by the theory, many sport psychologists began to question its validity for a number of conceptual and methodological reasons. To them it was not clear whether the hypothesis proposes a correlational or causal relationship between arousal and performance. This situation paved the way for a number of new theories and models that endeavoured to address the inadequacies of the Inverted-U at measuring and conceptualising competitive anxiety.

The Multidimensional Theory

Primarily, the theory is based on the assumption that competitive anxiety is comprised of two distinct parts; a cognitive component, and a somatic component, both having dissimilar effects on performance. Hence, theoretically, the components can be manipulated independently of one another. The cognitive component has been defined as the negative expectations and concerns about one's ability to perform and the possible consequences of failure. Whereas, the somatic component is the physiological effects of the anxiety experience, such as an increase in autonomic arousal with negative physiological effects, like palpitations, tense muscles, shortness of breath, clammy hands, and in some cases even nausea. The theory makes a series of predictions:

- There will be a negative but linear relationship between cognitive anxiety and performance
- There will be an inverted-U relationship between somatic anxiety and performance
- Somatic anxiety should decline once performance begins but cognitive anxiety may remain high if confidence is low.

The first attempt to confirm the existence of somatic and cognitive sub-components as separate elements of state-anxiety was by Liebert & Morris (1967). Later attempts by Carron (1980), Park (1980), and Morris, Davis & Hutchings (1981) confirmed relationship between the two sub-components.

However, culmination of the recognition of a Multidimensional Theory of Anxiety, in relation to the field of sport psychology, came about through Martens et al.'s (1990) development of the Competitive State Anxiety Inventory-2 (CSAI-2), a multidimensional state-anxiety measure specific to sport. Martens et al. (1990) proposed that somatic anxiety had an Inverted-U shaped relationship with performance, whilst cognitive anxiety had a negative linear relationship with performance. In addition, Martens et al. (1990) utilised a time to event paradigm to assist in the demonstration of the dissociation of somatic and cognitive anxiety. Administering their CSAI-2 to a selection of athletes, forty-eight hours, twenty-four hours, two hours, and five minutes before a critical event, they affirmed that the cognitive component stayed stable before the start, but the somatic component began to increase prior to the onset of the event (Fig. 13.2).

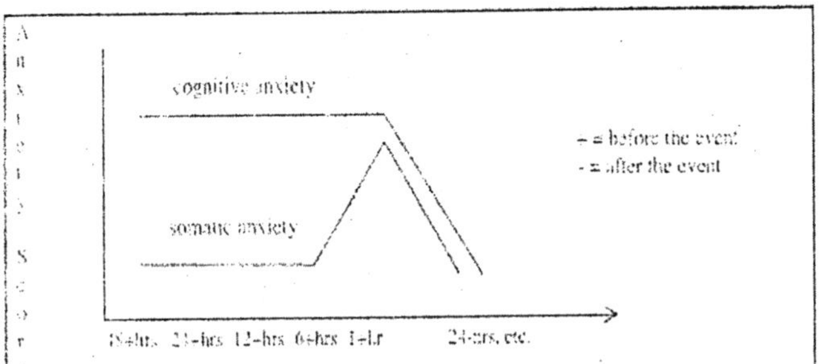

Fig. 2 An approximate representation of the time to event paradigm demonstrated by Martens *et al.* (1990).

Fig. 13.2 Cognitive and somatic components of anxiety

Scant initial research and questionable methodology used offered no full support for the Multidimensional Theory of Anxiety as a result there were a number of differing conclusions by researchers as to the specific effect that somatic and cognitive anxiety had upon performance. This lack of concordance between researchers was considered the greatest shortcoming within the theory. Another prominent shortcoming of Multidimensional Theory of Anxiety is its continued association with the outmoded Inverted-U hypothesis which underlines a two-dimensional approach to explaining competitive anxiety. The majority of research has made predictions about the interaction between cognitive and somatic anxiety with performance independently, with little or no emphasis on the interaction between the two sub-components. In reality a three-dimensional approach that will incorporate both sub-components simultaneously is required, says Krane (1992).

Catastrophe Theory

Using physiological arousal rather than somatic anxiety (as in multidimensional theory) as the asymmetry factor, Hardy & Fazey (1987) developed the catastrophe as an improvement on multidimensional theory. It suggests:

- stress and anxiety will influence performance,
- each athlete will respond in a unique way to competitive anxiety, and
- performance will be affected in a unique way which may be difficult to predict using general rules.

Vital differences exist between multidimensional theory and catastrophe model in relation to their effect on performance exist. The argument is that physiological arousal may have a direct effect upon performance through the suppression of crucial cognitive and physiological resources (Hardy et al., 1992). Further, physiological arousal may also cause an athlete to interpret their physiological state as either negative or positive, inadvertently altering their performance. Somatic anxiety, on the other hand, is believed to affect performance only if the extent of the somatic response is so large that the athlete becomes excessively concerned and distracted with their perceived physiological state (Martens et al., 1990).

The catastrophe model authors in their version state that physiological arousal follows the Inverted-U hypothesis in relation to performance. Nevertheless, that will only occur when the individual is exhibiting low cognitive state anxiety, e.g. they are not worried about their immediate performance. Alternatively, a catastrophe will occur if the individual is exhibiting high cognitive anxiety (e.g. concern over their immediate performance). This is typified by an increase in physiological arousal that will reach a threshold point just over the cusp of optimal arousal. Thereafter follows a steep and expeditious deterioration in the individual's performance, i.e. a catastrophe. Hardy (1990) further proposed that cognitive anxiety behaves as a splitting factor that causes the normal factor's (i.e. physiological arousal) effect on performance to be smooth and small, large and catastrophic, or alternatively falling somewhere within the two extremes. The model also predicts that if there is low physiological arousal present in the days leading up to an important event, cognitive anxiety will enhance the athlete's performance in relation to the baseline data that can be taken from his training session. The model will predict either positive or negative effects of physiological arousal upon performance when there is an elevation in cognitive anxiety. This depends upon how high the cognitive anxiety is at the time.

Fazey & Hardy (1988) suggested four additional proposals based upon their model:

1. Physiological arousal should (for the most part) only be deleterious to athletic performance when there is high cognitive anxiety.
2. Predictably, there will be a negative correlation between performance and cognitive anxiety when physiological arousal is high, and a positive correlation when physiological arousal is low.
3. An average level of performance is unlikely to occur when high cognitive anxiety is present. Moreover, performance is likely to follow two distinct modes under conditions of high anxiety, as opposed to being unimodal when cognitive anxiety is low.
4. Utilising a number of statistical methods, it is conceivable that 'real-life data' be applied to cusp catastrophes.

Optimum Arousal Theory

According to the Optimum Arousal Theory (Yuri Hanin) each athlete will perform at their best if their level of arousal or competitive anxiety falls within their optimum functioning zone. The challenge for the coach is to determine the athlete's zone and identify the techniques that will place the athlete in this zone prior to competition.

Despite its shortcomings, catastrophe model has been regarded by many as a plausible 'up to date' alternative to the outmoded multidimensional theory. Nevertheless, the multidimensional theory has been invaluable in leading the way towards the identification and establishment of cognitive and somatic anxiety or physiological arousal as two distinct sub-components of A-state.

Assessment of Sport Anxiety

A range of psychometric tests or sport anxiety questionnaires (SAQ) have been used by sports psychologists to understand and measure anxiety. The most widely used anxiety questionnaires these days are Taylor Manifest Anxiety Scale, Speilberger's Trait Anxiety Inventory (TAI), State Anxiety Inventory (SAI), CSAI-2 by Rainer Martens et al., (1990).

In 1966 Charles Spielberger argued that it was necessary to

make a distinction between momentary states and more permanent traits.

- Anxiety states (A-state) is our response to a particular situation (i.e. sky diving)
- Anxiety traits (A-trait) are the characteristics of our personality, our general anxiety level

Martens (1990) developed anxiety traits (A-trait) questionnaires that were tailored specially to sport known as the Sport Competition Anxiety Test (SCAT), briefly described below:

> It is a test measuring the tendency of an athlete to experience anxiety when competing in a sport. It is used to measure competitive trait anxiety. Test scoring is based on 10 questions that ask individuals how they feel when competing in sports and games. Each item is answered on a three-point scale (often, sometimes, hardly ever) and a summary score ranging from 10 (low competitive trait anxiety) to 30 (high competitive trait anxiety) is computed for each respondent

Martens recognized that any measure of sport anxiety must take into consideration cognitive anxiety (negative thoughts, worry) and somatic anxiety (physiological response). The Competitive State Anxiety Inventory or CSAI-2 takes into account the difference between A-state and A-trait and distinguishes between cognitive and somatic anxiety.

Summing up Sport Anxiety Issue

The following facts deduced from the theoretical discussion on and dynamics of sport anxiety might bring the issue to some logical conclusion:

- Only an *optimal* anxiety level facilitates the best performance; both high and low anxiety levels are debilitative.
- The optimal anxiety threshold *differs* from athlete to athlete, and from situation to situation in the same athlete.
- With rise in performance level and experience in a sporting event, the athlete is able to manage anxiety and convert it into a success factor.
- The optimal arousal level varies as function of task complexity and athlete's skill status. As an explanation, elite athletes performing simple tasks need a moderately high level of arousal for optimal performance; less skilled

athletes and those performing a complex task require relatively low level of arousal for maximum performance,

- A high skill and fitness level is helpful and conducive to anxiety reduction. A long-term engagement in sport is necessary for anxiety decrease, control and management.
- State anxiety is a situational variable, which with proper psychological conditioning and training, can be kept under check. A major difference between high and low performing athletes lies in their ability to control and manage anxiety.
- Pre-competition anxiety is natural and occurs inevitably in all athletes, but highly experienced athletes are much less influenced by it than novices, young athletes and those less experienced.

Anxiety Management

Coping with anxiety, whether in life or in sport, is a Herculean task. Consciously, or unconsciously people wrestle with anxiety in variety of ways; for instance, by reacting to the emotional situation(s) violently using a variety of defence mechanism or adopting a few cognitive and somatic relaxation techniques. The extent to which one succeeds in doing so largely depends on (1) intensity and frequency of anxiety situations encountered over time; (2) age, sex and mental makeup of the individual; (3) routine efforts to diffuse anxiety; and (4) attempts to adjustment lifestyle.

In sport, things are different. While it is important for an athlete to have some kind of internal-external stress without which he cannot perform with full vigour and the same time keep performance anxiety, arising out of stress, under proper control, not allowing it to go beyond permissible limits. In other words, every athlete has to *"psyche up"* (deliberately arouse himself physically and mentally so as to generate enough strength and power to perform); *calm down* (keep his cool and not emotionally arouse himself beyond certain limits); and *overcome performance anxiety* (be in control of himself by tacking external disturbing elements, and maintain a constant state of equilibrium). In order to attain this state of checks-and-balances, coaches and sport psychologists insist upon athletes to make use of one or other strategies (techniques) now available in great variety.

As anxiety has both somatic (physiological arousal) and psychic (feeling tone) manifestations, some of the anxiety management techniques are somatic, others cognitive. Reduction in physiological arousal often correspondingly results in decrement of anxiety tension. Muscular tension (not synonymous with anxiety but a component of it) is one of the factors that usually accompanies cognitive and somatic anxiety, says Cox (1994). According to Cratty (1989), anxiety-management techniques fall in three major categories: (1) ***Somatic Techniques*** (bodily processes), which include adjustment muscular tension, breathing and/or cardio-vascular functions influencing peripheral circulation and heart rate; (2) ***Visualization Methods***, e.g. visual imagery; and (3) ***Cognitive Adjustment Methods*** involving ways of changing thought processes (how and what to think – meta-cognition or quality of thought). Depending upon the situation, these anxiety-management techniques may be used singly or in combination.

(a) Somatic Techniques

Physical techniques of anxiety management are many and each one can be used for specific purpose in specific situation. Major techniques are described below:

Somatic Adjustment

Due to psycho-physical integration of the human organism, what happens in physical domain at once has its impact felt in the psychic domain and vice versa. Emotional reactivity during intense anxiety, anger, fear, or love recognizes no borders between what is physical and what is psychological. When an athlete is in a state of terrible anxiety or anger, the upheaval that follows is felt both in body and mind simultaneously and without exception. On the one hand, terrific changes occur in heart rate, respiration, muscle potential, metabolic functions, hormonal functions, etc., and on the other, there is utter confusion, loss of confidence, poor concentration, a feeling of heaviness in mind and limb, etc. The bodily and mental functions define and influence each other. Somatic adjustment necessarily brings about corresponding changes in the feeling tone associated with emotion (anxiety). However, control of observable behaviour is fairly impossible without exerting some deliberate control over cognitive process, for example, attitude. Even though called somatic, none of the techniques placed under this head is purely associated with bodily processes: in other words, it is not at all wholly somatic. The chief objective of the use of these strategies is to make the nerves and muscles relax by bringing about physiological changes that are diagonally opposite to the fight response of the sympathetic nervous system.

Progressive Relaxation

Edmund Jacobson (1929, 1938) argued that 'an anxious mind cannot exist in a relaxed body'. Resultantly, he came out with the *Progressive Relaxation Technique* with the underlying idea that if we learnt how to reduce the muscular tension, mental tension produced by anxiety could well be reduced and thus controlled. In this technique, the subject is first made to identify the highly tense muscle groups, then become aware of the degree of tension inflicting them, induce more tension in the affected muscle groups, and finally progressively relax them. According to Jacobson's premise, muscular system and emotional states are directly linked; when peripheral skeletal muscles are placed under conscious control, the inner state of the person comes under better self-control.

Progressive relaxation technique has been widely used by sportspersons, however with mixed results. Most researchers have found it highly useful in streamlining physiological functioning but its effects on psychological aspects of anxiety are yet to be monitored more accurately. If used in conjunction with other relaxation techniques, e.g. visualization, it yields better results.

Autogenic Training

In progressive relaxation, the athlete practices dynamic muscle contraction-relaxation, the autogenic training focuses on feelings connected with limbs and muscles. Based on the idea of auto-hypnosis, the autogenic training, in its simplest form, consists of a series of mental exercises designed to bring about sensations of (1) heaviness in limbs, and (2) a feeling of general warmth in the body, arms and legs. Though exercises intended to bring about relaxation differ from one another, the autogenic training primarily consists of (a) auto-suggestion to the mind of a feeling of warmth in the body, and heaviness in the limbs; (b) imagery or visualization of the relaxing scenes, and (c) specific themes such as self-sentiments - suggestion to the mind that the body is really relaxed or getting relaxed.

The use of autogenic training as an adjunct to sports training procedure has been ascendant over the decades for its capability to help athletes achieve a relaxed state of mind during stressful competition situations. However, direct relationship between autogenic training and athletic performance is still a matter of remote reckoning, requiring deeper investigations. Notably, controlling mental processes and also emotional feelings is the most difficult thing to achieve.

Meditation

Basically meditation is a yogic concept, practiced in conjunction with (or as part of) other sequential exercises, with the single aim achieve a state of utmost concentration (selective attention) on a specific thought, object or mind (especially *shunya* or nothing in particular), and eliminate the feelings associated with excessively heavy, useless, and troublesome thoughts or experiences, thereby achieving a calm and serene state of mind. Meditation may be practiced with or without chanting of a scriptural *mantra* (a magic word or sentence). However, the practitioners of yoga believe that meditation on the *Brahma* – the ultimate universal celestial power – or any described object may not be possible without exerting strict controls on such psycho-physical processes as *achara* (conduct), *vichara* (thinking), *vyavahara* (routine activities, behaviour), *ahara* (diet), and *nidra* (sleep). For the West, meditation means simply a mental relaxation device or a technique of developing selective attention, which is possibly not correct.

Benefits of mediation for athletes in terms of stabilized cardio-respiratory and autonomous functions are immense. Meditation inter alia helps sportspersons to effect thought-focusing, behavioural modification and achieve a state of one-pointed-ness. Cratty (1989) refers to subjective reports of athletic teams that have employed techniques of meditation indicating that athletes were well-focused on the game and aggressed appropriately without becoming overly aroused. Researchers, however, differ in their views about the use and efficacy of Zen meditation and transcendental meditation in sport contexts. Unless strict regulatory procedure and progression are maintained in the practice of mediation, no tangible results could be expected.

Benson's Relaxation Response

Benson's technique is a form of meditation that can be used to attain quite a deep sense of relaxation and can be ideal for staying calm in between rounds of a competition. It can be mastered with just a few weeks' practice and comprises of seven easy steps:

1. Sit in a comfortable position and adopt a relaxed posture;
2. Pick a short focus word that has significant meaning for you and that you associate with relaxation (e.g. relax, smooth, calm, easy, float, etc.);
3. Slowly close your eyes;
4. Relax all the muscles in your body;
5. Breathe smoothly and naturally, repeating the focus word;
6. Be passive so that if other thoughts enter your mind, dismiss them with, 'Oh well' and calmly return to the focus word – don't concern yourself with how the process is going;
7. Continue this for 10-15 minutes as required.

Letting go

Resembling Jacobson's progressive relaxation technique, "letting go" is a useful exercise in removing muscular tension. If you wish, you can also use this exercise to aid a restful night's sleep. Just lie down somewhere comfortable where you are unlikely to be disturbed. Close your eyes and let your attention wander slowly over each part of your body – starting from the tips of your toes and working up to the top of your head. As you focus on each part of the body, make the associated muscles tense for a count of five and then 'let go'. If this does not relieve the tension in a particular body part, repeat the process as many times as you need to. Once you have covered each body part, tense the entire body, hold for five and then 'let go'. You will feel tranquil and deeply relaxed.

The Five Breath Technique

This anxiety control exercise can be performed while you are standing up, lying down or sitting upright. It is ideally used just before competition, or whenever you feel particularly tense. You should inhale slowly, deeply and evenly through your nose, and exhale gently through your mouth as though flickering, but not extinguishing, the flame of a candle:

- Take a deep breath. Allow your face and neck to relax as you breathe out;
- Take a second deep breath. Allow your shoulders and arms to relax as you breathe out;
- Take a third deep breath. Allow your chest, stomach and back to relax as you breathe out;

- Take a fourth deep breath. Allow your legs and feet to relax as you breathe out;
- Take a fifth deep breath. Allow your whole body to relax as you breathe out;
- Continue to breathe deeply for as long as you need to, and each time you breathe out say the word 'relax' in your mind's ear.

Biofeedback

Biofeedback technique is based on the premise that with constant practice human beings are able to control and modify body's autonomic activity, which is generally considered involuntary. Using this technique the subject learns how to monitor auditory or visual signals about his heart rate and experiments with those feelings, thoughts and sensations which help him stabilize functioning of his heart especially under highly stressful conditions. Besides the heart rate, galvanic response, muscular tension, peripheral body temperature, brain-wave changes, etc., are also used as biofeedback information to monitor the activation-arousal level, with an aim to reduce it and ensure relaxation.

Biofeedback technique is being increasingly used with sportspersons with encouraging results in managing anxiety and keeping it at an optimal level during competition. Biofeedback is a good device for the athletes to get aware of their arousal level, reduce anxiety by a deliberate effort and thus improve ability to perform. The technique can also be used in the field-setting for an instant help to the stressed athletes. It serves as an objective parameter for providing direction to their attentional focus.

Other somatic techniques include 'physical exercise, hypnosis, autohypnosis, sexual intercourse etc.', (Cratty 1989).

(b) Visualization Methods

Visualization (Imagery)

Visualization, also called imagery, is based on a common notion that imagining a scene or "thinking" a thought consciously creates its, more or less, permanent image on our mind and helps us to use it as a raw material for (or to translate it into) its actual performance. Imagery is referred to as a "mental process", so important to mental practice, mental rehearsal, cognitive rehearsal, or visualization technique, used by athletes in their effort to improve skill, perform an activity exactly as it should be performed and manage anxiety.

One form of imagery is ***thought-stopping*** in which an athlete puts a sudden stop to a negative thought that has been troubling him, and to (better) replace it with a more useful and positive thought. Precisely, when you experience a negative or unwanted thought (cognitive anxiety) such as *'I just don't want to be here today'* or *'He beat me by five metres last time out'*, picture a large red stop sign in your mind's eye. Hold this image for a few seconds then allow it to fade away along with the thought. If you wish, you can follow this with a positive self-statement such as 'I am going to hit it hard right from the off!' Thought-stopping can be used to block an unwanted thought before it escalates or disrupts performance. The technique can help to create a sharp refocus of attention keeping you engrossed in the task at hand.

A second type of imagery is mind's ***"movement in space and time"*** wherein the athlete imagines cruising through, or in and out of space and time so that some positive changes are produced that effect anxiety reduction. The idea is to let the athlete mentally live through some previous positive (pleasant) experiences rather than focus on the current stressful situation and the pangs it gives. Moving forward and backward in time helps a person to manage anxiety. It is, more or less, a *stream of consciousness* experience.

Mental Skill Rehearsal is yet another type of imagery in which the athlete concentrates on a particular skill or a group of skills and their complex parts in which he finds himself deficient and is unable to perform them with full confidence. As an imagery exercise, the athlete is asked to perform certain tasks in certain imagined or actual situations in his effort to tackle anxiety and reduce its impact. Mental skill rehearsal strategy has such components as replication and elimination of social stresses.

Visual-Motor Behaviour Rehearsal is a combination of progressive relaxation and imagery techniques. In this, the athlete practices a skill mentally under social stresses spotted in actual competition situations. The practice (or life) situations are made competitive i.e. stressful, and skill-practice carried out in mind (imagination) so that when actual competition is played, the performance flow is natural and uninterrupted. Elite athletes benefit more from this strategy than less skilled or inexperienced athletes.

Centering

'Centering' involves focusing attention on the centre of your body, the area just behind your navel. This technique is particularly effective during sports that have breaks in the action, such as in between sets in tennis, or prior to a penalty in soccer. Centering has a calming and controlling effect, providing a simple but effective way to counteract the negative effects of anxiety:

- Stand with your feet flat on the ground, shoulder width apart, arms hanging loosely either side of your body;
- Close your eyes and breathe evenly. Notice that when you breathe in, the tension in your upper body increases, but as you breathe out, there is a calmer, sinking feeling;
- Inhale deeply from your abdomen and, as you do, be aware of the tension in your face, and your neck, and your shoulders, and your chest. As you exhale, let the tension fall away and focus on the feeling of heaviness in your stomach;
- Continue to breathe evenly, focusing all your attention internally on the area immediately behind your navel;
- Maintain your attention on that spot and breathe normally, feeling very controlled and heavy and calm;
- On each out-breath use a word that encapsulates the physical feelings and mental focus that you want, e.g. 'loose', 'calm', 'focused', 'sharp', 'strong' etc.

Positive thinking and positive mental practice of an action spur positive neurotransmission, thereby making the performance of observable action and activities smooth and flawless. Imagery as an anxiety-reduction strategy may have some limitations.

(c) **Cognitive Adjustment Methods**

Known as "psychic weapons", cognitive techniques are powerful tools of managing stress, anxiety and tension both in life and in sport. Using them without expert guidance, usually from a clinical sport psychologist or a mental health professor, could be dangerous.

Behaviour Modification

This strategy has the backing of the theories of association and conditioning. The idea is that an athlete can identify anxiety-producing situations and factors and deliberately learn to avoid or disassociate himself with them, he might be able to manage his anxiety to a great extent. When successful avoidance strategies and responses occur (avoiding a trick, a coach or a specific apparatus around when anxiety happened), it is motivating; avoidance and the resultant anxiety-reduction become mutually reinforcing.

Flooding

Flooding involves exposing oneself to anxiety-producing stimuli while preventing the occurrence of avoiding responses. Sometimes this method is called *paradoxical attention* the objective of which is to heighten fear-producing imagery and then carefully make an attempt to reduce anxious response to what is experienced or imagined. This technique has been successfully used in various athletic contexts.

Systematic Desensitization

This is an important cognitive strategy of managing anxiety systematically. The technique begins with muscular relaxation procedure. The scenes of low anxiety (fear) to high anxiety are created in a sequential manner. As the athlete passes through each scene in his mind and moves up the scale, his fear responses are monitored. It is presumed that each successful attempt brings down anxiety level. The technique, being highly complex, may not be within practice range of each and every athlete.

Hypnosis and Autohypnosis

The use of ***Hypnosis*** and ***Auto-hypnosis*** in anxiety-management process has found favour with many athletes and trainers. Some people claim that under the influence of hypnosis, a common individual or an athlete virtually finds himself in a trance-like state or an *altered state of consciousness.* Under the impact of hypnosis, argue others, the subject rationally follows the suggestion of another person on account of his willingness to do so. In fact, hypnosis is a combination of several somatic and cognitive relaxation techniques. Positive outcomes of expect-guided hypnosis practice have been reported in literature. Research studies show that the athletes perform best under altered state of mind (consciousness) – also called *special state* – and hypnosis is a means of producing this state. While *hypnosis* *is done by another person, autohypnosis is administered by the subject* (athlete) himself, who induces this state by using certain positive statements. In several studies, effects of autohypnosis were reported positive and rewarding. Nevertheless, the technique is used by highly experienced athletes who know their own mind better than any one else can.

Apart from this, ***Meditation, Cognitive Meditation,*** and ***Rational Emotive Therapy*** (RET) have also been mentioned as anxiety-management techniques. Importantly, cognitions and thoughts, i.e. internal behaviours are capable of being learned, unlearned, modified and changed by conscious effort if systematic practice is carried out for long. If the individual is helped to learn how and what to perceive, and how and what to think at will, he will get habituated to this practice and get deft in changing his negative thoughts, states, and behaviours into positive ones and engage in activities that help produce a healthy, relaxed and cool state of mind characteristic of a truly well-trained athlete. These cognitive techniques are fairly difficult to master even when practice for months, even years for controlling mind and thought processes is not and easy task.

Rational Emotive Therapy works well with those athletes who often complain about facilities, equipment, officials, coaches, etc., and try to shift the blame for any thing that goes wrong with their performance on to others' shoulders. Irrational thoughts like these have to be removed from the athletes' minds by teaching them how to talk to themselves (i.e. do internal taking), self-talk, restructure their thoughts, and make all-out effort to substitute anxiety-laden thoughts with one that are less disturbing, least demanding, or low-anxiety producing.

The use of anxiety-management techniques has a direct relationship with the status of the athlete, type of sport one plays and its demands, level of one's experience in the game, level of one's intelligence, the calibre of the coach, expertise for intervention programme available, and the like. No single technique is flawless.

Performance Anxiety Management

To reach an optimum psychological state, as an athlete you need to understand your own natural responses to stress and be sensitive to your bodily signals. Learning to handle the demands of competition involves learning to read your thought patterns and physical responses, and to develop the skills necessary to find your ideal arousal level. Stress management requires excellent self-awareness because, if you know yourself well, you will better understand the roots of your anxiety.

Anxiety is a reality in sport. It cannot be banished from the scene nor from the mind; it can not be controlled either as some would profess to do; it can only be handled carefully and managed skillfully so that what debilitates performance begins to facilitate it. Since anxiety is directly linked to the physiological arousal and is also a matter of *feelings* that arise at a given moment of time, it naturally reflects what goes on inside one's body and mind (akin to an *upheaval-like state* indeed). Therefore, learning to handle the demands of competition involves learning to read your thought patterns and physical responses, and to develop the skills necessary to find your ideal arousal level. How one can expect to perform well given such an internal environment, is a million dollar question the answer to which is not easy to find, but realizing the presence of the malady is the first step towards knowing its nature and diagnosing its cause. Athletic trainers may try to help the athlete understand why disturbing thoughts and feelings develop and then try to change or modify that process with limited amounts of success. Why such thoughts arise may be of interest, but knowing the answer is not always necessary to overcome them. Trying to explore the situation is an important step towards remedying it.

As sport competition draws near, anxiety begins to develop in the athlete, and it is encountered before the event, during the event and also after the event. It makes a vicious circle. Notwithstanding complex cognitive and relaxation anxiety management techniques suggested in literature, simple measures, as described below, could be taken to handle anxiety.

Before the Event

Understand that pre-event jitters are normal and accept them. Don't fight the nervous energy you feel. Don't misinterpret it by thinking that it is fear. The *adrenaline rush* you feel is normal and it is part of your body's natural preparation for the competition. Notice it, but don't focus on it. Once the event starts, that feeling will subside, as it always does. Prepare both mentally and physically. Arrive at the event with plenty of time so you aren't rushed, which only increases your stress. Get a thorough warm-up. Do some easy stretching. Know the field. Dress for conditions.

Allow a few minutes to *visualize* yourself doing everything right. Breathe easy, close your eyes and use mental imagery to visualize yourself performing well. This positive self-talk can change your attitude. While athletes need to be flexible enough to react during the event, you should enter the event with a general strategy of how you want to race. Your strategy can be simple (maintain a steady heart rate) or complex (catapult yourself into action straight away.

During the Event

Focus on the task at hand, not on the outcome. Stay present in the moment and avoid thinking too far into the event or thinking about the finish.

If you find yourself thinking negative thoughts or negative self-talk, stop and focus only on your breathing. Focusing on your breathing rhythm will automatically pull you back into the present. Force a smile, for sure. If you are struggling with negative thoughts and can't break out of the cycle, simply force yourself to smile, even if only for a few seconds. This simple action will change your attitude in a split second. Perhaps that is all the time you need to relax back into your performance.

Perform the action like you don't care about the outcome. If you find yourself caught up in negative thoughts and find that you suddenly expect the worst it will be impossible to perform at your peak. If you begin to perform like you don't care about the outcome, you may relax and enjoy the event for what it is - another day in your life. Not the most important thing in your life.

After the Event

Review the performance and recall the things you did well. Focus on actions, thoughts and behaviours that helped you perform. Acknowledge, but quickly dismiss things that hindered your performance. This is the same principle as avoiding an obstacle while driving - *look where you want to go, not where you don't.* When you focus on the pothole, you invariably hit it. Focusing on the negative aspects of the event will not help you improve in the future. Rather, you want to focus on the times when you 'got it right.' This is a form of mental rehearsal where you practice skills that will be used in the next event. Design a training programme that mimics event-like conditions. Teams and clubs often do such training. If you always train alone, consider joining a group so you can do this type of simulation. Practice is most effective if you can mimic the conditions you will be faced with in competition. Coaches can also help or hinder an athlete's ability to overcome choking during competition. Coaches often inadvertently reinforce a pattern of choking when trying to encourage ("the next shot is critical"). Such talk only increases the pressure an athlete feels to perform.

Remember that choking can be dealt with if you are aware of the pattern of negative thoughts that snowball before and during competition. If you find yourself in such a downward spiral, simply acknowledge those thoughts and let them go. Focus on your breathing and play as though you are enjoying it. Chances are you will realize that you are enjoying it despite the occasional less than perfect performance.

SELECTED REFERENCES

Bird, Anne Marie & Cripe, Bernette K. *Psychology and Sport Behaviour*, St. Louis; Time Mirror/Mosby, 1986.

Burton, E.C. In *Res. Quart.* 42: 139-144, 1971

Carron, A. V. *Social Psychology of Sport*, Ithaca, NY: Mouvement, 1980

Coakly, J.J. *Sport in*, 1994.

Cratty, Bryant J. *Psychology in Contemporary society: Issues and controversies* (7th Ed.), St. Louis: Mosby, 2001

Cox, Richard H. *Sport Psychology: Concepts and Applications* (Third Ed.) Madison, Wisconsin: WCB Brown and Benchmark *sport* (Third Ed.), Englewood Cliffs, NJ: Prentice Hall. 1989

Cratty, Bryant J. *Psychology and Physical Activity*, Englewood Cliffs; NJ, Prentice Hall. 1968

Crooks, Robert L. & Stein, Jean *Psychology – Science, Behaviour and Life*, New York; Holt, Rinehart and Winston, Inc., 1988

Endler, N.S. The interaction model of anxiety; some possible applications. In D.M. Landers & R.W.Christine (Eds.) *Psychology of Motor Behaviour*, Champaign, Ill: Human Kinetics, 1978

Fazey, J. & Hardy, L. The Inverted-U Hypothesis: Catastrophe For Sport Psychology. *British Association of Sports Sciences Monograph No. 1*. Leeds: The National Coaching Foundation, 1988

Hardman, J.M. & Johnson, W.R. The emotional readings of college athletes, *Res. Quart*, 23: 391-397., 1952

Hardy, L. A Catastrophe Model of Performance in Sport. In J. G. Jones & L. Hardy (Eds.), *Stress and Performance in Sport* (pp. 81-106). Chichester, England: Wiley, 1990

Hardy, L. & Fazey, J. *The Inverted-U Hypothesis: A Catastrophe For Sport Psychology?* Paper Presented at the Annual Conference of the North American Society For the Psychology of Sport and Physical Activity. Vancouver. June, 1987

Hardy, L., Parfitt, G. & Pates, J. Performance Catastrophes in Sport: A Test of the Hysteresis Hypothesis. *Journal of Sports Sciences*, 12, 327-334, 1992

Harris, D.V. & Harris, B.L. *The Athlete's Guide to Sports Psychology: Mental Skills for Physical People*, New York: Leisure Press, 1984

Ikegami, K. Character and personality changes in athletes, In J.E. Kane (Ed.) *Contemporary Psychology of Sport*, Chicago: Athletic Institute, 1970

Jacobson, E. *Progressive Relaxation*, Chicago: The University of Chicago Press, 1929, 1930

Johnson, W.R. Psycho-galvanic and word association studies of athletes, *Res. Quart*, 22: 427-433, 1951

Kamlesh, M.L. *Athletic Personality: A Psychological Probe*, Delhi; Surjit, 1990

Kane, J.E. Personality and physical abilities, In J.E. Kane (Ed.) *Contemporary Psychology of Sport*, Chicago: Athletic Institute, 1970

Krane, V. Conceptual and Methodological Considerations in Sport Anxiety Research: From the Inverted-U Hypothesis to Catastrophe Theory. *Quest*, 44, 72-87, 1992

Kroll, W. The stress in high performance athletes, In P. Kalavora and J.V. Danial (Eds.), *Coach, Athlete and Sport Psychologist*. Ontario; University of Ontario, Canada, 1979

Liebert, R. M. & Morris, L. W. Cognitive and Emotional Components of Test Anxiety: A Distinction and Some Initial data. *Psychological Reports*, 20: 975-978, 1967

Lingis, A. The void that awaits the force of anxiety, *Jr. Phenomenological Psychology*, 6 (2): 51- 1963), Sept, 1976

Link, W.A. *Der Stress. Institute für Menschen und management*, expert-verlag, Ehningen-Hamburg, 1993

Lorenz, K. *The Eight Deadly Sins of Civilized Man*, New York: Horcourt Brace Jovanorich, 1974

Loy, J.W. *The nature of sport: A definitional effort. Quest*: 10-15, 1968

Martens, R. *Sport Competitive Anxiety Test*, Champaign, Ill: Human

Kinetics, 1977, 1982

Martens, R. Anxiety and motor behaviour: A review, *Jr Motor Behaviour,* 3: 151-179, 1971

Martens, R., Burton, D., Vealey, R. Bump, L. & Smith, D. The Development of the Competitive State Anxiety Inventory-2 (CSAI-2). In R. Martens, R. S. Vealey & D. Burton (Eds.). *Competitive Anxiety in Sport* (pp. 117-190). Champaign, IL: Human Kinetics, 1990

Morris, L., Davis, D. & Hutchings, C. Cognitive and Emotional Components of Anxiety: Literature Review and Revised Worry-Emotionality Scale. *Journal of Educational Psychology,* 73, 541-555, 1981

Park, R. J. *Citius Altius Fortius.* The Academy Papers. Reston, VA: American Academy of Physical Education, No. 14, 1980

Picunas, Justin *Human Development: A Science of Growth,* New York; McGraw hill, 1969

Rethlingshafer, D. *Motivation as Related to Personality,* New York; McGraw Hill, 1963

Skubic, E. Studies of little league and middle league basketball, *Res. Quart;* 27: 97-110, 1986

Spielberger, C.D. Theory and research and anxiety, in. C.D. Spielberger (Ed), *Anxiety and Behavior,* New York, Academic, 3-22, 1966

Speilberger, C. D et al. *The State-Trait Anxiety Inventory,* Palo Alto, California; Consulting Psychological Press, 1966

Vandar-Zwaag, H.J. *Policy development in sports management* (2nd Ed.); West Port; C.T. Praege, 1998

Aggression is common in sport because it is common in life. Sport is meant to be a socially acceptable means of expressing aggression and many promote its cathartic effect.

- Unknown

CHAPTER - 14

AGGRESSION IN SPORT

Both animals and human beings have biologically inherited aggression as an emotional expression to the instinctive tendency of pugnacity or *fight* - a survival reaction meant to perpetuate organism's struggle for existence. While aggression in animal has limited biological motive, aggression in man has psychological and social orientation with chief motives being *possession* (acquisition of wealth, property, territory, etc.), *expansion* (making the self, community and society grow in dimensions), and *domination* (showing oneself as stronger, more important, and more effective than others). To achieve these objectives, man would not mind harming man physically and/or psychologically. In this sense, aggression is bound to be defined as *the act or practice of attacking without provocation especially beginning a quarrel or war.* Aggressive behaviour - a mild form - is socially approved and could be deemed necessary for individual's personal progress and social uplift but when human *greed* for anything crosses limits of decency, behaviour is bound to become hostile, showing up as aggression.

Etymologically, aggression stems from the Latin word *aggressio* or *aggredi* meaning "to attack". It is defined as *a forceful action or procedure, especially when intended to dominate or master.* Characteristically, it must be aimed at another human being with the goal of inflicting physical or psychological harm. "Aggression", says Cratty (1989), "is behaviour and actions that usually seek to inflict psychological and/or physical harm, either on another person or an individual's possessions or dear ones." According to social psychologists, aggression is often due to a conflict between the interests of two or more individuals or groups. Conflicts generally arise over limited resources such as territories, food and mates.

To some people, the use of the word *aggression* seems to be confusing in itself and with assertiveness. The term aggression is employed to describe angry violent behaviour with intent to hurt a person or cause damage to property. Aggressive behaviour is also used to depict a strong and somewhat adventurous effort. Thus an aggressive sales person or athlete, for example, may be perceived as obnoxious or violent by some and motivated and hard working by others. According to Baron (1977): "Aggression is any form of behavior directed toward the goal of harming or injuring another living being who is motivated to avoid such treatment." Thus, aggression:

- is an act not a cognitive state
- is not accidental, it is an intentional act to harm
- acts involve both bodily and psychological harm
- acts involve only living beings; harm to objects does not count as aggression
- The receiver of aggression does not want to get hurt.

Assertiveness, on the other hand, involves legitimate physical, or verbal force to achieve a goal. There is no intent to harm; therefore, it is not aggression.

NATURE AND TYPES OF AGGRESSION IN SPORT

Nature of Aggression

In psychological sense, aggression is often referred to "hostile or destructive behaviour" - the act of initiating hostilities or invasion, the practice or habit of launching attacks, or hostile or destructive behaviour or actions. Nature of aggression is no difficult to understand from several facts connected with it.

- During aggression, attack is initiated with the intent of injuring or intimidating the other person. Hence, aggression is deliberate and intentional. An inadvertent collision between two opponents in a soccer match while coming to head a descending ball, is no aggression, whereas slapping, forcefully pulling or pushing, or abusing the opponent, whether or not he is physically hurt, falls within the definition of aggression.
- As aggression is aroused, a sequence of behaviour (gesturing, abusing, pushing the opponent, etc.) is started in which the goal is to harm another person in some way.
- Most often the aggressive behaviour is directed against a *living* target (a human being), in which there is a probability greater than zero of imparting a noxious stimulus (such as hitting or striking another individual with a limb, a stick or an implement).

- Aggression constitutes any form of behaviour that is directed toward the goal of harming or injuring another person who is motivated to avoid such a treatment by guarding against the act in some way.
- For an action to be overt aggressive behaviour, it must be directed against a living target, thus excluding hitting a desk with a fist.
- There must a reasonable expectation that the aggression will be successful and that the target harmed. Thus, this excludes behaviour where the victim cannot be harmed, i.e. aggressor and victim are separated by bars or teammates.

Types of Aggression in Sport

Aggression has long been a part of the sport domain. Russell (1993) suggested that outside of wartime, sports is perhaps the only setting in which acts of interpersonal aggression are not only tolerated but enthusiastically applauded by large segments of society. In recent years, however, violence in sport, both on and off the field, has come to be perceived as a social problem. Infliction of an aversive stimulus, physical, verbal, or gestural, by one person upon another constitutes aggression in sport. It is 'not an attitude but behaviour and, most critically, it is reflected in acts committed with the intent to injure' the other person. Wide ranging acts, engaged by athletes, coaches and/or spectators, as physically hitting another individual and verbal abuse, fall within the definition of sport aggression. According to Bredemeier (1983) aggressive behaviour in sport means "the intentional initiation of violent and or injurious behaviour." By 'violent' is meant 'any physical, verbal or nonverbal offence, while 'injurious behaviours stand for any harmful intentions or actions'. Thus, an accidental foul or injury inflicted on another athlete resulting from inferior skills will not be considered as aggression. However, an intentional foul, although not resulting in any harm or injury, is considered as sport aggression.

Aggressive behaviour can be classified according to the primary reinforcement sought via the act. Leonard (1988) and Cratty (1989) identified two forms of aggression in sport, viz. (1) hostile, reactive or retaliatory aggression, and (2) instrumental aggression or non-emotional and task-oriented.

Hostile aggression is where the principal reward, or intent, is to inflict harm (physical or psychological or both) upon another for its own sake. It has an underlying emotional component, the outcome of which often is violence, with harm as its goal. Violence refers specifically to the physical component of aggression. It is defined as "harm inducing behavior bearing direct relationship to the competitive goals of sport, and relates, therefore, to incidents of uncontrolled aggression outside the rules of sport, rather than highly competitive behaviour within the rules of sport, rather than highly competitive behavior within the boundaries of rules of sport ." (Terry & Jackson, 1985). In other words, violence is equated with physically inflicted illegal and hostile aggressive acts. In retaliatory (hostile) aggression the aggressor aims to inflict injury on the opponent and make him suffer from the pain and injury resulting from aggressive acts/actions. This is accompanied by anger, sometime wrath, in the aggressor. On this account only, it is known as angry or reactive aggression.

Instrumental aggression, in contrast, is where the major reinforcement is the achievement of a subsequent goal. In this case, an athlete may intend to injure the opponent, but the most important goal to be achieved by the aggression acts is to win the competition, to be acknowledged by the coach, and the like. Instrumental aggression denotes actions that reflect simply trying-hand and employing strong effort without accompanying desire to injure to another person.

It may reflect (or even involve) a violent action but not necessarily hostile behaviour; its primary aim lies in gaining some material or psychological advantage over the opponent, and not to harm or hurt him. It is tantamount to "snatching" away the external reward or goal from the opponent who wanted to possess or enjoy it. Instrumental aggression truly is a "veiled" threat posed to the opponent through seemingly hard effort or legitimized hostile behaviour, in a way. In sport, such acts/actions as pitching at a terrific speed, kicking or hitting the ball hard or violently, charging, grunting etc., reflect instrumental aggression and are part and parcel of legitimate sport behaviour, violating no rule.

In nutshell, a comparison between the two kinds of aggression can be made in the following way:

Hostile Aggression "impulsive-reactive-hostile-affective"

- <u>Goal</u>: To injure another human being
- <u>Intent</u>: To make him/her suffer

- Reinforcement: The pain and suffering caused
- This type of aggression is always accompanied by an angry aggressor.
- Example: After being angered by being accidentally hit while sparring, the student purposely strikes the opponent.

Instrumental Aggression "controlled-proactive-instrumental-predatory non-impulsive aggressive"

- Goal: To receive some other external goal
- Intent: To harm the opponent
- Reinforcement: The external reward
- Example: During competition, student sees winning as important and uses unnecessary force to intimidate the opponent.

Overall, as the distinction between hostile aggression and instrumental aggression has been made evident, by no means should there be confusion as to which type of aggression is appropriate for natural game behaviour. On the face of it the relevance of the hostile aggression and instrumental aggression is outlined distinctively. When hostile aggression dominates play, performance would appear to wane in light of the aggressor being more concerned with harming the opponent than defeating the opponent. On the other hand, when instrumental aggression begins to possess mind, performance is more likely to improve given that the player harms the opponent in order of gaining an advantage.

The third behavioural tendency often treated at par with aggression is ***assertiveness***. Too much assertiveness is considered to lie on the borderline of hostile behaviour. Being assertive in a contest means using legitimate physical or verbal force to achieve a purpose, for example, scoring a point or goal, giving a power-packed punch to the adversary in boxing, tackling violently in soccer or intimidating an opponent in field hockey. In such cases, the intention of the asserting player may not be to hurt the opponent but he cannot restrain himself from causing some physical or mental hurt to the opponent, though accidentally. In the heat of the moment, the athlete may or may not be aware of whether he is asserting himself on the situation or retaliating. The discretion to categorize an athlete's behaviour as an act of aggression or assertiveness in a field situation lies with the referee or umpire, who inflicts penalty according to how he perceives situation and interprets it.

The relationship among hostile aggression, instrumental aggression and sport assertiveness (Fig. 14.1) is more a matter of rational interpretation of aggression as a general tendency with athletes in certain sports, the situation in which aggression dominates the scene and the intention with which aggressive behaviour is resorted too. Seeking an empirical explanation for this is a difficult proposition because several areas of ambiguity among the three exist.

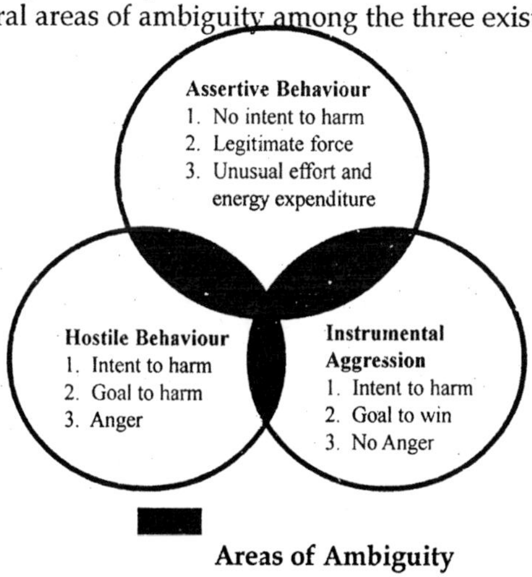

Fig. 14.1 Sport aggression and sport assertiveness relationship - areas of ambiguity

Possibility of aggression, as also perception of it, may differ from sport to sport and also from player to player, as is the intent to aggress. "Intent of action" in any sport and in a sport at any point of time will determine whether a player is indulging in hostile behaviour, using instrumental aggression to score a point or showing assertiveness in his attempt to dominate the play proceedings.

There have been attempts to distinguish between types of aggression based upon *antecedent* conditions i.e. conditions that *precede* or lead up to the aggressive behaviour. For example, while Moyer (1968) distinguished among (a) predatory, (b) inter-mate, (c) fear-induced, (d) irritable, (e) territorial, (f) maternal, and (g) instrumental; Brain (1981), divided aggression into (1) predatory attack, (2) self-defensive behaviours, and (3) parental-defensive behaviours - social conflict. In sport context, this categorization would mean going too far.

Like anxiety, aggression too is sometimes categorized as a personality trait and a situational phenomenon. ***Trait Aggression*** is an inherited relatively stable personality characteristic or disposition (an innate behavioural tendency) which makes a person respond to environmental stimuli with acts of aggression. Self-reporting (questionnaires) are usually employed to monitor it both in life and athletic contexts. ***Situational Aggression*** (state or episodic aggression) is a transitory state of emotional reactivity characterized by consciously perceived feelings of aggression, often resulting in some sort of physical or psychological hostility beyond ethically permissible limits. Precisely, a person may possess aggression as a general trait as part of his nature due to which he generally gets provoked by any situation and vents his anger in some way. Such a person is over-sensitive, touchy, emotionally unstable, and has low physical energy level. On the other hand, any danger situation may provoke even a perfectly normal person to react violently when he perceives an impending harm or threat to his self. The quality of response given to a particular situation, will determine whether an act constitutes retaliatory or instrumental aggression, or is simply assertive behaviour.

Sources of Sport Aggression

According to Terry & Jackson (1985), reinforcement for acts of violence may come from (1) the athlete's immediate reference group - coaches, team-mates, family, friends; (2) structure of the game and implementation of rules by officials and governing bodies; and (3) attitudes of fans, media, courts, and society.

Psychologists, by and large, agree that aggressive behaviour in all probability is learned for which the foundation is laid in childhood and during early sporting experiences. The first show of aggressive behaviour is seen in a child's violent reactions to ordinary life situations. Some children, who by birth are more aggressive, often fall into tantrums over trifles forcing parents to accede to their demands for toys, clothes, eatables, etc. Reinforcing aggressive behaviour greatly depends on what rewards and encouragements or deterrents and discouragements children receive from parents for behaving aggressively.

At school during intramural and extramural competitions and in club sport fixtures teachers, athletic coaches, team-mates, peers, friends, seniors and even parents become the source of children's aggressive behaviour because they want to see them "winning", excelling every one else all the time. That way aggressive behaviour may be inherited in one sense and acquired in another. Cratty (1989) observes: "Some young athletes who possess varying degrees of aggressive tendencies, perhaps, learnt in youth, may tend to select sport that requires a compatible degree of aggression". Reinforcement may take the form of rewards, such as praise, trophies, starting position, respect of friends and family. 'Vicarious reinforcement may be derived from seeing professional or top amateur players *lionized* and paid huge salaries, in spite of, or because of, their aggressive style of play' (Leonard, 1988). Players who do not display the desired degree of aggressiveness may receive negative reinforcement through criticism from parents and coaches, lack of playing time, harassment by team-mates, opponents, or spectators. Fear of retaliation too adds to aggression and counter-aggression, resulting in heightened aggression and circular effects.

The structure of a sport and implementation of the rules by officials and governing bodies constitute another potential factor in generating aggressive behaviour among athletes. In some sports, aggression is inbuilt in the play dynamics itself, and in others its intensity may rise with rise in competition. For instance, there is (1) direct and strong aggression in boxing, American football, wrestling, martial arts, etc., (2) limited aggression in basketball, handball, soccer, hockey, water polo, etc.,(3) indirect aggression in volleyball, tennis, badminton, table tennis, etc., (4) aggression directed only against objects as in golf, throwing events in track & field, and (5) little observable aggression as in gymnastics, figure-skating, aesthetic events, etc. Sports violence is most prevalent in professional sports.

Cox (1995) has listed several factors associated with occurrence of aggression in sport-specific contexts:

- *environmental temperature*
- *perception of opponent's intentions to aggress* (the athlete who perceives that the opponent is trying to inflict harm will respond in the same way)
- *fear of retaliation* (a victim of aggression will retaliate even more aggressively)
- *structure of the game* (closer the physical contact between the opponents, greater the chance of retaliatory aggression)

Game variables which often lead to aggressive behaviour summarily include: (a) *point difference* or *point spread potential* (aggression is most likely at the mid-point between a close game and a clear lead by one of the teams; conversely, closer the score of the opposing teams, lesser the chance of aggression; in such a critical situation where penalties for aggressive behaviour are very severe, neither players nor coaches take the risk of behaving unduly aggressively); (b) *playing at home (turf) or away* (every cock fights best on its own dunghill is a wise saying; it can happen in reverse order also; however, it is well-known that visiting teams foul more often while the home teams have more steals, rebounds and blocked shots as in basketball); (c) *outcome of participation* (defeat in a fixture makes athletes behave more aggressively towards themselves, opponents, officials, and/or coaches), (d) *league standings* (the lower the standing of rating of a team, the more aggressive it is in its struggle for improvement of its standing; in other words, as per the general trend of the current evidence, the leading teams in any sport fixture exhibit less aggression than trailing teams); and (e) *periods of play* (aggression intensifies as the game proceeds, the period of play and intensity of aggression are found related). Research evidence points out that acts of aggression occur more frequently among teams that lose, during games that are not close or too far apart, on the part of the visiting team, and after the first quarter of play.

Athlete behaviour is aggressive because in sports contests, the opposing individuals or teams try to assert their superiority in skill, fitness and playing ability over the other, and dominate proceedings on the field. The effect of victory and defeat in sport contests is not the same on all individuals depending on what aggressive tendencies they have inherited or acquired and what skills they have been taught to deal with the provocative stimuli.

Mass media also contribute to the acceptability of sport aggression. In fact, media occupies a paradoxical position. On the one hand it affords ample exposure to sports-related aggression via television, magazines, newspapers, and radio, thus providing numerous examples to children who may imitate such behaviour. It glamorizes players, often the most controversial and aggressive ones. Its commentary is laced with descriptions suggestive of combat, linking excitement to violent action. On the other hand, the exposure given to sport aggression by the media has stimulated increased efforts to control and prevent such behaviour.

In a two-way traffic of sport aggression, the media too profits quite a lot from its own practices such as writing feature articles and producing documentaries about sport and competitions. In fact, sport now is a primary source for the media industry to focus on. The exploitation of professional athletes in feature stories still secures TV ratings and sells newspapers, magazines, and books, especially when it comes to the issue of sports aggression. Generally, violent and rough play is highlighted in media more than general play. To make the news sensational, the focus is on sport violence in many of our print and TV news. Rough play guarantees interest and facilitates enjoyment presumably because of the fierce competitiveness it exposes and the aggression it generates all around.

For example, most sports telecasts prominently highlight the day's scores (e.g. in cricket, tennis); they also take time to recognize the scuffles, brawls, fisticuffs, etc., that may have occurred in a particular soccer, hockey, or basketball fixture. Similarly, on the *Sports Page* of a daily, firsthand accounts of such noxious happenings can easily be seen underlined. Whenever a fight occurs in a soccer game, it is so emphatically reported that one forgets who played how but carries the impression who assaulted whom and how and with what outcomes. An even better example is World Wrestling Federation contests. For anyone who has seen the WWF bouts on TV, they could obviously notice that violence is the name of the game here. Excessive replay of violent incidents (car or boat crashes; fights among athletes, fans etc...), and showing of a clip of a multiple collision and burning cars as a promotion for a racing programme. Everyone realizes that what is seen during the broadcast is scripted and "fake". The show is marketed with the fans' interests in mind (i.e. what spectators wish to see or read about – broken bones, bleeding noses, teeth knocked out, or severing players, limping players and badly injured players being carried out on a stretcher). Those packing the stadiums are a thrill-hungry lot who thoroughly enjoy aggressive play and add fuel to the fire.

No matter how you look at it, the media realizes that violence, to a certain degree, is tolerable and extremely profitable. So, it is going to be a long time before we see the extinction of violence in sports. The fact remains that violence is a well-established safety valve for players (i.e. fighting in soccer). If violence ceases to exist, it will not be the same game. There is no doubt that the media profits from violence, and therefore, in the interest of society, we learn to tolerate it and bring it under disciplinary control that will satisfy our needs.

Spectator violence is a reality of modern sport, and the research evidence is inconclusive as to 'whether fans incite player violence or reflect it' (Debenedotte, 1988). Spectators do take cues from players, coaches, cheer leaders, and one another. Spectators often derive a sense of social identity and self-esteem from a team. Emulation of favourite players is an element of this identification. Group solidarity with players and coaches leads to a view of opposing teams as enemies and fosters hostility towards the "out-group" and, by extension, its supporters, geographical locale, ethnic group, and perceived social class.

Aggression occurs in sports where an athlete's generalized expectancies for reinforcement for aggressive behaviour are high, (e.g. receiving praise from parents, coaches or peers) and where the reward value outweighs the punishment value (e.g. gaining a tactical and/ or psychological advantage with a personal foul). "Expectancies of reward (or punishment) for aggressive acts may be learned by previous reinforcement (or punishment) or by modelling/imitation of significant others such as coaches, parents, or sport heroes", say Tenenbaum et al., (1996). The winning has become an essential part of sport and increased professionalism creates an atmosphere of winning at all cost.

In nutshell, sport-specific factors influencing aggression in sport include:

- Reciprocity (we respond to being "attacked")
- Rivalries (traditional or "territorial") and "Protection" of team-mates
- Use of drugs (e.g. steroids, alcohol)
- Using sports equipment (e.g. hockey sticks, helmets, etc.) as "weapon"
- Athletic environment (e.g. a crowded, noisy, hot indoor stadium or gym; obnoxious fans)
- Taunting by opponents or fans
- Nature of the game (contact)
- Inconsistent officiating (leading to frustration)
- Media effects

THEORETICAL EXPLANATION OF AGGRESSION

Aggression is known to be the oldest instinctive tendency with animals including man. While working and expression of aggression in animals has remained almost unchanged ever since the origin of life, aggression in man has been influenced by wide-spread socio-cultural developments in human society. A few proposed theories for the explanation of aggression in life as in sport include biological, psychological and social learning theories.

Instinct Theory of Aggression

According to social-biologists, aggression (a racially old behavioural tendency), both in animals and human beings, is a legacy of the biological evolution, and is closely related to *struggle for existence* or survival mechanism. The instinct theory is based on the works of Sigmund Freud (1950) and Konrad Lorenz (1974) who considered aggression as an innate drive similar to hunger, thirst, love, or sex.

Explaining his psychoanalysis theory, Freud (1950) referred to aggression as an integral part of our existence; being inborn and innate, it is unavoidable. Like any other drive, it may be regulated through discharge or fulfilment. As a part of "death instinct" (*Thanatos*) - an urge for destruction - it gets directed outward or inward, depending upon the situation and state of the organism. When directed outward, it may cause harm to others (individuals, objects, materials, etc.) or expressed in activities that reflect extremely hard effort; when directed inward, it may become a potential cause for distress, mental disequilibrium, illness or physical disorders, and even lead to suicidal behaviours. Social constraints (societal rules and ethical codes) block aggressive impulses from getting released. Freud emphasized that expression of aggression effects catharsis (from the Greek word 'katairein,' meaning 'to cleanse) - a "purging-up" or "cleansing effect" - of the psyche, facilitating maintenance of homeostasis or internal equilibrium. The expression of aggression in a controlled sport environment, according to cathartic model is an acceptable avenue for the release of accumulated aggressive energy.

Lorenz (1966) argued that aggression has great survival value and evolutionary significance for the animals as well as human beings. For example, we are predisposed to protecting our safety and possessions. The instinct theory portrays humans as aggressive mammals that are driven by a biological instinct to fight, flight, or guard their mate, offspring and territory. Animals express their aggression freely in mating, fighting, mauling one another over spoils, etc. When the males of many species, for example, fight for mates, the strongest one(s) prevail, signifying that the *fittest* will reproduce, not the weakling.

An innate inhibition prevents animals from killing members of their own species, but Lorenz (1966) claims that human beings never developed this inhibition, probably because with neither lethal claws nor sharp teeth, they were unlikely to inflict serious damage on one another. Mechanical weapons of war (automatic guns, bombs, etc) supported by intelligence, make human beings the most dreaded of all living creatures. Lorenz suggested that the situation is worsened by social norms that suppress our fighting instincts, thus causing our aggressive urges to build up on to the point that they explode into extreme acts of violence. Some researchers have tried to link genetic factors with aggression.

"The main function of sports lies in the cathartic discharge of aggressive urge" (Lorenz (1966). He believes that sports are one example of a safe and socially acceptable outlet for pent-up aggression. However, Berkowitz (1969, 1972) pointing out the contentious points in the instinct theory and instinct hypothesis, provided the following arguments:

- inadequate controlled systematic research (research does not support the catharsis theory)
- use of ambiguous terms
- gross analogies and oversimplifications
- certain societies do not display aggressive behaviour or include aggressive games in their culture

Frustration-Aggression Hypothesis

Originally. proposed by Dollard & associates (1939), the frustration-aggression model is a variation of catharsis theory. It posits that aggression is a universal reaction to frustration. Initially the F-A hypothesis predicted that (a) "aggression is always a consequence of frustration" (or some drive), and (b) frustration always leads to aggression". The frustrated individual, assert the theorists, generally behaves aggressively because aggression stems from frustration. The inference here is that every time we are thwarted in the fulfilment of a need (or a drive towards some goal), we are expected to behave in an aggressive manner, venting out our anger on the object of our frustration or anything that comes our way at a moment our feeling of frustration is at its peak. For example, after losing in a football match, we may indulge in blame-game, have a tiff with our team-mates, brawl with the opponents or officials, yell at our dog, hit every object on our way home, or quarrel with family members at home.

The frustration-aggression theory is a psychological theory which differs from Instinct theory in that aggression may be the result of instigators other than biological instincts, such as environmental situation. Aggression, according to this hypothesis is situational and results when one's efforts to reach a particular goal are blocked (Leonard, 1988). In sports, frustration can be caused by questionable calls by officials, failure to make a particular play, injuries that interfere with optimum performance, heckling from spectators, or taunts by coaches or players. A more recent view of the F-A hypothesis suggests that the magnitude of the expressed aggression is dependent on:

- the amplitude of the frustration
- the individual's threshold for frustration
- the amount of frustrating incidents, and
- the magnitude of the anticipated retaliation to one's expressed aggression

(For example, consider a "yellow" or "red" card for rough play or an altercation between two or more players during a soccer match. The "yellow" card acts as a warning and the "red" card signals the ejection of the offender from the current, and in some cases future games. Now, compare foul behaviour in sport to foul conduct in every day life situations where the penalty may be decided in a court of law based on criminal assault charges. In which of the above described environments would you expect to observe more restraint? The soccer field or the side-walk behind the soccer field's stands? A crucial question in the F-A hypothesis researcher's mind is whether it is a biologically driven expression or is it a learned one?)

Based on the view that all behaviour is a by-product of various degrees of natural and environmental influences on the living organism, Berkowiz (1978) reformulated the initial F-A hypothesis. Thus, frustration does not automatically invoke aggression. Neither does exposure to aggressive models always lead to expressed aggression. Instead, Berkowitz (1978) postulated that frustration acts as a "readying mechanism" for an aggressive reaction. Frustration, and more frustration, gradually argues one's likelihood to display an aggressive response. He suggested that two conditions generally instigate aggressive behaviour: (1) readiness to act aggressively which is often associated with the anger (an emotion); and (2) presence of external (environmental) cues such as presence of individuals who are perceived as accepting aggressive behaviours, weapons, and certain objects an acceptable target for aggression. Berkowitz (1978) stressed that while we may respond to frustration by getting angry, our anger is not likely to be translated into hostile aggression unless aggression-facilitating external cues are present. Frustration is not the only cause of aggression; some other environmental factors might cause it.

Berkowiz (1978) does not entirely dismiss the acute cathartic effect of expressed aggression. In his view, an aggressive reaction to a real or perceived provocation results in a temporary feeling of relief. To describe the urge for a feeling of satisfaction following vented aggression, Berkowiz (1978) coined the term "completion tendency." Continuous reinforcement of one's completion tendency will lead to a learned expectation to "complete" each F-A cycle. This, however, is a vicious cycle; each completion cycle leads to a future expectation of the ability to vent one's frustrations. Thus, acute displays of aggression and a following relative calm lead to long term recurring incidents of gradually escalating "competetion" needs. Finally, Berkowitz (1978) agreed that an act of aggression triggered by frustration may prove cathartic. If the aggressive act, however, results in a learned behaviour, further acts of aggression may persist.

Berkowitz's conclusion that biological instincts and learning are closely intertwined is crucial to the derivation of solutions to the problematic infiltration of aggressive behaviours into all levels of sport participation and competition. Young athletes promptly learn that they can get away with certain foul behaviours that they would otherwise find quite difficult to justify in an every day, off-the-field situation. In some cases small, and in other cases significant modifications to the existing rules would gradually inculcate newly learned, more restrained reactions to incidents of on-field (erroneous calls by contest officials, fouls, etc.) frustration provoked aggression.

Berkowitz's distinction between "legitimate" (no fault) and "illegitimate (at fault) aggression is an important dichotomy to a better understanding of aggression in the sport context. Hitting in football, choking in judo, and/or punching in boxing are all examples of legitimate, within the rules acts of aggression in sports. Yet, despite the physical and aggressive nature of sports, such as boxing and football, neither sport's rules would tolerate choking. On the other hand, the rules of judo or wrestling allow a variety of aggressive acts, such as, pinning down, throwing, choking etc., but do not permit hitting or punching. Soccer players legally engage in rough shoulder to shoulder contact but risk a warning or ejection for pulling on another player's shirt or pants.

The "threshold of tolerance" toward aggressive acts that fall within the twilight zone of the continuum between "legitimate" (no fault) and "illegitimate (at fault) aggression is an area that requires close and careful inspection. When, or under what circumstances, for example, may a hit in football be regarded as "legitimate" force and at what point, if any, it may be construed as "too much" and thus represent "illegitimate" force. There decidedly is a constant apparent abuse of the thin, and invariably clear-line between "legitimate" and "illegitimate" aggression by athletes very frustrating. Most competitors are serious students of their game or sport. They are trained to push the limit, reach new heights - further raising the bar on the "legitimate" to "illegitimate" force continuum not excluded.

Two concrete examples of soccer rules that create fertile grounds for stretching the "threshold of tolerance" are the shoulder check and the slide tackle. Redefining the slide tackle in soccer as an illegal game strategy may not eliminate it from occurring in the game, but it may definitely help reduce excessively aggressive defensive play. A positive side effect resulting from such a change in game rules may be an added advantage to the offensive players. A less vulnerable attacker may be able to score more often—a sorely needed feature in the present game.

Social Learning Theory

Social psychologists repose no confidence in drive theory and innate nature of aggression. Instead, they believe that aggressive behaviour is largely learned and that social environment is the chief agent responsible for provoking, propagating, maintaining, weakening (diminishing) or strengthening aggression in human beings. The social learning theory has received the most empirical verification (Leonard, 1988). While acknowledging the existence of physiological mechanisms for aggression and rage, Albert Bandura (1973, 1986) was strongly critical of the instinct and the frustration-aggression hypothesis. Calling catharsis hypothesis "utter nonsense", he emphatically stressed that learning and experience modified and shaped aggressive behaviours; they seldom represent the work of isolated biological instincts. Successful, unchallenged aggressive acts, according to Bandura, lead to further aggression. The circular pattern of aggression may continue and escalate until this vicious cycle is interrupted by a counteracting reinforcer.

The aggressive act an individual will express depends on the range of aggressive responses the individual has acquired, plus the consequences (possible punishments and/or rewards) that the individual anticipates for expressing some hostile act. An act of aggression, when reinforced, leads to another aggressive act, and possibly stronger than the one given on previous occasion. People usually learn to be aggressive by observing others' behaviour, if it is tolerated, eulogized, appreciated, awarded or rewarded.

The social learning theory maintains that aggressive behaviour is learned through modelling and reinforced by praise, trophies, starting positions, rewards and punishments. Young athletes take sports heroes as role models and imitate their behaviours (mannerisms, attire, modes of walking and talking, styles of play, etc). Other models demonstrating support for aggressive styles of play may include parents, coaches and team-mates. According to Cox (1990), the social learning theory "provides the single most viable explanation for the continued rise of aggression and violence in amateur and professional sports."

Physiological and Psychological Constructs

Numerous researchers have attempted to explain aggression phenomenon by combining physiological-arousal-activation and psychological (cognitive) processes. In this new approach, variables generally considered are physiological arousal, moral reasoning, and aggression-performance relationship. It is hypothesized that physiological or undifferentiated arousal is a pre-condition for arousing hostility feelings, i.e. there being a cause present in the environment to aggress the other person. It is not unreasonable to believe that when a person is passing through feelings of aggression he is usually over-aroused physiologically where in sympathetic nervous system is in a state of high activation. This goes perfectly in line with the existence of two known aspects of an emotional experience - physiological arousal or activation, and feeling tone (intensity of feeling). It is, therefore, clear that an overly aroused person is in a state of frustration, and in the presence of an aggressive stimulus would naturally give an aggressive response. Relationship between arousal and reactive aggression is difficult to rule out.

High arousal in players, coaches and spectators may be one strong reason for sport aggression. Cratty (1989) observes:

> Activation together with the instigation of an obviously intentionally aggressive act by an individual, who may be easily retaliated against, will generally trigger direct aggression. This particularly is true if the aggressor is not likely to suffer any sanctions for the aggression and if the victim has, in the past, been awarded and seen the utility of direct personal aggression ("fighting hard wins games").

But activation itself is positively not a valid reason for the aggression to occur, some environmental factor must exist to inflame it. We are aware that oxygen itself does not burn but it helps burning the inflammable object. So activation may not cause aggression in sport; it may aid it to occur. In conjunction with some situational factor, it may help spread it.

On the basis of certain research reports it is speculated that sports that involve high levels of arousal, and a substantial amount of contact, will also result in increased levels of hostile aggression. Physical factors such as climate, season, heat, temperature, noise, crowd, alcohol, presence of opponents or some other unknown individual, etc., are facilitators of aggressive behaviour in sport. They interact with other variables to produce aggression in situations in which the likelihood of violent behaviours is high. Any object, situation or person may trigger off aggression if it stands in the way of an athlete's drive for a goal-directed action, i.e. attainment of an important objective or progress of an on-going activity important in some way. The role of media as an aggression catalyzing agent cannot be brushed aside especially in the case of younger athletes who are passing through an impressionable phase of life. Acquired comparatively at a young age, aggression is perpetuated in adulthood and carried out almost through out life.

Cox (1995) referred to several research studies that support the notion of a relationship between a person's promptness to engage in aggression and his state of moral reasoning. The high level of morality necessary for every day life is often suspended (or gets moved to backstage) during acts of aggression. This can happen during highly competitive sport fixtures also. Sometimes, assertive athletic behaviour, i.e. playing a dominating role, is misconstrued as aggression. Keeping "winning" as the central focus of attention all the time athletes have to be assertive on the environment, on the game and on the opponents without transgressing the boundaries of social ethics and personal morality.

Research generally does not support the belief that observing violence on the television screen or otherwise has a cathartic effect on viewer's mind. The reality, however, is that aggression increases over the course of the game and aggression begets aggression if no stringent measures are used to contain it.

MANAGEMENT OF AGGRESSION

Aggression is inherent both in man and in sport. Brushing it aside as a trivial issue would mean underplaying its implication for the health of the individual and that of the society. It is impossible to root out aggression altogether from society as well as sport soil; however, some serious efforts should be made by all concerned to reduce its incidence both in severity and frequency by using effective methods and means. The two-pronged strategy to tackle aggression include: (1) well-planned deliberate vigorous efforts on the part of the sport management (organizers, coaches, team managements, game officials, supporting personnel, sport federations, etc.) to create conditions in which the occurrence of aggression is minimal, and to take stringent possible measures to deal with it, should it raise its ugly head in any situation; (2) proper education and training of athletes and their coaches to control their aggressive impulses and cope with over-arousal, frustration and anger both on and off the field. The approach to the tackling of sport aggression menace has to be both long-term and short-term.

As a long-term measure, aggression control should become a part and parcel of the athlete's training right from young age. Unfortunately the thrill-hungry spectators (like the gladiatorial contest watchers in ancient Rome), the victory-maniac coaches, the money-minded organizers, the crazy media, the overly-psyched athletes, and other stakeholders may not be willing to oblige humanity by exerting necessary control over their emotions and keep sports an "aggression-free" zone, on account of their vested interests. The short-term measures include curbing or eliminating aggression-prone conditions, situations, and occasions on the basis of previous experience. Forearming to prevent and handle aggression on the field is an important aspect of strategic planning.

The ***International Society of Sport Psychology,*** in its position statement, has recommended to the sports managements to take the following effective steps to contain athlete and spectator aggression and violence in sport:

- Make fundamental penalty revisions so that rule violating behaviour results in punishments that have greater punitive value than potential reinforcement. (*There must be low tolerance and severe and swift penalties for athlete to athlete aggression, athlete to referee, coach to referee, and for coaches who support and promote aggressive play*).
- Ensure proper coaching of teams, particularly at junior levels, which emphasize a fair play code-of-conduct among all participants.
- Ban the use of alcoholic beverages at sporting events.
- Make sure facilities are adequate regarding catering and spacing needs and the provision of modern amenities at the sporting venues.
- Impress upon the media to place in proper perspective the isolated incidents of aggression that occur in sport, rather than making them "highlights".
- Make it incumbent on the media to promote a campaign to decrease violence and hostile aggression in sport which will also involve the participation and commitment of athletes, coaches, management, officials, and spectators.
- Organize workshops on aggression and violence for coaches, managers, athletes, media, officials, and authority figures (i.e., police) to make them understand aggression, its causes, the cost of aggressive acts, and the ways and means to control the aggressive behaviour.
- Assert on the coaches, managers, officials, and the media to encourage athletes to engage in pro-social behaviour and punish those who perform acts of hostility.
- Organize such programmes for the athletes as aim at helping them reduce behavioural tendencies toward aggression. The tightening of rules, imposing of harsher penalties and changing of reinforcement patterns (of awards, rewards, encouragements, punishments, etc.) are only part of the answer to inhibiting aggression in sport. Ultimately, the athlete must assume responsibility for his/her behaviour.

Guidelines for Physical Education Teachers and Coaches

Physical educators and coaches are in a key position to lay the groundwork for positive attitudes in sports. Guidelines for teaching children to abstain from or shun violent behaviour in sports include:

(a) *Put sports in perspective.* Coaches should not emphasize winning at all cost; rather they should make enjoyment and the development of individual skills as the major objective. They need to be alert to and praise improvement. Athletic performance should not be equated with personal worth (Coakley, 1982). Players should not be encouraged or allowed to play when injured or ill, as a demonstration of stoic virtue.

(b) *Place emphasis on participation.* Several studies show that many children 9-14 drop out of sports because they spend too much time on the bench and not enough on the field. They perceive themselves as *unsuccessful* because their level of performance doesn't earn them more playing time. It is better for young athletes to play on a losing team than sit on the bench of a winning team.

(c) *Present positive role models.* Sports violence is most prevalent in professional sports. Coaches should avoid symbolic associations with professional athletes and teams, and they should not model their own coaching techniques on those of professional coaches. They should encourage input, permit participation in decision-making, and listen to player feedback. Feelings of team ownership foster team cohesiveness, which in turn leads to better performance.

(d) *Integrate values-oriented intervention strategies into the curriculum.* Teachers and coaches should commit themselves to actively teaching positive sports-related values, and devise curricula that do so; for instance, sportsmanship or fair play code of conduct. They should know what is okay in sport behaviour and what is not through curricular interaction.

(e) *Involve parents.* As the earliest and potentially the most influential role models, parents can have a critical impact on a child's attitudes towards sports. Physical educators and coaches should inform parents of curricular activities and goals, alert them to signs of anxiety or aggressive behaviour, encourage positive attitudes toward competition and physical activity, and promote realistic expectations for performance.

SELECTED REFERENCES

Bandura, A. *Social Foundations of Thought and Action: A Social Cognitive Theory.* Englewood Cliffs; N.J., Prentice Hall, 1986

Bandura, A. *Aggression: A Social Learning Analysis.* Englewood Cliffs; N.J., Prentice Hall, 1973

Berkowitz, L. Whatever happened to the frustration-aggression hypothesis. *American Behavior Scientist.* 21, 691-708, 1978

Berkowitz, L. *Roots of aggression: A re-examination of the frustration-aggression hypothesis,* New York; Atherton, 1969

Bredemeier, B.J. Application and implication of aggression research. In W.B. Straub (Ed.) *Sport Psychology: An Analysis of Athlete Behavior* (203-213), Ithaca, New York; Mouvement Publications., 1983.

Coakley, Jay J. *Sport in Society, Issues and Controversies* (2nd Edition), St. Louis: C.V. Mosby Company,1982

Brain, *Multidisciplinary Approaches to Aggression Research,* Brain & Benton (Eds.), Elsevier/North Holland, Amsterdam, 1981

Cox, Richard H. *Sport Psychology: Concepts and Applications* (Third Ed.) Madison, Wisconsin: WCB Brown and Benchmark, 1985, 1990

Cratty, Bryant J. *Psychology in Contemporary sport* (3rd Ed.), Englewood Cliffs, NJ: Prentice Hall. 1989

Debendotte, Valerie. "Spectator Violence at Sports Events: What Keeps Enthusiastic Fans in Bounds?" *The Physician and Sports Medicine,* 16 (4) 203-11: EJ 372 800.1988, March

Dulard, J., Dobb, L., Miller, N., Mower, O., & Sears, R. *Frustration and Aggression,* New Haven, C.T: Yale University, 1939

Freud, Sigmund Why war? In J.Strachey (Ed.) *Collected Papers,* London: Hogarth, 1950

Leonard, Wilbert Marcellus. *A Sociological Perspective of Sport* (3rd Edition). New York, Macmillan Publishing Company, 1988

Lorenz, K. *The Eight Deadly Sins of Civilized Man,* New York: Horcourt Brace Jovanorich, 1974

Moyer, *Communic. Behav. Biol*. A, 2, 65-87, 1968

Russell, G.W. Aggression in sport. In P.F. Brain & D. Benton (Eds.) Multi-disciplinary Approaches to Aggression Research (431-446), Amsterdam; Elsevier, 1993

Terry, Peter C. and Jackson, John J. The Determinants and Control of Violence in Sport. *Quest,* 37 (1) 27-37. 1985

Personality is the essence of a human being.

- Gordon Allport

CHAPTER - 15

PERSONALITY AND SPORT

Personality is a household word. In our everyday conversations we generally refer to personality traits of people we know. For instance, we often say so and so is well-built, healthy and looks impressive; so and so is frail and weak, but reflective and serious, he is more like a philosopher; so and so is disciplined, terribly confident and assertive, so he shows himself up as an army officer; so on and so forth. In literature, philosophy, education, psychology, dramatics, politics, and in the tinsel movie world, the term 'personality' is used with breathless rapidity usually with reference to certain key figures - litterateurs, artists, writers, characters, actors, poets, heroes, villains, comedians, leaders, etc., all in different contexts. This way, it is natural for the personality to be understood as 'the characteristic blend of characteristics that make a person unique', or label it as "what makes one individual different from another".

The term personality is derived from the Latin *persona,* meaning "mask", which the ancient Greek dramatis personae (actors) in a play wore not as a device to *disguise* their own identity but to represent or *typify* particular characters. Later this term was used by Romans. The credit for using *mask* to denote observable aspect of personality goes to Gordon Allport. The concept was later embodied in more modern personality theories by Carl Jung, in whose view 'persona was at the outer edge of the self, a mask worn by the person in response to the demands of social civilization'. It was a role given to the individual by his culture - the part he was expected to play in life; in other words, his public personality (or image).

Since then, the notion about personality has been fairly flexible. The question whether personality is something fixed or dynamic, inherited or acquired, concrete or abstract, etc., is yet to be resolved in terms acceptable to all those who deal with it. At one stage, personality was conceived of as "the pattern of behaviour in a certain way", at another, it referred to an '*attribute that people possess in varying amounts*'.

Some people thought that all the stuff of which personality is made, was supplied by "intelligence of mind". Allport (1973) argued: "The term personality refers to both mind-in-particular and the mind-in-general. If we wish to study personality, we must be ready to shift our attention rapidly from the particular to the general, from the concrete person to the abstract person, and back again". Obviously, the expression "concrete person" refers to an individual's overt features such as his body-build, limb-proportion, complexion, posture, movements, activities etc., the "abstract person" imbibes intellectual, mental, spiritual, and social qualities, attributes, etc., which usually emerge from individual-environment interaction and experience. In order to understand a person wholly, it would be necessary to have an overview of him in general as well as particular measures.

Making comparisons is in man's blood, for it seems to be a good way to understand what you are in relation to others. Other way round, probably the best way to get to know other people is to know yourself, not as you imagine yourself to be, but as other people see you. Your character attributes can best be judged by your actions. You may think that you are generous, but others may view you as stingy. You may think that you are easy to get along with, but others may think that you are domineering and pushy. Your yardsticks of judging your own self and those used by society are always at variance. However, Kluckholn & Murray refer to three different norms of setting judgment on your personality; they contend: "Every man is in certain respects: (a) like other men (*universal norm*), (b) like some other men (*group norm*), and (c) like no other men (*idiosyncratic norm*)". In what proportion do *generality* and *particularity* combine to create a unique individual, is a mind-boggling puzzle. In social context, an individual (personality) is a complex whole of (a) *what individual considers himself to be*, (b) *what he is in the estimation of others*, and (c) *what actually he is.*

DEFINITION OF PERSONALITY

In dictionary, personality means "the quality or condition of being a person". It is defined as *the totality of qualities and traits, as of character or behaviour that are peculiar to a specific person*. No two psychologists ever agreed on the definition of personality. This is evident from some of the early definitions of personality, given hereunder:

- "Personality is the entire mental organization of a human being at any stage of his development. It embraces every phase of human character: intellect, temperament, skill, morality, and every attitude that has been built up in the course of one's life." - ***Warren & Carmichael***
- "Personality is the dynamic organization of interlocking behaviour systems that each of us possesses, as he grows from biological new born to bio-social adult in an environment of other individual and cultured products." - ***Norman Cannon***
- Personality is "the effect upon others of a living being's appearance and behaviour so far as they are interpreted as distinctive signs of that being." - ***Carl Pearson***
- Personality is "the more or less stable and enduring organization of person's character, temperament, intellect and physique, which determine his unique adjustment to the environment." – ***H.J. Eysenck***
- "More or less stable, internal factors ...make one person's behaviour consistent from one time to another, and different from the behaviour other people would manifest in comparable situations." - ***Child***

With fast widening personality perspective, modern definitions of personality have placed greater emphasis on external influences determining patterns of individual's behaviour than inherited traits. From a philosophical viewpoint, Dr. S. Radhakrishanan observed: "Personality is the union of our acts and potentialities, a complex unity of body, mind and spirit. It is the symbol of human integrity, of a constant and unique form created in the midst of incessant flux." Maddi (1988) pleaded that personality "is a stable set of characteristics that have continuity in time and may or may not be easily understood in terms of the social and biological pressure of the immediate situation alone." With Buskist & Gerbing (1990) personality came to be defined as "a particular pattern of behaviour and thinking prevailing across time and situations that differentiate one individual from another." Ryckman (2004) defined personality as "a dynamic and organized set of characteristics possessed by a person that uniquely influences his or her cognitions, motivations, and behaviors in various situations". Continuing this assertion, Mayer (2005) presented a more modern view of personality: "An individual's pattern of psychological processes arising from motives, feelings, thoughts, and other major areas of psychological function. Personality is expressed through its influences on the body, in conscious mental life, and through the individual's social behavior."

The concept of personality is dynamic because human *self* is dynamic – always acting, interacting, adapting, adjusting, assimilating and integrating, i.e. incessantly struggling for actualization itself. This fact assumes great significance when it comes to understanding, defining, explaining, evaluating and helping personality development.

The key points in personality definitions can be summed up as under:

- Personality is a dynamic concept, comprising of inherited and acquired traits, characteristics, dispositions, behaviours, tendencies, expressions, moods, attributes, feelings as perceived by others, etc.
- While the observable facet of personality is characterized by the differences in physique, complexion, postures, movements, activities, and behaviours among people, its core is made up of psychological qualities, characteristics, typical responses and traits peculiar to each individual.
- Individuality, being the *essence* of personality, makes personality psychology a complex "study of individuals – their distinctive characteristics, and traits, and the manners in which they integrate all aspects of their psychological functioning as they adapt to their environment".
- Personality is a *unique* organization of an individual's psycho-physical systems. Its complexity is thought to be shaped by genetic factors, family dynamics, social influences, and personal experiences.
- Physical, mental, intellectual, emotional, social and spiritual aspects of personality are mutually interactive and perfectly integrated; it is little gainful to discuss and develop one without reference to the other(s). Eysenck rightly pointed out that "the unique individual is simply the point of interaction of a number of qualitative variables".

To study generality (common human stock) and make generalizations about personality is far easier than understanding individuality (particular individuals) because no one is sure about how various "abstract variables" interact with one another and shape the growth and development of a particular individual. Uniqueness is impossible to understand, explain, and compare. Allport (1961) quotes Sherlock Holmes (the hero of the great detective stories from Sir Conan Doyle) telling his friend Watson: "While the individual man is an insoluble puzzle, in the aggregate he becomes a mathematical certainty. You can never tell what any one man will do but you can say with precision what an average number will be up to. Individuals vary but percentages remain constant".

With an essentialist's approach, Allport (1961) concludes the personality debate:

> Personality is what a person really is regardless of the way other people perceive his qualities or the methods by which we study him. Our perceptions and our method may be in error, just as an astronomer may fall short in studying the constitution of a star. But the star is still there, a changing object of study. My definition (of personality), of course, does not deny that a person is variable over time or that his behaviour may change from situation to situation. It says simply that the person has an internal structure and range of characteristics (variables, to be sure) ascertainable, and it is the structure that we hope to study.

DIMENSIONS OF PESONALITY

Personality is an integrated whole having concrete (the body hardware) as well as abstract dimensions (the mind software). Its different aspects are interdependent and so meticulously integrated that what happens in one compartment has inevitable direct or indirect bearing on the other compartments. Compartmentalization of personality into physical, mental, intellectual, emotional and social aspects, does not, in any way, preclude the concept of personality as an integrated whole; it is done for the sake of understanding this complex phenomenon more succinctly.

Physical Dimension

Our body, with a peculiar upright posture, is distinctively different from those of animals nearest to us. Physique is the starting point and a concrete basis of personality. Each one of has received this rare gift of nature from our parents through a process of biological inheritance. We are what our parents have made us – tall, short, bony, crane-necked, parrot-beaked, dark-haired, brown-eyed, fair-skinned, ebony-black or dark complexioned, awe-inspiring, timid, mongoloid, Negroid, stout or soft in build, and so on. Nothing can be added or subtracted from the physical features (traits) our genetic endowment has determined for us. The body is the plinth of our personality. Our physical profile is truly unique to us only; it gives us a distinct identity. Along with body, we also inherit from our parents the basic quality of our health, morphology (the capability of being a sprinter or a long distance runner), physiological capacities and physical attributes - looks of a jackal or a tiger, swiftness of a steed or steadiness of a tortoise, tendency to be a glutton or frugal eater, etc. Our body, its dimensions, and looks cast on others the first spell of our personality wherever we might be. A layman's vision about personality is usually restricted to its physical aspect - the bodily dimensions, outward appearance, i.e. what appeals to the human eye. The primary and instant assessment and evaluation of our personality comes from people on the basis of our physical characteristics, and we are meted out treatment by others accordingly in the classroom, on the playfield, in the market place, in the club, or else where. Most of our physical features are permanent, so difficult to alter even with surgery. Therefore, physical structure is the most stable dimension of personality - of course, fixed and non-modifiable.

A shapely body, a blooming face, and a towering physique instantly attract others' attention consciously or unconsciously. A frail body-build, a shabby look, and a sullen face generally repulse. No doubt, we cannot change or alter our physical features including our physiology, certain attributes like health, fitness, functional efficiency, strength, endurance, lifestyle, etc., can be improved through education, training, and positive social interaction. Plastic surgery, use of cosmetics and beautification devices may help us put up a better outward image of ourselves but this virtually adds nothing to our personality. Since ancient times, all great civilizations - Greek, Roman, Aryan, Chinese, etc. - have placed great emphasis on the development of a strong, healthy and aesthetically attractive body, capable of serving man equally well in war and peace. Plato considered body as the servant of the soul. 'A good servant', said he, 'ought to be robust and healthy in order to obey the master (the soul)'.

Mental Dimension

Human beings are the only species that is capable of thinking.

Nature has blessed them with a highly intelligent brain and complex nervous system, the two important causative factors for cognitive activity characteristic of intelligence. All humans are in possession of the same sensory-perceptual and cognitive processes, but they are not alike in mental abilities, i.e. the level and the kind of intelligence; some are good at music, some in art; some possess high lingual fluency, others high mathematical ability; some have tremendous aptitude for science, others can perform mechanical operations better and faster; and still others can carry out life routines hundred times better than others. We generally inherit basic intelligence and the aptitude for certain things from our parents.

Body without sharp mental processes is like a headless horseman that knows neither its direction nor objective. The powers of our mind (mental faculties) - reasoning, cognition, memory, judgment, intuition, imagination, decision-making, etc. - raise personality from the earthly level and give it a godly touch. Human beings behave intelligently because they possess mind - the psychological core of personality in the form of most basic and deepest attitudes, values, interests, and motives. Only human mind could create super-super computers and could make man run the most gruelling Marathon race just in about two hours. Only *superior minds* make superior personalities. If there were no mind man would neither be a rational nor a social being.

Intellectual Dimension

While mental dimensions of personality underline psycho-physiological abilities, intellectual dimensions refer to highly complex thought processes, rational thinking of the highest order and creativity. Our intellectual functioning largely covers such faculties of the mind as wisdom, intelligence, imagination, knowledge, artistic sense, finesse, creativity, etc., reflected in the behaviours, writings and works of great writers, intellectuals, academics, scientists, philosophers, statesmen, and others. We grow intellectually by interacting with learned people, great men and powerful minds, and intellectual giants and assimilating their wisdom. Some individuals may be quick-witted and possibly may exhibit mental sharpness very often but they are not necessarily intellectual because such people often lack the capacity for deep rational thinking. So they keep floating on an ordinary plain through out life only bothering to fulfill their biological needs and attend to life routines. Their contribution to the intellectual domain of life is negligible. Intellectual inadequacy is a serious lag in the growth of a harmonious personality. Intellect is not a matter of inheritance; it grows out of individual-environment interaction. Basic intelligence does certainly play part in the growth of the intellect.

Emotional Dimension

Apart from our mind and intellect, our passions (deepest feelings) and longings are essential guides to our character and personality. Human beings owe much of their existence to the power of these in their life affairs. Psychologists today have begun to believe in the dichotomy of mind into rational mind and emotional mind, and the exquisite coordination existing between the two in most moments of life. "In a sense," says Goleman (1996), "we have two brains, two minds – and two different kind of intelligence: rational and emotional. How we do in life is determined by both – it is not just IQ, but emotional intelligence that matters. Indeed, the intellect cannot work at its best without emotional intelligence". The feelings, psychologists argue, are essential to thought, and thoughts to feeling.

A life without passion (emotion) would be dull wasteland of neutrality, cut off and isolated from the richness of life itself. But, as Aristotle observed, what is wanted is *appropriate* emotion, feeling proportionate to circumstance. When emotions (anger, fear, love, sex, repulsion, disgust, frustration, hate, etc.) are too muted, they create dullness and distance: when out of control, too extreme and persistent, they become pathological, as in immobilizing depression, overwhelming anxiety, raging anger, maniac agitation. An emotionally controlled or balanced individual puts up a far brighter image of his personality than does the one hijacked by emotions.

With training and education, human beings learn to bridle and tame emotions. Notably the development of human personality is greatly influenced by emotional ebb and tide in life. In the discussion of personality, man's emotional life cannot be brushed aside. Emotionality is an important trait of personality; it affects our decision-making ability in crucial moments. Emotional stability means control over emotions. The individual is emotionally stable if he does not lose his head (reasoning, intuition, judgment) when under the upsurge of emotions. Emotional stability indicates good mental health, which is an important ingredient of personality. Emotionality, psychologists believe, may be an inborn characteristic to an extent, but the ability or the skill to exert control over emotions can be acquired by self-awareness and training.

Social Dimension

The role of environment in the shaping human character and personality has been discovered to be more crucial than that of genetic factors. This way, social dimension of personality assumes great significance. Man is a social animal and his growth as a human being is squarely dependent on the society in which he is born and brought up. Humanization and socialization of man occur only in society, and society only accords due recognition to human personality. The *individual self* and *social self* of man have to fit into one single mould and becomes indistinguishable. In the absence of such social attributes as character, competence, cooperation, coexistence, adjustment, honesty, integrity, sportsmanship, spirit de corps, etc., personality become a non-entity; it does not remain a concrete reality. A physically healthy intellectual giant living like a recluse in the inaccessible caves of the Himalayas, contributing nothing to the wellbeing of man and the society is no better than a temple idol – cold, insensitive and inert.

In the beginning, all children are egocentric; growth and interaction with environment makes them socio-centric, responsive and sensitive to the social influences. This facilitates development of the social dimension of their personality. Social norms and standards guide their conduct and behaviour. The way they typically adjust or respond to the environment determines what kind of social personality they would be developing – happy-go-lucky, shy, dominating, or submissive.

PERSONALITY TYPOLOGY

Personality typology, in vogue since the ancient times, refers to a technique of *classifying people on the basis of "shape, size, and body-form"*. ***Hippocrates*** (400-377 B.C.), a physician and an acute observer, was, perhaps, the first typology theorist who claimed that different personality types are caused by the balance of imaginary body fluids or humours viz. black bile, yellow bile, blood and phlegm. He attempted to classify people according to the predominance of one or the other humour, and attributed certain peculiar characteristics to each one of them. For example, individuals with an excessive of black bile were classified as *melancholic* (depressed and pessimistic); those with an excess of yellow bile were *choleric* (quick tempered and easily irritable); those with a predominance of blood were *sanguine* (cheerful, optimistic); and those with excessive phlegm were classified as *phlegmatic* (slow, impassive, unresolved). The Ayurvedic Body-humour Theory of *Kafa* (phlegm), *Vata* (wind), and *Pitta* (water) stands on the same assumption as that of Hippocrates, and still highly prized in understanding the temperament of a person and treatment of variety of ailments, disorders and diseases.

Though Hippocrates' theory was discarded long ago, some of its essential elements were retained by the succeeding typology theorists. In due course, ***Hall*** (1779) recognized four body types: abdominal, muscular, thoracic (long and slender), and nervous (cephalic). ***Rostan*** (1828) published a famous treatise describing three essentially different types of body-builds or physical constitutions viz. *type digestif, type musculaire,* and *type cerebral,* dominated by digestive, muscular and neural systems respectively. Rostan also hinted at some relationship between body-build and temperament. ***Viola*** differentiated three distinct morphological types calling them *microplanchnic* (individuals with small trunks and relatively short limbs), *macroplanchnic* (persons with large and heavy structure; bodies with relatively long limbs), and *normoplanchnic* (people with well-proportioned medium muscular frame). These names are just descriptive. ***Bean*** described three extreme variants viz. *hypo-ontomorph* (literally under-developed or un-evolved individual having a fat, round body, short extremities, and a relatively enormous predominance of visceral mass); *neuro-ontomorph* (person with a strong, massive, powerful body, with a relatively small forebrain or cerebrum, but a large cerebellum); and *hyper-ontomorph* (individual with a light linear physique with extremely small cerebellum). ***Kretchmer,*** whose body-classification technique achieved eminence in 1925, revived the Greek terminology and described three body types: *Pyknic* (compact and round), Asthenic (slender without strength), and *Athletic* (robust, and heavy musculature). Later he added to this classification *Dysplastic* (undifferentiated).

A German philosopher, ***Spranger*** (1928) published a treatise called *Types of Man* in which he classified human beings according to six basic interests and values they cherished:

Theocratic or Cognitive	Philosophers, scientists, explorers, lovers of knowledge and truth, etc
Aesthetic	Lovers of beauty, artists, connoisseurs of art, etc
Economic	Utilitarian people, businessmen, merchants, industrialists, tradesmen, etc
Political	Statesmen, politicians, diplomats, etc
Religious	Saints, mystics, priests, spiritual heads or leaders, yogis, etc
Social	Preachers, social workers, reformers, etc

Apart from this, very widely known personality classifications came from ***Carl Jung*** (introvert, and extrovert), and ***Sigmund Freud*** (oral and anal). Later, while explaining dimensions of personality – introversion, extroversion, neuroticism and psychoticism, Hans Eysenck remarked: "Human beings differ with respect to the speed with which excitations and inhibitions are produced, and speed with which inhibition is dissipated. These differences are properties of the physical structures involved in making stimulus-response connections".

Sheldon's Constitutional Typology

Also known as Constitutional Psychology, the Constitutional Typology – *the study of body-structure and personality* – became popular in 1940 with the efforts of an American psychologist William Sheldon (1898-1977) and his associates, and came be known as Somatotyping.

This so-called scientific system of body-classification was based on external appearance and, perhaps, the first ever empirical approach to understanding personality in a new perspective. In the beginning, approximately photographs of four thousand young men in nude were judged with regard to important physical variables. In his 1954 book, *Atlas of Men*, Sheldon recognized three components (fat, muscle and bone) for body-classification, using Endomorphy, Mesomorphy, and Ectomorphy as respective terms. He used a 7-point scale to evaluate each component, with extreme body types being 7-1-1 for an *Endomorph* (spherical, round, soft-bodied, under-developed muscles, difficult to lose weight, etc.), 1-7-1 for a *Mesomorph* (cubical, rugged, muscular, athletically-built, hard-bodied, mature muscle mass, excellent posture, thick-skinned, etc.), and 1-1-7 for an *Ectomorph* (linear, fragile, delicate, flat chest, lean, and lightly-muscled). The early two-polar classification techniques were discrete where as the distribution of Sheldon's components is continuous and unimodal. With 7-point rating scale for each component and also by applying intermediary ratings such as 4½–5 -5½ etc., Sheldon observed, that the entire world population could possibly be classified into 343 categories. Sheldon himself identified some seventy six somatotypes of which fifty are fairly common. Compound terminology is used to describe mixed somatotypes, the dominant type being used as the second (half) term so that an individual who is highly mesomorph with a strong endsomorphic component, for example, is identified as endo-meso.

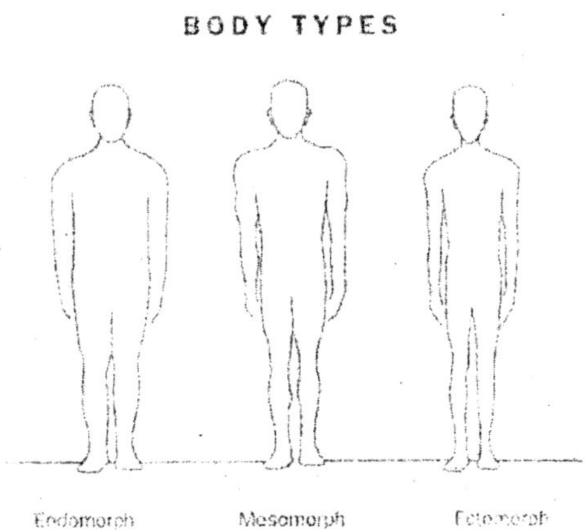

Fig. 15.1 Sheldon's three somatotypes

It is now believed that Sheldon's original purpose was to study the relationship of personality, temperament, and body measurements. He was seeking an answer to the question *whether those who look alike behave alike*. In this process, Sheldon rated the subject for temperament, which involves emotionally toned aspect of personality, such as joviality, moodiness, tenseness, and activity level. Hundreds of terms describing temperament were selected and eventually reduced, through statistical procedures, to three temperament types, i.e. *Viscerotonia, Somatotonia,* and *Cerebrotonia*. Endomorphy was correspondingly came to be related to viscerotonia (love of comfort, slow reaction, relaxation, love of eating, sociability, complacency, affectionateness, etc.); mesomorphy to somatotonia (assertiveness, love of physical venture, vigour, energeticness, need for exercise, love for dominance, risk-taking and chance, directness of manner, courage, general noisiness, need for action when in trouble, etc.), and ectomorphy was related to cerebrotonia (restraint in posture and movement, rapid reaction, over-tension, anxiety, secretiveness, action-inhibition, thought-introversion, need for loneliness , etc.)

The idea that these general body-types may correlate with general psychological types did not originate with Sheldon. In general outline it resembles ideas found, for instance, in the *Bhagawat Gita* (the Song Celestial of the Hindus) and Plato's "Republic" and propounded in the twentieth century by George Gurdijeff. Sheldon's ideas may also owe something to Aristotle's concept of the soul. Roughly the three corresponding personality types proposed by Sheldon are somewhat akin to Carl Jung's categorization of *thinking, feeling* and *sensing* types. As such they correspond quite closely to popular stereotypes of the skinny nerd, the jolly fat man, the slow-witted tough.

Despite an inherent powerful appeal, the constitutional psychology became a subject of big controversy and several objections were raised on its theoretical assumptions and the procedures involved. For instance, the research findings seemed to be contaminated because the ratings on the body and temperament were made by the same research scholars who admitted bias. Secondly, temperament is only a limited aspect of personality, even if it does show some relationship with physical characteristics. In fact, somatotyping is not a theory of personality in real sense of the term. Predictions from constitutional typology seem related little to a person's interests, attitudes and motivation.

THEORIES OF PERSONALITY

The approach of the psychologists to the study of personality has undergone a sea change in recent times. From speculative and rational it has become highly scientific, thereby contributing a lot to the building up of a very sound theoretical framework. Since Freud's psychoanalysis, a variety of viewpoints have come into existence each one with a distinct line of action, focus and explanation on the structure and dynamics of personality. The personality theories can be grouped into four distinct categories: Trait theories, Psychoanalytic theories, Behavioural theories, and Social Learning theories.

Trait Theories

Traits are descriptors for personality, which have their origins in everyday language, and used to label personality. Trait psychologists believe that behavour is determined by relative stable traits that are fundamental units of personality. These traits - known to be more or less permanent characteristics or building blocks of personality - predispose one to act in a certain way, regardless of the situation. For example, a person high in intelligence will behave intelligently wherever he or she is, and the one who by nature is less confident, will find it difficult to show up to be confident whether in a lecture class or on the soccer field.

Modern theorists view traits as continuous rather than discrete entities. So, rather than being divided into categories, people are placed on a continuum representing high or low each individual is on any particular dimension. The assumption is that we all possess each of these traits to a greater or lesser degree, and that comparisons can be made among people. For example, categorizing people into separate groups of 'sociable' versus 'unsociable' is considered meaningless. Instead, it is considered more useful to determine the amount of sociability each individual exhibits. Personologists regard most traits as forming a normal distribution, so some people will be high in sociability and others very low, but most people be somewhere in the middle.

The Idiographic Approach of Gordon Allport, and Nomothetic Approach of Raymond B. Cattell occupy the central stage in trait theories. The idiographic approach proposes that each individual is unique and there are some traits that may be possessed by only one person. So, according to the idiographic approach, comparing one person with another becomes meaningless. On the other hand, the nomothetic approach allows us to make comparisons between people. Its basic premise is that we are all governed by the same behavioural principles – so we all have the same traits and differ only in the extent to which each trait is present. While the idiographic approach defines traits by studying individuals in-depth and focusing on the distinct qualities of their personalities, the nomothetic approach has had its focus on the groups of people in an attempt to identify traits that tend to appear in clusters.

Allport's Idiographic Approach

Using long-term case study as the major tool of in-depth study of individuals, Gordon Allport (1897-1967) argued that all people have certain traits (personal dispositions) that are *building blocks* of personality (Allport, 1937, 1961, 1965, 1966). Calling these traits as *"pre-dispositions to respond"* or *"generalized action tendencies"*, Allport maintained that it is these "bona fide mental structures in each personality that account for the consistency of its behaviour". Traits, according to Allport, are both enduring and broad in scope and they act to unify person's responses to a variety of stimulation situations. For instance, an individual having the trait of friendliness might be expected to be pleasant and sociable when meeting strangers, helpful and supportive on the job, and warm and sensitive when relating to family members. Allport firmly believed that personality traits determine unique patterns of response to environmental events. The same stimuli might be expected to have a quite different impact on different people.

Allport described three classes of traits: cardinal, central and secondary traits. A ***Cardinal Trait*** is a powerful dominating behavioural predisposition that seems to provide the pivot point in a person's entire life such as competitiveness or money mindedness. Only a small number of people, recognized Allport, possess cardinal traits. Less pervasive than cardinal traits but generalized and enduring are ***Central Traits;*** they are the major building blocks of personality such as sensitivity, honesty, and generosity. Allport found that most people could be characterized by fairly a small number – usually five to ten – of central traits. Finally, the ***Secondary Traits*** such as the styles of dress, preferences for things and dishes, physical exercise, etc., are less generalized and far less enduring. They affect our behaviours in specific circumstances. These traits are often changeable and have less prominent part to play in the dynamics of personality.

Cattell's Nomothetic Approach

Cattell's approach to personality traits was just opposite to that of Allport. Unlike Allport, Cattell studied groups of people, not individuals. After identifying certain explicit (clear cut) traits such as integrity, friendliness, tidiness, etc.), he called them dimensions of personality or *Surface Traits* (Cattell, 1950, 1965, 1973, 1982). Cattell used both direct observation of behaviour in every day life situations and a variety of questionnaires to collect three types of data, which he categorized as follows:

- L-data - life record data, in which personality assessment occurs through interpretation of actual records of behaviour throughout a person's lifetime (e.g. report cards, ratings by friends and military conduct reports);
- Q-data - data obtained by questionnaires (e.g. asking people to rate themselves on different characteristics); and
- T-data - or objective psychometric test data (e.g. the thematic apperception test).

Applying statistical procedures called factor analysis, he found certain surface traits occurring in clusters which probably indicated the operation of a single underlying trait. The exercise ended up in a model of personality describing 16 trait dimensions as shown below:

Reserved ———— Outgoing
Less intelligent ———— More intelligent
Stable, ego strength ———— Emotionality/neuroticism
Humble ———— Assertive
Sober ———— Happy-go-lucky
Expedient ———— Conscientious
Shy ———— Venturesome
Tough-minded ———— Tender-minded
Trusting ———— Suspicious
Practical ———— Imaginative
Forthright ———— Shrewd
Placid ———— Apprehensive
Conservative ———— Experimenting
Group-dependent ———— Self-sufficient
Undisciplined ———— Controlled
Relaxed ———— Tense

Cattell called them primary or surface traits and considered them as at the centre or core of personality. He then developed a questionnaire to measure these traits. Cattell listed each of these traits as a pair of polar opposites, such as trusting versus suspicious, submissive versus dominant, tough-minded versus sensitive, etc. The Sixteen Personality Factor Questionnaire (16PFQ) facilitates researchers to prepare individual as well as group profiles. The 16-P.FQ has served as a landmark in the study (assessment) of personality fairly objectively.

Eysenck's Supertraits Approach

The best known for his work in personality and the most cited psychologist in the world, Hans Eysenck (1916-97) (and his wife Sybil), like Cattell, used a complex statistical technique developed by Charles Spearman, *factor analysis*, to distill out the broadest sets of related traits (thus revealing underlying factors) and classify them. But he (1967) began with a theory of personality which he based on two *supertraits–extraversion–introversion* and *neuroticism*–stability.

The Eysencks reduced the number of traits to two dimensions: extraversion and emotional stability (level of neuroticism), which they viewed as independent, and believed that different personalities arise from differing combinations of the two supertraits. The world-famed Eysenck Personality Inventory (EPI) was constructed using these two supertraits only. According to Eysenckian theory, people who are highly extraverted are sociable and outgoing, and crave excitement and the company of others. People who are highly introverted are quiet and introspective; they tend to prefer spending time alone and to be cautious in the way they plan their lives. People who are highly neurotic tend to be anxious, moody and vulnerable, whereas people who are low on neuroticism tend to be stable, calm and even-tempered. People who are high in both neuroticism and extraversion tend to exhibit quite different traits than someone who is low in both, or a combination of low and high. So people who are high on both extraversion and neuroticism tend to be touchy and aggressive, whereas people who are high on extraversion and low on neuroticism tend to be carefree and sociable.

A further supertrait identified by Eysenck (1982) is *psychoticism* (propensity for aggression and loss of touch with reality). People scoring high on psychoticism are described as 'egocentric, aggressive, impersonal, cold, lacking in empathy, impulsive, lacking in concern for others and generally unconcerned about the rights and welfare of other people'. As a consequence, Eysenck revised EPI and developed a questionnaire designed to measure his supertraits – the Eysenck Personality Questionnaire, or EPQ (Eysenck & Eysenck, 1975).

Trait theories developed by Eysenck and Raymond Cattell exerted a considerable impact on research in personality.

The Big Five Theory

Although trait theories were well established by the 1960s, the consensus concerning the number or nature of the traits that make up personality was still badly lacking. Replications of Cattell's work in factor analysis often failed to find the original factor structure he described. Instead, a number of studies using Cattell's variables came up. As is the case with many ideas in science, so in personality studies, more than one set of researches contributed independently to the notion of the specific personality dimensions. In recent years, Lewis Goldberg proposed a *five-dimension model personality model* which he nicknamed as "Big Five", which might represent evidence of a universal structure for personality. McCrae and Costa (1990) developed the *five-factor model* (FFM), and Goldberg (1993) presented the *Big Five Theory*, which comprised of the same personality dimensions. The psychologists who proposed the five dimensions, built upon the work of many psychologists, from their own contemporaries all the way back to Allport. The acronym OCEAN makes it easy to remember these factors (Table below).

The "Big Five" Personal Traits

Dimension	A person is relatively.....	Or tends to be more.....
Openness	Receptive to new ideas, creative, broad in interest, interested in variety HIGH IN OPENNESS	Conventional, practical, narrow in interests, comfortable with what is familiar LOW IN OPENNESS
Conscientiousness	Responsible, organized, disciplined, achievement-oriented HIGH IN CONCENTIOUSNESS	Careless, disorganized, impulsive, lazy LOW IN CONCCIENTIOUSNESS
Extraversion	Outgoing, fun-loving, assertive, talkative HIGH IN EXTRAVERSION	Shy, serious, passive, quiet LOW IN EXTRAVERSION
Agreeableness	Warm, trusting, helpful, easy-going HIGH IN AGREEABLENESS	Cold, suspicious, uncooperative, argumentative LOW IN AGREEABLENESS
Neuroticism	Emotionally unstable, insecure, anxious, moody HIGH IN NEUROTICISM	Emotionally stable, confident, even tempered LOW IN NEUROTICISM

Openness (the tendency to be imaginative, independent, and interested in variety vs. practical, conforming, and interested in routine) to experience/intellect refers to receptivity to new ideas and experiences. People low on this trait prefer the familiar, practical and concrete, whereas those high on this trait are open to new experience, curious and imaginative. ***Conscientiousness*** (the tendency to be organized, careful, and disciplined vs. disorganized, careless, and impulsive) relates to organization and achievement. Highly conscientious individuals are ambitious, hard-working, competent and organized, and those low in conscientiousness are easy-going, low in self-discipline and not goal-driven. ***Extraversion*** (the tendency to be sociable, fun-loving, and affectionate vs. retiring, somber, and reserved) and ***Neuroticism*** (the tendency to be calm, secure, and self-satisfied vs. anxious, insecure, and self-pitying) are defined in the same way as Eysenck defined them. ***Agreeableness*** (the tendency to be softhearted, trusting, and helpful vs. ruthless, suspicious, and uncooperative) means the extent to which people are trusting, generous and concerned for others. Those low on agreeableness are viewed as antagonistic, tough-minded and hard-headed.

The Big Five Factor model is, in no way, a simplistic generalization of trait theory. As in Eysenck's (1967) model, each of the five factors is made up of a number of more specific traits. A questionnaire designed to measure traits within a five factor framework, the NEO-PI (Costa & McCrae, 1985), consists of 300 items. Respondents decide how characteristic each item is of themselves, rating each item on a five-point scale as well as scoring on the five factors, respondents receive scores on six sub-scales associated with each of the factors.

However, the Big Five/five factor model has been criticized for having a relatively unscientific, non-empirical (hard data) basis because its roots lay in Allport's working from dictionaries rather than in actual observations or assessments. Several researchers have identified other possible trait dimensions not accounted for in the model such as masculinity-femininity. Though the cross cultural support for it is mixed, the model provides an overall reasonably good way to organize and describe personality. It appears to have little predictive power as compared to situational factors, and tells us nothing about how people develop these traits. Still, the Big Five forms the basis for trait assessment of personality at the beginning of the twenty-first century, with questionnaires such as the NEO-PI and subsequent revisions (NEO-PI-R, Costa & McCrae, 1992) being used widely in occupational psychology.

Trait models have been criticized as being purely descriptive and offering little explanation of the underlying causes of personality. Eysenck's theory, however, does propose biological mechanisms as driving traits, and modern behaviour genetics researchers have shown a clear genetic substrate to them. Another potential weakness of trait theories is that they lead people to accept oversimplified classifications, or worse offer advice, based on a superficial analysis of their personality. Finally, trait models often underestimate the effect of specific situations on people's behaviour. It is important to remember that traits are statistical generalizations that do not always correspond to an individual's behaviour.

The Psychoanalysis Theory

Sigmund Freud's psychoanalysis theory, which later was endorsed and modified by his disciples - Adler and Jung, is considered as an important milestone in the personology history. Generally believed to be more a method of structure-investigation of personality and psychotherapy than a theory, psychoanalysis draws its basic substance from psychiatric and clinical studies. Using Breur's Cathartic Method (hypnotizing the patient) in the treatment regimen (of nervous disorders) in the beginning and later modifying this technique *into free association,* Sigmund Freud formulated a concept of the unconscious mind which ultimately became central to his personality theory. He likened mind to an iceberg, with most of it hidden beneath the surface in the vast reservoir of the unconscious. According to Freud memories, desires, and feelings are repressed and suppressed into the unconscious mind because they are too painful or anxiety-producing to be tolerated in the conscious thought. To Freud, the conscious was not the true reality. To understand a person's personality, we must tap his or her unconscious.

Freud argued that occasionally thoughts and ideas normally confined to the unconscious, find their way into the consciousness. This simple fact made him consider the study and interpretation of dreams as "the royal road to the knowledge of the conscious activities of the mind". Freud also emphasized that our personalities are determined by both conscious and unconscious powers with unconscious exerting considerable influence on the conscious. Specifically repressed ideas, thoughts and wishes covertly influence how we consciously think and behave. Occasionally these repressed intentions surface in dreams and slips of the tongue or pen (*Freudian slips*) the study of which can provide a deeper insight into the unconsciousness.

Freud was much influenced by Charles Darwin's views in considering human beings as biological organisms dominated by biological needs, especially sexual ones that must be controlled in order to civilize man. Man's struggle, claimed Freud, to *tame* these impulses leads to emotional conflicts that so profoundly shape human personality. Freud placed great stress on neurosis - defined as "the faulty resolution of a conflict between an individual's drives and his efforts to keep these urges and impulses from reaching the conscious level". Considering unconsciousness as the key factor in the understanding of mind and shaping of personality, Freud made it abundantly clear that 'overt' (outer, observable aspect of behaviour or personality) could not be properly explained without reference to the 'covert' (inner, unobservable). He asserted that childhood experiences played a major role in moulding personality. The psychoanalysis theory is an attempt to explain how personality shapes up by a continuing conflict by people's primary drives, particularly sex and aggression, and the social pressures of the civilized society.

With regard to the structure, Freud postulated that personality is made of three primary interactive and often conflicting components called the id, ego and superego. These components do not actually correspond to physical parts of the brain but represent the *basic principles regarding how mind works in shaping personalities*. The fundamental theme of Freudian theory is that the mind, especially its unconscious part, is a perpetual battle ground in which the id, ego and superego are engaged in an unceasing and unending conflict. The structure of personality, as envisaged by Freud, shows somewhat like this (Fig. 15.2).

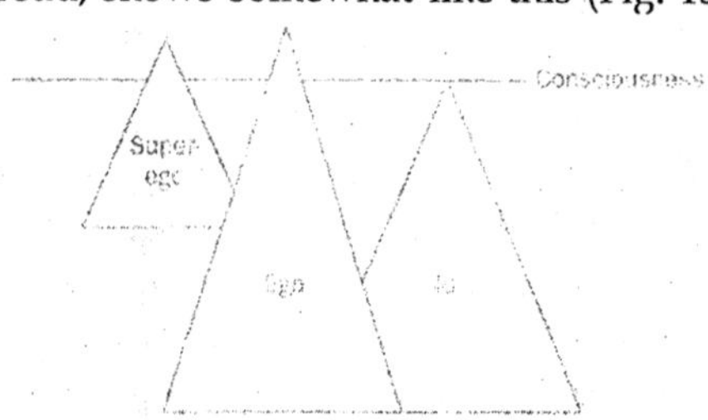

Fig. 15.2 Freud's structural model of human psyche

The three aspects of personality occupy different levels of awareness. The id is completely unconscious; its contents are normally inaccessible to the conscious mind. The influence of the superego can be exerted both at the conscious and the unconscious levels as also at preconscious level, which is the level of the mind that contains ideas, memories, etc., and can be brought into consciousness through attention. The ego, like the superego, transcends all three level of conscious, although it does not penetrate the unconscious to the extent superego does. The unconscious portion of the ego houses the ego-defence mechanisms, which protect the ego from threatening ideas, perceptions, emotions and instincts. A brief discussion on the qualities and functioning of the three states of mind (three components of personality) – Id, Ego and Superego – is important to understand the development and dynamics of personality.

The Id

According to Freud the *Id* is the biological component of personality, and is obscure, primitive and inaccessible. It can be reached only through the analysis of frame-work and diagnosis of neurotic symptoms. Much of its structure is of negative character and can be described as being all that the ego is not. We can move nearer to the *Id* through images. The *Id* is often called "a chaos, a cauldron of seething excitement, repressions and suppressions". It may consist of everything psychological that is present at birth. It is in close touch with the body pressures and is the unconscious reservoir of *libido*, the psychic energy that feeds inherited biological instincts and operations of the ego and superego. The *Id* operates according to the *pleasure principle*, seeking immediate gratification of all instinctive drives regardless of reason, logic, rationality or impact that the behaviour it motivates shall have. There is nothing corresponding to ideas on time, no recognition of the passage of time: it is timeless. Values, morality and ethics are unknown to the *Id*.

Freud recognized that there are two basic instinctual drives: ***Eros*** or life instincts such as hunger, thirst, sex, etc., and ***Thanatos*** of death instincts such as hate, anger, aggressiveness, destruction etc. The *Id* cannot tolerate any tension arising out of the non-fulfillment of the instinctual drives, and seeks release from it at once unmindful of what will follow as the consequence of this. Since it operates essentially at an unconscious level, it is unable to interact effectively with the external reality to achieve gratification. Freud claimed that the *Id* seeks to discharge tension by conjuring up mental images of the objects it desires. For example, a hungry baby might form an internal image of the mother's breast or might dream about sex. This wishful mental imagery, according to Freud, is called *primary process thinking*. While the life-instinct is manifest in positive, constructive and life-preserving and maintaining activities such as food-seeking, love, shelter, sex, etc., the death-instinct - sometimes referred to as hate instinct - is noticed operating in homicidal and suicidal tendencies which aim at destruction of the individual, in other words, a universal tendency of the organism to return to the inorganic state of existence, taking specific forms in the hates of man.

The *Id*, precisely, is the store-house of largely unconscious, biologically-based instinctive drives that provide the basic energy sources for the total personality system. Of the three components of personality, only the *Id* is present at birth. Later, it serves as foundation-stone for the growth of ego and superego.

The Ego

The appearance of *Ego* in man is really a strange phenomenon. The child is dependent on the mother for the gratification its needs. He uses crying, screaming and weeping as powerful tools to attract mother's attention, but it might not necessarily bring immediate solution to the problem it faces at the moment. During this process, the child comes in contact with the reality. According to Freud, discovery of the reality prompts the development of *Ego* as an outgrowth of the id. The *Ego* develops gradually as the child interacts with the external environment and learns to cope with the external reality. So, *Ego* functions as an intermediary between the instinctual demands of the *Id* and the reality of the world. Also acting as an interface between the individual and the environment, it is responsible for our self-awareness. In fact, the *Ego* serves as the *executive* (general manager) of the personality, making decisions regarding the pleasures that will be pursued at the urging of the *Id*, and the morals dictates of the super ego that will be followed. The *Ego* is part of the *Id*, and never becomes completely independent of it.

The *Ego* operates by the *reality principle*, carrying the tendency to satisfy *Id*'s demands realistically, yielding to and accounting for the demands of reality, sometimes delaying the gratification of the desires springing forth from the *Id* and sometimes relaxing (transgressing) the rules and regulations by the superego. It tries to strike a balance by integrating the conflicting demands of the *Id*, the superego and the external world. Freud says:

> The poor ego.... feels hemmed in on three sides, threatened by three kinds of danger, which it is hard pressed, it reacts by generating anxiety. Thus, the ego, driven by the Id, confined by the superego, repulsed by the reality, struggles to master its economic task of bringing about harmony among the forces and influence working in and upon it, and we can understand how it is that so often we cannot suppress a cry; life is not easy.

The *Ego* deals with these competing forces by resorting to the use of primary strategies called defence mechanisms. Defence mechanisms are unconscious mental tactics (such as worry, anxiety, rationalization, substitution, repression, suppression, etc.) that the ego uses to insulate itself from threatening ideas, perceptions, emotions and instincts. The most fundamental of these defence mechanisms is repression which involves obstructing from awareness the instincts of the *Id* and the emotions entailing guilt and regret of the superego. To carry out managerial functions of screening the *Id*'s impulse, the ego-system must involve cognitive processes such as abilities to perceive, think, learn and remember.

The Superego

While the *Id* is known to be the biological aspect of personality, the *Ego* is its psychological facet. The *Ego* has no moral sense, only practical sense. It is a third structure, the superego, which, according to Freud, provides moral guidance, embodying parental and societal values. Therefore, *Superego* is personality's social component - the internal representation of the ideas of the society, the moral judge of conduct. It emerges as an infant grows up into a child; and is a composite of the moral values and standards of parents and society that incorporate into our personalities as we advance in years. The major concern of the *Superego* is to decide whether an act is right or wrong by norms and standards of morality. Perhaps, the most difficult task of the *Superego* is to exert control over powerful sexual and aggressive impulses of the *Id*; these are the impulses the (wanton) expression of which is most likely to be condemned by the society. The superego reflects the social conscience of the individual. Being diagonally opposite to the *Id*, it does not drive the individual to seek pleasure but to strive for perfection. When the *Id* urges "do it now", the *Superego* counters with "do not do it if it is morally wrong".

According to Freud, the *Superego* is composed of two parts - called subsystems: the conscience and the ego-ideal. The ***conscience*** consists of the moral inhibition ("*should nots*") of behaviour which stems from punishment (either parental punishment or punishing ourselves through guilt). The ***ego-ideal*** is made up of "*shoulds*" of behaviour, for which we often receive approval and/or awards, rewards, and for which we aspire ardently. In the conscience reside the moral sanctions which the *Superego* uses to counter aggressive and sexual promptings of the *Id*. The conscience is a sort of substitute parent. The ego-ideal contains the standards of goodness and virtue, which a person strives to achieve. "As the moral arm of the personality, superego tries to prevent the *Id* from expressing its primitive impulses. Even though it shares some characteristics with the *Id* (it is non-rational) and the *Ego* (it is controlling), it nevertheless stands in opposition to both of them. Unlike the *Ego*, which merely suppresses the *Id* long enough to find a rational way to satisfy its needs the superego tries to block *Id* impulses totally", observe Crooks & Stein, (1988). In this sense, it is the original "spoil sport". If the ego is too successful in its task, the end-result is a rigid, guilt-ridden, inhibited personality but if the superego constantly plays a weak hand, the result is a self-centered, self-indulgent, and anti-social personality.

Dynamics of Personality in Psychoanalysis

Dynamics refers to the interplay of forces that shape up personality. The three-cornered continuous clash among the impulse-driven *Id*, the guilt-inducing *Superego*, and the intermediary *Ego* is at the centre of the strife constituting personality dynamics, which represents an unending struggle among conscious, pre-conscious and unconscious regions of the mind (individual self). The conscious level represents present awareness, the fore-consciousness (pre-consciousness) is the level at which past experiences and incidents, names, dates, etc., are available for ready recall. On the unconscious level - the most inclusive of the three - are materials and stuff that cannot be reached so easily and recalled on demand from others or ourselves yet which are brought to the memory automatically (in most cases just accidentally) at times, through hypnosis, or some other technique. Mind's unconscious region has in it both strivings from the *Id* which have never been conscious and other urges which were once conscious but have been forced out of consciousness into the dark abyss of unconsciousness. All the functions of the self (pertaining *Id, Ego,* and *Superego*) have share in the three different levels of the self (unconscious, conscious and pre-conscious) and none of the three aspects of personality is to be regarded as exclusively significant at any one of the three levels.

Importantly, the three levels are not markedly compartmentalized and shown different from one another. No single function is screened off from others. The self (i.e. its focus) shifts in degrees to which it is conscious, fore-conscious or unconscious. Apart from this, various functions of the self tend to dominate the whole at different times so that the individual's behaviour is largely *Ego, Superego,* or *Id* dominated. The interplay among *Ego, Superego,* and *Id* – the all powerful forces of personality – is always in a fluid state, but maintaining a subtle balance, often so difficult to effect. Despite utmost efforts by an individual to maintain a steady state or balance among the external stark realities of life, their primitive urges (desires, wants, needs), and society's moral impositions (codes) by making adjustment in each and every situation, the conflict among *Ego, Superego,* and *Id* is impossible to resolve for good. The unresolved conflict is the root of all behavioural problems that makes people suffer from psychosomatic disorders in these times.

Defence Mechanisms

When the ego is faced with conflicts that threaten to disrupt the balance among the systems of personality, it sounds an alarm all over in the form of anxiety, in which situation the ego calls upon various *face-saving devices* called defence mechanism designed to control this anxiety (a kind of free floating irrational fear with no identifiable source) or release tension. Defence mechanisms are the less rational protective methods; they protect the ego from anxiety by denying, altering or distorting (falsifying) reality. They operate unconsciously so that we are not aware that a distortion of reality, in any way, has taken place or is taking place. Defence mechanisms are not subject to any checks and balances of rational, conscious reasoning. Some of the important defence mechanisms are briefly described as under:

Compensation: Compensation is an attempt to make up deficiency by directing one's energies to such other aspect(s) of personality in which no deficiency exists.

Rationalization: It is a process of fallacious thinking intended to justify an adjustment that is emotionally desirable but not intellectually justified and often socially disapproved.

Projection: Projection is misplacement of blame, i.e. projecting the threatening thing on to others. For instance, making team-mates or officials responsible for one's defeat in an athletic competition.

Identification: This enables a person to achieve satisfaction from the success of other people, friends, groups or organizations.

Substitution: Substitution is an attempt to evade failure or to lessen the effect of natural failure by selecting a new goal or a new situation which is easier to attain.

Repression: Repression means holding back or banishing from consciousness a variety of unacceptable impulses and disturbing memories. (*Freud describes repression as a primitive mechanism in which our strong emotional ideas and unpleasant memories which do not fit in with our social values and norms are split off from consciousness and thrown out into the unconsciousness.*)

Regression: It is reversion to infantile or childish level of behaviour.

Negativism: Negativism is identified as anti-behaviour. It means refusing to do what one is told to do just because one is told.

Sympathism: It is trying to get sympathy from others for one's failures rather than making a genesis of the real causes.

Withdrawal or Evasion It is attempting to remain obscure. The individual hopes to protect the integrity of the ego.

Displacement: It is substituting an acceptable behaviour for anxiety-inducing one.

Reaction Formation: It is creating an attitude opposite to the one that you hold. For example, whatever the coach tells the top athlete does exactly the opposite.

Intellectualization: This is transforming emotional or affective drives into rational intentions.

Worry (feeling too much concerned about something to the point of distress), ***anxiety*** (irrational fear), ***fantasy*** (living in cloudland), and ***day-dreaming,*** are all defence mechanisms.

Psychogenic Model of Development

Freud believed in determinism. He was convinced that certain elements of personality were determined at the time of conception, and others "within the first few years of life". The actual personality of a person emerges from out of the struggle for existence and strivings for adjustment in the environment. So, the interplay between genetic factors and environmental forces occupies an important place in the total personality development process. Freud proposed that child development proceeds through a series of stages related to physical development, and that adult personality is influenced by how crises are resolved at each stage. As Freud considered libido as an all-permeating powerful force, psychosocial growth became crucial to the development of personality. He challenged the traditional view that sexuality remained unexpressed during childhood. Rather, he asserted that a child was very much aware of the body stimulations leading to sexual pleasure; Several body parts, contended he, manifested sexual urge and played key role in the arousal and gratification of the sexual drive.

According to Freud, a child progresses through *five* stages of psychosexual development (oral, anal, phallic, latency period, and genital stage) in which the focus of sexual gratification shifts from one body part to another. The way a child moves through these developmental stages, argued Freud, becomes a crucial factor in the determination of the direction of personality development. Each psychosocial development stage is named after an erogenous zone, or area of the body that can experience pleasure from the environment. Excessive gratification or frustration at any one stage can result in the fixation of libido and subsequent disruption to normal personality development. These stages are briefly described below:

Oral stage (Birth to 18 months)

At the beginning of this stage children are highly dependent on their mothers and derive pleasure from sucking and swallowing. Freud suggested that children who become fixated at this early oral stage derive pleasure in adulthood from activities such as overeating, smoking, drinking and kissing. Such people, according to him, were *oral-incorporative* or *oral-ingestive*.

Later in the oral stage, children begin to cut teeth and experience pleasure from biting and chewing (lips and mouth being the erogenous zone). Fixation at this later part of the stage results in chewing objects and nail-biting in adulthood, as well as being sarcastic and critical. Freud called those fixated at this level oral-aggressive or oral-sadistic.

Anal stage (12-18 months to three years)

At this stage pleasure is gained from the expulsion and retention of faeces. This is also a stage at which children start to explore their environment but experience control and discipline from their parents. According to Freud, fixation at this stage may result in people being messy and generous - anal expulsive characters, or being mean and orderly - anal-retentive characters. Freud believed that the nature of toilet-training during anal stage could have serious implication, rather complication, for the later adult personality.

Phallic stage (3 to 5-6 years)

It is at the phallic stage that children discover pleasure from touching their genitals; the focus of sexual gratification shifts to genital stimulation. They also become aware that they are in competition with siblings and their father for their mother's attention. The peculiarity of this stage is the emergence of "family romance" in which the child begins to become sexually attracted to the parent of the other sex, and also experience some kind of jealousy of the same-sex parent. Freud referred to *Oedipus Complex* (attraction of the male child towards the mother), and *Elektra Complex* (attachment of the female child with the father), both being crucially important in the development of a child's personality. He was emphatic that most children find this situation extremely stressful, so they try to resolve it by repressing their feelings of sexual attraction and identifying with the same-sex parent.

Latency Period (6-12 years)

According to Freud, personality is formed by the end of the phallic stage, and sexual impulses are re-channelled during the latency period into activities such as sport, learning and social activities.

Genital Stage (13 years to adulthood)

As young people approach the age of reproductive ability, they begin to focus their libido, or sexual energy, towards the opposite sex. If the earlier psychosexual stages have been successfully negotiated, the individual should now begin to form positive relationships with others.

Freud strongly felt that a child may possibly experience some kind of growth retardation at one of the early stages of psychosexual development due to over or under exposure to gratification. This is technically known as *Fixation*, which can influence the adult personality development. Children thwarted from experiencing oral stimulation (sucking, biting, eating, etc.), for instance, might take to smoking or eating excessively. Verbal hostility may also be traced back to frustration encountered by a child during oral stage. Excessive gratification also influences personality development. For example, infants who get milk bottle or any other pacifier at the slightest indication of need may become overly dependent on adults in later life. Obsession with cleanliness or over-consciousness about sanitation has also their origin in the toilet habit-formation in the toddling stage.

Freud has not explained well as to how fixation takes place, but his reference to it, generated much interest among researcher for further investigation into the realm of personality development. Freud's analysis of mind, behaviour and personality was based on his clinical (largely subjective) observation of his patients. He could not produce any empirical evidence in support his hypotheses, observations and largely inference-based findings. His vague pronouncements about personality fell short of even normal scientific requirements. Some of the terms used by Freud were difficult to define operationally. Secondly, Freud's theory did not have the strength to predict development of personality on the basis of childhood experiences. The psychoanalysis could reveal which factor played a dominant or dormant role in shaping individual personality, but not which factor will do so. Thirdly, Freud interacted with and made observations on mentally disturbed people (sexually repressed Victorian society); healthy personalities never served as subjects his of study. Consequently, Freud's conclusions about personality are difficult to generalize. Finally, some of Freud's observations about sexual development of people, especially women, are very strange, a masterpiece of creative imagination without little scientific explanation.

Contributors to Psychoanalysis

A number of theorists carried forward Freud's views. Some of them were his associates and students who followed his line of action for some time and then developed their own theories by modifying Freud's original ideas.

Carl Jung was one of the first prominent psychologists to break away from Freud's classical psychoanalysis. He saw humans as being guided as much by aims and aspirations as by sex and aggression. His new approach came to be known as *analytical psychology*. According to him, personality consists of competing forces and structures within the individual that must be balanced. Unlike Freud, he emphasized conflicts between opposing forces within the individual, rather than between the individual and the demands of society, or between the individual and reality.

Alfred Adler, Freud's another disciple, agreed with his *Guru* that early childhood experiences are important to development, and that birth order may influence personality development. He believed the oldest was the one that set high goals to achieve to get the attention they lost back when the younger siblings were born. According to Adler, the middle children were competitive and ambitious possibly so they are able to surpass the first-born's achievements, but were not as much concerned about the glory. He felt that the last born would be more dependent and sociable but be the baby. Adler believed that the only child loves being the centre of attention and matures quickly, but in the end fails to become independent.

Concurring with Freud's idea of transference, *Heinz Kohut* used narcissism as a model of how we develop our sense of self. Narcissism is the exaggerated sense of one self which is believed to exist in order to protect one's low self esteem and sense of worthlessness. Kohut had a significant impact on the field by extending Freud's theory of narcissism and introducing what he called the 'self-object transferences' mirroring and idealization. In other words, children need to idealize and emotionally "sink into" and identify with the idealized competence of admired figures such as parents or older siblings. They also need to have their self-worth mirrored by these people. These experiences allow them to thereby learn the self-soothing and other skills that are necessary for the development of a healthy sense of self.

Karen Horney, still another Freud's disciple, is credited with the development of the "real self" and the "ideal self". She adopted a more optimistic view of human life, emphasizing human growth and self-realization, and believed that all people have these two views of their own self. The "real self" is how you really are with regards to personality, values, and morals; but the "ideal self" is a construct you apply to yourself to conform to social and personal norms and goals. Ideal self would be "I can be successful, I am CEO material"; and real self would be "I just work in the mail room, with not much chance of high promotion". One of Horney's major contributions was her challenge to Freud's treatment of women. She countered that, in the early part of the twentieth century, women were more likely to be affected by social and cultural oppression than the absence of a penis.

Despite serious lacunae, the psychoanalysis theory was able to open new windows on human behaviour and set stage for a serious probe into the structure, dynamics and development of personality, more specifically functioning of the unconscious aspect of mind and the interplay of unresolved conflicts. Today, only a small number of people are in agreement with Freud's postulates and premises, but no one dared deny that Freud's ideas were bold, creative, highly courageous and revolutionary considering the cultural context in which they were made.

Behavioural Theories

While the psycho-analytic viewpoint attached greater importance to internal mechanism in explaining the structure and dynamics of personality, behaviourists explain personality in terms of the effects external stimuli have on behaviour. It was a radical shift away from Freudian philosophy.

Behavioural Theory

The behaviourists (John Watson, Charles Skinner, and others) maintained that identifiable characteristics of personality are merely products of the interplay of various external environmental forces in the form of reinforcing stimuli, rather than the internal stressors as assumed by the psychoanalysis theory. They argue that it is futile to rely on abstract internal concepts as determinants of personality and ignore visible, realistic and concrete external variables. Skinner (1953) argued:

> The practice of looking inside the organism for an explanation of behaviour has tended us to obscure the variables which are immediately available for a scientific analysis. These variables lie outside the organism in his immediate environment and its environmental history.

Considering personality as the sum total of overt and covert behavioural responses, Skinner emphasized that our patterns of responding to environmental stimuli are a direct growth of the reinforcement we have experienced in the past. He believed children do bad things because the behaviour obtains attention that serves as a reinforcer. For example, a child cries because its crying in the past has led to attention to him from some one. These are the *response,* and *consequences.* The response is the child crying, and the attention that child gets is the reinforcing consequence. According to this theory, people's behaviour is formed by processes such as operant conditioning. Skinner put forward a "three term contingency model" which helped promote analysis of behaviour based on the "Stimulus - Response - Consequence Model" in which the critical question is: "Under which circumstances or antecedent 'stimuli' does the organism engage in a particular behavior or 'response', which in turn produces a particular 'consequence'?"

Behaviourists do not trace individual differences to any innate source (or a cluster of any inherited traits), but to unique histories of operant and classical conditioning in childhood. They challenge the notion that enduring traits are an evidence of some underlying behavioural dispositions. Instead they argue that seemingly stable traits stem from varied consistent patterns of reinforcement contingencies. The change in external reinforcements can dramatically alter certain enduring aspects of personality. That way, behaviourists seem to be more concerned with changes in behaviour with behavioural consistencies.

Social-Cognitive Theories

Social-learning theorists also give greater weight-age to environmental factors as the determinants of personality but they are not in agreement with behaviourists over the issue of cognitive processes. Charles Skinner considered internal cognition incidental to behaviour and personality, social-learning theorists emphasize our cognitive interpretations of external events to fit our memories, beliefs and expectations. Cognitive theories are theories of personality that emphasize cognitive processes such as thinking and judging. However, according to social-learning perspective, cognitive processes – mediating between external environmental events and behaviours – influence the shaping of personality. Our thoughts, perceptions and feelings profoundly influence the development of our behavioural patterns, i.e. personality. The central point of social-learning theory, also known as social-cognitive theory, is the interaction between cognitions and environment in shaping personality. Albert Bandura, a social learning theorist, suggested that the forces of memory and emotions worked in conjunction with environmental influences.

Bandura (1982, 1983, & 1986) forcefully argued that observational learning strongly influences our behaviour, and personality development. He maintained that through out childhood and adulthood, our observations of which behaviours are rewarded and which are punished or ignored, provide us certain cognitive representations that serve as models to our own actions. Our personality, therefore, reflects our observational learning. Besides this, Bandura proposed the concept of reciprocal determinism, which means that our behaviours (personalities) are shaped by the interaction between cognitive factors, such as thoughts, perceptions, feelings, etc., and environmental factors. Each of these two factors, emphasized Bandura, can influence and modify the other, and the direction of change is typically reciprocal rather than one-way.

Later, Bandura came out with the concept of *self-efficacy* – a central component of his theory. Self-efficacy is described as the belief that *we can perform adequately and deal effectively with a particular situation.* Bandura believed that our sense of self-efficacy greatly influences personality development by affecting whether or not we will even try to behave in certain way. For example, we think we are socially inept and boring, we are inclined to avoid social interactions with people and thus become withdrawn or aloof, thereby further reducing our sense of self-esteem as some psychologists believe. He views self-efficacy as a collection of specific evaluations that we make about our sense of adequacy in a variety of situations. Self-efficacy is, therefore, situation-specific. A person who feels socially inept may at the same time have a strong sense of artistic self-efficacy. According to Bandura, self-efficacy arises from several experiences, including our past successes or failures, our observation of the performance of others, and our own particular feelings as we contemplate a task. Besides influencing what activities or situations we become involved in, our self-efficacy judgments are likely to influence the amount of effort we exert. For example, if one perceives one-self to be a good athlete, one would make more serious efforts to do still better than a person with a lower self-efficacy.

Both behavioural and social-learning approaches attach greater importance to external events that give shape to personality. Through rigorous research, the social-cognitive schools of thought have fostered a climate of empirical science which other approaches to personality development have often lacked so badly. The behavioural and social-learning theories have also attempted to answer the head-sapping question 'why behaviour changes from situation to another and why certain presumably enduring aspects of personality fail to remain enduring at all'.

Despite convincing arguments about external factors shaping personality, these theories have failed to account for such internal factors as motives, drives, tendencies, traits, etc. Besides this, human dimensions such as creativity, spontaneity, love, and strivings for fulfillment cannot simply be discounted from the concept of personality while emphasizing the role of external reinforcements, observational learning, and imitation in personality shaping.

Humanistic Theories

The humanistic perspective on personality is relatively a recent one. Discarding the age-old model of behaviour, the humanistic approach stresses upon the unique characteristics of humanity in the interpretation of man's nature. The humanistic views on personality are divergent but not without agreement on certain points. First, all humanistic theorists argue that the primary motivation for behaviour comes from each person's striving to develop, change and grow in pursuit of the full realization of an individual's potential. Second, the human personality is not at all shaped by baser impulses as postulated by Freud, and his followers. Third, humanistic theories also tend to be *phenomenological* emphasizing a subjective view of reality as seen from the individual's own frame of reference. The "material stuff" of personality consists of our own subjective personal view of the world including our attitudes, beliefs, and feelings.

The theories of the most influential humanists, Carl Rogers and Abraham Maslow, need special brief explanation here because they illustrate the broad features of the humanistic school of thought.

Self-concept Theory

Freud and Carl Rogers (1902-1987) applied clinical observation as major tool of study of human mind and behaviour. However, their observations on this issue differed considerably. Where Freud found "sexual and aggressive impulses" as the basic motivators of behaviour, Rogers saw in every man "inherent potential for good". The latter was convinced that the most enduring (driving) force in people's life is their *constant striving toward self-fulfillment* and *the realization of their own unique potential.* He considered this striving to be a positive, constructive force that motivates us to engage in healthy behaviours that enhance our sense of self.

'Self' is the core of our being and that of Rogers' theory. It is the central organizing, all-encompassing structure that accounts for the coherence and stability of our personalities. According to Rogers, each one of us tries to know "who I am" and this striving leads us to the formulation of self-concept or self-image that determines how we perceive and respond to the world. Rogers maintains that the key to healthy adjustment and happiness is a consistency or *congruence* between our self-concept and our experiences. In addition to the inter-relationship between the self and the external world, Rogers suggests that all of us are possessed of sense of an ideal-self, i.e. what we would like to be. Just as maladjustment can be caused by experiences that contradict our self-concept, it can also be caused by a discordance between the *ideal-self* (what we wish to be), and the *real-self* (what actually we perceive ourselves to be).

Self-actualization

Abraham Maslow (1908-1970) proposed the *self-actualization* theory which explains human motivation and personality. The central focus of thecry is a 'need hierarchy'. Human needs spiral up from the basic needs of hunger, thirst, sex, etc., at the baseline through psychological needs to the need for self-actualization at the top. Maslow derived his ideas about motivation and personality from the study of "self-actualizing persons", those who are "fulfilling themselves and doing the best they are capable of doing", and not disturbed individuals observed in clinical settings. Most probably his keen interest in creative, vibrant, well-adjusted people led him to place a strong emphasis on such positive qualities as joy, love, enthusiasm, creativity, and human relationship while largely ignoring other forces like guilt, anger, shame, conflict and hostility. Maslow was influenced and inspired by the study of a number of historical and contemporary public figures who, he believed, exemplified his concept of self-actualization. Characteristics of self-actualizers, according to Maslow, include the four key dimensions:

- *Awareness* - maintaining constant enjoyment and awe of life. These individuals often experienced a "peak experience". Maslow defined a peak experience as an "intensification of any experience to the degree there is a loss or transcendence of self". A peak experience is one in which an individual perceives an expansion of his or herself, and detects a unity and meaningfulness in life. Intense concentration on an activity one is involved in, such as running a marathon, may invoke a peak experience.
- *Reality and problem centered* - they have tendency to be concerned with "problems" in their surroundings.
- *Acceptance/Spontaneity* - they accept their surroundings and what cannot be changed.
- *Unhostile sense of humor/democratic* - they do not like joking about others, which can be viewed as offensive. They have friends of all backgrounds and religions and hold very close friendships.

Characteristically, the humanistic approach considered the positive dimensions of personality, viewing the individual as an active, creative, experiencing human being who lives in the present and subjectively responds to current perceptions, relationships, and encounters. Maslow and Rogers disagree with the dark, pessimistic outlook of those in the Freudian psychoanalysis ranks, but rather view their theories as positive and optimistic proposals which stress the tendency of the human personality toward growth and self-actualization. This way, they made a valuable addition to our understanding of personality in its widened dimensions.

Humanistic theorists have been criticized for their vague and subjective conceptualization, which they seem to have based on often non-verifiable observations on people in certain situations. Rogers' concept of the self and Maslow's principle of self-actualization both are purely subjective terms, defying objective, operational descriptions. What cannot be defined operationally may not stand a test of sustainability and effectiveness to prove its validity. The humanists have also come under fire for focusing so closely on the individual and the role of the self, almost ignoring external (environmental) factors so crucial to the shaping of personality. Some psychologists consider the humanistic approach much more philosophic than psychologic because of its undue emphasis on the self - an obscure and vague concept, so difficult to understood and investigate objectively.

PERSONALITY ASSESSMENT

Descriptive and explanatory approaches project personality as a very complex phenomenon, not so easy to deal with. It encompasses both subjective and objective elements, constructs and subject content. Several aspects of personality are genetically determined and, therefore, fixed and non-modifiable; others are influenced by environment, and hence dynamic and modifiable in relation to time and space. Moreover, psychologists are still not in complete agreement over what exactly constitutes personality. All this places hurdles in the measurement and assessment of personality. To judge a person's overt actions and activities and set norms and standards for them is relatively easy, but so difficult to penetrate their mind - his traits, dispositions and unconscious mental processes, etc. - and evaluate the real stuff of personality viz. psychological abstractions like repression, anxiety, introversion, dominance, submission, self-confidence, self-actualization, and so on. Still by developing various techniques to understand the structure and dynamics of personality, psychologists have really hit a jackpot.

Techniques employed by psychologists to assess personality include: (1) Observation, (2) Interviews, (3) Paper-and-Pencil questionnaires (self-reports), and (4) Projective tests. Each one of them has its relative merits and demerits. While observation and interview techniques are largely subjective and beset with difficulties of data collection, recording and objectification as also result generalization, paper-and-pencil instruments are objective and easy to use on individuals as well as groups. Most paper-and-pencil tests require the subjects to rate as *true* or *false* series of statements about their thoughts, beliefs, feelings and activities. Some of these questionnaires are designed to measure a very limited range of traits or only a single personality characteristic such as anxiety, self-concept or introversion-extraversion; others are constructed to produce more global measures of personality.

Paper-and-Pencil Personality Questionnaires

Paper-and-pencil questionnaires are multiplying fast. Some of them such as MMPI, 16PFQ, EPI (EPQ), CPI, etc., have proved their worth in education, psychology, management and sport.

Minnesota Multiphasic Personality Inventory

Originally designed to help diagnose and classify persons with psychological disorders, the MMPI today is 'the best known and most widely used objective personality inventory' (Hathaway & Kinley, 1942). Since its origin, it has undergone several transformations, alternations and modifications in terms of its contents, processes, procedures of administration, response-evaluation and behaviour analysis on the basis of the data its administration yielded. In its final version, the MMPI contains 566 statements about behaviour, thoughts, and/or emotional reactions that subjects rate as "true" of themselves, "false", or "cannot say" (undecided about the truth of the statement). There are ten clinical scales designed to measure such conditions as depression, social introversion, schizophrenia, paranoia, and psychopathic personality. It also includes four validity scales designed to assess whether the subjects have falsified or faked their answers.

Despite its popularity as a diagnostic tool, it is charged with geographical bias in its construction. The original criterion-keyed test (MMPI) has also been questioned for its validity and reliability because the decision-process by which diagnosis of the sample cases were made has not been documented. Because some of its items particularly those dealing with sex and religion, intrude into the private domain of individual' personality and disturb their privacy, the questionnaire is criticized on ethically grounds. The excessive length of the MMPI causes at least some subjects to get sloppy in their haste to get the process over with. Although the inventory seems to be a good device for differentiating disturbed and normal individuals but it lacks the capacity to differentiate reliably within each of these categories; it fails to monitor individual differences.

California Psychological Inventory

Authored by Gough (1957-1975), CPI is one of those personality inventories that have been standardized on normal population samples. In format, it resembles MMPI and is based upon fifteen "normal" personality traits: dominance, sociability, self-acceptance, social presence, self-control, achievement via conformance, achievement via independence, responsibility, intellectual efficiency, flexibility, socialization, capacity for status, psychological mindedness and tolerance. Additionally, the CPI also includes three response-bias scales. The inventory was standardized on much larger group than MMPI and care was taken in controlling factors such as social status, geographical locale and age. The inventory has been cited to have 'a test-retest reliability of .90 which is much higher than that of the MMPI' (Ross, 1987). In predicting school and job success, leadership, conformity, and reactions to stress, CPI has proved itself as a highly reliable instrument.

16-Personality Factor Questionnaire

Like MMPI, the 16-PFQ also received wide acclaim and popularity in personality domain. Its author Raymond Cattell believed that (a) personality may only be understood when the individual is viewed in given situations; (b) personality traits exist in at least two levels; and (c) personality testing should not only be employed to obtain group data, but also individual information by using what he termed a technique. The individual should be assessed repeatedly over time in order to determine trends and patterns in behaviour, feelings and motives. Considering traits as the building blocks of personality, and using actor analysis technique, Cattell identified 12 primary factors (as a result of factorial analysis technique), and 4 secondary factors (higher level qualities), which he finally wove into an inventory called 16-Personality Factor Questionnaire. The factors are not just unique to the test but instead rest within the context of a general theory of personality. Each factor listed with its alphabetical designation (for example, outgoingness, A; intelligence, B; ego-strength, C, etc.) and brief descriptions of low and high scores (for example, score 1-3 on factor B shows low intelligence, and score 8-10 high intelligence, on factor I, it shows tough-mindedness and tender-mindedness respectively, and so on).

As per 16-PFQ manual, the essential elements to be considered in evaluating personality are the ones given below:

(1) the test is embedded within the broader fabric or network of general psychological theory;

(2) in its present form the test rests on an empirical foundation of more than ten factor-analytic investigations across a pool of several thousand items;

(3) psychometric properties of the scales (e.g. reliabilities, validities, etc.) have been explored and reported for a variety of samples and conditions: and

(4) research findings involving the test provide the test user with a rich base of criterion evidence in industrial, clinical, social and educational psychology.

For analysis of personality, the raw scores derived on each scale are converted into sten scores (standard ten) and profiling done. For comparison purposes, norm tables are available for general adult population and various other chunks of population (men and women) separately.

Eysenck Personality Inventory

The Eysenck Personality Inventory (its latest version is called Eysenck Personality Questionnaire) is a modified version of Maudsley Personality Inventory, which "sets out to measure two major dimensions of personality, extraversion and neuroticism" (Eysenck, 1959a, 1960a). The inventory consists of two parallel forms, facilitating retesting after experimental treatment without interference from memory factors. Apart from Extraversion and Neuroticism Scales, the EPI also contains a *Lie Scale* (in EPQ, it is called Social *Desirability Scale* or Psychoticism), which may be used to eliminate subjects showing "desirability response set". Direct evidence is available of the validity of the EPI as a descriptive instrument of the behaviour manifestations of personality. For the analysis of date the procedure is very simple because raw scores are not at all converted into any standard scores. The raw scores themselves show the presence or absence of the major personality dimensions. Norms for general and special slices of populations are available for comparison purposes.

NEO-PI

A questionnaire designed to measure traits within the Big Five Model framework, the NEO-PI (Costa & McCrae, 1985), consists of 300 items. Respondents decide how characteristic each item is of themselves, rating each item on a five-point scale. As well as scoring on the five factors, respondents receive scores on six sub-scales associated with each of the factors. Most of the early work on the Big Five model was conducted in North America using the English language. A recent review of studies involving European languages found general support for the Big Five. Evidence from studies conducted in non-Western cultures is less widely available, but does show some support for a five factor structure. The Big Five forms the basis for trait assessment of personality at the beginning of the twenty-first century, with questionnaires such as the NEO-PI and subsequent revisions (NEO-PI-R, Costa & McCrae, 1992) being used widely in occupational psychology.

Projective Tests

While paper-and-pencil questionnaires have a closed-ended response, the projective tests contain open-ended response patterns, facilitating tapping of subjects' unconscious thoughts and feelings. Because the projective tests do not obviously carry correct and socially more or less desirable responses, it is assumed that subjects *project* their own feelings or thoughts through the responses they make in their typical styles. The projective technique derives its strength from the theory of psychoanalysis which predicts that will people resort to hidden (inner processes) to "project" structure onto ambiguous stimuli. The two most commonly used projective tests in psychology are the Rorschach Ink-blot test and Thematic Apperception Test (TAT).

Rorschach Ink-blot Test

Harmine Rorschach, a Swiss psychiatrist developed this test, which consists of 10 cards hosing ink-blots that are presented to the subject individually one at a time in a prescribed sequence. The subject is asked to examine each of the blots and tell what it looks like or what brings to his mind by looking at it. Scoring of the response is extremely complex, requiring extensive training in one of the several systems by which the responses are coded, scored and interpreted. However, all the different systems agree that the major scoring categories for each of the responses includes its *location* (where the subject focus attention), its *determinants* (colour, implied movement, shading, particular form, etc.), and its *content* (human, non-human, animal, or object). Subject's response can be interpreted in various ways. Because the interpretations are subjective, even highly experienced psychologists using this test are not in agreement with one another about responses interpretation.

The validity of the Rorschach Ink-blot Test as a diagnostic tool has often been questioned. Most clinical psychologists use this test in conjunction with other tests (or data collection device), and interpret the subject response with reference to information collected from different sources. This makes it difficult to truly assess the capacity of the instrument by itself to provide valid personality assessments and accurate behavioural predictions. Despite claims and counter-claims on the effectiveness of the Rorschach Ink-blot Test, its use has not diminished through the world.

Thematic Apperception Test (TAT)

Developed by Henry Murray, the Thematic Apperception Test measures the need for achievement and other human motives. Later McClelland (1953) refined the test, making it an effective psychological instrument. The TAT asks the subjects to make up stories about a series of ambiguous pictures, the idea being that people will project their own motives, interests and values into the stories. Precisely, the test consists of 30 cards that depict various scenes and one blank card. Though recognizable, all pictures are vague and ambiguous. In the standard administration of the test, the tester selects 20 cards on the basis of the sex and age of the subject, who is then shown the cards one at a time and asked to describe what is going on in each scene, what the characters are thinking and feeling, who led to the portrayed situation, and what its outcome will be.

Disclosing the underlying assumptions in developing the TAT, Murray (1938) remarked: "The test is based on the well-recognized fact when a person interprets an ambiguous social situation he is apt to expose his own personality as much as the phenomenon to which he is attending". Even though formal systems for scoring and interpreting TAT responses are available, most clinical psychologists prefer to rely on their own impassionate and subjective assessments. Undoubtedly, there are limitations in the total procedure of the TAT, but the test seemingly has shown sufficiently high validity when used as a research instrument under controlled conditions.

Despite the existence of a wide range of personality evaluation procedures, most psychologists agree that there is a scope for refinement in techniques geared to understand distinctive needs, values, and patterns of behaviour that characterize individuals' adaptation to the situations of their lives. Life situations are very fluid and dynamic; they make both the individual-environment interaction and personality testing a really difficult task.

Do's and Don'ts of Personality Testing in General and in Sport

In order to measure and interpret people's behaviour and personality, experts prescribe the following do's and don'ts in personality testing.

- *Do* inform participants about the purpose of the personality test and exactly how it will be used.
- *Do* allow only qualified individuals who have an understanding of testing principles and procedures of measurement error to give personality tests.
- *Do* integrate personality test results with other information obtained about the subject.
- *Do* use sport- and exercise-specific tests whenever and wherever possible, giving them in consultation with a trained (sport) psychologist.
- *Do* use both state and trait measures of personality.
- *Do* provide the subjects with specific feedback concerning the test result.
- *Do* compare individuals against their own baseline levels rather than against normative information.
- *Don't* use clinical personality tests that focus on abnormality to study an average population of sport and exercise participants.
- Don't give or interpret personality tests unless you are qualified to do so by the APA or another certifying agency or organization.

- *Don't* use personality tests to predict behaviour in sport and exercise settings without considering other sources of information.

PERSONALITY AND SPORT PERFORMANCE

Over the decades, psychologists have shown great interest in the study of personality in sport context obviously for two major reasons: (1) this new area of interaction has immense research potential; and (2) relationship between personality and sport has been reported to be quite thick, so important for developing strategies for performance-enhancement. As a subject of study and application, the area is both interesting and exciting, in which the discussion has often taken place at several levels and contexts; for example, personality as related to participation in sport, personality as predictor of athletic performance, personality of athletes and non-athletes, etc. The athletes of today, whether recreational or elite, run and swim faster, throw farther, and jump higher than their competitors from the past. These improvements have been attributed to several factors related to smarter nutrition; a greater understanding of biomechanics of sport movement, better training techniques, advances in psychological support, improvements in coaching education, and above all psychological inputs.

With the rise of sport psychology as a distinct field of research and study of athletic behaviour in various contexts of sports participation, the sport psychologists and researchers (along with coaches, trainers, medicine specialists, etc.) have begun to focus their attention on and possibly exploit each and every mind factor – whether genetic or environmental – that contributes, in some way, to performance-enhancement and success at the competition. Both in sport and psychology, personality is an important region of research, interaction and manipulation that can address several questions pertaining to sport talent selection, grooming of athletes and preparing them for top sport competition.

Highways to Athletic Personality

Often a question is raised as to what kind of people participate in sport, meaning whether those born with certain propensities or qualities of behaviour conducive to sports participate in sport and become successful or it is sport participation that makes them the type of personality and character they are. Millions play a sport, say tennis or soccer, at various levels but only a few reach the pinnacle. Whether being at the top is due to their inherited personality traits or external factors such as skill, fitness, training and hard work, needs head-scratching and heart-searching. Kroll (1967) argued: "There is a possibility that a discrete set of personality factors exists which is related to causing some people to select and participate in sport. Perhaps those possessing the strongest and the most fortuitous combination of these salient personality factors tend to persist in sport and become successful as outstanding athletes". Alderman (1974) makes the picture clear:

> At any one time, the group of best athletes in the world is a finite population consisting of only a few individuals in each sport. In various levels below these select groups exist thousands upon thousands of other participants; some good, some not so good, and some in-between. Because of the obvious differences that exist between these participants in terms of the quality of their performance, one can be interested exactly in what factors contribute to the differentiation.

What makes an elite (outstanding) athlete is a million dollar question, but its answer is not easy to find due mainly to mysterious genetic potential and the individual differences that exist among people. However, there is a general agreement among researchers that outstanding sportspersons are a "special breed" (Cofer & Johnson, 1960), and that 'a rare combination of genetic endowment, generally good environment and a very special training can produce an Olympic athlete" (de Garay et al.1974). The question whether characteristics of an outstanding athlete are inborn or acquired, wholly or partially, drags us into the age-old inconclusive debate over the role of nature and nurture in shaping personality both structurally and functionally. It is so difficult to draw a demarcating line between what is inherited and what is acquired. However, scientists are convinced that characteristics like body-build, limb measurements, morphological structure of the muscles, physiological capacities and functioning including that of the glands, etc., are inherited, while skills and strategies of the game, fitness, interpersonal relationships in a team, personal attributes such as confidence, resoluteness, courage, etc., are acquired through individual-environment interaction in which education and training play a crucial role. Placing too great a reliance either on genetic endowment or on the external factors as determinants of performance in sport will just be a simplistic approach to defining athletic personality. In making of an outstanding athlete, it is the best combination of the two that settles the issue. Some people are blessed with some inborn qualities more than others of developing into elite athletes, but they may not be able to realize their full potential without sustained and fruitful interaction with the environment.

Surveys on the personality of superior athletes over time have, more or less, convinced the sport scientists that:

- out of millions practicing a particular sport at a given moment of time, the elite ones (those forming the topmost layer) are a few but certainly the best in terms of physical, physiological, and psychological characteristics;
- acute inter-sport and intra-sport variations in somatotype distribution exist among them, making it an impossible task to develop an athlete template for a particular sport, e.g. volleyball, tennis or soccer;
- elite athletes are extraordinarily fit physically and mentally tough;
- top athletes are so meticulously trained that they become master of their sport as they move up in their performance standard; and
- psychologically, elite athletes are a distinct category of people, capable of performing under most stressful conditions.

Researchers have hinted at the possibility of existence of a "football" or "wrestling type" individual but presence of a "unique athletic personality" is still a matter of remote reckoning probably for two reasons: (1) human beings are not born as "football" or "tennis" types; (2) physical and mental requirement for each sport are different. Perfect matching between the two is almost impossible. In the same sport, all individuals are not alike in physical and psychological characteristics.

Personality and Performance Prediction

Research on personality of elite performers and prediction of success in athletics on the basis of identified personality traits makes an interesting study. As in psychology and education, so in sport the study of personality began with the traditional trait approach. Individual differences in traits (generally considered to be genetically inherited) could be subdivided into *competencies* (e.g. some technical sport talent), *affective dynamic traits* (e.g. sensation-seeking tendency), *cognitive traits* (beliefs), and *formal traits*, referring to formal aspect of human behaviour (e.g. aggressiveness). Personality traits, both in life and sport, have been subjected to investigation, evaluation and analysis through the administration of traditional self-reporting questionnaires/ personality inventories (for example, 16-PFQ, CPI, EPQ, etc.) used by psychologists for various purposes.

The traditionalist non-athletic trait psychologists share three assumptions: (1) people are cross-situationally consistent; (2) our behaviour displays a temporal stability; and (3) there is co-occurrence of behavioural manifestations referring to the same underlying trait. They do not pretend that people will have the same way in all situations. As time went by, the absoluteness of the traits was frowned upon and more psychologists begin to get convinced that traits could not predict behaviour. As a result, the trait research either slowed down or was abandoned, and the researchers turned to studies on the predictability of behaviour from situational variables – considered the actual dynamics of behaviour. But proponents of the trait theories prefer several arguments in defence of their views. For example, they contend that the behaviour of only some people (those low in self-monitoring or high in self-consciousness) is predictable from measures of traits. Secondly, only some traits are useful for describing and predicting how people will behave. Finally, trait measurements could serve as predictors of future behaviour only in situations low in constraints or weak in pressure to conform. Today, greater emphasis is placed on external factors (individual-environment interactions) than on traits as the true predictors of behaviour in general, and performance in sport. The trait psychologists also do not doubt that behaviour is a function of environmental as well as person variables. The interaction between the two kinds of variables is a two-way traffic (reciprocal interaction) meaning that person variables influence and modify environmental variables and vice-versa. Besides this, proponents of dynamic interaction hypothesis argue that exposure of the individual in certain situations is a function of personality characteristics of that individual. By his overt behaviour the individual can create a situation which, in combination with personality traits, elicits the consequential behaviour.

Inter-Group Personality Comparisons

Traditionally, personality comparisons by athletes versus non-athletes, successful versus less successful, and men athletes versus women athletes have often been made. Inter-sport comparisons have also been there. The goal here obviously is performance prediction and selection of athletes on teams. Extent to which these attempts have been really very successful is difficult to know. The instruments used for this purpose were traditional non-athletic trait inventories/ questionnaires like 16-PFQ, EPI, CPI, etc.

During 1960s and 1970s more than 1000 sports personality studies were reported across the Globe, however, with "far from consistent" result findings and conclusions. Some sport personality research reviewers like Martens (1975) and Rushall (1975b) went on record that 'general trait measures are worthless for the purpose of predicting relevant sport behaviour'. A contrasting viewpoint was defended by Morgan (1980) who argued that 'elite athletes display unique personality characteristics." He observed: "An athlete who is neurotic, depressed, anxious, schizoid, introverted, confused and fatigued and scores low on psychic vigour will tend to be unsuccessful in comparison to an athlete who is characterized by the absence of such traits." In numerous studies successful athletes were reported to be characterized by such traits as emotional stability, high need for achievement, assertion and dominance (Kane, 1964; Cooper, 1969; Ogilvie, 1976; Tuto, Lyon & Ogilvie, 1969 cited in Alderman, 1974). According to McKelvie, Simpson-Housley, & Valliant (1981), there are important differences between an athlete and a non-athlete in terms of personality. Bailey, Moulton, & Moulton (1999) found that athletes experienced higher levels of self-esteem than non-athletes, and psychological factors such as personality can play an important role in athletic participation. Raglin (2001) showed that psychological factors and athletic performance worked hand in hand, suggesting that as much as 85% of athletic success or failure could be attributed to some psychological factor. Some research has revealed that personality can be an effective predictor of athletic performance. Blanco, Hill, & Piedmont (1999) evaluated the effects of the five-factor model of personality on athletic performance. Reiss, Sherman, & Wiltz (2001) suggested that, not only is personality an effective predictor of athletic performance, but that combined with motivational theory, individual differences can be addressed in more detail. They showed that no one personality trait can be shown to "predict" personality.

The inclusive findings about sport personality can be traced to two major reasons: (1) "lack of conceptual or theoretical framework"

(Martens, 1981); and (2) use of varied psychological tests with varied groups of subjects" (Singer, 1988). Besides, serious methodological short-comings were reported by several reviewers of personality research (Caron, 1980; Hardman, 1973; Heyman, 1982; Martens, 1975; Morgan, 1980; Silva, 1984). First, critical variables such as elite and non-elite athletes, anxiety etc., have *not* been operationally defined. Second, sampling techniques employed in the studies are poor. For instance, the use of intact sport teams with inevitable skill-level heterogeneity, made generalizations of the conclusions impossible. Third, inappropriate statistical analyses are employed. Fourth, personality tests were selected without regard for their origin or for the rationale of their development. The MMPI, for example, was not developed for measuring the normal person's personality. The inappropriate use of personality inventories in athletic context has not only complicated the issue but also invalidated the conclusions of the research conducted. Finally, where the data of between group comparisons are rational, some have assumed them to be casual.

Athletic Performance - Situational Variables

It is evident that research in sport personality began with identification of traits (internal dispositions) considered to be highly conducive to performance-improvement in sport and activity. Gradually, myths attached to it were shattered and more sport psychologists began to evaluate the influence of external (situational) variables on athletic performance. This experiment too did not succeed because when behaviour is seen as an exclusive product of environment, the belief in genetic factors determining behaviour receives a setback and the centre of gravity of the personality concept gets disturbed. The pure situationalism, i.e. environmental variables as the determinants of behaviour, neglecting individual differences among people, has not received approbation almost every where including sport psychology. Martens (1975) saw situationalism as an "overreaction to trait psychology". In contemporary psychology, greater importance is being attached to interaction between internal (inherited) traits and external situations as the chief determinant of the quality and kind of behaviour, and so personality, both in life in general and sport in particular.

Psychologists from various academic schools today are employing, rather developing, more precise techniques and strategies of evaluating the relationship between personality and athletic performance. The use of POMS (Profile of Mood States) on elite groups of athletes, statistically integrated data on personality and performance (for instance, the existence of extraversion trait differences between elite and non-elite athletes through met-analysis) and multivariate analysis of complex nature of human functioning and prediction of performance have added new dimensions to personality research in sport setting and yielded information hitherto not much known to the sport psychologists. Precisely, the POMS studies have greatly confirmed findings of Morgan (1980) that elite athletes showed reduced scores on the scales of labelled Tension, Anger, Depression, Fatigue and Confusion and elevated scores on Vigour. Interestingly, most studies of this nature reported and reviewed were generally found to have been conducted on male American elite athletes who typically displayed the iceberg profile (Fig.15.3), especially during training periods, sometimes before competition.

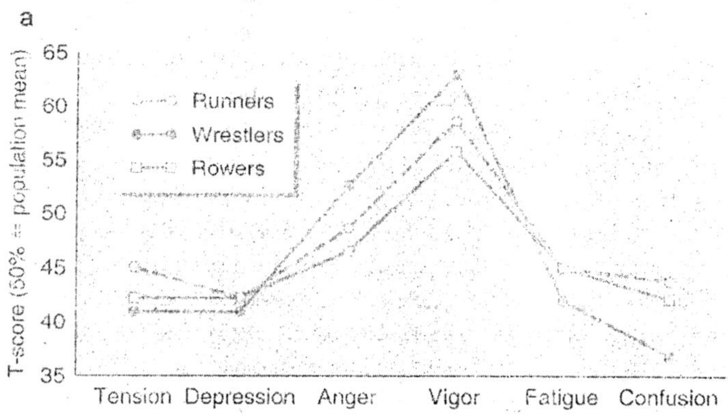

Fig. 15.3 The Iceberg Profile

Turning to studies on extraversion with meta-analysis, it is reasonable to remark that the chief purpose of this exercise was a quantitative integration of research findings taken from different studies when the original data were not available. An important problem, when considering a meta-analysis on personality data from elite athletes is the variety of research designs, reflecting divergent goals and hypotheses. For example, successful elite athletes are typically compared (1) with non-successful athletes, or athletes at a lower performance level, (2) with a control group or with non-athletes, (3) with the test norms of the general population, (4) across sport disciplines, or (5) by gender. The meta-analysis was conducted on a single trait extraversion-introversion because it has been argued that this is the trait for which elite sportspersons score higher than is expected (Eysenck, Nias & Cox, 1982; Hardman, 1973) as compared with normative data. Most studies were conducted using 16-PFQ, EPI or EPQ. The meta-analysis, by and large, confirmed the no-difference (null) hypothesis when athletes and normal population were compared on extraversion as trait of personality. Hardman (1973), who examined reports on 42 elite athletic populations (dated 1952-1968), was proved right. The sweeping claims that extraversion is an essential element of the sportsperson's personality, is difficult to accept. The use of multivariate and multidimensional mode in research on elite athletes is a recent phenomenon the major objective of which is to predict performance on the basis of empirical data on a variety of psychological variables in addition to physiological (e.g. heart rate, blood lactate), morphological (e.g. weight, body fat, muscle type), and skill (e.g. skating speed, stick handling) variables. The idea is to deal more adequately with the complex nature of human functioning and the multi-factorial determination of performance. It is now being argued that top level athletes in a specific sporting discipline are, to a great extent, homogenous on physiological, technical and tactical parameters, the differentiation in performance might be attributed mostly to psychological variables. Inadequacy of samples in various studies, and variation in the characteristics required for each sport, makes the existence of a unique set of characteristics for elite athletes across sports somewhat questionable.

Selected Findings in Personality Research

- Morgan's (1980) mental health model shows that successful athletes exhibit greater positive mental health than do less successful athletes
- However, precise predictions have not been achieved and should not be used for team selection
- POMS has been raked over the coals as far as applicability to sport & healthy populations
- Huge problem is that there are only correlation data,

especially between personality differences and athletes/ non-athletes (no causation!)

Characteristics of Champion Athletes

Jack J. Lesyk, clinical and sport psychologist at the Ohio Centre for Sport Psychology, observed that *successful athletes* characteristically (1) choose and maintain a positive attitude; (2) maintain a high level of motivation; (3) set high, realistic goals; (4) deal effectively with people; (5) use positive self-talk; (6) use mental imagery. (7) manage anxiety effectively; (8) manage their emotions effectively; and (9) maintain concentration.

After an extensive review of the literature, Williams & Krane (2001) identified a number of psychological characteristics of highly successful (champion) athletes, as well as the mental skills these athletes used to achieve optimal psychological states. Characteristics included self-regulation of arousal, high confidence, better concentration and focus, an in control but not forcing it attitude, positive imagery and self-talk, and high determination and commitment. Skills used to achieve peak psychological states included imagery, goal setting, thought control strategies, arousal management, well-developed competition plans, well-developed coping strategies, and pre-competitive mental preparation plans. The quantitative and qualitative results collected with these Olympic champions paralleled these results almost exactly. Specifically, as a group these Olympians were found to be characterized by:

- The Ability to Focus
- Mental Toughness
- Hope/Goal Setting Ability
- Sport Intelligence
- Ability to Cope
- Competitiveness
- Confidence
- Coachability
- High Drive
- Intrinsic Motivation
- High Optimism
- Adaptive Perfectionism
- Automaticity : The Ability to Click into Automatic Performance
- Emotional Control: Ability to Relax and Activate

SELECTED REFERENCES

Alderman, R., B. *Psychological Behaviour in Sport*, Philadelphia; W.B. Saunders, 1974

Allport, G.W. *Personality. A Psychological Interpretation*, New York: Holt, Rinehart & Winston, 1973

Allport, G.W. *Pattern and Growth in Personality*, New York: Holt, Rinehart & Winston, 1961

Allport, G.W. *Letters from Jenny*, New York: Harcourt, Brace and World, 1965

Allport, G.W. Traits revisited, *American Psychologist*; 21, 1-10, 1966

Bailey, K., Moulton, M., & Moulton, P. Athletics as a predictor of self-esteem and approval motivation. *The Sports Journal*, 2(2), 1, 1999

Bandura, A. Self-efficacy mechanism in human agency, *American Psychologist*: 37, 127-147, 1982

Bandura, A. Temporal dynamics and decomposition of reciprocal determinism: a reply to Philips and Orten, *Psychological Review*: 90, 166-170, 1983

Bandura, A. *Social Foundations of Thought and Action; A Social Cognitive Theory*, Englewood Cliffs, NJ: Prentice Hall, 1986

Blanco S., Hill D. C., & Piedmont, R. L. Predicting athletic performance using the five-factor model of personality. *Personality and Individual Differences*, 27(4), 769-777, 1999

Buskist, William & Gerbing, David W. *Psychology: Boundaries and Frontiers*, Glenview, Ill: Scot, Foreman/Little Brown Higher education, 1990

Carron, A.V. *Social Psychology of Sport and Physical Activity*, London: Mouvement Publications, 1980

Cattell, R. *A Systematic Theoretical and Factual Study*, New York: McGraw Hill, 1950

Cattell, R. *The Scientific Analysis of Personality*, Baltimore: Penguin Books, 1965

Cattell, R. Personality Pinned Down, *Psychology Today, July, 40-46, 1975.*

Cattell, R. *The Inheritance of Personality and Ability*, New York: Academic Press, 1965

Cofer, C. & Johnson, W. Personality dynamics in relation to exercise and sport, In W. Johnson (Ed.) *Science and Medicine of Exercise and Sport*, New York: Harper, 1960

Cooper, L. Athletics, activity and personality: Review of literature, *Research. Quarterly*: 40, 17-22, 1969

Cratty, B.J. *Psychology in Contemporary Sport* (Third Edition) Englewood Cliffs NJ; Prentice Hall, 1989

de Garay, A.L., Levine, L., & Carter, J.E.L,. *Genetic and Anthropological Studies of Olympic Athletes,* New York: Academic Press, 1974

Eysenck, H. J. *Manual of Maudsley Personality Inventory,* London; University Press, 1959a

Eysenck, H. J. *The Structure of Human Personality,* London; Metheun, 1960a

Eysenck, H. J., Nias, D.K. & Cox, D.N. Sport and Personality, *Advances in Behaviour Research and Therapy;* 1, 1-56, 1982

Goleman, Daniel *Emotional Intelligence,* New York; Bantam Book, 1996

Gough, H. *California Psychological Inventory Manual* (revised, 1975), Palo Alto, C.S.: Counselling Psychologists Press, 1957, 1975

Hardman, K. A dual approach to the study of personality and performance in sport, In H.T.A. Whiting, K. Hardman, L.B. Hendry, & M.G. Jones *Personality and Physical Education in Sport* (pp 77-122), London: Kimpton, 1973

Hathaway, S. & Mc Kinley, J. *Minnesota Multiphasic Personality Inventory,* Minneapolis; University of Minnesota, 1942

Heyman, S.R. Comparison of successful and unsuccessful competitors: A reconsideration of methodological questions and data, *Journal of Sport Psychology;* 4, 295-300, 1982

Kroll, W. Sixteen personality factor profiles of collegiate wrestlers, *Research Quarterly,* 38: 49-57, March, 1967

Kretschmer, E *Physique and Character,* New York: Harcourt, Brace and World, 1925

Martens, R. The paradigmatic crisis in American sport personlogy, Sortswissenchaft, 5; 9-24, 1975

Martens, R. Sport personlogy, In G.R.F. Wichen & G.H. Sage (Eds.) *Handbook of Social Science of Sport* (pp 492-508), Champaign, Ill., Stripes, 1981

Maslow, A. *Towards a Psychology of Being* (2nd Ed,), Princeton, NJ; Van Nostrand Reinhold, 1968

Maslow, A. *Motivation and Personality,* (2nd Ed.), New York; Harper & Row, 1970

Mayer, J. D. A classification of DSM-IV-TR mental disorders according to their relation to the personality system. In J. C. Thomas & D. L. Segal (Eds.), *Comprehensive handbook of personality and psychopathology (CHOPP) Vol. 1: Personality and everyday functioning.* New York, NY: John Wiley & Sons, 2005

McClelland, D. *The Achievement Motive*, New York; Appleton Century Crafts, 1953

McKelvie, S. J., Simpson-Housley, P., & Valliant, P. M. Personality in athletic and non-athletic college groups. *Perceptual and Motor Skills*, 52(3), 963-966, 1981

Morgan, W.P. The trait psychology controversy, Research *Quarterly for Exercise & Sport*, 51, 50-76, 1980

Raglin, J. S. Psychological factors in sports performance: The mental health model revisited. *Sports Medicine*, 31(12), 875-890, 2001

Reiss, S., Sherman, M., & Wiltz, J. Trait motivational correlates of athleticism. *Personality and Individual Differences*, 30(7), 1139-1145, 2001

Rogers, Carl *Becoming a Person: A Therapist's view of Psychotherapy*, Boston; Houghton Mifflin, 1961

Ross, A. *Personality: The Scientific Study of Complex Human Behaviour*, New York, Holt, Rinehart and Winston, 1987

Rushall, B.S. Psychodynamics and personality in sport: status and values, In H.T.A Whiting (Ed.) *Readings in Sport Psychology -2*, (pp 72-84), London; Lepus, 1975b

Ryckman, R. *Theories of Personality*. Belmont, CA: Thomson/ Wadsworth, 2004

Skinner, B.F. *Science of Human Behavuour*, New York: McMillan, 1953

Homo Olympicus – the elite Olympian – is a product of superior genotype and of a favourable milieu.

- Unknown

CHAPTER - 16

HEREDITY AND ENVIRONMENT

Organisms are a product of *Nature* called heredity, and *Nurture*, meaning environment or external factors. These terms were coined by Francis Galton who was very much influenced by Charles Darwin's book *The Origin of the Species*. While nature refers to a person's innate qualities – nativism or innatism - determined, demarcated and delimited by genetics, nurture underscores personal experiences (empiricism or behaviourism) and environmental interactions, so importantly responsible for determining or causing individual differences in physical and behavioural traits.

The nature-nurture interplay, a very complex process to explain, is a more realistic and dynamic approach towards answering the intricate question "which, nature or nurture, contributes more to personality?" Our moods, thoughts and behavioural patterns are largely shaped by the long-drawn interaction of the forces of nature and nurture. Psychologists know that innate traits may not exhibit themselves in the form of behaviours, movements and activities unless there is environment around to facilitate this process. While heredity supplies the basic material of our personality and behaviour, environment encourages it to take a concrete shape by which a human being performs all functions of life. The entire growth process – physical, mental, intellectual, social, emotional and spiritual – that influences development of personality is subject to laws of inheritance and environmental influences.

Biologically, all organisms have a similar beginning but they become different as they grow. While some scientists attribute the consequential differences largely to heredity, others to environment, which in their view is a modifier. Both could be right in one way, and wrong in another because neither nature nor nurture can singularly bring an organism into existence and determine its destiny as an animal or a human being, a man or a woman, an athlete or a non-athlete, a scientist or an artist, and so on. Variations and similarities, exceptions and commonalities, and generality and uniqueness are caused neither by heredity nor by environment alone single-handed but by a powerful sustained interaction between the two in varying degrees under varying conditions.

Psychologists are baffled over the effects, which the mind-boggling genetics-environment interaction produces. Some believe that the actual determinant of personality characteristics is heredity; environment is only the modifier or modulator. While the heredity characteristics are transmitted from parents to children, acquired traits have no transmission channel. There is little doubt that the basic building blocks of personality are supplied by heredity, the work of shaping personality is left to environment. An organism is a toy in the hands of the circumstances. Neither the same or similar persons produce the similar individuals, nor do the same or similar persons inherit the same traits and characteristics even if they are progeny of the same parents.

Much of psychologist's interest in biology lies in the relation between people's physical and intellectual capacities and the extent to which these shape up and determine our routines and behaviours in general. The basic question, defying solution, pertains to the extent to which nature or nurture contributes to shaping of human behaviour and personality. Meaney (2004), Herschkowitz & Herschkowitz (2002), and Scott (1995) quote psychologist Donald Hebb replying this question posed to him by a journalist with a counter-question "Which contributes more to the area of a rectangle, its length or its width?" This indicates that nature versus nurture tangle is not easy to resolve because the influences of these two fuse into each other in such a matter that it becomes virtually impossible to pinpoint where heredity ends and environment begins or where environment ends and heredity takes over. Still a ray of hope lies in three important factors: (1)'both nature and nurture influence the expression of traits such as intelligence, (2) the surrounding environment must make it possible for an inherited trait to be expressed in behaviour, (3) the complex and constantly changing relationship between biology and environment affects behaviour' (Lefton, 1985). Notably, the genetics provides a framework for behaviour and personality, and experiences (external interactions) give it a form it possibly is capable of.

The question whether Olympic (exceptional) athletes are born or made is directly ascribed to nature-nurture role in producing people with towering characters in art, science, literature, technology, education, philosophy, sport, etc. While there is a general agreement among sport scientists that a "rare combination of genetic endowment, generally good environment and a very special training can produce an Olympic athlete" (de Garay et al. 1974), it has not as yet been possible to ascertain the extent to which each of these three major factors (having a large number of observable and non-observable variables) is prepotent in ensuring athletic success at the apex level. Psychologists and geneticists assume that the genetic material, which carries exceptions and commonalities, is evenly distributed over the entire mankind human races, and yet certain sub-culture or ethnic groups have produced more athletic giants and in greater number than others.

HEREDITY (Nature)

Heredity is '*transmission of traits from parents to offspring through genes, the functional units of heritable material that are found within all living cells*'. In biological sense, it is nature's act of passing on of physical and mental characteristics genetically from one generation to the next. It is what we inherit biologically from our parents, grand-parents, great grand-parents and so on in the dynastic lineage. Sandiford (1933) says:

> Heredity to some is a mysterious force which moulds off-spring in the likeness of parents, to others it is the antithesis of variation that is heredity consists in the resemblances, and in the dissimilarities between progenitors and descendents. Heredity is not a force. Neither is it merely the likeness between offspring and parents; it includes all traits both like and unlike.

In other words, heredity is the growth potential every individual receives from their parents through the transmission of genes. It is the sum-total of inborn characteristics, both similar and dissimilar, to those of the parents. With rare exceptions, perhaps barring monozygotic twins, every human being is genetically unique. Each one of us shares traits with brothers, sisters, and parents, but none of us is exactly alike to any of them or any one else in the family. In the propagation of animal species, the invisible force that guides the reproductive process and determines each individual's characteristics, in terms of genetics, is called heredity. Transmission of heredity characteristics from parents to children is no mechanical process meant to produce run-of the-mill units, exactly alike in structure and function, but a unique process governed by peculiar laws of mysterious nature that determines both likeness and unlikeness. In nutshell, heredity is that imperceptible force which is at the root of resemblances and dissimilarities among parents and their offspring. It is an agent that demarcates the boundaries of one's physical growth and sets limits in terms of one's potential for overall growth and development.

Genetic Secrets

As one lamp lights another, so does one life ignite another. A new life begins as a single cell – a fertilized ovum or female egg – technically known as *zygote*, created by the fusion of the spermatozoon (male sex cell) with the ovum. Heredity (the unique characteristics carried by an individual) is determined by a complex organization of chemical materials with the nucleus of the fertilized cell. The sperm, a stripped down cell shaped like a tadpole, is 3,00,000 times smaller than the ovum which is relatively enormous and one of the largest cells in the body – so large that can be visible to the naked eye. Although the ovum weighs only a millionth of a gram, it contains considerable amount of cytoplasm and also a small amount of yolk needed to nourish the fertilized egg in its earliest days of growth. The female ovaries contain an estimated 4,00,000 eggs of which from 300 to 400 are released during a woman's fertility life. In this regard, the male partner of the offspring has been so abundantly supplied with that in one ejaculation about 300 million to 500 million sperms get released to meet the egg to lay the foundation for a new life. The sex of the new child is determined right at the moment of the fertilization and is governed by precise laws of genetics.

All cells in the human body except the sex cell – sperm or ovum - contain 46 chromosomes, a definite number of bodies, arranged in the nucleus in 23 pairs. Only sperm and egg contain 23 chromosomes each. Each female cell sex has identical chromosomes called XX, and each male sex cell carries XY chromosomes. When the two opposite cells fuse, the resultant zygote contains 23 paired chromosomes. Chromosomes are strands of DNA (deoxyribonucleic acid). Along with some proteins, they carry the vital genetic information in their basic functional units called genes. Genes are lined up on the chromosomes in the nucleus (the centre) of the sex cell. In the body, every cell is thought to contain up to six hundred feet of DNA which adds up to 17 billion miles (27 billion kilometres). One scientist has described DNA as an "exquisitely thin filament" so light that a thread of it running all the way from the Earth to the Sun, 93 million miles away, would weigh only 50 grams. In human beings, a little more than 40 percent of the DNA governs cell function. The remaining 60 percent of it, the function of which is yet to be understood, is specific variations. In this regard, DNA carries tentatively repeated sequences which occur again and again. The number of such repeating units is highly variable. Every individual in this world can be differentiated and identified at the molecular level on the basis of their DNA, the genetic material which it inherits from his biological parents, and which is identical in every cell. With the exception of identical twins, no human child has identical sequences. At the moment of conception, a sperm and an ovum, each containing half of each pair of the parent's chromosomes, combine to form a new individual and the chromosomes join to form new pairs. There are 8,388,688 possible re-combinations of the twenty three with a colossal 70,368,000,000 possible re-combinations of genes. Thus, although many people look alike and have common characteristics no two individuals, except identical twins, are exactly alike genetically. Each member of the parental generation transmits only half its genes to the offspring, and different offspring of the same parents receive different combinations of genes. Many characteristics are polygenic (i.e., influenced by more than one gene). Many genes exist in numerous variations (alleles) throughout a population. The polygenic and multiple allelic nature of many traits gives a vast potential for variability among hereditary characteristics.

The combination of good genes from both male and female parents makes really good heredity, while poor combination results in inferior inheritance. Genetic scientists believe that we do not, in fact, receive our bodies from our parents but only a germ-plasm – the seed, an aggregate of characteristics – which by mysterious force transforms into a human being. Interestingly, the germ-cell which produces a dog may be similar to the one producing man yet the one gives rise to puppy, the other to a child. In 1875, Francis Galton had pointed out that the child, in a sense, is as old as the parent, indeed as old as the remotest parent : "the parent is rather the trustee of the germ-plasm than the producer of the child", said he. The reproductive part of the germ-plasm is passed on from generation to generation as if withdrawn from one bank and deposited in another. The fusion of the material from the male and female parents seals the fate of the foetus by determining once for all its traits and characteristics it would exhibit as a human being. Significantly, a person's heredity and the potential it carries is fixed at the time of conception. Nothing can be added or subtracted from it, and changed or modified later.

Biologists have shown that genes create certain gross common features for all representatives of the *Homo Sapiens*, for example, an upright posture, a pair of eyes and a pair of ears, a pair of arms and legs each, and a bilaterally symmetrical body. They have the same body chemistry and a capacity for feeling and thinking, for speaking, imagining, remembering and reproducing. Exceptions in this arrangement are rare. Our genetic heritage is unaffected by our day-to-day experiences and routine. It is noteworthy that due to physical and physiological adaptations to changing environment over millions of years, humans have evolved a highly organized brain that allows learning to influence their behaviour. Our brains act as libraries of information. Every new enriching experience affects our later behaviour (Rosenzweig, 1984). Proponents of nurture position, however, suggest that human beings are not limited by their genetic heritage because experience, training and a little hard work can stretch their potential to amazing limits.

Though the body structure, body chemistry, size, colour, physiological functioning, temperament, and intelligence, to an extent, are closely related to heredity, they too are influenced by external forces. Lefton (1985) argues:

> Love for other animals, desire to be good and ability to develop high levels of creativity, communication and technology, all reflect human genetic endowment. Especially important are the abilities to remember, think, combine, recall and invent new ways of thinking. Genetic makeup may limit potential but it also confers the ability to think about the future and to respond to environment changes in adaptive ways. A person's genetic makeup is the foundation on which all his or her behaviours are built. Experiences in the environment act in collaboration with the inheritance to shape day-to-day behaviour.

Laws of Heredity

The imperceptible most powerful process of heredity trait transmission is governed by precise laws of nature. Geneticists and heredity position holders cite numerous experiments and observations to emphasise that basic traits of species do not alter at all unless mutation, i.e. sudden catastrophic change takes place in the genetic material of the animals. According to biologists, the process of transmission of characteristics genetically is govern by three fundamental laws: (1) like begets like (similarity), (2) like also produces unlike (variation or dissimilarity), and (3) regression (getting back to averages).

Like Begets Like

The assertion *like begets like* signifies that a corn seed produces corn plant; a dog, a puppy; a cat, a kitten; a horse, a foal, and a man, a child. No mango tree can bear peaches or pears, and vice versa. In basic biological characteristics such as body structure, limb length, form, shape, complexion, etc., children go after their parents and family lineage to a great extent. In mental traits such as intelligence, memory, reasoning, judgment, temperament, etc., the basic stuff (the tendency to be superior, average, or inferior in a given trait) is also liable to be transmitted from parents to children. Children who do not resemble their immediate parents broadly are likely to have resemblance to some one up the family stream. Some people do believe that stupid parents have stupid progeny; intelligent parents, intelligent offspring; and athletic parents, athletic children. But William Shakespeare wrote 'good wombs have also born bad children'. Sandiford (1933) observed: "That children are bound to resemble their parents some what closely is due to the continuity of the germ-plasm (the essential germinal material) that part of the substance of the parents which does not die with them but perpetuates itself in the offspring".

The germ-plasm theory was brought to prominence by Weisman and Francis Galton who attempted to show that a part of the germ-plasm contained in the present egg-cell is not used up in the constitution of the body of the offspring but is reserved unchanged for the foundation of the germ-cells of the following generation. *Likeness*, as per this assumption, is there because both the parents and the offspring possess the same germ-plasm. Parents, in this sense, are mere custodians or storehouse of the germ-plasm, and not its producers.

The 'likeness' theory emphasizes that traits that are encased in the germ-plasm itself are transmitted from one generation to the next, but not the ones that are acquired by an individual during its life time. A blind couple does *not* necessarily produce blind children nor does one-handed woman give birth to a one-handed off-spring. Similarly, the acquired knowledge, skill, art, technique of doing something and experience of a father or mother bears little likelihood of automatic transmission to the progeny because such characteristics are no part of the germ-plasm. 'Like begets like' principle fully illustrates the biological phenomenon of *racial propagation.*

The early bio-psychologists explored the family histories of famous as well as notorious individuals to substantiate their assumptions about the likeness theory. Today, the principle of likeness is illustrated through personality or trait studies of the twins, siblings, etc., reared in the same and different environments. Personality studies of monozygotic (identical) and diazygotic (fraternal) twins by Loehlin & Nicholls (1976), Loehlin (1992), and others have shown genetic influence and confirmed that monozygotic twins have exactly the same combination of genes and they are much more similar than diazygotic twins on personality traits.

Like Produces Unlike

Sound arguments and intuitive appeal have been found short of strength to compensate for the lack of empirical evidence supporting likeness theory. The common observation shows that likeness between parents and their offspring is never complete, nor perfect. Mentally inferior children are born to mentally sound people, short children to tall parents, ugly children to handsome parents, and vice versa, confirming the assumption that "although like begets like, there are variations". In the explanation of the theory of heredity, the term variation may mean *modification.* According to a section of biologists, variation, if ordained by Nature, is the result of certain set of principles while modification is more or less, extraneous. A psychologist made a distinction between variation and modification thus:

> Technically defined a variation is a filial departure from the parental type which is founded on germinal change ..... variations are inheritable, they are passed on from one generation to another. Being due to potentialities of the cell, variations are expressed from within. Modifications, on the other hand, are impressed upon the structure acquired in the life-time of an individual as direct result of environment - chiefly use, injury, or training.

For instance, difference in complexion among parents and children may be due to variation, but difference in physical prowess is on account of the modification in the working/living environment. The thoroughly-cultured parents may not necessarily have cultural offspring unless reared in a good cultural environment. The same way athletic parents may not have athletic children despite the genetic material being passed on to them. Variations are genetic, permanent and unchangeable; modifications are caused by the individual-environment interactivity and are temporary. Forced modifications on successive generations may, perhaps, bring out some variation in the germ-plasm but this process is terribly slow – a matter of millions of years.

Variation is an impeachable law. Life's existence and beauty lie in variation, not in stupid similarity. Evolutionists say that the protoplasm – cell's living material, the fourth state of matter) has an innate tendency to vary. Without it, the evolution and propagation of a wide variety of species of fauna and flora would be impossible. Variation is the essence of evolution, no matter whether or not we can understand it fully and explain it convincingly.

Departure of the offspring from the parental stock in some traits has been explained with the help of different theoretical models and hypotheses. In the early stages of evolutionary theory, Lamarck, a noted zoologist, assumed that variations in the species are chiefly caused by (1) the existence of inner urge, (2) use and disuse of organs, and (3) transmission of acquired traits. He felt that every living character possesses an "inner urge" for continuing life activities. Striving for the fulfilment of biological needs (food, sex, shelter, etc.) compel living beings to either adapt to the environment or alter their own surroundings (which is rare in animals as compared to man). In this process, certain body parts are used more frequently than others, some not used at all over long time at a certain stage of life. Hence, use and disuse is the main cause of variation in the long run and modification in the short run.

According to Lamarckians, modifications are transmitted generation to generation causing species and their members to vary in some way. By citing growth of the fur on the animal skin in colder regions (or in cold seasons), increase in the wing-size of the long-distance flying birds, change in the structure and form of giraffe, horse, man and other animals due to change of movement patterns or food-seeking habits, Lamarck wanted to gather support for his argument. Weisman and William McDougall disapproved Lamarckian theses. Pavlov's and Harrison's experiments with some animals revived scientist's faith, to some extent, in the theory of transmission of acquired traits. The whole thing is so intricate that scientists find it difficult to distinguish between acquired traits and those transmitted genetically with 100% accuracy. Further research on this issue shows that change in hereditary characteristics is either very slow or abrupt and catastrophic.

In Darwin's view causes of variations among animals are: (1) the principle of salutatory mutations and small chance variations; (2) struggle for existence; (3) survival of the fittest due to favourable variation; (4) natural selection; and (5) transmission of natural variations, and not of the acquired variations. Darwin observed that fecundity of animals in nature is prolific and subsequently their progeny is enormous. In Nature, there is no adequate food for all and hence there is a struggle for existence. Animals vary in physical and mental characteristics and these variations are, sometime slight and sometime big, and mostly innate. A process of natural selection is always at work in Nature, due to which those born with favourable variations survive and other perish. These variations are natural, not acquired, as Lamarck had contended; they are transmitted to the offspring in course of time to produce a new species of animals. The emergence of new species of animals from the same stock is at the nucleus of the biological evolution. Therefore, variation law as it applies in nature may be stated as: (1) If a large number of unselected, homogenous individuals of a given species is measured for a varying trait, the measures are found to be distributed according to the curve of chance or probability; and (2) in successive generations variants tend to move toward the average of the species which they form a part. Technically, this is called law of regression.

Law of Regression

In dictionary, regression means "a return to a former state", and in statistics, it is 'a process for determining a line or curve that best represents the general trend of a data set'. Francis Galton made an attempt to give a mathematical explanation to genetic trait transmission phenomenon. This effort resulted in Law of Regression which Galton explained as given below:

> Each peculiarity in man is shared by his kinsman, but in a less degree. It is reduced to a definite fraction of its amount, quite independently of what its amount might be. The fraction differs in different orders of kinship, becoming smaller as they are more remote. When the kinship is so distant that its effects are not worth taking into account, the peculiarity of the man, however,

remarkable, it may have been, is reduced to zero in his kinsman. This apparent paradox is fundamentally due to the greater frequency of the mediocre divisions than extreme ones, occurring between limits separated by equal widths.

The explanation importantly reveals that heredity trait transmission is never total but partial. While dwelling upon his law of ancestral heredity, Galton argued that "an individual derived, on the average, one half from his parents, one quarter from four grand parents, one eighth from his eight great grand parents". On the face of it, this might look good and interesting but empirical evidence for such an assumption is hard to come by even through longitudinal studies to be conducted on generations of a family in chronological order.

Trait transmission (regression equation) phenomenon has often explained on the basis of Gregor Mendel's experiments. Mendel called certain traits to be dominant and others recessive after categorization of genes as dominant and dormant or recessive. He claimed that both kinds of traits (dominant and recessive) are transmitted by a set of laws and appear in the offspring accordingly. According to him, there are three basic elements responsible for the transmission of traits: (a) *Independent Unit Characteristics,* (b) *Dormant Characteristics,* and (c) *Purity of Genes* (reproductive cells) or *Segregation.* Variations in offspring are due to recessive traits which are implicit in the parents but present in the germ-plasm and appear in the succeeding generation. On the strength of Mendel's experiments, it is believed that diseases like haemophilia (inability of the blood to clot), colour blindness, etc., are hereditary in character and are transmitted from one generation to the next.

Chromosome Theory or *Genes Hypothesis* has provided further explanation to Mendel's expostulations. This hypothesis considers gene or the chromosome as a unit of inheritance rather than the unit character as Mendel said. There is a definite number of chromosomes in the body cell of each animal, which happen to carry a definite number of genes (both dominant and dormant) - considered as the true unit characters of inheritance. As the fusion between the male and the female sex cells takes place, there occurs struggle for dominance among genes from the two parental streams. Whether the child will have a fair complexion or a dark one; whether he will be tall or short, intelligent or dull, temperamental or strong-nerved, submissive or dominant, will ultimately depend on the gene-combination in which case *chance* plays a very crucial role. Restak (1988) observes: "Although many presumably acceptable sperm are available for the egg, only one actually fertilizes it. Why this sperm and not another? Problems like this, formerly considered unresolvable, or credited simply to "chance" or "fate", are new potentially answerable because of what scientists are learning about selection, choice, and discrimination at the cellular level".

Ever since James Watson and Francis Creek discovered the complex structure of DNA in 1953, geneticists have been able to decode the genetic code and identify each gene and also its function(s). Besides the chance-combination of genes in determining a factor of traits, a variety of hormones, neurotransmitters, peptides, even mother's behaviour and mood have been shown to influence this process at the time of fertilization. Nature *selects* and *makes choices*, so do cells, chromosomes and genes at the cellular level to produce a trait or decimate the chances of its being produced.

Likeness or variation in the off-spring is, therefore, a direct result of similarity or dissimilarity in the genetic structure of the parents and new combinations caused at the time of the union of the two sex cells. The entire mechanism of transmission of hereditary characteristics is very complex and governed by variety of possibilities and impossibilities, certainties and uncertainties, and oddities and idiosyncrasies. Allport (1965) subscribes to this fact in this way:

> Now in the human germ cells are 46 chromosomes. Each cell is marked with about 30,000 genes. One or more genes are required for an inherited trait. At a certain stage in the development, the germ-cells undergo "reduction fission", and come out with 23 chromosomes, thus discarding many possibilities of inheritance, because chromosomes possess different combinations for various genes. A further hazard - an enormous one - concerns the chance that one particular gene variant will unite with a given ovum to result in the conception of a new life. It is preposterous to suppose that any two individuals on earth (except only identical twins formed from the same ovum and same sperm) can have a common pattern of inheritance. The number of possible combinations of human genes with the respective mutations, Dobzhansky estimates as 'vastly greater than the number of atoms in the entire universe. Obviously an infinitesimal fraction of the possible gene-combinations are, or even can be realized anywhere in the world..... every human being is then the carrier of unique genotype.

Genetic scientists are now in a position to tell with a fair amount of accuracy as to what genes are dominant, and what recessive. They also can identify the "rogue genes" considered responsible for certain inheritable diseases and deformities. Attempts are also being made to synthesize genes artificially in the laboratories so that defective genes in the genetic structure of a child could be replaced.

Even though scientists today claim to have understood the secrets of genetic traits, and the mechanism of their transmission, eyebrows are being raised on the unethical practice of gene therapy to cure certain physical and mental disorders. Cloning of animals has become a reality; cloning of man is in the offing. Moralists, however, are dead set against creating *A Brave New World.*

ENVIRONMENT

Environment refers to all external factors and forces that substantially influence man's growth, development, behaviour, character and personality. It neither adds to nor subtracts from man's genetic endowment (what he has received from his parents), but affords it opportunity to unfold its potential to every extent possible within the limits and limitations put on it by nature. Only environment makes an individual's "self-actualization" a reality. This way, environment is simply a correlative of heredity; it merely determines which genetic trait can possibly be developed and to what extent.

From growth perspective, environment can be divided into prenatal (before birth) environment, and postnatal (after birth) environment.

Prenatal Environment

The influence of the environment begins very early in life, with *prenatal* or *intrauterine* environment having a crucial role to play in the normal development of child right from the moment of conception. The environment influences the faetus in various ways. To begin with, the sperm in the female genital tract encounters a variety of conditions. A woman's hormonal status may affect the consistency and thickness of the mucus in her uterus and cervix. Her central nervous system may affect the strength of uterine contractions. Each of these factors may influence the speed of sperm transport. This has all the appearance of *behaviour* at the cellular level.

There are many other environmental influences that can help determine the genetic make-up of an embryo. Besides affecting the selection of sperm, genes exert influences on each other as well. In one environment, certain genes may be "turned on" to influence development along a certain line. Alter the environment and another aspect of that vast genetic potential will be activated. Thus, the development of our mind - how we think; the behaviour we display, the emotions we experience - is affected in important ways by the formative influence of the environment.

Much myth surrounded the intrauterine environment earlier; for example, some people wondered how the "waters" (amniotic fluid) within the womb nurtured faetus, and how a faetus , could be contained within the body of another, the mother, etc. Generally, great emphasis was placed on the mother's emotional state. A mother was required to ponder only "elevated thoughts". lest her infant develop along malevolent lines. Fright, sudden shock, dependency, and other unsettling emotions were held to exert an influence on the timing of the birth process, the infant's personality, and some extreme instance even to cause the death of the faetus. However, with the advent of new discoveries in the biological sciences, many of these early concerns about the influence of the mother on her developing faetus are being taken seriously. It has become clear that a variety of hormones, neurotransmitters, peptides, even the mother's behaviour and mood, are understood to influence fertilization and growth of the embryo. Alcohol, malnutrition, and tobacco are now known to cause faetal malformation, pre-maturity and gross of subtle learning disabilities. So, the mother's experiences - what she drinks, eats, and breathes - can have profound influence on the development of the infant mind. Expectant mother who smokes during pregnancy, really expose her embryo to a variety of disorders.

The mother's thoughts, feelings i.e. emotional states,) can modify neural networks within her faetus (in several ways.) One path, of course, is the placenta, the organ that directly unites the faetus to the maternal uterus. The mother is also able to influence her faetus through the same sense that enables us to palpate our environment, for to a limited extent the faetus too is able to hear, see, smell, and feel in the intrauterine world. The featus' development can proceed in normal way only when the liquid which surrounds the growing foetus inside mother's womb has proper thermal and chemical properties. Added to it is the expectant mother's own state of body functions and mind. Compared to postnatal (external) environment, the prenatal environment is constant, simple and limited in terms of time and space; nevertheless, the developing organism is susceptible to a variety of changing conditions within the mother including nutritional deficiencies, infections, chemical changes in the maternal blood resulting from mother's emotional states, and exposure to radiation.

A lot more implications and complications of the prenatal (internal) environment are well-documented in the medical science literature, but which may not be of much interest here. In any case, the importance of prenatal environment cannot be under-estimated though the specific ways in which it influences later development of a child are largely unknown.

Postnatal Environment

Postnatal environment means the external environment – the earthly surroundings in which we all live, grow and interact with others. The most obvious environmental influences are those which serve as external stimuli for the organism to respond to; for example, a variety of physical, chemical and human energies, which influence organism's growth and development in hundred ways. This external environment, in our day-to-day terminology, is referred to 'environment', and is the most important factor in the shaping of personality. Environment as such can be categorized into (a) physical environment, and (b) social environment.

Physical Environment

Physical environment refers to the physical surroundings and ecology comprising vegetation, fauna & flora, rivers, landscape, mountains, hills, the sun, the air, the water, varying climate, soils, mineral deposits, plains, forests, mountains, lakes, rivers and rainfall, insects, bacterial life, wild beasts, and the whole gamut of geography of nature plus the adaptations and constructions of man represented in such items as sky scrapers, apartment house clusters, highways and subways, exploited coal mines, use of electricity, radio, television, and motion pictures, elevated trains, honking horns, motor exhausts, newspapers, gigantic industrial machinery, satellites, nuclear devices, and a countless number of implements, equipment and blessings of an industrial age. They affect our growth and development significantly.

Our physical features and physiological functioning show clear traces of the environmental influence. The complexion, colour (of the skin, the hair), capacity for work, endurance, etc., of the people living in colder regions is significantly different from that of those living in hot climates. Living and working conditions of a place greatly impact the development of number of our abilities, for example, capacity to endure heat and cold, to carry out certain kind of jobs, etc. Biologically, either the living beings adapt to the environmental conditions or face extinction threat. Both human beings and animals can adapt to the environment but only human beings are capable of altering their environment within certain limits to suit their needs and accomplish their objectives. Using their mental faculties, humans have put in efforts to make their environment more conducive to the growth of the self and the society.

Social Environment

Social environment is comprised of people and their ideas, beliefs, thoughts, experiences, convictions, prides, prejudices, customs, traditions, laws, rules, regulations, etc. - almost everything that regulates life. With the growth of human mind, the social environment has changed dramatically over hundreds of millennia of civilized life. Change and more change, and too fast too, is the order of the day. Our growth, development, behaviour and performance in all fields of interaction and knowledge bear the impress of our culture especially our ethics, philosophy, economics, etc. Increasing life stresses due to rising competition in job-market, trade, commerce, business, industry, technology, education, sport, etc., are rendering human behaviour more complex and difficult to deal with. The swift means of transport and communication, the all-pervasive electronic media, the information technology, the push-button lifestyle, and the sky-rocketing consumerism are all producing such sets of values as are no match with those that have guided human destiny for ages. Resultantly, the life-value system itself and human mind are under severe strain, having serious implication for the health of man and that of the society.

The external forces - both physical and social - are terrifically dynamic and least under human control. Their potential to influence every activity and endeavour of man is tremendous. We are what our environment is making us today. Notably, therefore, the definition of "nurture" is expanded to include influences arising from prenatal, parental, extended family, and peer experiences, and extending to influences such as media, socio-economic status, larger inter-personal interaction, and so on. The speed of social transformation of man is much greater than that of the physical transformation sweeping over the great Globe.

Interestingly, if no two persons inherit the same genetic material, no two human beings also have exactly the same environment since they cannot be exactly at the same place at the same time. On its face value, it might look the same for a while, but not always, but from the viewpoint of effects of environment on their personal development of the two individuals, things will always be different. For example, in a family with two sons, one child has older brother and other a younger brother, and the parents may treat the older and the younger children quite differently. Besides, these children will have different friends, and will be inclined to develop different interests, skills, aptitudes, and attitudes. Later they may identify themselves with different religious, political, social, and athletic groups and organizations. A single external factor, how so insignificant, is capable of pushing one's behaviour, character and personality development into divergent directions. Depending upon how the genetic-environment interaction takes at any point or period of time in one's life, the developmental pendulum can swing to either direction - positive or negative.

HEREDITY-ENVIRONMENT INTERACTION AND SPORT PERFORMANCE

Heritability

According to Buskist & Gerbing (1990): "Heritability is a technical term developed by geneticists to refer to the amount of variability in a trait in a given population that is due to genetic factors. The more that a trait in a given population of individuals is influenced by genetic factors, the greater the heritability is. This does not mean, however, that heritable traits may not be modified by environmental factors." Heritability is sometimes confused with inheritance, the tendency of given trait to be passed from a parent to individual offspring. *Heritability does not apply to individual; it pertains only to the variation of a trait across a specific population at a particular point in time.*

In simple words, heritability quantifies the extent to which variation among individuals in a trait is due to variation in the genes those individuals carry. In animals where breeding and environments can be controlled experimentally, heritability can be determined relatively easily. Such experiments would be unethical for human research. One way to determine the contribution of genes and environment to a trait is to study twins. In one kind of study, identical twins reared apart are compared to randomly selected pairs of people. The twins share identical genes, but different family environments. In another kind of twin study, identical twins reared together (who share family environment and genes) are compared to fraternal twins reared together (who also share family environment but only share half their genes). Another condition that permits the disassociation of genes and environment is adoption. In one kind of adoption study, biological siblings reared together (who share the same family environment and half their genes) are compared to adoptive siblings (who share their family environment but none of their genes).

A few scientists have rightly pointed out that environmental inputs affect the expression of genes. This is one explanation of how environment can influence the extent to which a genetic disposition will actually manifest. The interactions of genes with environment, called gene-environment interaction, are another component of the nature-nurture debate.

In only a very few cases is it fair to say that a trait is due almost entirely to nature, or almost entirely to nurture. In the case of most diseases now strictly identified as genetic, such as Huntington's disease, there is a better than 99.9% correlation between having the identified gene and the disease and a similar correlation for not having either. On the other hand, Huntington's animal models live much longer or shorter lives depending on how they are cared for (animal husbandry). At the other extreme, traits such as native language are environmentally determined: linguists have found that any child (if capable of learning a language at all) can learn any human language with equal facility. With virtually all biological and psychological traits, however, genes and environment work in concert, communicating back and forth to create the individual.

The scientists holding heredity position as well as those holding environment position, have not been able to resolve the nature versus nurture tangle. The genetics-environment interaction is not a simple mechanical procedure to allow any one to draw definite conclusions and predict the quality and direction of one's development as a human being. The heredity, no doubt, supplies the basic material in terms of potential with all the boundaries for growth fixed; environment facilitates its growth to maximum extent possible subject to exigencies of time and place. In comparison to heredity, which is a close-ended proposition, environment is an open-ended phenomenon with no demarcated boundaries of influencing factors. Therefore, assigning exclusive roles to heredity and environment is, simply preposterous.

Heritability measures always refer to the degree of *variation between individuals in a population*. These statistics cannot be applied at the level of the individual. It is incorrect to say that since the heritability index of personality is about 0.6, you got 60% of your personality from your parents and 40% from the environment. To help to understand this, imagine that all humans were genetic clones. The heritability index for all traits would be zero (all variability between clonal individuals must be due to environmental factors). A highly genetically loaded trait (such as eye colour) still assumes environmental input within normal limits (a certain range of temperature, oxygen in the atmosphere, etc.). A more useful distinction than "nature vs. nurture" is "obligate vs. facultative" — under typical environmental ranges, what traits are more "obligate" (e.g., the nose — everyone has a nose) or more "facultative" (sensitive to environmental variations, such as specific language learned during infancy). Another useful distinction is between traits that are likely to be adaptations (such as the nose) and those that are byproducts of adaptations (such as the white colour of bones), or are due to random variation (non-adaptive variation in, say, nose shape or size).

Developmental psychologists find it hard to pinpoint with absolute correctness as to which of the personality traits is exclusively due to heredity and which one due to environment alone. No doubt, several physical characteristics such as a person's height, form, morphological structure of muscles (i.e. predominance of red fibres or white fibres), etc., have genetic orientation, situations abound where distinction between what is genetically determined and what is a product of environment, seems to disappearing. For example, no one, for sure, can say that blue eyes are inherited and a coat of tan is acquired because nutrition in infancy and childhood may significantly affect the eye colour and tan would not occur at all unless pigments in the skin were prepared by nature to respond to the sun-rays. Similarly, we cannot say that a dog's bark is inherited but response to his name is learnt. Reared in isolation, a dog may fail to bark and unless an inherent teachability exists no dog will learn to come when called. Receptivity of the protoplasm to training is neither exclusively due to nature nor because of nurture; its gravity lies somewhere in the middle of the two positions extremes.

The proportion of heredity and environmental roles required to produce a *like* individual is impossible to fix, or even estimate in the complex scheme of things in the universe. Till today scientists have literally not been able to come out with a precise technique or formula, which could help resolve this issue; in other words to accurately specify as to how much heredity and how much of environment are required to produce an ideal personality. The situation here is very much analogous to that of a plant in whose case the heredity is hid in its seed – the carrier of the germ-plasm. The bigness or smallness of the plant's size, the bitterness, or sweetness of the fruit it will bear, the shape and colour of its flowers, the size, shape and quality of its leaves, and many other characteristics of this nature are all encased in the germ cell or seed which is a gift of nature (a product of heredity). The nurture which causes the tiny seed to exhibit its characteristic potential in terms of its growth may constitute (i) the season and weather conditions in which the seed is sown, (ii) the kind and quality of the soil (the quantity of necessary chemicals it contains), (iii) the atmosphere (right amount of sunlight, water, air, temperature, moisture, etc.), (iv) external growth facilitators (fertilizers, manure, pesticides, etc.), and (v) protection and security against environmental hazards. A poor quality and/or supply of any of these elements will tilt the balance of plant's growth. In sum, nature supplies the internal constituent material; nurture provides support for its qualitative and quantitative growth. Apart from this, to complete the process, a good gardener uses all his experience, knowledge and intelligence in selecting a good quality seed, sowing it in proper season at an opportune time, taking care of all the environmental factors influencing plant growth, and protecting it against all possible external onslaughts so as to enjoy the fruit of his labour in the form of good fruit crop. Still chance – the invisible hand of nature especially calamities and hazards – plays its inevitable role. The growth and development of human personality and behaviour are subject to the same process and laws of nature, as does the plant. Likenesses and variations are imperceptibly directed both by nature and nurture alike, but it is impossible to explain which of the two does it more, better and how.

Genetics and Environment as Influencers of Athletic Performance

The question whether elite athletes are born or made has a direct reference to the roles genetics and environment play in the total process of sport - talent identification, skill acquisition, training, selection, participation and success at competition. It is now established that Olympic athletes are "a special breed" (Cofer & Johnson, 1960), and "a rare combination of genetic endowment, generally good environment, and a very special training can produce an Olympic athlete", (de Garay et al., 1974). Elite athletes undoubtedly possess outstanding qualities of body, mind and spirit. At the outset, they come from genetically healthiest stock of the humanity and are *gifted* in some way. Their anthropometric, physiological and psychological profiles perfectly match the *requirements* of the sport or the event they chose to play. Most of the characteristics under these performance-related subheads are genetically determined, while others require a favourable environment to develop optimally. Along with the prerequisite genetic endowment, the external performance-enhancing variables such as *smart* nutrition, highly *specialized* training (including excellent trainer), exotic infrastructure, sophisticated equipment, top-class health care facilities, sport-science backup, enhanced exposure in competitive environment, reinforcers in adequate and qualitative measure, and so on, have an important role to play in the success of an elite athlete.

The statement - *'if you want to be an Olympic athlete, choose your parents carefully'* - though a light-hearted one, is pregnant with the greatest truth of sport that outstanding athletes, like great scientists, litterateurs, and artists, are born; they are rarely made. It also puts a message across to sport scientists and athletic trainers to identify the *genetically gifted* children as early as possible and put the selected ones under systematic training at an opportune time. To illustrate the genetic aspect of the issue, take for example, height as a high performance variable. Height, as we know, is genetically determined and that tall individuals, all other things being equal, have an edge over those comparatively shorter in height in sports like volleyball, basketball, swimming, etc. But if the tall person is not well-coordinated; he is poorly skilled or ill-trained, the advantage of height to him will be rendered ineffective. On the other side, a comparatively short-stature player, who is better skilled and better trained, will excel the taller one. This shows that advantage in some genetic trait is of use only when none of the other factors varies.

Consistent research has revealed that several motor abilities such as speed, agility, explosive power, coordination, endurance, reaction time, etc., considered fundamental to success in sport, are by and large inherited. They need congenial climate to develop to optimal potential and get integrated with the athletic skill acquisition programme at a young age. Most physical qualities (also called fitness components) viz. strength, flexibility, stamina, body composition, etc., develop chiefly through individual-environment interaction, i.e. fitness training. Developmental scientists are still not very sure as to which of these qualities or abilities bears a greater imprint of heredity, and to what extent. However, they have begun to believe that well-planned play and activity programme during infancy and early childhood contributes a lot to the making of champions in due course. Most athletically advanced nations have exploited this fact very skilfully to excel in Olympic sport over the decades.

Athletes, trainers and scientists can manipulate and exploit maximally the external performance-related factors such as nutrition, training load, learning, transfer effect, facilities, equipment, sport-science backup, etc., in order to enhance chances of success, it is beyond their scope to meddle with the genetics. It would be disastrous to make a choice between heredity and environment as the highroad to success in sport, but to have both in appropriate combination. Nature's plan of growth for each and every individual is different and no one can know the exact proportion in which heredity and environment will interact with each other to produce a champion athlete. Out of hundreds of thousands individuals playing a sport at the top or near top level in the same environment, who will shine as a star in the final analysis is impossible to predict because several observable and non-observable factors and forces play their roles in their own characteristic ways.

At the baseline of human development, there are hundreds of fixed (genetic), as well as flexible (environmental) factors - physical, physiological, nutrition, social, training, psychological, etc. - common to all individuals and all activities. However, as the performance curve begins to move up several physiological and psychological abilities become specific in terms of their strength and quality, often raising hurdles in the athlete's way to success unless he or she is trained harder and fine-tune his performing ability. Champion athletes are easily distinguishable from those of lesser ability by such qualities as increased receptivity to higher training load, extraordinary cardiovascular efficiency, pain-tolerance, risk-taking, mental toughness, high drive, firm resolution (determination), cool-mindedness, confidence, ability to focus, ability to cope, etc.

Logical analysis of performance variables and empirical evidence from research and observation strengthen sport scientists' belief that superior athletes are both and made. The genetic studies of outstanding athletes have not revealed any substantial relationship between any specific gene(s) and exceptional performance ability although a variety of single genes have been segregated which most probably renders an individual dwarf or giant, intelligent or idiot, feeble-mindedness or intellectually strong, etc. While one *wrong* or *rogue gene* may ruin the chances of an individual to become an outstanding athlete, an astronomer, an astronaut, a mathematician, painter or a poet, etc., a multitude of favourable genes must combine to endow him with extraordinary potential for excellence in a particular field of interaction or knowledge. It may not be correct to say that a single gene is capable of producing an Olympic giant. Similarly no amount of balanced nutrition, technically sound training, and ultra-modern facilities can transform a genetically inferior urchin into an outstanding athlete.

Our cultural practices, religious beliefs, values, attitudes, interpersonal relationships, social intercourse, and life-style too have bearing on our participation in sport and rising to the level of an outstanding athlete. Our being a right-handed or a left-handed is related to our career in life and sport. Right-handedness or left handedness is largely acquired even though many scientists do not rule out the possibility of its being genetically determined. Roughly estimating that 80% of the individuals are right-handed, Howell (1945) felt that "these presumably are individuals who by nature are potentially ambidextrous. The brain structure permits to favour either hand but culture is right-handed. Therefore, the parents and the society teach the child to favour his right hand". The left-handed batsman or bowler may have some advantage over the right-handed one during a game, but it needs to be understood that left-handed batsmen or left-handed bowlers are not made by a deliberate effort of the parents or coaches; they are simply born. No one impressed upon them to change their handedness. Being ambidextrous, perhaps, may be a learned behaviour, because some people deliberately put in effort to acquire skills that way; for example, hitting tennis ball with left hand and right hand or kicking a soccer ball with right or left foot with the same efficiency.

A sport, say soccer or badminton, may produce hundreds of outstanding sportspersons but each one of them can be distinguished from others in some unique trait or attribute, in which the secret of his or her success lies. One athlete may owe his performance to a given trait, for example, aggressiveness or cool-mindedness, speed or agility, primarily to inheritance; another may attribute his success to better skill, technique or intelligence. Scientists believe that there seems to be a *compensatory mechanism* in human physiology and psychology, which can help an individual, having deficit in one trait to get compensated in some other. For example, a long-legged athlete may have greater stride-length but lesser stride frequency, and a short-stature person greater stride frequency, to finish a race clicking same time. One athlete may be reclusive and retiring, easy-going with a devil-may-care attitude because of his innate nature (temperament); another may be too sensitive, highly aroused and over-stimulated (overexcited) due chiefly to long-drawn struggle with life and in sport. Generalities and specificities with regard to the influence of heredity and/or environment on athletic performance are not difficult to make out.

In the opinion of Borma & Habbelink "…..studying Olympic athletes is a unique challenge from several different points of view: they are best; they exemplify the optimum combination of heredity and environment to produce peak performance; they stem from different ethnic background". With increasing number of cross-sectional and longitudinal studies being undertaken on different groups of performing athletes - ordinary, mediocre, pre-elite and elite - across sports and different sport settings, more interesting facts about the influence of heredity and environment on performance are pouring in to make things clear. For example, a survey by de Garay at al. (1974) found "birth order" of the Olympic athletes unexpectedly to be significant factor in their performance, i.e. there was an excess of second-births among the Olympic athletes. In addition, an astounding discovery was the presence of sickle-gene carrier among the Olympic athletes, signifying some inborn potential for outstanding athletic performance. After reviewing a large number of genetic and anthropological studies, Carter (1984) concluded:

> ...research on the genetics of high level performers must consider not only their genotypes but also their response to training...... athletes of Olympic calibre are well endowed individuals with

respect to sport-specific phenotype and most probably also have inherited the genotype characteristic of high response to training.

Every individual's phenotype is the result of the interaction between the genotype and the environment. In sum, the genotype determines the extent to which the environment can influence an organism's development and behaviour, and an athlete's ability to move up the performance ladder reaching the top position in Olympics.

SELECTED REFERENCES

Allport, G.W. *Pattern and Growth in Personality,* New York: Holt, Rinehart & Winston, 1965

Buskist, William & Gerbing, David W. *Psychology: Boundaries and Frontiers,* Glenview, Ill: Scot, Foreman/Little Brown Higher education, 1990.

Carter, J.E.L. (Ed.) *Physical Structure of Olympic Athlete,* Basel; Karger, 1984

Cofer, C. & Johnson, W. Personality dynamics in relation to exercise and sport, In W. Johnson (Ed.) *Science and Medicine of Exercise and Sport,* New York; Harper, 1960

de Garay, A. L., Leveine, L., & Carter, J.E.L. *Genetic and Anthropological Studies of Olympic Athletes,* New York; Academic Press, 1974

Herschkowitz, N. & Herschkowitz, E.C. *A good start in life: Understanding your child's brain and behavior.* Joseph Henry Press, 2002

Howell, T. H. The Obsolete Dogmas of Heredity, *Psychological Review;* 52, 23-24, 1945

Lefton, Lester A. *Psychology* (3rd Ed.), Boston; Allyan & Bacon, 1985

Meaney M. The nature of nurture: maternal effects and chromatin remodelling, in *Essays in Social Neuroscience,* Cacioppo, JT & Berntson, GG eds. MIT press, 2004

Meaney, Michael J. Nature, nurture, and the disunity of knowledge. *Annals of the New York Academy of Sciences,* 935:50–61, 2001

Restak, Richard M. *The Mind,* New York: Bantam Books, 1988

Rosenzweig, M.R. Experience, memory and the brain, *American Psychologist;* 39, 365-376, 1984

Sandiford, Peter *Educational Psychology,* London; Longman Green, 1933

Scott, A. *Stairway to the mind: The controversial new science of consciousness.* Springer, 1995

Tanner, J., & Gordon, R.T. *Growth,*Time/Life International; Netherlands, 1963

No two persons are born exactly alike; but each differs from the other in natural endowments, one being suited for one occupation and the other for another. - **Plato**

CHAPTER - 17

INDIVIDUAL DIFFERENCES

Nature has not made two individuals exactly the same or even similar. People differ from one another in height, weight, colour, appearance, speed of reaction, character, personality, behaviour, and the like. That people differ from each other is obvious. How and why they differ and what impact do the differences among them has on their behaviour, learning, ability to acquire various skills and career-selection in life is less clear. This subject of individual differences is generally dealt with under individual differences in psychology or *Differential Psychology*. Psychology studies people at three levels as Henry Murray & C. Klukhohn (1953) believed: "Every man is in certain respects (a) like all other men, (b) like some other men, (c) like no other man." However, the focus of individual differences psychology particularly is on this second level of study, the researchers studying the ways in which people differ in their behaviour. Individual difference psychology examines how people are similar and how they differ in their thinking, feeling and behaviour. No two people are alike, yet no two people are unlike. So, in the study of individual differences we strive to understand ways in which people are psychologically similar and particularly what psychological characteristics vary between people.

The enduring differences among individuals have been one of psychology's central concerns over the past 100 years or more. Psychologists and educationists generally study and deal with, though for different reasons, differences among children in their personality, motivation, intelligence, values, self-concept, self-efficacy, self-esteem, emotionality, etc., to name a few areas. Physical educators and athletic coaches, on the other hand, look beyond these areas and, besides this, take cognizance of differences among children in motor qualities, abilities, skill educability, age, sex, body size, etc., as they are critical to participation, performance and success in sport.

Individual Differences – A Biological Viewpoint

Although to study individual differences seems to be a study in variance, i.e. how people are different, it is also to study central tendency, how well can a person be described in terms of an overall within-person average. Indeed, perhaps the most important question of individual differences is whether people are more similar to themselves over time and across situations than they are to others, and whether the variation within a single person across time and situation is less than the variation between people. A related question is that of similarity, for people differ in their similarities to each other. Questions of whether particular groups (e.g., groupings by sex, culture, age, or ethnicity) are more similar within than between groups are also questions of individual differences.

The human species are born with similar gross biological characteristics, but each member of the species possesses a variety of physical and psychological characteristics, traits, abilities and qualities which make him look and behave differently from others. The process of inheritance continues to be a jigsaw puzzle for the scientists, and so is the mechanics of variation among groups and individuals. Developmental psychologists are still in the dark about how genetics and environment interact with each other to produce individuals alike in some respects, but unlike in most others. Personality psychology addresses the questions of shared human nature, dimensions of individual differences and unique behaviour patterns of individuals. Research in individual differences ranges from analyses of genetic codes to the study of sexual, social, ethnic, and cultural differences and includes research on cognitive abilities, interpersonal styles, and emotional reactivity.

Individual differences or variations include the differences that could be seen across individuals of any given species in terms of their biological characteristics such as strength, speed, size, body-build, etc., as well as in intelligence, sociability, group cohesion, inter-personal relationship, social adjustment, and the like. According to biologists, variations exist at two levels: first, an organism's genetic makeup – its genotype which typically differs from that of other members of the species; and second, the organism's physical appearance and behaviour – its phenotype which varies from individual to individual. Every individual's phenotype is the result of the interaction between its genotype and the environment. Precisely, the genotype determines the extent to which the environment can influence an organism's development and behaviour, observe Buskist & Gerbing (1990). Notably, a person's genotype and phenotype are subject to *biological laws*, which have governed evolutionary process all through, and *cultural influences* - adaptive changes of culture to recurrent environmental pressures over millennia. In terms of these two conditions, some individual differences are innate and non-modifiable, while others may be due to socio-cultural influences.

Individual Differences - Beyond Biology

Biological evolution created humans in the same mould but not without variation at individual level, *Cultural Revolution* added more differential to it. Widening or closing the gap in individual differences is a function of the individual-environment. It is so because human beings possess an immense capacity for interaction, learning and behaviour modification as a result of experience and reinforcement. Cultural effects, responsible for individual differences, are not inheritable unlike the genetic variation in traits or characteristics. Cultural inheritance is an important phenomenon with human society but not cultural heritability. Individual differences resulting from ongoing social-cultural process are skin-deep and are possible to remove. For instance, if some one is socially or economically backward, their status can be improved by employing a few remedial measures, but nothing can be done to improve the height of a short-stature or a crane-necked individual. On the whole, the cultural differences are peripheral, and the biological differences vital.

Variations are observed in individuals of the same age in height, weight, body build, growth pattern, temperament, etc.; some individuals are short, some tall; some lean and thin, some stocky and hard; some are fair-complexioned, some dark; some early maturing, some late maturing; some gluttons and obese, some frugal eaters and weaklings; some intelligent, some moron; some have musical ear, some have no ear for music; some highly receptive to training, some simply indifferent; some enthusiastic and motivated, some dull and sloppy; some are aggressive, some submissive; some athletic, and some averse to sport, and so on. Some of these differences among children might be innate, some socially-culturally oriented, but nonetheless important and cause for concern for teachers and academic administration.

Research in individual differences addresses three broad

questions: (1) developing an adequate descriptive taxonomy of how people differ; (2) applying differences in one situation to predict differences in other situations; and (3) testing theoretical explanations of the structure and dynamics of individual differences.

NATURE OF INDIVIDUAL DIFFERENCES

There are infinite ways in which individuals differ in terms of observable physical characteristics, abilities and capacities; a limited number of latent or unobservable constructs. The innate differences among individuals are generally seen in such concrete variables as sex, age, ethnicity, body-build, physiological functions, and psychological makeup. The superficial differences are mostly caused by environmental factors and they exist in social status, economic condition, living standards, education, knowledge, achievement, etc.

Sex Differences

Except for certain sex-based innate abnormalities, for example those found in eunuchs, all normal human beings are born either as male or female. By biological laws, the gender of a foetus is determined right at the moment of conception. No force - celestial or terrestrial - can alter this status. Sex specialists believe that man in some respects is a bio-sexual organism, because every man or woman has "some" percentage of character of the opposite sex. The degree to which an individual is male or female is largely based on and measured by certain physical and behavioural characteristics only. The reproductive anatomy clearly defines male and female, and concretely distinguishes them. The two genders differ significantly in physical structure, average height, size of the internal organs and limb measurements, physiological capacities, biological functions, temperamental traits, etc. These innate differences between the sexes influence their behaviour, character and personality, giving them a distinct identity and roles to play. It is impossible to do away with gender-differences in the scheme of things in life.

Sex differences have biological, psychological and social implications for man and the society; they have bearing on our life-style, motivation, course preferences, choice of career, performance, achievement, etc. From educational viewpoint, until the age of puberty, not much significance is attached to gender differences. However, as children step on to the threshold of puberty, the fast appearing secondary characteristics completely change their physical profiles, and push them into divergent directions of life. Their thought, emotion and action exhibit an irreversible change. Lindhard (1949) rightly pointed out that at this stage (with the onset of puberty), the "object of their education must differ in the same degree because the boys must be brought up to be men and girls to be women".

Obviously, gender differences are not merely superficial but significant because even a layman considers them to be so profound that it is regarded as an insult to refer to a person to the other sex than that to which he or she rightly belongs. Gender role-play has immense social significance because society expects the two genders to take up responsibilities prescribed for them by traditions, customs, religious books, ethical norms, oral conventions, etc. Traditionally, certain fields of activity, for example, entry into armed forces, hazardous industrial sections are considered the male bastion, not deemed suitable for women because of certain inherent *deficits* (constraints and/or limitations) in their anatomy, physiology, temperament, etc.

In physical activities and sports, where too close body contact between boys and girls (men and women) is impossible to avoid, the fair sex is always at the receiving end, which is both physically and ethically hazardous for the individual and the society. Apart from this, in many other regions of physical ability such as physical prowess, physiological capacity, endurance, etc., women are no match to men. All this has significant influence on their job selection, deployment at work, economic activity, social status, and so on. In most psychological variables - memory, intelligence, cognition, judgment, motivation, trainability, etc. - gender differences are negligible, and of little consequence.

Age Differences

Like gender, age is also an unalterable variable because time moves in one direction only. Well-defined growth stages are demarcated in terms of time only. Human beings are categorized into neonates, infants, children, adolescents or adults, and seniors, juniors or sub-juniors on the basis of their chronological age, reckoned in years, months and days.

Each stage of growth is marked by distinct physical, physiological, emotional, psychological and social characteristics, considered so significant in educational and sport process. From physical education and sport perspective, individuals of varying age cannot be closeted in one learning situation, nor can they be encouraged to compete in the same athletic events without suitable adjustment in standards and other arrangements as they vary significantly in skill, fitness, experience, playing ability, etc. Juniors stand no match to seniors in any compartment of the game. Importantly, each year of growth during childhood and adolescence adds something to the learning and performing ability of the individual in education, sport and any other endeavour in terms of skill, experience, and mental maturity. The quality of individual-environment during childhood-adolescence span determines the kind of character (personality) shall an individual have – athletic or academic - as they step onto the wide world of adulthood. Developmental psychologists do not consider age as a significant differential after adolescence by which time the developmental processes are almost complete.

A section of psychologists does not recognize age a reliable index of a person's growth especially until the adulthood threshold. They believe that curves of the development of physical and mental abilities do not necessarily move up concurrently and with the same speed. Along with chronological age, they use also use mental age as a supporting yardstick for evaluating growth effects. Dentition and anatomical age (ossification of skeleton) are used as authentication criteria of chronological age.

In school setting age differences among children are of utmost importance. They facilitate placing children into different groups, temporarily or permanently, on the basis of their physical or mental abilities either to serve certain exigencies of time or achieve certain activity or academic programme objectives. Age differences also help or obstruct other psychological processes in learning and training. They have telling effect on the planning of curricular activities, organization and conduct of competition in tasks involving more advanced physical and mental abilities, measurement and evaluation of almost all traits of personality, and standardization of physical ability and mental ability (aptitude) tests required to set norms and standards of performance for different groups and slices of population.

The concept of age is relevant to male and female alike. We know that growth is a continuous process and its effects are invariably carried forward from one age level to the next without any impediment. The academics and physical educators need to understand that greater the age-difference among pupils, the greater shall the difference be in their physical and mental abilities to acquire various kinds of skills and perform different tasks both in the classroom and on the playing fields.

Physical Differences

Physical differences among people are vital and important for us all, because our identity is directly related to our body, and the peculiar features we have. Body is the most concrete and observable part of human personality. Individuals are distinguishable primarily on the basis of their physical characteristics such as body build, height, weight, complexion, colour of the eyes, skin and hair, etc. In critical situations, dermatoglyphic features (lines and patterns on the one's palm and fingers), shape and size of various body parts, etc., are also used to identify individuals. Differences in height, size and shape of body parts, quality of muscles, etc., of the people are well-established; they, by and large, are traced to ethnic, racial and family affiliations. Except body size, height and weight, which are subject to change due to natural growth process, no major physical feature gets altered as one passes through various developmental stages.

In most body-type classification technique such as somatotyping, physical characteristics are of primary consideration. Physical characteristics like shape of the nose, head or ears, complexion, shape of the skull might be helpful in distinguishing one person from another only but physical characteristics such as height, limb-length, bone-shape, bone-quality, and muscle type have significant relationship with performance in all skill-based activities and sport. For example, a tall individual has an advantage in basketball and volleyball and a medium-height person in gymnastics. Certain physical features suit certain sports fairly well.

Physical differences due to genetic variation are difficult to discount even if one backward in a certain characteristic may have compensating feature (advantage) elsewhere in the personality trait-fabric. For example, a long-legged athlete may have longer strides in running in comparison to an athlete shorter in height, but the latter may have greater stride frequency to compensate for the disadvantage in height, with advantage in speed. Extreme tallness without corresponding limb-coordination is meaningless; it may rather be a debilitative factor. In order to bring down the impact of individual variation in physical characteristics, physical educators generally match individuals and groups on certain abilities. When physical characteristics vary a great deal, people learn to make adjustments as exigencies of time and place dictate.

Matching individuals on a single physical trait is no educationally sound practice. It leads to several administrative bottlenecks and problems. That, perhaps, is the reason why classification of students, necessary for different reasons, must be guided by sound philosophy, scientific principles, proper ethical standards and norms, and administratively viable procedures. Several techniques of categorizing students are well-documented in measurement and evaluation literature. In most sports, players are classified as colts, sub-juniors, juniors, youth, and seniors solely on the basis of chronological age. In sports like boxing, wrestling, judo, weight-lifting, etc., player classification-criterion is weight, a physical variable.

Student-classification techniques are employed to dilute the influence of individual differences in physical characteristics and to restrain the physically superior individuals to have psychological edge over others. If there were no physical differences among people there would be far more social problems than we have today.

Physiological Differences

Physiological differences – inter-gender and intra-gender – usually refer to differences in various physiological parameters such as cardiovascular and/or cardio-respiratory efficiency, vital capacity, metabolic functioning, cardiac output, stroke volume, aerobic capacity, hormonal functioning, etc. These differences between men and women are well innate, while those among individuals of the same sex may be inborn or due to external factors like nutrition, exercise, growth effects, external (climatic) conditions, living conditions, etc. Innate physiological differences cannot be zeroed at all. However, certain physiological capacities can be optimally developed by adjusting life-style, i.e. factors such as diet, exercise, health care, routines, etc. The extent to which physiological capacities can be enhanced is related to genetic factors, not environmental. It is absurd to think that physiological differences among people could disappear if environmental conditions were uniform and ideal for all.

Physiological differences among people have least educational significance, but they have serious implication in physical activity and sport programmes. Out of millions of performing athletes, only those with superior physiological status, so importantly related to their fitness, shall have the edge over others in sustaining and succeeding in sport. This is greatly true for endurance (long distance running) and speed sports (sprints). The roots of physical fitness both for life in general and sport in particular lie in various physiological efficiencies and capacities - some trainable, some non-trainable. Winning or losing at an athletic contest is closely related to "fitness" - vastly a physiological phenomenon.

Today, the closing gap in male and female performances in certain track & field and swimming events is due largely to better techniques (especially weight-training) of improving physiological efficiency and achieving higher standards of physical fitness by women athletes.

Psychological Differences

Intelligence, memory, perceptual-cognitive ability, temperament, trainability, emotionality, aptitude, sentimentality, motivation, and many more, are psychological variables in which differences in people are existent; sometimes the differences could be acute. Most psychological variables have genetic orientation though they are profoundly influenced by external factors. From psychological perspective individual differences include the study of intelligence, IQ, and personality. In our everyday experience we find people different in their motivation, approach to problems, interest, ability to learn, aptitude, attention span, emotional reactivity, adaptability to changes in the environment, general mood, attitude, ability to transfer training, and so on.

Even identical twins too are found to differ in aptitude, inclination, intelligence, motivation, self-confidence, etc. While physical differences are observable to the naked eye due to the profundity attached to them, psychological differences are subtle and implicit in behaviours; they surface under favourable conditions. William Sheldon assumed that 'those who look alike behave alike', meaning that physical characteristics (mostly inherited) have a very close relationship with temperamental traits. Implicitly this shows that physical differences among individuals can also cause psychological differences among them, more or less. For instance, an endomorph (big-bellied person) is a power-packed action-oriented individual – the one who acts first, and thinks later - where as an ectomorph (crane-necked all-bone physique) is comparatively more reflective and calculating – the one who thinks much before he acts.

One of the methods used in educational psychology to measure individual differences is the use of psychological tests. Assessing intelligence, personality, interest, creativity and other attributes with the help of psychological tests has become an established practice. In selecting people for jobs, diagnosing of mental handicap and monitoring psychological development have provided impetus to develop a variety of tests to suit different groups of people (e.g. children, adults, educated, illiterate). The term IQ has now become a common word and people often want to know their IQ and personality. A wide variety of psychological tests – paper-and-pencil questionnaires and performance tests, personality inventories, projective tests, etc. - are available to distinguish abnormal individuals from normal ones, inferior and superior, and backwards from forwards on one or more psychologist traits or parameters. Individual as well as group testing is possible in psychological domain.

As compared to physical and physiological variations that exist in people, psychological differences among them are considered critical to motor skill learning. Dominance or submission, cowardice or courageousness, intelligence or stupidity, tender-mindedness or tough-mindedness, introversion or extraversion, etc., have a lot to do with a child's ability to acquire motor skills, groom himself into a good performer and achieve excellence in activity and sport. Subject teachers, physical educators and athletic trainers often have to sweat profusely to tackle children with superior psychological characteristics such as intelligence, dominance, and risk-taking.

Sometime early life experiences at home and/or at school can also cause psychological differences among children. This affects the programming of the soft-ware of the mind of a child so that in adult life he shows divergence in behaviour. Psychologists believe that being docile or stubborn, aggressive or submissive, timid or bold, and coy or courageous could be due to early childhood experiences.

CAUSES OF INDIVIDUAL DIFFERENCES

Individual differences among people are traced to heredity, environment, or both genetic and external factors. At the time of conception and in early embryonic stages, all foetuses look more or less identical. As growth continues, differences become increasingly apparent. Even neonates show significant differences in their behaviour. Some are quiet, others cry a lot and loud; some are more active, others less active; some have better appetite, other crave less for feeding, and so on. As time passes, individual differences become so pronounced that it is difficult to classify them. How do these differences originate, when every one has a similar beginning? The answer is due to heredity and environment.

Heredity

Our biological inheritance is determined by the chromosomes and genes. Sets of chromosomes from different persons, of the same sex look very much alike but actually they differ a lot internally. These differences are most pronounced in unrelated individuals. The heredity factors hidden within the chromosomes are called genes. They are assumed to be *"packets of chemicals"* strung along the chromosome like small beads on a thread. Action of the genes on cytoplasm changes the shape and other characteristics of cells. The heredity basis of individual differences lies in almost unlimited variety of possible gene combinations which may occur. No two siblings get an identical heredity, as they do not get the same genes from parents. Fraternal (dizygotic) twins, born to the same parents, at the same time, are different from each other in several characteristics because of different pairs of germ cells. On the other hand, identical (monozygotic) twins developed from the same sperm and ovum, have exactly the same set of genes, hence they resemble each other in most characteristics.

Heredity, therefore, is the basic cause of individual differences. It determines a person's gender - one being either a male or a female with peculiar sex characteristics. The two sexes have innate differences in body build and physiological functioning and other characteristics directly related with them, for example, physical prowess, suppleness, peculiarity of gait, etc. While determining a child's sex nature follows its own laws, entertaining no interference from any quarter. The birth of a freak child is due to some unusual activity in nature; it is no usual practice. The primary gender characteristics (for example, reproductive anatomy with external and internal arrangement of sexual organs) are inborn, subject to no modification or alternation except by surgery. Secondary sex characteristics that begin to appear in young people with the onset of puberty gradually become more pronounced during adolescence transforming girls into women and boys into men. This inevitable transformation in human physique and the characteristics that go with it is governed by individual's biological clocks, and regulated, to an extent, by external factors such as nutrition, climate, season, place, time, etc. Later, these differences between the two sexes determine the course of their lives and demarcate the boundaries of their biological activities and social responsibilities.

Apart from the variation heredity causes in an individual's body-build, features (phenotype), complexion, body chemistry, anthropometric measurements, temperament, physiological functioning, intelligence, etc., it also sets limits in terms of their potential for growth and performance in different physical and intellectual activities. Being athletic or reflective is by birth alone. Even though scientists today know quite a lot about genetics (and its mechanism), yet trait inheritance continues to be a mind-blowing puzzle. It is impossible to predict the trait profile of a newly born. Whether a trait exhibits itself in a generation or an individual and to what extent is the biggest secret of nature. In one respect, individual characteristics may be a simply mathematical calculation; in another, it is nature's most intricate process beyond any calculation.

A person inherits family characteristics as well as certain racial traits also, e.g. being Negroid or Mongoloid. When a certain characteristic appears in a group of people and is passed on from one generation to another in succession, it takes the form of a racial trait. Racial traits are equally powerful causes of individual differences.

Physical Environment

Environment refers to external factors and forces that cause temporary or permanent variation among people. Unlike heredity, it is dynamic and its influences are felt even in the intrauterine life of a developing organism, and later from the time of birth. In the mother's womb, the nucleus, chromosomes and genes are surrounded by a jelly like substance known as cytoplasm. The cytoplasm is an intracellular environment, because the genes surrounded by it are influenced by and in turn influence its characteristics. The growth of the organism is determined by cytoplasm as well as its heredity. A new internal environment comes into existence, after the interaction of genes and cytoplasm has produced several cells. The actual structure of a cell depends upon its relation to other cells. Development in specific location determines the part of the body. Later endocrine glands and hormones produce another intercellular influence. Many congenital deformities are the result of overactive or under-active endocrinal functioning. The growing organism is surrounded by amniotic fluid and attached to the mother by umbilical cord. Hereby the growth of the embryo depends on nourishment provided by the mother. Foundation for a good growth as well as several individual differences is laid in this internal environment. The mother's nutritional status, emotional condition and lifestyle have an indelible mark on the development of the embryo.

After birth, as the child comes in contact with the earthly environment, in which both objects and human beings are important ingredients, influences on its growth, behaviour and personality development become extremely varied. The social psychological environment in which the child happens to be born provides social heritage. The customs, socio-economic status, family environment, interaction amongst the family members and later peers and school environment cause variety of conditions to determine individual differences.

The physical environment has distinct role to play in individual differences among people. If people happen to migrate from one geographical environment to another, e.g. cold region to temperate or hot region and vice versa, their physical and physiological characteristics will be greatly influenced by this change. Those who live in equatorial region are significantly different from those in the polar region in terms of their physical and physiological characteristics, capacities, complexion, etc. Dietary habits, seasons, climatic conditions – all contribute their share to creating individual differences. Environmental change sets in motion the process of physical, physiological, and psychological adaptation in the organisms, which in due course becomes a potential cause for individual differences. Short duration shift from one environment to another may cause a temporary change in some physical, physiological and behavioural variables but long settlement leads to permanent adaptation, which may take even generations.

Realistically, external factors cause no individual differences but create conditions in which people are forced to adapt to the changing conditions of life. For example, if each of the twins is lodged in a different environment from the other, say rural urban, each is certainly to develop different personality characteristics. The one doing manual labour right from the beginning will develop a tough body, strong musculature as well as rugged features. The other child brought up in luxurious atmosphere will develop a soft, delicate and smooth physical frame prone to injury at the slightest instance. With different environmental backdrop and physical and physiological capacities, both will develop different interests, attitudes, aptitudes, dispositions and inclinations.

Social-Cultural Environment

Cultural inheritance, social attitudes and practices, religion and economics influence human growth and cause individual differences. Broad mindedness or narrow mindedness, religious tolerance or intolerance, frugality or lavishness, etc., are not genetically inherited but acquired forms of behaviour as outcomes of traditions, customs, etc. Given a different socio-cultural environment, people will change their attitudes, lifestyles, behaviours, and develop a different outlook on life. Some communities do not, for example, have a favourable attitude towards sport, especially participation of women in athletic competitions on account of certain peculiar religious beliefs and social attitudes. Until recently, even celebrated social reformers and philosophers had divergent views on this issue, but now the attitudinal change is sweeping over the world very fast.

The economic status of family influences a person's personality development. Quality education is difficult to have without adequate resources. Nor is it possible to earn a better social status without a better economic status. As the economic status looks up or slides, the social status corresponding goes up or comes down. Two brothers living under different economic atmospheres - one being rich and the poor - have different social status and social circles, and are meted out different treatment on most occasions. Both develop different attitude towards life, people and towards important issues concerning family, children, relations and even themselves. Life scenario is changing fast, and so are differences among people.

Many social behavioural modes are acquired by people from cultural practices. For example, one's being right-handed or left-handed is said to be related to the culture in which an individual is born and brought up. Etiquettes, manners, mannerisms, and civilities are determined culturally and transmitted from one person to another by observational learning process. People differ in lingual eloquence, pronunciation, gestures, gesticulation, walking, talking, dressing and addressing styles, etc., due to cultural variation. Along with biological adaptation, there is cultural adaptation occurring in individuals and societies.

INFLUENCE OF INDIVIDUAL DIFFERENCES ON SPORT

Individual differences are a stern reality of education and psychology. For sure, they cannot be decimated but put in a proper perspective and understood to serve as way-finders in the dense jungle of learning-teaching problems. In educational setting, understanding of individual differences helps in designing curriculum, planning course material and training programme both for students and teachers. It is now being recognized with greater understanding that all students do not learn in a similar way. Some are fast learners, others slow in grasping; some have scientific bent of mind, so they are interested in science subjects, others prefer humanities or arts subjects; some can concentrate on a task for long hours, others require more frequent rest pauses; etc. Some are in-depth readers while others surface readers, and yet others mixed type. Individual variations mark teachers too. Some are goody-goody, while others really good; some are grand teachers, and a few master teachers. For some teaching is a formality, others enjoy teaching. There is no dearth of teachers who are dull and drab, and there is shortage of teachers who make even the dullest subject as the most interesting thing to learn. Understanding individual differences between the teacher and the taught can help in matching teaching styles and learning procedure for best educational outcomes.

The situation in physical education and sport is no different from that in education. Here also the physical educators and coaches have to teach and students have to learn, less in the classroom but more on the playing fields. The individual differences among physical educators and among students are obvious. Starting with infant's natural pranks and a child's free play, sport shows itself up at various growth stages as an enjoyable pastime and recreation for one and all, and competitive endeavour for the talented and well-trained. The boisterous adolescent play is a source of great achievement for the individual and the community. Spread over a widest possible activity range, sport may be as active as tennis or badminton or as passive as chess or carom, organized indoors or outdoors, and played on recreational or competitive basis. Sports are, perhaps, the best media to engage a large number of people with diverse individual differences in age, sex, body build, psychological makeup, physical prowess, social and economic background, cultural affiliation, etc., in most productive, mentally stimulating and socially sound activity.

Until puberty, age and gender differences in children are of little significance as far as physical activity and sport are concerned. Even though children differ significantly in their aptitudes, interests, likes and dislikes individually, their group activities involving vigorous physical effort are not much influenced by these variations. However, this fact would serve an anchor to guide physical educators and athletic coaches to design curricular programme to suit interests and aptitudes of the two genders, diversify objectives of their physical activity and engage them in activities involving contact among the opposite sexes for reasons of social ethics and mental health.

Ideally both education and physical education & sport ought to be child-centred activities in which every child must get adequate opportunity for an optimal development of his or her potential. Individual satisfaction has to be the primary objective of all physical activity programmes with reference to children's interests, aptitudes, and abilities. A good strategy to play down the impact of individual differences among children is to offer them such activity programmes as are of general nature and could be organized in mass, rather than class. Highly specialized and specific type of sports must be reserved for a talented few.

One great advantage of physical education and sport is that individual differences in the strengths and weakness of children in a wide variety of their abilities – physical, motor, psychomotor and psychological – can be spotted in a twinkle as children learn, practice and participate in physical activities. In education and psychology, the procedure for knowing individual differences among children with regard to their abilities is circuitous; in sport and physical education it is simple, straightforward and objective. For example, making a boy or a girl run a 50m dash will tell you how speedy he or she is; and asking him or her to do as many as possible sit-ups in 30 seconds will reveal how strong his or her back and abdominal muscles are. All simple activities like running, jumping, hitting, kicking, etc., serve as good yardsticks of measuring physical abilities of children and spotting out differences among them. The data thus obtained are objective and fit for statistical treatment, allowing teachers to draw enduring conclusions.

Physical, anthropometric and physiological differences among people seriously affect their performance in sport as well as in life. They cannot be removed from the scene even with best of the scientific and managerial techniques available with man. Athletic coaches and physical educators need to deal with the individual differences with care and caution. One of the effective alternatives to grapple with the problem of individual differences is to facilitate fixing square peg in square hole and round peg in round hole, meaning to match individuals' abilities with requirements of each sport or event. For instance, tall children suit basketball, volleyball, or swimming, and muscular short stature individuals, gymnastics without sacrificing their aptitude. Anthropological and genetic studies of the Olympic athletes have revealed a close relationship between body-build and sport. For example, Olympic sprinters have been found to be endo-mesomorphic in body-build. Similarly, certain physical and physiological characteristics have also been identified which most suitably match with sport requirements. Considering human variation as a biological fact in the context of Olympic sports, Ross & Ward (1984) argue that "......event selectivity reflects concomitant genetic and environmental influences on physique. For this reason, the Olympic Games provide an anthropological macrocosm which permits human biologists to delineate 'prototype' with special structural and functional capacities to excel at highly defined, ritualistic, physical performance tasks or combination of tasks in orchestrated play". Notwithstanding individual variation, those who are closest to the prototype of the athletic personality such as football type, wrestling type, etc., may presumably give outstanding performance and occupy top spot. This, however, does not mean that all outstanding athletes in a sport are hundred percent alike in their personality profiles. The proximity of elite athletes to the prototype – a hypothetical ideal image of perfection – is much greater at the general characteristics and qualities and gradually tapers down as we move towards specifics. For example, in cricket, one player is incomparable in spin bowling, the other in fast bowling, another in batting (further a batsman may be a good stroke player, another, a hard hitter). In basketball, one player may have no parallel in shooting, the other in pivot play or ball making.

Training, practice, and exposure to competitive situations not only afford opportunity to the people to narrow the gap in gross individual differences in health, fitness, skill, and performance but also bring to surface individual differences in psychological strengths and weaknesses, which the performing athlete and their trainer must necessarily know. The outstanding athletes may not be much different from people of similar or same physical and physiological characteristics, but they have no parallel in such qualities as mental toughness, grit, resolution, risk-taking ability, one-pointed concentration, pain tolerance, etc. Some of these are exceptional and, in a sense, inborn. Many other psychological qualities and characteristics can be developed through psychological skill training, and specially prepared intervention programmes.

In exercise and sport, the individual differences is another important principle of training which underscores the fact that optimal benefits are achieved by devising training programmes to suit the specific needs of individual athletes. The principle applies equally well to exercisers. Ideally, each exerciser should have an individualized exercise programme. This would ensure that the exercises are tailored to meet the requirements of the individual, and would minimize the risk of overtraining and overuse injuries.

SELECTED REFERENCES

Alderman, R. B., *Psychological Behaviour in Sport*, Philadelphia; W.B. Saunders, 1974

Buskist, William & Gerbing, David W. *Psychology - Boundaries and Frontiers*, Glenview, Ill; Scot Foreman/Little Brown, 1990

Kamlesh, M.L. *Physical Education: Facts and Foundations*, Faridabad; P.B. Publications, 1988

Kamlesh, M.L *Athletic Personality: A Psychological Probe*, Delhi; Surjit, 1990

Lindhard, J. *The Theory of Gymnastics*, London; Methuen, 1949

Ross, J.S. *Ground work of Educational Psychology*, London; George G. Harrap & Co., 1955

Ross, William D. & Ward, Richard Proportionality of Olympic Athletes, in J.E.L. Carter (Ed.) *Physical Structure of Olympic Athlete*, Basel; Karger, 1984

True enjoyment comes from activity of the mind and exercise of the body; the two are ever united.

- Alexander von Humboldt

CHAPTER - 18

PSYCHO-PHYSICAL UNITY OF THE HUMAN ORGANISM

While an organism is "a living individual consisting of a single cell or a group of interdependent parts sharing the life processes" (Reader's Digest Oxford Word-finder), man is defined as 'a highly complex, intelligent and social being' - the Crown of Creation. Biologically, man is not much different from many other organisms near to him. He undergoes the same biological processes - birth, growth, development, decay, and death - and his behaviours (movements, actions, reactions and interactions within and outside his body with external environment) are almost like them. What fundamentally makes man different from animals is "his ability to think, assimilate experiences and engage in intellectual pursuits." Even though functions of the nervous system are common to most organisms, the concept of mind (synonymous with *intellect, intelligence, brain, wit, reason)*, referring broadly to the capacities for thought, perception, memory, and decision, is conspicuously unique to man and relevant to his activities - both individual and social.

The ancient Greeks believed in the dichotomy of body and mind. For centuries their influence has been so strong that even today most people consider body and mind as two separate domains. Those days the philosopher was comparatively a more dominant force in the society than the scientist (biologist); he focused on mind as the subject of his study and left the body to the physician's care. As a result, it was the philosopher who came out with the concept of the *material self* (body) and the *mental self* (mind) and allowed no integration of the organism concept to progress beyond a certain limit. The body and mind dichotomy became a gospel truth for formulation of most educational policies and programmes through the ages emphasizing cultivation of mental faculties like memory, intelligence, reasoning, knowledge, judgment, logic, etc., as an important objective of formal schooling.

The body development was considered an *odd-man-out* curricular content. Since the advent of the scientific era, myths about dichotomy of man into body and mind have been shattered by interdisciplinary research approach. Today, philosophers, scientists, educationists, psychologists, sociologists and others have firm belief in integration of man, and they make use of this principle for various reasons.

Physiological-Psychological Confluence

In fact, categorizing man into muscle and mind is arbitrary, but convenience of study kept the issue alive much longer than needed even against scientific evidence. Basically, man is all physiology – a typical complex structure in movement or action; processes of sensing, perceiving, feeling, thinking, memorizing, analyzing, synthesizing information, etc., are all ultimate aspects of physiology. However, typical physiological studies are concerned with digestive and metabolic processes, the chemistry and circulation of blood, and mechanism and characteristics of the muscular contraction. In comparison to physiologists, psychologists are more closely concerned with the activities which are covert and least observable but involve organism as a whole, typical of which are motivation, instincts, emotions, personality, etc. No psychological activity (perceiving, feeling, thinking, etc.) may be understood correctly without the knowledge of physiological and chemical processes that produce and underlie it. Conversely, no physiologist can fully understand physiological processes and their effects without accounting for the imperceptible affective and cognitive processes, considered so powerful in altering, modifying and adaptation of physiological responses under certain conditions.

Biologists have all through upheld the notion of structural and functional inter-connectivity of the organ systems and their functions so prominently reflected in observable (overt) and non-observable (covert) behaviours. Sherrington rightly viewed muscle as "the cradle of recognizable mind" which "seems to have arisen in connection with the motor act. Where motor integration progressed and where behaviour progressively evolved, mind progressively evolved." In common parlance, mind and mental processes refer to cognitive activity of the cerebral cortex (the thinking part of the brain) one aspect of which is interpreted as physiological and the other as psychological. The distinction between what is physical, and what is mental disappears altogether when the organism and its behaviour are studied as a whole. Walking may seem to be a physical activity but it does involve some thinking; similarly thinking may be a purely cerebral activity but implicit in it inevitable neural activity.

The relationship between *psyche* (mind) and *soma* (body) may best be illustrated in the affective (intense emotional) states in which both the psychological and physiological processes are so deftly fused that it is impossible to pinpoint as to which is the cause and which, the effect. According to *Sankhya Darshan* - the Hindu dualistic philosophic thought - the matter and the mind, and their effects, are various aggregates of all the *gunas* or qualities in the *Prakriti* - the material cause of the physical universe. This philosophic system recognizes three levels of existence: (1) the *inorganic* at which there is no growth or reproduction; (2) the *organic* at which there is metabolism, the capacity to grow and reproduce; and (3) the *psychological* at which there are thoughts, emotions, and feelings. In human beings, whom the great Biological Evolution has provided the most sophisticated apparatus of sensation, perception, cognition, the psychological level includes awareness of the cognitive (psychological) phenomena and inference of their occurrence in others. Even though these three levels of organization of matter - physical, biological and psychological - are merely abstractions, they, nevertheless, are manifestation of the same ultimate reality - the *Prakriti* - with its inherent *gunas* or qualities. This establishes the contiguity between body and mind.

BEHAVIOUR MECHANISM

Understanding the mechanism of behaviour facilitates understanding body-mind relationship a great deal. This technique is far easier than seeking philosophical explanation for the issue. Structurally and functionally, a human being is a unity - an integrated organism. Our body is composed of roughly 7 trillion cells with a mind boggling level of physical and biochemical coordination. These cells are of various kinds organized into fibres, organs and organ-systems meticulously arranged in a hierarchical order. All of them perform highly specialized functions for certain objectives. The entire structural and functional organization is immaculate and efficient. The interdependence of organs and organ-systems is an established fact of physiology. The body also encases mind and soul, called abstractions, not concrete physical organs. Where there is *no* body, there is no mind. Mind is the essence of man's being – an instrument of consciousness, an abstract reality that can be understood only through human thought, action and behaviour.

Behaviour is not simply a series of mechanical movements or actions; it is a complex but subtle process of sensory stimulations (external and internal), perceptions, cognitions, conations, motivations, physiological processes, motor functions, etc., deftly interwoven into a fine texture The observable and the implicit aspects of behaviour are so intimately related, inter-dependent and intertwined that there is least possibility of explaining and discussing one without reference to other(s). In real sense of the term, human organism is a unitary system which reacts to various stimulations as a whole, not in parts.

Behaviour is primarily explained as a stimulus-response phenomenon. When an external stimulus impinges on the organism, it causes it to react in some way. A special receptive apparatus is usually provided for each kind of stimulus to which the body is sensitive, namely, the sense organ and receptor. Our sense organs – eyes, ears, tongue, skin and nose – also known as *gateways of knowledge*, are specialized anatomical structures, having equal importance in research and study of physiology and psychology. They perform both physiological and psychological functions. So they are categorized as organs of the assumed psycho-physical system. (*A sense organ is usually regarded as a part of the nervous system though it may contain a very complex assortment of non-neural accessory tissue*). The sensory neural pathways connecting sense organs to the brain transmit the excitatory impulses from the respective receptors to a centre of coordination and correlation there. The nerve-centre in the brain is the central adjustment centre (cognitive activity or information processing centre) which transfers the impulses to the efferent pathways or motor nerves with or without, more or less, complex modification of the excitation of the centre itself. The peripheral organs of response receive the impulse through the efferent pathways. The specific apparatus of response is termed as the effectors which is usually not a part of the nervous system, e.g. muscles, glands, etc.

For convenience sake, behaviour is categorized into observable movement and non-observable (what transpires in and between the nerves and muscles) activity. The observable movement is performed by muscles, bones, joints, etc., and the non-observable activity, like an undercurrent in an ocean, occurs inside the sensory-motor organs connected with the response mechanism such as afferent nerves, cerebral cortex and efferent nerves. This intra-nerve activity, called neurotransmission, constitutes cerebral behavioural mechanism and is hidden from our eyes. The observable movements, also called motor activity, are impossible to occur without discharge of excitatory impulse from the efferent nerve system into the muscle-fibre structure. The entire mechanism of behaviour, from stimulus impingement to information-processing in different parts of the brain, and to external observable response, is a continuous chain of actions-reactions involving both body and mind functions. Therefore, compartmentalization of behaviour into internal and external parts is arbitrary. Wenger, Jones & Jones (1956) observe:

> We become aware of our external environment and aware of some aspects of our bodily states and functions; we remember and learn and thus are able to control many of our body functions and many aspects of our environment. We develop concepts for both concrete objects and abstract symbols, and finally we utilize these concepts and other memories in various manners which we call thought, imagination, ideation, reminiscence, etc. All of these activities, of course, are called mental. If we are unaware of them, they are called unconscious. But so far we know, all essentially are activities of the cerebral cortex.

The cognitive and motor processes are so wonderfully interwoven that it is almost impossible to call a particular function of the organism as either purely physical or completely mental. "No act", says Singer, "purely motor, perceptual, conceptual or cerebral rather the degree of emphasis in any act allows us to refer to it in a certain way". In a motor skill learning experience, no cognitive element can be discounted, nor can motor element be pushed aside while acquiring conceptual or perceptual skills. When over-learning (i.e. automatization) of motor skills takes place as a result of constant stimulus-response repetition the learner has a feeling that the cognitive element has been completely eliminated, which is not correct. In fact, no motor skill can be learned and/or performed without involvement of mental processes, more or less. Observing a skill, developing its correct image in the mind, performing the skill at the mental level, focusing intently on the action-sequence over and over again, etc., constitute mental activity.

Mind is no organ of the body; it is "an organized group of events in neural tissue occurring mediately in response to antecedent intra-psychic or extra-psychic events which it perceives, classifies, transforms and coordinates prior to initiating an action whose consequences are foreseeable to the extent of available information" (*Webster's Dictionary*). In general, thinking, memory, reasoning, etc., are called pure mental activities which do not necessarily require any external input (environmental stimulation) for them to work. However, these internal processes become meaningful only in relation to the external realities, and their functional utility depends on how organism transforms them into observable activities. What we receive from the external environment in the form of impressions, symbolic concepts, ideas, skill or performance techniques, etc., is stored in our memory for use in the time of need. The concept of mind, therefore, is unthinkable without the existence of sense organs, muscles, nerves, glands, etc., which are the virtual instruments of our behaviour – internal and external.

The evidence against body-mind dichotomy comes from research studies on individuals with deviant behaviour and those having frequent emotional breakdowns. We know that emotional states like fear, anger, anxiety, love, sex, etc., not only alter our physiology but also leave some residual effect on the nerves, muscles and glands that leads to serious health complication. Mental stress can cause muscular tension, stage-fright, loss of proper words and inability of the organism to smoothly move. *Freeze response* to the terrifying situation is an evidence for the fact that physical immobility is caused by too intense bombardment of the nerve-impulse (neurotransmission) on the muscular system. Conversely, severe body-ache due to too intense and chronic fatigue may not allow a person to react to a stimulus which requires purely cognitive response such as solving a mathematical problem. Bualch suggests that the intellectual, spiritual, emotional and physical components of human personality are inseparable. Plato believed that "any defect of psyche or soma is the occasion of the greatest discard and disproportion in the other".

THEORETICAL VIEWPOINT ON PSYCHO-PHYSICAL UNITY OF MAN

Our knowledge of human anatomy and physiology today is unbelievably great yet several psycho-physiological processes of our body are not clear to us. They are subject to a great deal of surmise, inference and conjecture. For instance, we are well aware as to what part of the brain does what, and relation different parts of the brain among them. However, what produces thinking and how, where the memory is stored, how retrieval of facts becomes possible, how endlessly we can talk without thinking, etc., continues to be a big mystery even to best of the scientific minds today. Several regions of the mind are still inaccessible to us, and so it is difficult to talk about them and discuss them. A variety of our mental processes have become a subject of theoretical assumptions. While philosophers try to understand *what* mind thinks, scientists are attempting to reveal *how* the brain thinks and performs certain functions (calculations, analyses, syntheses, etc.) with tremendous accuracy and speed. This is the domain in human physiology, neuroscience and psychology, which continues to pose great challenge to the scientist; the philosopher has the answer to several mind-boggling questions on the issue but they are more speculative than scientific.

Philosophers have long found the relation between mental and physical phenomena problematic. Descartes gave a modal argument for supposing that mental and physical phenomena are distinct. He argued that if it is possible for one's mind to exist without one's body, then one's mind is distinct from one's body. He further claimed that it is possible for one's mind to exist without one's body, for one's mind to exist disembodied. So, he concluded, one's mind is distinct from one's body. There are non-physical minds and non-mental bodies: dualism is true.

Most theoretical viewpoints on the body-mind integration are rational, with little empirical evidence.

Idealistic View

With Plato as its progenitor, the idealism theory recognizes mind as spirit and body as matter. In Plato's view mind is the focus of man's being and the body a product of mind, spirit or being. Realities about things originate from mind whose existence does not wholly depend upon the body or the material self. In observable behaviours, mind makes use of the body parts to express itself, but in variety of intellectual functions such as contemplation, reasoning, imagination, decision-making, etc., does not depend on body nor makes use of any of its parts. Plato argued that the mind had nothing to do with sensation as intellection and sensation were two different domains, with nothing in common between them. He viewed sensation as a function of the body, chiefly the sense organs. For him intellectual activity was different from and higher than sensation.

The philosophers of the later generations differed with Plato, stressing that in routine activities mind utilized the body, but in highly intellectual and purely spiritual activities, it abstained from doing so. The most obvious problem for dualism is that if minds and bodies are such radically different things, then it is difficult to see how they could causally interact. How could damage to physical bodies cause pain in non-physical minds? And how could perceptual experiences in non-physical minds causally affect the movements of physical bodies?

As related to body-mind relationship, the idealistic theory, therefore, is, more or lees, primitive, illogical and unscientific.

Materialistic View

The materialistic theory claims for itself a scientific status. Endorsed by naturalists and biologists, it considers mind to be an outcome of evolutionary process, in which the nervous system of some animals gradually became more complex both in structure and function, thereby making these animals rise to a higher level in the hierarchy of kingdom of the living beings. In his *Descent of Man* (1871) Charles Darwin 'rejected Aristotle's basic distinction between the human mind and the mental life of other species. He proposed that all minds adapted to their environment over time. His theory of evolution said that the human mind has its roots in the past shared with other animals, evolving as part of a continuum.' As a sequel to this process, the greater sensitivity of the nervous system enabled these higher placed animal species especially the primates to interact with the environment with more productively, monitor more varied sensory information, and process it more meaningfully, thereby making their behaviour more complex than that of other animals. The development of human mind and behaviour is a part of this developmental continuum. Dr. Desmond Morris, a zoologist, says: "Although chimps are much closer to us than some people would like to admit, we are somehow over a whole new threshold, even a whole new world. The human mind has become just that little but more complicated than the chimp's mind. And that was enough to take us not ten degrees but a million degrees further. We can sit down and close our eyes and think for two hours, and when we open our eyes at the end of that time, apparently having done nothing, we are different people".

Further evolutionary processes went a long way in developing in man consciousness or self-awareness, symbolism, language, introversion, self-reflection and formation of mental models, which we call mental and/or intellectual activity. All these and many more mental functions, in fact, are functions of the body - the matter in organic state of existence. So, the materialistic theorists consider mind as the product of matter at the highest level of organization. While attempting to explain the relationship between matter and mind, philosophic psychologist Descartes declared: "I think, therefore, I am." He made mind-brain (or body-mind) dualism explicit and placed the site of the mind in the brain like Plato but unlike Aristotle who believed that the mind rested in the heart. Descartes asserted that existence of matter depended on the existence of mind; he, however, did not digress from the concept of body-mind *dualism*, which has influenced the concept of mind ever since. Many of our contemporary ideas about mind and brain can be traced back to Descartes.

As a matter of fact, existence of things, objects, and events does not depend on mind alone. Rocks may not possess mind, but they exist. The matter, in one form or another, exists whether or not human mind is aware of them. Descartes' philosophical postulates about mind may have some validity, but when judged objectively, they seem to be fading out in the dazzle of scientific facts.

Psycho-physical Parallelism

Psychophysical parallelism is the theory that the conscious and nervous processes vary concomitantly whether or not there be any casual connection between them (Heidelberger, 2003). In other words, modifications of consciousness emerge contemporaneously with corresponding modifications of nervous process. The theory is the third possible alternative in considering the relation between mind and body, the others being interaction and one-sided action, for example, materialism. It should be observed that this theory is merely a statement, not an explanation.

Spinoza, Pillsbery, Tichtner, and other contemporary philosophers believed that bodily functions and mental processes are neither dependent one each other, nor do they have any interaction between them; they are independent and run as parallel processes. These parallelists respond to the problem of dualism by simply denying that minds and bodies causally interact. They hold that physical events have only physical effects, not non-physical mental ones, and that non-physical mental events have only mental effects, not physical ones. Like the two banks of a river or two lines of a railway track, the physical and mental events move side by side and simultaneously. Proponents of parallelism cite thinking and talking as parallel processes having neither anything in common between them nor brooking any antagonism. Arguably, thinking is a mental activity and talking is a physical one. The one does not cause the other nor interfere with the other, but both occurring simultaneously. This example illustrating psychophysical parallelism needs little proof of its existence.

Research has disproved the parallelism hypothesis. Though obviously a physiological activity, talking is nevertheless controlled by our brain (mental processes such as memory). We know no deep thinking is required when one is talking, but it does not negate the possibility of a tape-like stream of consciousness working behind the talking phenomenon. What we talk at any moment of time is a long-conditioned speech-response data stored in our memory in the form of bare facts, symbols and images. Long established stimulus-response patterns, frequently repeated expressions and dialogues, over-learnt thought processes, perceptions, cognitions, apperceptions, etc., embedded on the memory tape are always in readiness to get transformed into words, sentences and/or actions in a flicker (as electrical impulses get converted into sounds and photo images in a television) as soon as an appropriate stimulus signals the sensory-perceptual apparatus to come into action. The thinking-talking process is so precisely automatic and continuous that a slightest hint makes us articulate words and sentences with little stress or distress. Sometime we do pause to select from the memory appropriate words, ideas or images to continue talking but this is all natural and unconstrained. In the entire thinking-talking mechanism, word associations, symbols and memory-chunks have a critical role to play. The articulations and gesticulations (gestures and body language) that are made emerge from no pre-thought. Talking and thinking process is carried on simultaneously on parallel lines. The higher brain centres intervene only when (a) some sudden interference interrupts the process, and/or (b) lower brain centres dealing with conditioned stimulus-response patterns at their own level find it difficult to cope with the strong stimulus bombardment.

An experienced speaker, with fairly good retention and recall power, large vocabulary, better language control, smooth articulation, etc., encounters little stumbling, fumbling, thought vacuum, speech blocks, etc., when addressing familiar or unfamiliar groups of people – big or small. The perfect coordination in his thought and expression of it, i.e. what he thinks and what he talks, can be attributed to his or her experience, practice, knowledge, excellent memory, lingual efficiency, emotional stability, etc.

Thinking and talking or talking and thinking are highly coordinated psycho-physical experiences, not dichotomous processes. The discovery of a site at the base of the brain called the neuromuscular conjunction holds the key to a real scientific understanding that the body mind connection isn't only one-way traffic. It is in fact two-way system because the neuromuscular conjunction acts as a kind of switch box for neuro-chemical exchanges between the two.

Psycho-Physical Interactionism

Our body is a brilliant piece of machinery that outperforms even the most advanced computer. None of its processes are the subject of any speculation but scientific investigation and experimentation. Now scientific laboratory studies are producing increasing evidence that our mind and body interact - there is a continuous flow of information between them causing them to affect each other. Our every thought has a physical effect and every physical state we get into affects our thinking. It is now well-recognized that when you feel physically tired or less-than-well, this affects your mood. For example, it is very hard to be cheerful and humorous when you are exhausted. Similarly our thinking affects our physical state. If we spend a while going around telling ourselves that we can not cope or that we are a failure this will tense our self up and drain our energy.

How the body balances and harmonizes the functioning of the brain, which contains the mind, with that of the body, is a subject of study and investigation under the theory called *psycho-physical interactionism, psycho-somaticism* or *psycho-physiological interactionism.* This purely scientific viewpoint proclaims that a mental attitude or modified situation, at any moment of time, is good-enough to produce modified physiological state or physical functions. In other words, a discomfort state like injury, fatigue or muscle cramp may create a state of emotional turmoil which suddenly brings change in our thinking, perceptual and cognitive processes.

The psycho-physical interaction is a two-way traffic. To

illustrate body-mind interaction and conjure up how the bodily and mental processes influence each other, compound terminology such as psychosomatic, and/or somato-psychic (relationship) is used. The term ***psychosomatic*** refers to a condition where the real cause (stimulation) is psychic or mental, i.e. the perception is internal usually in the form of recollection of or mentally going over a previous experience of highly alarming nature. The perception of the situation and its accompanying feelings (dream state or loneliness) may be so intense as to cause changes in the physiological, glandular and neural activity reflected in external or observable signs and symptoms. These affective states are neither purely psychic nor completely somatic; they are psychosomatic. Conversely, ***somato-psychic*** condition is one in which the cause (stimulus) is external and its impact is seen or felt on various organs leading to a modified internal state and activity such as injury, insect bite, uncomfortable body posture, etc.

The body-mind interaction is best exemplified in the affective states caused by intense feelings during anger, fear, love, hate, repulsion, disgust, etc. The greater the intensity of emotional upsurge, the more intense will be the psycho-physical reactivity. A child who had a bad fall and an adult who lost his job will be terribly upset and afraid, though for different reasons. In the former case, the cause is external (physical), and in the latter, the cause is internal (psychic). Research on the causes and mechanics of psycho-somatic diseases and disorders such a peptic ulcer, hyper-tension, diabetes, hay fever, etc.; confirms the body-mind interaction theory. Wenger, Jones & Jones (1956) observe:

> For most of these psychosomatic disorders there is no known organic basis other than tissue changes initiated by mental changes. For some tissue-change facilitates the development of a disorder, such as stomach ulcer. Apart, however, from the apparent absence of organic basis, there is another essential criteria for a designation of a disorder as psychosomatic. It must be demonstrated that the disorder can be intensified or reached through psychological intervention (e.g. psychotherapy or hypnosis).

The Behavioural School considers stimulus-organism-response process as the basis for psycho-physical relationship, stressing that the organism reacts to a stimulus as a whole. There is no response categorically physical or psychic; body and mind respond together and simultaneously. However, depending upon the kind of activity involved, we might perceive a response to be largely physical or mental. Different organ-systems perform their specialized functions, but all of them are so well-connected that any hurdle in the functioning of one, creates ripples almost in each of the other systems. In both overt and covert behaviour muscles, glands, nerves, viscera, etc., are partially or wholly involved. That is why, functions of one system are difficult to explain and discuss without reference to other(s).

It needs no reiteration that pains and pleasures are not simply physical or psychic phenomenon; they are psycho-physiological. For example, if you hurt your little finger while driving a nail into a plank, the pain caused is no physical problem, it has serious mental repercussions and emotional reactions too, because it produces stress-tension syndrome which engulfs the entire organism. The same way, the effect of physical exercise is not just physical, it is mental too - a "satisfying mind state" and emotional catharsis. Williams (1964) rightly pointed out: "Thinking may be affected by the condition of the digestive track, the amount of haemoglobin in the blood and secretions from various glands." Herrick supported Williams: "We do not think with brain alone. The term mind is name not for a separate mental substance but for a function of the individual".

The body-mind connection (or interactionism) theory has a strong backing of the evolutionary theory, according to which movement has been a major factor in toning up the brain. One of the great steps in the evolution of advanced organisms was the ability to move. Simpler organisms simply wait for food to come along. The ones that evolved ways of moving themselves around to go and get food had more going for them. Eventually the movers developed techniques for anticipation, timing, stalking, hunting, recognition, remembering, learning from mistakes and passing information on to others of their species. In short, they developed brains of various kinds.

PSYCHO-PHYSICAL UNITY - ACTIVITY AND SPORT PERSPECTIVE

The laws of nature, the laws of living, and the laws of activity and sport are the same, confirming that the discipline nature imposes on all living beings and non-living things, has the same import in life and sport. If the body-mind unity is essential for harmonious development of an individual, it is essential in sport and activity too. There is a unity in the universe and in the human organism. The universe appears to be essentially inseparable whereby everything interpenetrates everything else. As odd it may seem, it appears that all divisions and boundaries are simply matters of our thought's construction. Bewildering and as counterintuitive as it sounds, nothing appears separate from anything else in the quantum world, much less in body and mind. Moreover, the same principle seems to apply in our everyday macro world. If we proceed from this underlying assumption of the emerging sciences, then the word connection loses its basis. If there is no separation, there is no need for connection. We have the body, and we have the mind no doubt, but they are no separate entities; they are two aspects of the organism. Although the notion of a mind-body connection is a far cry from traditional medicine, which views the mind and body in a dualistic dichotomy, it does not go quite far enough. Mind and body appear to be simply differing aspects of the same whole. As the head and tail of a coin are not separate, but differential points of the same coin, mind and body are thoroughly entwined and inseparable. Where one leaves off and the other starts is a consideration rooted in the outdated belief of cause and effect.

Movement, which forms the basis of life and also the essence of sport, accepts no body-mind dichotomy for in education and sport, the *whole* child learns and performs; neither its body nor its mind alone. Thinking and doing, and doing and thinking are highly integrated processes, so important in human education. Centuries ago, the wise Greeks had realized that there could be no *Man of Wisdom* (the brainy individual) without there being *Man of Action* (the brawny person), signifying the growth of qualities of muscle and mind in equal measure, i.e. a harmonious development of personality, so essential for war and peace. Aristotle gave to the humanity the concept of *sound mind in sound body* based on the principle of body-mind integration. Millennia later, commenting on the objective of education, Jean Rousseau argued: "it is not mind only that we are training nor the body but the whole man". In his opinion, the "whole man" meant the complete man - a perfect combination of body, mind and spirit. Rousseau stressed that education should strengthen this triad and assist every child to shape himself into a balanced personality without losing individuality. His liberal and progressive views on body-mind relationship had a salutatory effect on the contemporary education through out Europe. From then onward, dramatic changes were noticed in the concept, content and methodology of education almost every where in the world.

According to Millman (1979) athletic training, which throughout has placed utmost stress on training of physical abilities largely, should better be called *psychophysical training* because every athlete today is called upon to train both body and mind in equal measure without which he or she would find it hard to click at the competition. This new concept underlines harmony of body and mind. In order to achieve or realize his natural unity with his universe (of sport), man (athlete) must first attain unity with himself - by balancing and harmonizing body, mind and emotions - all so important as stepping stones to top performance.

Motor activity is vital to play; without it play is a wanton pursuit. Through activity only our mental faculties keep themselves in fine fettle. Strengthening of the apparatus of intellect and intelligence - nerves, muscles, brain, etc. - takes place only through the medium of physical activity and sport (not be confused with highly competitive sporting endeavours meant for a talented few). It is now very well realized by all and sundry that regularly exercising the body to keep the muscles, lungs and heart trim does not just create the "body beautiful" and facilitate longevity. By keeping the cardio-vascular system (heart, lungs and blood vessels) hard at work, the oxygen supply to the brain is kept in good working order to help maintain brain power too. It is a win-win situation when regular exercise not only keeps people healthier and looking good, but also helps the brain to appreciate the body's new lease on life to the full. Considering activity (exercise) a vital link between body and mind, Williams (2000) desired physical education to strengthen "integration of man" by providing activity experiences that are, "physically wholesome, mentally stimulating and socially sound."

But now some new discoveries about how the body's very own built-in "PC" (personal computer) goes about its business are surprising the brain chemists, neurologists, physiotherapists and fitness experts alike. The discovery of a site at the base of the brain called the neuromuscular conjunction holds the key to a real scientific understanding that the body-mind connection is not only one-way traffic. It is in fact a two-way system because the neuromuscular conjunction acts as a kind of switch box for neuro-chemical exchanges between the two. Not only is the traffic two-way, but it can now be shown that various forms of mental and physical activity can interact to have observable and measurable effects on the brain, muscles and other organs. Better learning, improved judgment and understanding, self-discipline, high self-esteem, etc., are also inevitable outcomes of physical activity, making the individual self-confident, emotionally-controlled, self-dependent and sentimentally stable. Megill (1990) asserts that physical activity 'reduces the risk of depression, and promotes healthier life-styles'. In totality, the emphasis in physical education and sport is the integrated development of the child through the supreme physical effort.

SELECTED REFERENCES

Bucher, Charles A. *Foundations of Physical Education*, St. Louis; C.V. Mosby, 1974

Gerber, Ellen, W. *Innovators and Institutions in Physical Education*, Philadelphia; Lea, Febiger, 1977

Heidelberger, Michael, Paolo Parrini & Wesley Salmon. (Eds.) *The Mind-Body Problems in the Origin of Logical Empiricism: Herbert Feigle and Psychophysical Parallelism*, Pittsburg PA: Pittsburg University Press, 2003

Megill, Lewis, J.O Do it right to perform right, *International Journal of Health, Physical Education & Recreation*, XXVI (4); 11-14, 1990

Millman, Daniel *Whole body FITNESS: Training, Mind, Body and Spirit.* New York, Clarkson N. Potter, 1979

Wenger, M.A., Jones, P.N. & Jones, M.A. *Physiological Psychology*, New York; Holt, Rinehart & Winston, 1956

Williams, J.F. *Principles of Physical Education*, Meerut; College Books, 2000

Wilson, John Rowan *The Mind*, Netherlands; The time-life Internationals

Wherever you are right now in your life, there lives within you an urge to go deeper. To be useful. To be alive. When you resist that urge, you kill any chance of living a life of purpose.
*- **Unknown***

CHAPTER - 19

INTELLIGENCE IN LIFE AND SPORT

Intelligence is a household word, so commonly used by us in a variety of contexts, and yet no subject in psychology has provoked more intense public controversy than the study of human intelligence, because it, perhaps, 'means different thing to different people' (Lefton, 1985). The term intelligence remained almost an obscured topic of discussion until Sir Francis Galton (1822-1911), British biologist, who was influenced by Darwin's *Survival of the Fittest* theory, championed its cause. Galton assumed that from economics viewpoint, "the most fit" individuals were those with high intelligence. To test his hypothesis, he designed a few procedures such as tests of sensory activity, reaction time, and very precise skill measurement technique to measure attributes which, in his perception, constituted the content of intelligence. Although Galton could not succeed in proving his thesis, his insistence that intelligence was a biological entity that was inheritable, and normally distributed in populations, persisted, and became linked to a very different method of assessing intelligence devised by Binet who like Galton played a key role in developing the modern conception of intelligence. With so much study, discussion and research ever since, intelligence still continues to be an enigma - a conundrum.

DEFINITION OF INTELLIGENCE

Defining intelligence in concrete terms has all through been a challenge with the psychologists, philosophers and educationist over centuries probably because the list of attributes, functions, operations and activities attached to it is so exhaustive. In common parlance intelligence is defined in hundred ways such as *the capacity to acquire and apply knowledge; *success in adapting to new situations; *the faculty of thought and reason; *skill in reasoning or producing abstract ideas or problem-solving; *the superior powers of the mind; the number and originality or mental associations; *capacity of our rational mind to consolidate and evaluate external stimuli by integrating sensory input with our memory and our programming; and so on. Various all-time greats have defined intelligence as:

> "the application of intellectual abilities in handling a situation or accomplishing a task." - ***Woodworth***
>
> "... judgement or common sense, initiative, the ability to adapt itself, to judge well, to understand well, reason well" - ***Alfred Binet***
>
> "... the aggregate or global capacity of the individual to act purposefully, to think rationally, and to deal effectively with his environment" - ***David Weschler***
>
> "To my mind, a human intellectual competence must entail a set of skills of problem solving—enabling the individual to resolve genuine problems or difficulties that he or she encounters and, when appropriate, to create an effective product—and must also entail the potential for finding or creating problems - and thereby laying the groundwork for the acquisition of new knowledge" - ***Howard Gardner***
>
> the "...goal-directed adaptive behaviour." - ***Sternberg & Salter***
>
> "...innate general cognitive ability." - ***Cyril Burt***

Though behavioural scientists still differ in what constitutes intelligence, at least two major "consensus" definitions of intelligence have been proposed during 90s. First, from ***Intelligence: Knowns and Unknowns***, a report of a task force convened by the American Psychological Association in 1995:

> Individuals differ from one another in their ability to understand complex ideas, to adapt effectively to the environment, to learn from experience, to engage in various forms of reasoning, to overcome obstacles by taking thought. Although these individual differences can be substantial, they are never entirely consistent: a given person's intellectual performance will vary on different occasions, in different domains, as judged by different criteria. Concepts of "intelligence" are attempts to clarify and organize this complex set of phenomena. Although considerable clarity has been achieved in some areas, no such conceptualization has yet answered all the important questions and none commands universal assent. Indeed, when two dozen prominent theorists were recently asked to define intelligence, they gave two dozen somewhat different definitions.

A second definition of intelligence comes from ***"Mainstream Science on Intelligence"***, which was signed by 52 intelligence researchers in 1994:

> a very general mental capability that, among other things, involves the ability to reason, plan, solve problems, think abstractly, comprehend complex ideas, learn quickly and learn from experience. It is not merely book learning, a narrow academic skill, or test-taking smarts. Rather, it reflects a broader and deeper capability for comprehending our surroundings—"catching on", "making sense" of things, or "figuring out" what to do.

Commenting on the definition of intelligence, Cratty (1972) said: "Some writers have attempted to define intelligence by outlining the type of mental operations purportedly carried out by the individuals assumed to be mentally capable. Some theoreticians have only searched for the meanings of words denoting some aspect of intelligence and others have seemed to probe deeper and seek the essence of intellectual activity, while still others have apparently been tied to the supposition that intelligence is composed of qualities that thousands of psychologists agree upon as emanating from purportedly valid tests of IQ."

We all have some idea about intelligence and what it means but defining it in operational terms is a tough job especially when we are not clear about expressions like "think abstractly", "act purposefully", engage in a "goal-directed adaptive behaviour" used in several definitions. Crooks & Stein (1988) remarked: "Virtually all intelligence researchers agree that intelligence is not precisely a measurable commodity that we possess. Rather it is a concept or label invented to explain why some people behave in a more effective and adaptive manner than others".

NATURE OF INTELLIGENCE

Human behaviour is intelligent for human beings can perform a variety of physical activities and mental operations which no other animal species is capable of. Psychologists differ greatly on the general nature of intelligence. For some intelligence is a *general ability* of the organism to perform certain acts in 'certain' ways; for others it is what constitutes the core of personality - thinking, reasoning, processing information, decision-making, and so on. Sandiford (1933) explicitly said: "Intelligence is the ability to undertake activities that are characterized by (i) difficulty, (ii) complexity, (iii) abstractness, (iv) social value, (v) the emergence of originals and to maintain such activities under conditions that demand a concentration of energy and resistance to emotional force". Explaining intelligence as an inherited quality, Allport (1965) remarked:

> Intelligence is the raw material of personality because intelligence in some way is closely related to the central nervous system, and the nervous system is as much a matter of native endowment as is the neuro-glandular system underlying body-build and temperament....No one can say in how many ways at the start of life one human nervous system may differ from another. There are wide variations in the number of brain cells existing, in their arrangement, metabolism, conductivity, connectability, and the general ability for use. When the combinations are favourable, a person is endowed with high intelligence, when unfavourable with intelligence low and when conditions are mixed, the results are intermediate.

Intelligence is considered both a process and a product. A fool may differ from a philosopher in the degree of interaction, rather than in kind. Some authors believe intelligence to be an 'innate potential of a person for meeting adequately new problems and conditions of life'. There is some truth in what Allport (1965) contended:

> Certainly there is something that distinguishes an idiot from a genius and this factor we call 'general intelligence'. There seems to be likewise 'special intelligence'. Even a generally stupid person can have limited regions of special ability (idiot savant), and many geniuses are virtually imbeciles in some respects. One near-genius has no sense of direction and can scarcely leave home without becoming hopelessly lost. One other feeble-minded boy is a 'whiz' with machinery.

Whether intelligence is wholly inherited or acquired, is still not clear. However, Thorndike regarded it as a combination of individual's "general and specific abilities". Reading a road map upside-down and generating synonyms for the word "brilliant" are two very different skills. But each is a measurable indicator of general intelligence, a construct that includes problem solving abilities, spatial manipulation and language acquisition. Scientists generally agree that intelligence can be captured by psychometric tests. But the study of intelligence is dogged by questions of just how much IQ contributes to an individual's success and well-being, how genes and environment interact to generate smarts and why the average IQ score rose throughout the world during the twentieth century.

In order to get closer to the idea of the nature of intelligence, we must see how intelligence is generally understood and defined in some selected areas of knowledge.

- In ***Children's Health Encyclopaedia,*** intelligence is understood to be *an abstract concept whose definition continually evolves and often depends upon current social values as much as scientific ideas.*
- In ***Education,*** intelligence refers to *the ability to learn or understand or to deal with new or challenging situations.*
- In ***psychology,*** the term intelligence may more specifically denote the *general mental ability involved in calculating, reasoning, perceiving relationships and analogies, learning quickly, storing and retrieving information, using language fluently, classifying, generalizing, and adjusting to new situations,* or *to think abstractly as measured by objective criteria (such as the IQ test).*
- In ***Encyclopaedia of Science and Sports Medicine,*** intelligence is generally regarded as *an ability to act purposefully, to think rationally, and to deal effectively with the environment; it is often measured by an intelligence test.* A highly intelligent person has the ability to adapt to new situations that often involves the ability to utilize abstract concepts and to learn, to grasp novel relationships.
- According to the ***Food and Fitness Encyclopaedia,*** although there is no universally accepted definition of intelligence, it is generally regarded as *an ability to act purposefully, to think rationally, and to deal effectively with new situations.*

Modern psychologists precisely refer to intelligence as a property of the mind encompassing a variety of related mental capabilities, including the ability to reason, plan, solve problems, think abstractly, comprehend complex ideas, learn quickly, and learn from experience, as well as the potential to do these things. It is usually thought of as deriving from a combination of inherited characteristics and environmental (developmental and social) factors. The subject remains hotly debated, and many have tried to show that either biology (especially genes) or environment (especially conditions reflecting socioeconomic class) are, more or less, exclusively responsible for producing differences in intelligence. Particularly contested have been studies purporting to show links between ethnic heritage and intelligence, most of which have not been accepted in the scientific community. General intelligence is often said to comprise various specific abilities (verbal ability, ability to apply logic in solving problems, etc.), but critics contend that such compartments fail to reflect the nature of cognition and that other models, perhaps, based on information processing, are needed.

APPROACHES TO INTELLIGENCE

Like mind, intelligence is a complex concept to unfold and understand. Theoretically, it is a mysterious faculty of the mind; in practice, it is what exhibits itself in our overt behaviour distinguishing itself clearly from instinctive behaviour. As a process and a product, intelligence has been approached variedly. The two prominent approaches to get at the heart of intelligence include: (1) the Implicit Approach, and (2) the Explicit Approach.

Implicit Approach

In implicit approach, the meaning of intelligence, in fact, resides in the mind of the people who attempt to define it. Since the ideas and meaning already exist, psychologists need only to discover them through rational thinking, not create or invent them. The implicit approach relies on qualitative data viz. people's ideas, concepts, beliefs and notions as a consequence of their understanding and experience concerning intelligent behaviour. For example, in the third decade of twentieth century, a few psychology celebrities were asked to define intelligence as they understood it. As expected, their answers differed greatly.

- *The power of good response from the point of fact* -Thorndike
- *The capacity for knowledge and knowledge possessed* –Herman
- *A biological mechanism by which the effects of a variety of stimuli are brought together and given somewhat unified behaviour* – Paterson
- *The capacity to inhibit an instinctive adjustment* –Thurstone
- *The ability to carry on abstract thinking* – Terman
- *The ability to adapt oneself adequately to relatively new situations in life* –Pinter

- *The capacity to acquire capacity* –Woodrow
- *The capacity to profit by experience* –Derrback

Based on simple reasoning, the implicit approach is *an open-ended approach* and does not stand in the way of the individual who would try to define intelligence the way one likes to, nor does it contradict others' views about it. The consensus falls on defining intelligence as (1) *the capacity to learn from experience*, and (2) *the ability of the individual to adapt to his environment*. Many psychologists feel that intelligence, in fact, needs no definition because it underlines no single special ability of a person to do something but a variety of abilities.

Piaget (1972) envisioned the growth of intelligence as reflecting simultaneous processes of adaptation to the environment which involve equilibrium between organism and his world through various mental operations. ***Adaptation***, in Piaget's view, includes two sub-processes: (1) ***Assimilation***, and (2) ***Accommodation***. While accommodation implies that human beings require to modify their physiological functioning in response to demands placed upon them by the environment, assimilation refers to the tendency of the organism to incorporate elements of the environment directly into itself in various ways. Organization of behaviour, therefore, said Piaget, underscores the tendency for all the species to systematize their behaviour into coherent and meaningful system of increasing complexity as maturation takes place. With stimulus-response bond theory as the backdrop. Thorndike diversified the concept of intelligence. He argued that intelligence was at least of three types rather than one: (1) ***Social Intelligence*** – ability to understand and deal with persons; (2) ***Concrete Intelligence*** – ability to understand and deal with objects or things, as in skilled trades and scientific apparatus or appliances; and (3) ***Abstract Intelligence*** – ability to understand and deal with verbal and mathematical symbols. In fact, Thorndike tried to demonstrate various types of intelligence and also paint a complete picture of intelligence.

The implicit approach takes cognizance of the interaction that occurs between genetic endowment and environment through the process of maturation. Following the implicit approach, Neisser (1978) prepared a "prototype" – an ideal case around which intelligence is organized. According to him, intelligence is defined by the degree of resemblance to this prototype. Since there are multiple prototypes, so a valid concept of intelligence would be difficult to find. The implicit approach is a long winding journey into the realm of intelligence. It may possibly reveal what people mean by intelligence but not what intelligence actually is. Lack of empirical support, has rendered implicit approach ineffective in defining and explaining intelligence.

Explicit Approach

Explicit theories have a more direct, systematic and scientific approach to the understanding of intelligence in various hues. Under this approach, some basic *units of ability* have been proposed which explain individual differences in intelligent behaviour. The three basic units of ability as identified by various scholars include: (1) Stimulus-Response (S-R) Bond, (2) The Factor, and (3) the Component (Cognitive).

S-R Bond Theories

The S-R bond theories were propounded by E.L. Thorndike and his associates (1928), who viewed intelligence primarily as "the ability to learn", i.e. building up and strengthening the stimulus-response bonds (as explained at length in Chapter-8 on learning). While explaining the basic tenets of the Theory of Connectionism (trial and error method), Thorndike proposed that learning, which reflects the elements of intelligent behaviour, is largely a matter of connection between the stimulus and the response under certain favourable conditions. Gagne (1970) identified at least eight kinds of learning which vary from one another both in quantity and quality of S-R bonds involved. From the simplest to the most complex these are: (1) *Signal learning* (Pavlovian conditioning), (2) *S-R learning* (operant conditioning), (3) *Chaining* (complex operant conditioning), (4) *Verbal association,* (5) *Discrimination learning,* (6) *Concept learning,* (7) *Rule learning,* and (8) *Problem-solving.*

According to S-R bond viewpoint, there is nothing like general intelligence but many specific acts, the number of factors depending upon how refined a classification we might wish to make and are capable of making. Many elements which involve intelligent (efficient) working of the mind are grouped together. Verbal meaning, arithmetical reasoning, comprehension, visual perception of relationships, etc., exemplify grouped (clustered) elements involved in intelligent behaviour.

Factor Theories

In explaining the nature of intelligence, traditional theorists have considered factor as the basic unit. The paradigm has been called differential, psychometric or factorial on the basis of the tetrads – a set of correlations – worked out by finding interrelations among mental tests placed in columns and rows in order.

In this regard, Charles Spearman's (1923) Two Factor Theory presents almost diagonally opposite view to S-R bond theory. Spearman thought that all intellectual activity is dependent primarily on and is an expression of a general factor common to all mental activity. He called this factor as 'g' (factor) which is present in all individuals in varying degree depending upon the type and complexity of the activity. Spearman characterized this general factor as mental energy because, in the intelligence domain, it has a similar role as physical energy has in the physical world. Relationship and correlation are the basis of a factor. Spearman had his own intelligence test constructed on the premise of general ('g') and specific ('s') factors, the framework of which he derived through factor analysis. According to this rationale, if all questions on an intelligence test require similar intellectual abilities, intelligence may be viewed as a general capacity of the individuals. On the other hand, if different questions on the test require different abilities, then intelligence may be viewed as a variety of specific kind of capacities. So, to determine whether intelligence is a general or specific capacity every question of the intelligence test is correlated through factor analysis with every other test question. Weakly correlated questions point to different intellectual capacities. Tests designed to measure 'g' factor necessarily provoke an individual to establish relations and correlations existing among diverse sorts of perceiving, knowing, reasoning, and thinking. The amount of general factor operating in each activity will determine the size of the correlation between the two essential activities being measured. Meaning, arithmetical reasoning, sentence completion, reasoning by analogy, paragraph interpretation, perception of relationship in geometrical forms, picture completion, etc., constitute the stuff used in current tests of intelligence. Although all these show positive relationship with one another, inter-correlations are by no means perfect.

Spearman's insistence on specific factor ('s' factor) specific to certain activities brought a revolution in the concept of intelligence. According to Spearman's views, say Crooks & Stein (1988), all of us have a certain level of general intelligence ('g' factor) probably genetically determined, that underlies all our intelligent behaviour.

We also have specific abilities ('s' factor) that are more useful on some tasks than on others. This theoretical perspective leads to the prediction that a person with high 'g' factor will score higher on most skill tests than will a person with an average level of general intelligence. It would not be particularly surprising, however, for individuals with average general intelligence to score higher on some specific skills because of a particular strength in their 's' factor.

Theoretical explanations given by Thorndike and Spearman touch two different poles standing wide apart. There emerged some intermediate theories oscillating between the two. For instance, Thompson (1939) disputed Spearman's claim that the 'g' factor represented a single underlying source of individual differences. Instead he proposed that the appearance of a general factor was due to the working of a multitude of mental bonds including reflexes, learnt associations between stimuli and the like. Performance of any particular task activates a large number of these bonds. Some bonds will be required for the performance of virtually any task requiring mental effort and these bonds in combination will give rise to the appearance of a general factor.

Louis Thurstone (1938) accepted in principle Spearman's hypothesis of a 'g' factor but he argued that it is only a second order factor or phenomenon, one which rises only because the primary or first order factors are related to each other. Thurstone's theory emphasizes that certain mental operations have in common a "primary" factor that gives them psychological and functional unit and that differentiates them from other mental operations. According to this theory, mental operations have been organized into various groups each of which has its own primary factor, giving the group a functional unity. Each primary factor is relatively independent of other factors. Using the differential method of factor analysis, Thurstone devised seven primary factors: (1) ***Number Factor*** (N) – "ability to do numerical calculations rapidly and accurately"; (2) ***Verbal Factor*** (V) – "found in tests involving verbal comprehension"; (3) ***Space Factor*** (S) – "involves any task(s) in which the subject manipulates an object imaginably in space"; (4) ***Word Fluency Factor*** (W) – "involves whenever the subject is asked to think of isolated words at a rapid rate"; (5) ***Reasoning Factor*** (R) - "found in tasks that require the subject to deliver a rule for a principle involved in series or groups of letter"; (6) ***Perceptual Speed***; and (7) ***Rote Memory Factor*** (M) – "the ability to memorize quickly".

Realizing that it was fallacious to think of intelligence comprising only these seven primary factors, Thurstone added certain "second order factors".

Guilford (1967) refused to acknowledge the existence of general factor in human intelligence. Instead, he (1977, 1982) believed that any intellectual task can be analyzed in terms of three major intellectual functions: (1) the ***mental operations*** that are used (*how to think*); (2) the ***content*** upon which these operations are performed (*what we think about*); and (3) the ***products*** of applying a particular operation to a particular content (*the end result of thinking*). Each of these three functions is divided into a number of sub-functions, and there are 150 possible interactions and combinations of these sub-functions. Guilford thus maintains that he had identified 150 kinds of intelligence.

The most widely accepted factorial description of intelligence, however, is hierarchical one. Johnson (1969. 1970) viewed intelligence as comprising two levels - associative learning ability (called level I), and conceptual learning and problem-solving (called level II) both largely hereditary. Associative abilities are those that associate certain stimuli and even, for example, short-term memory and information task on I.Q. tests. Cognitive abilities are those that deal with learning and problem-solving. Accepting Spearman's 'g' factor, Vernon (1971) proposed that intelligence can be described as comprising abilities at varying levels of generality. At the highest (most general) level is a general factor, encompassing all tasks. This is followed by (1) major group factors including a verbal educational factor and practical mechanical factor, (2) minor group factors, and (3) specific factors.

Cattell (1971) subdivided Spearman's 'g' factor into (1) ***Fluid Intelligence,*** and (2) ***Crystallized Intelligence.*** While fluid intelligence is defined as the ability of the individual to see relationships as in analogies and letter, numerical series, crystallized intelligence refers to acquired knowledge and skill (Murphy & Davidshafer, 1994). Where fluid intelligence deals with reasoning ability, crystallized intelligence is concerned with one's state of factual knowledge. As one might expect measures of fluid and crystallized intelligence tend to be highly correlated reflecting the fact that people high in fluid intelligence find it easier to quickly build up a large store of factual knowledge. Nevertheless these two types of intelligence are conceptually distinct and there is evidence that they show different developmental trends.

Extending the boundaries of Cattell's work in collaboration with

Cattell himself, Hakstian (1978) added higher stratum capacities of visualization capacity, general perceptual speed, memory and general retrieval capacity besides crystallized and fluid intelligence.

Cognitive (Component) Approach

The cognitive approach does not, in fact, address any specific theory. A common element, under this approach, is a unit of analysis that can be described as elementary information process or component which operates upon internal representations of the objects or symbols. The component may translate a sensory input into a conceptual representation and transform a conceptual representation into a motor output. What is labelled as a component depends upon the desired level of theorizing. Under this approach, researchers attempt to analyze directly the processes involved in intellectual behaviour rather than try to find behavioural correlates of such behaviours.

Minimizing the importance of traditional intelligence tests, Sternberg (1980) proposed that factors could be understood in terms of three components: (1) ***The cognitive Component*** – the specific cognitive processes that underlie intelligent behaviour; (2) ***The Experimental Component*** – the situation in which previous experience with a particular kind of problem affects the way that problem is solved; and (3) ***The Contextual Component*** – the environmental context within which the problem-solving occurs. To Sternberg, intelligence is illustrated by a continuum anchored on one end by the ability to solve novel problems and on the other end by the ability to automate frequently encountered tasks. In nutshell, to understand general intelligence is to understand each of the three specific components of intelligence as they operate together. Sternberg's theory (1979, 1981, and 1982) focuses on how people process information in order to solve problems and deal effectively with the environment. Sternberg firmly believed that if we can analyze how people use various steps (mechanisms) to process information and solve problems, it may be possible to teach them strategies for improving their performance.

Multiple Intelligence Approach

Not being satisfied with the psychometric approach (traditional IQ tests), since about 1970, towering psychologists like J. P. Guilford tried (1982), and Howard Gardner (1985) developed the concept of multiple intelligence. While Guilford talked of 150 kinds of intelligence,

Howard Gardner in his landmark book *Frames of Mind: The Theory of Multiple Intelligence* unveiled ***Theory of Multiple Intelligence*** in 1983, famously rejecting the traditional and the long-held view of aptitude solely as the ability to reason and understand complex ideas. Gardner broke intelligence down into at least eight different components or categories, thereby giving a completely new interpretation to its concept. His theory is based on studies not only on normal children and adults but also studies of gifted individuals (including so-called "savants"), of persons who have suffered brain damage, of experts and virtuosos, and of individuals from diverse cultures. He argued that *psychometric tests address only linguistic and logical plus some aspects of spatial intelligence*; other forms have been entirely ignored. Moreover, the paper and-pencil format of most tests rules out many kinds of intelligent performance that matter in everyday life, such as giving an extemporaneous talk (linguistic) or being able to find one's way in a new town (spatial). The eight different categories of intelligence are briefly described below.

- ***Linguistic Intelligence*** meaning that a person is good with words, either in a spoken or written language. People with high linguistic intelligence are good at reading, telling stories, doing cross-words (or other puzzles) and *writing* and learning foreign languages. They learn best by reading and taking notes, and usually are very good at explaining something clearly to other people. Politicians, writers, teachers, lawyers, etc., are linguistically very intelligent.
- ***Logical-Mathematical Intelligence*** is reflected in the *ability to efficiently analyze information and work with numbers*, which scientists, researchers, detectives, mathematicians, economists, etc., possess typically to a high degree. They are interested in patterns, categories, and relationships, and are also very good at investigating and then drawing conclusions about some object, activity or phenomenon, as in scientific research.
- ***Bodily-Kinesthetic Inteligence*** involves *physical activities, fine motor movement, and athletic prowess*. People possessing this kind of intelligence process knowledge through their senses and tend to excel at physical activity, sports, dance, crafts, performing arts, exploration, etc. They prefer learning things by physically doing them, and are generally

active and animated people.

- ***Interpersonal Intelligence*** refers to one's *ability to understand people, how they feel, what motivates them, how they interact with one another*. Individuals with interpersonal intelligence are good communicators and tend to be good at reading and understanding *other peoples' feelings and motives* and get along very well with other people. They feel comfortable in social situations, enjoy speaking in pubic and are usually recognized as being a "popular" person (leaders among peers) at school or at work. Politicians, managers, diplomats, social workers, etc., possess fairly high standard of interpersonal intelligence.
- ***Naturalistic Intelligence*** involves *a love of nature and the outdoors*. It allows people to distinguish among, classify, and use features of the environment. Typically these people *love animals* and will have them as pets. They may also enjoy plants and are likely to have them in their home, and grow them in *the garden*. Scientists, conservationists, farmers, naturalists, gardeners, etc., are the kind of people who belong to this category. They tend to be very spiritual. Naturalist adolescents can often name and describe the features of every make of car around them
- ***Intrapersonal Intelligence*** is *the ability to see oneself, to develop a sense of self-identity*. Almost complete opposite of the interpersonal intelligence, it is found in philosophers, psychologists, theologians, writers, etc., who are deep thinkers, usually self-motivated and self aware of who they are and their *emotions*. These people tend to be perfectionists though shy or feel uncomfortable in social situations, such as speaking in front of other people.
- ***Spatial Intelligence*** is *the ability to find your way around an environment, to form and think in mental images and pictures of reality, and to transform them readily*. It is being generally good at mazes and jigsaw puzzles, and also making things. Spatially intelligent people are good at thinking something in their head, and then creating it in reality. They spend time in daydreaming and have good hand-eye co-ordination, and are very efficient at drawing, building (with blocks) giving directions. Dominant in this form of

intelligence are more often men than women. Builders, architects, pilots, artists, etc., belong to this category of people.

- *Musical Intelligence* refers to *the ability to perceive and create pitch and rhythmic patterns.* Being a domain of the musicians, singers, conductors, composers, etc., the musical intelligence involves being good with music, rhythm and learning. Musical people typically are discriminating listeners, i.e. they are aware of sounds others miss. They play a musical instrument and/or sing and are always seen singing or taping out a beat.

Referring to Sternberg (1994), Allix (2000), Gardner & Connell (2000) and Gardner (2004), Waterhouse (2006a) reported the absence of "published studies that offer evidence of the validity of the multiple intelligences." Gardner is said to have conceded that "MI theory has few enthusiasts among psychometricians or others of a traditional psychological background".

Taking an expanded notion of intelligence, the American psychologist Robert Sternberg (1985) developed the ***Triarchic*** (three-part) ***Theory of Intelligence*** containing three fundamental aspects of intelligence - analytic, creative, and practical - of which only the first is measured to any significant extent by mainstream tests. His investigations suggest the need for a balance between analytic intelligence, on the one hand, and creative and especially practical intelligence on the other. According to Sternberg's theory behaviours must be viewed within the context of a particular culture; it asserts that a person's experiences impact the expression of intelligence; and that certain cognitive processes control all intelligent behaviour. When all these aspects of intelligence are viewed together, the importance of *how* people use their intelligence becomes more important than the question of "how much" intelligence a person has. Sternberg has suggested that some intelligence tests focus too much on what a person has already learned rather than on how well a person acquires new skills or knowledge.

The EEG Recording and Error Information Approach

On the groundwork of psycho-physiological theories and cybernetic (information processing) another line of thinking developed, culminating in more subtle discoveries about intelligence. Galton, probably, was the first person to also suggest that reaction time and intelligence were inter-related. In the beginning and for a long time, most researchers did not distinguish between reaction time and movement time; both "underlie different processes" and have correlation over repeated trials for an individual. Researchers, however, have found reaction time and intelligence related; "....intelligent people tend to have faster reaction time than less intelligent people", is a highly useful finding because it points to a possibility of using a quick simple test instead of long and arduous test to measure intelligence. Pursuing Galton's line (relationship between reaction time and intelligence), Hendrickson (1982) obtained results using electro-encephalogram (EEGs) that do link properties of brain wave activity with intelligence as measured by standard intelligence test. The property that was measured is an evoked potential, a brain-wave generated in response to the presentation of a specific stimulus. In Hendrickson's study, the evoked potentials were recorded with the EEG machine as the person listened to a tone that lasted for 20 milliseconds. Hendrickson showed greater consistency in their EEG pattern. The theory is concerned with errors of transmission as neurons communicate with one another. Basically, Hendrickson argued that the brains of more intelligent people work more efficiently in the sense that they have fewer transmission errors, which means that the EEG wave-forms are more consistent from trial to trial for more intelligent people. The key aspect of the EEG data that follows the theory to be tested is that the final wave-form for each individual is the average wave form computed over many trials. The result is that the final averaged wave-form is jagged and complex for those with high intelligence and more smooth and rounded for those of lower intelligence.

Critics of Hendrickson's theory maintain that EEG recordings may have less to do with the biological meaning of IQ than they do with "the ability to maintain concentration on a remarkably tedious test". However, on the other hand, part of being intelligent may be the ability to do well as "remarkably tedious" tasks.

The Emotional Intelligence Concept

Harvard psychologist Dr. Daniel Goleman (1996) authored a book titled ***Emotional Intelligence***, after a decade of research on how the mind produces emotions. He saw a need to redefine what "intelligence" means. His conclusion from his research: when we try to determine what produces success, it is character, or the ability to resist temptation by developing will power, self-control and empathy, which is more important than the intellectual power of the brain as measured by standard IQ tests and SAT exams.

Goleman claims emotional intelligence to be as important as more traditional sorts of intelligence. It is *a form of social intelligence that involves the ability to monitor one's own and others' feelings and emotions, to discriminate among them, and to use this information to guide one's thinking and action* (Salovey & Mayer, 1990). The four core abilities underlying emotional intelligence include: self control, zeal and persistence, self motivation, and empathy for oneself and others. Emotional awareness of one's being as well as cognitive processing and behavioural decision-making (e.g. to act or not to act in a given situation) is an important factor in intelligence. In simple terms emotional intelligence explores your feelings, thoughts, and actions in relation to the world around you. The higher your emotional intelligence the more effectively you are able to react to the world about you.

Factors affecting Intelligence

Since ancient times psychologists have viewed intelligence as matter of inheritance, but now those holding interactionism and humanistic viewpoint, have begun to believe that intelligence is influenced by environment. Stephen (1996) says that intelligence is alterable by a number of factors, including diet and schooling. Consider these facts, for example.

- ***IQ scores are correlated with the speed of some simple mental processes*** such as accurately figuring out which of two lines is longer when lots of other things are going on in the visual field. Possibly the nervous systems of high IQ people are more efficient, better able to screen out background noise.
- ***School attendance counts.*** It elevates IQ or, more accurately, prevents it from slipping because you learn in school how to organize information categorically. This negates the widely held view about IQ as a measure of innate intelligence. Missing school means missing the stimulation it provides, ultimately lowering one's IQ as the schooling deficit is cumulative. There is a systematic

decline in IQ scores over the summer (vacation) months. With each passing month away from school, children lose ground from their end-of-year scores on both intellectual and academic tests. Dropping out of high school can diminish IQ by about 8 points. Educational attainment not only boosts IQ, it also boosts earning power.

- ***IQ has nothing to do with birth order.***
- ***IQ is related to breastfeeding.*** Breast-fed infants grow into children with higher IQs than their non-breast-fed siblings - 3 to 8 IQ points ahead by age three. Immune factors in mother's milk may prevent children from getting diseases that impede early learning.
- ***Intelligence is plural, not singular.*** Apart from general intelligence universally present, all researchers agree that other, independent mental abilities exist - spatial, verbal, analytic, and practical intelligence. The skills of practical intelligence, such as common ***sense,*** are important in predicting life outcomes but are distinct from IQ-type analytic intelligence. Consider emotional intelligence, which has a long reach and ultimately leads to more successful life-course outcomes.
- ***Intelligence scores are predictive of real-world outcomes.*** Even among people with comparable levels of schooling, the greater a person's intellectual ability, the higher that person's weekly/monthly earnings. Workers with the lowest levels of intellectual ability earn only two-thirds what workers at the highest level earn.
- ***Intelligence is highly context-dependent.*** Most skills of intelligence are connected to a specific domain. Whizzes at handicapping horses at the racetrack, calculating odds and predicting winners can be abysmal at reasoning outside the track. *A genius at the track can be a dolt in the stock market, even though both pursuits require many comparable mental activities.* It turns out that the knowledge is organized differently in different domains, and so what a person knows about the track can lie fallow on Wall Street. [*Gordon Allport rightly stated that in situations a genius finds himself acting as a fool, and an idiot is a whiz at machinery.*]

- ***Intelligence is on the rise.*** There has been a steady increase in performance on IQ tests - by approximately 20 points every 30-year generation born since 1889. The largest gains appear on nonverbal IQ tests.
- ***IQ can be influenced by diet.*** Mother was right. Eat your fish; it is brain food.

We all have different forms of intelligence, and different people are intelligent at different things; for instance Lata Mangeshkar, Bhimsen Joshi or Zubin Mehta (*musical intelligence*), Mandira Bedi, Shah Rukh Khan or Amitabh Bachan (*interpersonal intelligence*), Osho, Ravi Shanker or J. Krishna Murti (*Intrapersonal intelligence*), Vishwanathan Anand or Karpov (*logical intelligence*), Dalai Lama or Satyasai Baba (*existential intelligence*), M.F. Hussain or Pablo Picasso (*visual-spatial intelligence*), Ayn Rand or Panini (*linguistic intelligence*), Charles Darwin or Dr. Salim Ali (*naturalistic intelligence*), and finally Don Bradman, Sachin Tendulkar or Usain Bolt (*bodily kinaesthetic intelligence*). To illustrate the point further, a person acknowledged as highly intelligent in one component of intelligence, may not necessarily be equally intelligent in another. For example, David Beckham, the great English footballer, is someone extremely intelligent. .... (Some people might feel laughing at this statement), but he is exceptionally good at football (soccer). So it is obvious that his dominant form of intelligence is bodily-kinesthetic. However, David is not very good at mathematics, but focusing his dominant form of intelligence (i.e. sport) he eventually became very successful doing something he enjoyed.

MEASUREMENT OF INTELLIGENCE

The Background

Once developed, intelligence becomes a stable attribute and always remains an important consideration when taking decisions about individuals, particularly if these decisions have a long-term implication or far reaching consequences for people. It is believed that individual differences in general intelligence are manifest in the performance of cognitively demanding tasks. The primary scientific basis for asserting that 'general intelligence exists and that individual differences have some impact on the behaviour is the observation that there is a positive correlation between every reliable measure that calls for mental processing, retrieval or manipulation of information and almost any other measure that involves cognitive ability', remark Murphy & Davidshafer (1991).

The testing and measurement of intelligence comprehensively have probably been the greatest challenge for psychologists because principally (1) intelligence is a construct, not a thing; (2) it cannot be defined strictly in terms of one type of behaviour, but rather in terms of a variety of behaviours that pose cognitive demands such as calculating, reasoning, perceiving relationships and analogies, learning quickly, storing and retrieving information, using language fluently, classifying, generalizing, and adjusting to new situations; and (3) intelligence, by its very definition, should be related to success in a variety of cognitively demanding endeavours, e.g. work, school, training programme.

As explained above, measurement of intelligence began with Francis Galton, whose early efforts were somewhat disappointing. Since his times, the concept of intelligence and also its testing procedure have undergone tremendous change and transformation at the hands of Alfred Binet, J.P. Guilford, Wechsler, and others. In fact, intelligence testing has evolved itself gradually coming out of the confusion and chaos which existed amongst the psychologists about its nature, and its constituents. Today, numerous very high rated devices (tools and instruments) of measuring intelligence are available.

Psychometric Approach to Intelligence

Around the turn of the last century, a French psychologist Alfred Binet, out of necessity, made a successful attempt in developing an objective test to identify 'above average' children from out of a vast majority of ordinary ones. Binet and his collaborators - especially Theodore Simon - reasoned that virtually all children follow essentially the same course of intellectual development but that some progress more rapidly than others. Those with sub-normal intelligence were presumed to be merely "retarded" or backward in their development. Going a step further, Binet theorized that a child of low intelligence should perform on tests of intellect as would a normal child of a younger age and conversely, that a precocious child should perform like an older child of average intelligence. Binet came out with the concept of *mental age* which corresponds to the chronological age of the children, who, on the average, receive a similar test score. Binet and his colleagues argued that it would be possible to obtain accurate estimates of children's abilities to profit from the standard school curriculum by comparing their mental age to their chronological age (Binet & Simon, 1905). They developed a series of subsets covering a range of reasoning and problem-solving abilities and were successful in evaluating level of children and predicting children's success in regular school work. Since then, this first ever valid test of intelligence underwent tremendous change and transformation.

In 1916, Lewis Terman at Stanford University expanded and reworked Binet's Stanford-Binet test. He revised many original items, and added some new questions and calculating new age norms to suit American ecology. Later revisions called the Binet Test as Revised Stanford-Binet Intelligence Tests that were published in 1937, 1960, and 1985. The individually administered Stanford-Binet test is made up of subsets that are graded by age level. Although the test is used primarily for children, there are also some subsets for adults. The test has been used widely for a longer time than any other test of intelligence, and it is still highly regarded by most psychologists and academicians in psychology and education. The test possesses impressive predictive ability to do well at school. The Stanford-Binet test has come under criticism on two major grounds. First, it places too much emphasis on verbal abilities such as word knowledge, sentence interpretation, etc. Second, it was originally designed for children and still remains for more applicable to children than adults.

> The ***Stanford-Binet Intelligence Scales*** consist of questions and short tasks arranged from easy to difficult, measures a wide variety of verbal and nonverbal skills. Its fifteen tests are divided into the following four cognitive areas: verbal reasoning (vocabulary, comprehension, absurdities, and verbal relations); quantitative reasoning (math, number series, equation building); abstract/visual reasoning (pattern analysis, *matrices*, paper folding and cutting, copying); and short-term memory (memory for sentences, digits, and objects, and *bead* memory). A formula is used to arrive at the intelligence quotient, or IQ. An IQ of 100 means that the child's chronological and mental ages match. Traditionally, IQ scores of 90–109 are considered average; scores below 70 indicate mental retardation. Gifted children achieve scores of 140 or above. The Stanford-Binet intelligence test can be used with children starting at age two. It is now widely used to assess cognitive development and often to determine placement in special education classes.

The work of Binet, Terman, and Wilhelm Stern paved the way for a method of classifying intelligence in terms of a standardized measure, with standardization ensured by the large number of individuals of various ages taking the test. German psychologist L. Wilhelm Stern was the first to coin the term *intelligence quotient* (IQ), a figure derived from the ratio of mental age to chronological age. He devised a simple formula to avoid the problem of needing to deal with fractions that arose when mental age was compared to chronological age. This formula – mental age x chronological age divided by 100 – yielded an intelligence quotient or IQ score which provided a rough index of how dull or bright a child was compared to his peers.

For a long time, psychologists considered IQ score a valid index of a person's intelligence but gradually it became clear that interpretation of intelligence scores using this formula was not flawless. While there is evidence that many adults continue to add to their store of factual knowledge throughout their lives, it seems apparent that the rate of development in basic cognitive abilities declines sharply with advancing age. In effect, an IQ score based on mental age penalizes the older examinee. While chronological age is progressing at a steady rate, the mental age levels off fast. As a result the IQ formula reveals that as people advance in age, they steadily become less intelligent. Apart from this, mental age is no longer used in computing IQ scores these days. In the modern tests, a *deviation IQ score* is worked out by computing standard scores on a specific intelligence test and then converting these scores to a scale with a mean of 100 and standard deviation of 15.

In order to overcome problems inherent in Stanford-Binet test, David Wechsler developed a new kind of test, which is known as ***Wechsler Adult Intelligence Scale*** (WAIS) and was designed exclusively for people in late adolescence or adulthood.

> The test includes eleven subsets or scales, arranged according to the aptitude being tested rather than by age level. They are divided into two sections: verbal (six) and nonverbal or performance (five), with separate scores for each. Verbal intelligence, the component most often associated with academic success, implies the ability to think in abstract terms using either words or mathematical symbols. Performance intelligence suggests the ability to perceive relationships and fit separate parts together logically into a whole. The inclusion of the performance section in the Wechsler scales is especially helpful in assessing the cognitive ability of children with speech and language problems or whose first language is not English.

The test can be of particular value to school psychologists screening for specific learning disabilities because of the number of specific subtests that make up each section. It is possible to identify individuals with special strengths in non-verbal area and to detect superior intelligence even in people who might have had limited opportunities to develop verbal skills.

Kaufman Assessment Battery for Children (KABC) is an intelligence and achievement test for children ages 2.5–12.5 years. It consists of 16 subtests, not all of which are used for every age group. A distinctive feature of the test is that it defines intelligence as problem-solving ability rather than knowledge of facts, which it considers achievement. This distinction is evident in the test's division into two parts - intelligence and achievement - which are scored separately and together. The test's strong emphasis is on memory and lesser attention to verbal expression are intended to offset cultural disparities between black and white children..In addition, the test may be given to non-native speakers in their first language and to hearing impaired children using American Sign Language.

The Standard Progressive Matrices, for children as well as for adults, by Raven (1977) are culture-fair tests designed to evaluate subject's ability to comprehend relationships between geometric figures and designs and to perceive the structure of the design in order to select the appropriate part (from out of several given) for completion of each pattern of relations.

> The scale consists of 60 problems divided into five sets of 12. In each set, the first problem is nearly as close as possible to the other, is self-evident. The problems which follow become progressively more difficult. The author claims that the SPM cover "the widest possible range of mental ability and to be equally useful with the persons of all ages, whatever their education, nationality or physical condition". The test is regarded as test of innate educability and a measure of the general ('g') factor of intelligence. With Stanford-Binet test, the validity of SPM has been found to range from .50 to .91. When correlated against verbal and non-verbal tests, it came closer to measuring the forms of abstract and conceptual intelligence rather than functions involved in other non-verbal scales.

Apart from this, the ***Army Alpha Test*** (for recruits who could read) and the ***Army Beta Test*** (for illiterates and non-English speaking individuals) were developed in the United States. These tests, with their initial objective being different, were enormously helpful both as models of group intelligence test and an impetus to developing more effective measures. Today, group tests of intelligence are globally available in a great variety and are used in a variety of settings. These group tests have certain obvious advantages over individual tests. They are cheaper and quicker, and easier to administer. Since group norms are available for these widely used group intelligence tests, they can be scored quickly and accurately, with little need for the kind of clinical interpretation by trained testers that individual tests demand. In group testing, variables like motivation, situational disposition, etc., are difficult to control.

Aptitude and ***achievement tests*** are directly used as measures of intelligence because many test items in a test of intelligence are actually measures of what one has already learnt or achieved. For example, a person's ability to define words (vocabulary) or figure out what is missing from a picture (picture competition) is related to how much has been learned by exposure to previous information. Classroom tests are good examples of achievement tests. Aptitude tests are more general in nature and designed to measure cumulative knowledge, skills and abilities that have developed as a result of the subject's life experience. The distinction between aptitude and achievement is now recognized as being one of emphasis rather than as the fundamental distinction as was once assumed.

There have been attempt to construct tests to measure "pure" intelligence, i.e. a person's basic capacity to behave intelligently rather than a reflection of how much that person has learnt from previous experiences. Unfortunately, these efforts have fallen short of expectations, and to date there is still no clear measure of people's aptitude as distinct from what they have already learnt.

BODY-MIND INTERACTION AND INTELLIGENCE

Like the body-mind dichotomy, intellectualism and athleticism have, since earliest times, been considered two different domains of organism's activity with nothing common between them. Now that several concepts in education, psychology and sport have undergone cataclysmic change with the emergence of the age of reason and science, unity of the organism and body-mind interactionism have become ineffaceable truths. It is impossible to deny that Plato – the most venerated Greek philosopher – had been a successful Olympic wrestler completely falsifying that an athlete is a fool "to whom Heaven denied of soul, is well-compensated in limbs" (John Armstrong, 1962). Modern research has removed age-old dust from the muscle-mind relationship and shown that an athlete is *no* dullard, and a genius, *no* athletic fool. Being athletic or being intellectual is not categorical, but attitudinal.

In the changed scenario of epistemological advancement, intelligence is being viewed not simply as a gamut of non-observable cerebral functions, but a multi-coloured spectrum of cognitive, affective and motor processes, inter-related and inter-dependent. The overt and covert behaviours are immaculately interwoven in the intelligence fabric. Getman (1952) and Kephart (1960) considered body-mind interactionism "expounded on the rationale that not only were sound intellectual and perceptual functioning dependent upon good motor functioning but that (a) if one was clumsy, perceptual difficulties including inaptitude in various academic skills were inevitable outcomes, and (b) that to improve perceptual functioning one merely had to engage in a prescribed set of sensory motor (perceptual motor) tasks". Cratty (1974) argued that "movement is a powerful tool and for the most part constitutes a highly emotional experience in the life of children. Physical experiences are seldom likely to have a neutral effect upon the mind and psyche of the maturing child". He quoted Getman: ".....movement is learning..... learning requires movement...... foundational to every activity of the human being is the skill of motor control and coordination. Thoughts which do not get into muscles, never fully possess the mind".

Psycho-physiology research points out that neurons and nerves - the major instruments of intelligent behaviour - derive their strength from the action-potential of the muscles, the instruments of observable behaviour. The more efficiently are the muscles exercised and trained, the more effectively they supply nutrients and oxygen to various body organs especially the brain and the nervous system – the material cause of intelligent behaviour. Sherrington (1940) rightly observed: "The muscle is the cradle of recognizable mind which seems to have arisen in connection with the motor act. Where motor integration progressed and where motor behaviour evolved, mind progressively evolved". As there is no reason to compartmentalize *intelligent behaviour* as purely physical or purely mental, there is no reason either to look at athleticism and intellectualism as two poles apart than two points on a behavioural continuum.

INTELLIGENCE IN ACTIVITY AND SPORT

The relationship between physical activity and intelligence has often been a matter of serious debate among sport psychologists. Play, exercise, athletics, sport, etc., are skill-based activities varying in movement complexity. However, they all derive vitality from motor abilities, which develop in increasing complexity over time as the child grows in years maintaining quality interaction with the environment. Since all skilled behaviour is intelligent, relationship between athleticism and intelligence is undeniable. The nature of this relationship, however, often depends on how close the physical and the intellectual elements are embedded in an activity. On this issue, Digiovanna (1937) said:

> ..... intelligence is exercised in the analysis of skilled movement; the more complex, (and) the more interpretative the movement, the greater the amount of intelligence necessary to comprehend it. Educability in such a case is dependent on practice in the movement and the greater the intelligence, the greater the possibility for educability. Intelligence, in athletics is also exercised in the strategy in the various games......Given a series of athletic tasks, administered under the same conditions and with all other factors influencing athletic achievement to two individuals, identical in physique but differing in intellect, it is reasonable to believe that the more intellectual will prove superior. The assumption, thus, is that intelligence plays a part in athletic achievement.

The relationship between academic achievement and athletic success and between general intelligence and certain parameters of athletic performance such as motor ability, physical efficiency, body-build, success in certain games/sports, playing ability, etc., is well reported and documented in literature. Reviewing several studies on this issue, Kamlesh (1990) found (1) great variation in the investigative designs covering samples, variables and instruments; (2) contradictory findings of almost equal magnitude; and (3) a need for an entirely new level of conceptual precision with a "more sophisticated vision of the methodological requirements, and theoretical possibilities" (Ismail, 1972).

Intelligence is a multi-faceted variable that operates in hundred one ways. A person considered intelligent in mathematics may not be impressive in literary or mechanical endeavours. It can be vice versa also. Sport is no exception to this principle. An elite athlete may or may not score high on a test of intelligence, and a highly intelligent individual may or may not be too good at sport. Being athletically successful does not mean being intellectually high or vice versa. This is what makes intelligence to be a big puzzle both in life and sport. Much of the research on intelligence as a relative component of athletic performance is "more suggestive" than empirically significant. Cratty (1972) says:

> It has been found for example that most superior athletes in Olympic competitions, in Eastern Europe possess at least average intelligence, and that IQ scores are well above average. But clear vision exists between intelligence quotient of sportsmen practicing activities they had been exposed to in college and the intelligence test scores of men practicing sport usually not associated with a college.

Athletes are reported to differ in intelligence on game to game basis. For example, athletes in team sports like soccer, basketball, ice hockey, etc., will score higher on standardized measures of IQ than others participating in activities in which force and power dominate more than strategy, i.e. shot put and boxing. Sports are classified according to their skill structure, play dynamics, physical requirements, organizational pattern, etc. Classification of sports based on the psychological stress they impose, includes (1) sports requiring strategy and interaction with others, (2) those involving imminent physical harm, (3) those in which all-out effort dissipates stress, (4) those in which stress builds up as the competition progresses such as archery, shooting, etc., and (5) those in which there is a strong aesthetic element, e.g. gymnastics, diving, figure skating, etc. An extensive review of studies on the relationship between physical activity and mental activity in sportspersons, Cratty (1974) concluded:

(a) Fit individuals exposed to moderate exercise will improve performance on the test of mental ability;
(b) Unfit individuals will, if over-stressed in exhaustive exercise, evidence decrement in ability to carry out mental operations;
(c) Both fit and unfit (individuals) are likely to perform on tests of academic and intellectual ability equally well, all things being equal and held constant (as they seldom are)......

Rail, writes Cratty, also advanced several hypotheses on the inter-relation between physical fitness and intellectual advancement: (1) early in the school years dull children channel their energies into physical activity to compensate for their lack of intellectual ability; (2) high intelligence implies a greater ability for self-amusement, primarily available to the intellectually less capable children; (3) with increasing age, bright children become better able to deal with games of increase complexity with which they are confronted.

CONCEPT OF ATHLETIC INTELLIGENCE

Ever since Thorpe & West (1969) coined the metaphor "sports sense" in athletes, sport psychologists began to take interest in intelligence as a correlate of athletic performance. No doubt, criticality of intelligence in sport performance is yet to be highlighted through empirical approach, it is, more or less, established that no motor (sport) skill or performance is devoid of perceptual and cognitive processes, which constitute intelligence. Every skilled activity of man - whether in life or sport - is an outcome of perfect combination of certain physical, psychic, motor and environmental ingredients in certain proportions and brought into play as a function of time, place and objective.

An important question that continues to defy solution even today and which needs to be addressed with an open mind is: Are superior athletes also intellectually superior when assessed on the conventional general mental ability tests or do they possess intelligence which is different from general intelligence? Tackling such a ticklish question would require sport psychologists to approach the subjects of intelligence and sport from a radical angle, for which some background has already been prepared. The induction of idea-motor, psychological skill training (Mahoney, 1989, 1987, 1984) besides greater emphasis tactical training in the general training regimens of sportspersons indicates a sort of realization on the part of the sport psychologists and athletic trainers that intelligence is a crucial variable which needs serious attention and proper treatment in the scheme of things in athletic training programmes.

The concept of athletic intelligence is not a new one but it has recently become an important area of research and study. In its simplest form, athletic intelligence is defined as ***thought in action***, for which corroboration comes from Jesse Owens, the Quadruple Gold Medallist at 1936-Olympic Games at Berlin:

> "In the end, it's extra effort that separates a winner from second place. But winning takes a lot more than that, too. It starts with complete command of the fundamentals. Then it takes desire, determination, discipline and self-sacrifice. And finally, it takes a great deal of love, fairness and respect for your fellow men.
> "Put all these together, and even if you don't win, how can you lose?"

While general intelligence involves certain mental skills, sport intelligence encompasses several physical skills already considered as ingredients of general intelligence: for example, how intelligently your body moves on the floor or any athletic court and/or in the air when you are playing a particular sport. To all this, mental processes like perception, attention, concentration and cognition are vital at some stage of learning, skill-perfection and muscle-mind fine-tuning.

Both Spearman (1927), and Thurstone (1938) considered attention and perception as part of intelligence, today this agreement is no longer unequivocal (Tenenbaum & Bar-Eli, 1992). Sigler & Richards (1982) maintained that the skill of perceptual and motor identification is important in the early assessment of intelligence and that this skill had not been analyzed in the sport setting. The most important variable for sport is ***perceptual intelligence.*** Coding and accessing are the mechanisms with a close relationship to perception and attention. Behaviour is an external representation of neural competence. Behaviour may be no more intelligent than the way in which events are perceived in the brain. Categorization and organization are the most important mechanisms for the collection of information. It is more important to be able to utilize knowledge stored in the memory than to contain a great amount of knowledge (Sternberg & Salter, 1982).

Bodily-Kinesthetic Intelligence

The possibility of considering bodily-kinesthetic intelligence and athletic intelligence as synonyms is impossible to rule out as several features of intelligence universally accepted as essential are common for individuals to be kinaesthetically and/or athletically intelligent.

Briefly defined as *the capacity to use your complete body in expressing ideas and feelings,* the kinesthetic intelligence has much to do with bodily movement and physiology. Theoretically, using muscle memory and movement the kinesthetically intelligent people often learn best by "doing" things physically, i.e. getting up and moving around into the learning experience. They generally remember things through their body such as verbal memory or images; would rather touch than just look; enjoy the outdoors; can't sit still for long; like to be active and love movement; enjoy exhilarating experiences; have abundant physical energy, etc. Highlighting the ability to use one's body in a differentiated ways for both expressive (e.g. dance, acting etc.) and goal-directed activities (athletics, working with one's hands), the bodily-kinesthetic intelligence is governed by the following criteria:

- Highly developed coordination (harmonious functioning of muscles), balance, dexterity (grace in physical movement), muscle strength, speed, flexibility and sensitivity of touch.
- Expertise in using the entire body to relate thoughts and feelings.
- An ability to manipulate objects skilfully, using both fine and gross motor movements.
- Dancers, athletes, and gymnasts are examples of bodily-kinesthetic intelligence.

In sport context, the bodily-kinesthetic intelligence could better be defined as *our capacity to perform a given physical task with minimal energy expenditure and minimal stress.* (It doesn't take a 400 m runner or a marathon runner to see how valuable this capacity might be over the course of his or her race.) Until now the two greatest assets for the disciplined athlete have been *genetic potential* and a *comprehensive training programme* to maximize that potential. At this moment, with emergence of sport psychology as "buzz word", sport scientists have begun to recognize and develop a new resource, one that promises to revolutionize any sport. This new asset is *bodily-kinaesthetic intelligence,* or, in short, kinetic intelligence. It is really no new discovery at all. We all exercise kinetic intelligence (most often unconsciously) every time we walk, climb the steps, pick up an infant child or open the refrigerator door and reach for a snack. In our daily lives, we take this form of *intelligence* for granted. We assume our motor-skills are fully developed by the time we are "grown-up".

What elements constitute bodily-kinesthetic intelligence and how these elements can be improved to enhance athletic performances *and* our functional daily lives is the next important consideration. Importantly, some of the specific elements constituting bodily-kinesthetic intelligence identified so far include the speed of our movements, the duration required to accomplish the task, the physical and environmental characteristics – such as weight, size, distance, temperature, elevation slope, etc. – and the complexity of the task. Trainable as these elements are, they can be improved through training. Developing kinesthetic intelligence in sport training system would require focusing on and performing a sport *intelligently* – with more efficiency, grace and economy – to reduce exertion levels and time investment in training, and yet improving performances and further minimizing recovery time and rate of injury.

Distinction between Kinesthetic and Logical Intelligence

Surely, there is a profound difference between logical intelligence and kinesthetic intelligence. The latter is radically different from our conventional notion of intelligence as the "purely mental" power of reasoning and logic. The logical form operates through a linear sequential format – surfacing in our brains as an endless string of verbal commentary produced by that "little voice" in the back of the brain that somehow disassociates itself from the body. Because this commentary is relentless, our kinesthetic intelligence is overshadowed and relegated to some unconscious level in our brain. When the serious athlete comes to fine-tuning their mental faculties in the process of improving their performance ability after their game skills have reached a level of near perfection, they and their trainers realize that performance-enhancement is as much a matter of kinaesthetic intelligence as it is of logical intelligence. It is simply impossible to do with one without the other. While we may regard logical intelligence as *the* most essential tool for success, security and survival in our modern world of economics, business and information, we could not function in our daily lives or improve our sporting ability without basic bodily-kinesthetic intelligence.

The Content of Athletic Intelligence

According to Fisher (1984), *athletic intelligence is an interactive construct that is related to the capacity to cope with specific environmental demands.* Intelligence depends on perception and memory (coding and perceiving). These are essential for the performance of skilled movements of athletics. There is clear proof that *motor proficiency in its basic sense, is an intelligent action.* The characteristics of the task are related to athletic intelligence in that tasks are performed successfully when cues are oriented and processed in such a way that appropriate actions are performed at the end of the process (Robb, 1972). According to Fisher (1984) the athletic tasks with which the athletes should cope are:

1. Locating, finding and perceiving the characteristics of the environment (important cues).
2. Searching for and finding essential cues for the task (distinguishing essential from nonessential stimuli).
3. Identifying cue patterns (identifying passive, internal situations as opposed to external ones).
4. Using short term memory to plan the game, for time-out strategy, and for previous defence tactics (these are examples of the strategies that exist in memory and precede given response patterns).
5. Using long term memory (movement patterns can improve if warning signs are coded and identified in the brain).
6. Decision-making.

There is not much time left for information processing and reacting. The need for excellence creates a potential for failure accompanied by thoughts of disaster. Despite this, exceptionally outstanding performances are executed by athletes according to the process described. Starkes & Deakin (1984) maintain that the best basketball player is not necessarily the best dribbler, the fastest runner or the most accurate shooter. He/she also does not necessarily have the best spatial visualization or information processing characteristics. In spite of this, it is possible to determine the nature of the cognitive dimensions (software) of athletes, and how they differ from sport to sport. The skilled athlete *selects processes* and *retrieves* construct information of the situation differently from the inexperienced player.

Analysis of the actions athletes perform in their specific kind of sport makes its possible to understand their action better. Using a specific paradigm, it is possible to examine the cognitive actions the skilled athlete undergoes and to hypothesize that he/she has an appropriate visualization, and neurological ability, since otherwise such action would not be successful.

The content metaphor raises the questions such as "Do skilled athletes encode and retrieve information related to the environmental construct differently and at different speeds from lesser skilled athletes?", "Do skilled athletes understand visual search of the environmental stimuli differently from non-athletes?", "Do skilled athletes have a different diagnostic attention for details of information in the environment than others?", "How are speed and accuracy in decision-making in games demonstrated differently in skilled athletes and in lesser skilled athletes?", or "What is the nature of perceptual anticipation in game situations?" At the same time there remains the basic question "Is intelligence in a game (i.e. the ability to solve problems) related to general intelligence, or is the general intelligence in a game one specific characteristic of the range of characteristics that is typical of general intelligence (g)?"

From the review of literature on athletic intelligence, three propositions could possibly be visualized:

(1) sport (athletic) intelligence is the same as general intelligence;

(2) bodily-kinesthetic intelligence is the much hyped athletic intelligence; and

(3) athletic intelligence is a delicate but intelligent mix of bodily-kinetic intelligence and logical intelligence or general mental ability.

Gardner's *Multiple Intelligence Theory* and Sternberg's *Triarchic Intelligence Theory* overrule compatibility between athletic intelligence and general mental ability hinted in the first proposition. Further, various features and properties of bodily-kinesthetic intelligence draw some parallel between it and conceptualized athletic intelligence, but they hardly allow one to serve as a substitute for the other, thereby refuting the second proposition. The third proposition has a substance to highlight the psycho-physical reality of the performing art like sport.

Cratty (1973) suggested that athletic intelligence could possibly be a combined effect of the matching between elements of general intelligence such as memorization, evaluation, divergent-convergent thinking, analysis-synthesis, flexibility in problem solving, social intelligence, etc., and athletic skills and abilities such as remembering and incorporating skill-components, rules, tactics in total act, evaluating one's own and that of the team mates, and opponents' abilities; coach's tactics, components of training regimen, analysis of the mechanical principles of the game, visible game strategies, deciding upon tactics, analysis of the team interactions, personal relationships, etc.,

While developing the theoretical framework of athletic intelligence, Cratty (1972) identified (1) Cognitive abilities, (2)

Adjustment, (3) Tactics and Strategies, (4) Anticipation of and Responding to tactics, (5) Analyzing opponents' moves, (6) Quick decision-making, (7) Analyzing skills of team interaction, (8) Exploiting opponents' moves, (9) Ability to change tactics when new situations arise, (10) Personal relationships, (11) Forcing the opponents to play to your tune, (12) evaluating one's own and opponents' abilities, and (13) Remembering rules of the game as possible constituents of this new construct. Cratty emphasized that the identified 'athletic skills and abilities, when appropriately developed and tested', could give very valuable clues to the "intellectual dynamics and mental status" of the athletes.

As research continues, the mist enveloping athletic intelligence is gradually disappearing, apparently revealing that highly coordinated intelligence and communication between the brain and the rest of the body characterize those with high athletic intelligence. Until recently, this skill was not considered "mental". Now, however, more scientists are accepting the idea that it is the brain's superior capacity in this area that permits, for example, athletes (as well as dancers) to calculate the time, length and strength of their movements. Those who have this particular ability can easily coordinate all kinds of actions – large muscle and fine muscle – showing potential for superior performances. Further analysis of the situation shows that at the gross root (basic skill) level sport is predominantly physical both in thought and action; however as the level of performance rises, more psychological variables begin to appear more prominent hinting at greater precision, accuracy and speed in skill execution. At this skill-performance level, bodily-kinesthetic intelligence dominates the scene. Finally, when almost every single skill is executed as an automatic routine, performance is predominantly guided by cognitive-perceptual factors and directed by athletic sense, which is neither a physical variable nor an intellectual one, but a dynamic complex of physical, mental and emotional factors.

In any game situation, all things being equal and all opponents having the same time and energy to devote to their training, the key element that will unleash a new realm of power and performance is the understanding of the neural aspects of athlete adaptation. We all think of the mind/brain as a psychological tool that has to be managed as you approach competition. In truth, it is the mind/brain that is the ultimate being, the true leader of performance on the field of play, and understanding how the brain manages your performance is the key to the future of high end performance in sport.

Testing Athletic Intelligence

To make athletic intelligence testing a viable proposition, sport psychologists would require to: (a) concretize its concept, and (b) find operational definition for it. A few options suggested could possibly be tried.

School Intelligence Testing Yardsticks

At school, intelligence is defined and tested by exams. If you do well on the exam, you are then considered as "smart". Often society associates intelligence with success in academics or life in general. If this procedure is replicated in sport, it could perhaps be possible to test an athlete's intelligence by evaluating his or her success or achievement in his or her chosen sport both objectively and subjectively. The higher the achievement or the score in sport, the higher the rank in athletic intelligence, could be the yardstick used. A rational assessment of the situation points out that from skill-acquisition stage to the ultimate winning performance at the Olympics, athletic performance is a complex phenomenon of perceptions, cognitions and motor actions guided and directed by a variety of inherited qualities and environmental factors (correlates) that cogently reflect human thought (intelligence) in action.

It is least contestable that success in sport is a combined effect of all the inter-related and interactive physical, mental, emotional and social variables constituting personality dynamics. That way, there could be no better way of testing athletic intelligence than just by success in sport. While general intelligence involves certain mental skills, sport intelligence encompasses several physical skills besides the mental skills falling within the purview of general intelligence, for example, how intelligently your body moves on the floor or the athletic court and/or in the air while playing your sport.

This is easily said than done for the path of athletic intelligence testing is strewn with variety of thorns and thistles. At first, success in a physical activity (athletics) is yet to be recognized by psychologists as a measure of intelligence almost exactly as academic success. Secondly, the success (achievement) of a track & field athlete, a gymnast, an archer, or a shooter can be objectively measured and recorded, but that of a soccer player, a cager, a shuttler, or a cricketer is impossible to measure objectively. Usain Bolt or Carl Lewis in track and David Beckham or Ronaldo in soccer may be extremely intelligent individuals in their own way but the success of the one is easy to quantify, that of the other too difficult to reduce to an objective score. Finally, activity or athletic success measures are predominantly physical, physiological and biomechanical; the intelligence measures are mental and intellectual.

The Bodily-Kinesthetic Intelligence Measure

If kinesthetic intelligence is defined as *the capacity to perform a given physical task with minimal energy expenditure*, then some of the variables relevant to each physical task include the speed of our movements, the duration required to accomplish the task, the physical and external factors – such as weight, size, distance, temperature, elevation slope, etc. – and the task complexity. Obviously, bodily-kinesthetic intelligence is an integrated effect of the interaction between our physical capacities [muscular strength, metabolic (aerobic) capacity and neuromuscular coordination], and (often overlooked) mental attributes such as *perceptive* capacity – our ability to accurately observe the conditions relevant to accomplishing the task and their interrelationships, along with our body's relationship to those conditions.

The focus of current athletic training programmes is largely on improving muscular strength and aerobic capacity. Hardly does it directly address the neurological system. However, according to Dr. Phillip Maffetone, this neurological system responds and improves much more to training than the metabolic or muscular systems. (In fact, the muscular system responds and improves the *least*.)

In conventional athletic training, the emphasis is on strengthening the metabolic system through aerobic activity, muscular system through resistance training and neurological system through sport-specific drills to improve form and technique. Notably, these three physiological systems are interdependent – we do not train one without affecting the other two. *Integration* is the key – training and developing an integrated neuromuscular system is the foundation of bodily-kinesthetic intelligence, which is an intimate and harmonious integration of mind and body – *mind in matter*. This is profoundly different than our conventional logically-based approach of *"mind over matter"*.

By devising ways and means to measure the neurological response of the body to the athletic situations along with testing of aerobic capacity and muscular strength as essential in each sport, we might be able to have a measure of bodily-kinesthetic intelligence, generally considered equivalent of athletic intelligence. ***Time*** (speed at which something happens, the duration - lasting through time, and viewing time through rhythm); ***Shape*** (design, symmetry and asymmetry, letter and number shapes, and geometry); and ***Space*** (three-dimensional space concept - height-weight-depth), are fundamental elements of kinaesthetic intelligence. Developing techniques to measure human response as the body moves through time, in certain shapes and through the space the possibility of measuring athletic intelligence could not be impossible.

The cellular intelligence of the body extends far beyond the linear sequential format of our logical intelligence. Our bodies beg for opportunities to demonstrate the functional brilliance of kinesthetic intelligence and the opportunity to re-format the evolution of human intelligence.

Testing the Typical Athletic Intelligence

The overall perspective depicted above underlines one important fact - while general intelligence involves certain mental skills, sport intelligence encompasses several physical skills besides the mental skills falling within the purview of general intelligence, for example, how intelligently your body moves on the floor or the any athletic court and/or in the air when you are playing a particular sport. The assumption here is that athletic intelligence is neither success at athletics, nor efficient bodily movements in relation to time, space and shape: it is a construct applied to the particular types of mental abilities needed to complete the demands of a sport task successfully. Considering the psychometric aspects of it, the essential elements of *Sporting Intelligence* could include:

- ***complete knowledge of the sport;***
- ***knowledge of where and when important cues are likely to occur*** during skill-acquisition stage and actual play;
- ***the ability to search for and detect task-relevant cues;***
- ***identification of cue patterns;***
- ***skill of perceptual and motor identification*** (Sigler & Richards, 1982), not analyzed in the sport setting so far;
- ***short-term memory recall;***
- ***perceptual intelligence*** (perception and attention);
- ***collecting*** (categorizing and organizing) ***processing*** (coding and accessing) ***information,*** and utilizing it speedily and efficiently (Most people usually have more than enough

knowledge to cope with tasks in particular situations, but few are capable of accessing the appropriate knowledge stored in the memory so that it is specific and successful for coping with particular situations.); and

- ***decision-making ability.***

Macak (1955) developed a number of laboratory stimulation tests to assess athletes' ability to solve problems in real game situations Same way, psychologists in Czechoslovakia, the former East Germany and Poland also contrived an array of more than 20 visual situations to test ***problem-solving ability*** of the athletes in sports like volleyball, football, ice hockey, and others (Vanek & Hosek, 1967). The method of evaluation was found to be effective in predicting athletic performance (Macak, 1963). However, Vanek & Cratty (1970) concluded that instead of abstract pictures, real and concrete game situations are required in each type of sport to distinguish among various levels of sportspersons. These attempts were aimed at assessing some specific elements of intelligence, rather than the whole of it.

A survey of some correlational studies made Kamlesh (2007) conclude that certain specific athletic abilities carrying higher percentage of intellection are easy to test and measure objectively; however, a large number of abilities reflecting both bodily-kinaesthetic intelligence and logical intelligence (general mental ability) especially those involving ***tactics and strategies used in dynamic play situations of a sport, at-the-spur-of-the-moment decision-making ability, ability to use several response options, exploiting opponents' weaknesses etc.***, are difficult to evaluate as objectively as motor and/or psychomotor abilities can be.

SELECTED REFERENCES

Allport, G.W. *Pattern and Growth in Personality*, New York: Holt, Rinehart & Winston, 1965

Binet. A., & Simon, T. *The development of intelligence in children.* Baltimore, Williams & Wilkins. (Reprinted 1973, New York: Arno Press; 1983, Salem, NH: Ayer Company), 1916

Buskist, William & Gerbing, David W. *Psychology – Boundaries and Frontiers*, Glenview, Ill; Scott Foreman Little Brown Higher

Education, 1990

Cratty, B.J. *Physical Express of Intelligence*, Englewood Cliffs, NJ; Prentice Hall, 1972

Cratty, B.J. *Psychomotor Behaviour in Education and Sport*, Springfield; Charles C. Thomas, 1974

Crooks, Robert L. & Stein, Jean *Psychology – Science, Behaviour and Life*, New York; Holt, Rinehart and Winston, 1988

Digiovanna, Nicent G. A comparison of intelligence and athletic ability of college men, *Research Quarterly*, 8(3): 96-106, 1973

Gagne, R.M. *The Conditions of Learning*, New York; Holt, Rinehart & Winston, 1970

Gardrner, Howard *Frame of Mind: The Theory of Multiple Intelligence*, Luvene; Research Publication, 1985

Guilford, J.P. *The Nature of Human Intelligence*, New York; McGraw Hill, 1967

Guilford, J.P. *Way Beyond the I.Q.*, Bufallo, New York; Creative Education Foundation and Bearly Unlimited, 1977

Guilford, J.P. Cognitive psychologists' ambiguities: some suggested remedies, *Psychological Review*, 89: 48-59, 1982

Hakstian, A.R. & Catell, R.B. High stratum ability structure as a basis of twenty primary abilities, *Jr. Educational Psychology*, 1978

Hendrickson, D.E. The biological basis of intelligence, Part-II: Measurement, In H.J. Eysenck (Ed.), *A Model of Intelligence*, New York; Springer-Verlag: 197-226, 1982

Ismail, A.H. Integrated development, In J.E. Kane (Ed.), *Psychological Aspects of Physical education and Sports*, London; Routledge and Kegan Paul, 1972

Jenson, A.R. How much can we boost I.Q. and scholastic achievement, *Harward Educational Review*, 39: 1-123, 1969

Jenson, A.R. Hierarchical theories of mental ability, In W.B. Dockrell (Ed.), *On Intelligence*, Toronto, Ontario; Institute for Studies in Education, 1970

Kamlesh, M.L. *Athletic Personality: A Psychological Probe*, Delhi; Surjit, 1990

Kamlesh, M.L. On the question of relationship between intellectual dynamics and athletic dynamics, *Research Biannual for Movement*, 5 (2), 1987

Kamlesh, M.L. A studying relationship between general intelligence and body-kinaesthetic intelligence, *Paper presented at the IX National Conference of Sports Psychology*, Nagarjun University, Guntur, May, 1984

Lefton, Lester A *Psychology* (3rd Ed.),Boston; Allyn & Bacon Inc (P284), 1985

Macak, I *The education of attention in volleyball games.* Teorie a Praxe Telesne Wchovy, Prague, 3, 8, 1955

Murphy, Kevin R. & Davidshafer, Charles O *Psychological Testing: Principles and Applications* (2nd Ed.), Englewood Cliffs, NJ; Lawrence Eribaum Associates, 1991

Piaget, Jean *The Psychology and Intelligence*, Totwa, NJ; Littlefield Adams, 1972

Raven, J.C., Court, J.H. & Rave, J. *Manual for Raven's Progressive Matrices and Vocabulary Scales,* London; H.K. Lewis & Co., 1977

Robb, M.D. *Dynamics of Motor Skill Acquisition.* Englewood Cliffs: NJ, Prentice-Hall, 1972

Sandiford, Peter *Educational Psychology*, London; Longman Green, 1933

Sigler, R.S. & Richards, D.D. The development of intelligence. In R.J. Sternberg (Ed.), *Handbook of Human Intelligence* (pp. 897-971), New York: Cambridge University Press, 1982

Spearman, C. *The Abilities of Man.* New York: Macmillan, 1927

Starkes, J.L. & Deakin J.M. Perception in sport: A cognitive approach to skilled performance. In W.B. Straub & J.M. Williams (Eds.) *Cognitive Sport Psychology* (pp. 115-128), Lansing, NY: Sport Science Association, 1984

Sternberg, R.J. The nature of mental abilities, *American Psychologist,* 34: 214-220, 1979

Sternberg, R.J.Sketch of a componential sub-theory of human intelligence, *Behavioural and Brain Sciences,* 1980

Sternberg, R.J. Testing and cognitive psychology, *American Psychologist,* 36: 1181-1189, 1981

Sternberg, R.J. Reasoning, problem-solving and intelligence, In R. Sternberg (Ed.), *Handbook of Human Intelligence,* New York; Cambridge University Press, 1982

Sternberg, R.J. & Salter, W. Conception of intelligence. In R.J. Sternberg (Ed.), *Handbook of Human Intelligence* (pp. 3-28), New York: Cambridge University Press, 1982

Tenenbaum, Gershan & Bar-Eli, Michael Decision making in sport: a cognitive perspective. In Robert N. Singer, Milledge Murphey, & L. Keith Tennant (Eds.), *Handbook of Research on Sport*

Psychology. New York: Macmillan: 171-192, 1993

Terman, L. In symposium: Intelligence and its Measurement, *Journal of Educational Psychology*, 12, 127-133, 1921

Thompson, G.H. *The factorial Analysis of Human Ability*, London, 1939

Thorndike, E.L., Brengman, E.O., Cobb, M.V. & Kloodyard *The Measurement of Intelligence*, New York; Teachers College, 1928

Thorpe J. & West C. Games sense and intelligence, *Percept. Motor Skills*: 20, 326, 969

Thurstone, L.L. *Primary Mental Abilities*, Chicago; University Chicago Press, 1938

Wechsler, D. *The Measurement and Appraisal of Adult Intelligence* (4th Ed.), Baltimore; Williams & Wilkins, 1978

Wechsler, D. Intelligence defined and undefined: A retrospective appraisal, *American Psychologist*, 30: 135-139.

Vanek, M. & Cratty, B.J. *Psychology and Superior Athlete*. London: Macmillan, 1970

Vanek, M. & Hosek, V. Tachistoscopic investigations of players as indicators of the quality of their judgment. *Paper read at the Meeting of Sport Psychologists in Hrachove*. Czechoslovakia, 1967

Thurstone, L.L. Primary Mental Abilities. *Psychometric Monograph*, I, 1938

"If you win one Olympics, you become famous. If you win two Olympics, you become great and if you win three Olympics, you become history."

- Alexander Popov -
The Legendary Russian Swimmer

CHAPTER - 20

ATTENTION AND INTEREST

Attention and interest, though two different processes, are inter-related like the obverse and reverse of a coin. We often attend to things, subjects and situations which interest us and conversely we get interested in things which, intentionally or unintentionally, happen to come within the focus of our attention. Both interest and attention play a significant role in teaching-learning process. Pupils pay much greater attention to a teacher whose lessons interest them; they hate attending the class of a teacher who they find least interesting in terms of his or her appearance, lesson content, and teaching style. Absence of attention and interest both on the part of the teacher and the taught makes teaching-learning a dull affair, and substantially brings down the quality of pupil-teacher interaction and ultimately ends up in poor performance on both sides. Closely related to the system of human motivation and performance in academics, physical activity and sport, attention and interest call for special treatment as a topic of study in psychology and as an applied principle in educational process. When students lack attention and show little interest in the lesson or activity, teachers and physical educators have moments of anxiety and feel concerned. They try every conceivable strategy up their sleeve to control elements of distraction around in the learning situation and boost up students' interest in the lesson/activity.

Attention and interest are no inherited traits; they are developmental variables - a product of individual-environment interaction largely training and self-discipline. People greatly vary in attention span; every one cannot attend to every thing like every other person. Their interests are varied; some are interested in studies, some in sport; some like to grow as business executives, others as professionals; some like to eat fruit, others hate doing so, and so on. Children, in general, have a short attention span, and their interests in objects, things, events, activities, sports, peers and people wax and wane often very quickly. Performance in academic activity and sport greatly depend on the extent to which attention and interest have been developed in children right from the beginning. Commenting on this issue in the context of sport, Cratty (1989) says: "The young child must attend to instructions when skills are taught, and the team athlete must focus attention on numerous variables when playing, including visual and verbal information emanating from mates and coaches, as well as internal self-instruction and kinaesthetic cues coming from his or her own exhibition of skill".

ATTENTION

Everything in life responds positively to attention. People, objects, stocks of inventory, and money are but a few examples. For example, the best way to give attention to money is to account for it very accurately and promptly. Keeping accurate and up-to-date accounts of money is a powerful mechanism for attracting more of it from life. Education, activity, sport, business, and so on, are no exception to this principle. A focus on "attention" creates an environment of efficiency and economy as the task of learning, whether in classroom setting or on the playfield, competes with a range of distraction. A lack of attention is due to a lack of skill on either the part of the teacher or the students. Attention is "within" the student, or something that a student "has." Attention is one of the most intensely studied topics within psychology and cognitive neuroscience.

Definition of Attention

The word "attention" comes from the Latin *attention*, itself derived from *attendere*, which means "to turn one's mind towards"— to turn one's mind or perhaps one's senses. In general, attention is concentration of consciousness upon an object or an idea. It is the cognitive process of selectively concentrating on one aspect of the environment while ignoring other things, e.g. listening carefully to what someone is saying while ignoring other conversations in a room (the cocktail party effect) or listening to a cell phone conversation while driving a car. A cricket fan attentively watching an India-Pakistan encounter on television, an adolescent listening the Michael Jackson musical number, and a yoga-practitioner sitting in *Padamasna* (lotus pose) fixing his gaze (and thought) on *Shuniya* – nothing in particular –

unmindful of the things around, exemplify attentional focussing on something of interest and values to each of them. In dictionary, attention means *concentration of the mental powers upon an object; a close or careful observing or listening.* The processes by which you were able to spot your friend, hear your name despite the noise of the party, and then quickly turn toward and then away from the sound of the breaking glass involved attention.

In the context of human information processing, attention is the process that, at a given moment, enhances some information and inhibits other information. The enhancement enables us to select some information for further processing, and the inhibition enables us to set some information aside. The best definition of attention so far has come from James (1890):

> Everyone knows what attention is. It is taking possession by the mind, in clear and vivid form, of one out of what seem several simultaneously possible objects or trains of thought. Focalization, concentration, of consciousness are of its essence. It implies withdrawal from some things in order to deal effectively with others, and is a condition which has a real opposite in the confused, dazed, scatterbrained state which in French is called distraction, and Zerstreütheit in German.

This definition conveys intuitive feeling for the subject. However, it is common to break the subject down into two subdivisions: (1) arousal and (2) selection of information. The processes involved in *arousal* involve achieving and maintaining an alert state sufficient to remain in contact with environmental stimuli. This sense of attention separates the waking state from conditions such as sleep or coma. *Selective attention* refers to the processes involved in selecting information for consciousness, for immediate response, or for storing information in memory. The conscious content of selective attention is only a small subset of the information that could be available at any given moment. Thus, the ability to switch or orient one's attention is critical to the successful use of attention in any environment.

Along with selectivity, attention involves, in general, control of the visual and auditory processes. Three groups of 6-grade students watching a movie, attending a class in geometry, and listening to the radio commentary on a soccer match, respectively - when questioned individually at the end of the session as to what each of them saw or heard - will reveal variation in their focus of attention to the same stimuli. This situation may have no link with the intellectual status of the child – their brightness or dullness – but, of course, with their interest.

A fundamental characteristic of human cognition is our *limited capacity* for processing information. We cannot see, attend to, remember, or react to everything that we encounter in our environment. Nowhere does this limited capacity play a more central role than with attention. This attentional bottleneck implies that paying attention to one source of information causes the processing of other things to suffer. For example, when a driver of a motor vehicle begins to chat on a cell phone, his performance degrades as attention is withdrawn from driving and directed toward the phone conversation. Often this becomes a potential cause of accidents. Attention involves conscious diversion of the perceptual processes and control of flux and fluidity of the mind. Freud (1891b) discusses the divided attention in an interesting manner:

> When I read proofs with the intention of paying special attention to the letters and other symbols, the meaning of what I am reading escapes me to such a degree that I require a second perusal for the purpose of correcting the style. If, on the other hand, I read a novel, which holds my interest, I overlook all misprints and it may happen that I retain nothing of the names of the persons figuring in the book except for some meaningless feature or perhaps the recollection that they were long or short, and that they contained an unusual letter such as x or z. Again, when I have to recite, whereby I have to pay special attention to the sound impressions of my words and to the intervals between them, I am in danger of caring too little about the meaning, and as soon as fatigue sets in I am reading in such a way that the listener can still understand, but I myself no longer know what I have been reading. These are phenomena of divided attention which are of particular importance here.

Characteristics of Attention

Cognitive theorists attach great importance to attention considering it a pre-condition for learning. Characteristically, attention:

- is a selective process because of the limited capacity of the sensory-perceptual channels.
- works on a priority principle – first things happening first.
- plays more dominant role in cognitive tasks than in affective and conative (motor) activities.

- has a narrow aperture, so its range is limited.
- shifts from one object or event to another very quickly.
- is related to interest closely.
- is drawn to new, unfamiliar and more interesting objects or events than to those that are familiar, similar or the same.
- is value-based and exploratory in operation, allowing us to attend to items, issues and events that have importance for us.
- makes the incoming information clearer and its details more elaborate, when it is deeper and sustained.
- facilitates strengthening or weakening of S-R connection and determining the motor adjustment that follows depending on the quality of sense-perception about the task, event or object.

Mechanics and Nature of Attention

Attention is a selective activity of the mind. Due to limited information processing capacity of our brain and nervous system, all events that occur and all objects present in the environment around us are *not* attended to with the same amount of concentration. Several things happen simultaneously and in quick succession within us and around us but not all of them attract our attention in the same measure. Some get in the focus of our consciousness vividly; some remain in the periphery of consciousness, and others remain out of focus. Even in a particular situation, we attend to one object or one aspect of an event more than other(s).

At any point of time, a great variety of external stimuli impinge on our sensory apparatus, which transmit the information in the form of electrical impulses to various brain centres. This sensory-perceptual process is the cause of experience that we have and determines our state of consciousness in a particular situation. Obviously, sense-perception is a multi-channel mechanism constantly feeding external data to our brain especially the cortex. Sometime, one channel, for example, visual feeds more powerful signals than auditory or olfactory. The selective filter at the opening of the consciousness is very narrow; it does not allow the entire sensory-perceptual input to enter the memory store. Only new important information is allowed into our memory and the insignificant one blocked. As a result, there is no confusion in having a clear and vivid view of all the assailing sense-perceptions at one and the same time. The narrow-window (aperture) of consciousness is known as ***focus of consciousness***. The sensory-perceptual inputs not attended to instantly, remain in the periphery (margin of consciousness) until the opportune moment. Attention is focused on to important sense-impressions which are brought into sharp focus of consciousness.

Likened to a *'search light'*, attention is focused on one thing after another in succession, i.e. it shifts from one object to another quickly or slowly as situation dictates. The entire process is selective process. Attention-span, i.e. the amount of time attention remains focused on one particular object varies from situation to situation and from individual to individual. Moray (1970) alludes to the "input space", meaning that attention must be directed either consciously or inadvertently to specific areas (points) of display. For instance, while looking at a painting the focus is either on the form, contours, design, or colours at a time; it moves from one aspect to another. Besides, James (1973) says: "Knowing what information in the display is worth attending to will depend on the past experience of the person in relation to the skill (task) being performed".

It is difficult to have conscious control over sense perception except in a natural way. Sensory input is a continuous activity when we are in a conscious state. James (1890) compared consciousness to the flow of a river whose waters keep moving - sometime fast, sometimes slow, sometimes in a thin stream, and sometime in torrents, but never stopping even for moment depending on inflow. Ideas and sense-perceptions float and flow in our mind unceasingly, keeping the information system in a pliant state working efficiently.

Interest plays a vital role in attention selectivity. Referring to the relationship between these two, James (1890) said: "Millions of items of the outward order are presented to my senses which never properly enter my experience. Why? Because they have no interest for me. My experience is what I attend to. Only those items which I notice, shape my mind - without selective interest, experience is utter chaos". Ideas floating in the margin of consciousness always struggle to move to the focus of consciousness and disturb (or push aside) those already etched there. A person intently scanning a charming figure in a painting is also conscious of its colour scheme, contours and background seen in the margin of attention (consciousness). The same way, another individual watching a dance recital is not only focusing his attention on the bewitching movements of the artiste but also the stage background, accompanists, and the surroundings. In both cases, the attentional focus shifts from one aspect of the object/event to another, sometime gradually, sometime quickly, and sometime it gets pointed longer on an important feature. The ultimate experience, then, is the cumulative effect of the attentional focus shifting consciously, subconsciously or unconsciously back and forth.

Priority principle governs attention phenomenon. Stimuli that demand expedient and immediate response (or action) on emergency basis are attended to first that those carrying secondary importance. Priority is established by taking into account value and importance of the items received at any given moment. James (1890) observes: "Generally speaking the *successful* information is that which is considered important or interesting or else is that which the observer has been told to look for, but there are also other determinants, e.g. limited capacity of the channels in the nervous system to transmit information".

Attention is teleological in nature, its major objective being fulfilment of a goal. Many things enter our attentional focus randomly; they too have some purpose, though not clear to us immediately. No cognitive, affective and conative aspect of a learning experience can be carried out unless the attention is goal-directed. Ross (1955) argued; "it is better to say I attend to my work than my attention is directed to my work". Attention is essentially a mental activity which, consciously or unconsciously, is focused on some definite task.

Types of Attention

Primarily attention is classified as Objective Attention (due to external conditions and factors, i.e. what happens in the environment), and Subjective Attention (due to a person's internal psycho-physiological states or conditions).

Objective attention is based on the notion that any stir in the environment by an object, individual or event attracts our attention by force of circumstance irrespective of its value to us biologically or socially. A sudden flash of light, a crashing sound, an offensive smell, an insane man walking about in nude, etc., instinctively draw our attention. This is an innate reflex mechanism that serves as a protective shield for the organism. Even under normal circumstances, the moving human beings, the speeding vehicles, the hanging multi-coloured banners advertising products, the huge billboards on the roadside, the rising mobile towers over residential buildings, young children playing cricket in the lanes, and so on knowingly or unknowingly come into attentional focus. Turning attention away from them is literally impossible. This kind of attention psychologists call objective attention because we have no control over what we see or hear.

Subjective attention may be volitional or non-volitional, i.e. acquired (learnt) or spontaneous (inborn) reaction. *Volitional Attention* is based on acquired interests of concrete sentiments, abstract sentiments and self-regard sentiment. *Non-volitional Attention* is spontaneous - an outcome of instinctive drives. A thirty crow's attention is drawn to water, a hungry dog's attention to food, and a hospital patient's attention to medicine or doctor. This attentional phenomenon is natural and simple. Same way, blooming flowers, beautiful paintings, well-designed dresses or costumes, lilting melodies, etc., attract our attention spontaneously. There is little constraint in the effort. Our interest and desire to accomplish to some goal serve as a backdrop to volitional attention. Subjective attention may also be categorized as voluntary and involuntary. *Voluntary attention* is one which is guided by our own will power and *involuntary attention* is a compulsive process in which we cannot restrain ourselves from paying attention to an object or event. Further, the attention paid to ideas, thoughts, reasoning, imagery and imagination is called *Ideational Attention*. Analytical or *Discriminative Attention* is one when consciousness utilizes energies for analyzing various situations. In *Synthetic* or *Associative Attention* consciousness utilizes energies for synthesizing ideas, thoughts, situations, etc., and establishes relationship among objects, occurrences, and events. Attention may be differentiated according to its status as 'overt' versus 'covert'. *Overt attention* is the act of directing sense organs towards a stimulus source. *Covert attention* is the act of mentally focusing on one of several possible sensory stimuli. Covert attention is thought to be a neural process that enhances the signal from a particular part of the sensory panorama.

Besides this, attention can also be classified in many other ways depending on the context in which it is used. For example, *General Attention* is usually a less alert state of mind from which responses are made slowly and the focus is also not narrow. *Closed Attention* is accompanied by a higher state of arousal-activation. It requires more energy and resources than general attention. Sometimes general attention is also referred to as *Passive Attention*, and *Closed Attention* as *Active Attention*. Mention has also been made of *Flexible Attention*, the one which quickly shifts from one aspect of a thing to another, and *Rigid Attention*, the one which is fixed and one-pointed.

In clinical setting, attention is best described as the sustained focus of cognitive resources on information while filtering or ignoring extraneous information. It is a very basic function that often is a precursor to all other neurological/cognitive functions. In a recent clinical model, five different kinds of attentional activities of growing difficulty are described as given below:

- ***Focused attention***: This is the ability to respond discretely to specific visual, auditory or tactile stimuli.
- ***Sustained attention***: This refers to the ability to maintain a consistent behavioral response during continuous and repetitive activity.
- ***Selective attention:*** This level of attention refers to the capacity to maintain a behavioral or cognitive set in the face of distracting or competing stimuli. Therefore it incorporates the notion of "freedom from distractibility"
- ***Alternating attention***: It refers to the capacity for mental flexibility that allows individuals to shift their focus of attention and move between tasks having different cognitive requirements.
- ***Divided attention***: This is the highest level of attention and it refers to the ability to respond simultaneously to multiple tasks or multiple task demands.

Application of Attention in Real-World Setting

Based on recent research studies, the varieties of attention and related concepts are applied to real-world settings under such subheads as selective attention, divided attention, sustained attention, mental workload, effects of practice, executive control, and individual differences.

Selective Attention

Selective attention refers to the ability to selectively process some sources of information while ignoring others (Johnston & Dark 1986). Given that we cannot process all the information that is constantly bombarding our sensory systems, it is important to be able to select the information that is most important to our current set of goals for further processing and exclude irrelevant sources of information from analysis. A compelling example of the efficiency of selective attention in excluding irrelevant material from further analysis is provided from the sport field.

> In a research study, participants were asked to watch a short video clip of two teams passing a basketball back and forth and report the number of times that the team wearing white jerseys passed the ball. Midway through, a person dressed in a gorilla suit walked into the scene, stood in the middle of the basketball players, beat his chest, and then sauntered off the screen. Amazingly, 58 per cent of the people watching the video failed to see the gorilla! This *inattentional blindness* indicates that the mechanisms of selective attention are actually quite effective in filtering out highly salient, but irrelevant, information.

Several factors contribute to the efficiency of selective attention in searching for information in visual displays such as colour or shape, onset stimuli or cues (e.g. flash code used by air traffic controllers to rapidly draw attention to situations requiring immediate attention, blinking cursor on the computer monitor), object movement (moving display of information on new electronic billboards with bright images, flashing messages, and moving objects), expectancy (an owner of a new car suddenly noticing many of the same vehicles on the road), etc.

Divided Attention

Divided attention refers to the ability to perform two or more concurrent tasks or activities. In this context, attention has been conceptualized as a commodity that can be flexibly allocated between different tasks, based on the *processing priority* assigned to each (Kahneman 1973; Narvon & Gopher, 1979). Both facilitative and debilitative effects of dual-task conditions on performance have been reported in research. For example, some skills may become so automatic that they can be combined with another activity with little or no cost. The second category of dual-task combinations includes situations in which performance of a task in dual-task conditions varies as a function of the processing priority allocated to the two tasks. As more attention is allocated to one task, performance on that task improves and performance on the concurrent task deteriorates; cell-phone/driving dual-task combination is a good example of dual-task interference in which the driving and cell phone tasks compete for limited capacity attention.

Further, intuition might lead you to suspect that walking would be a task that is automatic and could be combined with other activities without costs. While some people are reported to have difficulty in walking and chewing gum at the same time, others can perform two tasks with the same ability. Finally, in considering divided attention it is worth examining how finely attention can be divided; that is, how many *independent* things can be attended to at the same time. James (1890) suggested the range to be between four and six. The current estimates are within James' proposed 4–6 range.

Sustained Attention

Sustained attention situations are vigilance task situations in which an observer must sustain attention for prolonged period of times. In a typical vigilance task, the observer searches for target signals (e.g., enemy planes on a radar display, tumours in a radiograph, hidden weapons in a luggage X-ray, etc.) that are unpredictable and infrequent. Vigilance tasks are often quite taxing, performed under time pressure, associated with high levels of mental workload, and have levels of performance that are less than desirable. Airport baggage screening provides a good example of successive discrimination. Because the list of prohibited items is quite large and there is considerable variation in the features within each category, the screening task places a considerable load on working memory. As with the other variants of attention, there are important individual differences in the ability to sustain the focus of attention Researchers suggest that providing consistent practice to make critical target information automatically capture attention, and offering incentives to increase the motivation of the observer can improve sustained attention; for example, a baggage screener could get a bonus for detecting prohibited weapons.

Mental Workload

The stream of our thought is like a river. On the whole, easy simple flowing predominates in it, the drift of things is with the pull of gravity, and effortless attention is the rule. But at intervals, an obstruction, a set-back, or a log-jam occurs, stops the current, creates an eddy, and makes things temporarily move the other way. There is a relationship between attention and mental effort. Trying harder means allocating more attention to a task, often with corresponding increases in the mental workload experienced by the operator. In general, there is an inverted U-shaped function relating mental workload and performance (Yerkes & Dodson, 1908). If workload is too low, then fatigue and boredom can set in and performance will deteriorate. If workload is too high, then the operator will be overloaded and performance will suffer. The "middle ground" of mental workload is a situation where the task demands are high enough to keep the operator alert and functioning at high levels of performance, but not so high as to overtax the individual. For example, as the mental workload of drivers increases, they may exhibit greater difficulty in keeping the vehicle in the centre of the lane. The workload is often assessed using *subjective* assessments of the individual performing the task. Primary task measures, secondary task measures, physiological measures, and subjective measures all capture important aspects of mental workload and each is associated with different strengths and weaknesses.

Effects of Training

The wise saying *practice makes perfect* means that performance improves when people perform a task routinely. Indeed, one of the most important characteristics of human cognition is the ability to acquire new skills and expertise. Novices and experts differ greatly in performance quality. A novice performance is typically slow, effortful, and reliant on limited capacity attention, and that of an expert fast, effortless, and automatic. Research shows that performance improves with certain types of practice, not with other types even with tens of thousands of trials of practice. When there is a *consistent mapping* of stimulus to response over trials, performance will improve with practice and may eventually be characterized as automatic (e.g., free of capacity limitations, autonomous, ballistic). Contrarily, when the mapping of stimulus to response varies across blocks of trials (i.e., *varied mapping*), performance does not improve with practice and remains subject to the capacity limitations of attention. When tasks (skills) become more automatic, they place fewer demands on limited capacity attention. Anyone who watches an expert gymnast in action on the bar or the floor cannot help wondering at the mastery of his/her skill. Experts can make a seemingly impossible task for a novice look routine and effortless. At high levels of automatization, attention can be withdrawn from the task and the skills can be performed autonomously (i.e., without attentional control). There is also evidence to show that paying too much attention to the automatic components of a skill can interfere with the performance of an expert. Consistent practice no doubt improves performance; however, much will depend on the complexity of the task (skill) and whether it can be fragmented and extensively practiced in parts before it is practiced as a whole.

Executive Control

A general consensus among psychologists is that there is an executive system based in the frontal cortex that controls our thoughts and actions to produce coherent behaviour. This function is often referred to as executive function, executive attention, or cognitive control. Working memory capacity, as measured by counting, operation, and reading span tasks, is thought to play a critical role in helping to keep task-relevant information active and accessible during the execution of complex tasks. From this perspective, working memory capacity reflects an executive attentional system reliant upon prefrontal cortical brain regions in which "the memory representations are maintained in a highly active state in the face of interference, and these representations may reflect the action plans, goal states, or task-relevant stimuli in the environment" (Kane & Engle, 2002). The executive attentional system appears to be a critical component in people's ability to successfully perform a task when confronted with distraction or interruption. Indeed, in the workplace we are often interrupted by ringing phones, beeping emails, queries from colleagues, alarms, etc., and it is often a challenge to resume the interrupted task at the appropriate place in the sequence. These interruptions can have harmful consequences if the task is resumed in such way that an important item is omitted.

Individual Differences

As with all aspects of human cognition, individual differences are found in diverse varieties of attention and, in the extreme, deficits in attentional processing. In applied settings, an important goal is to select the right people for the right job. Individuals differ in their abilities (e.g. general ability, perceptual speed ability, psychomotor ability, reaction time, etc.) and each job has unique requirements. As consistency of a task increases, the role that these ability differences play in skill acquisition grows. It needs no reiteration that not all ability differences can be practiced away and differences in attention can have important consequences for performance in applied settings. Several investigators have demonstrated that individual differences in attention are predictive of real-world performance. In a research study, performance on a sustained attention task were found related with measured intelligence, and that the correlation grew in strength as the cognitive demands of the sustained attention task increased (Schweizer *et al.* 2000).

ATTENTION IN PHYSICAL ACTIVITY AND SPORT

Performance in physical activity and sport greatly depends on attention, because all psychosomatic processes such as sense perception, cognition, motor memory, intelligence, etc., are closely associated with it. This makes incumbent on young boys and girls at school to be very attentive during the activity lesson so that they miss no vital cues which govern performance of an important skill or series of skills. Similarly the competitive athletes have to acquire the ability to combat distracters during practice and competition and develop one-pointed concentration - a state in which all bodily and mental energies are brought to a flashpoint. It is established beyond doubt that the success of the archers, shooters, divers, gymnasts, boxers, wrestlers, track athletes, jumpers, throwers, and others largely depends on their attentional ability because in a split second the performance sky changes. Inability to pay attention especially when it is needed the most makes one miss the boat, e.g. scoring a point so vital for one's team to be declared as the winner.

The learning of new motor (sport) skills requires comparatively more attention so that relevant inputs can be stored. The storage of such information rests upon structures that lie deep within the motor memory. Attention appears to play a decisive role at several stages of motor skill acquisition. It is important for young learners to be able to convert visual and auditory inputs into certain constituent mental images, action sequences and performance frames by being utterly attentive during the activity class. The attentional networks play a key role in accessing the important cues of the skills.

Physical educators and coaches are usually aware that maintaining an alert state in the activity and sport environment is dependent both upon factors that are intrinsic to the child - e.g. adequate rest, good nutrition, and high motivation - and those that can be controlled by the teacher/coach himself, such as the use of innovative and involving movements and exercises at an appropriate level to challenge the student. As attention is closely related to interest, capturing the child's interest is important in fostering achievement, but effortful control allows the practice of skills that can lead to new interests, and the developing goal structures of children will allow the development of interest in activities or skills that will lead them to their chosen (predetermined) goals.

The athletic trainers and physical educators need to be aware of individual differences in the development of the mechanisms of selective attention important in the storage and retrieval of information relevant to various tasks (skills). Assessment of attentional capacities may be very useful for this purpose. Children can then be encouraged by exercises appropriate to their level to sustain the effort necessary for effective skill-acquisition, problem-solving, and decision-making. Assessment of the school environment may also be useful in considering children's attentional capacities. The application of effortful control can be tiring, and the opportunities for skill learning and for active play may be important in supporting its activity.

Attention is also important in the development of children's social skills, for sport is no physical activity performance alone, it is a wide and varied area of social interaction among all kinds of children. When physical education teachers point out aspects of other children's experiences and focus on the welfare of others, they can train the direction of a child's interest and concern. Again, this activity will be easier with some children than with others, but it can serve the goal of encouraging empathy and discouraging aggression in a child's development.

From cognitive perspective, the attention span of children is very short. They cannot concentrate on a task longer and get distracted easily. Long skill practice bores them and impinges on their attention. Possibly, the teacher's unusually long boring talk or repeated skill demonstration is replete with numerous irrelevant elements that strike at students' attention. Robb (1972) asserts:

> When a student says that he cannot 'see' or 'understand' what he is to do in a movement-pattern sequence, it is quite obvious that he is, in fact, 'seeing' something different from what the instructor wants him to see. Several students may see a demonstration and

> have several different perceptions of what they are to do. The teacher may believe he is showing one thing and the students are actually seeing something else. For example, the teacher may think that he is demonstrating how to shoot a basket; the student may see only whether or not the basket is made.

Individual differences among children in attentional capacity are a reality which teachers need to be aware of. Individuals perceive things differently even under the same conditions. Eysenck (1987) ascribed this situation to internal psycho-physiological process rather than to external factors, as many people believe. He states: "….. for every task an optimal level of arousal for efficient performance is proposed but the level varies for different individuals, Extroverts have shown higher threshold of arousal than introverts". This way, arousal (activation) level and input seem to be closely related, indicating that learners (as also performers in sport) who are optimally aroused have better attentional control and precision than those who are under- or over-aroused.

Many children fail to show remarkable progress on motor-skill tasks because (1) they do not have an optimal arousal level, and (2) their attention in the initial stage is directed to *other* things than the major task already in progress and the cues related to it. For example, when the gymnastic instructor demonstrates a stunt many students concentrate less on the movement mechanics and sequence and more on the gym's interior setup, teacher's attire, and so on. Similarly, referees and umpires fail to supervise the game well if they concentrate on who plays how. The basis for attention is focusing. When failing to focus attention, players miss their target, lose control of the ball as in soccer or basketball, react slowly to the situation, exhibit poor judgment, and commit more fouls and rule violations.

Children unable to control distraction, often attend to *other things* in a skill-learning class, resulting in poor show of performance. The concept of *selective attention* is critical to sport. A basketball player who is not concentrating on the ring while making a free throw, and a volleyball player who is not concentrating on the next serve are lacking in selective attention, which can play havoc with their performance. Selective attention is an outstanding cognitive quality of successful athletes. Interestingly, it is not an inherited characteristic. With proper mental skill training it can be developed to a desired level of proficiency.

According to Kahneman (1973) a person's limited ability to do several things at the same time seems to indicate that the total amount of attention that can be displayed at one time is limited. Different tasks impose varying demands on the limited capacity. Any deficit in demand and supply of attention will make learning and performance suffer. The concept of limited information processing capacity is synonymous with the concept of *available space* (Keele, 1970). If a motor task cannot be performed simultaneously with another motor or verbal task, then one of or both tasks are said to take space. Conversely, if several tasks can be performed at the same time, then apparently some or all of them require space. This principle impresses upon physical educators and coaches to be discrete in giving children inputs so that they do not trespass the limits of their innate information processing capacity.

Attentional Focus and its Measurement

A player's ability to attend to appropriate stimuli during learning and/or competition is known as *attentional focus*, which requires the athlete "to narrow and to broaden his/her attention when necessary". For example, in soccer, when initiating a move, the defence player or linkman has to keep the up-moving team-mates (forward players) within his visual orbit or periphery by broadening his attentional focus. The same player has to narrow down the focus of attention while making a free throw or a penalty kick. The concept of *attentional narrowing* is best understood in terms of *cue utilization* (Cox, 1984). Attentional narrowing is a function of available cues provided to the athlete from the environment during performance. In any sport, environmental cues are available to the athlete in abundance, some of which relevant but most totally irrelevant. Some cues may even be dangerous and debilitating.

Research shows that under conditions of low arousal, the athlete picks up both relevant and irrelevant cues. As arousal increases, the athlete's attention span begins to narrow. At some optimal point, attention-narrowing gets out of the relevant cues and allows the irrelevant cues to remain. At this point, performance ought to be at its best. The increase in arousal beyond the optimal level causes the loss of relevant cues and results in deterioration of performance. High levels of arousal lead to attention distraction, adversely affecting athlete's ability to selectively attend to one stimulus at a time. Attentional distracters include: actual physical distracters (e.g. light, sound, people's movements, etc.), task difficulty and reduction in information-processing capacity. They cause distraction in performance but their debilitating effects can be countered effectively by attentional focus training.

Being a dynamic phenomenon, attentional focus shifts awfully fast from one abject to another and from one situation to another. Under the circumstance, one is not sure whether or not the athlete is attentive at a given point of time; if yes, how much? Psychologists, however, have evolved certain techniques which help measure attentional focus in order to facilitate some intervention programme, if needed.

The primary ways of measuring attention have been identified and used by sport psychologists (Landers, 1988). First is *behavioural assessment of attention through reaction time* probe technique. In this procedure, demands of a primary task are estimated based on a subject's performance on a secondary reaction time task. Second technique is physiological indicators in which *attention is measured through physiological arousal* that is known to be very closely related to attention. It is based on the notion that as an individual's level of arousal increases (not beyond optimal), his attentional focus tends to narrow. Third is *self-report* (questionnaire) technique. The first two methods allow psychologists to measure attentional abilities at a specific point of time; the self-report tends to indicate attentional focus as a personality trait or disposition. The primary originator of the self-report for assessing attentional focus is Nideffer (1967, 1968b, 1980a, 1980b).

The Test of Attentional and Interpersonal Style (TAIS) developed by Nideffer is a popular psychological inventory which tends to assess individual attentional strengths and weaknesses in a range of performance settings, including sport. This 144-item paper-and-pencil test is structured on two theoretical premises. The first, derived from the work of Silverman (1964) and Wachtel (1967), is that the attentional requirements of task can be adequately represented along two independent dimensions - a *width dimension* which refers to the number of concurrent stimuli that can be effectively attended to, and a *direction dimension* which refers to the extent to which attention is directed externally to environment stimuli or internally to cognitions and emotions. Collectively these dimensions allow the attentional requirements of different tasks to be positioned in one of four possible quadrants (Fig.20.1).

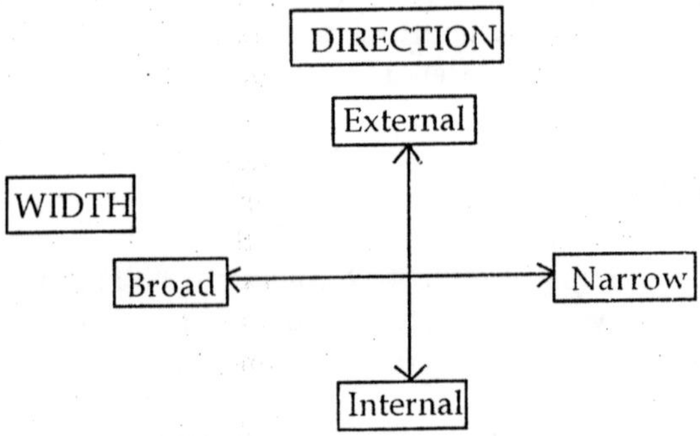

Fig. 20.1 Dimensions of attention

The width dimension of the athlete's attentional focus ranges from broad to narrow, and the direction dimension varies from internal to external. The second premise is that individuals, like tasks, can be classified with respect to some enduring attentional styles, and measurement of these styles is sought primarily through six attentional scales with the TAIS, three measuring elements of effective attention, and three complementary aspects of ineffective attention. The six subscales that reflect attentional processes are: (1) broad attentional focus (BET), (2) overloaded by external stimuli (OBT), (3) broad internal attentional focus (BIT), (4) overloaded by internal stimuli (OIT), (5) narrow attentional focus (NAR), and (6) reduced attentional focus (RED). High scores on three of the six attentional subscales reflect positive attentional traits (BET,BIT, and NAR), while high scores on the remaining scales reflect negative attentional traits (OBT, OIT, RED).

Despite questionable construct and predictive validity, the TAIS have been have been persistently used by researchers. Factor analysis of data collected by using the TAIS on sport groups do not appear to reveal the two dimensional structure of attention on which the TAIS was developed, the attentional breadth (band width) dimension in particular appearing to be multi-dimensional rather unidirectional. Through the use of sport-specific rather than general items, some predictive value of the test may be achieved but on the whole, the TAIS has been generally shown to be a poor demonstrator of experts and novices in sports in which selective attention is known to be important. One of the reasons why TAIS have not demonstrated a high degree of predictive value is that it is not sport-specific or situation-specific.

Attention Improving Techniques

Attention is very fleet-footed variable. Like quick-silver it is fluid, and always moving. Spiritualists and yogis claim to achieve attentional control by practice. Sport psychology research also indicates that with proper knowledge, education and training athletes can acquire the ability to increase their attention-span, process information efficiently and pay selective attention to their objectives. Several ways of improving athletes' attention have been suggested by Cratty (1989) and Cox (1994).

Physical Conditioning

A competitive athlete must be highly conditioned and fit. This is a pre-requisite for skill-acquisition and competition. The one with poor fitness and conditioning is sure to tire too soon and too often, rendering himself liable for physical and psychological harm. An unconditioned body is a great attention distracter. Even apprehension of fatigue adversely affects skill-learning and shortens attention-span. Under chronic fatigue condition, the athlete is bound to suffer from mental distraction due to disturbing impulses arising from body aches and pains. Conditioning replenishes physical energy; keeps the athlete legitimately psyched up and mentally alert; and instils him much needed self-confidence, so important for better attentional control. Getting physically exhausted and being mentally fatigued are two different phenomena though closely related. In sport, physiological fatigue often precedes mental fatigue (the one may not be the cause of the other). Therefore, the primary focus of the athlete and the trainer ought to be on muscle-mind conditioning leading to total fitness - an excellent device to resist undue fatigue and injury. A well-conditioned and fit athlete is highly confident and least distracted. Poor conditioning is an open invitation to early fatigue and injury, and, of course, poor attention.

Effective Skill Instruction

Skill-practice spells are often long and tiring, causing interest and attention to slide precipitously. Budding athletes and young school children feel the impact of this the most. They crave for rapid change in routines to sustain motivation. Novelty of skill and innovative teaching technique positively affect learners' interest and attention. To keep students' attention drawn to the activity, both physical educators and athletic coaches must (1) introduce novel element in skill-practice programme to ward off boredom; (2) give logical sequence to skills and their combination; (3) allow greater self-practice; (4) provide augmented feedback with emphasis on relevant cues; and (5) monitor progress too often to keep learners optimally attentive.

The coach's insistence on skill-perfection in a given time-frame often makes the athlete unduly anxious and his arousal level to race up. Significantly, too high or too low arousal causes attention distraction and is detrimental to skill-acquisition and performance at competition. This requires methodological innovation whereby the skill "wholes" are fragmented logically to effect skill-perfection in minimum possible time. Perfection in skills generates confidence, which, in turn, becomes a potent cause for better attention. Cratty (1989) points out that "an extrovert or an athlete who is typically highly aroused should be dealt with differently from one whose basic nature is calm when designing a concentration program intended to heighten the prolonged attention needed in sports like archery and pistol shooting". The over-aroused athlete may require relaxation training and an under-aroused (calmer) athlete may need special help in psyching up and activation in order to concentrate well (and also for a long time) on the intense competition ahead.

Practice under Stressors

'Introducing distracting stressors (e.g., crowd noise – recorded or live, multi-coloured ads.) in practice situations in order to habituate athletes to the distractions they will encounter in competition' is a good strategy to enhance athlete's attentional control. It is a kind of mental conditioning technique. Recent research has substantial evidence of positive benefits of artificial stressor-modelling attention along with other psychological variables. Sudden change in the competition schedule, equipment, competition venue, practice time, game officials, crowd composition, etc., serves as an effective attention conditioning stressor. Good coaches always resort to this technique without athletes' knowledge to see how they react to the change in situation and perform without getting disturbed. Players should be trained to face any eventuality any time. However, the stressors so used should be within tolerable limits and virtually serve as attentional training devices.

Cognitive Interventions

It is natural even for the top athletes to get distracted during competition due to one or other reason – internal or external. Sport psychologists suggest various attention training cognitive strategies called intervention programmes such as self-talk, thought-stopping & centring, mental rehearsal, meditation, imagery, etc. Using one or more of these strategies helps athletes either to develop a higher level of attentional control or to adjust their arousal/anxiety level.

According to Cratty (1989), 'informing an athlete of the theoretical information available might encourage positive attentional strategies' including:

(1) Switching from general to close attention at intervals in order to conserve attentional energy;
(2) Adopting useful strategies before competitions in order to either engage in specific attention-focusing techniques, or to devote time before competition to activities that will successfully save attentional intensity and effort for the contest itself;
(3) Learning to select relevant cues in a situation and to ignore or biock irrelevant cues;
(4) Successfully imagining skills with various kinds of distracters present.

It is important for athletes to develop a high degree of attentional control – 'a technique designed to keep athlete from slipping into a cycle of anxiety and self-doubt", says Nideffer (1981). Athletes often encounter problems of negative thoughts about performance and competition outcomes for which effective cognitive intervention is ***thought-stopping & centring.*** When negative thoughts come to overshadow consciousness, they have to be removed or displaced with the positive ones. "*The strategy of stopping a negative thought and replacing it with a positive one is known as thought-stopping*", says Ziegler (1980). Psychologists believe that a negative thought, which is often very troublesome, cannot be suppressed at all. The more a person tries to suppress it, the more forcefully does it rebound, making the situation worse. A better way is to replace it with a positive thought rather than to create void by banishing it. A positive thought helps the athlete to focus internally on selective basis. *Centring means directing thoughts internally.* This involves conscious awareness of the body's centre of gravity, while at the same time internalizing thought processes, feels Nideffer (1985). Immediately following the centring process, the athlete narrowly focuses his attention on task-relevant external cue. It is at this point that the skilled action is executed. Any delay in directing attention externally and skill execution will only invite distraction in the form of negative thoughts or unwanted environmental stimuli. The ***basic steps in thought-stopping & centring*** include the following:

(1) Displace any negative thought that comes into your mind with a positive thought.
(2) Centre your attention internally while making minor adjustments in arousal;
(3) Narrowly focus your attention externally on a task-relevant cue associated with proper form;
(4) Execute the sport skill as soon as you have achieved a feeling of attentional control.

Refocusing is another important attention-improving strategy archers, shooter, golfers, divers, gymnasts, etc., generally use. In refocusing process, the athlete should deliberately concentrate his/her attention on the task in hand, rather let it wander. Athletes who focus on errors already committed and distractions, instead of refocusing on the task ahead, often suffer a performance decline.

Attenional control strategies differ from sport to sport depending on the nature of sport. Even in the same sport, the attentional focus may differ from one position to another in a team sport (for instance, goalkeeper and forward line players, linkmen in field hockey or football) and situation to situation.

The attentional control training must be part of the total training procedure including psychological training, and relevant to the mechanics of the sport and objective. Certain yogic exercises such as *trataka, padmasana, meditation*, etc., when practiced under expert guidance facilitate attentional control improvement. Using more than one technique in combination is believed to be more effective.

INTEREST

No topic has received more attention from pedagogical writers than that of interest because educational process centred on the concepts of interest and attention. Learning and teaching take on deeper meaning when an emphasis is placed on "interest" rather than "attention." Erich Fromm said: "The interested person becomes interesting to others because interest has an infectious quality which awakens interest in those who cannot initiate it without help." "Interest" comes from the Latin *inter-esse*, that is, "to be in-between" or "it matters or concerns". If you are interested (in some thing), you must transcend your ego, be open to the world, and jump into it. Interest is based on activeness. It is the relatively constant attitude which permits you at any moment to grasp intellectually as well as emotionally and sensuously the world outside.

Definition of Interest

Interest is a *driving force* of attention, meaning what interest us, is attended to. Drever says: "Interest is a disposition in its dynamic aspects. It is a state of body and mind that keeps us attached to something." Finding no distinction between interest and attention McDougall (1949) said: "Interest is latent attention and attention is interest in action". Millions of objects, things, and living beings are present around us and hundreds of events occur every second, but not all interest us. According to Fromm, there is connection between our interest and sense of self. He recognizes that the "object" of interest may take on many forms ("persons, plants, animals, ideas, social structures") depending on the individual. In education, often the object of interest is guided or set by the curriculum, and physical education and sport by love for activity and sense of achievement. Some situations appeal to special instincts from the very outset, and others fail to do so until the proper connections have been organized in the course of the person's training. We say of the former set of objects or situations that they are *interesting* in themselves and originally. Of the latter we say that they are natively uninteresting, and that interest in them has first to be acquired.

Murphy & Davidshafer (1991) define interest as "response to liking", which is no matter of inheritance; it is *a learned affective response to an object or activity*. Interest is a simple phenomenon involving our liking. If we like something, we get interested in it. Our likings for friends, clothing, books, peers, teachers, careers and courses, etc., differ from others; even our own liking for something differs from situation to situation, depending upon what weighs on our mind when.

General Characteristics of Interest

In the documented literature, general characteristics of interest are enumerated as given below:

- Interest is matter of liking. I play sport because I like it.

- It is a driving force behind attention.
- It is generally a learned response, not an inherited trait.
- Interests vary with people and in the same individual in different situations.
- Our interest in objects, activities, events, and individuals fluctuate over time depending upon variety of internal and external factors.
- Interest and attention supplement and complement each other. Where we are wanting in interest, we are deficient in attention too.
- Interest can be used to predict choices, especially when there are few external constraints.
- Interests differ in their specific gravity, and importance.

The Interest Principles

The basic principle of interest is that *"If I am interested then I will pay attention"*. In life, in general, we are interested in those things that affect our needs and goals. When we are interested, we go to any extent to fulfill our needs and achieve goals using whatever ways and means possible. Interest can be explained from several perspectives.

- ***Interest leads to attention***: According to a sales model, the first step of selling is to draw customer's attention, without which it is impossible to have any kind of conversation with him. The same is true of any kind of persuasion. If you want to maintain attention, you will need to constantly play to their interests throughout any interaction. You can grab attention in crude ways, but shock tactics tend to have only a short-term effect. To sustain the conversation, working with interests is by far the most effective method.
- ***Bodily sensations are an index of interest in something:*** When interested in something, one experiences bodily sensations of some kind such as a hot flush rushing up your neck and around your face. When other people are feeling something, there are likely to be visible signs, such as skin colour changes and different facial expressions. Watch out for these signals, especially after you have done or said something that is intended to stimulate their interest. You can also discover their interests by observing them in everyday action.

- ***Interest is selfish:*** Each one of us is interested in our own self and the problems or products that concern us, not others'. If we are nice to other, we wish they be nice to us; this is again a selfish motive. Biologist Richard Dawkins, in *'The Selfish Gene'*, explained how, at the most fundamental levels, we are simply machines for propagating our genes, and all our actions can be explained in this light.
- ***Interests are in achieving goals:*** Our pursuit of goals in life is endless. Today we may be interested in achieving some goal, tomorrow another, and day after still another. This is the basis of our motivation. The teachers teach, and the students learn, both attempt to achieve certain goals, and engage in an activity that benefits both in some way. The basic principle, then, is that if you want to persuade someone to do something, then it helps a great deal if you can find out what they need, want or like.
- ***Interests are in avoiding suffering:*** We can have positive goals and also have negative goals, where we seek to avoid bad things. The degree to which people will choose one over another is affected by the attraction versus avoidance preference that people have. Bad stuff is usually more important and thus of greater immediate interest than good stuff. If you were in a bank and a robber came in, then most people would lie on the floor rather than tackle the man with the gun - discretion usually being the better part of valour.
- ***Interests are in stimulating pleasure:*** What we often consider as interest is stimulation of the pleasure zones in the brain. If one is interested in going to the movies, it is because all movies, as all entertainments, are designed just to cause that pleasure. This is a broad and general class of positive goals, where we are not particularly furthering our selves in life, rather the goals are about relaxation and the general seeking of immediate pleasures. Many people drift through life with few driving goals. They accept the pleasures that fall in their path and try to avoid less pleasant things (which often include the uncomfortable truth).
- ***Interests are different from abilities:*** Being interested in something is one thing and being able or competent to do

have it or do it, another. For example, you may be interested in cricket or golf but it does not reflect that you really are good club player. If you are gifted, have genuine interest in a sport like cricket and receive proper training to this effect, then, of course, sky will be limit for your performance and achievement. Interestingly, however, sometimes interest and abilities tend to show some kind of similar patterns. People often learn to like things they do well, and learn to dislike things they do not do well. This means that interests are cultivated. The more satisfying the outcome or consequence of an activity, the more liking do people develop for that activity. One practical distinction between abilities and interests is in terms of the variables that they tend to predict. Measures of ability tend to predict measure of performance or efficiency. Interests typically are related to satisfaction, (largely a psychological measure) rather than to performance.

Types of Interest

Since some objects are natively interesting and in others interest is artificially acquired, it is important for us to know as to how the latter and the former are connected. On this basis, interests are categorized as instinctive and acquired.

Instinctive Interests are natural and deeply rooted in our biological motivations. Much of our instinctive behaviour aims at fulfilment of our basic needs and achievement of life goals; for instance, we have natural interest for love and look for some with whom we can exchange amorous feelings as an expression of our innate drive. Similarly, our interest in food, water, social interaction and fellow feeling is natural; it is not learned at all. The driving force behind food seeking or a love partner, asserting on the environment, forming groups to protect our interests, etc., is the life energy that comes from our within. Therefore, what directs our instinctive interest are our innate needs, urges, desires and drives. Since these drives are specific, the satisfaction of one drive does not necessarily result in fulfilment of the other. For instance, a hungry individual will not be satisfied with a cold drink, nor a thirsty person with food. Immediate substitution for instinctive interests is rare. Non-fulfilment of the drive heightens interest and invigorates the physical and mental effort in the achievement of the objective. Once the objective is achieved, the drive dies down and the interest disappears until another occasion. The well-fed individual will be no more interested in food nor will he it pay any attention to even the presence of dainty dishes around. Therefore, the amount of attention to be paid to an object, event or an individual is directly proportional to the intensity of the physiological drive on the conative impulse.

Biologically, interest is no skin-deep sensation; it has its genesis in the chemical-physiological-psychological functioning of the organism. Both in interest and attention, contative factors are as important as cognitive factors. Simply viewing an object or an event does not make us interested in it; it requires some physiological or psychological urge or drive working in the background and the expectancy of its satisfaction in the foreground. Mere direct or indirect awareness of an object or an event has little importance for the organism; its biological value matters a lot. Further, if the object is perceived to have the capability of meeting some need of the organism, its value is enhanced. The objects, individuals and events that test well on this criterion are likely to engage our interest and attention more than others. This apart, a variety of natural attractions carry a strong psychological appeal for us viz. an object of beauty, a rhythm, a melody, free play, etc. It is natural for humans to tap foot or nod head when a musical number is being played, clap when a gymnastic feat is performed perfectly and fix gaze when a beautiful painting is displayed. Events like these may not have much to do with our physiology, they are directly linked to our instinctive feelings.

Acquired interests have environmental orientation. Our interest in movies, prestigious careers and courses, in certain types of clothes, toys, books, furniture, etc., are acquired. Hunger is inherited as a biological need (expressed in food-seeking), but tastes for different kinds of food are developed; some enjoy simple food, other relish junk food. We are innately interested in food, but where we feed ourselves (at home or at a hotel) is a matter of choice and interest. When born and brought in a particular environment, we develop variety of interests not originally present in us. All this is an outcome of varied individual-environment interaction, experience, education, learning, training, etc. Biological drives are inherited, likes and dislikes for objects, persons, things, events, etc., are largely learnt. With change in environment, our interests change influencing our lifestyle and effort for adjustment.

The interests of infants and children are guided greatly by their instinctive urges, those of an adult by knowledge, experience, social and economic needs, and cultural values. Murphy & Davidshafer (1991) believe that "values are regarded as more general and more resistant to change than interests.... Values are objective one seeks in order to satisfy a need, while interests are likened to specific activities through which values can be obtained." Although largely personal, values and interests are part of our social inheritance. All through their growth span, children acquire behaviours, concepts, ideas, beliefs, values, etc., as they see them operating in society around. As they mature, they cast a critical eye on them and become discrete in developing their likes, dislikes, interests, values, etc.

According to psychologists, acquired interests stem from absurd and concrete sentiments, most important among them being the "self-regard sentiment". McDougall calls it the *master sentiment* which gets strengthened as a child passes through various developmental stages and begins to locate his ego. Self-actualization, i.e. to achieve one's full potential, which according to Abraham Maslow, is on the top of the hierarchical structure of man's needs, is an outcome of self-regard sentiment and denotes man's constant struggle towards perfection, achievement and mastery over environment. We get interested in and our attention gets focused on objects (material possessions), ideas (values, thoughts, philosophic tenets, innovations, etc.), individuals (significant others, teachers, parents, etc.) and activities (performances, actions, movements) which facilitate our rise in life and hasten achievement of our ultimate objectives. Getting interested in good things of life – health, fitness, exercise, sport, recreation, respectable career, etc – needs some education, which must begin early in life. It needs constant reinforcement too.

Measurement of Interest

Interest measurement is an important activity in vocational guidance. In order to plan their careers, people must know their interests and aptitudes. No counselling psychologist can offer guidance to an individual unless he knows their interest, aptitudes and abilities. Like aptitudes and abilities, interests are measured through interest inventories, whose number today is approximately 200. Most of them are used for counselling after people's vocational interests are known. According to Holland (1973), vocational interests can be broken down into six basic types: *realistic, investigative, artistic, social, enterprising,* and *conventional.* Interests in specific occupations (occupational careers) can be predicted on the basis of those factors or themes.

The two basic approaches to the measurement of interest are (1) actuarial approach, and (2) trait and factor approach. In the *Actuarial Approach,* act-measures compare a person's interests to those of members of specific groups, and attempt to predict satisfaction with various activities and occupations. The first requirement for an actuarial measure is criterion-related validity. As far as *Trait and Factor Approach* is concerned, the most obvious pre-requisite for a good trait and factor measure is the existence of reasonably detailed theory or rationale that outlines the set of factors to be measured, the relations among them these factors, and the relationships between these factors and behaviours such as occupational choice.

In general, inventories prove useful when the questions span several domains and when scores are provided which illustrate several different kinds or levels of interests. All infants and children have fascination for activity, play and sport but with growth, their interests diversify and the focus of their attention begins to shift to other seemingly important activities of life. Every one is not interested in competitive sport. A few talented ones may rise to the level of national and international sportspersons. Some may even opt to join physical education as a profession.

Arousing Children's Interest in Activity and Sport

Without children taking interest in activity and sport, the standard of individual and national health, fitness and achievement can never improve. Play is a natural, spontaneous and pleasure-giving activity in which infants and children remain interested through out until they become (rather made to become) conscious of more socially important obligations and academic work. Due to lack of exercise and sport culture and career-consideration taking precedence over everything else in life in our society, neither parents nor teachers insist upon young boys and girls to be serious about their health and fitness for which attending activity and sport classes at school or club is a must.

Physical educators and coaches can address this problem by adopting various strategies based on the following generalizations:

- Interest is one form of emotion and emotions, on the whole, are contagious. In education, the emotion like interest travels from teacher to the student. An uninteresting teacher and an uninterested pupil make no headway. By using interesting methodological, communication, management and activity skills, interesting teachers make their subject/activity so interesting that pupils themselves get interested in it. Uninteresting teachers, on the other hand, make a mess of even most interesting programmes.

- Selecting appropriate curricular experiences in consideration of pupils' age, grade placement, ability and mental level is an effective strategy of augmenting students' interest in physical activity and sport.
- Teachers must arouse children's interest in play, activity and sport by explaining at length and logically the varied goals of the activity, skill, lesson, etc. Once aware of the incentives activity and sport offer, students will go all out to embrace them.
- Maintaining continuity in skills and skill-sequences enhances students' interest in the activity. Perfection in skills and excellence in performance are possible only through sustained interest in the activity and sport. Proper goal-setting and progression in activity lessons are additional interest-enhancing factors.
- Exercise/activity novelty and innovative teaching techniques never let students' interest sag. Stereotyped and prolonged skill-instruction classes often cause monotony, and impinge upon students' interest and attention. Interpolating a modified "whole" game or a short recreational activity in the lesson keeps the learning atmosphere interesting and invigorating.
- *Nothing succeeds like success* has to be the watchword. Success is the measure of all activity and sport endeavours. Outcomes of success in sport and activity are generally in the form of heightened confidence, interest and enthusiasm. Therefore, teachers must always aim at success.
- Motivation keeps interest sustained both among teachers and students. Effort of the teacher should be to strengthen intrinsic motivation rather than enhance extrinsic motivation. Effects of reinforcement are temporary.
- Providing correct feedback to the students goes a long way

in sustaining their interest in the activity and sport programmes. Giving positive feedback instantly and negative feedback discretely is better strategy in keeping interest in the activity/sport alive.

- Using reward and punishment with ingenuity and skilfully has a positive effect on children's interest. To produce salutary effect, these should be given instantly and only in deserving cases, not indiscriminately.

SELECTED REFERENCES

Cox, Richard H. *Sport Psychology – concepts and applications* (3rd Ed.), Madison, Wisconsin: WCB Brown & Benchmark, 1994

Cratty, B.J. *Psychology in Contemporary Sport* (Third Edition), Englewood Cliffs, NJ: Prentice Hall, 1989

Eysenck, H.J. *The Biological Basis of Personality*, Springfield: Thomas, 1967.

Freud, Sigmund *On aphasia: A critical study*. (E. Stengel, Trans.). New York: International Universities Press, (1891b), 1953

James, Marilyn Personality and perceptual characteristics, In HTA Whiting (Ed.) Personality and Performance in Physical Education and Sport, London: Henry Kimpton, 1973

James, William *The Principles of Psychology* (Vol. I), New York: Henry Holt & Co., 1890

Johnston, W. A. & Dark, V. J. Selective attention. *Annual Review of Psychology*, 37, 43–75, 1986

Kahneman, D. *Attention and Effort*. Engiewood Cliffs, NJ: Prentice-Hall, 1973

Kane, M. J. & Engle, R. W. Working memory capacity and the control of attention: the contribution of goal neglect, response competition, and task set to Stroop interference. *Journalof Experimental Psychology: General*, 132, 47–70, 2003

Keele, S.W. *Attention and Human Performance*, Pacific Palisades, CA: Goodyear, 1973

Landers, D.M. Cognitive states of elite athletes: Psychological studies of attention. *Paper presented at the meeting of the American Alliance for Health, Physical Education, Recreation and Dance* (Research Consortium Lecture) Kankas City, Missouri, April, 1988

McDougall, William *An Outline of Psychology*, Chapter-1, 1949

Morary, N. *Attention: Selective Processes in Vision and Learning*, London: Prentice Hall, 1970

Murphy, Kevin R. & Davidshafer, Charles O. *Psychological Testing: Principles and Applications* (2nd Ed.), Englewood Cliff, NJ: Prentice Hall, 1991

Navon, D. & Gopher, D. On the economy of the human processing system. *PsychologicalReview*, *86*, 214–255, 1979

Nideffer, R.M. *The Inner Athlete: Mind plus Muscle for Winner*, New York: Thomas Y. Crewell, 1976

Nideffer, R.M. Test of attentional and interpersonal style, *Jr. of Personality and Social Psychology*,34: 394-404, 1976b

Nideffer, R.M. Attentional focus - self-assessment, In R.S. Suin (Ed.) *Psychology in Sport: Methods and Applications*, Minneapolis Burgess, 1980a

Nideffer, R.M. *The ethics and Practice of Applied Sport Psychology*, Ithaca, New York: Mouvement Publications, 1981

Nideffer, R.M. *Athlete's Guide to Mental Training*, Champaign, Ill: Human Kinetics, 1985

Robb, Margaret *The Dynamics of Motor Skill Acquisition*, New Jersey: Prentice Hall, 1972

Ross, James S. *Groundwork of Educational Psychology*, London: George Harrap, 1955

Sandiford, Peter *Educational Psychology*, London: Longman's Green, 1933

Schweizer, K., Zimmermann, P. & Koch, W. Sustained attention, intelligence, and the critical role of perceptual processes. *Learning & Individual Differences*, *12*, 271–287, 2000

Sherington, C.S. *Integrative Action of the Nervous System*, London: Cambridge University Press, 1933

Silverman, J. The problem of attention in research and theory in schizophrenia, *Psychological Review*, 71: 352-379, 1964

Waschtel, P. Conception of broad and narrow attention, *Psychological Bulletin*, 68: 417-429, 1967

Woodworth, R.S. *Dynamics of Behaviour*, New York: Henry Holt & Co., 1987

Yerkes, R. M. & Dodson, J. D. The relation of strength of stimulus to rapidity of habit formation. *Journal of Comparative Neurological Psychology*, *18*, 459–482, 1908

Zeigler, S.G. An overview of anxiety management strategies in sport, In W.F. Straub (Ed.) *Sport Psychology: An Analysis of Athlete Behaviour* (2nd Ed.), Ithaca, New York: Mouvement Publications, 1980

INDEX

T

V

W

Z